Adorno

I dedicate this biography to my daughter Anna-Maximiliane because I would like my account of Adorno's life and work to help keep alive for future generations something of the thinking that was so influential for my own intellectual orientation.

Adorno
A Biography

Stefan Müller-Doohm

translated by
Rodney Livingstone

polity

First published in 2005 by Polity Press

Polity Press
65 Bridge Street
Cambridge CB2 1UR, UK

Polity Press
350 Main Street
Malden, MA 02148, USA

ISBN: 0-7456-3108-8
ISBN: 0-7456-3109-6 (pb)

A catalogue record for this book is available from the British Library.

The publication of this work was supported by a grant from the Goethe Institut.
Typeset in 10 on 11 pt Times
by Graphicraft Limited, Hong Kong

For further information on Polity, visit our website: www.polity.co.uk

Contents

List of Figures

List of Plates

To write history is to give the dates a face.

Walter Benjamin

Preface

Curiosity, the pleasure principle of thought.[1]

A biography of Adorno lays itself open to the objection that he had no liking for this genre of writing and in fact had grave reservations about the wisdom of exploring writers' lives in order to discover the key to their artistic or philosophical works. He expressed the hope that in his own case too readers would give preference to his writings rather than to the accidental facts about his life. Of course, he read and made use of biographies; the life of Richard Wagner is a case in point. But he never wearied of warning his readers not to scour musical compositions or literary texts for traces of the author's experience, subjective intentions or impulses. However, there is a constant temptation to do just that when thinking about Adorno himself. His texts contain many autobiographical allusions to happy childhood memories or sly references to local place names in Frankfurt or the surrounding area. What Adorno thought important was not such reminiscences, but the interplay between the objective content of his work and its historical context, i.e., what he called the force field consisting of the historical situation of the authorial subject, his life and his oeuvre.

This maxim has been the guiding principle of my life of Adorno, which has been completed forty years after his death and at a point in time when he would have been a hundred years old. During the six years and more that I have been working on this book I had a quotation from Adorno standing above my desk in a frame and visible at all times: 'Even the biographical individual is a social category. It can only be defined in a living context together with others; it is this context that shapes its social character and only in this context does an individual life acquire meaning within given social conditions.'[2]

The present biography attempts to reconstruct the context of Adorno's life with other people. It is based on the corpus of documents consisting of Adorno's publications, his published and unpublished letters, a variety of notes and the transcripts of his lectures and talks, as well as interviews with key contemporaries. A large number of other sources and texts belonging to Adorno's intellectual contemporaries have been consulted. Despite the sheer quantity of the material referred to, it should be borne in mind that there remain documents that have not been made available in the archives or where legal restrictions have prevented access. This applies especially to his correspondence; some letters have been blocked, in particular the highly significant correspondence with Siegfried Kracauer which is preserved in the Deutsches Literaturarchiv in Marbach.

Biographies are sometimes distinguished by an emotional distance from their subject. This would be inappropriate in my case. Both as a schoolboy and a student, I had the good fortune to experience directly something of the fascinating intellectual power of this protagonist of critical theory. 'The only relation of consciousness to happiness is gratitude: in which lies its incomparable dignity.'[3]

Acknowledgements

Thanks to the financial support of two projects by the Deutsche Forschungsgemeinschaft, it was possible to establish the Adorno Research Centre at the Carl von Ossietzky University in summer 1998. Under my direction my colleagues have helped to create the framework which has made it possible to write the present biography. I wish to thank the DFG for its financial support and also for the financing of a replacement professor for the whole of the winter semester 2002/3. It was only this support that it made it possible to complete work on this manuscript.

My personal thanks go to the members of the research group: Dirk Auer, Thorsten Bonacker, Thomas Jung, Jascha Rohr and Christian Ziegler. Without their productive collaboration and vigorous assistance this book could not have been written.

A part of the research consisted of interviews that I conducted with contemporaries of Adorno who were more or less closely associated with him. These interviews were recorded on tape and then transcribed. The two extended interviews with Ute and Jürgen Habermas in their house on the Starnberger See were not only highly instructive but also warmly sympathetic to my project of writing a life of Adorno. I am indebted to both of them for their patience with my questions and for their many suggestions.

I wish to thank a number of other people with whom I was able to conduct highly informative conversations: Hans-Magnus Enzensberger, Marianne Hoppe, Ludwig von Friedeburg, Lore Kramer, Elisabeth Lenk, Rudolf zur Lippe, Elfriede Olbrich, Klaus Reichert, Elisabeth Reinhuber-Adorno, Rolf Tiedemann, Alfred Schmidt, Herbert Schnädelbach, Wolfram Schütte and Bernhard Villinger.

In order to refine my own picture of Frankfurt University in the 1960s, I took the opportunity to speak with Uta and Hans-Dieter Loeber, Christa and Walter Siebel and also Eberhard Schmidt. I would like to thank them as well as my friends, whose curiosity over the years has helped me to keep on going.

I was also able to obtain good advice from other people during my work on the biography. In particular, I wish to thank Tom Huhn,

Martin Jay, Robert Hullot-Kentor, Alexander Kluge, Wolf Lepenies, Thomas Levin, Ahlrich Meyer, Klaus Neumann-Braun, Jürgen Ritsert, Hartmut Scheible, Rolf Wiggershaus, Gisela von Wysocki and Harro Zimmermann, as well as the universities of Princeton, Berkeley and Columbia (New York) for their hospitality.

This project could not have been carried out without the support of the Theodor W. Adorno Archive in Frankfurt and the assistance of its director and her colleagues: Gabriele Ewenz, Christoph Gödde, Henri Lonitz and Michael Schwarz. I owe thanks also to Jochen Stollberg, the director of the Horkheimer, Marcuse and Löwenthal archives in the Stadt- und Universitätsbibliothek in Frankfurt am Main, who helped me in the friendliest way.

In addition, I was assisted in my work by the following archives, to whom I also owe a debt of gratitude: the Bodleian Library, Oxford; the Archive of the Academic Assistance Council, London; the Leo Baeck Institute, New York; Deutsches Literaturarchiv, Marbach; Institut für Stadtgeschichte, Frankfurt am Main; Thomas Mann-Archiv, Zurich; Archiv der Johann Wolfgang Goethe Universität, Frankfurt am Main; Stadtarchiv Dettelbach; and Institut für Sozialforschung, Frankfurt am Main.

Since I have the old-fashioned habit of writing my first drafts by hand, Elke Glos had the difficult task of transferring the text to the computer, which she did with endless patience and great understanding. Barbara Vahland made use of her great expertise in pre-editing important sections of the text.

Gertrude Meyer-Denkmann showed great understanding and competence in advising me on the sections of the biography dealing with musical matters.

Thanks to their professionalism, the editorial department of Suhrkamp Verlag headed by Bernd Stiegler have helped to ensure that the manuscript could be completed and available in the bookshops in time for the centenary of Adorno's birth. I am especially indebted to the cooperation and exchange of ideas with Bernd Stiegler, who has meticulously edited the entire book chapter by chapter.

My increasingly close cooperation with Reinhard Pabst (our almost daily briefings provided emotional support as well as practical help) turned out to be a particular stroke of good fortune. I am indebted to him for a large number of valuable ideas as well as enthusiastic assistance in collecting the photographic materials, a task he finally took over completely.

My wife Heidi encouraged me to make the formulation of many of my ideas more comprehensible at the manuscript stage, and she generously overlooked the months during which I had retreated to my desk.

Oldenburg, April 2003

Illustration Acknowledgements

Günter Adolphs, Bonn: Plate 5
Theodor W. Adorno Archiv, Frankfurt am Main: Plates 11, 12, 14, 16, 20; figure 5
Archiv Günther Hörmann, Ulm: Plate 19
Bildarchiv Preußischer Kulturbesitz/Tüllmann-Archiv, Berlin: Plate 28
Deutsches Literaturarchiv, Marbach: Plates 9, 13
Deutsche Presseagentur, Frankfurt am Main: Plate 30
Historisches Archiv des Hessischen Rundfunks, Frankfurt am Main: Plate 27
Horkheimer-Archiv, Frankfurt am Main: Plates 17, 18; figure 4
Hotel Waldhaus, Sils Maria: Plate 21
Barbara Klemm, Frankfurt am Main: Plate 29
Stefan Moses, Munich: Plate 25
Reinhard Pabst, Bad Camberg: Plate 6; figure 1
Elisabeth Reinhuber-Adorno, Oberursel: Plates 2, 4; figure 2
Stadt- und Universitätsbibliothek, Frankfurt am Main: Plates 1, 7
Lotte Tobisch, Vienna: Plate 22
Bernhard Villinger, Weissach: Plate 3
Rüdiger Volhard, Frankfurt am Main (photo: Ilse Mayer-Gehrken): Plate 23

All other illustrations come from the collection of the author or Suhrkamp Verlag.

Part I

Origins:
Family, Childhood and
Youth: School and
University in Frankfurt
am Main

Family Inheritance:
A Picture of Contrasts

Reflection shows us that our image of happiness is coloured through and through by the time to which the course of our own existence has assigned us.

Walter Benjamin[1]

Every human being has his own way of dealing with the chance nature of historical events. But equally, individual lives are determined by the gifts bestowed on them by the fairies, both good and wicked, operating through the culture of their time.

Thomas Ludwig Wiesengrund-Adorno, who was born on Friday 11 September 1903 in Frankfurt am Main, was no exception. At his cradle there was a profusion of gifts of the most varied kind. Symptomatic of this abundance was the fact that his mother, whose maiden name was Calvelli-Adorno, toyed with the idea that her son should bear the name Adorno in addition to his father's name Wiesengrund. Thus right from the start the baby, who was baptized a Catholic, was the meeting point of two opposed cultural traditions. On the one hand, there were the Jewish origins of his grandfather and his assimilated father. Oscar Alexander Wiesengrund owned a successful wine-exporting business and identified with the open-minded, liberal values of the Frankfurt middle class. On the other hand, for Adorno, who was an only child, his mother's view of the world was of the very first importance. Maria Calvelli-Adorno della Piana was a devout Catholic who believed fervently in an ideal of artistic self-realization. Before her marriage to Oscar Wiesengrund she had made a name for herself as a singer who could boast of having performed in Vienna at the Imperial Court Opera. Her younger sister Agathe, to whom she remained close throughout her entire life, had made a name as a singer and pianist. She also had highly developed literary interests. Maria was the offspring of a Franco-German marriage that was itself highly unconventional for the time between the well-bred daughter of an established master-tailor in Frankfurt, who was herself musically gifted, and a roving Corsican officer and fencing master who had settled there. It is likely that Maria had something of a bohemian streak and that she was susceptible to a variety of cultural influences. For what could be more remote from the adventurous wanderings of a patriotic Corsican than the educated bourgeois outlook of a Jewish businessman who had been quietly minding his own business like his father before him in the commercial and trading metropolis on the River Main?

1

Adorno's Corsican Grandfather: Jean François, alias Giovanni Francesco

In the nineteenth century, Corsica, the island in the Tyrrhenian Sea, was still strongly marked by its native traditions. Nor did much change under the French constitutional monarchy, when Louis Philippe, the 'bourgeois king', built roads on the island and launched a programme to enlarge the harbour. The same might be said of Napoleon III, the nephew of the great Napoleon, who had come to power through a *coup d'état* in 1851. He followed a pro-Corsican policy in the hope of gaining the allegiance of the island with its rebellious population.

Corsica, the stubborn mentality of its inhabitants and their internal feuding were looked on with fascination in the imperialistic France of the Second Empire. This emerges clearly from the writings of Prosper Mérimée, one of the most popular authors of the decade of the July Monarchy. In 1840 he published his story *Colomba*, which opens with the return to Corsica of Lieutenant Orso della Rebbia, 'poor in hope, poor in money'. Back at home, he meets his sister Colomba. Her exotic appearance represents for him the true nature of the island. Although he is an upright citizen who identifies with law and order, she inveigles him into helping her to avenge the death of their father many years previously, for which they blame the Barricini brothers, a family from the same neighbourhood.

The French public of the day was fascinated by this exotic story with its vivid contrast between civilization and savagery, even though the dominant ethos of its own bourgeois industrial aristocracy was one of material gain.[1] When *Colomba* appeared, Jean François was scarcely more than twenty years of age and was well on the way to a career like that of Lieutenant Orso della Rebbia in Mérimée's story. There was even a certain physical resemblance between the two men. 'His face was bronzed by the sun, he had sharp, black eyes and a frank, intelligent expression.'[2] That is a description of the literary character Orso della Rebbia. But what do we know about that other Corsican, Jean François Calvelli, who, like his literary doppelgänger, tried his luck in the French army and must surely have read and valued Mérimée's picaresque story?

I have referred to the exotic figure of Jean François not because of the evident similarity between fact and fiction, but because he is one of the grandfathers of Theodor W. Adorno.

Jean François Calvelli was born on 14 April 1820 in Afa, Corsica.[3] Afa was part of the municipality of Bocognano, situated 650 metres up in the mountains. Today, it is a village surrounded by chestnut forests at the foot of Monte d'Oro, around 25 miles from Ajaccio. The inhabitants' lives were determined by the seasons and the consequent changes in the pastures for the herds of sheep and goats. Afa was scarcely more than a *paese*, a collection of houses, that came together with others of the same sort to form a church parish, a *pieve*. By the late eighteenth century, the Calvelli clan had settled in Afa and built a *torre*, the visible sign of a modest material security. This little stone house was the birthplace of Jean François, the only son of the *pastore*, Antoine Joseph Calvelli (1787–1822), and Barbara Maria, *née* Franceschini (1790–1846). The birth certificate in the town hall in Afa records the name in its Italian form: Giovanni Francesco Calvelli. His parents had married thirteen years before the birth of their son. They already had a daughter, Agatha, who was two years older than her brother. Their mother, Barbara, was eighteen when she married Antoine Joseph. He came from a family of some importance regionally. Her mother-in-law, Angela Orzola Calvelli, was already a widow. Her pride in her family, which was called Boldrini, was taken for granted. She was particularly proud of what were claimed to be close connections with the family of Napoleon Bonaparte, who in 1806 had promoted her brother to the rank of captain in the French army. She was of course present at the wedding, as were other near relatives. In all probability it was a close-knit family, as was customary in Corsica, and Jean François was more dependent on it than most. For when he was only two he lost his own father, likewise a fervent Bonapartist. The death certificate does not make clear whether the 35-year-old had died of natural causes, whether he was the victim of a stabbing, or even whether he had been condemned for political reasons. At any rate, Barbara had the sole responsibility for the upbringing of the two children. Their education, however, lay in the hands of the local priest whom the French prefect had entrusted with the task of teaching the children of the community, among them the bright young Jean François.

At the age of twenty, Jean François applied, evidently with success, to join the French army in Ajaccio. He began his career as a 'chasseur' second class in the Second Infantry regiment. After a brief interlude as an ordinary recruit in St Omer, he was sent to Africa, in December 1845. Following the French conquest of Algeria in the 1830s, there had been a number of uprisings under Abd el Kader against the colonization of the country. Troops were sent out to the colony to suppress the rebels, among them the young Corsican Jean François Calvelli. In the years to come he was in the habit of telling anyone who would listen about his exploits at this time; his grandson, too, would hear about them in due course.

After two years' military service in Algeria, which seems also to have resulted in a dose of malaria, Jean François was finally released from the army in Ajaccio, and in accordance with the rules prevailing at the time he was retired as an officer on half pay, just like his literary doppelgänger, Orso della Rebbia. We are also reminded of Mérimée's dashing lieutenant in the personal description of Calvelli that was produced at the end of his seven years' period of service. For his outward demeanour he was given the mark '*de bonne conduite*', and the testimonial continued: 'Height 1.66 m, oval face, broad brow, brown eyes, average nose and mouth, rounded chin, hair and eyebrows, very dark.'[4]

Calvelli returned home to the island to discover that his mother and sister had died shortly before. What was left to keep him in Corsica? In the following years he kept moving from one place to the next; he spent time in Italy, France and even Spain, as far as it is possible to trace his movements. He left France following the political events in Paris during the February Revolution in which Louis Philippe was forced to abdicate by the mass demonstrations and battles at the barricades in Paris. His departure was interpreted there as a sign that the Corsican Bonapartist had little liking for the revolutionary events in Paris in 1848. He doubtless felt greater sympathy for the rise to power of the despotic Louis Bonaparte. Karl Marx, one of the most perceptive witnesses of these events, published a brilliant analysis of the elimination of the parliamentary republic brought about by this change of government. Once the revolutionary proletariat had left the historic scene, an account of the social and political causes of the plebiscitary dictatorship could be followed in Marx's series of articles entitled *The Eighteenth Brumaire of Louis Bonaparte*.

What had happened? In December 1848, Napoleon's nephew was elected president of the French Republic. As early as 1851, he organized a *coup d'état*, dissolved parliament and had himself crowned emperor. At the point in time when Calvelli turned his back on France his path might in theory have crossed that of the author of *The Eighteenth Brumaire*. For, when Marx was expelled from Brussels in 1848, he spent some of the February in Paris before going on to Cologne. If we imagine Calvelli laying hands on *The Communist Manifesto*, we can be certain that the restless Corsican would have found it quite alien. He might easily have found more to interest him in Heinrich Heine's *De l'Allemagne*, a book that Heine, who had been living in Paris ever since the July Revolution of 1830, had written specifically with French readers in mind. Not the least of Heine's intentions was to provide a corrective to the idealized picture of Germany that had been offered by Madame de Staël. He wished to make the complex situation of German intellectuals comprehensible, but also to warn about the dangers that might result from the intellectual capture of the romantic movement by the politically conservative restoration after 1815:

If we were to compare the history of the French Revolution with the history of German philosophy, we might easily come to the conclusion that the French had requested us Germans to sleep and dream on their behalf, and that our German philosophy was nothing more than the dream of the French Revolution.[5]

While Heine, the champion of the Enlightenment, remained in Paris and gradually saw his hopes fade, and while the stateless Karl Marx finally saw himself forced to emigrate to Britain, the thirty-year-old Calvelli took the burdens of constant travel and change of locality upon himself in order to earn his living as a fencing master. Since he was anxious to work only for reputable and affluent families, he must have been very eager to preserve his own good name. His visiting card had to be impressive enough to open the doors of the best houses of the nobility. Just as Lieutenant Orso, a member of the *nobile*, had enhanced his name by calling himself 'della Rebbia', Jean François embellished his own surname by adding 'della Piana'. This addition refers to a *paese* in Corsica that Calvelli either regarded or claimed as his original birthplace.[6] But how are we to explain the further addition of 'Adorno'? From the little information that we have, it is likely that he came across the name in Genoa or perhaps even Turin. He was fortunate enough to spend a longer period of time in one or other of these towns, where he perhaps lived in a Villa Adorno or else with an Upper Italian family of that name to whom he gave fencing lessons. However that may be, when around 1859 or 1860 he made his way to Frankfurt on the recommendation of the Russian consul, Nicholas Wertheim, whom he had met in Stuttgart, he travelled under the impressive name of Calvelli-Adorno della Piana. At that time, in the post-Napoleonic period, Frankfurt had regained its old status as a free imperial city and was therefore an autonomous political entity. This meant that, since its territory was small, it imposed correspondingly restrictive conditions of entry. This explains why Calvelli took up residence in Bockenheim, a suburb to the west of the city that was actually part of Hesse-Nassau. For most of the nineteenth century Bockenheim was an independent town that was increasingly industrial in character. Not until 1895 did it become an integral part of Frankfurt itself.

Fencing master Calvelli-Adorno in the Frankfurt suburb of Bockenheim

Calvelli's connection with the respected Wertheim family helped him to obtain a lodging in the house of a worthy master-tailor, Nicolaus Henning (1801–71), and his wife, Maria Barbara (1801–72). Here he met their musically talented daughter Elisabeth, who was able also to speak French. Their relationship developed with a certain romantic inevitability. They fell head over heels in love. They married as early as February 1862, despite the opposition of the tailor, who was concerned for his family's good name and who had placed all his hopes for the future on making a more advantageous match for his daughter. The official papers that Calvelli had sent for to Bocagnano proved insufficient for a wedding in Frankfurt. For this reason it was decided to celebrate the wedding in London. The marriage was registered in the district of St Pancras in the county of Middlesex. The profession of Calvelli-Adorno was given as 'fencing master'. The witnesses were Victor Alexander and Henriette von Erlanger, who came from a reputable Frankfurt family belonging to the Jewish commercial and financial middle class. In February 1865, the registry office wedding in London was supplemented by a religious ceremony in Frankfurt Cathedral. At that time, Elisabeth had already given birth to two children, both of whom, however, had died in the year of the religious wedding. When the ceremony took place in Frankfurt, the bride was pregnant once again. In September of the same year she gave birth to her daughter Maria. The following year Louis was born. When he was baptized his parents added the name 'Prosper' to his French Christian name – proof that the writings of the Parisian author held a special place in the young couple's affections.

In the years after Louis' birth the couple continued to live in Frankfurt, which had once again become part of Prussia. They lived in what were evidently straitened circumstances and during this period Elisabeth Calvelli-Adorno gave birth to another four children. Of the four the only one to survive was Agathe, who had been given the same name as Jean François' sister. Agathe was born in 1868 and, as if the fact of her name had a symbolical significance, a deep relationship developed with her sister Maria which lasted the whole of her life, even after the marriage of the older sister in July 1898. Providing for the daily needs of his wife and three children was no easy task for the fencing master. He only ever spoke French and Italian. In all his years in Frankfurt Calvelli was never able to earn the 5000 guilders annually that were needed to qualify for the rights of a free citizen of the city. But he worked as hard as he could to secure an income for his family befitting their standing. When the viceroy of Egypt came to take a cure in Bad Homburg, Calvelli-Adorno offered his services as a fencing master. He also submitted a petition to Louis Napoleon in 1867.[7] In his letter to the emperor's *chef de cabinet*, Calvelli-Adorno referred to the good relations that once obtained between his own family and the emperor's. After describing his own unfortunate financial situation, he went on to ask for assistance. He was very willing, he wrote, to appear in person in Paris to give an account of his conduct as a French patriot. He gave the name of His Majesty's ambassador in Italy, Monsieur Nigra, who would testify to his probity. In his letter to the emperor, who as the nephew of Napoleon I had established the Second Empire in December 1852, Calvelli-Adorno gave a detailed description of the friendly relations between the Bonaparte family and his own. He pointed out that, when the Bonapartes had found themselves in difficulties at the time of the British occupation of Corsica, they had asked the Calvellis for help and this had been freely granted. This was the basis for ever closer bonds between the two families. Calvelli claimed that after the Egyptian campaign Napoleon spent some time in Corsica and that he had promised to give the Calvelli family property and the title of count. Because his father had been a Bonapartist the whole of his life and had even been the leader of the Bonapartist faction in Corsica, Louis XVIII had decreed that after Napoleon had been captured Calvelli should be interned and sentenced to death as a supporter of the emperor. Calvelli's letter ended with a description of his present reduced situation in Germany which compelled him to recall the contributions of which his family could rightly be proud.[8]

There is no evidence that a reply was ever received to this petition. Presumably, the French Empire failed to respond generously, since the circumstances of the Calvelli-Adornos remained as difficult financially as before. It is true that Elisabeth, Calvelli's wife, played her part and attempted to improve the financial situation by giving singing lessons and by occasional engagements as a singer herself. She went on concert tours, to Brussels on one occasion, accompanied by her husband. We know this because he needed a passport which was issued by the French Consulate General in Frankfurt. The personal description records his brown eyes and skin, the greying hair and beard and a height of 1.72 m.

Calvelli was of course primarily committed to his French background. How did he react, then, when the Franco-Prussian War broke out in the summer of 1870? Although – or perhaps because – his family represented a burden, an obligation and a responsibility, he resolved as a patriot to join up on the French side. The passport that he had issued to him in June 1870 contains the entry '*Pour se rendre directement en France*'. He later told his children that in order to reach the French army he had left Germany disguised as a peasant. His grandson subsequently reported that his grandfather had been a professional officer and 'had been seriously wounded' in 1870 near Lille.[9]

After the war there were still eight years of life remaining to Calvelli-Adorno. Together with his wife and children, the stubborn survivor evidently continued to battle with poverty. His methods were not always on the right side of the law. On one occasion he was found guilty by the royal court of having tapped his neighbour's water supply. Can it have been petty problems of this sort, including perhaps difficulties in paying the rent, that explain why the family moved house eight times in Frankfurt? A number of legends grew up around the Corsican officer and ensured the survival of his name among the following generations. The story was told, for example, that he had once halted a runaway horse in the middle of Frankfurt with a smart tap of his cane. He liked whiling away the time in the Italian coffee house Milani in the city centre. This was perhaps the place where he made notes for his little booklet on the art of fencing. He had an especially close relationship with his son, Louis Prosper. While his two daughters profited from the above-average musicality of their mother and one of them was to make a name as a musician in her own right, the only son made use of his father's connections with the Erlanger banking family. He made his career in their bank, which was subsequently taken over by the Dresdner Bank, and was thus in a position to help keep the family's head above water. This was particularly important since his father was no longer able to provide for them. When Jean François died in May 1879 – his tombstone in Frankfurt cemetery records his Corsican birth and his captain's rank in the French army – he had just celebrated his fifty-ninth birthday.

After her husband's death, Elisabeth tried to improve her financial position by giving public concerts together with her children, Maria, Louis and Agathe, who were all still quite small. Newspaper reports describe them as musical prodigies whose talents would, it was hoped, continue to be fostered. In the arts section of the *Frankfurter Zeitung* of 21 November 1878, Maria, who was thirteen at the time, was singled out for her 'exceptional talent as a singer'. The review highlighted her performance of 'the revenge aria of the Queen of the Night, the Proch coloratura variations . . . and the rondo finale from Bellini's *La sonnambula*. The young singer does indeed warrant the highest expectations for the future, for if we consider the exceptional sound of her voice . . . and her skill with coloratura arias we may say that she will surely earn a place among the outstanding stars of the concert hall.' Her two siblings were also praised for their contributions. The twelve-year-old Louis 'produced a trill at the end of his *Sonnambula* aria and a staccato passage from the serenade from the *Barber* . . . which would have done credit to an adult *primo cantatore* of the Rossini school. Agathe, too, sang an aria from *Sonnambula*, "Tutto è gioia", in a very pleasing manner.' The evening edition of the *Frankfurter Zeitung* of 24 February 1880 likewise contained a report of the 'three prodigies par excellence' and their mother, the exceptional singing teacher Calvelli-Adorno. It came as no surprise, then, that Maria Calvelli should have made a very respectable career as a singer under the supervision and guidance of her ambitious mother. The *Illustrierte Wiener Extrablatt* certainly thought it worthwhile to devote space to the debut of Miss Adorno in the Hof-Operntheater in Giacomo Meyerbeer's opera *Les Huguenots*. As a mezzo-soprano, she sang the part of the Page to the Queen of Navarre. In the edition of 14 August 1885, the newspaper reported:

> The youthful novice whom we have already heard from time to time in such roles as the Shepherd in *Tannhäuser* or the Woodbird in *Siegfried* tackled the role of the Page very resolutely, and successfully navigated past the cliffs and other perils of the coloratura aria. . . . Miss Adorno's voice is strong and harmonious . . .

She also received praise in the *Wiener Allgemeine Zeitung*, at least for her singing achievements: her 'resonant singing' showed her to be 'mistress of her voice'. 'Once Miss Adorno learns how to exercise the same control over her arms and legs . . . , her appearance on the stage will be an even greater pleasure.'

Later on, Maria was engaged to sing at the Municipal Theatre in Riga. Here, she received enthusiastic reviews. 'The way she moved, her fresh face and flashing eyes, everything, in short, was so expressive of youth that we could only conclude that this singer must have begun as a child to train her voice and to practise the arts of staccato, trills and the astonishing interval leaps of which she was capable.' This extremely favourable review ends with the comment that Miss Adorno was a 'song-bird' who aroused great expectations, since she was also very pretty.

The mother of these successful and attractive daughters survived her husband by only eighteen years. She died on 28 November 1897. In view of Maria's strict Catholic upbringing she could contemplate marriage only after a suitable period of mourning. She waited, therefore, until the following summer before marrying Oscar Alexander Wiesengrund. She was already thirty-three years old and her prospective husband was five years younger.

2

Wiesengrund: The Jewish Heritage of his Father's Romantic Name

The Jewish family of Wiesengrund moved from the village of Dettelbach in Franconia and settled in Frankfurt towards the end of the nineteenth century. At that time, the inhabitants of Frankfurt normally drank cider, but even then the pleasure-loving citizens did not confine their enjoyment to that somewhat sour drink. They knew very well how to profit from the fact that they were surrounded, to the west and to the south-east, by two important traditional wine-producing regions that still produce wine today. The long-necked bottles brought Riesling from the Rheingau, while the slopes of the bends in the River Main around Würzburg were the source of wine from the Sylvaner grape that was sold in large-bellied bottles. It was natural for a businessman who had grown up in one of these regions to earn his living by dealing in the produce of the Riesling or Sylvaner grapes.

The Wiesengrund wine-merchant's business was first established by Beritz David-Wiesengrund in 1822 in Dettelbach am Main, close to Würzburg with its bishopric and princely residence. He appeared on the scene in Dettelbach as a merchant together with his brother Abraham David, who was six years his senior. Jews had been actively engaged in trade in Dettelbach since before the end of the sixteenth century.[1] Both brothers founded families and increased their already considerable possessions. Each owned his own house; they were actively engaged in cattle-dealing to begin with, and then in dealing in land and property. The wine-merchant business was a later addition. In 1817 the prince bishop of Würzburg decreed that the Jews of the region should change their names. The name David was now abandoned in favour of Wiesengrund.[2] His first son, Bernhard, was a cooper by trade, and in 1837 he took over his father's wine-merchant business. The younger brother, David, inherited his father's imposing house, but soon afterwards moved to Würzburg, where he died in 1861. The well-established wine business belonging to the young merchant and master-cooper Bernhard Wiesengrund (1801–71) evidently had a bright future. However, since he was able to increase his already considerable inheritance, and had become wealthy, and since there were too many competing

```
•••••••••••••••••••••••••••••••••••••••••••••••••••••••••••••••••
:                                                               :
: Bernhᵈ Wiesengrund, Frankfurt a. M. :
:  Weingroßhandlung                                             :
:     Gegr. 1822   Schöne Aussicht 7   Tel. I. 1153      [16 :
:  ladet die p. t. Festgäste freundlichst ein.  :
:                                                               :
•••••••••••••••••••••••••••••••••••••••••••••••••••••••••••••••••
```

Figure 1 Bernhard Wiesengrund, wine wholesaler of Frankfurt am Main (estd 1822), extends a hearty invitation to its honoured guests

wine-merchants in the vicinity, he soon abandoned the small-town milieu and moved together with his wife, Caroline, *née* Hoffmann (1812–89), in order to set himself up in a major centre of commerce and free trade: the city of Frankfurt, with its important trade fairs. In 1864, the energetic businessman was canny enough to settle in one of the most favoured residential quarters of Frankfurt. The house, number 7, Schöne Aussicht, did its owner proud. The four-floor neoclassical building which contained both the shop and the wine cellar was extremely impressive. The Schöne Aussicht was part of the old town and hence a purely residential quarter, free from the noise made by commercial activities of whatever kind. Nevertheless, Wiesengrund was able to ply his wine-merchant's trade in this select area. The house was ideal for his purposes, since to the rear of the building there was a spacious internal courtyard, and the cellar vault was over 3 metres high.[3] A photograph from around the turn of the century gives a picture of the shop. Standing in front of it is the owner, together with three master-coopers or cellarmen, the latter recognizable by their large leather aprons; the picture also shows two women workers and two other employees. The street ran along the north bank of the Main and was generously laid out and planted with a row of trees opposite a row of bright middle-class houses. In one of them, number 16, Arthur Schopenhauer had lived during his years in Frankfurt. Next door Felix Mendelssohn-Bartholdy had stayed as a guest in July 1836: 'The view really is enviable, especially now in the splendid summer weather when you can look down the River Main with its many cranes, barges and ships, and the pretty shores over on the other side.'[4] The houses in the Schöne Aussicht were all more or less on the same scale, but some were occupied by several families and others by only one. They were built in a modern style on neoclassical principles: three-storey rendered buildings divided horizontally by cornices, with tall, narrow windows and an attic. They were lived in for the most part by merchants, brokers, bankers and diplomats. It was slightly out of the ordinary for the house next door to the Wiesengrunds to have belonged to a painter, Friedrich Wilhelm

Delkeskamp, a well-known figure at the time, whose paintings of views of Frankfurt have come down to us.[5]

David Theodor Wiesengrund was born on 3 July 1838, after his father had transferred the business to this enviable view. At the time when he was growing up the little world on the River Main was probably not much different from Mendelssohn's description of it. As an adult, the eldest son of the founder of the firm took over the flourishing wine-merchant's business. As the second son, his younger brother Benedict (1843–1903) was traditionally in the weaker position. He married Johanna Offenbach, who came from Mannheim and was nine years his junior. Together they had three sons. Initially, they lived nearby in 13 Schöne Aussicht. Later, they moved to Württemberg, where Benedict died at the early age of sixty. His youngest child, Fanni, who was born in 1846, married in Würzburg in 1867 and subsequently emigrated with her husband to the United States.

There is no doubt that the eldest of the three siblings fared better. At the age of thirty, David Theodor married Caroline Mayer (1846–94), a banker's daughter from Worms. The marriage resulted in the birth of six children, three boys and three girls, although one of the girls lived for only two years. The second son, Oscar Alexander, became the designated successor to the business, although he was frequently absent from Frankfurt and had of course to come to terms with his father. With what feelings did he enter into this inheritance instead of his elder brother? For the latter, Paul Friedrich (1869–86), had died at the age of seventeen and his younger brother, Bernhard Robert (1871–1935), emigrated to Britain soon after completing his course in engineering. He had graduated from Rostock with a study of refrigeration and began by working for large German companies until he was able to start his own firm in 1907, not far from London. Seven years later, having become a successful businessman, he acquired British citizenship along with his wife, Helene, *née* Richter, and his three children.[6]

A generous father and two musical mothers

Oscar Alexander Wiesengrund conducted his business affairs with great flair during the last years of the nineteenth century. He exported wine to Britain and the United States and established a branch of the company in Leipzig. He also owned a share in the wine-merchants Friedrich Daehne GmbH. This firm had been registered since May 1923 and was situated at different times in various locations in the city centre. Oscar Wiesengrund and Carl Feuchter were officially registered as its directors, both of them being listed as resident in Frankfurt am Main.[7] In addition, the Wiesengrund family owned a property in the little Odenwald town of Seeheim. The fire register of Seeheim shows that Oscar Alexander Wiesengrund owned a house there in the years

1918–38.[8] The wine-export business expanded considerably under his management and created a solid foundation for his marriage. The cosmopolitan wine-merchant was not yet thirty when he made up his mind after a lengthy stay in London to settle down and marry. This was all the easier as his sister Alice Betty (1873–1935) had set him a good example by making an excellent match the year before. She became the wife of Paul Epstein, a mathematician and subsequently professor of mathematics in Strasbourg. He was the son of a well-respected, cultivated middle-class family in Frankfurt. The couple had four children, one of whom later became a musicologist and another a historian. Oscar's other sister, Jenny (1874–1963), married Arthur Villinger. Her wedding took place the same year as her brother's.

Oscar Alexander Wiesengrund was an enthusiastic participant in the city's cultural life. He frequently attended performances at concerts and the opera. This had led to his introduction to two somewhat unusual ladies who were part of Frankfurt society. There was scarcely a single musical event in the city from which the inseparable sisters with the somewhat exotic, and even mysterious, name of Calvelli-Adorno della Piana were absent. They were well thought of as musicians. What must the reaction of the family have been when Oscar's marriage to the already somewhat mature singer was announced? After all, such a union fell well outside the expectations of the affluent Jewish commercial middle class. The business orientation of such families suggests that there may well have been objections and reservations. However, Oscar was man enough to get his own way, and in all probability his sisters would have given him moral support. It was surely necessary for him to assert himself, since his new family was intended to include not just his fiancée, Maria, but also her younger sister Agathe, who became a member of the new Wiesengrund household from the outset. For, not satisfied with introducing two socially respected but nearly penniless artists into the house, Oscar discovered that even the formalities of the wedding were not without their complications. There was no denying that Maria Calvelli-Adorno della Piana had a sensational name.[9] But there was the legal difficulty that she possessed French rather than German citizenship because, in all his years in Frankfurt, her Corsican father had never succeeded in satisfying the property requirements needed for him to be granted official recognition as a citizen of the imperial city. That explains the couple's decision to take the same route that her own parents had taken before her. They thus brought into being an amusing family custom, and in the summer of 1898, after a suitable period of engagement, they went to London where, like the bride's parents, they celebrated their marriage in the register office of St Pancras.

The couple had to wait almost five years before any children made their appearance. Not until Friday 11 September 1903 did the day arrive when a son was born, at around 5.30 a.m. As was customary in those days, the birth took place at home. How did the family react to this event? No doubt with a special joy, since three years previously Maria had had a stillborn child.[10] David Theodor, the 65-year-old grandfather of the newborn baby, must have regarded him as his son's predestined successor in the successful business, the preserver of the family tradition. Oscar must have been happy and relieved that his wife, who was no longer young, had survived the labour so well and that he had a son. The two women, his mother and his spinster aunt Agathe, joyfully rose to the challenge of educating this highly promising child. They were particularly eager to take charge of his musical education and of developing his mind more generally. From his earliest childhood, the boy grew up surrounded by a world of music. His mother or his aunt would sing him to sleep with Brahms's Lullaby, a sleep protected by 'the curtain round the cot'. He found it unforgettable that he could dream on 'until milking time'. He would also remember that other lullaby: 'Sleep in gentle ease / little eyes shut please, / hear the raindrops in the dark, / hear the neighbour's doggy bark. / Doggy bit the beggar-man, / tore his coat, away he ran, / to the gate the beggar flees, / sleep in gentle ease.' Later, he kept a note of these lines. They may have reminded him of a vivid illustration by Ludwig von Zumbusch in the family copy of Schott's *Song-Book* of 1900, but in any event they were of the greatest importance to him and he even intended to base an entire theory on these verses.[11]

On 4 October 1903, the Wiesengrunds took their son to Frankfurt Cathedral and had him baptized into the Roman Catholic faith. This fact emerges from personal documents belonging to Franz Calvelli-Adorno and also from the baptismal book of the Catholic parish of St Bartholmew's.[12] While his mother's religion is given as Catholic, the entry for his father states: 'Oscar Alexander Wiesengrund, merchant, Israelite'. The ceremony was conducted by Chaplain Perabo.

Family lore narrates that Adorno's mother, a woman proud of her origins, wanted her son's paternal surname to be supplemented by the addition of her own name: Adorno. As an adult, her son retained the double-barrelled name Wiesengrund-Adorno, and used it at the start of his writing and academic career. But later on it was subjected to a slight modification. In his formal application for US citizenship in exile in California, he gave his name as Theodor W. Adorno, and it was under this name that his publications appeared thenceforth. His decision to jettison the Jewish name Wiesengrund in favour of the North Italian name Adorno, which his Corsican grandfather had once adopted because it sounded so impressive, tells us where his preferences lay. We know from the memoirs of Peter von Haselberg, a friend of the same age with whom he often played music, that, even as an adult, Adorno was fascinated by the magic of his mother's name, 'Calvelli-Adorno della Piana'. He seems in general to have had a definite penchant for families with aristocratic titles. Once the two had come to know each other better, the recently qualified lecturer proudly told Haselberg that

his mother's ancestors had been doges of Genoa and were related
to the princely Colonna family. 'He never explained this in greater
detail . . . He was astonished and scarcely able to conceal his delight
when I told him that in that case he must be a direct descendant of
Jupiter, whom the Colonnas claimed as their ancestor. He admitted that
he had not known this.'[13]

It is unclear whether he had an ironic relation to the etymological
origins of the name 'Adorno', which derives from the Italian word
'adorno' = 'adorned, decorated'. As an adult, he was conscious of such
personal foibles as his inexhaustible urge to communicate and a degree
of vanity that bordered on narcissism. He never made a secret of it, any
more than he denied the satisfaction he derived from the fact that
his name, Theodor W. Adorno, had become the symbol of a way of
thinking that was made famous under the name *critical theory* and that
has exercised a sustained influence in philosophy, in sociology, and in
musical and literary criticism.

Adorno's two first names, Theodor Ludwig, establish a connection
with his father's family as well as his mother's brother. By giving him
these names, his parents passed on an inheritance of divergent family
traditions. On the one hand, there was his father's search for material
security, with its reliance on the virtues of persistence and calculation;
on the other hand, there was his mother's gift for empathy, with its
emphasis on the creativity and spontaneity of art. We may ask whether
Adorno was conscious as he grew up of the complex nature of this
heritage. The question is not one we can answer, but one illuminating
fact is that his whole life long he preferred to use the affectionate
diminutive form of his name. As a child, an adolescent and an adult
he liked to be known as Teddie, and would often sign his letters 'Your
old Teddie'.

As the family grew in number, the need for a change of dwelling
became more pressing. They moved from the Schöne Aussicht to 19
Seeheimer Straße. Seeheim lies south of the River Main in the suburb
of Oberrad, a district that was absorbed into Frankfurt in 1900, but
retained its village character for many years thereafter. The family moved
here – *Dribbedebach*[14] – in 1914, shortly after the outbreak of the First
World War. They now occupied a two-storey detached house in a quiet
side road. There was a nearby tram stop, and it was easy to reach the
centre of town on the number 16 tram.

> Anyone who entered the house in Seeheimer Straße in Oberrad in
> which Adorno spent his youth experienced an environment to
> which he owed a protected childhood in the best sense of the
> word. The traditions that came together in his parents' house, the
> commercial spirit of Oscar Wiesengrund, his Jewish father from
> Frankfurt, and the aura of music that surrounded his mother
> Maria . . . , the shining eyes of her sister Agathe who was like a

second mother to him, are all preserved . . . in Adorno's thoughts and feelings.[15]

The larger family context, too, was highly ramified, just as the background of his mother and father was many-layered. His father's lifestyle had an Anglo-Saxon flavour, something that had rubbed off from the contact that was maintained with his brother Robert in London. In addition, he himself had spent some time in Britain, having lived there for a period before his marriage. In religious terms, he had become assimilated, a process that was facilitated by the liberal Frankfurt tradition. But this assimilation was not without its more problematic side, since, by detaching himself from Judaism, he surrendered an aspect of his own identity.[16] This may explain his somewhat ostentatious aversion to everything that was consciously Jewish. This hostility was directed in the first instance at the so-called Eastern Jews, i.e., East European Jews who had fled to Germany from the pogroms in Russia and Poland, and who had settled for the most part in the eastern part of the town. His son Teddie, too, was on his own testimony not immune to the arrogance assimilated Jews felt towards the East European Jews.[17] Siegfried Kracauer, who was to have considerable influence on Adorno's intellectual development later on, describes the East European Jews in his novel *Ginster*:

> Blank house façades, behind them courtyards from which the Jews poured out. They wore kaftans and flowing beards, they talked together in pairs as if there were four of them. They were Jews who looked so authentic, you thought they must be imitations.[18]

There was a huge gulf between the circumstances of these Jews and the elegant lifestyle of the Frankfurt Westend with which the Adornos identified, even though they did not live there. This sense of belonging to a relatively affluent and socially elevated stratum of society was very marked in the case of Oscar Alexander Wiesengrund, the successful businessman. As Peter von Haselberg remembers him, 'he was a short, slim, determined man. It was easy to see why he might have been an enthusiastic Anglophile, though it should be added that such enthusiasm was very widespread in Frankfurt before the First World War and was even fashionable as a gentle rebuke to the Prussians.'[19] Within the family what his father represented for Adorno was a form of individualism that was typical of the commercial ethos of the city, an individualism based on private means and experience of the world. The resulting self-confidence and attitude of tolerance seems to have been absorbed instinctively by his son. In addition, a kind of sober, secular attitude towards everything religious, and especially everything concerned with the Jewish religion, appears to have been transmitted from father to son. Like his father, Adorno had no real commitment to Judaism, or indeed to any other religion, although he flirted from time to time with Catholicism, perhaps from sympathy with his mother.[20] The Jewish *Lehrhaus* (house of learning) that was so influential in Frankfurt at the time was always alien to him.[21] On one occasion, he referred to his friends Erich Fromm and Leo Löwenthal, who were active in the *Lehrhaus*, as 'professional Jews'. And he ostentatiously kept his distance from the great Jewish scholars at the *Lehrhaus*, Martin Buber and Franz Rosenzweig. Indeed, to the horror of right-thinking people he even referred to Buber as the 'religious Tyrolean', or so Peter von Haselberg reports. Wiesengrund travestied Buber's *Legends of the Hassidim* under the title 'Stories of Rabbi Misje Schmal'. In his version the stories took the form of pointless jokes – folksy anecdotes that seemed like a blend of the writings of Peter Altenberg, Robert Walser and Martin Buber.[22]

In the early years of his childhood, Teddie's relationship with his father was marked by the latter's great tolerance and kindness. During adolescence Adorno may have come to regard his father as the embodiment of bourgeois values, the businessman interested in nothing but economic efficiency and profit, a man whose way of life was entirely unconnected with his own. In this sense it is likely that he had little time for his father and his father's ideals. However, this did not mean that he was lacking in respect or that he failed to recognize his father's achievements. Moreover, he had every reason to think highly of him. For Oscar Alexander's sense of loyalty to both his wife and his son knew no bounds, and he fully sympathized with the latter's artistic inclinations and his early intellectual ambitions. Oscar Alexander's proverbial generosity emerges clearly from the letters he wrote to different members of the family and from his selfless readiness to give his son both financial and moral support right up to the time of his emigration to the United States.

This literally uncomplicated relationship between father and son suggests that Oscar Alexander did not play a dominant role in the running of the household. As a businessman, he was not only out of the house all day long, he also had to make numerous time-consuming business trips. He was not only successful as an exporter; his wholesale business found plenty of customers in Frankfurt itself. In 1912 he presented his best wines at the Golden Jubilee Shooting Festival – bottles from the Rhine and the Palatinate, from the Saar and the Moselle. He even produced champagne for the marksmen. 'Frankfurt's wine trade had fully justified the confidence placed in it since the numerous wines on offer were all of outstanding quality.'[23] For Adorno as a boy, the several floors of his father's wine cellar were 'spookily pleasurable' places where he could play 'with school friends from the tough pub world of Sachsenhausen'.[24] Oscar Wiesengrund's function was to secure the economic foundations of the family's upper-middle-class standard of living. This he did. In addition, he took obvious personal pleasure in the concerts given at home, the frequent guests and the lively discussions on such topics as the current productions in the city theatre, the 'rather questionable performance of Beethoven's Violin Concerto' in the concert series put on by the Museumsgesellschaft in the Saalbau, or the current programme in the famous opera house. His precocious son took an active part in these discussions as he grew older and his curiosity increased. In his devotion to music, his love of art and his youthful curiosity he could rely on his mother's support, and such interests also found a ready listener in his beloved aunt.

Following her marriage, Maria Calvelli-Adorno found that she had moved a step upwards in society, and this success strengthened her self-confidence. With her half-Italian, half-French Catholicism, she represented a combination of romanticism and idealist devotion. As a former singer in the Imperial Viennese metropolis and also in Riga, she seemed to stand for an insecure world of art that may well have had bohemian overtones. The house in Seeheimer Straße was one in which visitors were welcome and to which they frequently came (partly because of the culinary skills of Anna, the maid). It was natural to have a gramophone in the living room, even though the educated classes tended to look down their noses at such innovations.[25]

From the very outset Maria's sister Agathe was a member of the inner circle of the family. Adorno always spoke of her as his 'second mother'. She made a major contribution to the musical life of the household, which echoed from morning to night with singing, and with keyboard sonatas by Bach, Mozart and Beethoven. It was thought natural for the ten-year-old boy to go to concerts, and the adult always had fond memories of his first encounters with Mozart, Beethoven or Mahler.[26] Agathe Calvelli played an important part in Adorno's literary education, as well as his musical upbringing. The few surviving letters between the two show very clearly how close they were and how their relationship was based on complete trust. Adorno admired both his mother and his aunt. He remembered how as a small boy he 'went to hear his mother sing at a charity concert. Because he identified with her so completely, he clambered up uninvited onto the stage after the applause and began to recite poems. He describes his precocious fluency as a mark of his ability to concentrate, the urge to speak as exhibitionism.'[27]

We may regard Adorno's basic sense of emotional and material security, together with the way he was surrounded by music, as of crucial importance for his personality. Music was the primary medium through which the intensity of his feeling for the two women was created. At the same time, his intensive preoccupation with music was an early source of highly personal experiences of achievement.

> The child who thinks he is composing when he plays around on the piano endows every chord, every dissonance and every

MATINÉE

zum Besten der hiesigen Stadtarmen

im Saale der Loge zur „Einigkeit"

Alte Rothhofstrasse 8

am 22. Februar 1880, Vormittag 10½ Uhr

PROGRAMM.

1. Ouverture zu „Idomeneo" . . . . *W. A. Mozart.*
   für Streichquartett.
2. Nocturne für Violine . . . . *J. Field*
   vorgetragen von **Carl Sidler.**
3. Trio in G für Clavier, Violine & Violoncello *J. Haydn.*
   vorgetr. von **L. G . . Philipp Heyl & Hermann Kolb.**
4. Die Fischer, Duett . . . . *C. M. Gabussi.*
   gesungen von **Agathe & Louis Calvelli Adorno.**
5. Romance aus der 8 Sonate für Violoncello . *B. Romberg.*
   vorgetr. von **Hermann Kolb.**

6. Andante religioso . . . . *P. Köhler.*
   für Doppelquartett.
7. Souvenir de Haydn, Fantasie für Violine . . *H. Leonard.*
   vorgetr. von **Ludwig Pörtner.**
8. Schmetterling setz dich . . . . *F. Abt.*
   gesungen von **Agathe Calvelli Adorno.**
9. Romance in F für Violine . . . . *L. v. Beethoven.*
   vorgetr. von **Philipp Heyl.**
10. Quartett in A für Clavier, Violine, Viola u.
    Violoncello . . . . *W. A. Mozart.*
    vorgetr. von **L. G . . L. Pörtner. W. English &
    H. Kolb.**

Herr **L. Hachenburger** war so gefällig sowohl die Proben als die
Leitung unseres Concertes zu übernehmen.

Figure 2 Programme for the charity concert in which there were
performances by Agathe and Louis Calvelli-Adorno

surprising turn of phrase with infinite importance. They have a freshness as if they were being heard for the first time, as if these particular sounds, formulaic though they are for the most part, had never existed before; as if they were pregnant with everything he imagined.[28]

In the family there were scarcely any doubts about the talented nature of the young boy who was evidently superior intellectually to most of his contemporaries and whose gifts were confirmed by his achievements at school. Thus during his childhood and youth the family bonds were confirmed by mutual admiration. Adorno's precocious behaviour and artistic talents seemed to confirm his mother's expectations, and by the same token they enabled him to develop the self-confidence to mature into the person he wanted to be.

No doubt, the adventurous life of the father of these 'two mothers' would have had its place in the imaginative world of the child. His legendary maternal grandfather, the officer in the French army from the country of *Colomba*, whom the Arabs had left unscathed during his military service in Algeria, who had wandered through the lands of Southern Europe and who bore such a magic-sounding Italian name, must surely have haunted the childhood dreams of the imaginative child like the hero of a fairy-tale. The 'two mothers' would no doubt have made their contribution to the story-telling about the hero in the family, for Adorno himself spoke of his grandfather with admiration.

But what about the other grandfather, the one on his father's side, with whom Teddie had dealings right up to the age when he left school? Belonging as he did to the generation of the period of the founding of the new German Empire, he may be supposed to have identified more with the Kaiser and the empire than the rest of the family. We do not know whether and to what extent David Thomas still abided by the rules governing Jewish life. But if he did, he would have done so as a Reform Jew. In any event, he would have been the only relative in a position to convey to Adorno an impression of the practices and religious rituals of the Jewish people, and an idea of their uniqueness. And he may perhaps have conveyed to his grandson in his own person the most authentic idea of the tensions that arose from emancipation: the conflict between the economically active citizen's wish to assimilate into the dominant society and his desire for freedom and enlighten-ment, on the one hand, and the persistence of such religious traditions as keeping the Sabbath, circumcision and the dietary laws, on the other.

The wider circle of the Wiesengrund family included, lastly, Teddie's various aunts and uncles, who lived mainly in *haute bourgeoise* circum-stances. Among these were Alice Betty Epstein and Jenny Villinger, who lived in Frankfurt, and the London uncle, Bernhard, whose family played a significant part in Adorno's life when he was forced to begin a second course of studies in Oxford after escaping from Germany following the Nazi takeover. We shall return to this phase of his life in due course.

The family in which Adorno grew up, and which formed an important element of his mental and emotional horizon as both a youth and an adult, can be seen to be unusually varied and stimulating: a collection of different socio-cultural models and ideas about the world. The test of the durability of these family links and interconnections came three decades later when he found himself defined as being 'of half-Jewish origin', a verdict that condemned him to permanent unemployment in Hitler's Germany. He then had to place his entire trust in this family network and rely on its selfless generosity. In later years, looking at the bourgeois nuclear family as a sociologist, he criticized it as an 'irrational natural relation'. Nevertheless, this criticism did not seduce him into denying the human value of this primary form of life that was so threatened with destruction. 'Under extreme conditions and their long drawn-out consequences, such as we see them in the case of refugees, for example, the family has shown itself to be strong despite everything, and frequently to be a powerhouse of survival.'[29]

3

Between Oberrad and Amorbach

In one's youth many things are taken as a promise of what life has to offer, of anticipated happiness.[1]

'One evening, in a mood of helpless sadness, I caught myself using a ridiculously wrong subjunctive form of a verb that was itself not entirely correct German, being part of the dialect of my native town. I had not heard, yet alone used, the endearing misconstruction since my first years at school. Melancholy, drawing me irresistibly into the abyss of childhood, awakened this old, impotently yearning sound in its depths.'[2] Childhood memories like these transmitted the sense of things irrevocably lost, but they also had a stimulating effect on Adorno's mental world. In other words, his artistic sensibility and critical mind fed on two principal sources.

On the one hand, it is not possible to overestimate the importance of the happiness that Adorno experienced in his parents' house in Frankfurt. The family in which he grew up corresponded in most respects to the picture of the bourgeois family that Horkheimer later described in his study *Authority and the Family*: 'The development and happiness of others is what is sought in the family. This gives rise to the conflict between the family and a hostile reality. In this respect, the family points the way not to bourgeois authority, but to the presentiment of a better human condition.'[3] Adorno frequently spoke of this presentiment of a better human condition during his own childhood and youth. For example, in response to the question of why he had returned to Germany after 1945 despite the barbarity of National Socialism and his forced emigration, he declared,'I wanted simply to return to the scene of my childhood, ultimately with the feeling that what we can achieve in life is little other than the attempt to recapture our childhood in a different form.'[4]

On the other hand, the particular social, cultural and political climate that predominated in Adorno's home town during this part of the 1920s down to his forced emigration created a sense of security that seemed self-evident, as was perhaps hinted at in his aperçu about the wrong subjunctive, which he wrote during his years in America. But, in addition, the specific urban culture of Frankfurt acted as a stimulus to intellectual autonomy and independence of thought.

Adorno's childhood years were spent in the period up to the outbreak of the First World War in a big-city environment rich in contrasts. On the one hand, the age of guards regiments, imperial manoeuvres and naval parades was not yet a thing of the past. At the same time, thanks to the sustained period of economic growth from the end of the Franco-Prussian War up to the turn of the century, a collective awareness that Germany was now a power in the world was becoming more prevalent. This was self-evident not just to the old and new power elites – the officers, the large landowners, the bankers and big industrialists. It was true also of the higher reaches of the civil service and the newly wealthy middle class. On the other hand, in contrast to the predominant ethos, a sceptical attitude towards national megalomania began to make itself felt, above all among the liberally inclined economic and cultural bourgeoisie that was particularly strong in a town like Frankfurt which could look back on a tradition of civic republicanism. It was by no means unusual to encounter a liberal and socially concerned outlook on the part of men close to the National and Social Association of Friedrich Naumann, a Frankfurt clergyman,[5] an outlook that outlasted the lost world war and may have made it easier to identify with the parliamentary democracy of the Weimar Republic.[6]

In 1928 Siegfried Kracauer published his novel *Ginster*. Kracauer, who was now the editor of the culture section of the *Frankfurter Zeitung*, had developed ties of friendship with Adorno while the latter was still in the sixth form at school, ties that had become closer with the passage of time. *Ginster* contains a vivid contemporary description of

> the metropolis that had grown historically, situated on a river between low-lying hills. Like other towns, it exploited its past to encourage the tourist industry. Imperial coronations, international congresses and a nationwide shooting competition took place within its walls, walls long since transformed into public parks. A monument has been erected to the landscape gardener. A number of Christian and Jewish families trace their origins back to their ancestors. But even families without a history have created banks that have connections with Paris, London and New York. Cultural institutions and the stock exchange are separated only in spatial terms.[7]

The process of industrialization was slow to develop in Frankfurt and the surrounding area in the nineteenth century. Barriers arising from the traditional economic function of the town and its cultural image could be overcome only with difficulty. Frankfurt had always been a centre for services in banking and commerce.[8] This meant that over long periods of time preferential treatment was given to the needs of commercial and finance capital at the expense of industrial capital. This feature determined the future of the town for a long time, both in its underlying economy and in its appearance. During Adorno's childhood there were still horse-drawn carts and hansom cabs. Public transport had just undergone electrification: the horse-drawn coach and the steam-driven bus gave way to the tram. Motorized transport started slowly to develop alongside a pulsating metropolitan life. The streets were filled primarily with businessmen and merchants, tradesmen and journeymen, rather than factory workers. Schoolchildren poured into the twelve high schools, eight middle schools, thirty primary schools or four private Jewish schools. Fashionably dressed society ladies strolled along the splendid streets wearing their Paris hats, contrasting sharply with the housewives and also with the country folk in their traditional costume who flocked to the city, particularly on market days. The maze of little streets around the Römer, the Schirn and the cathedral contained many little squares and niches where you could hear people gossiping in their usual Frankfurt dialect.[9] Adorno had mastered the dialect over the years, and sometimes spoke it. Building beyond the centre was on a generous scale; the different quarters of the town each had their own particular character. In the mornings, the iceman went round the suburbs ringing his bell and delivering the heavy blocks of ice for the iceboxes of the well-off. In the summer, the bilberry women from the Taunus and the Spessart regions would cry their wares in the streets, as did the potato sellers from the Wetterau, often in competition with the rag-and-bone men who were skilled in drawing attention to themselves with their cries of 'Iron, bones, rags, bottles, paper'. Every morning, the milkman delivered directly to the house, as did the grocer.[10]

The living conditions of the Wiesengrunds were a cut above the average. They were not those of the *haute bourgeoisie* typical of the patrician villas of the Westend, the villas near the Palmengarten, but the newly built house in Seeheimer Straße with its sandstone window surrounds was a perfect expression of the upper-middle-class standard of living of the wine exporter. In their house the family could live in the spacious comfort of their two-and-a-half floors, and in the summer they could enjoy the garden behind the house in which as a child Adorno could play and give his imagination free rein. The interior of the house may also have stimulated his imagination since, in tune with the taste of the time, its furnishings combined the styles of a variety of periods.

The house of the Wiesengrund family was designed with two purposes in mind, as was typical of middle-class dwellings of the time: to guarantee internal intimacy, on the one hand, and to make possible a certain outward show, on the other. So alongside the working areas and the kitchen, there were the private living rooms and bedrooms, and in addition there were rooms for entertaining in public, such as the salon with its obligatory oil paintings, with what Adorno remembered as

Böcklin's 'Island of the Dead over the sideboard', and the music room with the piano in the middle. It is questionable whether, as Kracauer put it, the furniture 'was supposed to mind its manners in front of the piano, and whether the only people allowed to approach it were those who knew how to respect the emotional life that could be ascribed to the instrument.'[11] In the case of the Wiesengrund family, the piano was anything but a mere ornament designed to show that the businessman whose time was limited could nevertheless be interested in the world of music. The piano was an integral part of the family life, and music-making was part of their daily activities. From going to concerts Adorno was familiar with 'the last movement of Haydn's Farewell symphony, the F sharp minor piece in which one instrument after another ceases to play and departs, until finally only two violins remain to extinguish the light.'[12] Adorno himself, who could already play pieces by Beethoven on the piano at the age of twelve – before that he had learnt the violin or viola[13] – is a witness to this life in and with music. His experience of music as a child includes 'lying in bed at night and pricking up my ears to listen to a Beethoven sonata for violin and piano when I was supposed to be asleep.'[14] Looking back at the age of thirty on his childhood, he remembered very clearly that, in his parents' house,

> there was very little symphonic and chamber-music literature that was not introduced into the family circle. This was thanks in part to the large volumes in landscape format that the bookbinder had bound uniformly in green. They seemed to have been made for the express purpose of turning their pages, and I was allowed to turn the pages long before I could read the notes, just following my memory and my sense of hearing. They even included Beethoven violin sonatas in curious adaptations. I have internalized many pieces, such as Mozart's G minor symphony, so deeply that it still seems to me today that no orchestra can ever reproduce the excitement of that introductory quaver movement as perfectly as the questionable touch of the child on the piano. Music like this fitted better than any other into the domestic environment. It was produced on the piano as if it were just a piece of furniture, and the performers who played it without any fear of false notes or awkward pauses were all part of the family.

The common practice of playing duets was a good aid to discipline. For, with duets, a young person 'who lives for the dream that he is himself an artist is not able to modify tempo and dynamics according to his own whims, as he is in the habit of doing with Grieg's *Lyrical Pieces*, but is forced to follow the letter and the instructions of the work.'[15]

In his early years, Adorno came into contact with the aura of art, and especially music, through the holidays the family frequently spent in the little town of Amorbach in the Odenwald.[16] The Wiesengrund family was friendly with the Spoerer family, the owners of the Post House Inn. Adorno's memories of Amorbach, which he wrote down and published some four decades after these happy times, convey movingly the powerful affection he retained for this magical place with the monastic buildings of the former Benedictine abbey in the midst of a hilly landscape, just to the south of the little town of Miltenberg on the River Main.

The walk over the long ridge path from Amorbach to Miltenberg comes to an end at a gate 'that is known as Chatterhole [*Schnatterloch*] because it is so cold in the forest [that your teeth chatter]. When you go through the gate, you suddenly arrive at the most beautiful medieval market-square, without any transition, just as in a dream.'[17] When the family stayed at the Post House Inn, Adorno would be woken up in the morning by the 'thunderous hammer blows' from the smithy next door 'that echoed the long-forgotten past, the prehistoric world of Siegfried.' In the Post House you could not only find excellent food and drink; in addition, the innkeeper and his family tried to satisfy the musical needs of their distinguished guests. Together with the piano there was a guitar, and, even though it had two strings missing, Teddie strummed on it, 'intoxicated by its dark dissonant sounds, probably the first I had encountered with so many notes, years before I heard a note of Schoenberg. My feeling was that music should be composed to produce the sound of that guitar. When, later on, I read Trakl's line "traurige Gitarren rinnen" [mournful guitars trickle on], what it reminded me of was that broken guitar in Amorbach.'[18]

Adorno was fascinated by the artists and musicians he encountered in Amorbach, a fascination that survives in the memoir he wrote late in life:

> In fact I came into contact in Amorbach with the circle around Richard Wagner. The painter Max Rossmann had his studio in an extension to the abbey buildings. We often sat on his terrace in the afternoons, drinking coffee. Rossmann had built the decor for Bayreuth productions. He was the true rediscoverer of Amorbach and used to bring singers from the festival ensemble there. Something of the luxurious Bayreuth style of life with its caviar and champagne transferred itself to the Post House Inn. At any rate, the kitchen and cellar surpassed everything that was to be expected of a country hostelry. I have a very clear memory of one of the singers, although I cannot have been more than ten at the time. He readily engaged me in conversation once he had noticed my passion for music and the theatre. . . . At a stroke I found myself swept up into the world of the grown-ups and in the world I had dreamt of, not yet realizing that the two were irreconcilable.[19]

   Enjoyment was not confined to the summer holidays in the idyllic
setting of Amorbach. The Wiesengrunds also entertained frequently at
home. Visitors were a daily occurrence and Adorno retained a clear
memory of many a house guest:

> When a guest comes to stay with his parents, a child's heart beats
> with more fervent expectation than it ever did before Christmas.
> It is not presents that are the cause, but transformed existence.
> The perfume that the lady visitor puts down on the chest of draw-
> ers while he is allowed to watch her unpacking has a scent that
> resembles memory even though he breathes it for the first time.
> The cases with the labels from the Suvretta Hotel and Madonna di
> Campiglio are chests in which the jewels of Aladdin and Ali Baba,
> wrapped in precious tissues – the guest's kimonos – are borne
> hither from the caravanserais of Switzerland and the South Tyrol
> in sleeping-car sedan chairs for his glutted contemplation. And,
> just as fairies talk to children in fairy-tales, the visitor talks
> seriously, without condescension, to the child of the house.[20]

This memory can be contrasted with a different one from his
childhood:

> In early childhood I saw the first snow-shovellers in thin shabby
> clothes. Asking about them, I was told they were men without
> work who were given this job so that they could earn their supper.
> Then they get what they deserve, having to shovel snow, I cried
> out, bursting uncontrollably into tears.[21]

There can be no doubt that, as an only child who was pampered
and protected by his mother and aunt, Adorno was highly sensitive.
According to his later testimony, the fact that he was given space to
develop his individuality suggests that his own experience must have
been the quintessence of a happy childhood. Leo Löwenthal recollects
that Adorno's was 'an existence you just had to love – if you were not
dying with jealousy of this beautiful, protected life – and in it Adorno
had gained the self-confidence that never left him his entire life.'[22]
   We must ask, however, how he went about internalizing the reality
principle, in other words, how did he manage to cope with growing up?
After all, that was what he aspired to, even if he was to say in later
years that the price of growing up was a loss of spontaneity and sensibility. The mature Adorno continually returned in his reflections to this
theme of the contradictory nature of the process of growing up. In the
1960s, he wrote an essay about his friend Siegfried Kracauer on the
occasion of Kracauer's seventy-fifth birthday. He describes there what
happens when a child takes his first step into adulthood and becomes
conscious of the pain of this transition:

The childhood image survives in the futile and compensatory determination to be a real adult. For it is precisely the adult that is infantile. All the more reason for the sadness whose lament can be heard in the mimicry, the more emphatically the smile assures us that everything is in the best of order. For a temperament like this, remaining a child means holding on to a way of being in which less happens to one; the expectation, however disappointed, that such ineradicable trust will be rewarded.[23]

Adorno's expectation of living in a humane world based on mutual respect and solidarity was frequently disappointed in the course of his life without his ever having armed himself against potential disillusionment. On the contrary, his thought was influenced from the outset by the perceived need to face up to reality without illusions and to anticipate its constraints.

Was this aspect of his personality the paternal inheritance of which I have already spoken? This inheritance – 'the earnest conduct of life', as Goethe phrased it – was something he had already benefited from in school. Here too the young Adorno showed himself to be extremely talented and of above-average intelligence. From the age of six he attended the Deutschherren middle school, which he could easily reach by tram. His 'two mothers' were concerned about him. They accompanied him to the tram stop and made sure he safely caught the number 16, which later on would also take him to the Kaiser-Wilhelm Gymnasium, to which he soon switched and where he remained from 1913 to 1921. Once when he was in the tram he was attacked by a neighbour as he was deep in conversation with a fellow pupil:

You goddamned little devil! Shut up with your High German and learn to speak German right. I had scarcely recovered from the fright Herr Dreibus gave me when he was brought home in a pushcart not long afterwards, completely intoxicated, and it was probably not much later that he died. He was the first to teach me what *Ranküne* [from the French, meaning rancour or spite] was.[24]

Looking back on his youth, Adorno described his behaviour in his early years at school as 'well-behaved and obedient', but as the behaviour of a child 'who purchases through his compliance the freedom to think independently and to join the opposition.'[25] His scope to do as he pleased sprang from the fact that he was protected by the dubious aura of precociousness. Nevertheless, at the age of forty, he recorded his reflections on the complicated situation of the precocious child. The early maturer finds himself oppressed by the painful compulsion to deliver on his promise. This leads him to anticipate in the imagination experiences that subsequently have to be laboriously lived through again in the shape of real encounters and challenges:

Contact with the non-self . . . becomes for the early maturer an
urgent need. The narcissistic direction of his impulses, indicated
by the preponderance of imagination in his experience, positively
delays his maturing. . . . He is struck down by passion; lulled too
long in the security of his autarky, he reels helplessly where he
had once built his airy bridges. The infantile traits in the handwriting of the precocious are not an empty warning.[26]

School experiences of a precocious youth

At grammar school Theodor did not have good handwriting, but it must
have been passable. For he received good marks in all subjects and top
marks in most subjects, except for mathematics, physics and handwriting (in those days pupils were still given marks for the neatness of
their handwriting). He was exempted from gym lessons and religious
instruction. In his leaving certificate, on 2 March 1921, he was even
given high marks for 'behaviour' and 'diligence'. His dealings with the
teachers were almost entirely unproblematic, as was his grasp of the
demands of the curriculum. Nevertheless, as a boy who played music
and wrote poetry he had mixed feelings about school as an institution.
This had nothing to do with the teachers and their approach to teaching
a humanist syllabus. What he found difficult was the school's insistence
on discipline and the emphasis on classification and standardization in
the teaching process, as well as the conformism that was bound up with
the idea of loyalty to the class and the school.

He wrote about this in an essay for the *Frankfurter Schülerzeitung*
(Frankfurt School Magazine), whose first issue appeared in October
1919. This essay discussed the 'teacher–pupil relationship' in an unmistakably precocious tone. Nevertheless, it reflected the experiences of
a youth of seventeen, which it summed up in the words, 'From the
outset, there is a disharmony of the soul between teacher and pupil.'[27]
Although this was a youthful piece of writing, and in fact his first published text, its linguistic form and mode of argument tell us something
about the author's mental attitude and way of thinking. He began by
discussing the topicality and relevance of his subject against the background of current trends and ideas, and went on to look at fundamental
problems of education and teaching. He thought it encouraging that
at such a turbulent time – it was the end of the First World War – 'the
profoundest questions of our lives were the subject of debate, instead
of being ignored in a cowardly and complacent apathy', and that new
approaches were being entertained. The youthful author attempted
to give a precise account of the teacher–pupil relationship in schools
without following the fashion of blaming one side or the other. The
frequently lamented deformation of the personality of the teacher
that was so often depicted in contemporary literature, the tendency to

stereotyping and standardization, was a product of his profession: 'Man becomes a teacher through his profession. His strict pedagogical objectives find themselves confronted by the warmth of the pupil who is in search of something to hold on to, who has a powerful sense of self and many demands on life.'[28]

This fundamental critique of the pupil–teacher relationship must be contrasted with Adorno's many positive experiences during his eight years at grammar school, in particular in his relationship with his German teacher. This man was a committed teacher, full of pedagogical ideals and devoted to his profession. Reinhold Zickel was a man with literary ambitions who in addition to his teaching activities wrote poems, dramas and novels. His ideas, which were a blend of Protestantism, idealism and expressionism, made a powerful impression on the young Theodor Wiesengrund. Although the latter strongly resisted his teacher's 'impetuosity and categorical assertiveness', Zickel

overturned the complacent liberal assumptions that had informed my childhood. I shall never forget a conversation in which I talked about tolerance and he countered by giving me for the first time an idea that there could be an objective truth lying beyond a kind of intellectual laissez-faire. He literally brought my burbling fluency to a halt. The B+ that he gave me for an essay, instead of the A I had come to expect, cured me of any modest ambition. In an essay on the subject What do we expect from poetry?, I had used the word 'total', and, with incorruptible love, he put his finger on the clichéd and purely formal comment and on its amateurishness. Experiencing this at the age of sixteen leaves an indelible mark.[29]

In his autobiographical conversations, Leo Löwenthal says of his school years in Frankfurt that the teachers rarely lived up to the ideal of this German teacher, but that for the most part they were not nationalistic. 'A "Wilhelmine" tone was hardly in evidence . . . Many of my fellow pupils came from prosperous Jewish households. There really was an *esprit de corps* among internationally orientated young people who often, encouraged by their parents, got together after school to read and discuss.'[30] In contrast to this, Adorno saw his own schooldays at the Kaiser-Wilhelm Gymnasium in a less rosy light, despite the encouragement of his German teacher. This was because, as the boy who came top of his class, he was subject from time to time to bullying by his fellow pupils, 'who set upon a single schoolfellow, thrashed him and, when he complained to the teacher, denounced him as a sneak.' Adorno regarded such behaviour as an omen of the latent receptivity to the ideology of National Socialism, a tendency he expected from those of his contemporaries 'who could not put together a correct sentence but found all of mine too long. After all, did they not abolish

German literature and replace it with their own writ?'[31] A reminiscence
of Erich Pfeiffer-Belli,[32] who was two years older than Adorno, may
throw light on the general impression made by the obviously gifted
younger boy.

> He was the pampered child of his family.... At home he was
> called Teddy and this nickname had somehow become known at
> school. ... During break the older boys would wander round slowly
> in a circle, while we, the younger ones, played our boisterous
> games. Teddy had a few close friends who, like him, failed to
> notice that some enemy or other had stuck a piece of paper on his
> back with the word 'Teddy' in large letters. In a trice there was
> a howling mob after him shouting 'Teddy' at their unsuspecting
> victim. At the time, Teddy was a slightly built, shy boy who simply
> did not realize what was going on. We all knew that he was
> Jewish. But the uproar in the playground was not an anti-Semitic
> demonstration. Its target was this unique person who outshone
> even the best boys in the class. It was a stupid boys' trick, nothing
> more.[33]

This anecdote shows that the young Wiesengrund was seen as a person
who was accustomed to live in an individual world of his own and
therefore occupied an almost exclusive position. The esteem he enjoyed
as a clever boy attracted the barely concealed hostility of the larger
group. His tendency to withdraw into himself appeared to them as
arrogance, shyness or perhaps awkwardness. It is not surprising that, in
his contribution to the school paper, Adorno was more critical of his
schoolmates than of the teachers as a group. According to the sixth-
former's account, the pupils as a 'plurality of human beings' tend not
just to fail to appreciate 'that in life the human aspect has priority over
the intellectual', but, in addition, they end up 'hating and condemning
the teacher without the pupil being capable of seeing him as a human
being.' The constraints of school are converted to a mood of resistance
in the pupils that is shot through with envy and the desire for revenge.
This explains why the pupils band together against the teacher as the
many against the one, why they 'form a community of interests in order
to oppose him – frequently under the banner of "comradeship" – in
order to destroy him psychologically.'[34] Only when a pupil grows older
will he develop some control over such psychological reactions, thanks
to an awakening 'sense of shame'. Such an older pupil will be interested
first and foremost in the teacher's mastery of his subject. Nevertheless,
'the intellectual aspect of this question is ... no more than a cloak that
covers the sense of shame about his original feeling.'[35]
   It is hard to say how much of Adorno's own personal experience
entered into these sensitive reflections. But we can say that what he
writes evinces an acute self-consciousness. Enough indeed to give us

pause when the few authentic descriptions of him at this time, like the one by Erich Pfeiffer-Belli, emphasize his introversion and timidity. Could this picture of him be a projection? Adorno did not lack self-confidence and this is why he appeared to be precociously grown up. Could it not be the case that his self-confidence induced an insecurity and embarrassment in his fellow pupils that they were reluctant to admit? It is perfectly true that he could not be described as boisterous. He appeared frail and was exempted on health grounds from taking part in the hated sports lessons. However, there is nothing to support the view that he was timid or melancholic or that he suffered from inhibitions or anxieties. Thus a photograph of 1917 shows a slim youth standing in a relaxed pose with one hand on a chair rest and the other round the neck of a large dog, the Great Dane of his childhood and adolescent years.[36] His face, above all the nose and eyes, appears strikingly sensitive. There is no hint of a smile, as if such a gesture would be quite out of place. His gaze can be interpreted as reflecting an attitude that is directed inwards, calmly expressing the question What experiences and encounters will the world have to offer me? His pensive look is mixed with a kind of dreaminess. He seems to be untouched by such contemporary events as had already been revealed by the violent excesses of the First World War. How could such a person know that his would be the face of one of the many victims of the century?

Adorno experienced the four war years from the perspective of a schoolboy who had grown up in a family that kept its distance from the wave of patriotic war fever and rampant nationalist arrogance. Nevertheless, like other boys of his age he read the *Pocket Guide to the World's Navies* and dreamed of becoming the captain of a warship. 'We bought the models of the different ships in the school stationery shop.'[37] His father had received his call-up papers. Years later, he would be honoured for his war service.[38]

During the winter of 1918–19, Frankfurt, like everywhere else, was not spared the food shortages, plundering, mass excesses and uprisings that followed the victory of the revolution that was celebrated in the streets and the city squares. In November 1918, armed sailors and dockworkers, the 'storm petrels of the Revolution', arrived at the central station. Preparations had been made to use territorial reserves to disarm the revolutionaries from Kiel. But the political tide favoured the revolutionaries, who at once joined forces with the workers' councils in the factories. For a time they had their headquarters in the exclusive Frankfurter Hof Hotel. From there, under the leadership of the sailors' leader, Hermann Stichelmann, they authorized Georg Voigt, the left-leaning liberal mayor, to continue in office.[39] Despite the mass demonstrations of tens of thousands of people that the Council of Soldiers and Workers had called for, despite the red flag waving from the central station and the Römer, the influence of the revolutionaries in the town was no more than a passing episode. After the elections to the city

council in March 1919, of the ninety-six seats, the majority Social
Democratic Party received thirty-six, the USPD (Independent Socialists)
eight, the Democratic Party twenty-three, the Catholic Centre Party thirteen, the Deutsche Volkspartei nine, the German National Party five
and the Middle Class Alliance two.[40] The traditions of St Paul's Church
in Frankfurt might be thought to have made it the ideal location for the
Constituent Assembly,[41] but in the event the government of the Reich
opted for the small town of Weimar in central Germany. Undaunted by
this affront, the citizens of Frankfurt decided to take advantage of their
favoured geographical position as a trade centre. A mere eleven months
after the end of the war, the city witnessed the opening of the Frankfurt
International Fair, and none other than the Reich president, Friedrich
Ebert, was welcomed at the opening ceremony by Ludwig Landmann, a
town councillor and subsequently mayor.

When the document authorizing the Weimar Constitution was finally
signed on 11 August 1919, Theodor Wiesengrund-Adorno was just four
weeks short of his sixteenth birthday. This was a time when he was
reading with fascination *The Theory of the Novel* by Georg Lukács.
This book, which had appeared only shortly before, was a philosophically orientated tract inspired by Hegel's objective idealism. Lukács
was a Hungarian philosopher who became an orthodox Marxist soon
after the publication of the *Theory of the Novel*. He had a significant
influence on Adorno's intellectual development, even though in later
years fundamental disagreements were to open up between them. Lukács
had begun by attempting to marry Georg Simmel's *Philosophy of Money*
and Max Weber's analysis of capitalism with the philosophy of Karl
Marx. Later on, he was concerned with the synthesis of Hegel and Marx
on the basis of a dialectical materialist philosophy of history. At the
heart of his influential book *History and Class Consciousness* of 1922
lay the proletariat, which was regarded as the identical subject-object of
world history, as well as such concepts as 'reification' and Marx's notion
of 'commodity fetishism'. According to Lukács, the solution to all the
problems of the development of society was to be found in the riddle of
the commodity form, which led to a reified structure of consciousness
for every member of society.[42]

Ernst Bloch's *Spirit of Utopia*, a book that appeared in 1918, had
a similar value for the young Adorno, who described it later as the
author's *magnum opus*. In this book Bloch explores the idea of yearning as the foundation of a messianic design of history. He called his
utopia 'concrete' because according to Marx's history of philosophy the
proletariat was defined as the active agent of historical change. It was
concrete, moreover, because it undertook to explore the art, music and
painting of the West, as well as the works of popular culture, in search
of the image of a society free from domination.[43] The enthusiasm the
seventeen-year-old Adorno felt on reading Bloch comes through even
in retrospect:

The dark brown volume of over 400 pages, printed on thick paper, promised something of what one hopes for from medieval books, something I had felt as a child at home, in the calf leather *Heldenschatz* [Treasury of Heroes], a belated eighteenth-century book of magic full of abstruse instructions many of which I am still pondering. The *Spirit of Utopia* looked as though it had been written by Nostradamus himself. The name Bloch had the same aura. Dark as a gateway, with a muffled blare like a trumpet blast, it aroused the expectation of something vast, an expectation that quickly rendered the philosophy with which I had become acquainted as a student suspect as shallow and unworthy of its own concept. . . . I had the feeling that here philosophy had escaped the curse of being official . . . Bloch's was a philosophy that could hold its head high before the most advanced literature; a philosophy that was not calibrated to the abominable resignation of methodology. . . . The book . . . seemed to me to be one prolonged rebellion against the renunciation within thought that extends even into its purely formal character.[44]

Adorno's reading of these books shows that, at a period when a re-volutionary mood was widespread, he was preoccupied with the theory of the decay of bourgeois culture as well as with the philosophical Marxism of his age. Of course, the discussion of Marx's philosophy of history was in the air at the time. To anyone in Frankfurt it was impossible to overlook the fact that the transformation of society went hand in hand with the polarization of social living conditions.

Arousing philosophical interests in the musical soul: Kracauer's influence on Adorno

During this phase of social upheaval and extreme political tension between right-wing and left-wing radicalism, Theodor Wiesengrund met an unusual Jewish intellectual who was to turn out to be a meticulous, sociologically trained observer of that age of far-reaching changes and who believed that the survival of the still very young Weimar democracy, caught as it was between an extreme individualism and a reactionary fixation on authorities, depended on reconciling opposites.

While at the Gymnasium, Adorno, who was still almost as young as in the photograph I have described, met Siegfried Kracauer through a friend of his parents. This encounter made such an impact on Kracauer that he recorded the impression it made on him in his autobiographical novel *Georg*:

He wore a green jacket made from loden cloth which, together with his red tie, was a rough cloak in which he looked like a little

prince. Leaning on his mother's chair, he answered the questions
I put to him in a dull tone that contradicted the large, mournful
eyes that gazed out from beneath long lashes. Their expression
hinted at a mystery that lay hidden in the youth in the same way
that he was concealed in the coarse material.[45]

For Adorno too, who is called Fred or Freddie in the novel, the meeting
was of considerable importance.

> I was a student at the Gymnasium when I met him towards the
> end of the First World War. A friend of my parents, Rosie Stern,
> had invited the two of us to her house. She was a teacher at the
> Philanthropin, where Kracauer's uncle, the historiographer of the
> Frankfurt Jews, was a member of the faculty. As was probably our
> hostess's intention, a close friendship sprang up between us.[46]

The friendships of the so carefully guarded child of the Wiesengrunds
developed in proportion to his ability to free himself from his parents'
overprotectiveness as he grew older. Music was one way to achieve
this. Whenever possible, he looked for and found partners to play duets
by Haydn, Brahms, Schubert and Mahler. 'Playing duets made me a
present of the geniuses of the nineteenth century at the beginning of
the twentieth.'[47] This almost daily music-making had nothing to do with
what used to be known as 'edification'. Adorno was already deadly
serious about music. He even entertained thoughts of becoming a professional musician or composer. So it is not surprising that as early as
his final year in school he started to attend the Hoch Conservatory. This
conservatory was established by a citizen of Frankfurt, Dr Joseph Hoch,
who grew up in a wealthy family that later fell on hard times. Thanks
to an inheritance in later life, Hoch came into the possession of a considerable capital. His will provided for the foundation of a conservatory
that would enable young people to enjoy the same thorough musical
training that he had been denied in his youth. As early as four years
after his death, in September 1878, the conservatory was inaugurated
initially in the Saalhof opposite the Eiserne Steg, the iron footbridge
over the River Main, and then, ten years later, it was housed in its own
new three-storey building on a larger scale.[48] This important foundation
was clearly modelled on the Leipzig Conservatory that had been established by Felix Mendelssohn-Bartholdy. It provided the commercial city
of Frankfurt with a sustained and enduring stimulus to its musical life,
not least through the additional opportunities for performances in the
framework of the concert series organized by the Museumsgesellschaft.
After the First World War, the Hoch Conservatory fell on hard times; it
was badly affected by the hyper-inflation of those years. This crisis phase
coincided with the time in which Wiesengrund-Adorno studied composition with the respected Bernhard Sekles and piano with Eduard Jung.[49]

He also took private lessons from both men. The string quartet he composed during his training was performed by the Lange Quartet in 1923. This was by no means unusual, for in the 1920s Frankfurt had the facilities to provide an outstanding forum for new music. One of its most active advocates was the young Hermann Scherchen, who directed the museum concerts and was responsible for the 'New-Music Week'. The beginning of his friendship with Adorno dates back to those years.

Did Adorno even notice that, from the summer of 1922 on, inflation had begun to transform urban life in Frankfurt? According to Rolf Hilbrunn, with whom Adorno was friendly at the time, people were overcome by a boundless search for pleasure:

Dance halls (known as '*Dielen*') sprang up everywhere, decorated with the outlandish colours and confusing curves that were typical of amateurish attempts at expressionism. Nightclubs competed with each other to put on the most risqué shows. Gambling clubs opened up everywhere in the wealthier suburbs where the impoverishment of the middle classes had started, and many a worthy pensioner eagerly seized the opportunity of improving his financial position by renting out some of his seven-room apartment by the evening. The purchasing power of the Mark fell from week to week, and then from day to day, and even from hour to hour.[50]

Although no end was in sight to the collapse of the currency, the eighteen-year-old youth whom Leo Löwenthal describes as 'the pampered young gentleman from a well-to-do family' could embark on a journey to the south, to the South Tyrol and the Dolomites. It appears that he could afford a style of life that set him apart from the general poverty and misery of the inflation years. His father's business was unaffected by the all-too-common closures and bankruptcies, evidence that the cautious Wiesengrund had invested part of his fortune in material assets. As an only son, Adorno was the main beneficiary of the relative prosperity of the family which survived through the precarious postwar years. He could not only finance the trip to Italy, but could also take every opportunity to retreat with his family or with friends to Amorbach, where he spent his time reading or talking.

There was no lack of topics for such discussions. Chief among these were events from the cultural life of Frankfurt, such as lectures at the university, authors' readings, a concert in the Saalbau or a stage performance at one of the five city theatres. A visit to one of the last was the occasion of a clever article about expressionist drama, written while Adorno was still in his last year at school. This article, entitled 'Expressionism and Artistic Truthfulness', was published in *Die neue Schaubühne* in 1920. It was one of the first articles of his career as a writer and contained his critique of the expressionist currents of the day. It expressed his distrust of the exaggerations of the self that thinks itself truthful. This glorified individual was said to confront a world which he rejected as degenerate, alien and depraved. The expressionist gesture that viewed individual experience as a reflection of the whole world was false. 'The symptom of the ultimate untruthfulness of expressionism is the disintegration of realities – the world robbed of its reality becomes a plaything in the hands of one who takes it up only for the sake of duality and not to explore its meaning through this duality.'[51] What Adorno articulates here, albeit in a fairly rudimentary way, is the idea that art is not confined either to the realm of the beautiful or to the expression of an artist's personality. Instead, it claims to express the truth, and this is the source of its ethical power. Whether or not a work of art satisfies this claim to truth is to be measured in the first instance not by the contents or the political message of, for example, a play, or by the world-views of its protagonists, but by what is expressed through the artistic form of the work. This aesthetic form has to be embedded in the historical state of development of the artistic material. Only by such means can an artist overcome the limitations of his own self and give artistic shape to typical realities lying beyond the individual.

Adorno sharply criticized the literary forms of late expressionism as typified by such works as Reinhard Sorge's play *Der Bettler* (The Beggar) because here too the literary subject matter was derived from the suffering individual and his personal ideological conflicts. At the same time, he objected to Fritz von Unruh, a writer who enjoyed great esteem in Frankfurt, because in his play *Platz* he had failed to portray his characters' individuality as rooted in their historical context. On the contrary, they simply embodied abstract ideas, something scarcely compatible with the erotic obsessions that Unruh had foregrounded.

> Because the author is too weak to turn the hero into the bearer of a historical event on the basis of his own egotistic erotic fixation, because he necessarily fears that the pettiness of his content may cause him to appear trivial and commonplace against the sharply chiselled forms of a background historically articulated in any way, he lets his drama drift in a mist of an irony distant from reality. ... Hence the drama lacks any possibility of crystallization; no artistically convincing form emerges from it.[52]

In tune with this opinion, and with striking self-confidence, Adorno ends up on this note: 'One will have to ask oneself whether Fritz von Unruh is to continue being taken seriously as an artist.'[53]

This uncompromising sentence may explain why Adorno's review was not published at the time, unlike his essay on expressionism. After all, following the production of the pacifist play *Ein Geschlecht* (A Generation) in the Frankfurt Theatre towards the end of the war, Unruh had been regarded as the outstanding representative voice of the younger generation. The theme of the play, topically enough, was the situation of the individual who sacrifices himself in order to keep the wheels of modern technical warfare turning. In the culture section of the *Frankfurter Zeitung*, Heinrich Simon, the editor, published a euphoric account of a performance of the play. Adorno did not allow himself to be deterred from expressing an opinion that went against the prevailing judgement. Under the general direction of Karl Zeiß, innovators such as Georg Kaiser could gain a hearing, with plays such as *Die Bürger von Calais* (The Burghers of Calais), and plays by Carl Sternheim and Paul Kornfeld could be produced. Such writers were without exception social critics who denounced the double morality of a declining bourgeoisie, while proclaiming the self-discovery of an ethical, unaccommodated subjectivity which often took the form of an impassioned expressionism. Adorno's highly nonconformist judgements on these plays show that he engaged in a very personal way with the artistic questions of his day and that his self-confidence deserved to be taken seriously. He was deeply involved in the culture of his native city, its theatre, its concerts and the opera.[54] But also his early membership of exclusive groups of artists and intellectuals and the generous funding of his own individual interests did not prevent him from taking note of political events during the Weimar Republic. Quite the reverse. In a discussion of the concerts of the Chamber Music Festival in Frankfurt in the summer of 1923, at a time when of the half a million inhabitants of the city some 70,000 were unemployed, he began his article with the observation that the catastrophic economic and political situation of the German Reich had deteriorated to the point where it was no longer bearable. He commented further on the Franco-Belgian occupation of the Ruhr after the suspension of reparations payments to the Allies. It was all the more astonishing, he noted, that despite these grave difficulties and despite the city's chronic financial problems it had been possible to organize an outstanding programme of seven chamber concerts. Indeed, this was perhaps even more remarkable given that 'it had been necessary to curtail expenditure on externals.' The only cause for regret was that no modern French music could be included because of the political complications with Germany's western neighbour. The concert-going public was nevertheless richly compensated by the performance of works by Schoenberg, Schreker, Stravinsky, Bartók, Busoni, Delius and Hindemith.

> Everything was ruled out that might have distracted the public's attention – from sumptuous theatrical decorations to the numerical power of the arrogant modern orchestra and the cult of the virtuoso conductor. We owe it to Hermann Scherchen that the festival was able to be held at all and that it could concentrate on serious artistic matters without needing to make concessions to the coarse pleasure-seeking needs of the larger public.[55]

What is notable about Adorno's position here is not just the already noted criticism of a self-satisfied culinary attitude towards so-called serious music, but also the youthful author's asceticism. This may have been based on his disapproval of a style of life that became common, particularly in large cities like Frankfurt and Berlin after the currency reform of 1923 and the so-called miracle of the *Rentenmark*.[56] Heilbrunn recollected that 'the delight about the recovery of the economy expressed itself in the intensified desire to enjoy the beauties and pleasures of the world. The balls and parties of the winter season allowed people to forget the sacrifices that had been made to bring the new order into being.'[57] Denouncing this ostentatiously happy-go-lucky approach to life as a sign of the decadence of the bourgeois world was very much the fashion among left-wing intellectuals. Adorno was not alone in his disapproval when he opposed the continuation of the classical bourgeois tradition of music for its own sake and attacked the cult of pleasure as superficial. What he wanted from music was human seriousness, a strict attention to form and the superseding of the old and familiar by the techniques of atonality.

Adorno's musical *tour d'horizon* as occasioned by the Chamber Music Festival in the difficult year of 1923 remained unpublished at the time. This should not prevent us from reading it as a testimony to his personal perception of the contemporary intellectual situation. As in other texts, cultural phenomena are read and judged in relation to the circumstances of the postwar years, to the wretched condition of Germany. At the same time, his hopes for a completely different phase were expressed clearly enough. Adorno longed for change; his thoughts were concerned with a radically different state of affairs, particularly in music and literature.

Adorno's image of himself was that of an intellectual, not necessarily an isolated intellectual, but a mind willing to assume the personal risks associated with being provocative. While he was still at school he already thought of himself as belonging among those who are interested in learning and culture, and he behaved, wrote and talked in ways appropriate to his image of this group of people. His self-definition as an intellectual contrasted with a youthful tendency to snobbery which he made no attempt to conceal. A symbol of this 'was the fact that he never wore a wristwatch but, as if practising to become an old uncle of the previous generation, he would regularly take his gold repeater out of his waistcoat pocket and listen to it chime on the hour and quarter-hour. He would leave the lid shut since he wanted only to hear the chime that relieved him of the necessity of reading the dial. He occasionally referred to himself as Dapsul von Zabelthau, the magician in a story by E. T. A. Hoffmann.'[58] Highly sociable by nature, he had the cultivated manners of the middle class and was always meticulous and polite; in other words, he had mastered the conventions of his social milieu. It was this mastery that enabled Adorno, who regarded himself as the advocate of the avant-garde, to arrange for private performances of works of the Second Viennese School in middle-class Frankfurt houses. These works would be performed by the quartet led by the violinist Rudolf Kolisch, whom he personally thought outstanding. And when his initiatives met with success his commitment knew no bounds. Even while he was still at school, he would let no opportunity pass for a conversation about philosophical or literary subjects. Siegfried Kracauer is just one of those, albeit one of the most important, who would discuss philosophy with him at school. 'For years Kracauer read the *Critique of Pure Reason* with me regularly on Saturday afternoons. I am not exaggerating when I say that I owe more to this reading than to my academic teachers.'[59]

This statement confirms that, while still at school and during his early years as a student, Adorno was strongly influenced by Kracauer's opinions. Kracauer, who, like his pupil, never respected the boundaries between the different disciplines, was born in 1889 into the family of a Jewish businessman in modest circumstances. He grew up in the home of an uncle who taught at the Philanthropin, the Reform Gymnasium of the Israelite community, and who also documented the history of the Jews in Frankfurt. In order to have a profession that would give him material security, Kracauer first studied architecture in Darmstadt and subsequently philosophy and sociology in Berlin, where he came into contact with Georg Simmel.

There was an age difference of fourteen years between Kracauer and his protégé. This difference was no obstacle to their lifelong friendship, difficult though the relationship became at times. The correspondence between the two men extends over almost forty years and shows in quite a painful way that, despite their mutual attachment, there were repeated disagreements and conflicts triggered by feelings of jealousy. Hurt feelings and differences of opinion led to their breaking off contact from time to time. These disagreements had little to do with the age difference between these two highly self-willed men, but rather with the fact that neither liked to give way on a point of principle. In an article entitled 'Thoughts on Friendship', Kracauer reflects on friendships between people of different ages:

> The young man who is still developing looks to his friend for confirmation of his plans, of his spiritual nature. He leans on the older man even as he contradicts him. His as yet undefined character experiences pleasure at encountering fixed boundaries. . . . He speaks without restraint, expresses his opinions in lengthy monologues . . . ; he places himself at the centre of interest.[60]

For the older man, in contrast, the urgent questions of his younger partner are a constant challenge. They 'keep his mind alert, free him from the fetters of his daily concerns and lead him back to his own roots, to the core of his own nature.'[61] The fundamental disagreements between Kracauer and Adorno were primarily aesthetic. At issue was the question whether or not the gulf between mass culture and authentic works of art could be bridged. In the middle of the 1920s, when Adorno first broached this question in connection with music, the two men quarrelled for the first time, since it brought into focus the real divergences of opinion about their respective critical or sociological approaches to everyday cultural phenomena.

As is well known, Kracauer and Adorno met regularly in the 1920s to work through philosophical texts together. They began with Kant's *Critiques*, but these were followed by Hegel and Kierkegaard. Adorno was very much the learner in this situation. As he later said, Kracauer made philosophy 'come alive for me'. Under Kracauer's guidance, philosophy became a set of 'coded texts from which the historical situation of mind could be read.'[62] The key idea in their discussions was to interpret the different philosophies as force fields: 'Without being able to account for it fully, through Kracauer I perceived for the first time the expressive moment in philosophy: putting into words the thoughts that come into one's head.'[63] This involved a process that Kracauer described as 'seminal dialogue'. In an essay written for the *Frankfurter Zeitung* in March 1923, Kracauer gave a slightly precious account of his ideas. He maintained that the 'truth is to be sought in a struggle between different figures', a process that results in 'acts of spiritual procreation'.

> None of the participants in the discussions emerges from them exactly as he entered them. . . . The fruits of discussion have been engendered by the talking process, by the existential attachment between the interlocutors. . . . The creation of dialogue becomes a form of living together, and both partners advance in their own existence by each acting as midwife to the other.[64]

One of Kracauer's friends at the time was Leo Löwenthal, who met Adorno through him just as Adorno was finishing his school-leaving examinations.[65] Löwenthal describes Adorno from memory as 'the classical image of a poet, with a delicate way of moving and talking.'[66] Löwenthal himself had been born in Frankfurt in November 1900. He came from a background rather like that of Adorno, who was three years his junior. His father was a doctor, but Löwenthal, having passed the wartime school-leaving examination in 1918, ignored his father's wishes and studied almost anything but medicine in Frankfurt, Heidelberg and Gießen. His socialist views did not prevent him from working at the Free Jewish *Lehrhaus* in Frankfurt while he was still a student. The *Lehrhaus* was a kind of 'Jewish centre for adult education; its spiritual fathers were Franz Rosenzweig and Martin Buber'.[67] In 1923 he took his doctorate at Frankfurt University with a dissertation on the social philosophy of Franz von Baader.

Shortly after Kracauer and Adorno had been introduced to each other in Frankfurt, Kracauer published his epistemological study *Sociology as Science*, on which he had begun work in 1920. One of its strands of thought is concerned with his conviction that the dissolution of meaning in a chaotic world forces the isolated subject to rely on himself. 'The breakdown of meaning brings about men's descent into the hell of historical time; meaning, which was once a given, is now sought by individuals ... in different ways.'[68] For sociology, whose task is to penetrate the concrete mass of phenomena, this loss of meaning creates the necessity to 'find a path back to the sphere of individual reality.'[69] These ideas evidently made an impression on Adorno, who was just embarking on the first term of his university studies and was familiarizing himself with academic culture. For in the same year in which Kracauer wrote those sentences, Adorno wrote a music review in terms that came very close to his friend's ideas. 'Only from the vantage point of the self and the decisions it makes is it possible to transcend the self. No objective home shelters us; we must build our own home.'[70]

These sentiments could serve as the motto for the astonishingly well-defined intellectual position of the young philosophy student. At the time, he was still studying composition at the Hoch Conservatory while tirelessly writing concert reviews and pieces of music which he tried to have published. He was able to call on an array of distinguished journals for this purpose. Examples are the *Zeitschrift für Musik*, the *Neue Blätter für Kunst und Literatur* and, later on, the *Musikblätter des Anbruch*, which appeared in Vienna, as well as *Pult und Taktstock*. What strikes the reader as unusual is the extremely self-confident, elitist, and yet highly nuanced analysis of pieces of music and their performance. Adorno reviews works performed during the regular seasons of contemporary chamber music in the Verein für Theater und Musikkultur, as well as the concerts put on by the Museumsgesellschaft and the productions of the Frankfurt Opera. His views on the musical life of the city suggest that he rarely missed a concert or an opera production. This experience enabled him to pass judgement on the compositions of such men as Schoenberg, Hindemith, Jarnach, Bartók, Krenek and Stravinsky, as well as less prominent composers such as Weill, Hoff, Sekles and Wolpe. To give one example, he dismissed Bartók's *Bluebeard's Castle* with the scathing comment that it was a 'late bloom of soulful impressionism',[71] while he had no qualms about pronouncing Bartók's Sonata for Piano and Violin the best contemporary chamber sonata.

Anyone who felt confident enough to make such unequivocal judgements could have no difficulty in distinguishing between good music and bad. In fact, Adorno drew a sharp dividing line. On the one side stood music as commercial art, as a mood creator, music with false pathos and sentimentality appropriate to the level of the friends of 'musical comfort'. On the other side, we can find the rare but significant exceptional instances of an unconventional, radically modern style of composition. What such composers have in common is the abandonment of any harmonic sequence. This avant-garde music – we are speaking here of Schoenberg, Hindemith, Bartók, Jarnach, Krenek, etc. – convinces by virtue of the consistency of its structuring principles which enable 'its form to conquer time'.[72] Adorno frequently contrasts this rational mode of construction with 'the merely organic work of art that deludes the blind soul.'[73]

Admittedly, Adorno refused to applaud music that thought itself modern or up to date just because it used different rhythms or new motivic material. 'Faith in constant artistic progress may be evaporating today even in the minds of people who have a right to think of themselves as the champions of progress against the diehard traditionalists.'[74] While he placed himself unequivocally on the side of the avant-garde, he was sensitive to the inconsistencies of musical modernity. He attempted to expose these inconsistencies, just as he was determined to prove that simply to continue the tradition would inexorably lead to the blind alley of classicism, works of art as museum pieces. He demonstrated that the two trends went hand in hand in the review of a concert in August 1923 in which he discussed Stravinsky, a composer towards whom he developed a polemical, negative view from this time onwards. There had been a performance in Frankfurt of *The Soldier's Tale*, which Adorno tore to pieces, just as he would condemn other works by the same composer at the Stravinsky festival two years later. In Adorno's view, Stravinsky was trying to go beyond traditional musical form. But his attempts did not lead to fully constructed forms that offered a convincing alternative.

> The old forms have been destroyed; the formless soul refreshes himself amidst the ruins. Vive Stravinsky! Vive Dada! He has torn down the roof, now the rain pours in on his bald pate. This modernity does not go beyond the externals of the Paris artists' ball, a cigarette-filled atmosphere and bogeyman of the middle classes. It will serve as a dismal Bohemian prank; but, taken seriously, it is no more than a musical version of civilized literature, as distinct from true art.[75]

The young critic did not mince his words when making public statements about the value of internationally acclaimed composers and virtuosos. He likewise refused to allow himself to be overimpressed by the bustling activity of Frankfurt's musical life, of which he had by now become an integral part. In a concert review of December 1924, he stated bluntly that there was little good to be said about Frankfurt musical life, that chamber music in particular was in a poor way, and that the Opera had sunk to the level of a medium-size provincial stage

Figure 3 Title page of the *Musikblätter des Anbruch*

– as could be seen from a superficial production of *Die Zauberflöte*. How was this sterility to be explained? By the fact that musical culture in Frankfurt was geared to 'existing conditions, the true authority here to which everyone must bow if they wish to remain here.'[76]

Even so, there were rare exceptions to which Adorno repeatedly drew attention. Chief among these was Hermann Scherchen, the conductor of the orchestral concerts put on by the Museumsgesellschaft. Adorno found his 'earnest dedication to the matter in hand' captivating. Or, again, he singled out Erich Kleiber, the conductor of the student orchestra of the Hoch Conservatory. He thought that Kleiber, who 'as a conductor belonged to the same type as Bruno Walter, possessed a similarly relaxed naturalness and a crystalline love of detail, only harder, less dreamy and tender. If such conducting was the product of routine, then routine cannot be as bad as its reputation.'[77] In the same way, now forgotten conductors such as Reinhold Merten and Ernst Wendel received favourable notices, as did the soloists of the Rebener, Amar and Lange quartets.

Adorno's opera and concert reviews were remarkable, and not just for their trenchant judgements. The language used by the critic signalled that, over and above his musical concerns, he also had philosophical intentions. His rather forced use of obscure images, such as 'lack of commitment', 'the homelessness of the soul' or 'the disastrous age into which man has been born', pointed to an attitude critical of cultural trends even though their youthful author whose academic studies were only just beginning had not yet fully internalized them. Such phrases revealed a belief current among intellectuals at the time that religious values had collapsed and all hope of transcendence and also of a substantive ethic had to be abandoned. For this reason, every promise of a new metaphysics was no better than a swindle. 'No cathedral can be built if no community desires one.'[78] These reflections on the historical situation of mankind were shot through with elements of a particular philosophy of life. This arose not just from his reading of thinkers such as Nietzsche, Kierkegaard and Schelling, but seemed to point to the influence of Siegfried Kracauer, who at the same period had arrived at a pointed criticism both of Max Scheler's recent publication, *Of the Eternal in Man*, and of Ernst Bloch's *Thomas Münzer*. For the existential inference that Kracauer drew from the universal chaos he had diagnosed was – according to an article in the cultural section of the *Frankfurter Zeitung* in March 1922 – the attitude of 'waiting' as a 'hesitant openness'.[79] In Kracauer's view, this attitude of waiting resulted from a general philosophical insecurity. It arose because people suffered from the meaninglessness of existence and the isolation of individuals responsible for themselves: 'Isolation and alienation from the absolute leave their mark in an extreme form of *relativism*. Since people affected by this have nothing firm to hold on to, their minds drift without direction; they are at home everywhere and nowhere.'[80] There is no path leading out of this spiritual impasse to unambiguous truths. It is no more possible to find refuge in obsolete religious traditions than in substitute religious doctrines, not even of the quality of the ideas of Stefan George or Rudolf Steiner. Nor is salvation to be found in the messianism of the Communist Party. Admittedly, Kracauer had no wish simply to endorse the attitudes of a principled sceptic and intellectual desperado. He preferred at the beginning of the 1920s to make a plea for sobriety and a lack of illusions, for the ability to 'hold out' and the 'courage with which to face the terrors of the prevailing emptiness'.[81]

A few weeks after his programmatic essay had appeared, Kracauer spent the Easter holidays in Amorbach with his friend Wiesengrund-Adorno. Perhaps the two friends went on excursions to the remoter parts of the Odenwald. In May 1923, Kracauer had published a report of his experiences and his impressions of the landscape in the *Frankfurter Zeitung*. In this 'sentimental suite of the Bergstraße', he wrote, travellers felt as if they were wandering along paths in Provence or Tuscany.

> For here was the south, the genuine south. We grew into it more and more. We were like figures in a painting in which we strutted around wonderfully. Cool rooms, shaded by blinds, opened up for us, and later we sat at the large table in the hotel garden, astonished only that the waiter did not speak Italian.[82]

The narrator's companion, who like him was overwhelmed by the region and its atmosphere, bore the Italian name Gianino. When he saw a piano in a café, he could not 'resist playing his beloved melodies and, to the noisy counterpoint of clinking crockery, merriment welled up from the black keys in a viscous flow, filling the deserted world.'[83]

Since the two friends liked nothing better than arguing about philosophical questions, there can be no doubt that the younger of the two must have been familiar with the books and articles, as well as the manuscript drafts, of his older mentor. This applies in particular to a text by Kracauer demonstrating his interest in popular literature. The detective novel, the subject to which he turned his attention around 1922, was rarely discussed at the time. Both he and Adorno enjoyed reading detective novels in the evenings, but they were not just in search of entertainment. Unusually, Kracauer looked at the genre from a philosophical point of view, as the subtitle of his essay reveals: A Philosophical Treatise. He dedicated it to 'Theodor Wiesengrund-Adorno, my friend', who at that time had just made a start on his philosophy course and had written those confident theatre and concert reviews already mentioned. Kracauer focused on the interaction between the detective, the police and the criminal. 'Without being a work of art, the detective novel reveals to a society stripped of reality its own face in a purer form than it is otherwise able to see it. In such novels the agents of this society account for themselves and their functions and yield up their hidden meaning.'[84] Kracauer's essay barely even hints at the personal pleasure felt by anyone reading such trivial writings. From the very first page, his discourse moved into the abstract realms of the philosophy of religion – no less a thinker than Søren Kierkegaard is invoked. Kierkegaard's polemical writings, such as *The Concept of Dread, Fear and Trembling* and *Either/Or*, were destined to be the source of many headaches for Adorno in the years to come. In fact, Kierkegaard's ideas on aesthetics were to become a central theme for him up to the start of his academic career as a lecturer. He may have been encouraged in the choice of subject for his second doctorate by ideas like the following from Kracauer's essay:

> Sin, which is a determinate of being in a higher sphere, danger, which threatens symbolically from outside, mystery, which intervenes from above – everything that explodes our provisional sense of security is uniformly represented in the lower regions by characters drawn from realms beyond the law. Such characters dominate a space empty of mind and meaning but infinitely expanded by rationality [*ratio*], and play their games in amongst the atoms with their regular movements. . . . The characters representing the law fail to recognize that the same ethical acts that have taken fright can manifest themselves in infringements of the moral code, that murder may be not just murder, but also the negation of a definitive human constitution by a superior mystery.[85]

Adorno's first book publication was his second doctoral dissertation. Its subject was Kierkegaard's philosophy of existence. When it was published in 1933 by J. C. B. Mohr (Siebeck) under the title *Konstruktion des Ästhetischen* (The Construction of the Aesthetic), Adorno took the opportunity to repay the compliment Kracauer had paid him six years previously, and dedicated his book to 'My friend Siegfried Kracauer'. Thematically, too, there were links. Thus Adorno talks of Kierkegaard's doctrine of different spheres and his idea of man as an 'intermediate being'. Man's precarious situation lies in the fact that he is equidistant from a state of nature and from the uniqueness of God, while possessing a conscious relation to his own existence.

When Kracauer wrote his *Detective Novel* he too profited from his reading of Kierkegaard. But he could not have guessed at the extent to which it would inspire his diligent pupil. Kracauer was able to publish only a fragment of his book-length study in his collection of essays *The Mass Ornament*: the part entitled 'The Hotel Lobby', perhaps its most original section. In Kracauer's eyes, the hotel lobby was the antithesis of the House of God, and the favourite place of the detective – who as the representative of a higher reason was himself a godlike figure. The final section of *The Detective Novel* contains some remarkable ideas which reappear in Adorno's critique of popular culture. Kracauer pointed out, for example, that every detective story ends 'without tragedy', but is instead 'combined with the sentimentality that is an aesthetic constituent of kitsch. There is no detective novel which does not end with the detective shedding light in the darkness and joining up all the mundane facts in a logical fashion; and there are few which do not end with some couple or other being united.'[86]

The first product of Adorno's interest in popular culture, the 'Schlageranalysen' (Analyses of Hit Songs), was published in the March issue of the journal *Anbruch* in 1929. Here he made use of the concept of the 'shop girls' that Kracauer had introduced in the context of his study of white-collar workers. Furthermore, his comments on kitsch have an unmistakable affinity with the arguments put forward in Kracauer's *The Detective Novel*. The happiness that hit tunes promised showed them to be a form of 'treasured kitsch' with which the shop girls identified and which enriched their daily lives. But the enrichment turned out to be imaginary because, while listening to hit tunes, the shop girls were tricked out of that promised fulfilment in the real world in which 'the full individual is no longer alive.'[87] Adorno's criticism of music is unmistakably close to Kracauer's social criticism when he writes about a song called *Valencia*:

> Ever since concrete reality vanished from human life, the white-collar workers have come to resemble one another without distinction, spending six days at the typewriter and the weekend with their girlfriend. Hence the concrete reality, without which it is not possible to live, must be sought elsewhere.[88]

This reality is introduced in the text and music of this kitschy popular song. The very name *Valencia* was a mark of the exotic world that the 'excluded, impoverished, shattered bourgeoisie' yearned for as its members struggled to find their feet again in the post-inflationary world. Their desire for traditional security, for convention and for order was encapsulated in the popular song 'I kiss your little hand, Madame'. 'There were plenty of people to whom it had never occurred that it was possible to kiss anyone's hands until they heard this song. What was a feudal mode of showing respect was thoroughly democratized by this hit. Except the democracy of hand-kissing . . . is an illusion, for the new bourgeois only kiss a lady's hand so that they may be thought better than they are.'[89] But who did not want to be thought better than he was? Could not the same thing be said of the young Wiesengrund-Adorno who was as yet unsure which was more important, his artistic ambitions or his philosophical interests? But quite independently of a decision on this question, one which he basically left open his whole life long – in no man's land – he had yet to become the person who, apart from being a success in music or philosophy, wished for nothing more than to kiss the ladies' hands.

4

Éducation sentimentale

'Don't forget Monette!'[1]

The winter of 1923 had begun with an unusually cold spell. The temperature had fallen sharply in December. The people of Frankfurt, who were being buffeted by the bitter economic and confused political conditions, were now confronted with the rare sight of the River Main covered with huge ice floes. The painter Max Beckmann was so impressed by this bizarre winter weather that he made it the subject of his painting *Drift Ice*, one of his many paintings of aspects of the city. As in his picture *The Synagogue*, which he had painted four years before, or his well-known *Eiserne Steg* (The Iron Footbridge), Beckmann's concern in his paintings of the city was to bring out the unique features of the place where he lived and had his studio between 1915 and 1933. In the 1920s Beckmann was one of the most striking personalities of cultural life in Frankfurt at the same time as the young Adorno was emerging as a critical observer of the city, in particular through his contributions to the *Frankfurter Zeitung*. At that time, Benno Reifenberg was about to become editor of the cultural section of that distinguished paper, and it is natural that he should have felt inspired to react to Beckmann's winter scene:

> The city cowers as if it were freezing, as if it were afraid of the violence of the river, as if it were shrinking from the cold, inexorably grey sky. Frankfurt's cathedral squats red behind the houses. The bridge is a blue-steel line from shore to shore, beneath the bare trees there are bare wisps of green. But the gently swinging arc lamps, tinged with cinnabar and blue, are like late night revellers, staggering home with collars turned up. How grey the world is, how cold and grey. The wan morning soaks up the crescent moon. Only with effort does it creep over the roofs that stretch out like a black line, binding the city to the earth. – The ice floes glide down the dark river. They resemble strange fish with broad backs and pointed snouts. They pour out of the bend in the Main. They float

silently past the city, as if propelled from afar. They barely brush against the reddish quay, making a fearsome grinding noise.[2]

The expressionist tone of this description matched the aesthetic trends of the period: an expressionism that Adorno viewed critically but which predominated in literature and pervaded everyday forms of culture. This expressionism was an amalgam of protest, yearning and an exalted culture of the self that manifested itself as a defiant outcry against egregious economic problems, unemployment and terrible conditions in general, as well as a proclamation of the new that people were longing for in the period following the currency reform. In Frankfurt, life soon began to pulsate once more and people learned how to combine the search for pleasure with the activity of social criticism, an activity pursued enthusiastically in literature or art. This can be seen from the numerous etchings, lithographs and oil paintings that Max Beckmann produced during this period. 'We live from day to day.'[3] With this sentence he ended the self-portrait he had published in the *Frankfurter Zeitung* in March 1923.

How did people live in the circles in which Adorno moved? Siegfried Kracauer did not confine his activities to such intellectual matters as the critique of Franz Rosenzweig's *The Star of Redemption*, a book he described as 'apotheosis philosophy', which 'starts with the void and ends with the "sun in its heart".'[4] And, for his part, Adorno did not spend all his time preparing papers for Hans Cornelius's philosophy seminar on such topics as 'Kant's critique of rational psychology'. Both intellectuals found ample opportunity for entertainment in Frankfurt. An entire chapter of Kracauer's *Georg* – which is principally a social novel and a novel of personal development – is devoted to the depiction of the excesses of the citizens of Frankfurt in their fancy-dress parties. The first-person narrator is sucked into the garish and noisy hurly-burly, 'and, in the midst of the roar of this swirling, glowing chaos, a mass of human beings dances to the sounds of jazz, and carries the lanterns, the colours and the din along with it until the entire hall whirls round unstoppably.'[5] Georg, the autobiographical hero of the novel, plunges into the midst of this frenzied crowd to prove to himself that he is able to enjoy life's pleasures despite being an intellectual remote from worldly matters. He is fascinated by the women, whose attractions are enhanced by their exotic disguises, whether as apache maidens, negresses, whores or pierrots. At the end of a night of dancing, the narrator, the editor of the most important local newspaper, concludes complacently that he was wrong to have believed that he was too inhibited to take part. He finds he had no difficulty in joining in wholeheartedly and feels enriched by the experience. He now knows something of the ebbs and flows of the erotic adventures in which he had been swept up at the masked ball. It must be added, however, that even before this he had experienced some of the difficulties that can arise not just from facile, superficial relationships, but from intense, serious ones. The novel also contains a frank episode describing the powerful attraction felt between the narrator and his friend 'Freddi', who is fourteen years his junior. During the travels of the two, the closeness they feel can be explored, although the narrator is forced to confess his disappointment that the promise of a friendship without reservation may turn out to be problematic. He describes an episode in their modest holiday hotel in the Black Forest in which Georg and Fred share a bed in order to chat together before each goes to sleep in his own room.

> The bed was narrow and they found it difficult keeping their bodies from touching. Their arms felt particularly awkward since they needed too much space. Since they couldn't just saw off the offending limbs, they did in fact keep coming into contact. They tried to obscure the risks inherent in these contacts by keeping up a lively conversation, which they both felt to be senseless. Because of the warmth of the bed, the artificial conversation soon dried up; the words seemed to fall asleep of their own accord, and then they kissed. As had happened once before, Georg muttered 'Freddi', to himself. As had happened once before, the forgotten name surfaced unbidden. Fred half raised himself in the bed.
> 'I must confess something to you. I wanted to tell you the whole time, but didn't really dare. The fact is that Margot was my lover.'[6]

We can only speculate whether 'Teddie' was present at the masked ball 'Timbuctu' in the pavilion of the Zoological Garden, or at other festivities of this sort. No doubt his experiences were like those of the hero of Kracauer's novel. What we do know is that he was no sad loner, but was highly sociable. Even in later years, in the 1950s and 1960s, when he was professor of sociology and philosophy, he enjoyed being present at the student carnival celebrations. He would waltz with gusto, showing that his talents were not confined to the exegesis of Hegelian texts. And, if we can credit the discreet hints in his letters to Siegfried Kracauer and Alban Berg, he seems to have been no stranger to the kind of erotic adventure that his friend Friedel describes explicitly enough in *Georg*. Georg's reminiscences in the novel seem clearly to be based on actual events, and, similarly, there can be no doubt that in 1923, the year in which that fictional scene is set and in which Adorno went with Kracauer to Amorbach and the Bergstraße, he had an important encounter with a woman, though the place and the circumstances are not known.

What we do know[7] is simply that there were business connections between the firm of Oscar Wiesengrund and the factory of Karplus & Herzberger, a leather-processing company that belonged jointly to Joseph Albert Karplus and a businesswoman from Neuenkirchen, Else Herzberger.[8]

In the course of time, the business connection between Berlin and Frankfurt had developed into close personal ties between the two families, and were fostered especially by Else Herzberger, of whom the Wiesengrunds were particularly fond. Notably, the fifteen-year-old Teddie even dedicated his first compositions to her. These were musical settings of Theodor Storm's poems *Schließe mir die Augen beide* (Close Both my Eyes) and *Die Nachtigall* (The Nightingale) for voice and piano.[9] The two families frequently exchanged visits. During one such visit the eldest daughter of the Karplus family was introduced to the son of the Wiesengrunds. This encounter was to form the basis of a permanent relationship in the years to come.

First love and a number of affairs

The fidelity exacted by society is a means to unfreedom, but only through fidelity can freedom achieve insubordination to society's command.[10]

We are speaking here of Margarete Karplus, or Gretel as she was generally known. She lived and studied in Berlin and, according to her own account, was fascinated by the young Adorno's temperament and intelligence from the time of their very first meeting. He and he alone was the man for her![11] This self-confidence, together with a pragmatic view of life, was typical of Gretel Karplus. Her grandfather Gottlieb Karplus had once been an industrialist in Vienna. She was born on 10 June 1902 and, together with her slightly younger sister Liselotte, her father Joseph and her mother Amalie, she lived in considerable middle-class style at Prinzenallee 82, not far from the Tiergarten. Later, as a businesswoman, Gretel Karplus lived in Berlin-Halensee, in Westfälischestraße.

When Kracauer learnt of Adorno's love for Gretel, he wrote to him that he was deeply pained by this new liaison, not least because it had been kept a secret and he had known nothing about it. He had to come to terms with it, of course, since it proved to be a long-lasting, even symbiotic, relationship, one that was soon formalized by an engagement. After fourteen years, during which they were separated geographically for lengthy periods, they were finally married in September 1937 in Britain, where Adorno's parents and grandparents had celebrated their weddings.

In the Berlin of the 1920s, Gretel Karplus moved in intellectual circles and was acquainted with Walter Benjamin, Ernst Bloch and Bertolt Brecht. She was a sought-after, attractive and fashionably dressed woman. At the age of twenty-three, she was awarded her doctorate in chemistry. Her sister Liselotte later became the second wife of Egon Wissing,[12] a cousin and friend of Walter Benjamin who was a well-known and much admired figure among Berlin intellectuals of the day. Gretel had had close contact with him from the mid-1920s. Adorno, too, had become friendly with Benjamin during this period, having met him through Kracauer. He thought highly of him from the outset. Later on, Adorno would meet Benjamin in the Café Westend on the Frankfurt Opernplatz. They would also meet after they had both attended the seminars of Gottfried Salomon-Delatour, who was working on the ideas of the historian Ernst Troeltsch. 'I would say', Adorno recalled subsequently, 'that we met at least once a week, probably even more often, throughout the entire time that he lived in Frankfurt. Even after that, we saw one another regularly, both on his visits to Frankfurt, and above all in Berlin.' Adorno was drawn to Berlin not just because it was a cultural centre, but also to spend time with Gretel.

This then was the circle to which the two belonged and within which they were perceived as a couple. In due course, Gretel Karplus started to develop an independent relationship with a number of intellectuals with whom Adorno was friendly. The many letters she exchanged not just with him, but also with Benjamin, for example – he addresses her as Felicitas, she calls him Detlef[13] – provide clear evidence of her independent existence. A further factor in this independence was her ability to earn her own living up to her emigration from Nazi Germany. From 1933 to the end of 1937, she managed the firm of Georg Tengler, a workshop in Berlin manufacturing leather gloves, in which she also had a financial stake.

Benjamin fled from Germany immediately after the Nazi takeover or, rather, after the Reichstag fire at the end of February 1933. It fell to Gretel Karplus to rescue as many of his numerous manuscripts as she could as well as large parts of his library. It was at this time that a relationship of mutual trust grew up between the two. In a letter he wrote in May 1933, at a time when he had withdrawn to Ibiza in the Balearics for a stay of several months, he describes his highly personal, indeed intimate, experience of smoking opium. He writes frankly about his own day-to-day moods and plans, and he shows himself to be equally interested in Gretel's life in Berlin. 'I let a little wind music sway the top of the pine under which I am sitting, and paint a four-leaf picture of thanks at its feet. I trust you will pluck it in exchange for your last letter.' In another letter Benjamin declares that he would like them to get to know each other even better. To facilitate this he intends to use his letters to give a more sharply delineated portrait of himself. Perhaps, he adds, this will result in 'a halfway adequate silhouette'. Gretel is equally forthcoming. She complains about the problems of her work in the leather factory, about her mental and physical well-being, and shares with him her thoughts about the future of their mutual 'problem child' (*Sorgenkind*), as she calls Adorno, of the value of whose resolute activity her friend Detlev seems firmly convinced.[14]

After their later marriage, Gretel supported her 'problem child' in a strikingly selfless way in his work as a writer, and made sure that Adorno could follow his pursuits relatively undisturbed by everyday chores. And she kept this up both during the years of emigration in the United States and subsequently, after his return to the University of Frankfurt. Only in this way did it become possible for him to create works that belong among the most important achievements of the century. Gretel was, for the most part, the first to hear of his ideas and to support him in his projects, but also to prevent him from going astray from time to time. It was not unusual for her to write 'Be careful, TWA' in the margins of his manuscripts. This might refer to flawed verbal expressions or to assertions that did not seem persuasive in a given context. Adorno had formed the habit, above all in his most productive writing phases, of dictating his ideas and preliminary arguments to her on the basis of a few written notes. For 'dictating', he comments at a later date, 'is not only more comfortable, more conducive to concentration; it has an additional substantive benefit. Dictation makes it possible for the writer, in the earliest phases of production, to manoeuvre himself into the position of critic.'[15] Whatever is tentatively arrived at by spontaneously following his own line of thought during the process of dictation is intended from the outset for complete revision. As soon as the text is fixed in typed form, the author can look at it and revise it from a distance, as if it were someone else's text. This process of revision, which may end up with every sentence having been changed, was a process Adorno called 'carrion-eating' (*lämmergeiern*). Why this word? Adorno, a keen visitor to Frankfurt Zoo, presumably saw lammergeiers or bearded vultures there (*Gypaëtus barbatus*). They feed mainly on carrion, but also on small mammals and birds. They are particularly partial to bones. Very large bones are dropped from a height onto rocks to break them; the marrow can then be devoured. This method of arriving at the kernel of a problem which at first appears too difficult or inaccessible, of 'cracking' it in order to extract its essence, may well have been the reason for choosing this word. This seems more plausible than the alternative idea that lammergeiers are fastidious in their choice of partner, to whom they then remain faithful for up to forty years.

For the 'lammergeier' Adorno, dictation was a 'technical aid to the dialectical procedure that makes statements in order to withdraw them and yet to hold them fast. But thanks are due to the person taking down the dictation, if at the right moment he jolts the writer out of his complacency by contradiction, irony, nervousness, impatience and disrespect.'[16] This aphorism from Adorno's *dialogue intérieur* is in the first instance an act of homage to his wife, who was not only directly involved in the majority of his writings, but was the first to say what she thought of them.[17]

Needless to say, Gretel Adorno was not just his closest confidante in the obsessive processes of what Heinrich von Kleist called 'the gradual production of ideas through talking'. There was a bond of love between the two that was based on complete trust, although of course a marriage of forty years is necessarily subject to a 'test of feeling'.[18] We do not know whether, and in what ways, the relationship between the two was marked by a certain obsessiveness. Their letters were lost in the confusion after Adorno's early death when Gretel fell ill in the flat they shared in Kettenhofweg in Frankfurt and required prolonged medical attention. The couple were dependent on letter-writing since they were separated for lengthy periods before their marriage. She lived for the most part in Berlin, he in Frankfurt, Vienna and then London and Oxford. In the early years they met on public holidays, at weekends and during their travels together. Naturally enough, they saw each other mainly in Frankfurt and Berlin. Nor did Adorno fail to introduce Gretel to his beloved Amorbach in the Odenwald. Destinations further afield included south Germany, the Dolomites, Italy both north and south, and, in France, Paris and the Côte d'Azur. They also followed in the footsteps of his grandfather in the spring of 1932, when they did a round trip through Corsica, visiting Ajaccio and going as far as Bonifacio.

When Adorno had known Gretel for about eight years his experience of meeting her again at the station after months of separation may have inspired him to reflections that he published in the *Frankfurter Zeitung* in 1931:

> A man tensely waiting for a train arriving late one evening in the depths of winter. He thinks to himself . . . at long last, she really is here, as she leaves the carriage, one of the last to emerge, a slim figure in a fur coat walking up to the ticket barrier, past the still steaming locomotive, with the little black hatbox in her hand, followed by the porter in his green uniform wheeling the larger leather suitcase: it really is her.[19]

As they leave the station arm in arm, talking as they cross the square, what makes the writer doubt whether the woman he has so longed for really is the woman he loves above all others is the presentiment that the yearning felt by the roving imagination threatens to evaporate with the fact of arrival. At the same time, he plays with the idea that the sense of yearning that feeds on the need for love is really the expression of desires rooted in childhood experiences. Elsewhere in these *Words without Songs*, he reflects on the need for fidelity to the woman he loves, a moral commandment that has become unfashionable, just as love relationships in general seemed scarcely able to bear external pressure. 'Only the best and happiest relationships succeed in reaching the point where conflicts break out.'[20] Even though Adorno asserts that, 'ultimately, what emerges inexorably from the inability of lovers to reach out to each other is loneliness', his own bonds to Gretel Karplus, and hers to him, were strong and enduring. Tolerance was a self-evident reality, and this explains why Adorno felt no need for secrecy about the fact that in his frequent visits to Paris in the mid-1930s he was strongly attracted by the famous *maison de tolérance* 'Le Sphinx', and that it was not only Monette but also Josiane whose services he came to value.[21] The attachment that developed between Adorno and his wife-to-be was one that sought to create a free space for spontaneity and the expression of feeling. 'Love you will only find where you may show yourself weak without provoking strength.'[22] Significantly, Adorno saw himself, projected into the animal realm, as Archibald the rhinoceros, while he thought of Gretel as a 'modern giraffe'. The understanding between the two of them included the respect each felt for the other's need for distance. 'We always sleep separately', Adorno the rhinoceros explained to Max Horkheimer, whom we encounter in this bestiary as a mammoth. The secret meaning of these affectionate nicknames was revealed to Horkheimer without embarrassment at the time of their wedding, shortly before the couple moved to New York, and Adorno combined this revelation with the request en passant that Horkheimer should find them a place to live with two separate bedrooms.[23]

The marriage remained childless. Gretel once told Benjamin that she would like to adopt him 'instead of the child I shall never have'.[24] In so far as it is possible to say anything on this subject, the Adornos' childlessness was the result of a conscious decision that was taken in the light of the dramatic nature of contemporary events and their vision of the future resulting from it. When Adorno sent congratulations to Ernst Bloch on the birth of his son Jan Robert in October 1937, he wrote, 'It is beautiful and brave to have a child at the present time, almost a little shaming for us who do not venture to take this step because one can never know with whom a child might have to march one day.'[25] Later on, a few months before his fiftieth birthday, in a letter to Max Horkheimer, Adorno expressed his regret that both couples had decided against having children. He linked this fact with the sentiments he had expressed in the letter to Bloch that, throughout their entire lives, they had never been in a position to hope that they might themselves 'be the subjects of a form of practice that could avert the catastrophe'.[26]

Even if the wedding ceremony was far from being a mere formality wished on the couple by their parents and friends, the marriage certificate was not the most important aspect of the business. They felt sceptical from the outset about the conventions of bourgeois marriage, even though it is 'one of the last possibilities of forming human cells in an inhuman universe'.[27] Adorno needed no personal experience of the traditional rules governing the relations between the sexes to enable him to state, in the frankest of his books: 'Marriage, living on as an abject parody in an age that has removed the basis of its human justification, usually serves today as a trick of self-preservation.'[28] Adorno reflected on the position of women in love relationships as these were regulated by convention. The femininity so admired by men was the mirror-image of men's specific deficiencies in a patriarchal society. This explains why 'Glorification of the feminine character implies the humiliation of all who possess it.'[29] And the fact that the immediate flaring up of attraction associated with the idea of love cannot function properly in reality has its roots in the exchange relationship that has come to dominate in late bourgeois society: 'Love is chilled by the value that the ego places on itself.'[30] For this reason, one partner is never willing to give more than he can realistically expect from the other. In this way, love is replaced by the social institution of partnership in which men attempt to estimate the value of women and vice versa, according to the categories of income, prestige and beauty. Adorno has no difficulty in illustrating his point here: 'The quality of every one of the countless automobiles which return to New York on Sunday evenings corresponds precisely to the attractiveness of the girl sitting in it.'[31] His observations tell him that this calculation is made at the expense of the erotic charge of the love relationship in which both parties 'no longer want ecstasy at all, but merely compensation for an outlay that, best of all, they would like to save as superfluous.'[32]

What were Adorno's relations with the opposite sex? What is attested is his always courteous treatment of women in accordance with upper-middle-class manners. For example, the charming habit of kissing a lady's hand always has an air of gallantry about it that evidently did not fail to make an impression on women. Adorno's women students testify that their teacher was a man whose 'interest was quickly aroused'.

> No sooner did he encounter a woman than he began to flirt with her. This sometimes seemed arbitrary, as if he were 'colour-blind' to the individual nature of a particular woman – he was aroused, seemingly automatically, by 'woman as such'. To be sure, erotic permissiveness was no male monopoly in his view – he conceded the same rights to women. But in my opinion Adorno was neither chauvinistic nor sexist. And I can say that because I felt close to him personally and I do not wish to deny the presence of an erotic undercurrent in our relationship. His approaches had nothing macho or virile about them, they were instead uninhibited and childlike – much as in other spheres of life Adorno always preserved a kind of natural spontaneity that went back to his childhood. But he could also be extremely timid, something that does not fit the image of the ruthless ladykiller at all. Moreover, I always found Adorno to be very dependable and affectionate in his behaviour towards women. The decisive factor for me was ... that I was able to be friends with both him and Gretel. I felt that the relationship between them was marked by the same tension: loyalty despite everything, reliability, an almost symbiotic mutual attachment on the one hand, and the ability to preserve one's freedom on the other.[33]

During a marriage that lasted over forty years, Adorno took the liberty of entering into relationships with other women, frequently engaging in casual affairs without ever concealing them from his wife. She knew of his passion for the actress Renée Nell, for whom he wrote an entire poetry album during the Los Angeles years:

> Forgive me, Darling, for inventing you:
> Who might dare create such a creature?
> Yet I could no longer bear the shame of the masks of
>   activity and the screen
> So, seeking help, I named your name
> To bring me hope for one last time
> With despicable pride from the wasted days.
> In your name I have always known you,
> It is you who resembles the words that have always
>   captivated my ears and dreams,
> And since you extend your hand to me,
> I must belong to her who brings such solace,
> The unapproachable one who is softened by the word –
> Only good spirits let themselves be conjured up.[34]

Adorno's wife knew too of another hazardous and lasting romance, with Charlotte Alexander, the wife of his friend and doctor, Dr Robert Alexander. Charlotte Alexander lived in San Francisco at the time, and Adorno frequently went there in connection with the Public Opinion Study Group of Berkeley University. Charlotte was in the process of getting a divorce. When the divorce came through, Adorno initially regarded it with mixed feelings. He did not wish to lose Charlotte, but neither could nor wished to stay with her permanently. Did the evidently complicated divorce proceedings between Robert and Charlotte provide the basis for his reflections on divorce?

> Divorce . . . is apt to stir up a dust-cloud that covers and discolours all it touches. It is as if the sphere of intimacy . . . is transformed into a malignant poison as soon as the relationship in which it flourished is broken off. Intimacy between people is forbearance, tolerance, refuge for idiosyncrasies. If dragged into the open, an intimate relationship reveals the element of weakness it contains, and in a divorce such outward exposure is inevitable. . . . professors, after separation, break into their wives' flats to pilfer objects from writing desks, and well-endowed ladies denounce their husbands for tax evasion.[35]

After the divorce of Charlotte and Robert Alexander, Robert married Anita Seligmann towards the end of 1947. She was a good friend of Adorno's and, as a student of sociology and philosophy, had attended his seminars in the brief period when he had been a *Privatdozent* in Frankfurt. When he learnt of her marriage he wrote to her and to

Robert on 3 January 1948: 'The few of us who are different have seen the question of marriage in quite a different light. If we rebel against the convention of marriage and go in search of an unregimented happiness, it is only to discover that because of the emphasis on externals marriage itself has fallen apart. Hence nowadays resistance to the despicable way of the world is to be achieved rather by freely choosing marriage, and committing oneself to it, instead of denying its worth in a spirit of "realism" and practicality.'[36] But in a letter to another close friend, Hermann Grab, he writes very differently. He talks there of his love for Charlotte: 'We have enjoyed six months of the most unclouded happiness imaginable – mainly when she came here at weekends.'[37] And in a letter written shortly after this, in May 1946, he describes the feeling of pleasure he experienced: 'The term "fornication", which by the way refers to something the reverse of contemptible, is a far from adequate description of what has taken place – terms such as "aura" or "magic" would be more apt. It was as if the long-forgotten childhood promise of happiness had been unexpectedly, belatedly fulfilled.'[38]

Hermann Grab was born in Prague, in the same year as Adorno, and he grew up there. He was ultimately forced to emigrate to the United States, but had been friendly with Adorno since the mid-1920s. He was a pupil of Alexander von Zemlinsky, a member of the Schoenberg circle. His first published story appeared in 1935. This was *Der Stadtpark*, which describes the unspoken love of a schoolboy for a girl of the same age in upper-middle-class Prague at the time of the demise of the Habsburg Empire. A volume of his collected stories did not appear until after his death in 1949. In his obituary for Grab, Adorno wrote that the guiding-light for his literary production had been Marcel Proust's 'picture-world of a child's wide-eyed astonishment'. When Adorno made his indiscreet confession, to use his own word, and told Grab of his innermost feelings, and even of the name of the woman with whom he was in love, he was engaged in writing down reflections with the title *Zum neunzackigen Krönchen* (The Nine-Pointed Crown), some of which appeared in revised form in the *Minima Moralia*, but which survived unpublished in their original state: 'Love is nothing but the momentary flash of a dream in the midst of the real, actually a déjà vu in a person's appearance. It becomes visible for only a fraction of a second.'[39]

Gretel Adorno's unstinting loyalty to her husband extended to her acceptance of his flirtations and affairs during the Frankfurt years, when he was at the high point of his career. This included an affair with a lawyer called Eva, a friend of the family, and with Arlette, who accompanied the couple on one of their trips to Switzerland.[40] Perhaps such affairs had the same importance for Adorno as he believed the numerous affairs of his Viennese teacher Alban Berg had for him, that is to say, they were 'part of the productive apparatus' and were 'desperate', but not 'serious'.[41]

In Adorno's eyes love was not simply the passionate conjuring up of an image from the past, but also a matter of immediate feeling which gives rise to 'tenderness between human beings'. It is sustained by the desire for a different life, for a life that differs from the life of bourgeois society with its means–ends rationality.

Adorno did not trouble to make a secret even of his dream fantasies with their frequently erotic overtones. For the personal notes that he recorded were typed up by Gretel. 'A. came to my bed in the depths of the night. I asked her whether she loved me, and she replied "Madly", in a voice that sounded so natural that it might have been true.' In another dream, he had 'an indescribably beautiful and elegant lover; she reminded him of Arlette, but had the air of a lady from high society. I felt very proud of her.'[42]

In a subsequent account of a dream, he records a different picture, one that had a particular importance for Gretel Adorno even after his death. 'I dreamt that I was unwilling to abandon my metaphysical hopes, not because I clung to life, but because I should like to awaken together with G.'[43] Gretel must have known about her husband's wish. Is this perhaps why she kept on loving him all her life with a love in which she could show herself weak 'without provoking strength'?[44]

Part II

A Change of Scene: Between Frankfurt, Vienna and Berlin: A Profusion of Intellectual Interests

Commuting between Philosophy and Music

When he was seventeen, Adorno left the Gymnasium; as the best student of his year, he was welcomed by the university with open arms. Did this mean that his course was now set for a brilliant academic career? Looked at topographically, his horizons were limited to the cultural milieu of Frankfurt, the city of his birth, where he had spent most of his first two decades. Here, in this independently minded city, which had always maintained a certain coolness towards the Germany of Bismarck and his successors, he experienced the tensions of tradition and modernity, the diversity of intellectual trends and cultural forms of life. Looked at historically, alongside the intellectually stimulating years of childhood and youth in his parents' house, the crucial experience of his life had been the progressive disintegration of bourgeois values. He was therefore unable to repress the question of whether the vestiges of tradition deserved to be salvaged. His scepticism about traditional ways of thought and forms of art went together with his hope for a radical break with the continuum of history, and the expectation that something fundamentally new would assert itself in both life and culture.

Adorno's exceptional intellectual energy and his self-confident openness to the world did not seduce him into blinding himself to the turmoil of his age at the end of the First World War. Needless to say, the war was not the traumatic experience for him that it had been for the intellectuals with whom he associated and who were around ten years his senior. This explains his relative indifference to the protests of the youth movement and the rebellious gestures of the expressionists of the early 1920s. He had little reason to challenge the world of the fathers. Nor was he tempted to join the fashionable trend for escapism or to avert his gaze from the here and now. For all his superficial melancholy about the irrevocable passing of childhood, and despite his scepticism about the future course of history, he not only faced up to the challenges of his age but also grasped the opportunities it presented to him. When he turned twenty, he finished with his philosophy studies, perhaps in the hope that 'He that loses his life shall save it.'[1] Scarcely had he been awarded his academic degree than he turned his back on the university, albeit not for ever, as we shall see. His boundless passion for music in no wise yielded to the fascination that philosophy had for him all his life. The die was cast after his first encounter with Alban Berg, whom he met after a production of Berg's opera *Wozzeck* in Frankfurt. Later on, after studying composition in Vienna, Adorno again found himself at a crossroads.

He began by returning to his home town. Because he firmly believed that aesthetic expression was a function of theory, he went on to pursue a completely independent line of thought: the idea of a *philosophy of music*. This synthesis of philosophy and music was no facile compromise; Adorno always abhorred the idea of a golden mean. After the victory of the Nazis and his move into exile in Oxford, he devoted his energies to what he thought of as a 'definitive' critique of Husserl's phenomenology. But simultaneously he concentrated with equal intensity on the interpretation of Berg's music in order to be able to convey to the public something of the importance of the composer who had died so prematurely.

5

Against the Stream: The City of Frankfurt and its University

As the best student of his year at the Kaiser Wilhelm Gymnasium, Adorno skipped a year in the summer of 1920 and entered the upper sixth form. He took the leaving examination before Easter 1921 and was awarded the certificate with the comment '*primus omnium*', confirming his fitness to begin his university studies. Decisions about his future course of study had long since been taken. As early as 18 April, he registered at the Johann Wolfgang Goethe University in Frankfurt to study philosophy, psychology and sociology. In his first term that summer, he enrolled in a four-hour-per-week seminar on epistemology, given by Hans Cornelius. He also went to the latter's introductory course in philosophy and attended a lecture course in psychology given by Adhémar Gelb. The following term, he took the opportunity of studying with the young sociology lecturer Gottfried Salomon-Delatour. There his subjects were not only the recent writings of Max Weber and Ernst Troeltsch, but also the ideas and times of the Russian revolutionaries of the nineteenth century and the workers' movement in France. Over and above that, he attended the lectures of Rudolf Kautzsch, who enjoyed an excellent reputation as an art historian, as well as being the current rector of the university. Kautzsch had a close working relationship with Georg Swarzenski, the director of the Städel Gallery and the man who had played a key role in establishing the reputation of its painting collection. Over a number of terms, Adorno also went to lectures in the Music Department, mainly those of Moritz Bauer, who treated such topics as the history of Passion music, the history of the *Lied*, and the aesthetics of music.

The few years in which Adorno studied in Frankfurt – seven semesters in all – were years of major crisis for the recently founded university. The city's wealth had melted away with inflation, and cuts had to be made in the funds available for the university. At the same time, donations from affluent citizens were drying up, an important factor for a university which had been founded and developed largely through the patronage of private benefactors.

Seven years before Adorno had embarked on his studies there, in October 1914, teaching had begun in buildings in the Senckenberger Anlage. In contrast to the state-funded universities, Frankfurt owed its existence to the generosity of a number of wealthy citizens, Jewish businessmen and bankers for the most part. They had been won over for the project by the charismatic mayor, Franz Adickes.[1] Adickes was able to rely on a broadly based civic culture that went back to the time when Frankfurt was a free city and in which there was a strong tradition of private sponsorship of public projects. Examples were the Senckenberg Foundation, the Deutsche Hochstift, and the Jügel, Merton and Speyer foundations. Wilhelm Merton, a businessman, had laid the groundwork for the future university in 1896 when he set up the Institut für Gemeinwohl in 1896. This was then absorbed into the Akademie für Sozial- und Handelswissenschaften that Adickes founded in 1901. This in turn became the nucleus of an unconventional project: the establishment of a civic university based on private endowments. In the context of the traditional Prussian university system this was entirely unprecedented in Germany.[2]

In the course of time this nonconformism served to attract a number of scholars with socially critical views. They included Martin Buber, the religious philosopher, Carl Grünberg, the Austro-Marxist economist, Max Horkheimer, the social philosopher, the sociologists Karl Mannheim and Franz Oppenheimer, philosophers such as Max Scheler and Paul Tillich, and Hugo Sinzheimer, the sociologist of law. Under the leadership of Walter Gerlach and Kurt Riezler during the Weimar Republic, the university followed a culturally open-minded and democratic course that was wholly in tune with the views of Ludwig Landmann, the mayor who was in office from 1924: 'As in the city in general at the time, an invigorating, agile, alert spirit pervaded the university. Frankfurt's institutions flourished even though the town was sometimes reviled by outsiders as liberal, democratic and "Jewish".'[3] It was above all the most recent disciplines, i.e., the social sciences, that benefited most from this forward-looking climate. This meant that, from the very start of the Weimar Republic, sociology 'not only had full academic recognition, but a reputation, and even an intellectual leadership that went beyond the discipline itself.'[4]

Against this background it was obvious that only an unconventional university such as Frankfurt could have satisfied the academic ambitions of a receptive and intellectually curious school-leaver like Adorno. In the course of the 1920s it had developed into a forum for intellectual discourse and a space in which culture, art and science enjoyed enormous prestige.[5]

Progressive as the university was during its early years in comparison with others, it did not prevent Adorno from developing a lifelong aversion to the division of labour in the organization of academic studies. Perhaps he felt himself to be too much of an artist to be satisfied with the degree of specialization that affected both teaching and research even in those days. However that may be, he identified this division of labour as the cause of the institutionalized drawbacks that he associated with the tendency towards excessive specialization.

His enduring dislike of the university's neglect of education in favour of training may explain why Adorno came to focus his studies increasingly on the figure of Hans Cornelius, the professor of philosophy. Cornelius was very far from being a narrow-minded specialist. He had an enormous sensitivity to art. Alongside his work in the university, he was active as a painter, sculptor and pianist. Cornelius was a somewhat unorthodox or, as Adorno put it, an 'ingenious' exponent of neo-Kantian philosophy, a philosophical trend with various strands, such as the Marburg school and the South-West school. What the different strands had in common was, on the one hand, their opposition to speculative metaphysics, and to the so-called *Lebensphilosophie* [of Wilhelm Dilthey, Rudolf Eucken and others], and, on the other hand, their defence of Kant's critical standpoint along with the strict relation to empirical reality. Cornelius was by no means one of the outstanding philosophers of the day, even though his book *Psychology as Empirical Science*, which had appeared in 1897, had provoked a polemical response from no less a thinker than Edmund Husserl. His chief work, the *Transcendental System* of 1916, and his *Introduction to Philosophy* had only a modest impact, even though the latter went through a number of editions.[6] Nevertheless, Adorno read the books by his supervisor and studied them to such good effect that he was fully conversant with his teacher's philosophical programme. That applies both to his writings on the pedagogy of art and to his contributions on the epistemological foundations of gestalt psychology.[7]

In the year in which Adorno obtained his doctorate, the early summer of 1924, a second, improved and enlarged, edition of *Contemporary Philosophy in its own Words* was published by Felix Meiner in Leipzig. Cornelius's own contribution to this volume contains an instructive account of his own life and thought.[8] Adorno's supervisor, with whom he originally intended to study for the *Habilitation*, the second doctorate, was evidently just as versatile as his pupil. Notwithstanding his marked interest in art, in particular the Italian Renaissance, Cornelius had begun his academic career as a natural scientist. But once he had read Schopenhauer, philosophy would not let him go. *The World as Will and Representation* had proved to him that an idealist position was the only sure foundation for a knowledge of nature that is free from metaphysics. Once he had successfully completed his *Habilitation* dissertation in philosophy and the aforementioned work of 1897, on psychology as an empirical science, he was surprised to receive an invitation to accept the chair in philosophy at the University of Halle – it came just as he was 'engaged in copying a Tintoretto in Venice'.[9] But for a variety of reasons unconnected with Tintoretto he was reluctant to accept this invitation, and instead he finally decided to opt for an alternative, very attractive offer from Mayor Adickes of a chair in the future University of Frankfurt. Here he was very happy, since it was not long before 'enthusiastic students of philosophy would meet of an evening in his country house in the Taunus Hills in order to discuss problems of the theory of knowledge.'[10] They were soon joined by the representatives of gestalt psychology who would later becomes famous: Friedrich Schumann and Adhémar Gelb, as well as an exclusive circle of doctoral students, among them Horkheimer and Adorno.

Even if we discount this somewhat anecdotal account of his career, it is nevertheless illuminating to see what Cornelius has to say about his own philosophy.[11] For it contains ideas that overlap with Adorno's thought and are all the more striking for their being few in number. Pride of place goes to Cornelius's critical attitude towards a purely defining procedure in the arts and the social sciences. According to Cornelius, the danger of an infinite regress can only be avoided if you define the subject whose meaning is to be grasped with the assistance of conceptually anchored reflections. Adorno may well have appropriated in his own way Cornelius's claim that the validity of a subject has to be tested in the context of its origins, and vice versa, as well as his conviction that judgements on matters of fact contain more than can be read off from individual perceptions. In opposition to Husserl's '*Erschauen*' [seeing, viewing], Cornelius insisted on the importance of reflecting on the knowledge that came into being from synthesizing the contents of consciousness as an *a priori* precondition of statements about experience. In his view, our act of thinking always adds a noumenon to the phenomenon. Cornelius's other claim, however, that 'the development of our stock of knowledge ... consists in progressively subordinating phenomena to new laws',[12] was one that Adorno came eventually to reject, though he did not do so at the outset. It is also unlikely that he was convinced by the social aspects of Cornelius's teachings. Cornelius argued that maintaining the social conditions of freedom was a rational duty. However, this duty depended for its fulfilment on the organization of power and justice by the state. 'What mankind lacks nowadays is an education in consideration for others, and clear objectivity, instead of the constant urgings of personal gain and vanity.'[13] No doubt the young doctoral student would have shared the critical attack on the 'wretchedness of our age'. But even then he would have thought it a fallacy to seek the cause of social pathologies in the 'short-sightedness' of selfish people. For, from his very first years as a student, he was familiar with a sociological perspective that focuses on human subjects in the context of their social relationships. The ideas he formulated in the *Minima Moralia* two decades later were already present in a rudimentary form then – in particular, the belief that conservative cultural criticism is mistaken when it blames individual human beings for the decline of the individual and the crisis of culture.

Reactionary criticism . . . places the ontological responsibility for this on the individual as such, as something discrete and internal. . . . Society is seen . . . as an unmediated community of men, from whose attitudes the whole follows, instead of as a system not only encompassing and deforming them, but even reaching down into that humanity which once conditioned them as individuals.[14]

Thanks to his discussions with Siegfried Kracauer, Adorno was familiar with sociological ways of thinking. He might not have achieved analyses as succinct as in these remarks, but he certainly believed that thinking in sociological categories was a specific legitimate method. He also had the opportunity of learning about the history of social ideas in the seminars given by the now-forgotten Gottfried Salomon-Delatour. Salomon-Delatour had taken his doctorate with Georg Simmel in 1915, and six years later he still passed for a youthful lecturer at Frankfurt University. He was attached to the Sociology Department, which was under the direction of Franz Oppenheimer. There he was responsible for the history of ideas and historical sociology. He took a special interest in the French working-class movement and also the development of socialism and historical materialism.[15] Since Salomon-Delatour came from a family that was both French and German, Jewish and Protestant, Adorno may have felt a certain affinity with him. A further attraction must have been the circumstance that Salomon-Delatour knew Walter Benjamin, who even took part in seminar discussions from time to time.

Between 1923 and 1925 Benjamin frequently visited Frankfurt, where he hoped to obtain the *Habilitation* with his study of *The Origin of German Tragic Drama*, a project which Salomon-Delatour had enthusiastically supported – in vain, unfortunately.[16] As philosophers, neither Cornelius nor Horkheimer could approve Benjamin's work, and it was also rejected by Franz Schulz, the only literature expert to be consulted.[17]

A further opportunity to become acquainted with sociology was provided by the seminars of Franz Oppenheimer, the professor of sociology and economics, who was already in his fifties. Oppenheimer, the son of a Berlin reform rabbi, was a practising Jew; he had a socially critical outlook, but no allegiance to any political party. Having qualified for the *Habilitation* in economics, he accepted the offer of the foundation chair in sociology that had been endowed by Consul Kotzenburg. This was the first chair in sociology to be established anywhere in Germany. At Oppenheimer's request the title of the chair was extended to include 'economics'. Oppenheimer's experience as a practising doctor, first in rural East Prussia and then in the slums of Berlin, meant that the social question and the link between socialism and land reform were always high on his agenda, a programme that was reinforced by his intensive study of Karl Marx's critique of political economy.[18] It is not known whether Adorno was familiar at least with

Oppenheimer's magnum opus, although Horkheimer did refer to it from time to time.

First meeting with Max Horkheimer
in the seminar on gestalt psychology

The young Max Horkheimer, who had just completed his doctoral thesis on a problem in epistemology, was Cornelius's assistant at the time, though he still managed to be independent enough to put forward his own ideas. 'What we must seek out are not formal laws of knowledge, which are basically quite unimportant, but material statements about our lives and their meaning.'[19] This statement stands in stark contrast to Cornelius and can scarcely have escaped the attention of the young philosophy student. Can it be Adorno who is being referred to in a letter Horkheimer wrote to his future wife in November 1921? 'Yesterday, I lectured a young philosopher about the task of philosophy. He was very enthusiastic. Unfortunately, I learned today that Cornelius was next door and must have heard my speech, which was entirely directed against his opinions.'[20]

It was around this time that Horkheimer, whose career was being so energetically promoted by Cornelius, must have first encountered Adorno, in a seminar of the gestalt psychologist Adhémar Gelb.[21] Horkheimer, who was eight years Adorno's senior, 'did not really look like a student, but rather, like a young gentleman from a prosperous family who took an interest in learning, but from a certain distance.'[22] Horkheimer was untouched by 'that *déformation professionelle* of the academic who all too easily mistakes a preoccupation with learned matters for reality.' Adorno also recalls his impressions after Horkheimer had given a paper on aspects of Husserl's philosophy:

> I spontaneously went up to you and introduced myself. Since then we have been together. Among my early impressions was my sense of a slightly daring elegance that set you apart both from middle-class respectability and from the appearance of the other students. Your face was passionate and ascetically lean. You looked like a gentleman, and like a born refugee. This applied also to your style of living. You had bought a house in Kronberg together with Fred Pollock and lived a secluded life there, but with an evident distaste for furnished rooms.[23]

The connection between the two men was limited at first to Horkheimer's encouragement of Adorno's philosophy studies. This included practical help in preparing for the various compulsory examinations. Adorno wrote about this in a letter to Leo Löwenthal in July 1924. He had spent, he says, ten days in Kronberg as the guest of

Horkheimer and his friend Friedrich Pollock, 'both highly unusual people who received me with the greatest kindness and who drilled me strictly according to the principles of Schumannesque psychology. Both, incidentally, are communists and we had lengthy and passionate exchanges about materialist views of history in which we each made concessions to the other.'[24] We may presume that Horkheimer was rarely of one mind with Adorno's intellectual restlessness and his habit of referring constantly to music and composition.

At the forefront of their discussions was the problem of what was the right philosophy for the modern sciences. What answer does philosophy have to the growing evils of society? The fact that they both asked such questions formed the foundation for the collaboration between them on philosophical issues. This steadily grew over time in the seminars that Horkheimer gave on such topics as the phenomenology of consciousness, historical materialism or the history of metaphysics. Although he could not compete with Adorno's musical expertise, his knowledge and experience in dealing with academic philosophy enabled him to hold his own.

Philosophy was anything but a natural inheritance to Horkheimer, whose family background was that of conservative Jewish businessmen. He grew up in Stuttgart, the capital of Württemberg, the son of Moritz Horkheimer, a textile manufacturer who had been given the title of Kommerzienrat [commercial councillor] by the king of Bavaria after the First World War for his services to his country. His father presided over a strict, patriarchal regime in the family that led to sharp conflicts with Max as he grew up. These were mitigated by his mother, who provided security and loving affection. As an only son, Max was expected to take over the business once he had completed his commercial training. With this in mind, he left the Gymnasium in the fifth form to acquire practical experience for his future career. Travels to Belgium and Britain as well as service in the First World War led him to doubt whether a primarily commercial career was morally defensible. Together with his boyhood friend Friedrich Pollock, who shared his intellectual ambitions and political views, he went to Munich after the collapse of the German Empire in order to catch up on his education and take the *Abitur* examination. He began to study in Munich, where he came into contact with the revolutionary socialism of men such as Erich Mühsam, Ernst Toller and Gustav Landauer. After a brief interlude in Freiburg, where he encountered Husserl and Heidegger, he went on to the newly established university in Frankfurt and took his doctorate under Hans Cornelius's supervision. He had almost completed a dissertation in the field of cognitive and gestalt psychology – psychology was formally his major subject in Frankfurt – when it had to be scrapped because a Danish colleague had conducted a similar study just before him and had at once published his results internationally. This precarious situation now led to one of the most important events of his life, as he himself records. Cornelius had learnt about the debacle and, 'when I had to produce a seminar paper for one of his classes, he said to me "Do you have a manuscript copy?" I said I did whereupon he said, "Give it to me and come to my room in a bit". I waited for around an hour and went to his room. My manuscript was lying there with some marginal comments. Very many, in fact. And Cornelius said to me, "If you follow my instructions, that will be your dissertation". I did as he suggested and obtained my doctorate in 1922. What he did was quite wonderful . . . and in general he had a decisive influence on my life.'[25] But this influence did not prevent Horkheimer from going his own way. He had successfully shown in his disagreements with his father that he knew how to challenge authority and defend his own interests. He not only resisted his father's express wish that he should adopt a career in business, he even went against his family in the choice of his marriage partner. In 1926 he married Rosa Christin Riekher, whom he had met in 1915 in the family firm in Stuttgart, where she worked as a secretary. She was unacceptable to his parents both as a Christian and as the daughter of a bankrupted businessman. Moreover, she was eight years older than their only son. Despite quarrels with his parents that went on for years, Max's love for her never faltered, as can be seen from the warm, affectionate letters that he wrote to 'his Maidon' his whole life long.

Like Adorno, Horkheimer evidently maintained a split between his personal political convictions, his view of life and his mental attitude, on the one hand, and his formal career as an academic, on the other. There is an obvious discrepancy between the sympathy he felt in his youth for the revolutionary communist Rosa Luxemburg, who was murdered by Freikorps officers in January 1919, for democracy and socialism, for the philosophy of historical materialism, on the one hand, and the academically approved topic of his dissertation and indeed of his thesis for the *Habilitation*, on the other. His doctoral dissertation, which led to his being the first person to qualify at Frankfurt University with philosophy as his major subject, treated the antinomy of teleological judgement. Anyone who imagines that he was concerned there with conflicts between idealism and materialism would be sadly disappointed. Instead, he dutifully focused on distinctions between mechanistic and non-mechanistic explanatory models; he discussed the relationship between the whole and its parts in the world of phenomena. In an attempt to delimit Kant's equation of scientific and mechanical explanations, he pleaded for the concept of gestalt qualities – quite in tune with his own academic teachers, who were decisively influenced by Wilhelm Dilthey's notion of structure.[26]

Thus Horkheimer's early writing formed part of the official alignment with the dominant philosophy of Cornelius that was characteristic of those early years at Frankfurt University. According to Horkheimer, the mark of that philosophy was that 'it bore the marks of its origins in the epistemological problems that arise from a preoccupation with the natural sciences.'[27] The same thing can be said of Horkheimer's *Habilitation* thesis of 1925 on *Kant's Critique of Judgement as a Link between Theoretical and Practical Philosophy*, as well as for his first lecture course, which he gave in the winter semester of 1925–6. As before, he argued with Kant against Kant in order to show that the congruence between theoretical and practical reason was not accidental. If there were a difference in principle between the two forms of reason, this was to be explained by circumstances arising from the nature of consciousness. He also remained within the confines of identity-philosophy in his early notes on the *concept of totality*. Totality, he noted, goes back to a structure of existence that the subjective mind perceives directly, resulting in a unity of object and knowledge.[28] In his years as a *Privatdozent*, there was as yet no insuperable abyss between Horkheimer's way of thinking and modern positivism. On the contrary, positivism's critique of metaphysics and its logical reduction of linguistic utterances to empirical experience came close to his own views.

Adorno experienced the relation between his personal inclinations and the nature of academic philosophy in much the same way as Horkheimer. Privately, he was fascinated by critically minded, anti-bourgeois writers such as Georg Lukács in his *The Theory of the Novel* and Ernst Bloch in his *Spirit of Utopia*. In his university studies, by contrast, as in his thesis on Husserl in 1924 and even the first draft of his *Habilitation* dissertation on *The Concept of the Unconscious in the Transcendental Doctrine of the Soul* of 1927, he remained within the self-enclosed world of academic philosophy. 'The epistemological standpoint that we presuppose . . . is the one adopted by Hans Cornelius in his books. . . . This standpoint is generally assumed and it is therefore not necessary to make explicit reference to it.'[29] Similar statements can be found in the dissertation that Adorno had finished in summer 1924 and for which he received the mark *'summa cum laude'*. In a letter of July 1924, Adorno gave Leo Löwenthal an account of this hastily written dissertation: 'I spent the latter half of April in Amorbach . . . working on Husserl. By the middle of May, I had planned my dissertation and on the 26th I presented the plan to Cornelius, who duly accepted it. By 6 June, the dissertation was finished; it was dictated on the 11th and handed in on the 14th.'[30] There were unforeseen formal difficulties with the final examination, however, because the discipline of sociology was not recognized by the Arts Faculty as a legitimate subject. Adorno told Löwenthal that the reason for this was to be sought in 'anti-Semitic rancour towards Oppenheimer and Salomon'. A further factor was that the regulations required him to choose a science subject as a minor element in the examination. Adorno's choice fell reluctantly on 'Professor Schumann's psychology, which is actually even drearier than Salomon's sociology, productive only as a source below the kitsch threshold.'[31] In order to learn in short order as much psychology as he would need for the examination, he sought help from Horkheimer, who was conversant with the methods of gestalt psychology that were dominant in Frankfurt at the time. However, with assistance or without, once the dissertation had been awarded the mark of '*summa cum laude*', nothing much could go wrong in the oral examination, which was held on 28 June 1924. And even if Adorno was rather presumptuous in his views on the state of sociology and psychology in the university, his own dissertation was far from containing a manifesto of original deviations from the main currents of thought in Frankfurt.

What was the subject of his doctoral dissertation? It was an analysis of contradictory elements in Husserl's theory of things and knowledge. He focused, first, on his concept of the noematic, that is, the phenomenological description of the object, the thing that gives a percept its meaningful unity; and, second, on the Kantian concept of the 'thing-in-itself' that he thought ambiguous in Husserl's interpretation. He focused on the problem of what he saw as a dubious contrast between reality and consciousness, between the contingent world and the absolute self. He thought that Husserl had failed to make clear whether objects could be grasped by reducing them to what was given, or whether they existed as 'absolute transcendent things', independent of consciousness. In a crucial passage of his account he asked: what is the relation between existence as consciousness and existence as reality? Husserl assumed, so he maintained, that intuition was the only valid form of knowledge. Adorno rejected this premise because it is in conflict with Husserl's distinction between the idea of a thing and the sensuously perceptible individual objects. Furthermore, Husserl was said to have overlooked the fundamental importance of gestalt qualities for consciousness. Entirely in the spirit of Cornelius, Adorno continued: 'Without gestalt qualities the laws governing the functions of cognition and expectation simply become a miracle that can do no more than posit the existence of a world of objects independent of consciousness, and to which experiences are related as if to something "transcendental".'[32] Adorno rejected the concept of intuition in phenomenology because it assumes that the ultimate explanation for the truth of judgements about things is contained in what is immediately given, 'an object to be apprehended by its different characteristics. No infinite transcendence stands behind the phenomena. They are constituted solely in accordance with the laws governing our consciousness.'[33] To talk about a thing's identity only has meaning, he claims, if it can be conceived of as both ideal and empirical, 'if a thing can be thought of as one and the same thing in a plurality of *experiences*; only where there is a plurality of events can we speak of the identity of an object, and the plurality of events in which the identity of a thing becomes manifest are the facts of our consciousness.'[34]

When Adorno speaks of 'us' and 'our', which he did frequently, what he had in mind was himself and his teacher. For Cornelius a thing was something 'ideal', but 'not in a vague way like Husserl's concept of a thing, but as something well defined as part of a nexus of phenomena governed by laws. As such it is subject to correction by experience.'[35]

Guided by Cornelius's point of view, the twenty-year-old Adorno engaged with Husserl's philosophy, setting up a confrontation between transcendental idealism on the one hand and Husserl's *Logical Invest-igations* on the other, as well as his *Ideas Pertaining to a Pure Phenomeno-logy and to a Phenomenological Philosophy*. As a doctoral student, then, he practised what he was to call 'standpoint philosophy', an approach he later rejected. The dissertation was divided into three succinct chap-ters and contained lengthy quotations from Husserl's writings, but other-wise referred only to Cornelius and Kant's *Critique of Pure Reason*.

A glance at both Horkheimer's and Adorno's early writings shows that the two disciples of Cornelius distinguished between their political opinions and their philosophical positions. It is unlikely that they were unaware of the difference. What then motivated them to turn away from the neo-Kantian strand of transcendental philosophy?

As a young man, Horkheimer had a strong sense of social justice and solidarity. We can see this clearly in his early efforts as a writer. During the revolutionary events at the end of the First World War, when the soviet republic was proclaimed in Munich and the proletarian masses went out onto the streets, his profoundly moral view of the world became increasingly politicized. During this brief phase, Munich became a laboratory for anti-bourgeois lifestyles and revolutionary politics. Horkheimer was even caught up in these political struggles for a time. He was briefly arrested in Bavaria after the police mistook him for the writer and revolutionary Ernst Toller.

Characteristic of the age was the fact that in Germany anti-Semitism went hand in hand with the hatred felt by right-wing fanatics for all socialist ideas. Horkheimer reacted to this by moving gradually from Ernst Toller's expressionist advocacy of human brotherhood, via Arthur Schopenhauer's philosophy of compassion, to Karl Marx's critique of ideology, and ultimately to Marx's idea of a practice that would change the world. In what Horkheimer described as his desire to find out about the world, Marx's theory provided 'the best critical account of history'. He hoped that he would be able to use the theory of historical materialism to develop a historically based model for changing society.[36] Towards the end of the 1920s, the process of philosophical clarification started to be reflected in his activities as a university lecturer.

How did Adorno change from a neo-Kantian to a Marxist? Unlike the slightly older generation to which Horkheimer belonged, he was spared any direct experience of the First World War. For him the hor-ror of the war must have consisted primarily in the fact of nine million dead in Europe and the absolute meaninglessness of many individual human lives.

Adorno was as aware as many other sensitive contemporaries that the bourgeois world now lay in ruins and that capitalism was discredited.

But this knowledge did not follow from any personal threat to his own well-being. He thought of the crisis of the age as a general disintegration of bourgeois traditions, as a collapse that he confronted in the context of avant-garde art, literature and philosophy. Supporting the achievements of cultural modernity had already become second nature to him. Collectivist ideologies did not have the slightest attraction for him. His generally critical view of the bourgeois world went hand in hand with an anti-capitalist attitude, as well as a tendency to embrace radical socialist ideas.[37] By the middle of the 1920s it was clear to him that the categories with which he had interpreted the world up to then had become unusable. Influenced by the intellectuals with whom he associated, he now went in search of a viable philosophy of history and political theory. This brought him closer to socialist and communist ideas and their philosophical underpinnings. He now believed that the catastrophes of the age were the product of the conflict-ridden dynamic of the capitalist economy and that the existing social order was doomed. This was linked with an interest in the philosophy of historical materialism, the critique of political economy and Karl Marx's theory of revolution, all of which were very much in tune with the times. In this respect he was influenced by ideas that Georg Lukács had introduced around 1920, the ideas of 'transcendental homelessness', the 'contingent world' and the 'problematic individual'. Of equal importance was Walter Benjamin's diagnosis of the age:

> Experience has fallen in value. And it looks as if it is continuing to fall into a bottomless abyss. . . . For never has experience been contradicted more thoroughly even than strategic experience by positional warfare, economic experience by inflation, bodily experience by mechanical warfare, moral experience by those in power. A generation that had gone to school on a horse-drawn streetcar now stood under the open sky in a countryside in which nothing remained unchanged but the clouds, and beneath these clouds, in a force field of destructive torrents and explosions, was the tiny, fragile human body.[38]

Adorno felt impelled to inquire how the sense of crisis of the age was reflected in its intellectual products, and how it could find proper expression in art. Art had to be nonconformist, it must signify the abolition of bad traditions and remind us of the possibility of something better. Confronted with a world stripped of meaning and with history in a turmoil, art must pose existential questions, and above all the question 'of the existence of the spiritual as such'.[39] Art that aspired to truth – and only radical modern art could do that – could articulate the contradictions of the age as these were expressed in the clash between oppositional and restorationist ideas. But such art could not be the mere impression of a chance experience, or the expressionist scream of isolated individuals in their youthful protest against traditional forms. Instead, art should seek valid expression as 'the dissolution of the self into a higher unity'.

Early on Adorno had come up against the limits of the sovereign human subject: 'What has become subjective and contingent remains subjective and contingent in its effect as well. We are all in danger of sinning against the human spirit.'[40] This was Adorno's conclusion in an early essay on expressionism. It was plain that from the outset intellectual activity had a fundamentally ethical streak in his eyes. His ideas might have seemed close to cultural conservatism, but he escaped this by his determination to liberate himself from traditional patterns of thought. Thus his critical stance followed from his experience that the traditional forms of art were as obsolete as the bourgeois way of life as such. There was no alternative to Rimbaud's credo '*Il faut être absolument moderne!*' And this modernity in the realm of art was linked to the spirit of opposition that brought him closer to left-wing revolutionary movements.

Of course, like many other intellectuals, he had to confront the question of how this open-ended future was to be achieved in practice. It was his belief that criticism was the only instrument that would work. It protects the mind from dogmatic sclerosis and promotes the willingness to risk innovation both in art and in forms of social community. The revolution Arnold Schoenberg had brought about in music provided Adorno with a model. What had to be done to make the spark leap from the realm of art to that of society?

6

A Man with Philosophical Qualities in the World of Viennese Music: The Danube Metropolis

What were the prospects towards the end of 1924, a few months after the inflation and the economic crisis had passed its highpoint, for a young doctor of philosophy who had attracted some attention as a music critic? Even for an unusually talented person, career opportunities at the university were anything but rosy. After all, there had been moments during the crisis when there was a real threat to the future of the university. Not only might it have lost its special status as an independent university; it might even have been forced to shut its doors for good. Without further infusions of money it was scarcely viable. In the event there was a concerted rescue campaign by the city, the founding institutions and the state. This proved successful, thanks in large measure to Carl Heinrich Becker, the Prussian secretary of state at the time, and subsequently the head of the Ministry of Education.[1] In the event, Frankfurt University was rescued by the injection of state funds and was still able to continue as a private foundation without having to surrender its autonomy to central control.

Adorno was able to benefit from this continuity. Following his *Abitur*, he was able to remain in Frankfurt and graduate in a relatively short time. However, his prospects of obtaining even a modest position in the as yet still small Arts Faculty were minuscule. The advantage of this, Adorno wrote, was that he was protected from 'salaried profundity' and was exempted from the need 'to be at each moment as naive as the colleagues on whom one's career depended'. On the other hand, a non-academic philosopher would be forced to adopt a bohemian lifestyle that would bring him 'too close for comfort to the world of commercial art, crackpot religion and sectarian pseudo-culture'. 'So great is the power of the advancing organization of thought, that those who want to keep outside it are driven to resentful vanity, babbling self-advertisement, and finally, in their defeat, to imposture.' But even the philosopher's apparent escape route of earning his living by writing is unsatisfactory because 'he is obliged at every moment to have something choice, ultra-select to offer, and to counter the monopoly of office with that of rarity.'[2] Since philosophical thought had been an integral part of Adorno's life from his early youth, he continued to devote himself to it for the time being as a writer forced into being original every day and in the absence of a position in the Philosophy Department that would guarantee him financial independence. He was not rescued from the fate of a private scholar either by his good relationship with Cornelius, or by the breadth of his intellectual interests, even though these brought him into contact with a number of professors and a variety of discussion circles. As a philosopher and musicologist who also knew about composing, a further difficulty for Adorno was the circumstance that his extreme intellectuality made many people think him altogether too exotic a creature. His versatility and eloquence were indeed marvelled at, but the run-of-the-mill university staff tended to regard him with suspicion and even went out of their way to avoid him.

It took people who were themselves out of the ordinary and intellectually self-confident to engage in a more intensive and lasting relationship with the extravagant son of a wine-merchant and a singer. In addition to Siegfried Kracauer and Max Horkheimer, these included a number of people of his own age, in particular Leo Löwenthal, Peter von Haselberg, Carl Dreyfus and, later, Walter Benjamin and Ernst Bloch. All these men had more or less direct interests in philosophy. At this period, Adorno may well have recognized that his experience and knowledge could not match that of older men like Kracauer, Benjamin and Horkheimer. Nevertheless, it is clear from the correspondence that he attempted to meet them on an equal footing. Despite his youth, he did not lack in self-confidence.

Apprenticeship with his master and teacher

Adorno's attitude was quite different with regard to another person who would be of great importance for his future. This was the Viennese composer Alban Berg, with whom he was to have a relationship of growing intensity over the coming months and years.

Berg was born in Vienna on 9 February 1885. His career as a composer in association with the circle around Arnold Schoenberg began around 1910, when he finished his String Quartet, op. 3, and after the *Five Orchestral Songs on Postcards from Peter Altenberg*, op. 4, had been performed in Vienna. These works were then followed by the *Four Pieces for Clarinet and Piano*, op. 5. Berg obtained celebrity and then recognition with his opera *Wozzeck*, for which he had completed the orchestration in April 1921. When the opera was given its first performance on 14 December 1925 in Berlin under Erich Kleiber, it triggered a huge controversy. Thanks to the furore, it received twenty-one performances. Adorno and Benjamin were present at one of them, and both were deeply impressed by the work.[3] Further compositions by Berg include the *Lyric Suite* for string quartet, first performed by the

Kolisch Quartet in January 1927 in Vienna; and the Violin Concerto, which he dedicated to the memory of Manon Gropius, a daughter of Alma Mahler's, who had died at the age of eighteen. The so-called *Lulu* Symphony that resulted from the reworking of extracts from Act 3 of the unfinished opera *Lulu* was performed for the first time in Berlin in November 1934. Once again Kleiber conducted, and the performance was a great success. The opera itself was not performed until June 1937 in Zurich. Its composer, however, had already died of blood poisoning on 23 December 1935, at the age of fifty.

The intensity of the relationship between Adorno and Berg can be seen from their extensive correspondence (amounting to 136 letters) between 1925 and 1935. An exemplary passage illustrating the reverence Adorno felt for Berg can be found in the letter of 30 March 1926: 'You must be aware that there is no one to whom I feel more deeply, definitely and gratefully attached than to you; and I could not imagine anything, absolutely anything, that would make me wish to part from you.'[4] After studying for six months in Vienna, Adorno had taken to addressing Berg with the words 'Dear master and teacher'.[5]

Adorno had met Berg in person in the early summer of 1924, at a time when he was completing his doctorate. The occasion was the premiere of Berg's *Three Fragments from Wozzeck*, op. 7, for voices and orchestra, in the context of the Frankfurt Festival of the Allgemeiner Deutscher Musikverein. The concert was a success, as was a performance of the entire opera some time afterwards, something that caused Berg some unease. According to Adorno, Berg had said that, if a modern piece of music could win the audience over so directly, there must be something wrong with it.[6]

The Frankfurt performance of the *Fragments* was conducted by Hermann Scherchen, who was always eager to promote modern music and whom Adorno already knew well.[7] So Adorno asked Scherchen to introduce him to Berg. 'Within minutes', he reported later, it was arranged 'that I would go to Vienna to study with him; I had to wait until after my graduation in July. In the event, my move to Vienna was delayed until the beginning of January 1925.'[8]

A few months after making Berg's acquaintance, Adorno wrote a brief study occasioned by the premiere of *Wozzeck*. After his first extended stay in Vienna, his review was published in the December issue of the *Musikblätter des Anbruch*. This was his first attempt to discuss Berg's music as a highly individual continuation of the type of composition created by Arnold Schoenberg. Before he put pen to paper Berg had asked him 'not to write in a difficult manner, but in a generally comprehensible way.'[9] In vain: in a linguistically complex text, Adorno interprets the particular motives and symphonic scope of Berg's music by providing an account of his entire extant output; the early piano sonatas, the String Quartet, the *Pieces for Clarinet and Piano*, as well as the *Three Pieces*, op. 6, and the Chamber Concerto. Although, according to Adorno, there was a certain affinity with Gustav Mahler's symphonies, Berg's will to construct negated the language of emphatic subjectivity peculiar to the nineteenth century. This 'renunciation of psychologism by consummating it' had its basis in the music's technical economy. 'In that economy it calls for the responsibility of the person in the face of the chaos of shattered forms. Their ruins are the material it works with.' In *Wozzeck*, Berg's music immerses itself in the abyss of mankind, by piercing its 'psychological outer skin'.[10] In terms of its conceptual grip and stylistic force, this piece is one of the most powerful that Adorno wrote as a young man.

In addition to the *Wozzeck* essay, Adorno wrote about Schoenberg's *Serenade*, op. 24, a piece he was able to publish in *Pult und Taktstock* in September 1925. Here, too, his starting-point was the end of expressive music and the disintegration of traditional musical forms. This was the source of Schoenberg's irony, which remains 'equidistant from bourgeois complacency and nihilistic polemic'.[11] He analysed the form this irony took in the music by examining the solutions Schoenberg provided to the emerging problems of the composition. For example, he refers to his hidden use of a march within the seven movements of the serenade. This enabled the piece to combine freedom of expression with the creation of new forms arising from the musical material itself.

Years later, on the occasion of Schoenberg's sixtieth birthday, Adorno undertook the task of exploring in detail how this music worked. In that study he begins by asking what the abolition of traditional harmony means for modern music:

> Schoenberg asks where this harmony is drifting, and goes on to investigate the 'instinctual life of sounds'; he distinguishes between what is ornament and what is integral – and does away with ornaments and symmetries that in this harmony and this counterpoint become separated out from the matter in hand; he considers how to eliminate the break between exposition and development, now that the disintegration of the tonal unity of the sonata has deprived it of meaning; how to do away with the false predominance of one note over the other in the harmonic and melodic structure, and how to prevent the collapse of horizontals and verticals. And as a succinct, precise answer, he develops the twelve-tone technique.[12]

Adorno immersed himself deeply in Schoenberg's oeuvre. He regarded him as the revolutionary who transformed traditional methods of composition, and always emphasized the importance of his achievement. Even so, it was Alban Berg whom he most esteemed and for whom he felt the greater personal sympathy. It was for this reason that he sought to demonstrate the individual qualities of Berg's music and to display them in their proper light. From the outset he rejected the idea of a Schoenberg school whose writ was binding on its members.

Adorno's recollections of his first impressions show Berg to have been a man of exceptional charm. Berg's shyness helped him 'overcome the trepidation I would otherwise have felt at the sight of a man I so greatly admired. If I try to recall the impulse that drew me spontaneously to him I am sure it was exceedingly naive, but it was related to something very essential about Berg: the *Wozzeck Fragments*, above all the introduction to the March and then the March itself, struck me as a combination of Schoenberg and Mahler, and at the time, that was my ideal of genuine, new music.'[13]

Adorno was encountering problems in his own attempts at composition. His efforts to break out of the confines of his training with Bernhard Sekles left him increasingly dissatisfied and he found himself facing difficulties he could not resolve on his own. Even so, he had quite a number of compositions to his credit, including string quartets, string trios, and piano pieces. To a degree, then, despite his youth he was familiar with compositional practice by the time he wrote to Berg asking to be allowed to become his student.

> Independently of tuition [i.e., with Sekles], I went on composing for myself. 6 *Studies for String Quartet* (1920) were performed privately by the Rebner-Hindemith Quartet in 1921, my First Quartet (1921) was performed by Hans Lange in 1923. In addition, I have written 2 string trios and songs for various performers. In recent years I have concentrated on scholarly and technical work, and on the piano. The only pieces I have written are 3 four-part choruses for *a cappella* women's voices (1923) and three piano pieces. I am dissatisfied with all this and in order to carry out my new plans I should like to entrust myself to your guidance and control. My interest is in finding the solution to quite specific technical problems which I feel are beyond my powers. I believe that I shall be in a position to tell you precisely where I am wanting. . . . With sincere admiration, Dr. Th. Wiesengrund-Adorno.[14]

In March 1925, by which time Adorno's letterhead had been proudly sporting the doctoral title for three months, he finally made the journey to Vienna, where he took a room in a boarding house with the dauntingly old-fashioned name of Luisenheim. However, this boarding house, which was situated in the ninth district, was anything but conventional. It was an imposing building dating back to the boom years of the late nineteenth century, complete with portal, marble interiors, art nouveau stained-glass windows and a lift built of solid wood with mirrors typical of the Vienna of the day. To reach Berg, who lived in Hietzing, a long tram ride was necessary.[15] The boarding house was also home to a number of curious and interesting people. Among them were the actress

Ellen Delp, a black woman with a son who was said to be a communist, with whom he quickly formed a friendship. By chance, Arthur Koestler, who was not yet famous, was also living in the Luisenheim. Adorno did not take to him. For his part, Koestler thought the young man from Frankfurt was a shy, esoteric person with a subtle charm that he was too callow to appreciate at the time.[16]

The 21-year-old Adorno had longed to move to the birthplace of twelve-tone music and to study with Berg, but this is not to say he left Frankfurt without regrets. He was reluctant to leave his family and also to be separated from Gretel Karplus in Berlin or from his close friend Siegfried Kracauer. To begin with at least, Vienna was terra incognita, and it took time for him to familiarize himself with it and to accustom himself to the Viennese sloppiness, the easy-going manners he so frequently complained about.

Vienna at the time was partly an aristocratic city and partly a centre of bourgeois capitalist commerce. Having left Frankfurt, Adorno may well have cherished the hope of being able to find there 'a bolt-hole in which to lead an acceptable existence'.[17] Ultimately, he did not succeed in this, although he came to feel at home there and there is no doubt that he profited from the Viennese way of life and its musical culture. Vienna had a lively intellectual scene, half bourgeois, half anti-bourgeois. This stood apart from both the established bourgeois commercial circles and the socially enfeebled aristocracy. To gain an impression of this artistic life we need only to remind ourselves of the so-called Secessionist artists, Egon Schiele, Gustav Klimt, Peter Altenberg, Oskar Kokoschka, and especially Karl Kraus, with his magazine *Die Fackel*. In addition, there was Sigmund Freud's Psychoanalytical Society, the writers who wrote for Ludwig von Ficker's literary journal *Der Brenner*, and the music journal *Internationale Gesellschaft für neue Musik*, which had an international reputation and was engaged in a campaign to win support for the Second Viennese School. Some of these intellectual groupings had already begun to break up while Adorno was in Vienna, and he came into contact with only a few isolated individuals, but he benefited all the same from the after-effects of this ferment.

This Viennese avant-garde met in a number of salons, chief among them those of Alma Mahler-Werfel and Lina Loos. It 'brought about a liberation in the very concrete sense of creating an independence from the institutions and people who impeded their access to the public. We are talking here about the organizers of exhibitions, publishers and art critics, etc. This meant also a liberation from the pressure to conform to assumed or experienced audience expectations. This was the true "material" foundation of that "great revolution" in the art of the turn of the century.'[18] When Adorno studied in Vienna in the mid-1920s, the scandals created by the Rosé Quartet's performances of works from the Second Viennese School lay firmly in the past. There had been tumultuous scenes in December 1908 when Schoenberg's Second String

Quartet, op. 10, had been performed. There was a further scandal during a concert of the Academy for Literature and Music in March 1913, when Schoenberg's Chamber Symphony, Berg's *Altenberg-Lieder* and Mahler's *Kindertotenlieder* were on the programme. Eberhard Buschbeck, the promoter of the concert, even came to blows with a member of the audience, who subsequently turned out to be a popular composer of operettas. When Adorno was told of these events by Lotte Tobisch von Labotýn, who had witnessed them, he noted the irony of the situation in which the low-brow culture of the operetta leapt to the defence of high culture as soon as the opportunity arose to denounce modern music as an attack on traditional artistic values.[19] Adorno and Schoenberg met for the first time when Anton Webern was conducting Bruckner's F minor Mass in the local church in Mödling, where Schoenberg was living. Schoenberg was fifty-seven and was regarded as the authority on twelve-tone music. He was well aware of the special place he occupied in the musical life of Vienna, and cultivated this exclusive position in his dealings with the outside world. With his teacher, Alexander Zemlinsky, he had already established the Society of Creative Musicians in 1904 in order to create a stable framework for the few people interested in modern music. The Society for Private Musical Performances which he created in 1918 provided a venue for introducing the compositions of the Schoenberg circle to a select audience of genuine enthusiasts.

During Adorno's stay in Vienna the general mood could not be called optimistic, either in politics or in cultural affairs. On the contrary, he found himself confronted with a peculiar mixture of Viennese 'conciliatoriness', 'fried-chicken culture' and a systematic anti-traditionalism based on tradition.[20] His moods alternated between boundless enthusiasm, dislike and nostalgia, as can be seen from his detailed accounts of the city and the people he met, above all of Berg, to whose house in Trauttmannsdorffgasse 27 in Hietzing he would repair twice a week. 'At the time I thought the street was incomparably beautiful. With its plane trees it reminded me . . . of Cézanne.' He could recognize the house from the dissonant chords that were being struck on the piano. 'The name on the door was designed by Berg himself in artistic script . . . with a trace of *Jugendstil*, yet clearly legible, and without annoying curlicues.'[21]

Adorno's tuition with Berg was frequently interrupted by the latter's travels to give concerts or for recreation. What stayed in Adorno's memory of it was its unconventionality. Neither counterpoint nor the study of form were given precedence. Adorno's own compositions were regularly subjected to critical discussion, which was so thorough that Berg worked his own ideas into his pupil's pieces, which were in themselves conceived basically on Bergian lines. 'Usually, he would take a long time looking at what I brought him and then come up with possible solutions . . . that never smoothed over difficulties or skirted them with facile answers, but always hit the nail on the head.' In this way Adorno learned from Berg everything about composition that was of import-ance to him. Berg's 'musical strength was that of intellectual imagina-tion and an acutely deliberate command of the possibilities, as well as a strong original inventiveness.'[22] During the lessons the two would often practise playing four-handed, which both of them loved. Joint exercises in composition could also take on an element of parody, as when they produced a perfect piece of mock-Webern 'consisting of a single quarter-note rest under a quintuplet bracket and garnished with every conceivable symbol and performance notation'.[23]

In addition to studying composition with Berg, Adorno continued studying the piano as he had done at the Hoch Conservatory. His teacher was Eduard Steuermann, a native Pole whom Berg had recommended. He too belonged to the Schoenberg circle; indeed, he was regarded as the specialist in interpretation in works of the Schoenberg school. The mutual sympathy between teacher and pupil soon developed into a friendship that lasted a lifetime, extending beyond the emigration of both men to the United States, and ending only with Steuermann's death in November 1964. In Adorno's judgement, Steuermann did not simply 'possess an open-minded receptiveness to radically modern music. It was more than that; it was flesh of his flesh, the corporeal refutation of the separation of contemporary composition and traditional music-making.'[24] Adorno's obituary continues:

> His music-making was at its best, its most spontaneous, in a small circle, at night if possible, in situations in which his aversion from musical life and official musical culture found no encouragement. Even then it was not easy to persuade him to play. . . . But once he had sat down to the piano, he forgot everything else and would not stop playing. . . . His playing technique was vigorous and highly virtuosic; but he never revelled in virtuosity for its own sake. He sacrificed a facility that had cost him no effort in favour of expres-sion and structure, and despised any mere playing for effect.[25]

At the time, Adorno had not yet met Steuermann's sister Salomé, or Salka, who had trained as an actress in Max Reinhardt's Deutsches Theater in Berlin, and had then appeared at the Neue Wiener Bühne and the Munich Kammerspiele. In 1918 she had married Berthold Viertel, the writer and director, who as a young man belonged to the circle around Karl Kraus and Peter Altenberg. However, through Steuermann, Adorno became a close friend of both Salka and Berthold Viertel, although not until the emigration years in California. But more of that in due course.

During his six-month stay in Vienna, Adorno sought contact with other people in musical circles, in addition to Steuermann. The violinist Rudolf Kolisch played an important role because Adorno and he made plans, in a preliminary way, to produce a joint theory about the correct performance of a musical score, about musical reproduction. Adorno had drawn up some initial ideas about this during his stay in Vienna, and he published them in the music journal *Pult und Taktstock*. In this early sketch we can discern the outlines of Adorno's approach to musical interpretation. He continued to reflect on this subject throughout his life, but stuck to his original ideas, although naturally he developed and refined them conceptually. The notes he made were recorded in his so-called *Black Book*. His intention was to bring them together in an independent publication, and he maintained this intention for years without ever being able to make it a reality. He left an extensive set of fragmentary writings which did not appear for years after his death.[26] In texts that he wrote when he was only twenty-one, he developed the maxim that the framework of every interpretation should be determined by the objective content, the structure of the work or score concerned. Once the coercion implicit in the external world of forms has disintegrated, the freedom to interpret can concentrate strictly on the limits of the actual text. Interpretation proves its worth in its strict objectivity, its exclusive focus on a work's structure. Such an approach creates a tense relationship with any talk of the composer's subjective intentions.[27]

Kolisch was the leader of the so-called Vienna String Quartet, one of the few ensembles that made a point of including the works of the Schoenberg circle in its repertoire.[28] At the end of the 1930s, Kolisch emigrated to the United States, where his friendship with Adorno continued to thrive. Kolisch repeatedly used his influence to encourage the performance of Adorno's own works, and in 1926 he rehearsed, and then introduced to the public, Adorno's recently completed Quartet Pieces.

Were there any composers in whom Adorno had failed to show an interest in the course of his life? There were few whom he ignored,[29] but, as the initiator of the new music, Arnold Schoenberg occupied a privileged place. All the more striking, then, is the mutual antipathy that characterized the relationship between two headstrong men who were fighting for the same cause. As early as April 1925, Adorno wrote to Kracauer from Vienna about Schoenberg's 'restless', 'obsessed' and 'uncanny' temperament.[30] Indeed, Schoenberg was said to suffer from paranoia, and not without justification, since he had recently been spat at in a coffee house. Schoenberg was said to be unable to bear being contradicted and to have imposed his own ideas on the compositions of all his followers. Schoenberg had spoken to him, Adorno, 'like Napoleon to his adjutant'. Later on, Adorno's judgement was more discriminating, but the discrepancy between the high value he placed on the music and his distance from the composer remained.[31]

What did the young Adorno find so fascinating about Vienna? In his recollections, he emphasized the opportunities for sensuous pleasure, the enjoyment of good food and fine wine. Such things were as yet unknown to the young German. Berg took him to a number of excellent restaurants which served the specialities of Austrian cuisine. 'Berg lent everyday things concerned with enjoyment an unassuming dignity.'[32]

The sensuousness of Viennese life was only one side, albeit an important one, of Adorno's life in Vienna. If we go by the letters in which he recorded his personal impressions during his months there, what is striking is the regular, ordered life he seems to have led. Would his family back in Frankfurt like to see this for themselves or to help mitigate his homesickness? Scarcely had he started to familiarize himself with the new situation and the unknown city – two female acquaintances tried to help him find his way around – than he received a visit from his mother Maria and Aunt Agathe. He introduced them to Berg, after which they resumed their journey onwards to Salzburg.

In the mornings, he busied himself with composition and played, whenever he could, on the piano that had been placed at his disposal in the boarding house.

In addition to his music studies with Berg and Steuermann, Adorno spent his evenings reading and discussing philosophical texts. He also devoted much time to his new acquaintances, friendships and loves. The relationship with Anna von Tolnay, whom he was to accompany on a trip to Marienbad and Prague, seems to have been of short duration.[33] There was also Lila, with whom he could discuss philosophical topics. He broke the relationship off when it became apparent that the friendship could not continue without developing into an erotic attachment. In contrast, his friendship with Ellen Delp, who was ten years older than him and lived in the same guest house in the Eisengasse, grew in intensity. This was at the time when she was attempting to establish herself as an actress. Later, she was to turn to writing.[34] Adorno took a liking to her and thought she was talented and cultured and at the same time childish in a lovable way, without ever showing off.

From Vienna, he travelled to Prague, where he was able to deepen his friendship with Hermann Grab, with whom he could discuss music and literature. The pretext for these holidays was that he had assumed the role of a 'postillon d'amour'. Berg had fallen passionately in love at first sight with Hanna Fuchs-Robettin, the wife of an industrialist and a sister of the writer Franz Werfel. He was busy arranging secret meetings and exchanging letters with her.[35]

Whenever there was an opportunity, Adorno accompanied Berg and his wife to concerts and, of course, to the opera. On one occasion, they heard Mahler's Eighth Symphony conducted by Anton von Webern. They became so excited about the music that they talked too loudly and 'were almost thrown out for rowdiness'.[36] They also met for a theatre visit for the premiere of Franz Werfel's *Juarez und Maximilian*, as Adorno recollected even decades later, perhaps because he detested its author so intensely. For similar reasons he may have remembered a visit to Alma Mahler. After an affair with Oskar Kokoschka, Alma

Mahler had a brief marriage with Walter Gropius before settling down with Franz Werfel. At any rate, it was through Berg that the visit came about. He was horrified by her, 'particularly by the aplomb with which she produced the most excruciating trivialities. . . . There is no need to add that she absolutely failed to match up to the image that a 21-year-old had of Mahler's widow.'[37]

Together with Berg, he also attended the spectacular readings by Karl Kraus. Both Berg and Adorno were captivated by Kraus's charisma and intellectual brilliance, though in Adorno's case this did not happen all at once, but only later when he had a chance to read his writings, in particular *Sittlichkeit und Kriminalität* (Morality and Criminality) of 1908 and *The Last Days of Mankind* of 1922. His initial reaction was rather reserved. But in the public lectures Adorno thought of Kraus as an actor who was half-priest and half-clown. Decades later, when *Sittlichkeit und Kriminalität* was reprinted, he devoted an essay to Kraus in which he described him as an anti-psychological psychologist, a master of textual criticism, which he carried out with a specific combination of commentary and a montage of quotations.

A further noteworthy acquaintance was that of the thirty-year-old Soma Morgenstern, whom he also met through Alban and Helene Berg. Morgenstern, who had studied law, did not always have an easy relationship with the Frankfurt philosopher. The two men found themselves in competition for Berg's favour, which was all the harder because Berg was attracting considerable public interest in Vienna following the success of *Wozzeck*. Morgenstern was a writer from Eastern Galicia who had been living in Vienna since 1912. He had already known Berg for two years, and he was also acquainted with Béla Balázs and Georg Lukács, with Robert Musil and Joseph Roth. Adorno readily conceded that Morgenstern had a gift for wit and repartee which he did not possess himself to the same degree. As a German, he hoped to impress Berg by his ostentatious philosophical earnestness.

Even after he left Vienna, Adorno stayed in touch with Morgenstern, who worked briefly as the cultural correspondent of the *Frankfurter Zeitung* at the end of the 1920s. Berg, however, was keen to remain on good terms with both Morgenstern and Adorno. In a letter he used the image of a 'four-leaf clover' to refer to the three of them and his wife. What they liked doing best was what Berg referred to erroneously as 'Teikizerei', referring to the Yiddish word 'daigetzen' that was current in Vienna and means something like 'to spout profound rubbish'. Morgenstern maintained 'that Dr Wiesengrund was the greatest daigetzer ever.'[38] While Adorno told Kracauer about Morgenstern's friendliness and openness, he wrote later to Benjamin that, despite all his good qualities, Soma 'had an unfortunate tendency to mediocrity, even towards himself'.[39]

Morgenstern was equally blunt in his references to Adorno. In an essay (about Alban Berg that appeared posthumously in 1995), under the heading 'A Jew Boy from Frankfurt', he described how Helene Berg became very agitated and had done everything in her power to protect her husband from the torrent of words that poured forth from the newly arrived Adorno. Even in the last few minutes before the start of a Mahler concert he had made use of every moment to overwhelm his teacher with his verbosity. Helene begged Morgenstern to rescue her husband. He attempted therefore to draw Adorno into a conversation and invited him to accompany him after the concert.

> He was slightly built. Although the weather was very mild, he wore an overcoat of indeterminate colour. He had a thin, bony face, a well-shaped head with short hair which, despite his boyish appearance, was already rather sparse. His eyes were large, brown, and protruded slightly. His hands were the most expressive thing about him: they were narrow, with long fingers, very delicate and attractively sensitive. Such hands were not uncommon among young Talmud scholars in Eastern Europe.... I asked him whether he came from a religious family. He took a deep breath and said, 'Yes, my father is a socialist', whereupon I decided to invite him to join me in a coffee house. I went on to ask him, 'Surely you didn't learn your Baudelaire [whose poems Adorno had been quoting in French] from your father?' He replied, 'No, I learned about him from my aunt. My Aunt Agathe is a great connoisseur of Baudelaire, and she told me all about him when I was still a child.' So I invited him to come with me to the coffee house, and realized even before my friends had joined us that this Frankfurt Jew boy with his twenty-one years was a very knowledgeable, well-educated man.[40]

If we are to believe Morgenstern, the epithet 'Jew boy' comes from Helene Berg. But he had no compunction in using it himself, despite its obvious anti-Semitic tenor. Ignoring this is obviously a way of expressing his own aversion to Adorno. Morgenstern goes on to find fault with Adorno's high-flown, Hegelian–Marxist jargon, as well as his use of terminology derived from phenomenology and psychoanalysis. From Morgenstern's description, Adorno must have displayed an extreme intellectuality. He is said to have spoken constantly in a language full of ambitious theoretical concepts. Adorno points to the accuracy of this observation himself when he recalls that Berg would describe him as a 'bore' (*Fadian*), referring to his custom of always speaking earnestly in that refined language that came across to the Viennese as 'boring'.

At the same time, Adorno also struck Morgenstern as being extremely devoted and eager to communicate. At their very first meeting, he told Morgenstern with pride about his friendship with Kracauer and

Benjamin, his acquaintance with Ernst Bloch, and even mentioned his Franco-Corsican background, to which he owed the name 'Adorno'.

Later, when they were both in American exile, Morgenstern reproached him bitterly for having 'shaved off' (*abgemäht*) his father's Jewish surname 'Wiesengrund' in his 'ruthless ambition' to be accepted as a writer in the Anglo-Saxon world.[41] This reproach evidently expresses his resentment towards Adorno. However, the truth is that, if Adorno published in the United States under the name of Theodor W. Adorno, this was simply the consequence of the process of naturalization in the United States in November 1943. It was not a symbolic act of emancipation from his Jewish father. He never attempted to distance himself from his Jewish origins, or to deny his paternal inheritance. Completely without foundation, moreover, is Morgenstern's claim that during the Weimar Republic Adorno belonged to the Communist Party. There is no evidence to substantiate such an assertion. On the contrary, throughout his life Adorno had a deep aversion to formal membership of any party organization.

During Adorno's first stay in Vienna, however, his relations with Morgenstern were free from the acrimony of later years. Their dealings with each other were cordial and characterized by mutual respect. Morgenstern went out of his way to put Adorno in touch with the famous Georg Lukács, whom he knew and who was living as an émigré in Hütteldorf, just outside Vienna, in what Adorno remembered as difficult circumstances in a frugal apartment. In a letter to Berg, he wrote that he 'greatly revered Lukács; from a human point of view he had a profound effect on me, but in terms of ideas there could be no meeting of minds, and because it was Lukács, I found this especially painful, since intellectually he had influenced me more than almost anyone.'[42] This influence came from the early writings of Lukács, who was now over forty years of age. They included *Soul and Form*, *The Theory of the Novel* and *History and Class Consciousness*.[43]

During these months in Vienna, towards the end of June, Adorno was surprised and also delighted to be offered the editorship of the music journal *Pult und Taktstock*, in which a number of his reviews had already appeared. The journal belonged to the respected music publisher Universal Edition directed by Emil Hertzka, who came originally from Budapest. The head of the opera section was Hans Heinsheimer, who was also in charge of the *Musikblätter*, where Paul Stefan was the editor. In a letter of 25 June Adorno proudly announced to Berg that he had been offered Stefan's post. No sooner had he agreed and proposed a number of innovations than the journal's editorial board seemed to go cold on the idea. Reading between the lines, it is evident that Adorno's disappointment is greater than he cares to admit; it was another four years before he was given the status of an unofficial director, a post he occupied for only a short time, having become embroiled in constant disagreements with the management.[44]

7

In Search of a Career

In mid-August Adorno left Vienna, initially to take a holiday in the Dolomites, as he had done the previous year. Else Herzberger, the wealthy friend of the Wiesengrund family, had invited him to Madonna di Campiglio. From there he went travelling for almost six weeks, taking in Genoa, Naples, Pompeii, Paestum and Capri. In Genoa, where he also went to see the Palazzo Adorno, he met up with Kracauer. The trip to the south had been planned as a joint venture. As he reported, not without irony, he thought Italy a wild country 'in which the volcanoes are an institution and the swindlers are saved'. This affronts his 'bourgeois sense of values just as fascism is incompatible with my rebellious instincts. Nevertheless, I feel very comfortable here.'[1]

Kracauer recorded some of his impressions of Italy in an article for the *Frankfurter Zeitung*. Here is his description of Positano, in the vicinity of Salerno:

> A vanishing sense of time, pathological conditions; such things are no rarity in Positano. The pernicious effect of mythological substances attracts outlaws as well as flirtatious exhibitionists . . . ; their disorientation seems to find a sanctuary here. In the evenings everyone comes together in the beach café, a versatile locality in which, operetta-like, the Camorra chieftain holds court to the backdrop of the thundering breakers. Gramophone records succeed one another, intimate couples dance by the light of the sooty gas lamps, their contours merge, relationships smoulder wordlessly.[2]

Adorno too was very taken with the beauty of Positano, as can be seen from a letter to Berg written shortly after his return to Frankfurt: 'the Positano landscape is one familiar only in dreams; the same can be said of the people there. The Byzantine Ravello – above Amalfi – vouchsafes a glimpse of the East for the space of an evening. . . . Naples seemed like an ominous chaos at first, the streets look like a forest, melons are up for sale beneath symbols of a heathen culture.'[3] In the context of Naples, he mentions that the two travellers had met Walter Benjamin there and had become immersed in a 'philosophical battle' in which they had been joined by Alfred Sohn-Rethel. The latter lived in southern Italy at the time and had many of the same social and philosophical interests as Benjamin and Kracauer.[4] He was also introduced to Adorno, and this gave rise to a lasting relationship between two lively thinkers, although Adorno expressed himself quite critically about Sohn-Rethel's doctoral dissertation, *From the Analysis of Economic Activity to a Theory of Economics.*

The philosophical discussions that formed the focus of the encounters between Adorno, Benjamin and Kracauer were just one of Adorno's activities. He threw himself increasingly into composing during his stay in Italy. Now that he had become familiar with the techniques of twelve-tone composition, he thought of himself as an outsider who had penetrated to the inner circle of the Second Viennese School, and this stimulated him to produce his own compositions. These included the *George Songs*, op. 1, the *Two Pieces for String Quartet*, op. 2, the *Songs* from texts by Däubler, Trakl and Heym, op. 3, the *Orchestral Pieces*, op. 4, and also the *Bagatelles*, op. 6, as well as two of the *Frauenchöre*, op. 8. We shall say more in due course about his fragmentary opera based on Mark Twain's *Tom Sawyer*, a *Singspiel* that he began in 1933.

No sooner had he returned to Frankfurt after his lengthy trip to Italy than Adorno and the entire family set off for Amorbach to celebrate his mother's sixtieth birthday, on 1 October 1925. For this occasion he dedicated to her two pieces for voice and piano based on poems by Stefan George and later his *Four Poems by Stefan George for Voice and Piano*, which he specified as his op. 1.[5] By the time of the birthday party the entire collection of *George Songs* was far from ready, and he continued to work on it between 1925 and 1928. The poems were chosen from a number of George's volumes and it was natural for Adorno to apply the techniques he had learnt in Vienna to the settings; in other words, he made use of twelve-tone rows for the most part. These were particularly prominent in the setting for no. 2, *Wir schreiten auf und ab im reichen Flitter.*[6] In addition to free atonality, this, the second George song from op. 1, exhibits certain features specific to Adorno's own approach, such as his very idiosyncratic use of the serial twelve-tone principle.[7]

Following the months spent in Vienna and travelling in Italy, Adorno settled down once more in his parents' house in the sober commercial city on the Main. He attempted to maintain his position as both composer and writer on music. He also tried to establish himself as a philosopher. But where was he to begin? Thanks to the tuition he had received from Alban Berg and the piano lessons from Eduard Steuermann, he had seen the advanced methods of composition of contemporary music at first hand. This entitled him to regard himself as belonging to the avant-garde art scene. His published music critiques and his own compositions from both before and after his meeting with Berg strengthened his claims. However, now that he was back in Frankfurt, he sorely missed the collaboration with Berg: 'It is very hard for me not to be able to be in Vienna the whole time. Being together with you [Alban Berg] and making music in our circle was the one thing that could enable me to keep my balance. Here matters are more confused than ever.'[8]

Adorno's achievement as a composer was by no means contemptible; nor did it pass unnoticed. In the small circle of Frankfurt music lovers there had been performances – sometime previously – of parts of the early works that had been written while he was still studying at the Hoch Conservatory. The First Quartet, which he had composed in 1921, was performed by the Lange Quartet in a concert in April 1923. Far more importantly, his *Pieces for String Quartet*, which had been written under Berg's supervision, were performed for the first time in December 1926 by the Kolisch Quartet, which had only just been formed. This performance was part of the programme of the International Society for New Music. In November, Adorno had sent the score to Universal Edition in Vienna, and directly to Kolisch, while he had also asked Berg to check the copying and in general to give the project his blessing.

In the event, Berg responded positively to the piece in a letter to Schoenberg, who, as always, had his doubts.[9] 'The performance of Wiesengrund's insanely difficult quartet was a bravura achievement by the Kolisch Quartet, which had managed to study it in eight days and articulated it clearly in their performance. I find Wiesengrund's work *very good*.'[10] At the same time, he wrote to Morgenstern that Adorno's quartet was 'a truly splendid piece; it has had great success here and can look forward to being taken up by Universal Edition as soon as possible.'[11] He also wrote a card to Adorno's parents, telling them of his enthusiasm. Needless to say, Adorno wanted to be present for the performance in Vienna, shortly before the Christmas holidays in 1926. 'The performance is literally *a matter of life and death* for me. . . . The mere fact of a public performance of something of mine that would normally be of no importance to me if only I could hear it myself, has assumed a highly distorted and exaggerated significance in my eyes.'[12]

When they met again in Vienna for a few days, Berg's impression of the 23-year-old Adorno improved still further. Writing to Morgenstern, he said that Wiesengrund had 'become significantly more manly, but was otherwise unaltered. We spent delightful afternoons and evenings in each other's company.'[13] As for Adorno, much as he enjoyed being with Berg, he also found reasons to complain, as he wrote to Kracauer. He explained that the situation in Vienna had changed to his disadvantage. What he had in mind was Arnold Schoenberg's blunt rejection of his published music reviews. Schoenberg made no attempt to conceal his dislike of Adorno's writings on music. He thought his style mannered and his theoretical ideas incomprehensible. In particular, he believed that Adorno's over-philosophical interpretations damaged his [Schoenberg's] pioneering contributions to the New Music in the eyes of the public.

For his part, Adorno was supremely unconcerned about the public and its approval. He insisted that 'the criterion of all my intellectual activity is truth . . . not its possible impact on the public.'[14] Unlike Schoenberg, Berg not only understood Adorno's aims, he even endorsed his rigorous strategy once he had familiarized himself with Adorno's approach to music analysis. An important marker of this change was his attitude to Adorno's discussion of *Wozzeck* immediately after the premiere in Berlin. Under the influence of Schoenberg, and somewhat to Adorno's annoyance, he had initially found fault with incomprehensible passages. But a little later, Berg wrote, '*You have completely won me over.* I know now that what you have written . . . could not be expressed better, more precisely or shed more light on the entire context than you have done.'[15] Berg went on to say that he was 'convinced that, in the sphere of the deepest understanding of music . . . , you are capable of *supreme* achievements and will undoubtedly fulfil this promise in the shape of great philosophical works.'[16] At the time, few of Adorno's contemporaries were as prescient as Berg.

In order to advance his philosophical prospects at the same time as his musical activities, Adorno resumed his contact with Cornelius with a view to writing a dissertation for the *Habilitation*. Since Cornelius thought highly of him not just despite his constant excursions into the realm of music, but because of them, agreeing on a subject was straightforward. The matter was not without urgency as only two years remained to Cornelius's retirement. Furthermore, Leo Löwenthal, a member of the same circle of intellectuals, had also declared his intention of approaching Cornelius to supervise his own proposed *Habilitation* thesis. For this reason, Adorno set to work briskly. As on the previous occasion, he took Cornelius's *Transcendentale Systematik* as his model. On this occasion, however, he was concerned not with Husserl, but with the question whether and by what means Freud's theory of the unconscious could be reformulated on the foundation of a transcendental theory of knowledge.

As early as December 1925, after some months of illness, he reported to Berg that he hoped to be able to come to Vienna now that the '*Habilitation* question was more or less clear'.[17] This could only refer to his agreement with Cornelius and the rough outline of the project. He did not start work on it properly until the first part of 1926, a labour of reading and writing that lasted until the autumn. Even so, by the middle of September 1926, he had roughed out the plan for the dissertation for which he was reading many books by Freud. He was particularly pleased about this because he felt he had to complete the thesis before Löwenthal, with whom he was in competition. Moreover, he could expect sanctions from the family if anything went wrong with the *Habilitation*.

He had been told that he would have to obtain a qualification in law. Was this a genuine threat? It may have been merely a ruse on Adorno's part to gain Kracauer's support, since the latter was on friendly terms with Löwenthal and welcomed his plans for the *Habilitation* as warmly as Adorno's. Indeed, he may well have believed that Adorno's true talents lay in the sphere of music. And so they did, but he had other talents too. Admittedly, these other talents would show themselves only after a number of bitter disappointments both in philosophy and in music criticism.

The year 1926 also witnessed Adorno's unhappy love affair with the Frankfurt actress Ellen Dreyfus-Herz. She was in the process of obtaining a divorce from Adorno's friend Carl Dreyfus. In a letter written to Berg in August 1926 from Staudach-Rotten on the Tegernsee in Upper Bavaria, where he was holidaying, Adorno complained that he was suffering from 'severe depressions' that he ascribed to 'erotic confusions without hope or way out'. The relationship between him and Ellen was 'very strange. For both parties it is a combination of the intimate and the alien. And it proves to me once again how terrible it is for human relationships that have great ambitions to be incapable of fulfilment.'[18] A few weeks later, in November, he told Berg despondently that this passionate affair had now come to an end. 'This woman, to whom I have been totally committed, has left me for someone else – and in a way that only Kafka could have endured.'[19]

Adorno's affair with Dreyfus's divorced wife appears to have disrupted the friendship between the two men for a time. A few years later, however, they jointly published so-called *Surrealist Pieces* that appeared in the *Frankfurter Zeitung* in November 1931 under the pseudonym of Castor Zwieback.[20] These prose pieces depict grotesque situations: at a funeral, a committee meeting or in the tram. Castor Zwieback's surrealist intentions were also highlighted by the motto by André Breton and Paul Éluard that preceded them: '*Frappe à la porte, crie: Entrez, et n'entre pas.*'

Morning
A young man went on holiday in a spa hotel in the south. In the morning, still in his pyjamas, he went to the lavatory. Opening the door, he saw an elderly woman sitting on the seat. Although he hastened to shut the door, he could not avoid seeing the woman. She was wearing an embroidered black dress, and beneath the skirt, which was pulled up, long white knickers and black boots. The woman muttered something. When she appeared on the veranda in the black dress at lunchtime, the young man bowed.[21]

The two writers had produced far more pieces than could be published in the newspaper at the time.[22] Adorno had already tried out such prose forms in other contributions to the *Frankfurter Zeitung*, such as the *Worte ohne Lieder* (Words without Songs). So these surrealist pieces are further evidence of his literary ambitions, without which he would have been unable to develop the style which was already becoming visible in the majority of his writings. Presumably, he had been encouraged in these literary experimentations by Dreyfus, who hoped to write a novel on white-collar culture.

Dreyfus was five years older than Adorno and had studied in Heidelberg. At the time of their collaboration he was the manager of a business that made him financially independent, so that for the duration of the Weimar Republic he was able to lead the life of an independent scholar with literary and artistic interests. This put him in the same category as Hermann Grab, with whom he was on friendly terms, as he was with Max Horkheimer and Siegfried Kracauer. But he was not only in contact with male intellectuals. About a year before the Castor Zwieback texts were published, Dreyfus had met the actress Marianne Hoppe, who was twenty-one at the time. She was regarded in Frankfurt as a rising acting talent, and had a contract with the Neues Theater. In the middle of 1920, the Neues Theater, which was managed by Arthur Hellmer, had Max Ophüls as its artistic director. The theatre acquired some notoriety in autumn 1928, above all with the production of Brecht's *Threepenny Opera*. Thanks to her love affair with Dreyfus, Marianne Hoppe met Adorno and others from the same left-wing circles. She recalls[23] that the political discussions at which she was present were a factor in preventing her from approving the ideas of National Socialism, either then or later, even though she spent the Hitler years in Germany and made her great career there at that time.[24] Shortly before the Nazi dictatorship came into being, Dreyfus, under the pseudonym of Ludwig Carls, had been involved in a project to produce what Adorno described as an avant-garde film of Theodor Storm's story *Der Schimmelreiter*. Adorno wrote to Berg in September 1933, asking him whether he would be interested in composing the music for the film.[25] This film was actually made, although not until 1934. The directors were Hans Deppe and Curt Oertel. The music was finally written not by Berg, but by Wilfried Zillig, a pupil of Schoenberg's, whose work Adorno had briefly mentioned in two concert reviews.

Between philosophy and music: no parting of the ways

In December 1926 Adorno had the pleasure of hearing a performance of his *Two Pieces for String Quartet*, op. 2, in Vienna. Even before that he had started work on the *Habilitation*. Having made up his mind to do it, hc found this ritual exercise something of a chore. The fact was that his mind was focused on his existing scores. He wished to improve them to the point where they were ripe for performance and then to compose further pieces. Over and above that, there were his ambitions as music critic. His task there was to maintain the position he had won and to extend it in Frankfurt and beyond.

Towards the end of the 1920s, Adorno played an increasingly active part in Frankfurt's cultural life. His role as music critic was just his official function; his activities went far beyond that. It can hardly have escaped his attention that the financial resources of private cultural institutions had been badly squeezed by inflation, and that middle-class benefactors had also suffered. During Ludwig Landmann's term of office as mayor (1924–33), these economic constraints led to a gradual shift in the relative importance of 'citizens' culture and a culture that was administered municipally'.[26] This shift was an object lesson for Adorno, since it showed him what can happen to culture when it becomes the object of administrative attention. He wrote later that what it led to was 'the neutralization of culture'. Nevertheless, he thought that, once the material foundation of traditional liberal and individualist culture had been undermined, there was no alternative to public sponsorship:

> The appeal to the creators of culture, that they should withdraw from the administrative process and keep it at a distance, rings hollow. It would rob them not only of every opportunity to earn their living, but also of any conceivable impact, of any interaction between their activities and society. This is something that even the most incorruptible work cannot forgo without withering. Those who boast of their purity, who keep themselves to themselves, make us suspect that they are the true provincials and petty-bourgeois reactionaries. The customary argument that creative minds – and they were always the nonconformists – always had a precarious existence, and that they nevertheless preserved their strength in defiant self-assertion, is threadbare. The fact that this situation is not new does not give us the right to perpetuate it if it is no longer necessary; and the idea that the best will always come out on top is no more than a pious gingerbread motto.[27]

The realization that civic culture needs the support of the municipal authorities derives from Adorno's experience of Frankfurt before 1933. Once the city had involved itself in cultural matters, building projects were undertaken under the influence of architects such as Ernst May and Martin Elsässer, who were both associated with the Bauhaus. The supporters of cultural modernity had gathered round the journal *Das neue Frankfurt*, and they opposed the traditionalists of the Altstadtbund who wished to preserve the past in general and a civic culture specific to Frankfurt in particular. The radical modernizers aimed to do away with historicism and the worn-out styles of Late Wilhelminian society. One representative of modernity was Franz Wichert, who had been director of the School for the Applied Arts since 1923. He had similar interests to Georg Swarzenski, an outstanding connoisseur and protagonist of contemporary art. Under his direction, the Städel Art Gallery flourished. Those teaching at the Städel included Max Beckmann, whose own paintings at this time featured portraits of members of the cultural elite, such as Heinrich Simon, Georg and Marie Swarzenski, Fritz Wichert, the art-dealer Battenberg, and the collector and patron of the arts Lilly von Schnitzler-Mallinckrodt.

One institution on the side of the modernists was the radio, which had been based in Frankfurt since 1922. Its programming was highly ambitious under the direction of Carl Adolf Schleussner, and more especially of Hans Flesch, who was keen to promote modern music, experimental radio drama and the radio essay. In addition, the *Frankfurter Zeitung*, which had been founded by Leopold Sonnemann and was run as a Jewish family business, was known for its liberal political views and its open-minded attitude in cultural matters. The literature section edited by Heinz Simon, in particular, stood out for its willingness to publish unconventional writers. These included Benno Reifenberg and Siegfried Kracauer and the reviews and essays of Walter Benjamin and Soma Morgenstern, as well as the reportages of Joseph Roth.[28] For a number of years, this paper was noted for a pluralism which enabled it to provide a platform for progressive developments in the arts. The same pluralism was evident in the theatre, both in the Schauspielhaus and the Neues Theater, where, alongside the classics, there were productions of modern dramatists, such as Fritz von Unruh, Carl Sternheim, Paul Kornfeld and Georg Kaiser. There were bold innovations, too, at the Frankfurt Opera under Clemens Krauss, Alwin Kronauer and Lothar Wallenstein. Even in the Friday concerts of the Museumsgesellschaft, which were always important social occasions during the winter season, the works of modern composers could be heard, as was also the case with the symphony orchestra's Monday concerts.

In 1927, the city authorities organized a music exhibition that set out to give a complete overview of current trends in music, an event that attracted a great deal of attention. During the summer, the exhibition was combined with a concert series. As a regular commentator on all major musical events, Adorno reviewed the exhibition, *Music in the Life of the Nations*, as well as the summer concerts. Of the exhibition he observed that it represented the vain attempt 'to replace the now-disintegrated cosmos for the ear . . . with an encyclopedia for the eye'.[29] While he praised the performances of the Vienna Philharmonic and the Orchestre du Conservatoire, he was scathing about the 'Negro revue: *Black People*' in the Schauspielhaus:

> This is said to be Josephine Baker's troupe, and this meagre show could easily be conceived as a foil to an impetuous temperament, one that makes use of uniformity to show off one's own great form. But Josephine Baker was not there and the meagre show

was left to cope on its own with its Black Bottom and Yes, Sir, that's my Baby. No sensation, then, for a public used to bars. A few girls with gold fillings, very few in fact, though at least one with a good figure. A show projected against eerily out-of-date backdrops, among them a New York street so senselessly empty that it recalls Kafka's empty spaces. With a star that isn't one, and that is visibly imitating another unknown star that may not be one either.[30]

His discussion of Hermann Scherchen was free of polemics. Adorno observed in a review that his approach to music 'penetrated to the heart of the ideological problems raised by the works'.[31]

Adorno sent detailed accounts of all these cultural events to his 'master and teacher'. He spent the summer of 1926 trying to prepare the first movement of his quartet for performance. At the same time, he was writing a third movement. In addition, he wrote the 'Piano Pieces in strict twelve-tone technique', as well as songs that were later integrated into the *Six Bagatelles for Voice and Piano*, op. 6.[32] And, as if that were not enough, he also wrote a number of musical aphorisms, a genre new to him, that he was able to publish in the *Musikblätter des Anbruch*, and later in the *Frankfurter Zeitung*. Typical of such aphorisms was one in which he compared Max Reger's works to contemporary interior design, while Debussy's music was said to come to an end 'as a picture comes to an end when we step away from it'.[33]

All this composing and writing about music could not but have an adverse effect on his *Habilitation*. For several months he had undertaken an intensive study of psychoanalysis and had produced a bulky manuscript on the subject. In November 1927, he presented it to Cornelius for a preliminary reading. It bore the title *The Concept of the Unconscious in the Transcendental Theory of the Psyche*. When Cornelius had read it, he advised Adorno privately to withdraw his application for the *Habilitation*. He subsequently wrote to the committee of the Arts Faculty, saying that Adorno's work was too close to his own way of thinking, that it was insufficiently original and that it lacked innovative content. Adorno's disappointment was all the greater since he had evidently hoped that taking over Cornelius's terminology in the *Transzendentale Systematik* would be a guarantee of success. A vain hope: he now felt 'shamefully let down'.[34] His only consolation was that a majority in the faculty had been in favour in principle of awarding the *Habilitation*, and he was able to persuade himself that this setback did not close the door to a university career in Frankfurt. What further conclusions did he draw from this debacle? It was the first and only time that Adorno compromised his intellectual integrity. He also made attempts to see what could be salvaged. It was little enough. Since he had cautiously not gone beyond submitting an *inquiry* about an application for the *Habilitation*, he was able to withdraw it in January 1928. In his letters to Berg he played down the whole episode, but it had bitter consequences for him nevertheless, since eighteen months' work had gone for nothing. And anyway, how are we to explain Cornelius's outright rejection of the thesis?

The text was 200 pages long and divided into three lengthy chapters. If we look back at it now, we can see that, despite many redundancies, it was closely argued. There can be no doubt that it contains independent work. It can certainly stand comparison with other *Habilitation* dissertations, among them Horkheimer's thesis of 1925, *Kant's Critique of Judgement as a Link between Theoretical and Practical Philosophy*. His epistemological interpretation of psychoanalysis still makes for stimulating reading today. It is by no means far-fetched to suppose that he was attempting to grapple with a problem that Horkheimer had formulated in the last sentence of his own *Habilitation* dissertation: 'What must be clarified is the doctrine of the original division of the rational human being into a contradictory juxtaposition of will and knowledge.'[35]

Adorno's approach took its lead from the widely read popular philosophies of the day that focused on the concept of the unconscious. In this connection, he briefly reviewed Fichte, Schelling, Schopenhauer, Nietzsche and Bergson. He drew a distinction between their vague metaphysical use of the term and the concept of the unconscious in Freud's theory, at least to the point Freud had developed it in the *Introductory Lectures on Psychoanalysis* of 1916–17. To clarify this, he employed Cornelius's transcendental philosophy, whose starting-point, as Adorno emphasized, was the principle that consciousness alone was the basis of all knowledge. The link between idealism and empiricism derives from a discussion of Kantian transcendentalism. More specifically, it arises from a critique of the concept of the transcendental thing-in-itself, the so-called intelligible world, of the concept of subjective spontaneity, and also of the relation of parts to the whole. Against this background, Adorno believed he was in a position to reject all attempts to salvage metaphysics by endorsing any doctrine of existence or essence that transcends consciousness. In the same way, he criticizes philosophical trends which set out 'to preserve the transcendental nature of the object, as opposed to its phenomenal appearance, by identifying the thing-in-itself with the unconscious.'[36]

Adorno goes on to argue that, although within the Kantian framework the unconscious cannot be separated from the phenomenal self, the transcendental method must nevertheless be retained. Cornelius should really have been delighted with this conclusion. For, Adorno's line of thought continues, from the standpoint of transcendental philosophy, we may describe as unconscious all things that are neither perceived in the present nor recollected as past, nor are to be found in space, but which must be said to exist according to the laws governing consciousness, even if they exist independently of a present perception. This conclusion is entirely in the spirit of Cornelius's own system!

Why was Adorno interested in psychoanalysis, a discipline that was so very controversial at the time? He concentrated on Freud's own theory because its epistemological status was still completely unclarified, even though it operated with a concept of the constitution of mental objects – quite unlike associative psychology, experimental psychology and gestalt theory. What made psychoanalysis attractive for a transcendentalist analysis of the unconscious was its assumption that '*all psychic phenomena have a meaning*, all psychic existence is determined by laws through the agency of personal consciousness or . . . alternatively, all our phenomena . . . are the phenomena of *unconscious objects*, knowledge of which depends on understanding their conscious context and its laws.'[37] To demonstrate the truth of this thesis, Adorno referred to the so-called parapraxes or Freudian slips: dreams and neurotic symptoms.

To reproach psychoanalysis with failing to distinguish between normal consciousness and events determined by the unconscious is to succumb to the naturalist fallacy that has its roots in an untenable ontological distinction between consciousness and reality. 'Doubtless, the facts of our waking life are determined in many instances by changes in the material world, but is not the material world itself built on the laws governing our consciousness?'[38] Perceptively, Adorno warned expressly against a naturalistic misinterpretation of the unconscious and of instinct. In Freud, he maintained, neither concept is ultimately primary; they are rather no more than conceptual tools with which to describe laws governing the psyche.

Adorno was not at all interested in the therapeutic aspects of Freudian theory. He treated it purely as an epistemology entirely concerned with the nature of the knowledge arising from analysis. This led him to regard Freud's theory as a turning point inaugurating the definitive '*demystification*' of the unconscious. It followed that psychoanalysis was 'a sharp weapon . . . against every attempt to create a metaphysics of the instincts and to deify dull, organic nature.'[39]

With this conclusion the 24-year-old Adorno adopted a radically enlightened position that he was to retain throughout his life. Towards the end of the thesis a further important point emerged. He attempted to link psychoanalytical insight to sociological knowledge. He argued that the causes of the psychic symptoms uncovered by psychoanalysis could be eliminated only if there were a 'change in our current social conditions'. The analysis of the psyche was a necessary but not a sufficient condition for any fundamental transformation of the 'material world' so as to make it less oppressive for human beings. This finding sounds materialist, but Adorno did not go beyond mere assertion. However, he did move to a critique of those organicist and vitalist currents in contemporary philosophy that appealed to the ominous effects of processes operating unconsciously in history and society.

Adorno evidently wished to pillory attempts to transfigure social facts into natural, fated necessities. The social impact of such ideological patterns emerges most clearly, in Adorno's view, in the policies of imperialism and fascism. 'Where theories of the unconscious are rooted in Nietzsche's philosophy of power they take a terrible revenge in the real world. In Spengler's philosophy the connection between the metaphysics of the unconscious, the philosophy of power and destiny, the critical state of society and of the political actuality is expressed in exemplary fashion.'[40] With this statement at the end of his discussion of the unconscious, Adorno moves beyond a purely epistemological analysis.

Was this concern with social implications the true reason for the rejection of his dissertation? Cornelius confined himself to the objection that Adorno had done no more than paraphrase his own ideas – an objection not without foundation. However, he could easily have countered this criticism by pointing to the illuminating reconstruction of psychoanalysis in the third chapter.[41] This did not happen, however, and there are signs that even Horkheimer, who as Cornelius's assistant had originally lent his support to Adorno's plans, was unwilling to cast his vote against the established professor.

Thus the beginning of the year 1928 was anything but auspicious for Adorno. Further troubles, partly professional, partly private, were to follow the blunt rejection by Cornelius. After the Frankfurt fiasco, he needed to distance himself so as to be with his fiancée, Gretel Karplus. However, he was not only in search of solace. He wanted to find out whether he would be able to obtain a post as music critic with the Ullstein Press. He had the support of Rudolf Kastner, who was in charge of the music column for the *Berliner Morgenpost*. Nothing came of this, however, since it turned out that there were no editorial vacancies. Even so, Adorno set to work producing numerous reviews of opera performances and concerts which he then published in the *Neue Musikzeitschrift* under the engaging title 'Berlin Memorial'. He reviewed a piano concert in the Beethovensaal; the soloist was Egon Petri, who was said to have played 'the swansong of the romantic piano'. A different view prevailed in his review of the concert in the Sing-Akademie under Hermann Scherchen. He praised both the conductor and the work he performed: Anton von Webern's *Six Orchestral Pieces*. According to him, they 'are among the greatest and most substantial works of the modern orchestral repertoire'. He also gave his approval to Otto Klemperer's productions of *Don Giovanni* and *Fidelio*, on the grounds that he combined an extremely down-to-earth approach with an ability to make traditional works appear relevant. In contrast, he sharply criticized Bruno Walter's interpretation of Mozart's *Il Seraglio* because his 'refined music-making' was aimed at 'connoisseurs'. He also pulled Stravinsky's *Oedipus Rex* to pieces. The only merit of Klemperer's production at the Kroll Opera was that it enabled everyone to see the complete failure of a composer who had wished to destroy the classical, but who was nevertheless sustained by it. 'Black masses are held here, and nothing shows more clearly that music has lost its way than the fact that they are celebrated as divine services.'[42] Adorno took a certain malicious pleasure in mentioning this review to Berg in the same letter in which he reported that nothing had come of the editorial post.

This rejection by Ullstein was not the end of his losing streak. His return home to Frankfurt for Easter in 1928 was blighted by a serious car accident. A taxi he was in collided with a bus. He had to be taken to hospital, where he was found to have concussion, a head injury and bruising. To his great distress, he was confined to bed for several weeks. After his recovery, he wrote at once to Vienna, saying that his greatest fear had been unfounded: 'my hearing is quite unaffected.'[43] This letter radiated self-confidence and energy for other reasons. Even before the accident, he reported, he had finished a song, a setting of Theodor Däubler's poem *Verloren*. This piece is one of the *Four Songs for Medium Voice and Piano*, op. 3, which he dedicated to Berg after completing the score.

Scarcely had he recovered than Adorno forced himself to face up to the question whether he ought to make a second attempt to obtain the *Habilitation*. Both Horkheimer and Kracauer urged him to do so, the latter even suggesting that this time he should propose a topic concerned with the philosophy of music. Adorno could not make up his mind. For, as he wrote to Berg, an academic career was not really so vital for him, 'since I am entirely focused on music, or rather composition, and even if I were to obtain the *Habilitation*, my academic duties would have to take second place.'[44] And this was where the matter rested. When he had completed the song-cycle dedicated to Berg, the premiere took place in Berlin in January 1929, in a performance by the singer Margot Hinnenberg-Lefèbre, accompanied by Eduard Steuermann on the piano. After that, Adorno threw himself with renewed energy into the business of composition. He reworked the songs based on poems by Stefan George that he had begun in Vienna, and added to them. This brought him up against a new kind of problem, one that would continue to preoccupy him. In a letter to Berg he raised the question of how 'the freedom of the imagination was to be reconciled with twelve-tone technique'. He had been looking, he said, for ways of shifting 'the organization of the material behind the façade [by means of the twelve-tone technique], i.e., behind the manifest sound of the music, in order to create scope for the imagination'.[45] By calling for the 'restitution of musical freedom', he came into conflict with Schoenberg, who nevertheless remained in his eyes the most important musical innovator of the twentieth century.

To lay bare the nature of Schoenberg's achievement was a principal intention of the course of lectures on recent works of the new music that Adorno gave at the invitation of the Frankfurt Musicians' Association. Alongside these lectures, he went on writing about music, as ever. He continued to experiment with the genre of the musical aphorism, producing a further series of texts of this kind, and publishing them in various issues of the *Musikblätter des Anbruch* in 1928. One of these aphorisms may well have reflected his own experience of composition. 'The child trying to pick out a melody on the piano provides the paradigm of all true composition. In the same tentative, uncertain manner, but with a precise memory, the composer looks for what may always have been there and what he must now rediscover on the undiscriminating black and white keys of the keyboard from which he must now make his choice.'[46] In another aphorism he surprisingly leaps to the defence of sentimental kitsch music with the no less surprising argument that it is ideal as an accompaniment to imaginary catastrophes in the theatre or film: 'Where the tap-dancing is at its most assured, the boiler threatens to explode. On the basses of *Gern hab ich die Frau'n geküßt* [How I've loved kissing women], the listing *Titanic* presses down like a shadow from which there is no escape.'[47]

What is noteworthy here about the prose of the 25-year-old Adorno is its striking use of metaphor. Similarly, his ironic tone is pervasive, as can be seen in his comments on Stravinsky. In the same way, he strives constantly to discover the right aesthetic language with which to do justice to the musical objects he describes. This explains the sometimes artificial nature of Adorno's early prose, and its tendency to degenerate into monologue.[48]

In the *Musikblätter des Anbruch* Adorno had published not just a collection of aphorisms but also numerous music reviews. Further, he developed a comprehensive, detailed plan to revitalize the periodical, which had been founded in 1930 and was published by Universal Edition in Vienna. Four years previously, Hans Heinsheimer had asked Adorno to join its editorial staff. The snub he had received was, if not forgiven, at least overlooked. After all, Adorno was a regular contributor to its pages. So even before the summer holidays had begun, he started to think enthusiastically, and perhaps not too diplomatically, about changes he would like to introduce in the *Musikblätter*.[49] His idea was to use the journal to champion the cause of radical modern music even more strongly, starting with Mahler and proceeding via the Schoenberg school down to Kurt Weill and Ernst Krenek. As far as organizational changes were concerned, he proposed that decisions about content should be taken by a largely autonomous editorial committee, making decisions on a democratic basis. This would ensure that the journal would cease to function as advertising copy for other publications by Universal Edition. It should aim at an aggressive and polemical style of criticism, but on the foundation of a solid grasp of composition and music theory. The target of such criticism would be what he called 'stabilized music'. By this he meant the reactionary music of Pfitzner and the later Richard Strauss as well as the new classicism of Stravinsky and Hindemith.

The journal should also welcome the new media: it would publish reviews of recent gramophone records, radio concerts and film music. By this, Adorno had in mind the entire complex of popular music, from jazz, through hit songs, to operetta. He proposed that such music should be discussed without condescension. Kitsch, he suggested, should be defended against the degenerate ideals of personality and culture, but criticized for being ideological and musically retrograde. 'The defence of kitsch should not be undertaken in the spirit of naive approval, but as it were despite itself. . . . Kitsch is an object of interpretation, but one of the greatest significance. I would be happy to propose guidelines for the detailed treatment of the problems of kitsch.'[50] He did not leave matters at the level of guidelines; he soon made it his task to develop an entire theory of mass culture.

The concept of 'guidelines' conveys the flavour of Adorno's programme as a whole. His aim was nothing less than to use the journal as a weapon to promote the music of the Second Viennese School and the type of music criticism he advocated, without paying much heed to the possibility that this programme might conflict with the interests of Universal Edition. It comes as no surprise, therefore, to discover that little of this forward-looking plan was adopted in practice.

The sheer quantity of Adorno's plans, ideas and activities shows that he remained undaunted by the failure of his *Habilitation*, the rejection by Ullstein or his car accident, and that he would not allow himself to be deflected from his path. On the contrary, he persisted in his efforts to reapply for the *Habilitation* at Frankfurt University. However, this time, too, he found obstacles in his way. At the suggestion of Kracauer and Horkheimer, he first thought of approaching Max Scheler, who had succeeded to Cornelius's chair (instead of Horkheimer, the favoured candidate). However, the change of professor meant that 'working conditions' had changed for Adorno as well. Scheler had been influenced by phenomenology and had made his name with his ethical theory of material values. Would he be willing to take on Adorno? Such questions soon turned out to be otiose, since Scheler died unexpectedly during his first term in Frankfurt.

Adorno now faced the necessity of looking for an alternative supervisor, and the likeliest candidate was Paul Tillich. Tillich was appointed to the chair in philosophy early in 1929, despite the initial opposition of the faculty. He stood for a type of Marxist thought with humanist overtones. It was equally remote from Cornelius as from Scheler, and the only person to have a certain affinity with Tillich was Horkheimer. A philosopher of religion, he was chiefly interested in the interface between the different arts disciplines.[51] By the time he was appointed in Frankfurt, he had already written numerous books, including the *Ideas on a Theology of Culture*, then *Kairos: The Situation and the Direction of Mind in the Present*, and *The Protestant Era*. Adorno basically had no one but Tillich to turn to, at least in Frankfurt, and he was under no illusions about this. His realism expressed itself in the speed with which he now abandoned his earlier project and turned to a new one. Instead of attempting to persevere with Freud, he immersed himself in the works of a philosopher who was no stranger to him: Søren Kierkegaard.

8

Music Criticism and Compositional Practice

Adorno's intensive and sustained study of the writings of the Danish thinker Søren Kierkegaard began towards the end of 1929 or early in 1930. He devoted just over a year to the laborious task of producing a second dissertation. This task still lay in the distant future in the summer of 1928, when he went touring on holiday with Gretel Karplus. As in the previous year, they headed southwards. In September 1927, they had travelled round Tuscany and the Ligurian coast, whereas on this occasion they stayed briefly in the Dolomites, in Cortina d'Ampezzo, before moving on to Naples so as to spend a few days on the isle of Capri. However, the journey took less time than Adorno would have liked because Gretel, who managed her leather-processing business in Berlin single-handed, did not want to stay away too long.

Between late autumn 1928 and early in 1930, Adorno was involved in editing the *Musikblätter*, though he was not the editor in chief. Despite this constraint, he was willing to put his dissertation on ice for the time being in order to devote himself to the journal. In this sense his preparatory work on the reform of the programme for the journal paid off. Where he had control, he tried to implement his ideas during the following months. He took immediate steps to enlist the help of Alban Berg, supported the publication of an essay by Ernst Bloch, and secured contributions from Ernst Krenek, Kurt Weill and Hans Redlich.

The first issue of the transformed journal, which was henceforth named simply *Anbruch*, contained an editorial that plainly bore Adorno's handwriting, but was couched in more defensive terms than the exposé of the summer of 1928. The truth was that he could not ignore the views of Paul Stefan and Hans Heinsheimer, who still had the final word on editorial matters in Vienna. In the first issue of 1929, the claim is made in an understated fashion that the journal's yardstick is the modern music that has *dawned* (*angebrochen*) with the emergence of free atonality and the twelve-tone system. Its contemporary relevance, however, remained to be demonstrated, it was claimed, through the medium of music criticism.

The external appearance of the journal was changed for the first two sets of issues of 1929 and 1930. It now contained headings such as 'Critique of Composition' or 'Music and Technique', under which a whole series of articles by Adorno himself appeared. Adorno now introduced an entire battery of arguments about compositional technique or the philosophy of music on behalf of ideas he wished to defend. The very first contribution, 'Night Music', dedicated to Alban Berg, was succeeded by 'On Twelve-Tone Technique' and, finally, 'Reaction and Progress'. What unites these three texts is his attempt to make a persuasive case for the radical constructivism of musical material and, in addition, to show that Schoenberg's twelve-tone method was the crucial innovation in the 'rationalization process of music'.

As is well known, Schoenberg had already composed pieces using the twelve-tone method before this. In addition, there were attempts to provide a kind of manual with which to explain the foundations of twelve-tone music.[1] Two years previously, Adorno himself had analysed a number of Schoenberg's works, including the *Five Orchestral Pieces*, op. 16, the Serenade, op. 24, the Wind Quintet of 1928, but as yet unpublished, the Suite, op. 29, and the Third String Quartet, op. 30. The emphasis in these early analyses of 1927 lay on the formal shaping of the works. Their tone was strikingly apodictic, as can be seen from the assertion that 'Criticism is inappropriate in the case of Schoenberg's recent works; they set the standard of truth.'[2]

The essays that Adorno published from 1928, initially in the *Musikblätter des Anbruch*, and then in *Anbruch*, concentrated on Schoenberg's methods of composition. He defined twelve-tone technique as a preformed way of varying musical materials that had absolute validity for him.[3] The article on 'Night Music' from the first number of *Anbruch* addressed an entirely different topic. It began with the question of how we are to imagine the substantive content of traditional works today, given that they are the manifestations of a past history. We can assume the existence of neither an intelligent listener, nor a universally valid, timeless yardstick to guide our musical interpretation. Parallel with the disappearance of a musically literate public, contemporary society has also witnessed the dissolution of the previous unity of music. While serious music is still consumed by the dominant social class, albeit merely as an enjoyable ornament, light music, by providing glossy entertainment and sentimentality, has allowed itself to be misused to deceive the oppressed classes about their true social situation.

Given this background, what meaning can the musical tradition still retain? According to Adorno, this meaning 'cannot reside in an ahistorical, eternal, unchanging, natural stock of "works".' Rather, their truth content must be elicited by examining them in the light of advanced compositional techniques which give us an insight into the nature of 'historically preformed material'. 'What is eternal about a work is whatever manifests itself forcefully here and now, and destroys its deceptive appearances.' For this reason it is reactionary to object to the disintegration of works of music in the course of history. This idea can be put even more strongly: the truth character of a work 'is tied to its disintegration'. This disintegration is expressed in the fact that purely subjective music, music that reflects only interiority, has now lost its credibility. In the current historical situation, only 'music's true exterior, pure form, can survive'.[4]

To elucidate this development, Adorno introduced the concept of 'musical material'. What he meant by it was clarified in the article on 'Twelve-Tone Technique' that appeared in the autumn issue of *Anbruch*. Twelve-tone technique was a novel, historically developed method for dealing with musical material in a purely constructive way. Its foundation was created not simply by Schoenberg's elimination of cadence and the freeing of chromaticism from tonality. Nor was the avoidance of the repetition of notes within the rows the decisive innovation. What was new was the technique of constructive variation, the complete freedom of variation of motifs and themes 'so that the same musical event hardly ever recurs, and that at long last – and this is the crux – musical events take place not on the surface, but behind the scenes.'[5]

At this point Adorno focused on a specific idea of musical material, a concept of great importance for the future development of music theory.[6] In his view, the material of music was not a natural, neutral phenomenon. Because it was moulded by the dialectics of a contingent historical process, this meant that there could be no universally valid musical method or process of composition. Instead, if they wanted to achieve the 'coherence [*Stimmigkeit*] that was objectively available in the work',[7] composers had to work with the existing stock of materials that varied according to the historical stage in which they found themselves. In his article 'Reaction and Progress', Adorno proposed a concept of progress that would be valid for every branch of aesthetics that was based on the assumption of 'historical appropriateness', something that would show itself in the 'coherence' of the individual work. What would be 'coherent' would be the created unity that has to be quarried from the diverse materials that lie to hand. This material was in his view the theatre of progress in art. It meant that the freedom available to composers was no mere figment of the imagination, but was embedded in the dialectic of the material. Only the composer 'who submits to the work and seemingly does not undertake anything active except to follow where it leads, will be able to add something new to the historical constitution of the work, to its questions and challenges, something that does not simply follow from the way it happens to have been handed down historically. And the power to resolve the strict question posed by the work, by giving a strict response to it, is the true freedom of the composer.'[8] At the end of his essay for *Anbruch*, Adorno comes to the conclusion that the present age has produced no composers of the stature of Bach or

Beethoven. Nevertheless, we cannot speak of a retrograde step since 'the musical material has become freer and brighter and has been liberated from the mythic bonds of number, of the harmonic series and tonal harmonics, for ever.'[9]

The essay on 'Reaction and Progress' arose out of a controversy with Ernst Krenek, and did not appear until 1930. Another essay, on the question of whether 'Music can be cheerful', owes its existence to a disagreement with the music critic Hans Heinz Stuckenschmidt. Stuckenschmidt had accused Adorno of equating modern music with pessimistic music. Adorno reacted to this with a brief statement in which he set down some of the postulates of his theory of art, and music in particular. Once again, in opposition to the romantic notion of spontaneous creation, he emphasized the rational and material nature of the process of composition and the constructive aspect of art. Mozart's works, he argued, did not just arise because the Muses smiled on him, but because he was able to put in the labour of shaping the natural musical material. And as for cheerfulness, 'there was no objective reason for it'.[10] This cryptic sociological comment links up with a sketch entitled 'Stabilized Music' that he wrote in 1928, although he neither wished nor was able to publish it at the time. Put simply, he derived stabilized music from the society of the imperialist epoch that was in the process of achieving economic stability. He distinguished between two types of stabilized music: would-be classical music and folklorist music, each of which he ascribed to a particular social interest group. The playful nature of would-be classical music was a response to the needs of the new bourgeoisie for luxury goods, while the variants of music based on folklore were exploited by nationalist ideologies.[11]

How successfully did Adorno put into practice in his own compositions the insights and postulates which were now beginning to give a sharper definition to his own philosophy of music? Following his studies with Berg, he had determined to place composition at the top of his own priorities. The cycle of *Six Short Orchestral Pieces*, op. 4, was perhaps intended to apply in practice the theory that he had been publicizing. These pieces were his first attempt at testing his theory through the medium of a full orchestra.[12]

What characterizes these orchestral pieces?[13] At first hearing, or glance at the score, you register three lively movements alternating with three quieter ones, two of which have the traditional names of Gigue and Waltz. Some of the movements are very brief; two have only twelve bars and the waltz has twenty-nine. The influence of both Schoenberg and Berg is obvious. Nevertheless, Adorno does not always adhere strictly to the rules of twelve-tone technique. Alongside a rather free use of the tone-rows, what characterizes the pieces is their concentrated density, the reduction of the musical material to its smallest elements.

The first, highly dramatic piece attracts the listener's attention with the 'forte' entry of almost all the instruments. This eruptive climax is broken off after only four bars. Following a powerfully articulated melodic middle section, the dramatic opening gesture is repeated. In contrast, the second movement, which is divided into prologue and epilogue, opens up a deep space that is produced ultimately by the contrast between the principal and secondary voices. The sound is not primarily that of the full orchestra. Instead, it is dominated by the subtle interaction of soloists. The third movement is lively and is characterized by contrasting groups. The twelve bars of the fourth movement are strictly divided into three parts and, again, the instrumentation is subtle. It is difficult to discern any motivic progression and all the principal melodies are limited to two-note motifs, but the melody and accompanying chords all come together in a complete twelve-note field. Nevertheless, this section is not simply an exercise in the pure twelve-tone system. That can also be said of the fifth piece, the waltz, the longest one of the series. At its core there is a twelve-tone melody on the clarinet that determines what comes after it, but in such a way as to conjure up the past form of the waltz as a form now irredeemably lost. At the same time, the waltz is dissolved and reshaped as something new. The last movement is very slow and very brief; it is defined by its simplicity and also by the appearance of tonal chords, triads typically, that somehow suggest a montage of alien elements.

As a whole, the instrumental pieces that Adorno composed at different times between 1920 and 1929 are exemplary in two different ways.[14] On the one hand, they share an explosive spontaneity. On the other, we are struck by the tendency towards atonal rigour, a fixation on twelve-tone technique. This tendency can also be seen in his *Two Pieces for String Quartet*, op. 2, of 1925–6, which was composed partly under Berg's supervision, or at least in consultation with him. In addition to the use of diverse motifs, the second movement, which he wrote while he was still in Vienna, is notable for a theme defined by a tone-row with twelve variations – based on the pattern of canon, retrograde, inversion and retrograde inversion. So although a twelve-tone row emerges the pattern is disrupted, since a number of notes break the taboo on repetition. Adorno also used serial technique in the first movement, a sonata movement or rondo, which he composed at a later date in Frankfurt. The violin melody of the first twenty bars with its sweeping intervals is a classical twelve-tone movement. It makes use of the twelve notes of the scale without repeating any of them before all the others have been sounded.[15] The main movement contains four different twelve-tone rows, a principal row and three secondary ones. Even so, the row can still be said to play a kind of pre-compositional role in this quartet. The coherence of the piece is really established by timbre and texture.[16]

This tendency to use timbre and texture to play down the importance of twelve-tone technique is a characteristic that can also be found in Adorno's songs for piano. In terms of sheer quantity, these are at the forefront of Adorno's oeuvre; the genre attracted him from the outset and continued into old age. Taken together, there are no fewer than five song-cycles with opus numbers. In addition, there are almost twice as many pieces for piano and voice from the unpublished works, as well as the setting of seven French folksongs for voice and piano. Stylistically, the texts Adorno uses vary little: poems by Stefan George, Georg Trakl, Georg Heym, Else Lasker-Schüler, Theodor Däubler, Oskar Kokoschka, Franz Kafka, Bertolt Brecht, as well as earlier poets such as Friedrich Hölderlin and Theodor Storm. The songs of his productive phase between 1925 and 1929 have the following characteristics: the principle of polyphony, the advanced treatment of different voices, many-layered rhythms and twelve-tone technique. A further important feature is what he calls 'complementary harmony'.[17] Without attempting at this juncture to give a more detailed picture of, say, the *George Songs*, op. 1, or the *Four Songs for Voice and Piano*, op. 3, it is worthwhile pointing to the parallels with his instrumental pieces.[18] What characterizes Adorno's compositions is a tension[19] between the total autonomy of free atonality, the refusal to abandon spontaneous expression on the one hand,[20] and compliance with the norms of the twelve-tone method on the other. Adorno was never an orthodox practitioner of twelve-tone technique, and nor did he adhere rigidly to its basic rules. In the same spirit and at the same time, his criticism of twelve-tone orthodoxy became steadily more outspoken.[21]

Theorizing the twelve-tone method: Adorno's debate with Krenek

The starting-point for Adorno's critique of twelve-tone technique was given by particular considerations of music theory that also make clear that early in the 1930s he was beginning to effect the transition from music critic to music theoretician. At the same time they reflect his own experience of composition.[22] In the article already referred to, 'On Twelve-Tone Technique', in the September/October 1929 issue of *Anbruch*, he explains: since there can be no metaphysical certainties and universally binding norms in a contingent history of modernity, contemporary music is forced to free itself from all pre-existing traditions. The recourse to the forms of the past, as for instance in the neo-classicism of Igor Stravinsky and Arthur Honegger, was simply reactionary.

Adorno reconstructs the history of music as a process of disintegration. In the course of it, first the fugue and the sonata, and then tonality, along with its harmonic structures and cadences, ceased to be sacrosanct frames of reference. In his view the dynamic nature of the progressive process of rationalization had led to the emancipation of human consciousness from the bonds of myth. As a result atonality became crystallized as the absolutely new and uniquely valid form of composition.[23]

But if atonality were not to become obsolete in its turn, it would be necessary to practise a 'free music style' whose point of no return could only be a constant process of varying the musical material by means of 'construction springing from the imagination' or 'through the freedom of the constructive imagination'.[24] And, in order to vary the musical material in a constructivist way, what was needed were the modalities of twelve-tone technique.

In this phase of his theoretical development, Adorno conceived of twelve-tone technique as a rational procedure concerned with the material of music, rather than with its aesthetics. In other words, he distinguished between technique and work. Twelve-tone technique is the only adequate contemporary method of shaping the material of music, but this is not to say that it can satisfy the aims of musical and poetic expression. He did not tire of emphasizing that to think of it as a reference system analogous to tonality was a crass misunderstanding. To think of twelve-tone technique in mathematical terms was to commit a similar error. Just as Adorno was no orthodox serial composer in his own works, so too he became increasingly uncertain about the importance of twelve-tone technique on a theoretical plane. Between 1925 and 1935 his views of twelve-tone technique kept shifting and were also being refined. Alongside his purely theoretical analyses of music, a document of particular importance for an assessment of his position with regard to twelve-tone music was the correspondence he had begun with the composer Ernst Krenek in the spring of 1929.

Krenek was born in Vienna in 1900. He had met Adorno as early as 1924 in Frankfurt, where his comic opera in three acts, *Der Sprung über den Schatten*, op. 17, was in rehearsal. His first reaction was that Adorno was an 'over-articulate youth'. Initially, he was unimpressed, but soon he became fully convinced of Adorno's 'critical temperament', his 'astuteness' and the 'originality of his formulations'.[25] Adorno had already heard Krenek's music a year before they met, at the Composers' Festival in Kassel. Adorno was there to write about the festival and he heard a performance of Krenek's Second Symphony, op. 12, which came as a pleasant surprise. Krenek's opera *Jonny spielt auf* of 1925 foreshadowed the style of Weill's *Mahagonny* and *Die Dreigroschenoper* and made him famous overnight, not least because of his incorporation of jazz elements in the work. Adorno had seen it in Frankfurt in December 1927. In his review of the production he wrote that 'Krenek has enough demonic energy to enable him to launch a general attack', but that this production of *Jonny* 'lacked the power of the absurd that had created that terrifying *fortissimo* at the end of the Second Symphony.' Moreover, the content of the opera was suspect because 'it portrayed America as the ideal society of the future.'[26]

In the next few years, the two met with increasing frequency. Adorno introduced Krenek to Kracauer and Benjamin. Topical questions about contemporary music brought both similarities and differences of opinion to light. Following the debate in *Anbruch*, which had led to the two controversial articles about the issues raised in 'Reaction and Progress', these views were aired in a radio discussion which was then printed in the *Frankfurter Zeitung* in December 1930. Adorno used the occasion to restate his ideas about progress in music. According to him, progressive modern music manifested itself historically in the musical material. The task of the composer was to grapple with the material and transform it from an inward phenomenon to one visible to the outside world. 'If talk about the struggles of the great artist are to amount to anything more than the trite glorification of genius, it can only refer to this interaction between the artist and his material. Only from such interaction has it ever been possible to generate musical coherence.'[27]

A different aspect of their dialogue was concerned with the social nature of music. Adorno insisted that the sociological elements of music could only be discovered in the musical material; the material was the sphere in which a historically changing reality became concretely embedded. It followed that a sociologically based music analysis must focus on analysing particular works. For its part, the interpretation of works had the task of extracting the social meaning of music from the material. Adorno's statements make it clear that focusing on the interpretation of particular works by no means excludes our historical experience of given social relations. As in his sketch on 'Stabilized Music', he did not hide his view of 'the present relations of domination' in capitalist society which 'simply do not allow art to have a socially authoritative function, particularly any art that has a truth-content.'[28] This specifically sociological approach to music was to move gradually to the centre of Adorno's attention.

In this radio discussion Adorno focused on the concept of musical material. However, the correspondence with Krenek which started up in 1929 was triggered substantially by problems of atonality and twelve-tone technique. From the very outset, in April 1929, he emphasized that the compelling need for atonal compositions did not require a composer to make a subjective decision, but was the consequence of the musical material 'once it is no longer preformed and I may no longer take its preformed state for granted without falsifying what the material demands from me.'[29] And for the radically free composer the material does not call exclusively for twelve-tone music. Twelve-tone technique is no authoritative canon for composition; it is 'not a new shelter in which one can take refuge now that the roof has fallen in on tonality.' He went on to explain: 'I do not regard twelve-tone technique as the only possible form of atonality, but believe that it is possible to make meaningful music independently of any such commitment, and I hope to be able to prove this myself in the not all-too distant future.'[30]

Five years later, Adorno once again had occasion to comment in a letter on twelve-tone technique. Although he made use of it himself when composing, he had reservations about it, particularly if it became audible as a technique and drew attention to itself. In the letter to Krenek on 29 October 1934, he gave a definitive and quite unambiguous statement about it. This was accompanied by the first expression of a critical view of Schoenberg's own practice as a composer at this time: 'Twelve-tone technique today is nothing but the principle of motivic elaboration and variation, as developed in the sonata, but elevated now to a comprehensive principle of construction, namely transformed into an *a priori* form and, by that token, detached from the surface of the composition.' The concrete danger of a commitment to twelve-tone technique was 'a certain impoverishment, as I am aware from my own work.'[31] This passage makes it very clear that in his compositions Adorno looked at what he was doing from above, as it were, from the vantage point of his own music theory. In addition, moreover, the abstract problems of twelve-tone technique had their echo in the compositions that he wrote in parallel to his attempts to refine that theory.

9

Towards a Theory of Aesthetics

Learning the trade of composition and how to write scores was one thing. Reflecting on the problems of musical theory and writing about them was quite another. Adorno had been working on a philosophically ambitious theory of music with increasing intensity since 1928 at the latest. It is surprising that, although this topic was touched on in his correspondence with Alban Berg, it never became the subject of an extended dialogue between them. And yet they might easily have been able to exchange ideas about such matters as the 'concept of musical material', the 'nominalism of serial technique', or 'technique and form'. As it turned out, Ernst Krenek proved to be, if not more competent, at least more interested in discussing such questions. Not only was he a contemporary composer, he was also an active commentator on music. Even before he and Adorno entered into correspondence, both writers had published articles, in the eleventh and twelfth numbers of the *Musikblätter des Anbruch*, in which each referred to the other. This took place in the months when Adorno essentially had editorial control of the journal.[1] This series of articles was followed by the controversy about the problems of composition broadcast by Frankfurt Radio.

This controversy, which was held to be of direct relevance to contemporary composers, was, however, just one of the issues with which the 27-year-old Adorno had to grapple. In fact, he was forced to confront quite different problems, namely those raised by a philosophical theory of aesthetics. He hoped to be able to define the basic features of such a theory by engaging with the writings of Kierkegaard. Since his doctoral dissertation, which had been completed four years previously, and since the failure of his plans for the *Habilitation*, philosophical questions had been forced to take a back seat in favour of his musical activities. Nevertheless, they were never totally extinguished, since Adorno had tried to develop his theories of music with philosophical issues in mind. It was precisely this synthesis of music theory and philosophy that explains why he had attempted to set out a clearly defined position on this subject, partly in response to criticisms that his writings were incomprehensible and that they were couched in an over-complex language. His early concert reviews and critiques of musical works, followed by his theoretical articles and miscellaneous writings towards the end of the 1920s, allowed the gradual build-up of a philosophical theory of contemporary music. This theory included certain fundamental elements, among them the maxim that truth in music is possible only when a composition is thoroughly structured. A further principle was his insistence that musical expression must oppose the constraints of tradition. This led to the conviction that artistic methods and social development are dialectically interrelated. This philosophy of *music* was very far from being the justification of a *philosophy* with which Adorno might have been identified. He had made an intensive study of Kant and German idealism as a whole even before he started studying and subsequently during his university course. For his dissertation he had made an initial foray into Husserl's phenomenology. And, of course, he had read a fair amount of Hegel, Feuerbach and Marx, as can be seen from the intellectual echoes in his published writings and his use of concepts. He was able to articulate his reservations about Schopenhauer and Nietzsche and also to apply the methodology and terminology of psychoanalysis. Finally, he was familiar with the various current trends in philosophy and was in a position to express strikingly trenchant judgements about them. Despite the breadth of his philosophical learning, however, it was no false modesty that led him to tell Alban Berg that his academic aspirations came second to his musical ambitions.

During the months in which he poured his energies into the debates, written and oral, with Krenek, as well as into the revitalization of *Anbruch*, he had to come to terms with two further setbacks, on top of those he had already suffered. The lesser of the two was that, after a year's interval, his hopes of an editorial position with the Ullstein Press's *Berliner Zeitung am Mittag* were dashed once more. In a letter of 29 April 1929, Adorno had again asked Berg to recommend him to Ullstein. His chief competitor this time was Hans Heinz Stuckenschmidt, and it was Stuckenschmidt who ended up as the preferred candidate. So, once again, an extended stay in Berlin (in which he lived in the Violetta guest house in the Joachimsthalerstraße) turned out to be fruitless, at least from the point of view of a career. Did Adorno really have to worry about money at this time? It appears that, in addition to what must have been rather meagre earnings from his fees as music critic, he could always depend on financial support from his parents. When he applied for the position in Berlin, his father wrote to him from Frankfurt telling him not to worry about money, and that Adorno could rely entirely on his father. The most important thing for him was to have the opportunity to spend as much time with his son as possible. In a language redolent of military imagery, he told his son to apply to 'headquarters' for 'reinforcements' should that prove necessary.[2]

Since it soon became clear that it would take Ullstein months to reach a decision, Adorno felt increasingly reluctant to expect too much from it. He wrote to Berg that he 'could scarcely believe' that 'I have any real chance if anyone there has read even a single line of mine. ... But I am more than dubious that I should enter into competition with Stuckenschmidt, who has all the qualities of a confidence-trickster (including the good ones).'[3]

While in this instance Adorno was able to accept his defeat with relative equanimity, a further disappointment, in October 1929, was less easy to endure. Hans W. Heinsheimer, who was the representative of Universal Edition in Vienna responsible for *Anbruch*, wrote him a blunt letter on 1 October 1929: 'Your editorship has hitherto enjoyed a certain degree of independence' which was no longer acceptable. The fee of 100 Marks per issue that Heinsheimer had agreed to pay was now to be cancelled. Heinsheimer gave financial reasons for this last decision, specifying above all the decline in subscriptions. This was regarded as proof that the policy Adorno had been pursuing was not in keeping with actual developments in contemporary music and with the expectations of the readers. 'There can be no doubt, Mr Wiesengrund, that the "stabilization" of music that you have tried to combat, understandably enough, has nevertheless become reality to an extent that could not have been envisaged even a year ago.'[4] Adorno may well have been able to put up with such comments, since he was able to counter flagrant ignorance with irony. But he was cut to the quick by Heinsheimer's observation that 'Schoenberg and his closest circle' had considerable reservations about the direction taken by *Anbruch* since Adorno's appointment, and especially its philosophical assumptions about the nature of music.

It was not difficult for Adorno to identify Schoenberg himself as the source of this proclamation of displeasure. He complained bitterly to Berg that, of all people, it was Schoenberg, whose music he had tirelessly worked to promote as the only right path, who had stabbed him in the back: 'This is clearly a case of that stupid and solipsistic "sovereignty" that imagines that its outstanding achievement absolves it from every human obligation.'[5] He begged Berg expressly to make it clear to Emil Herzka, the proprietor of Universal Edition, as well as Heinsheimer, that it was not the whole of the Schoenberg circle that had taken sides against Adorno. This letter conveys the very definite impression that he believed that all his efforts to transform the journal and to publish his own writings had been in vain. Only after an inner struggle, and much persuasion on the part of Berg, was he prevailed upon not to break off all contact with the Viennese publishers from one day to the next.

But as early as the letter of 23 October 1929, he wrote to Berg: 'A "capitulation" on my part is *absolutely* out of the question ... I insisted on editorial control because I was being pushed into a kind of consulting role in which I would be expected to give my ideas without any guarantee that they would be followed up properly.'[6] At this point the

Viennese publisher did agree to a number of concessions to Adorno –
they were obviously well aware of his outstanding qualities as a writer
on music. Nevertheless, the dispute between the two parties dragged
on through the whole of 1930, until November, when Adorno finally
gave up all editorial responsibility. The first number of 1931 officially
informed the readers of his departure. As before, what hurt him was
not the formal end of his collaboration with *Anbruch*, but this new
evidence of Schoenberg's reaction, which he interpreted as a betrayal
of the common cause. This disappointment continued to weigh heavily
on the relationship between the two men, even during the years in exile
in the United States, where they were neighbours and often met.

It is typical of Adorno that despite his injured feelings he did not
succumb to self-pity. As early as the October letter to Berg in which he
gave his own view of the scandal, he finished up talking about the
burden of work that kept him from composing new pieces. The work
he was referring to was his second attempt at the *Habilitation*, which
he talked about henceforth as his 'Kierkegaard book'.

Needless to say, philosophy was never reduced to a shadowy existence
in Adorno's mind. He was merely continuing to do in an institutional
framework what he had been doing anyway during recent years. The
end of his editorial activities in Berlin and the fact that the Viennese
had decided to dispense with his assistance – with scarcely a word of
thanks – probably gave a timely fillip to the Kierkegaard book.

Another factor that was of benefit to the book, or, rather, was truly
inspirational, was provided by Walter Benjamin in the autumn of 1929.
Benjamin had just launched into a new, unique project: a major cultural
and historical study of the Paris arcades. After a number of lengthy
sojourns in Paris between 1927 and 1929, he had started to take notes
together with the Berlin writer Franz Hessel, who like him had been
strongly influenced by the French surrealists. Benjamin read extracts
from his notes to a small group of people in Königstein, including
Horkheimer and Adorno, as well as Gretel Karplus and Asja Lacis.[7]
Adorno was fascinated by Benjamin's plan to write a primeval history
of the nineteenth century based on an examination of the Paris arcades.

> It is scarcely hindsight if I say that from the very first moment
> I felt that Benjamin was one of the most impressive men I have
> ever encountered. . . . It was as if his philosophy revealed to me
> what philosophy would have to be if it were to fulfil its promise.[8]

One particular postulate of Benjamin's stood out from the draft that he
had read out in Königstein: 'No historical category without its natural
substance, no natural category without its historical filtration.'[9]

In the middle of 1929, stimulated by Benjamin's ideas, Adorno finally
felt able to bring himself to accept Tillich's offer to produce a dissertation on Kierkegaard for the *Habilitation*. Scarcely had he started to

collect the material and put his first thoughts down on paper, than he took off for the summer holidays with Gretel Karplus. He celebrated his twenty-sixth birthday with her in the Hotel Genazzini in Bellagio on Lake Como.

Why did Adorno fix on Kierkegaard's philosophy as the subject of his dissertation? He had been interested in Kierkegaard's ideas since his youth, and, to quote his own words, he had 'for years ridden around on Kierkegaardian ideas' about 'the problem of personality and the inwardness of the individual'.[10] And a letter from Kracauer to Löwenthal as long ago as December 1923 reveals that Adorno had even studied Kierkegaard intensively while he was still at the Gymnasium. 'If Teddie ever decides to make a declaration of love so as to escape from the sinful state of bachelorhood . . . , he will be sure to phrase it so obscurely that the young lady concerned . . . will be unable to understand what he is saying unless she has read the complete works of Kierkegaard.'[11] At the start of the 1920s, there was indeed a widespread interest in the discussion of terms such as 'anxiety', 'inwardness', 'decision' and 'leap'. This entire aspect of existentialist philosophy exerted a powerful fascination, chiefly as the antithesis of idealism and Hegel's philosophy of history. A clue to Adorno's personal interest in Kierkegaard can be gleaned from his preface to the book, in which he remarks that Kierkegaard provides the attractive opportunity of confronting a philosophy based primarily on existential and theological questions and reading it against the grain so as to set aside its religious, theological contents and lay bare its ideas on the problems of aesthetics.

In Adorno's eyes, Kierkegaard, the 'grandfather of all existential philosophy',[12] was (alongside Schopenhauer and Nietzsche) a major thinker because of his critique of the academic philosophy of his time. He was reacting to the fact that 'the academic discipline of philosophy had ceased to have anything to do with people.'[13] These were ideas to which Adorno was strongly attracted, but from which, precisely because of this attraction, he felt the need to distance himself (in the same way as from Husserl and Heidegger).

Adorno thought of Kierkegaard as a highly distinctive philosopher of the aesthetic. He used his philosophy as a foil to enable him to develop in more concrete form his own ideas about art. What fascinated Adorno was Kierkegaard's refined literary style with its ironical turns of phrase, what Kierkegaard had called 'aesthetic writing'. Adorno had independently played with the idea of an aesthetic existence, a mode of life that Kierkegaard had designed for himself as a counter-model to the way of life of the petty bourgeoisie as well as to the collective life of the masses, a counter-model that even he had difficulty in sustaining. But what Adorno was able to latch on to was Kierkegaard's ideas about the self as the fundamental structure of the modern subject, the anti-systematic tendencies in his thought and Kierkegaard's love of paradox.

Scarcely had Adorno begun to focus on these central themes of Kierkegaard's thought than he wrote that he was enjoying this work, but that it cost him far greater effort than the more narrowly circumscribed essays he had been writing for music journals. Even so, he started with lofty ambitions: first of all, he wished to reconstruct Kierkegaard's philosophy following the kind of procedure Benjamin had employed in his *Origin of German Tragic Drama*. In that book Benjamin had developed the idea of an allegorical principle of knowledge. The truth content of the baroque tragic drama was to be decoded by focusing on seemingly peripheral individual elements.[14]

Second, however, he wanted to appropriate the dialectical structural analysis with which Georg Lukács had attempted to solve the riddle of the commodity form. Particular importance was attached to the idea that 'the structure of commodity relations can be made to yield a model of all the objective forms of bourgeois society together with all the subjective forms corresponding to them.'[15] Of equal importance was the 'theory of interiors'. The interior was interpreted as the 'model of Kierkegaardian inwardness'. Furthermore, a fundamental critical analysis of the 'concept of existence' was indispensable.[16]

In order to advance his work, his excerpting and note-taking, Adorno had retreated in spring 1930 to Kronberg, an idyllic little town at the edge of the Taunus Hills, not far from the centre of Frankfurt. In this secluded village environment he worked on a draft of the book in 'complete isolation'. He worked so intensively, night and day, that by the beginning of August, as he reported to Berg, he had 'a complete breakdown – something that had never happened to me in the whole of my life.'[17] Even if we take his sensitive, slightly delicate nature into account, this breakdown was no chance matter. It was the product not just of his strenuous work on the dissertation, but also of his countless other activities. For despite the intended retreat to Kronberg, to the Frankfurter Hof inn, he was still in contact with a large number of people. Horkheimer and Pollock lived in the same place, and there were frequent visitors from Frankfurt. For the Whitsun holidays Gretel Karplus came from Berlin. In addition, there were concerts to be heard in Frankfurt. And since Ernst Schoen, a childhood friend of Benjamin's, had a contract as arts editor with Frankfurt Radio, Adorno found himself being drawn increasingly into activities for the radio.[18] One such was the performance of Ernst Krenek's songs by Hilda Crevenna-Bolongaro. What proved decisive for Adorno's nervous breakdown, however, was the fact that, in addition to his Kierkegaard studies, he was producing so many other writings. Having complained to Kracauer about continual insomnia and strong palpitations because of the overwork, he frequently sent him miniature treatises arising from his work on Kierkegaard with the request that he use his influence as editor of the cultural section of the *Frankfurter Zeitung* to have them published in that paper. Kracauer's efforts were successful. Adorno's

'Beitrag zur Geistesgeschichte' (Contribution to the History of Ideas), a highly original and witty comparison of Kant and Nietzsche,[19] appeared in the *Frankfurter Zeitung* on 6 June. He also wrote a number of articles on music, very much in the spirit of his favourite proverb, one he used to repeat throughout his life: 'The leopard cannot change its spots' (literally: 'The cat never stops catching mice'; trans.). These writings included his articles for *Anbruch* and short concert reviews, as well as a portrait of Arnold Schoenberg for the programme notes for the Kroll Opera house. Previously, he had written a new interpretation of Berg's opera *Wozzeck* for a new production in Essen, and this appeared in the programme booklet *Der Scheinwerfer: Blätter der Städtischen Bühne.*

Rather more than a beginner's foray into philosophy

Of Kierkegaard's writings, Adorno focused chiefly on *Either/Or*, *Fear and Trembling*, *The Concept of Dread* and the *Philosophical Fragments.* Apart from these, he confined his study to a quite narrow field of secondary literature. In the notes, apart from Kant, Hegel and Husserl, he refers only to a few contemporary thinkers, such as Georg Lukács, Ernst Bloch and Martin Heidegger.

The title *The Construction of the Aesthetic* was a clear indication that Adorno intended to give Kierkegaard's philosophy an unconventional interpretation. For, of the latter's three stages on life's way – the aesthetic, the ethical and the religious – the aesthetic was conceived as the least authoritative and the most superficial mode of existence. In contrast to this, Adorno's programme was the salvaging of aesthetic illusion.[20] The provocative question he put was whether the aesthetic was the realm in which truth is made manifest.

In the 'Exposition', and in tune with the title, he sets out the plan of the following six chapters. The reader is at once drawn into his interpretation. From the very first page he is confronted with the crucial question whether Kierkegaard's writings are philosophy or literature. Adorno explains his own criteria and introduces his own definition of philosophy: 'Philosophical form requires the interpretation of the real as a binding nexus of concepts. Neither the manifestation of the thinker's subjectivity nor the pure coherence of the work determines its character as philosophy. This is, rather, determined in the first place by the degree to which the real has entered into concepts, manifests itself in these concepts, and comprehensibly justifies them.'[21] He defines Kierkegaard's philosophy as a strictly subjective mode of thought. Despite the speculative element that is fundamental to it, this type of thought differs from literature, he believes, because it forms its concepts dialectically. The central question Adorno raises is: what construction of the aesthetic do we find in Kierkegaard? He distinguishes a threefold semantics of aesthetics: as a term describing the realm of art in its totality, as a personal attitude, and as a subjectively intended mode of communication. He concludes that, against his own intentions, Kierkegaard's theory of the beautiful is idealist, that is, determined entirely by subjectivity. Adorno, in contrast, insisted that works of art are essentially temporal and particular in nature; they appear in 'figurated form', not in the universal form of ideas.

Adorno briefly sets out his methodology. The distinction he draws between literal meaning and metaphoric, philosophical content which is laid bare by criticism corresponds to the relation of commentary and criticism as expounded by Benjamin in his essay on Goethe's *Elective Affinities*. This notion of a two-stage interpretative process was strictly text-based: it proceeds from the author's writings, not his life. 'The person is only to be cited in the content of the work, a content that is no more identical with the person than the person with the work.'[22] This principle holds good for Adorno's epistemology as a whole. It applies also to the chief criticism he levelled at Kierkegaard: that in Kierkegaard's work subjectivity has no weight of its own because it is simply the stage on which the universal structures of existence are enacted. Adorno pointed to the implication that Kierkegaard conceives of inwardness as being entirely objectless since 'the "I" is thrown back onto itself by the superior power of otherness'. The world of objects only supplies the subject with the mere occasion for the deed. Because 'given objects' are eliminated, 'there is only an isolated subjectivity, surrounded by a dark otherness.'[23]

On the one hand, Adorno's analysis focused on Kierkegaard's failed attempt to eliminate identity philosophy.[24] On the other hand, he was attracted by the concept of dialectics, only to discover to his disappointment that Kierkegaard employs a concept of dialectics without objects, and limits it to the movement of individual human consciousnesses in opposites. His conclusion, one that constitutes a principal plank of the book as a whole, is that 'Kierkegaard did not "overcome" Hegel's system of identity; Hegel is inverted, interiorized.'[25] Kierkegaard likewise fails to understand 'the irreversible and irreducible uniqueness of the historical fact',[26] particularly since he devalues history on the grounds that it represents radical evil, a universal threat to inwardness. Kierkegaard's central concept of 'situation', defined as the decision taken by a man thrown entirely on his own resources, could not constitute a solution in Adorno's eyes. On the contrary, the 'situation' is the reflection of the 'reification of social life, the alienation of the individual from a world that comes into focus as a mere commodity.'[27] These topoi, reification and the commodity form, were to become permanent features of Adorno's theory of society.

Adorno's settling of accounts with Kierkegaard focused on the concept of the *interior* in which all objects would have no more than symbolic value. The 'interior' is the symbol of the illusory nature of a society based on exchange, and is therefore unsuited as a principle with which to oppose a history that has gone astray. He bolstered this criticism by holding up to the light the sociological and mythical contents of the interior. Under the heading of the 'sociology of inwardness', Adorno disclosed the links between Kierkegaard's written utterances and his economic situation.

Adorno agreed with Kierkegaard's rejection of idealist ontology (Fichte's I = I and Hegel's subject/object), but refused to accept the absolute value he placed on subjective existence in the name of a transcendental meaning. What Adorno was unable to stomach was Kierkegaard's obsession with the individual human being: 'The self, the stronghold of all concretion, contracts in its singularity in such a fashion that nothing more can be predicated of it: it reverses into the most extreme abstractness; the claim that only the individual knows what the individual is amounts to no more than a circumlocution for its final unknowability.'[28]

In conclusion, Adorno assembled once more a number of his interpretative strategies in order to show that the realm of the aesthetic is the genius loci of Kierkegaard's philosophy. This becomes apparent when Kierkegaard asserts that 'the original experience of Christianity remains bound to the image.'[29] Because all subsequent and prospective images perish in the image of Christ, this process of decay proves to be the salvaging of the aesthetic. 'The hope that inheres in the aesthetic is that of the transparency of decaying figures.'[30] In other words, the fall of historical figures opens up the vista of a completely different history, if only as a glimmer of hope. At this juncture, Adorno develops the idea of reconciliation in art which even at this stage proves to be an essential component of his aesthetic theory, and was destined to remain so. This also holds good for the idea that hope arises from the fragmentary ciphers washed up on the shores of history, 'disappearing in front of overflowing eyes, indeed confirmed in lamentation. In these tears of despair the ciphers appear as incandescent figures, dialectically, as compassion, comfort and hope.'[31]

Adorno followed Kierkegaard in the belief that truth exists only as 'encipherment and disguise' and is revealed 'only through the disintegration of fundamental human relations'.[32] Fantasy, which according to Adorno had to be 'exact',[33] is the organ enabling us to break free from the catastrophic course of history and to become conscious of the possibility of reconciliation. 'The moments of fantasy are the festivals of history.'[34] Finally, Adorno construed the doctrine of existence as a negative philosophy of history that reverses that of idealism. He interpreted the direction taken by that reversal in the spirit of Walter Benjamin: the entire course of history hitherto was that of a crime against nature. Messianic hope will blossom when this catastrophic process reaches its end. Hence reconciliation depends on the disintegration of existing conditions.

Adorno needed barely more than a year to write and complete this dissertation, with its highly idiosyncratic ideas and methods and a plethora of ingenious formulations. How did he manage to master the enormous daily burden of work required for this task? It was possible only because he was inspired by a feeling of enthusiasm that grew almost by the day. He was convinced that, in criticizing Kierkegaard, he was also aiming an annihilating blow at Heidegger. To Berg, Adorno wrote that his struggle with Kierkegaard was 'new and original' since, on this occasion, he had written without looking over his shoulder at the faculty professors who would examine his work. Does this explain why they objected so strongly to what he had produced? In his letter, Adorno dismissed their criticisms as insignificant, saying that they sounded very like the objections to modern music.

In the event, the two examiners' reports, by Professors Paul Tillich and Max Horkheimer, proved to be positive. Tillich stressed the prospect of a new view of Kierkegaard that had been opened up by Adorno's critical interrogation of existential philosophy. He also praised the 'combination of the highest abstraction and vivid concreteness' and the 'insertion of a concept into the constellation of related and opposing concepts', as well as the programmatic hints of a philosophy 'whose truth is to be found in the interpretation of the microscopic events of a historical moment.'[35] According to Tillich, Wiesengrund's thinking was 'not topological, but fabric-like'; the argument 'is spun out essentially without breaks from one end to the other.' In the main, Horkheimer agreed with Tillich's assessment. But he drew attention to the fact that the concepts of 'hope and reconciliation' were essential parts of the dissertation and that they were derived from theological convictions which were quite alien to his own way of thinking. 'Nevertheless, I know full well that this study is the product not just of a strong philosophical desire to uncover truth, but also of a mind with the power to advance philosophy at important points.'[36]

Those of Adorno's friends who were not integrated into the machinery of the university, Kracauer and Benjamin in particular, had rather different reactions to *The Construction of the Aesthetic*. Benjamin, when he saw the page proofs of the book, responded enthusiastically in a letter of December 1932: 'Whether I turn to your presentation of baroque motif in Kierkegaard, to the ground-breaking analysis of the "intérieur", to the marvellous quotations which you supply from the philosopher's technical treasure trove of allegories, to the exposition of Kierkegaard's economic circumstances, to the interpretation of inwardness as citadel or of spiritualism as the ultimate defining limit of spiritism – I am constantly struck in all of this by the wealth of insight, as well as by the penetrating character of your evaluation.'[37] Benjamin was well aware that the Kierkegaard book owed a debt to his own ideas and his methods of interpretation as these were expressed in his essays and books, especially the essay on Goethe's *Elective Affinities* and the *Origin of the German Tragic Drama.* He was evidently happy for Adorno to make these borrowings, since he wrote: 'Thus it is true that there is still something like a shared work after all.'[38]

Kracauer had already been sent a copy of the first chapter of the book in manuscript as early as September 1930. He had barely read the first few pages before telling Adorno of his favourable response. Since Adorno was only a few days away from handing in the dissertation, this was important encouragement.

The book version of the Kierkegaard thesis, published in March 1933 by Mohr-Siebeck, appeared 'on the very day that Hitler seized dictatorial powers'.[39] It was far from being identical with the 26-year old Adorno's dissertation which had persuaded Frankfurt University to confer on him the *venia legendi*, the right to give philosophy lectures, in February 1931. The original version was thoroughly revised for pub-lication. As he explained to Krenek, all the building-blocks he had used were still there, but they had been completely rearranged. Thus an entirely new version had emerged, one that could truly be said to have been 'through-constructed'. In comparison, the original version could be said to be no more than a plan for this one. He had very little time to revise the book but had managed to complete it in barely two months in autumn 1932, partly in Frankfurt, partly in Berlin.

Scarcely had the book appeared in spring 1933 than efforts were made by both Benjamin and Kracauer, despite the autos-da-fé organ-ized by the Nazis, to publish reviews that would show that the author was a young philosopher whom the readership of the *Vossischer Zeitung* and the *Frankfurter Zeitung* would be unable to ignore in future. How-ever, the events following Hitler's takeover of power rendered all these efforts nugatory overnight. Even so, copies of the book were sold during the dark years in Germany. By the time Benjamin's review had appeared, Benjamin himself had been forced to leave Nazi Germany. Kracauer's lengthy review was typeset by the *Frankfurter Zeitung*, and the galleys had even been corrected, but the review never appeared. As a left-wing Jewish intellectual, Kracauer had fled with his wife to Paris immediately after the Reichstag fire on 28 February 1933. He did so trusting to the promise that he would be given the post of a corres-pondent of the *Frankfurter Zeitung*, a promise rescinded by Heinrich Simon, the paper's director, after only four weeks.[40] Adorno, who had previously warned about the political direction taken by the newspaper, was proved right. Even before 1933, every attempt was made to avoid confrontation with the radical right. According to Ernst Bloch, when the left-leaning economics editor, Arthur Feiler, was sacked, Adorno's only comment was the laconic statement that 'the ships are leaving the sinking rat'.[41]

In his review Benjamin focused on the crucial aspect. The author's main achievement, he said, was that he placed Kierkegaard's philo-sophy in an intellectual and cultural context which transposed the mythical dimension of existentialist philosophy back into the picture world of the nineteenth century. Benjamin concluded his review with a perceptive remark. 'This book contains much in a small space. The author's subsequent writings may some day emerge from it.'[42] We shall be able to see the accuracy of his prognosis when we present Adorno's philosophical writings of the 1960s, above all his *magnum opus*, *Negative Dialectics*.

Adorno himself published an essay in 1966 that looked back at his Kierkegaard book. He observes that in fact it contains tracks that he subsequently retraced step by step in the course of his philosophical studies. In this brief retrospective, he recapitulates his objections to the conception of the unique individual as well as to Kierkegaard's subliminal ontologizing of subjective truth. He goes even further than in the book when he emphasizes the extent to which Kierkegaard misunderstood the category of mediation. 'For Hegel, mediation passes through the extremes. Kierkegaard, however, simply mistook Hegelian mediation for a middle term between two concepts, a moderate compromise.'[43] At the same time, Kierkegaard's philosophy was in the right against Hegel 'when it came to the defence of the non-identical, the element that was not absorbed into the Hegelian concept.'[44] In addition, he underscored the importance of Kierkegaard's insistence on the individual as an absolute because this idea mirrored the false totality as an absolute. Finally, Adorno achieves an almost total personal identification with Kierkegaard when he writes: 'By judging the whole, whether as totality or system, to be an absolute deception, Kierkegaard throws down the gauntlet to the totality into which he has been impressed, as have we all. That is what is exemplary about him.'[45] As it was for the author of those words.

When Kracauer wrote his review he felt the need to justify his venturing to review a book that had been dedicated to him. He argued that 'côteries based purely on personal relations are pernicious', but he thought it necessary for 'people who have identical or similar interests to demonstrate their solidarity'.[46] That was an unambiguous statement in an age when solidarity was anything but self-evident, as Kracauer soon found out in his dealings with his employer, the *Frankfurter Zeitung*. Like Benjamin, Kracauer concentrated on reconstructing Adorno's critical analysis of Kierkegaard's concept of inwardness, which in his view had been conducted in the light of sociological insights. Kierkegaard's retreat into inwardness 'is explained with reference to the emerging epoch of high capitalism in which all things and values are becoming increasingly commodified.' From a philosophical point of view, it becomes clear that Kierkegaard's 'inwardness without objects . . . cannot establish contact with commodified objects.' It is rightly decoded as a natural and mystical concept. Kracauer explicitly draws attention to the fact that Benjamin's philosophy of history had acted as godfather to Adorno's own approach. With hindsight, Kracauer's review, which remained unpublished, conveys the impression that he wished simultaneously to make a comment on Adorno's inaugural lecture as a *Privatdozent*, which he had given in May 1931 in the University of Frankfurt. This lecture had been something of a sensation, and I shall discuss its content and direction against the background of the development of the situation of the university from the early 1930s, above all in connection with the debates of the day about the causes of the crisis in the sciences and the future of a critical philosophy.

10

A Second Anomaly in Frankfurt: The Institute of Social Research

In 1931 Max Horkheimer became director of the Institute of Social Research. At that point, the institute, a scientific organization with special status at the university, was already over six years old. Characteristically, it had been established thanks to a foundation set up by Hermann Weil, a prosperous businessman.[1] His son, Felix José Weil, was born in Argentina in 1898, and had lived in Frankfurt since he was nine. His studies led him to concentrate on problems of the world economy, and economics in general. Unlike his liberal-conservative father, however, he stood on the left politically, and had a political and scientific interest in Marxism.[2] Despite the political differences between father and son, the latter was able to persuade Hermann Weil to give financial backing to the project of establishing a research institute connected to the university on the model of the institute in Kiel.

The negotiations between the registrar of the university and the relevant ministry about the establishment of an Institute of Social Research as an endowed foundation began as early as 1922. After successful consultations, the ministry and the university finally concluded an agreement with the Weil Foundation about setting up an autonomous research institute whose financial basis should be secured by the Gesellschaft für Sozialforschung e.V.[3] The financial framework included provision for the construction and equipping of the institute building, in addition to the payment of the sum of 100,000 Marks, and the endowment of a chair in the Faculty of Economics and Social Science to be held by the institute director. Ideas for the proposed tasks of an institute dedicated to pure research emanated from an exclusive group of no more than twenty young, left-leaning intellectuals. They ranged from prominent Marxists such as Georg Lukács and Karl Korsch to Friedrich Pollock and Felix Weil. At Whitsun 1923, this group[4] organized a so-called Marxist Study Week, to discuss the programme and possible lines of research of the institute. What was common to all these people, many of whom were members of the Communist (KPD) or Independent Socialist (USPD) parties, was their rejection of the different strands of reformist or dogmatic interpretations of Marx. They were united by the attempt to breathe new philosophical life into a Marxism paralysed by its own orthodoxy.[5] Weil and Pollock were already on friendly terms before the Whitsun meeting, both having taken their doctorates in economics at Frankfurt University. Their academic ambitions led them to give vigorous support to the foundation of the institute. Pollock even envisaged conducting his own research there.[6]

Kurt Albert Gerlach was a left-leaning Social Democrat who was receptive towards Marxist economic thought. He had been given a chair at Frankfurt in 1922 and Felix Weil had at once offered him the directorship of the future institute. However, Gerlach died unexpectedly in October of that year, leaving the founders of the institute with the dilemma of having to find an alternative. The negotiations with the Berlin historian Gustav Mayer came to nothing because of irreconcilable views about the scope of the powers to be assigned to Felix Weil.[7] Following this setback, it became possible to recruit the so-called academic Marxist Carl Grünberg, who was a professor of political economy in Vienna and who had made an international reputation for himself as the editor of the *Archive for the History of Socialism and the Workers' Movement*.[8] When he took up the directorship of the institute in Frankfurt, he was also appointed to a chair in the Faculty of Economics and Social Science. In the summer of 1924, the year Adorno obtained his doctorate, he made a speech to celebrate the opening of the newly built home of the Institute of Social Research. The architect, Franz Rödele, had designed a four-storey building in Victoria-Allee 17 in the style of the New Sobriety. In addition to the offices of the director and the administration, it contained a library, four seminar rooms and more than a dozen small workrooms. The rooms on the ground floor and the first floor were put at the disposition of the Economics and Social Science Faculty. In his inaugural lecture Grünberg insisted on the need for fundamental scientific research, something scarcely possible in the universities. By this he meant that the work of the institute was to be based on Marxist methods of research, which he interpreted as meaning that the Marxist view of history should be its theoretical foundation. However, Marxism was not to be regarded as a fixed canon of eternal truths, but had to prove itself through its explanatory power.[9]

Grünberg was suffering from ill-health and he was unable to cope with the burdens of the directorship while the institute was being built up. He had a stroke in 1928 which had a lasting impact on both his administrative and scholarly work, leaving the initiative in the hands of the younger members of the institute. For the first eight years of its life, the research carried out at the institute centred on questions posed from a Marxist point of view. They included questions about the crisis in capitalist economies, the socialization of the economy, and the nature of planned economies. The majority of the researchers, too, examined these questions from a Marxist standpoint. The dogmatism of the Second and Third Internationals did indeed meet with criticism in the institute, and Grünberg declared himself in favour of a more open form of Marxism. However, there were other members, for example, Karl Wittfogel, Richard Sorge, Henryk Grossmann and Franz Borkenau, who were convinced that socialism and communism provided the models of a more equitable social order, one destined by history to triumph over capitalism. Friedrich Pollock and Felix Weil, who were both committee members of the Society for Social Research, also endorsed such views. The majority of the assistants who worked for the institute in the mid-1920s were either formally members of the USPD or the KPD, or else in sympathy with the communist movement. A further move in this direction was the controversial attempt by Pollock and Weil to establish a publishing house for Marxist literature. Their idea was to set up a privately run organization within the institute, a move that led for a short time to major conflicts in the university. This publisher was to act as a Marx–Engels archive. Pollock and Weil intended to use it as the vehicle for a critical edition of the works of Marx and Engels, in cooperation with the Marx–Engels Institute in Moscow and its director, David Riazanov, who was in contact with Grünberg.[10] There was some collaboration between the Frankfurt and Moscow institutes, but it did not last, since the growth of Stalinism in Russia proved to be the downfall of Riazanov, who was sent into internal exile in the early 1930s. In a parallel development, some institute members became increasingly sceptical about the ability of the working class to take on the role of agents of revolution, despite their economic oppression and social privation.

Max Horkheimer attempted a kind of sociological summing up in the light of current events in 1930 with a study entitled *The Beginnings of the Bourgeois Philosophy of History*. The chapter entitled 'Utopia' contains a number of sentences that encapsulate the climate of the period – and a viewpoint that may well have been shared by the majority of institute members, particularly since they had chosen Horkheimer as Grünberg's successor. 'History has produced a better society from an inferior one, and in its course it can bring about one that is even better – that is a fact. But it is also a fact that the course of history passes over the suffering and misery of individuals. Between these two facts there exists a variety of explanations, but no meaning that can justify them.'[11]

Two inaugural lectures

Max Horkheimer was appointed to the chair in social philosophy in 1930 – having been a *Privatdozent* until then. The publication of his study *The Beginnings of the Bourgeois Philosophy of History* in the same year must have told in his favour, since an in-house appointment was not without its difficulties. This made it possible for him to be installed formally as director of the institute the following year. His appointment led to a clear shift of emphasis in the work of the institute.

His intention was to exploit more systematically the theoretical and methodological advances in the social sciences. The very title of the public address he gave in January 1931 to mark the assumption of his duties as director – 'The Present Position of Social Philosophy and the Tasks Facing an Institute of Social Research' – indicated the change in research priorities. At a number of points, Horkheimer's argument touched on the same themes that Adorno was to address in his own inaugural lecture three months later. It is of interest, therefore, to look at the similarities and differences. What were the relevant questions for the social philosopher who was about to take over the research apparatus of an entire institute, and how did he conceive of its organization?

Horkheimer begins by defining the future focus of the institute's research interests: the 'question of the connection between the economic life of society, the psychological development of individuals and the changes in the realm of culture in the narrower sense (to which belong not only the so-called intellectual elements such as science, art and religion, but also law, customs, fashion, public opinion, sports, leisure activities, lifestyle, etc.).'[12] The emphasis of future research in the institute would lie, on the one hand, on the subjective, psychological factors influencing the consciousness of social actors and, on the other hand, the institutional and cultural aspects of society. In other words, so-called superstructural elements were to be included in the research programmes. In addition to the critical examination of the explanatory power of materialist theory, Horkheimer stressed the need for 'concrete research into particular objects', the results of which would act as an important corrective to the rampant growth of ideological speculation in the social sciences as well as to the corresponding notions of reality. Future relations between philosophy and the individual disciplines should not be concerned with the primacy of the one over the others, but should be determined in Horkheimer's view by the mutual 'interpenetration' of factual research and philosophical reflection.

What was needed was 'to organize research projects stimulated by contemporary philosophical problems, in which philosophers, sociologists, economists, historians and psychologists are brought together in permanent collaboration.'[13] Horkheimer illustrated this programme of philosophy-led social research with reference to a topic particularly close to his own heart, and which actually became a core research interest of the institute both then and later. This was the analysis of the relations between objective class situation and consciousness, i.e., social position and subjective attitudes. He was convinced that such relations could be explored only on the basis of empirical material. In order to come by the requisite empirical data he proposed no fewer than six different methodological tools: together with the use of statistics and expert reports, he thought it absolutely necessary to initiate dialogue between experts, to conduct the content analysis of the politically and culturally influential media, and, lastly, to analyse documents. In addition, he called

for large-scale field research along the lines practised in American sociology, together with the use of questionnaires. 'Each of these methods
alone is completely inadequate. But all of them together, in years of
patient and extensive investigations, may be fruitful for the general
problem.'[14]

This idea of interdisciplinarity combined with a methodological pluralism was to prove decisive for the work of the institute in the coming
years. But in addition, under Horkheimer's growing personal influence
in the institute, it had already begun to take on embryonic shape in the
empirical projects that were already under way. The new trend was
strengthened by the arrival of Leo Löwenthal[15] as a literary scholar,
Erich Fromm[16] as an analytical social psychologist, and, somewhat later,
Herbert Marcuse,[17] who, as a former student of Martin Heidegger, had
been recommended to the institute by the registrar, Kurt Riezler.

A few months after the lecture given by the 35-year-old director of
the Institute of Social Research, another inaugural lecture was given,
one no less programmatic in its aims, this time by Adorno, who had
qualified as a lecturer in philosophy in February of the same year. Its
title was 'The Actuality of Philosophy'. If the audiences of the two
lectures, which must have consisted largely of the same people, had an
ear for the similarities and differences between the two speakers, they
must have noted with some astonishment that, if anything, Adorno was
sceptical about Horkheimer's programme of a philosophy-led conception of social research.[18] His scepticism might easily be overlooked on
a superficial reading. On the first page Adorno evidently shares many of
the ideas and ways of seeing discussed by Horkheimer. For example,
in his extensive *tour d'horizon* of contemporary philosophy he agrees
with Horkheimer's critique of the chaotic specialization in the different
disciplines and thinks of it as part of the crisis of modern scholarship
that has to be overcome. The two men likewise felt the same scepticism
about the revolutionary potential of the workers' movement. Moreover,
they agreed that no way out of the crisis of the sciences would be
forthcoming either from Marxism, whether orthodox or revisionist, or
from the dominant academic philosophies in the shape of phenomenology, metaphysics or positivism. Nevertheless, unlike Horkheimer,
Adorno did not regard the new discipline of the social sciences as a
phoenix arising from the ashes. In his critical view, the formal shape of
the sociology that predominated in the Weimar period had not gone
beyond an abstract conceptuality. Whereas the idealist constructs of
philosophy hovered above the real world, sociology runs the risk of
distilling its concepts from the given realities in a concretistic fashion,
and this results in a merely descriptive 'doubling' of the given. 'What
remains is an endless, pointless chain of determinants that docs no
more than point to "this and that", that renders nugatory every attempt
at organization through understanding, and fails to provide any critical
yardstick.'[19] As early as 1931 Adorno complained that sociology of this

type 'succumbed to a kind of universal relativism', abandoning such categories as class and ideology in favour of general concepts of a purely formal nature, such as social relations, social formation, social distinction, social group, social organization.

In the inaugural lecture, he refers to sociologists – and Horkheimer will undoubtedly have been irritated by it – as 'cat burglars' (*Fassadenkletterer*, literally, façade climbers), a concept evidently borrowed from Martin Heidegger. As a cat burglar, the sociologist tries to salvage the valuable remnants of a building erected by one of the great architects of philosophy, but now abandoned as derelict. At the time of the inaugural lecture Adorno was not unfamiliar with sociological ways of thinking. On the contrary, he was conversant with the principal modern trends of the discipline. Nevertheless, sociology in his view had to take second place to his primary philosophical objective of rendering the world visible as an *enigma* by *interpreting* individual phenomena. What was meant by this?

His initial premise had been to insist that we must abandon the illusion that thought alone will enable us to grasp the whole of reality as a meaningful world. For this reason, all attempts to comprehend empirical reality by refining our philosophical systems are doomed. Because reality remains enigmatic in principle, the philosophical theoretician faces the task of solving one riddle after another. As long as philosophers rise to the challenge of interpreting 'the riddles of existence',[20] philosophy will remain relevant even in the modern world which has been demystified by the rationalism of the individual sciences. To attempt to solve such riddles by interpretative processes, however, does not mean that Adorno is trying to track down truths through some occult knowledge, to discern beings hidden behind the world of phenomena, beings that explain everything because they are at the root of everything that exists. On the contrary, the 'function of riddle-solving . . . is to illuminate the puzzle in a flash.'[21] Such moments of perception are given to the interpretative mind because the questions arising in response to the riddles are gradually surrounded by possible answers that propose tentative solutions.

This point in Adorno's argument is of central importance for his own model of knowledge. He states that the models of philosophical interpretation must be introduced into 'changing constellations'. Such 'changing experiments' should continue to be conducted 'until they arrive at figurations in which the answers are legible, while the questions themselves vanish.'[22] For Adorno, who at this point brought a notion of dialectic into play, knowledge means that the particular nature of one interpretation comes into conflict with another one. The truth content, which is always provisional, appears in a sudden flash illuminating what has previously been thought. In the same way, philosophical interpretations can claim validity to the degree that they lead to better insights.

In this early text, which was not published at the time, Adorno tried to clarify his ideas about how critique might be thought of as a mode of knowledge that could be defined as a dialectical process. This process appeared to him to be one of rational construction. Such constructs consisted of a series of mental models that could be brought together in a set of changing constellations. And these constellations in turn pour the historical materiality of society – what he called, following Freud, 'the dregs of the phenomenal world' – into new forms.

Adorno drew a distinction between this specifically philosophical goal of knowledge and the independent logic of research. This too was a theme in the inaugural lecture. Research, in his view, was the concern of the individual disciplines, including the discipline of sociology. The interaction between philosophy and sociological research that he vociferously called for was to be achieved through 'dialectical communication'. What he understood by this was that the aim of a large-scale philosophical diagnosis of the age was 'to construct keys with which to unlock reality'.[23] To put this strategy into practice calls for an 'exact imagination' which can be protected against pure speculation only if 'it adheres strictly to the material provided by the individual disciplines'.[24] This is where sociology has its place, alongside the other social sciences. With the assistance of its research methods, it makes factual data accessible.

The great thematic framework of Adorno's inaugural lecture was comparable in its programmatic scope to Horkheimer's directorial address. Apart from this external similarity, the two lectures did not have much in common, particularly as far as interdisciplinarity and the place of the individual disciplines and their relation to philosophy were concerned, topics treated by both men.

For Horkheimer, social philosophy – another word for social theory – was the Queen of the Sciences because it involved the 'general', the 'essential', and 'is capable of giving particular studies animating impulses'.[25] At the same time, he advocated a strategy of interdisciplinarity, explaining its productivity by the fact that only through the collaboration of the individual disciplines could the great goal of 'a theory of the historical course of the present age', a 'theory of the whole', be arrived at.[26]

In contrast, Adorno proclaimed his scepticism towards interdisciplinarity from the start of his lecture. He thought it pointless, since he deemed it futile to strive for the 'totality of the real', given that the social world has collapsed in ruins. In the same way, he tried to derail the model of an interaction between philosophy and science by arguing that the logic of the individual sciences was absolutely incompatible with the concept of truth applicable to philosophy. In his view, there was an unbridgeable gulf between research and interpretation. Thus, in contrast to Horkheimer's interdisciplinarity on a philosophical foundation, Adorno took up a position of his own which he was able to define metaphorically only with the aforementioned image of the *exact imagination*.

Adorno evidently had his own view of the relation between social theory and practical change in the social world, and one that differed from Horkheimer's. Horkheimer believed that theoretical enlightenment about the irrationality of society and its internal contradictions could lead to different forms of practice. Adorno, for his part, did not direct his criticism at the *contents* of social theory, i.e., at class antagonisms, or findings about the mechanisms of economic exploitation and the results of social research. Instead, he started from the assumption that the frozen images of reality could only be dissolved by a different *approach* to thinking about them, one that would construct intellectual models in a concrete fashion. Adorno did indeed use the term 'dialectics' in this connection, but failed to show in detail how dialectical thinking might actually lead to specific results.[27] Some of his listeners appear to have registered the absence of content in his lecture, and the failure to demonstrate the analytical benefits of the dialectical method. For example, Willy Strzelewicz, an assistant in the Institute of Social Research at the time, reports that, when he discussed Adorno's lecture with Horkheimer afterwards on the train, Horkheimer spoke quite disparagingly about what he had just heard. 'His reaction to Adorno's views was: what's the point?' It was a clear indication of 'the disagreement between them'.[28]

Apart from Horkheimer's cool response, Adorno's lecture provoked widespread criticism. Kracauer, however, in a letter of 7 June 1931, went out of his way to praise the introductory section in which Adorno had criticized contemporary philosophy. He evidently based his comments on a typewritten version of the lecture that he had before him in Berlin. However, he followed up his praise with the remark that, instead of the abstract statement of a philosophical programme, it would have been preferable to 'give his audience a little real-life example of dialectical research'.[29] Moreover, Kracauer proffered the advice that in his future career as a lecturer he should cultivate the 'tactical astuteness' that was more indispensable for Marxist theory than for any other.

> You probably found yourself in a game of hide-and-seek because of the place you had to speak in. You wanted to trail your coat but were unable to do so. In fact, it would not have been possible to declare your Marxism openly right after the *Habilitation* and on such an official occasion. It would also have been tactically unfortunate since it would have conveyed the impression to other lecturers that you had only been willing to state your principles openly once your *Habilitation* had been approved. You presumably disguised your views in order to avoid the impression that you were acting in an underhand way.[30]

Looking back on the 'scandal' forty years later, Peter von Haselberg saw the situation quite differently. 'It was a genuine inaugural lecture, attacking as it did all the dominant philosophical fashions. . . . Moreover, in addition to the lecture, what we witnessed was the production of a verbal work of art by a skilled performer. There was no hint of a shy young scholar; on the contrary, the man who left the podium like a celebrated soloist was an enthusiast who knew how to get the best out of his text.'[31] Was Adorno's enthusiasm in his own cause the reason for the reservations of some of his audience? There can be no doubt that this was partly the case, since Adorno had made it perfectly clear how far removed he was from the ordinary style of professional academic philosophy, which even at that early date he thought purely formal and lacking in substance, as 'a department, a specialized discipline beyond the other specialized disciplines'.[32] Anyone who was so critical of academic philosophy, and who declared his opinion so openly, was of course under an obligation to produce what he regarded as an alternative approach to the traditional one. How well did he succeed in implementing his implied alternative methods in his own teaching?

Even before his inaugural lecture, Adorno had been charged by Tillich with the task of giving seminars at the university. This meant, whether he liked it or not, that he was increasingly drawn into the academic routine. Peter von Haselberg has also left an account of these early philosophy seminars. According to him, these classes had an air of exclusivity and 'something of the atmosphere of a confidence trick'. In the first seminar on aesthetics Adorno had among other things given a free paraphrase of Kierkegaard's philosophy.[33] The aesthetics seminar of the winter semester 1931–2, which was the first course that Adorno conducted on his own, focused on Johannes Volkelt's *System of Aesthetics*, a three-volume work published in 1905, containing a now-forgotten systematic account of the philosophy of art. The 27-year-old Adorno had carefully prepared this seminar, as can be seen from the notes which have been preserved.[34] For every session he prepared a detailed and systematic manuscript. His intention was to develop his critique of the aesthetic system internally, by demonstrating that a pure aesthetics founders on its own abstractness. According to his own judgement, 'aesthetic objects and problems can be seen to have been historically produced. The mark of the authenticity of all aesthetic problems is the fact that they have their origins in history.'[35]

These notes give us at least a rough idea of some of the important principles governing Adorno's own thinking as these were expressed partly at least in his writings on music or his *Habilitation* thesis. An example is the idea that works of art are constructed, that they embody valid formal laws, that artistic illusion anticipates reconciliation and that progress in the arts is expressed in the way their material is shaped. He objected to classifying modern art as abstract and referred to 'the ambiguity of the concept of the sensuous foundation of art, which is understood sometimes as concerned with the senses in isolation and sometimes, correctly, as constructing the object-world.'[36] He also rejected the idea of an ontology of the senses, arguing instead that the senses are historical in nature. According to the notes, the chief point of the eighth seminar was 'our feelings on recalling odours, the emotion we feel when eating – these things contain the promise of a true art that art has hitherto failed to make good, and that will perhaps only be made good at the price of its own demise. However, this route cannot be taken by reverting to the past, but only dialectically, by taking the art of the refined senses to the point where it is transformed.'[37]

The last seminar of the course was devoted to an interpretation of Goethe's poem '*So laß mich scheinen, bis ich werde*', which deals with the life of Mignon, the mysterious beggar-maid in *Wilhelm Meisters Lehrjahre*. Adorno interprets the character of Mignon as 'a historical model from prehistory, like every great literary artefact, and the idea of artistic illusion adheres only to her historical aspect. . . . Every encounter with Mignon is a rediscovery because only in this and other historical characters do we rediscover the prehistorical dimension that is usually hidden from us.'[38] With this assertion Adorno adroitly establishes a bridge to the aesthetics seminar for the following semester. His intention was to examine Walter Benjamin's *The Origin of German Tragic Drama*, and especially its 'Epistemo-Critical Prologue', which had already figured both in his inaugural lecture and his book on Kierkegaard.

Although Adorno carefully prepared his classes, it seems that this was not enough to forestall spectacular misunderstandings on the part of his audience, something that strengthened his belief that 'philosophy irresistibly attracts the mentally ill'. Thus von Haselberg remembers 'a man who had taken early retirement who appeared to take down every word in shorthand and whom he asked for a copy of his lecture-notes. There amidst a lot of incomprehensible twaddle was the sentence: *Volkelt tends quickly to go to extremes*. In reality, Volkelt's book was a standard work at the time and Adorno had been at pains to unmask its psychologizing approach in order to show that it could not lead to objective judgements.'[39] No doubt, the pensioner's reaction to Adorno was not the norm. Another student, Kurt Mautz, later incorporated his personal impressions in a novel, *The Old Friend* (*Der Urfreund*). The novel contains a semi-fictional, semi-authentic portrait of Adorno, who plays a leading role under the name of Amorelli:

> Amorelli had only just turned up this semester. In the Senior Seminar he sat beside Paulus [i.e., Tillich], with whom he had obtained his *Habilitation*. As a *Privatdozent* he gave classes on problems of aesthetics. Kreifeld and I, together with a handful of other students, had discovered this unknown new star. To our minds, his thinking was more logical, more critical and more radical than that of Paulus. His style of speaking was highly polished. Every sentence seemed to say: this is exactly how it is. . . . He gave his aesthetics classes outside the university, in a students' library.

This library was situated in a quiet villa in the Westend, comfortably furnished, evidently a foundation. In my eyes this library of modern literature was an oasis in which we often found refuge from the sterility of the lecture rooms and the dreariness of the student residences. Here we met with Amorelli every Thursday evening in one of the little seminar rooms; there were no more than a dozen of us. He would sit at the upper narrow end of the table. His roundish head with the curly black hair, already beginning to recede, and his large dark eyes behind the horn-rimmed spectacles gave him a frog-like appearance. Sometimes he was accompanied by a young lady with golden hair, gold-brown eyes and rosy cheeks. She would sit next to him like a princess in 'The Frog-Prince', but she never uttered a single word.

The students in this seminar did not have an easy time of it. Amorelli insisted that minutes should be taken of what had been said in every discussion, and he was particular about what was recorded and how it was phrased. Those who took the minutes were exposed to a rigorous and sometimes bitingly ironic critique. No one wanted to disgrace himself. So when at the beginning of the session Amorelli asked who would like to take the minutes, the Twelve Apostles would for the most part sit in silence looking down at the floor.[40]

Another student has similar memories from this period before the Second World War. This was Wilhelm Emrich, subsequently a major literary scholar and Kafka critic who developed his own method of text interpretation. What had stayed in his mind were the discussions with Adorno about the 'prehistory of history', and 'Theodor Storm's "Der Schimmelreiter" [The Dykemaster] and "Regentrude". Adorno was interested in them as myths that exhibited the strange clash of regressive and progressive trends. Further topics included the traffic island around the Frankfurt City Theatre around midnight as an allegory of explosive traffic jams and the vacuum at the heart of modern society; Mark Twain's *Tom Sawyer*; the bourgeois mystique surrounding fires . . . ; the traumas of inwardness in Johannes Brahms, etc. etc.'[41] In contrast to Emrich, Ernst Erich Noth was fascinated by the meetings after the seminars in the Café Laumer that were said to have contributed more to the students' education than the official teaching programme.[42]

These contemporary testimonies to Adorno's intellectual activity in the 1930s flesh out the picture of an unusually alert and cultivated literary mind. His nonconformism went hand in hand with a penchant for discussing philosophical trends. Because Frankfurt University was a focal point of competing intellectual tendencies, everyone who had a feel for these political and ideological controversies was courted by the different parties. The boundaries between the different intellectual groupings were vague and membership of the groups overlapped. Even so, there were distinctions between religious socialists such as Paul Tillich and Carl Mennicke and the followers of Stefan George (such as Ernst Kantorowicz and Max Kommerell), and both of these groups looked down their noses at the members of the Institute of Social Research (Felix Weil and Fritz Pollock). Colleagues assigned to the 'fashionable' subject of sociology were looked upon with particular suspicion, for they all inscribed the word 'critique' on their banner, but were unable to agree among themselves. The circle around the distinguished registrar, Kurt Riezler, thought of itself as standing above the opposing factions, and Riezler saw it as his task to act as conciliator.[43] In general, Adorno would scarcely have found the Stefan George circle much to his liking, with its mixture of elitism and traditionalism, but he did find himself attracted to the group of George followers in Frankfurt who were led by the literary scholar Max Kommerell and the historian Ernst Kantorowicz. Kantorowicz's inaugural lecture was a fashionable university event, one that Adorno was not going to miss. This led Karl Korn, who was also present, to comment on the young man 'with the unusually intense and intelligent eyes' and to mistake him for someone from the George circle.[44] On the whole, however, Adorno felt more attracted to the opposing camp, the philosophers and sociologists who thought of themselves as the radical critics of society and as staunch upholders of the achievements of cultural modernity. Even before reaching the lofty heights of the *Habilitation*, Adorno had been privileged to join that circle of committed, left-leaning intellectuals that met irregularly in the Café Laumer to discuss the burning issues of the day, but also such matters as university appointments, new books and the wrong decisions made by the city in cultural affairs. The predominant figures at these meetings were Kurt Riezler, Paul Tillich, Max Horkheimer, Friedrich Pollock, the newly appointed sociologist Karl Mannheim, the economist Adolf Loewe and the educationalist Carl Mennicke. Adorno remembered these meetings as a typical Frankfurt phenomenon of the 1920s: 'We frequently went for one another like wild animals; it is difficult to picture our lack of restraint, but the fact is that we did not scruple to assault one another with accusations of being too ideological or else too lacking in principles, but all of that took place without in the least damaging our friendships.'[45] Needless to say, different alliances were formed at various times, but quite soon Mannheim had the misfortune to become the main target and one who constantly left himself open to attack. According to Peter von Haselberg, 'his book *Ideology and Utopia* provided serious competition to the social philosophy that Horkheimer wished to inaugurate and fill with substance.'[46] Adorno did not hesitate to take sides against Mannheim, who had occupied the chair in sociology since January 1930. Adorno not only shared Horkheimer's reservations about Mannheim's concept of ideology, but he even attempted to outdo Horkheimer's criticism of it.

Adorno also took an aggressive role in the seminar that followed Horkheimer's lectures in the winter of 1931–2. This was a select seminar, restricted to advanced students, doctoral students and assistants who were there by invitation. In addition to Horkheimer and Adorno, the participants in these weekly seminars included Peter von Haselberg, Leo Löwenthal, Carl Dreyfus, Willy Strzelewicz and Kurt Mandelbaum.[47]

In these discussions Adorno kept coming back to two questions. First, what is true knowledge in the sciences? And second, what is the value of social theory for our understanding of the present? Taking the various competing philosophies in turn, he inquired which could provide the best explanation for the crisis in the sciences. The sciences were themselves to blame for the crisis because of their constantly increasing abstractness. On the other hand, the failures of the sciences should also be sought in the degree to which they were co-opted by society and subjected to society's supervision and control. According to Adorno, the integration of science into society led to the increasing division of labour, rendering it incapable of providing 'an overview of the total reality'. Science confined itself to 'specialist knowledge without relation to the whole of our existence'. The validity of a unified modern science had become questionable because a scrutiny of its origins made it plain that the preconditions of knowledge were set by society itself.

During the seminar, Adorno went a step further in trying to explain the state of science in terms of the state of society. The more clearly it was perceived that the state of society is a precondition of knowledge, the clearer it would become that science's claim to autonomy was an illusion. This perception should not be used, however, as a pretext to abandon the demand for freedom. Adorno explicitly warned of the danger of 'transforming the materialist dialectic into a kind of objective spirit'.

Adorno's contributions to the debates show that he was enough of an expert to move about with confidence among the conflicting schools of philosophy. In the course of a critical account of idealism, he was able to discuss the explanatory power of alternative modes of thinking, such as historical materialism. In this context he illustrated his personal understanding of materialism with reference to technique in music. Musical composition involved a progressive process of problem-solving based on pre-given material. The solution to such problems depended, he said, on the socio-historical stage of technical mastery. The relations between modes of composition and society should not be conceived either as a pre-established harmony or as a simple analogy. Instead, 'the problem was to show that the most minute facts, for example, of a new artistic or scientific technique, contained social elements.'[48] Adorno proposed the reconstruction of the history of philosophy with this idea in mind, so as to show that at different times different philosophical solutions reflected changes in society. For example, Marx's view of the relations between existence and consciousness, base and superstructure, could only be interpreted properly if they were seen as belonging to a dialectical process, rather than an automatic mechanism.

What emerges from these records of the debates of the period is that Adorno was attracted by historical materialism as a method of acquiring knowledge. In this respect he thought it quite different from a mere world-view. And, like Horkheimer, he refused to think of materialism simply as the opposite of idealism. His critique of idealism was directed at a philosophy 'that either ascribes existence merely to spirit, or else subordinates all non-spiritual existence to the spirit.' What emerges, further, from the shorthand records of these ten discussions is the picture of an active participant with a high profile, one who takes the lead in debate and takes it upon himself to pass judgement on the scope and the limitations of philosophies as varied as those of Kant, Fichte, Hegel and on down to Marx and Freud. These discussions were clearly extremely highbrow and abstract, and it must be admitted that they were not free from a wish to impress verbally. Even so, there can be no doubting the intellectual seriousness of the participants. While Horkheimer could lay claim to a certain interpretative authority, Adorno's role was that of a stimulating and creative mind; it was he who drove the debates forward and kept coming up with the novel ideas.

A *Privatdozent* in the shadow of Walter Benjamin

Records also survive of the two seminars on aesthetics that Adorno gave independently in the summer semester of 1931 and the winter semester of 1931–2.[49] These seminars were devoted to Walter Benjamin's *The Origin of German Tragic Drama*. The records give us a rough idea of the topics on which discussion focused in the twelve seminars which Kurt Mautz incorporated into the novel referred to above.

What were the topics that attracted Adorno in the book on tragic drama, as well as Benjamin's essay on Goethe's *Elective Affinities*? The 'Epistemo-Critical Prologue' from the tragedy book discusses the question of truth. In Benjamin's view, language is the medium in which the truth is made manifest. He distinguishes between a scientific truth which is based on the idea that the world of phenomena is transparent, and a truth that is based on a language of judgement, a truth aimed at the representation of ideas incorporated in the world of phenomena. The first truth, scientific knowledge, is a matter of 'possession', one 'that must be taken possession of – even if in a transcendental sense – in the consciousness.' The second truth, philosophical truth, is a matter of 'self-representation'.[50] With this distinction Benjamin aims to show that 'the object of knowledge is not identical with the truth'.[51] Truth, according to him, is 'an intentionless state of being, made up of ideas'.[52] This definition of truth as a matter of ideas raises the suspicion that truth is available only through conscious reflection, or, in Kantian terms, only through transcendental reflection on the *a priori* conditions of the understanding. Benjamin argues against this Kantian idea by insisting that in principle the truth is capable of being represented in language. The argument has two main points. Since truth expresses 'an intentionless state of being, made up of ideas', it is beyond the subject, and hence beyond its control. This is the theological side of Benjamin, since he positions the truth in analogy to revelation. Truth is not representable *in toto*. It appears as representation, never as the object of representation. Hence truth is never the product of scientific deduction or of induction from empirical findings. It results solely from a 'constellation'. It is not the phenomena that contain the ideas, but only their significant relation to one another. The constellation has three aspects: the representation of ideas as an intentionless state of being, the redeeming of phenomena by 'grouping them together conceptually' according to 'what they have in common', and, finally, the preservation of the 'distinct and the disparate' by means of a 'microscopic process'. According to Benjamin, a truth content can only be grasped through the most precise immersion in the detail of a thing. The philosophical intention of the 'Epistemo-Critical Prologue' amounts to a project of philosophical reconciliation that is opposed to an idealist notion of intuiting 'connections between essences'.[53] Adorno had made Benjamin's idea of defining truth as an intentionless state of being his own – at least since the inaugural lecture. As his philosophy developed, he worked to clarify this antagonism to both the philosophy of consciousness and empiricism and to elaborate it as a theory of unreduced experience.[54]

In his desire to develop a conception of truth that would serve as a corrective to idealist philosophy, he proposed to centre the idea of knowledge in the meaning of an object in its specificity. Instead of starting from the knowing subject and the categories of the understanding, Adorno wished to give priority to the object (repudiating the idealist priority of the subject). In the constitution of experience, the object of experience is granted a kind of right to resist the ascription of the intended categories of consciousness. The only way forward for the knowledge of an intentionless state of being is to achieve an insight into the limits of knowledge, i.e., the process of acquiring knowledge through self-reflection on a meta-level, what Adorno in his major philosophical work will later call thinking against oneself.[55]

The main section of the book on tragedy provides the example with which to test the truth theory of the Prologue. For Benjamin the tragic drama (*Trauerspiel*) is a baroque allegory. This allegory encodes the disintegration of the medieval world order, a collapse of which people had become conscious. What is expressed in the allegory of the tragic drama is the melancholy provoked by the decay of the order of divine meaning, and especially by its fragmentation, the disintegration of the world order. Corresponding to the allegory of mourning, of the decay of the world, its obverse as it were, there is hope, a redemption that breaks in on the despair of the earthly kingdom. The more that worldliness precipitates the loss of earlier hopes of salvation, the more the allegory of decay allows us a glimpse of the opposing element of redemption. In summary, three elements of Benjamin's thought come to the fore in the tragedy book. First, the dialectical process within the allegory. Allegory here combines two extremes, decay and redemption, in such a way that a countervailing moment becomes visible. Second, Benjamin introduces the fragment as a part of an original meaningful whole in such a way that the illusion of salvation is preserved in the fragment by way of contrast. For the fragment contains not only the idea of the original totality, but also its utopian truth content: the idea of perfect beauty. Third and last, Benjamin is concerned with the allegorical process itself in which the present sheds light on the past.

What is striking about Adorno's treatment of the tragedy book in his seminar is his focus on text interpretation. The thematic emphasis in the individual classes kept closely to the text, dealing with such topics as the definition of mourning, the concepts of allegory, intention, expression and melancholy. The discussions were concerned with such matters as the relevance of the concept of the fragmentary in Benjamin, the dialectical significance of mythic images or the absence of a perspective on the future in the baroque era. The class of 13 May was devoted to a discussion of how to interpret the tragedy book. Opinions on the epistemological problems were evidently so diverse, and the discussions so heated, that Wilhelm Emrich, then a student, was asked to prepare a record of two of the sessions alongside the official one.

In a discussion about the hero's silence in tragedy, Peter von Haselberg noted, 'The hero must be silent because he no longer understands the world and the world does not understand him. The silence is both a gesture of rejection and a step in the direction of a criticism of the community.'[56] This comment is noteworthy because the idea is further developed in Adorno's later theory of art.

Adorno made several attempts to invite Benjamin to attend his seminar in person – a gesture that would have been an affront to the faculty he was teaching in, as was indeed the subject of his seminar. For seven years previously Benjamin had tried to obtain the *Habilitation* in Frankfurt on the basis of this very book on tragedy, and had been frustrated by the opposition of Hans Cornelius and Franz Schulz. Had Benjamin not yet succeeded in coming to terms with that rejection when he wrote to Adorno, saying that other commitments prevented him from accepting the invitation? This may be hinted at in the letter he wrote to his friend Gershom Scholem, observing how much Adorno had borrowed from his own writings. The situation was said to be so complicated that he did not feel he could explain it in a few words. What was complicated about it, in Benjamin's view, was that Adorno had allegedly taken over Benjamin's ideas on several occasions, without drawing attention to their source.[57] This was also the tenor of the letter Benjamin wrote in July 1931 after reading the text of Adorno's inaugural lecture. If that lecture were to be published he would like a reference to his baroque book to be included, since this is the source of the idea of interpreting the 'intentionless character of reality'.[58] Adorno defended himself with the argument that there were fundamental similarities between Benjamin and himself that could not simply be ignored. As for his borrowings from Benjamin, apart from the inaugural lecture, which had not been published, he had acknowledged his debt in his published writings, such as his book on Kierkegaard.

In his discussion of Goethe's novel, Benjamin had dwelt particularly on its mythical component. Adorno, when writing about Kierkegaard, had taken over this idea and applied it to what he saw as the mythic construction of the aesthetic. Both men were interested in the relation between myth and truth. They agreed that myth and truth were mutually exclusive. Both are critical of myth, suggesting that it is incompatible with reason. Adorno developed his critique as a critique of the unbroken myth of the autonomous spirit. This runs parallel to Benjamin, who claims that truth in works of art is distorted by the presence of myth. The two also shared the intention of linking their critique with the concept of illusion or semblance [*Schein* means both]. For Benjamin, the illusion of beauty was a 'cover' in which the truth appeared 'cloaked'. For Adorno, on the other hand, the illusion was simply false because it failed in principle to grasp historical reality.

There were striking resemblances to Benjamin not just in the Kierkegaard book, but also in the inaugural lecture. Adorno intended to dedicate the printed version to him, but the lecture was not published.[59]

The distinction Adorno drew between knowledge and truth in the inaugural lecture is further evidence of a debt to Benjamin. Just as Benjamin connected the redeeming of truth with messianic redemption, Adorno assumed that truth is possible only when the knowing subject has developed his entire ability to experience in historical and social terms. In both men the truth is a horizon in which reality and interpretation are mutually interrelated. Of course – and this is where they diverge – in Benjamin this constellation referred to the intellectual opposites (of transitoriness and redemption) contained in the phenomena of reality. In contrast, Adorno conceived of the same constellation in more materialist terms because the intentionless elements of reality were to be gathered together so that they became the interpretable images of the real. He understood interpretation as a constructive procedure that would generate concepts that make reality accessible. For Adorno, philosophical interpretation should not only unlock the riddles of the real, but it should also restore to the minutest, most intentionless elements the language of their true socio-historical nature. He brought philosophical interpretation into the framework of a materialist epistemology which was concerned with both the interpretation and the changing of reality as part of the programme of an enlightened science.

In July 1932, Adorno gave a lecture to the Frankfurt Kant Society which gave him the opportunity and also a suitable forum to acknowledge Walter Benjamin explicitly as a source and inspiration for his ideas. The lecture bore the title 'The Idea of Natural History'. This topic – the relationship between nature and history – was cleverly chosen since it coincided with a dispute that had broken out in Frankfurt between the phenomenologists and the historical materialists about their respective conceptions of history. In addition, the idea of natural history occurred also in a little essay Adorno had written for the *Blätter des Hessischen Landestheaters* in Darmstadt.[60] The highly original sketches on such topics as 'Applause', 'The Gallery', 'The Stalls' and 'Boxes' were produced entirely in the style in which Benjamin had written about baroque tragedy; they were a further attempt by Adorno to appropriate Benjamin's allegorical way of seeing, as Benjamin noted with approval in a letter after reading the text.[61] Adorno's borrowings were not restricted to Benjamin's *The Origin of German Tragic Drama*. He also relied on Georg Lukács's *The Theory of the Novel*. As in the Kierkegaard book, he attempted to define his own conception of natural history by developing it from the contrast with these two other philosophies of history. He began by clarifying the concept of natural history, at first sight a bewildering amalgam of categories that are normally held to be incompatible. As against tradition, Adorno proposed to 'abolish the customary antithesis of nature and history'.[62] We do not understand nature if we think of it as pure factuality, nor, on the other hand, should we regard history purely as the world history of the spirit, a progressive or evolutionary process as was believed in the Enlightenment. Thus Adorno resisted a type of philosophical thinking that hypostatized existence and history in an existential fashion. He exemplifies this with reference to Heidegger's concept of 'historicity', to which he has a twofold objection. An ontological conception of historicity is unable to accommodate the problem of historical contingency. So as to escape the danger of ascribing an absolute value to existence, Heidegger gives priority to the overall design of history to which historical events must be subordinated. This solution, which was one of the ideas actively debated in Frankfurt at the time, is in Adorno's view no more than a new version of idealism. He pointed out that this just meant that the traditional idea of the identity of subject and object would recur in the form of the identity of a subjectively conceived history and of factual history.

In order to provide a foundation for his own view – the concept of natural history – he took from Lukács the Marxist concept of a 'second nature'. Lukács had introduced it, according to Adorno, to designate the idea that the world is a historical product: it is a world of things that has become historically alien to man. Adorno was not content simply to define the world of things as a history that had ossified into nature. What he wanted was to *interpret* these reified objects *philosophically* as the ciphers of an ossified natural history. This programme had already surfaced in the inaugural lecture, and once again it was Benjamin's concept of allegory that supplied him with its underpinning. In allegory the ossified phenomena of nature join together with their distorted meanings to form a constellation in which nature and history are intertwined. Adorno took over Benjamin's programme of brushing history against the grain, and added it to his own dialectical way of thinking. This made it possible to avoid the ontological hypostatization of history or of historical epochs. The point of this way of thinking about nature and history was to see history as an embattled totality of primal myth and the historical new. 'History is at its most mythical where it is at its most historical.'[63] The relation between history and myth does not mean simply that myth keeps repeating itself, but that the latest history transforms itself into myth by a natural process. Adorno had this process of reversal in mind when he wrote 'The dialectic of history does not mean simply taking up prehistorical events and reinterpreting them; it means that historical events are transformed into myth and nature.'[64]

Benjamin's influence on Adorno as seen in this talk also had a linguistic dimension. Adorno's own style was already highly individual. Nevertheless, his prose and his approach to essay-writing is highly reminiscent of his model. When Benjamin first gave a reading from his *Berlin Childhood around 1900* in Ernst Schoen's house in Frankfurt, Adorno was spellbound by the vividness of his style and the way in which Benjamin had described his childhood memories of his middle-class family home in the metropolis.[65]

The *Zeitschrift für Sozialforschung* and Adorno's ideological critique of music

The new direction of the Institute of Social Research taken by the institute director was revealed by, among other things, the replacement of Grünberg's *Archiv für die Geschichte des Sozialismus* by Horkheimer's new journal, the *Zeitschrift für Sozialforschung*. From 1932 on, this was the journal that published the studies on social theory and social research produced by the members of the institute. The journal also had an unusually large review section, which provided space not just for the chief members of the institute but also for many young scholars, as well as well-known figures from Frankfurt University more generally. Leo Löwenthal acted as editor-in-chief. All manuscripts submitted were scrutinized carefully by institute members before publication, and were often referred back to their authors for revision.[66] Löwenthal has described the journal as the 'collective denominator' of the critical programmes that were carried out over a period of years by the institute.

The contents of the first year were a reflection of Horkheimer's own objectives, since it was he who acted as the journal's *spiritus rector* during the nine years of its existence. These aims were 'to acquire an understanding of the general course of society in the present epoch'[67] through a combination of historically substantial theory construction and empirical research.

The breadth of theory to be covered by the *Zeitschrift* according to Horkheimer can be indicated by the fact that in the very first year three out of eleven contributions were devoted to technical sociological questions, such as the changing bourgeois image of the world, the US party system, and the use of leisure time. Two essays, one by Henryk Grossmann and one by Friedrich Pollock, were concerned with problems arising from Marx's theory of economics, his theory of crises and the planned economy as an alternative to capitalism. A contribution by Erich Fromm outlined attempts to integrate Marxism and analytical social psychology. Furthermore, Leo Löwenthal sketched the tasks facing a sociology of literature, while Wiesengrund-Adorno drew on his musical expertise and sought to develop new approaches to a critical, Marxist sociology of music. Horkheimer inaugurated the journal with the leading article, 'Observations on Science and Crisis', an article which took up a number of ideas that Adorno had presented in the framework of that exclusive seminar during the winter semester of 1931.[68]

Despite friendly or at least professional working relations with Horkheimer, Pollock, Löwenthal and Fromm, Adorno was not officially a member of the institute either before or after obtaining his *Habilitation*. His ideas diverged from those of Horkheimer and a majority of institute members on a number of quite fundamental points. Despite this, Adorno published regularly, if at intervals, in the *Zeitschrift* from the very first issue. With these publications in the 1930s he appeared for the first time as a sociologist. It was from a sociological point of view that he began to develop the conceptual and methodological foundations for the analysis of music. This analysis would be concerned not with the individual composer's intentions, but with the social content of their works. This meant that, following in Max Weber's footsteps, he was making his contribution to the establishment of the sociology of music as a special branch of sociology. Among the early contributions to this subject in the *Zeitschrift* we may mention 'The Social Situation of Music' of 1932, the essay 'On Jazz' that appeared four years later and the essay 'On the Fetish-Character in Music and the Regression of Listening', which appeared in 1938 and was followed a year later by the 'Fragments on Wagner'.

In his comprehensive analysis of the social dimension of music, Adorno relies on one premise: all music in the capitalist society of today bears the marks of alienation and functions as a commodity that must realize its exchange value in the marketplace. Given this background, what decides the authenticity or inauthenticity of a piece of music is whether it submits to market conditions or whether it resists them by finding a dissonant expression for the contradictions of society. Music that is not produced according to the rules of commodity production pays for its exclusivity with its social isolation, an isolation it is unable to eliminate by its own efforts or by purely internal musical methods.

Written in a dense style, this essay focuses on the social conditions governing the production, reproduction and reception of music. 'Not only is the consciousness of the audience dependent upon the change in social conditions and not only is the consciousness of those involved in reproduction dependent upon the state of the total musical constitution of society at a given time; the works themselves and their history change within that constitution.'[69] Adorno illustrates this process of shaping and changing by looking at the transition from pre-capitalist musical practice to the point where the capitalistic production of music came to dominate. Before this time, thanks to the traditions of music-making, there was a direct interaction between the composition of a work and listening to it. The mark of the production of music under capitalism is that the text becomes fixed, leaving no freedom for the virtuoso conductor or instrumentalist to interpret the music, any more than there is freedom for autonomous individuals in society. 'Now the text is annotated down to the last note and to the most subtle nuance of tempo, and the interpreter becomes the executor of the unequivocal will of the author.'[70] Adorno interprets this development as proof that the link has been broken between subjective expression in music and a society determined by individuals. Authentic music brings this breakdown to our consciousness through the use of atonality, which by this means processes the pathologies of society in the practice of musical composition. This is done exclusively in the non-ornamental music of modernity, of the kind composed by Schoenberg, Berg and Webern. Their music

> has annulled the expressive music of the private bourgeois individual, pursuing – as it were – its own consequences, and put in its place a different music, one to which no social function can be ascribed – indeed, a form of music which even severs the last communication with the listener. However, this music leaves all other music of the age far behind in terms of immanently musical quality and the dialectic clarification of its material. It thus offers such a perfected and rational total organization that it cannot possibly be compatible with the present social constitution.[71]

In Adorno's view, in contrast to atonal music, all other forms of music, from folk music via operetta to jazz, are to be regarded more or less as commercial art. Their ideological function consists in diverting the listener from class contradictions in society. The quasi-communal music of the petty bourgeoisie corresponds to the fascist world-view. 'The organic is played off against the mechanical, inwardness against vacuity, and personality against anonymity.' Internally, music of this kind is reactionary because 'it rejects the further dialectic movement of musical material as "individualistic" or "intellectual".'[72]

Adorno's reflections on the sociology of musical reproduction link up with his initial arguments on this subject from his days in Vienna. He uses the figure of the 'great conductor' or the 'celebrity performer' to show how the apparent subjectivism of such figures is in reality the mouthpiece of objective social imperatives. The critique of ideology that underpins the essay as a whole applies also to his sociological analysis of music consumption, which he sees as fixated on the external snob value of the musical commodities offered in the marketplace or on what is universally acceptable or fashionable. The fetishist nature of consumption is most clearly visible in the case of popular music, or 'common music' (*vulgär*), as he calls it: 'No matter how their products look and sound, they are "successes"; listeners are forced to sing them to themselves.'[73] Jazz, too, according to Adorno, is to be classified as 'common music'. Its claim to the liberty to improvise is purely ornamental and hence illusory. 'Beneath the opulent surface of jazz lies – barren, unchanged, clearly detachable – the most primitive harmonic-tonal scheme with its breakdown into half and full cadences and equally primitive metre and form.'[74] Adorno exposes critically the ideological contents of the musical surrealism of a Kurt Weill, as well as the progressive proletarian workaday music (*Gebrauchsmusik*) of a Hanns Eisler. The fact that this music aims to have a collective impact, to appeal to the consciousness of the working class, acts as a brake on musical creativity.

When the first part of his sociology of music appeared, Adorno sent offprints to both Berg and Krenek, among others. Krenek immediately responded, in March 1932, with a lengthy letter containing objections in principle. Adorno should not be surprised, he wrote, to find his basic premise questioned by the argument that this social dimension of music is essentially external to it. Music must be viewed as 'existing in its own right'.[75] Krenek also pointed out that the commodity character of music did not explain its social co-optation, since musical works have always been exchanged and payments have always been made to composers and performers. What was crucial in Krenek's view was that, along with the destruction of human dignity under capitalism, the interest in authentic music would necessarily die out. Referring to the creativity of the composer, he again attacked Adorno's conception of the laws governing musical material that are said to be realized in the successful composition.

Adorno was fully occupied with preparing his Kierkegaard book for the press and so was forced to delay his reply to Krenek for over six months. All the lengthier was his response when it finally came, on 30 September 1932. He wrote from Prinzenallee 60 in Berlin, so he was evidently living with Gretel Karplus. His reply to Krenek's first criticism was that the aim of a sociological analysis of music must be to trace the specific historical shape of the antinomies of society in actual modes of composition. The interest in this was far removed from a vulgar sociological curiosity about the function of music in contemporary society. Adorno went on to give a more detailed account of the exchange relation in music by giving his view of the total impact of capitalism on life: 'the commodity character of art as the objective side and the destruction of "human dignity" as the subjective side are equivalents and cannot simply be separated.'[76] Interestingly, on the question of how to overcome reification in capitalism, he had recourse to Kierkegaard's idea of 'despair as the sickness unto death . . . , the idea that dialectically the sickness is also the cure.'[77] Finally, Adorno once again leapt to the defence of his concept of musical material. It referred to the problems that the composer had to solve within the framework of what was historically possible. Composition was 'a kind of deciphering'.[78] Towards the end of the letter, he conceded that art, and hence music, had something ornamental, and hence illusory, about it. But he rebelled against the idea that art was superfluous in a classless society. Only the immanent perfection of art could be expected to lead to its abolition.

Not only this fundamental sociological analysis of music, but also Adorno's subsequent work on musical styles was conducted as ideology critique. His intention was to counter the study of music as part of the history of ideas with a sociology of existing musical genres based on historical materialism. This meant arguing within the framework of a materialist notion of ideological superstructures which he in fact thought inadequate, because it was mechanistic. On the one hand, he clung to his ideal of reflexive theory-formation as rational construction, to his desire to go against 'the order of things'[79] and create a (formal) language of his own for both artistic genres and philosophy in their relations to the sciences. On the other hand, in his writings at this time he made increasing use of the language of historical materialism, in particular of such concepts as reification and false consciousness. This gave rise to a tension with the idea of philosophical interpretation (as found in the inaugural lecture). Not that he had abandoned this approach entirely in favour of sociology. Instead, by carrying out the ideological critique of internal musical contents, he imported the concept of ideology into his philosophical interests. By ideology he meant socially necessary illusion, and this idea of making it productive for theory and above all for empirical analysis was of course part of the programme Adorno shared with the director of the Institute of Social Research. Adorno's interest in it was primarily in its potential use in the sociological analysis of cultural phenomena. Horkheimer, on the other hand, wished to conduct an empirical analysis of society based on Marx's critique of capitalism, and in this project he found himself forced to defend his position against a powerful personality and a rival in the same university. This was Karl Mannheim with his sociology of knowledge. Mannheim's conception of the sociology of knowledge was a highly individual, modern-sounding theory of research on ideology. This forces us to inquire: what is research on ideology?

In league with Horkheimer against a second school of sociology under the same roof

The differences between Adorno's language-based critique of interpretation and Horkheimer's interdisciplinary materialism did not rule out an alliance between the two men. Whereas Adorno had previously been strongly influenced by Benjamin, he now, in his new role as social theorist, began to adapt ideas he had found in Horkheimer – needless to say, he did so in his own highly individual way. The bonds between them grew in strength the more Adorno, who had his roots in a variety of intellectual positions, began to align himself with Horkheimer. This had the effect of putting him in opposition to Karl Mannheim, who had earlier disapproved of Adorno's inaugural lecture. This is hardly surprising, given that towards the end of his lecture Adorno had mounted an attack on Mannheim's 'nominalist' sociology, which was alleged to have deprived the concept of ideology of its point. 'It is defined formally as the ascription of particular ideas to particular groups, without inquiring about the truth or untruth of those ideas. Sociology of this kind becomes part of a kind of universal relativism.'[80] Despite this criticism, Mannheim's basic thesis never quite loses its grip on him. Only in that way can we explain the fact that, in the years to come, he keeps returning to the foundations of the sociology of knowledge.[81] The main bone of contention between the two schools of sociology was the question: Now that the great traditions of philosophy have fallen into decline, what is the right way to establish a social theory adequate to the crisis-experience of the modern age? Both Horkheimer and Mannheim had espoused the cause of criticism. This meant that, since the arrival of Mannheim from Heidelberg, there were now two sociologists in the same faculty, and even in the same building, competing to establish a discipline that aimed to be critical, and even critical of ideology. The newly created sociology seminar presided over by Mannheim, as the representative of a modern, value-free sociology, was housed at the time in the Institute for Social Research. The personal presence of Mannheim, together with his colleagues such as Norbert Elias and Günther Stern, was not regarded as an opportunity for cooperation by the dominant colleagues in the institute. On the contrary, Horkheimer felt sufficiently challenged by Mannheim's presence to greet him with an extremely pointed criticism of the central concept of his new colleague's theory of sociology. He launched a frontal attack on Mannheim in an essay entitled 'A New Concept of Ideology?',[82] in which he accused him of adapting Marx's concept of ideology in a wholly inadequate way. On the one hand, he maintained that, by confining himself to taking over only a few weapons from the arsenal of Marxist theory, Mannheim had converted the basic terms of historical materialism into their opposites. On the other hand, Horkheimer insisted it was an 'idealist illusion' to reduce all intellectual formations to systems of world-views. 'If all thought as such is to be characterized as ideological, it becomes apparent that ideology, just like "particularity", signifies nothing other than inadequacy to eternal truth.'[83] By conceiving of truth as tied to existence, Mannheim empties the concept of meaning. Horkheimer further claimed that, instead of analysing the material conditions governing the development of different forms of consciousness, Mannheim was obsessed with stylistic peculiarities of thought. The concept of 'attachment to being' (*Seinsgebundenheit*) is nebulous unless it is related to structures of domination with their economic foundations and political organizations.

This critical blast can be explained by the fact that Mannheim's thesis that all knowledge is ideological threatened to undermine Horkheimer's desire to produce a universally applicable theory of society directed towards practical change. But since Mannheim's concept of ideology implied in principle that Marxism itself was one ideology among others, the further development of Marxism in the Institute of Social Research could only be pursued with this reservation in mind. It was this that provoked Horkheimer to his attack, since he wished to retain a kind of monopoly of research on ideology. For the current and the future empirical projects of the institute were all concerned with exploring the ways in which the processes of transmitting false consciousness operate in capitalist society.

Adorno faced the same problem in the context of his sociology of music. Just how the concrete mechanisms mediating between music and society actually functioned, and how music actually functions as an ideology in society, were open questions.[84] In addition to the concept of ideology, the question of value judgements was a further bone of contention between Horkheimer and Mannheim. Horkheimer demanded that what counted in deciding on the truth value of a social theory was not its explanatory power in the abstract, but its potential for bringing about social change. In Mannheim's view, this idea offended against the idea of a value-free theory and went beyond the predictive capacity of the social sciences. In his opinion, sociology should aspire to provide people with 'an appropriate life orientation in industrial society, . . . leaving open the question whether that society was to be organized on a capitalist or socialist basis.'[85] He inferred this idea of the function of theory from two findings. First, from the diagnosis of the present: following the disappearance of traditional, universally valid interpretations of the world, modernity is experiencing a general loss of direction, resulting in a need for guidelines to political action. Second, he inferred from the history of ideas that sociology should take over the mission of enlightenment, replacing the dogmatism of world-views with the self-reflexive corrections of existing systems of thought and knowledge.

The claim that the task of sociology is to scrutinize critically all existing world-views so as to expose their ideological content and, at the same time, to offer a guide to meaning and action was the central assertion of Mannheim's successful book *Ideology and Utopia* of 1929. There he raised the question: 'How is it possible for man to continue to think and live in an age when the problems of ideology and utopia are being radically raised and thought through in all their implications?'[86] This question went to the heart of the intellectual debates of the day. World-views fought one another to establish their exclusive right to explain the world. The emerging discipline of sociology, which saw itself as the guardian of our knowledge of society, fell apart in the struggle between materialist and idealist foundations. Against this background, Mannheim proposed to make conscious the fact that competition in the realm of the mind was productive because intellectual competition exposes both the historical and the social bias of different world-views, and thus relativizes the different doctrines.

Adorno had worked on an essay critical of Mannheim since the early 1930s, albeit with lengthy interruptions. He focused on the problematic equation of world-view and ideology as well as, more generally, on the flaws in Mannheim's thinking. As he wrote in November 1934 to Benjamin, it was his 'most explicitly Marxist piece'.[87] He was concerned primarily with *Man and Society in an Age of Reconstruction*, a book that had appeared in 1935, after Mannheim had left Germany. Mannheim had put forward the arguments it contained in a lecture in London at which Adorno had been present. He wrote a critical commentary on it which he then read out to Mannheim in person. Adorno claimed in a letter to Horkheimer that for the first time Mannheim 'was somewhat disconcerted'.[88] Like Horkheimer earlier on, Adorno again reproached Mannheim for being insufficiently radical in his social criticism as well as for his neutrality on matters of ideological commitment, both of which were linked to his self-imposed restriction to 'formal sociological description'. Instead of employing dialectical concepts to help make transparent the antagonistic laws governing social dynamics by testing them out on such questions as class distinctions or the formation of monopolies, Mannheim enters his concepts 'in a defined system of co-ordinates'. This means that the dynamic laws governing society appear 'to be contingent or accidental, mere sociological "differentiations"'. Such generalizing sociology seems like a mockery of reality.[89] Adorno's dispute with Mannheim ended up in a global rejection that was completely in line with Horkheimer's: whereas sociology began as a critique of the principles governing society, the sociology of knowledge limits itself to reflections on 'egregious [*illustre*] social phenomena'.

Adorno's criticism of Mannheim was not published, as originally intended, in the last issue of the *Zeitschrift für Sozialforschung* for 1937. One reason for this was that Adorno did not really add anything to Horkheimer's criticism of Mannheim's concept of ideology seven years earlier. Adorno once again mapped out the differences between the two variants of ideology critique, without advancing arguments that might have led to a productive controversy between the two. Such a discourse might have suited Horkheimer better than the repetition of disagreements and the division into opposing camps. The sharpness of Adorno's critique may have served to cover up the affinities he felt for Mannheim. These included not only a similar intellectual attitude but also the point of view of the academic outsider. In his reflections on the role of the intellectual, Mannheim had expressed the hope that the different groupings might move closer together. 'We who have been scattered all over the globe are the only international flotsam without solid ground beneath our feet: we are the people who write books and read, and who, when they read and write, are interested only in where the spirit leads them.'[90] In fact, both men were intellectuals who wrote, using the essay form for preference. They shared the stylistic freedom it conferred, the one man more musically expressive, the other more restrained. Both reacted with a comprehensive critique of modernity, Mannheim with a critique of consciousness, Adorno with a dialectical critique of society.

At the point when Adorno had finished his 'Marxist piece' on Mannheim's 'bourgeois sociologism',[91] it was no longer appropriate for the times. Nor, towards the end of the 1930s, did it really fit any more into the programme of the *Zeitschrift für Sozialforschung* or the institute, since the émigrés in New York were now trying to establish themselves in America and to seek out opportunities to cooperate with American sociologists. When Horkheimer had read Adorno's article in New York, he reacted favourably in a letter to him, but was unwilling to publish it. Adorno could not understand this ambivalence. He was entirely convinced of the validity of his critique of Mannheim and felt cheated when Horkheimer explained his reservations about publication by saying that, as a whole, the article was too positive.[92] Adorno defended himself by return of post, justifying his text-immanent approach 'of taking the greatest nonsense seriously and forcing oneself to prove that it really is nonsense . . . while loading the *polemical* burden of proof onto his shoulders, . . . i.e., making him [i.e., Mannheim] speak and destroying him by quoting him.' That his criticism had struck the nerve of Mannheim's sociology of knowledge could be seen from Mannheim's reaction in what Adorno calls

> an infuriated, but also helpless letter. . . . He was unable to answer a single one of the arguments, and escaped from the situation by claiming that the mistakes I reproached him with did not affect the methodology, but only his handling of it. As if that were the issue; as if anyone but the Heidelbergers could distinguish between method and substance in that way. No, I truly believe that the *suavis modus* shows up the contours of the *res severa* in a harsher light.[93]

Horkheimer remained unconvinced, and he also refused to launch a debate about the sociology of knowledge in the journal which, as Adorno crowed, would enable him to 'slaughter Mannheim with complete equanimity'.[94] Nor did Adorno find the editorial board more sympathetic to his argument that his critique of Mannheim would qualify him as an expert on the whole field of sociology, and not just on the sociology of music. He complained to Horkheimer that he felt like a 'wounded deer', and that it was 'vitally important for a writer to see his writings in print', for otherwise 'even a truly enlightened and self-controlled man might feel paralysed.'[95] There are no signs of the symptoms of paralysis in Adorno. Instead, he acquiesced in the decision not to publish, albeit with gritted teeth, as long as this refusal was justified in terms of institute policy.

For his own part, he continued to think highly of the article. This emerges from the fact that he published it twice after an interval of fifteen years, once in the journal *Aufklärung* in 1953 and then again in *Prisms*, a collection of essays that appeared in 1955. This suggests that he clung to the idea of two divergent sociological traditions. From the point of view of his own sociology, we can see that the Mannheim critique of 1937 initiated an attempt to clarify a problem of method. How was it possible to establish a sociology that did not focus on the sum of individuals and their actions, but was concerned to explain the social nature of the contents of the social world, and to track down their origins and validity? How can it be explained, and what does it mean, that 'a society' should produce itself as 'a strictly logical *system* . . . in absolute unreason and unfreedom'?[96] This striking remark makes us wonder whether Adorno could have written this sentence without his experience of fascism. And of the victory of National Socialism, the triumph of Hitler's dictatorship and the enforced emigration of its author from Germany, the country that had shown itself in practice to be a *system of absolute unreason and unfreedom*.

The opera project: *The Treasure of Indian Joe*

The magical power to manipulate childhood is the strength of the weak.[97]

How long was Adorno's normal working day? Hugely ambitious as he was from early on in life, his immense productivity over a wide range of intellectual activities shows him to have been a highly disciplined worker. The fact is that throughout his life he concentrated all his efforts on the things that he found vitally important, living on his nerves and working to the point of exhaustion. Even while he was still very young, his letters were full of complaints about the lack of time, and about physical and mental strain. Even supposing that, in addition to his passionate desire to write, he possessed exceptional powers of concentration and the ability to keep to a strict timetable, we may still feel baffled by his ability to cope with all his other duties as well as his writing commitments. As soon as he became a lecturer (*Privatdozent*), he took on a growing number of academic duties, on the one hand as Paul Tillich's assistant, and on the other as a teacher in his own right in the Arts Faculty. He also took part in the sociologists' debates in the Institute of Social Research, presided over by Horkheimer – and not simply as an onlooker. These sociologists were attempting to produce a theory of the historical laws governing the age. His association with the institute also implied a willingness to publish in Horkheimer's new journal, the *Zeitschrift für Sozialforschung*. That was just one publishing commitment alongside many others.

Pride of place among them must go to the various music journals he wrote for: *Anbruch*, *Pult und Taktstock*, *Die Musik*, *Der Scheinwerfer*, and *23*, among others. Independently of the many articles that appeared in the *Frankfurter Zeitung*, the *Vossische Zeitung*, and periodicals such as the *Neue Blätter für Kunst und Literatur*, he gave a growing number of talks for Frankfurt Radio. Added to these were public lectures and talks on musical topics, as well as philosophy. During this period, he produced more texts than he could publish or than he wished to make available to a larger readership. Much of what he wrote took the form of spontaneous, improvised notes. They disappeared into his desk from which they were eventually to be retrieved for subsequent use. He scattered his hand-written notes among various octavo notebooks,[98] each devoted to a particular topic and with titles like 'Black Book', 'Coloured Book' or 'Green Book'. In contrast, he typed his completed manuscripts himself on his Underwood typewriter. Later on, after his marriage to Gretel Karplus, he went over to dictation, and this soon became his preferred method. Once the texts had been typed out, he would go through them several times, sentence by sentence. Over the twelve years up to his emigration, these writings came to include over a hundred opera or concert reviews, and a further fifty critiques of musical compositions. Even professional music critics would be hard put to keep pace with productivity on this scale.

Quite apart from the sheer quantity of his output, the diversity of the literary forms involved is very striking. In addition to the relatively large number of polemical concert reviews, all written in his highly individual style, he experimented with aphorisms and essays. Alongside the features written for radio, there were monograph-length studies of musical trends and composers. Qualitatively speaking, these critiques of varying length, taken together with his numerous articles, can be seen as the building blocks of an independent theory of music which their youthful author would only develop in the years to come. Despite their fragmentary nature, these formally diverse texts had one thing in common: they provided growing evidence of the philosophical focus of his thinking. This had developed, by the time of his inaugural lecture at the latest, into a specific programme of philosophical interpretation. Thus, Adorno did not conceive of music primarily as a distinct form of art whose different elements – tone, melody, rhythm – had to be analysed in isolation. Instead, he investigated the intellectual substance of different works of music and attempted to understand and to elucidate them in their historical and cultural context. The core theme of his detailed philosophical analysis was contained in two fundamental questions. One explored the historical nature of the material of music, while the other investigated what it was about musical form that made it possible for a work to cohere into a harmonious whole. He saw musical compositions as works created by the conscious shaping of material in a way that was appropriate to a given stage of historical development. What was expressed in the construction of musical form was a valid, objective, supra-individual truth. Adorno's postulate is that, if music aspires to be art, it must be historically true; in other words, it must contain cognitive qualities that make it possible for the good and the beautiful to shine through.

As an exceptionally prolific writer, Adorno worked tirelessly to expound his philosophical ideas in the form of concrete analyses. Admittedly, up to the end of the 1920s and the early 1930s, these attempts at exposition were still somewhat tentative, despite the sometimes impatiently assertive tone of his writing. Nevertheless, parallel to his increasing philosophical output, his writings on music became steadily more assured. His growing mastery stimulated him to write more and more music criticism and to speak out boldly on philosophical matters. When we consider his daily output, it is hard for us to imagine how, in addition to his strenuous activity as a writer, lecturer and public speaker, he could also have been a practising musician. For, as if all his other activities were not enough, he once again took up composing early in the 1930s. It did not come easily to him. In a letter to Alban Berg written late in September 1931, scarcely five months after his inaugural lecture and a few weeks after a holiday in Berchtesgaden and Salzburg, the 28-year-old Adorno complained that as a composer he was in an absolute crisis. 'For the last two-and-a-half years I have not succeeded in finishing any sizeable piece of work. . . . I cannot tell you how this weighs on me. It poisons my entire existence and fills me with hatred for the university that steals my time in this way.'[99] He explains this stagnation self-critically by saying that he has too little courage and no inspiration, a condition connected in his mind with the 'sterile imaginative horizon' to which people living in Germany were condemned, a sterility that 'robs me of all freedom and genuine productivity.' Despite his lack of confidence as a composer, this lecturer in philosophy 'thought of himself as nothing if not a composer' and a man who would willingly let everything else go to the devil.[100]

He did the opposite. In the very same letter to Berg he evidently relished giving a list of the different engagements and jobs of recent weeks: radio discussions and talks, the next instalment of the aphorisms and music reviews, etc. Always curious and restless, he tried to cope with all these obligations, and was soon able to go back to composition and satisfy the standards he had set himself. He now proposed nothing less than to write an opera. Taking his inspiration from Mark Twain's *The Adventures of Tom Sawyer*, he soon had the framework for a *Singspiel* which he entitled *The Treasure of Indian Joe* (*Der Schatz des Indianer-Joe*). He wrote the libretto between November 1932 and August 1933. At the same time, he started to set passages of the text to music. However, he only ever completed 'Two Songs for Voice and Orchestra'.[101]

The reason why this project remained fragmentary was not just a consequence of Adorno's existential insecurity, which arose from the difficulties with which a left-wing, so-called half-Jew had to contend in National Socialist Germany. A further factor was the reaction to the libretto of a single person whose judgement he particularly valued. Immediately after completing the text he seized the opportunity for a reading in a small, private circle. He then sent a copy to Walter Benjamin in summer 1933. As an oppositional thinker, Benjamin was among the first Jewish victims of the Nazi seizure of power. He fled initially to Ibiza, and from there went on to Paris.[102] Doubtless because of his extremely difficult circumstances, he took an unusually long time to respond to *Indian Joe*. He had to be reminded frequently by Gretel Karplus that he should write to Teddie, who was impatiently waiting for his opinion.[103] Despite her urgings, Benjamin, whom Adorno regarded as the ideal reader for his libretto, took his time and did not respond until February 1934. When he did so, he wrote very diplomatically, but his negative reaction was unambiguous. He complained in general about the choice of subject matter: the story of the friendship between two boys in rural America in the middle of the nineteenth century. He went on to criticize the 'reduction to the idyllic', which in his view was incompatible with the author's intentions.[104]

Was this global rejection of Adorno's libretto justified? Adorno had, after all, undertaken the task of coming to grips with a very relevant contemporary experience, that of fear. Both the actions and, implicitly, the dialogue of the two young protagonists are marked by fear. They witness a murder committed by Indian Joe, who kills from a wish for revenge and then tries to put the blame on another tramp. Fearing that they may expose themselves to retribution in their turn, the boys remain silent, a misdemeanour that frightens them all the more as they know their silence is the product of cowardice.

The central importance of the murder motif emerges clearly in the very first scene. Tom Sawyer mourns the death of his tom-cat, which he has on his conscience because he had fed the animal some medicine that was intended for him. Scene 2 is a midnight meeting in the graveyard. While Tom and his friend Huck lie in hiding, they witness a quarrel between Indian Joe and Muff Potter, on the one hand, and Dr Robinson, on the other. The three have met in the graveyard at this unusual hour in order to rob the corpse of 'Old Williams', who has only just been buried. While quarrelling about the spoils, Joe stabs the doctor in the belly. The scene ends with Tom and Huck singing the 'Song of the Bystanders':

Tom	A man has died No one saw it happen No one is guilty.
Huck	A man has died Another saw it happen One man is guilty.
Tom	A man has died Two saw it happen Both are guilty.
Huck	Whether anyone is guilty When a man dies Depends on whether someone sees.
Both	A man has died Two saw it happen All are guilty.
With emphasis	As long as they don't talk.[105]

The climax of the following scene is the song of Muff Potter, who is under arrest. The text of the song contains motifs to which Adorno was to return later on in *Minima Moralia*. Inside the tower where he is locked up, Muff Potter sings:

> In the woods, the lovely green woods,
> everything is lovely,
> the sun shines, the moon shines
> and they never set.
>
> The hunters go out hunting,
> the hares and deer abound.
> All of them are killed,
> The hunters all fall down.
>
> The snow lies on the green fields,
> All is so warm and cold,
> Nature lies quite still,
> When the bugle sounds.

> The girls sleep in the bushes,
> A beggar hurries to the gate,
> I wake them up in a flash,
> Sleep in gentle ease.[106]

The song of Muff Potter, who is about to be hanged, contains elements that are as alien to Mark Twain's original story as the Frankfurt dialect that, according to the libretto, some of the characters are supposed to speak. For this 'Song of the Innocent', Adorno has adapted lines from Wilhelm Taubert's 'Lullaby', a song which he once told Walter Benjamin was his favourite because of its use of the beggar motif.[107]

Muff Potter's song cuts the boys to the quick, since they know he is innocent. For this reason they do not just give him moral support. Tom Sawyer also resolves to speak up in the court hearings.

Scene 4 takes place on Jackson Island in the Mississippi. The friends fled there after Potter's release in order to escape the revenge of the malevolent Indian Joe. The highpoints of the scene include Tom's 'Song about Dying Needlessly', and also the antiphonal songs in the first finale when the runaways decide to return home to escape the dangers of a life of adventure.

> *Tom*   We must go back
> We're out of luck
> There are no adventures here
> In Hannibal we are freer
> You've heard it all before
> We must go back once more.[108]

Scene 5 is set in the notorious haunted house in Hannibal where Huck and Tom are looking for treasure. Once again, they see Indian Joe planning further dark deeds. He has escaped punishment and is now the owner of some treasure he has found near the fireplace of the abandoned house. He is just about to hide it in a nearby cave when, in scene 6, the three main characters suddenly find themselves face to face. The powerfully built Indian Joe hurls himself at Tom, but slips and falls to his death. They find themselves in utter darkness, but finally see a chink of light which enables them to escape to freedom. In the final scene Tom and Huck are welcomed back into respectable Hannibal society and acknowledged as the legitimate owners of the treasure. Whereas Tom reluctantly accepts his new role as an adult, Huck escapes from the constraints of a regular life.

The theme of the second finale at the end of the *Singspiel* – and at the same time the leitmotif of the entire piece – is futility. Huck's refusal to fit in is as great a delusion as Tom's decision to abandon his childhood dreams of a life of adventure in favour of bourgeois security.

We can't get away / from this old house . . . / And if we run in fear / We're still stuck here / We're full of fear / we can't get clear.[109]

Faced with Benjamin's wholesale dismissal, Adorno defended himself with the argument that a children's story could 'present some extremely serious things'. He was particularly concerned with 'the expression of fear'.[110] Benjamin did not comment on Adorno's remarks. This lack of appreciation led Adorno to attempt to clarify his intentions in discussions with other friends. In November 1934, he sent the libretto to Ernst Krenek in Vienna, with a detailed explanation of its central themes. He pointed out that Tom Sawyer frees himself from the irrational power of the oath and that this is a piece of 'de-mythologization'. The story of Tom Sawyer attracted him, he said, because it shows in an exemplary way 'how a truly human morality proceeds from a kind of psychological immorality'. His 'original intention' had been confirmed, he thought, by Richard Hughes's book *A High Wind in Jamaica*, 'one of the most important novels I have come across in recent years'.[111] He also explained his ideas about the work in some detail. Only the text passages written in verse were meant to be sung. Huck's role was to be performed by a girl soprano, while Tom's part was to be written for tenor.[112]

Unfortunately, Adorno only ever completed two songs from the first scene in manuscript form.[113] Huck's 'Entrance Song' and Tom's 'Dirge for a Tom-Cat' were essentially written in twelve-tone rows combined with free atonality. Thus in Huck's song, every note used relates to the twelve-tone row, although it is not obvious because of the overall shape of the music. Tom's dirge is like a children's song, with a strong rhythm. Taken together, the two songs suggest that Adorno envisaged a medium-sized symphony orchestra. The libretto shows that he planned choruses and intermezzos, and intended to add two finales and a quodlibet.[114]

Having been forced by political events to leave Germany in 1933, Adorno shelved the entire opera project. This was partly due to the discouraging response to his attempts at music drama, but above all because the future prospects of the 'non-Aryan' intellectual in National Socialist Germany lay in ruins. The music he had envisaged for the opera was evidently no match for the experience of genuine fear and the trauma of expulsion.

Part III

Emigration Years: An Intellectual in a Foreign Land

A Twofold Exile: Intellectual Homelessness as Personal Fate

There is no longer any homeland other than a world in which no one would be cast out any more, the world of a genuinely emancipated humanity.[1]

Horrified by the Nazi takeover, Adorno found himself unable to speak when he became a witness to the ghastly events in Berlin in the first few months of 1933. On the winners' side, shouts of 'Heil Hitler' in the intoxicated sense of unity, victory celebrations with the Horst Wessel song, an oppressive sea of flags with swastikas, mass meetings, vows, ceremonies of consecration, all accompanied by anti-Semitic outrages and book-burnings in many German university towns. On the losers' side, the flight in panic of Jewish fellow citizens, left-wing politicians and oppositional intellectuals trying to make their escape across the frontiers of the Third Reich, their exodus triggered by waves of arrests, torture in the cellars of the Gestapo and the arbitrary violence of the first concentration camps of the SA.[2]

Overwhelmed by shame at his impotence in the face of the bestial events unfolding before him, Adorno felt paralysed. But, even more significantly, his distance from them also enabled him to register 'the lethal sadness' that arose from the presentiment of the disasters to come. He was not unaware that the monumental productions of the new masters, as well as their talk of a 'national community' (*Volksgemeinschaft*), were designed to camouflage any awareness of the approaching catastrophe. Behind the pomp and ceremony, the rumblings could already be heard. 'Everyone and nobody was too stupid to perceive' the destructive nature of National Socialist power politics.[3]

It was easier to grasp the situation a good ten years after the events – that was the time lag between this reminiscence in *Minima Moralia* and the triumph of collective folly – than under the weight of the impressions that crowded in on him at the time. Adorno, as a 'half-Jew' and left-wing intellectual, had no alternative to the passive role of an observer who gradually becomes conscious of the threats facing him. For a brief period he still thought he might be able to lead a private life as a composer, but this belief soon proved illusory. He was quickly disabused of the naive hopes so characteristic of an intellectual innocent of politics and of the confidence that a minimum of civility would still survive under the Nazis. He might have been able to come to terms with humiliations such as the withdrawal of the *venia legendi*, the right to give lectures. But what finally induced him to leave Germany, in autumn 1934, was the fact that, in addition to acts of discrimination, the authorities were trying to silence him. Condemned to impotence! According to his own explanation, that was the decisive reason for his emigration.

The threats he faced in Germany and the experience of expulsion could not fail to affect him. However, in the long run his will to resist was fortified by the arbitrary actions of the National Socialists, which he interpreted as examples of the decay of the bourgeois order. Later, after the four years and more in Oxford and London and the two years he spent in New York, he finally began to settle on the west coast of America, close to Los Angeles. There, even though the sight of the unfolding historical catastrophe reinforced and sharpened his critique of social irrationality, he never ceased to be an outsider.

Thus, despite being stigmatized as an émigré, Adorno was able to preserve his integrity, and he was also adept in avoiding the pitfalls to which exiled intellectuals frequently succumb if they let themselves be seduced into closing their eyes to their own uprootedness. 'Every intellectual in emigration is, without exception, mutilated, and does well to acknowledge it to himself, if he wishes to avoid being cruelly apprised of it behind the tightly closed doors of his self-esteem.'[4] This process of ruthless self-knowledge preserved Adorno from forgetting that the exile remains rootless even when he is able to assimilate. 'His language has been expropriated, and the historical dimension that nourished his knowledge, sapped.'[5] On the other hand, his reflections on his own status as outsider enabled him to conceive of exile as the mark of an entire epoch. In this epoch alterity was demanded even of the critic in matters of practical living. When Adorno described himself as 'a quasi-professionally homeless person',[6] he was voicing his conviction that the bitter experience of the alien in exile was congruent with the general experience of the intellectual as an outsider. He assumed in principle that 'inviolable isolation is the only path' for the intellectual who wishes to hold up a mirror to society.[7] 'In other words', he wrote to Thomas Mann, 'one is nowhere at home, but of course anyone who is engaged in the business of demythologization should not complain too much about it.'[8] Such a person is condemned to live in a state of suspension. As a homeless person, the intellectual finds that 'writing becomes his home', but the social critic is 'not even permitted to set up house in his text'.[9]

Even though Adorno procrastinated for months during the first phase of the Nazi dictatorship in 1933 before taking the decision to emigrate, the complex situation of the exile was no novelty to him. For having become clearer in his own mind about his own philosophical intentions, he had become increasingly conscious that his own programme isolated him intellectually. His focus on dialectical interpretation placed him outside both the historicizing tradition in the arts and philosophical scientism. He had long since become familiar with Lukács's concept of 'transcendental homelessness', and he agreed with Benjamin that history was a 'history of catastrophe'. As a philosopher, Adorno was convinced of the contingent nature of historical reality. To his mind, the apparently 'organic' nature of society was an illusion. The personal experience of being an alien during his years in emigration was a subterranean component of his way of thinking. Even before his expulsion from his homeland, the intellectual's experience of individual loneliness, isolation and marginalization was part of his make-up. Thus he underwent a *double* exile; it was not merely a physical exile in the culturally distinct countries to which he was forced to emigrate, first Britain and then the United States. We can say that his place had always been between two stools; his spiritual exile matched his experience of actual, physical exile. In this sense, Adorno was both an existential and an intentional outsider.[10]

In this way, the exiled Adorno's gaze, fixed as it was on the catastrophic course of history, found appropriate expression in his 'Reflections from Damaged Life'. These reflections drew much of their concrete material from the 'unhomely' situation and the distancing it entailed that inevitably accompanied life as a foreigner. Despite their subjective starting-point and their personal tone, these attempts of an uprooted intellectual to find his bearings were not motivated either by his personal experience of enforced emigration or by the shock of having to adapt to the social and cultural realities of the countries that gave him refuge. This explains why he applied to himself the commandment 'to deny oneself the ideological misuse of one's own existence, and for the rest to conduct oneself in private as modestly, unobtrusively and unpretentiously as is required, no longer by good upbringing, but by the shame of still having air to breathe, in hell.'[11] This metaphorical description of bourgeois society as hell points to Adorno's general belief that the world was in a desperate state. Even if the experience of exile was not a precondition for this belief, it was a situation in which his self-definition as an intellectual was mirrored: the identical situation internally and externally.[12] This intermediate position was a necessary if not a sufficient condition for his intransigent style of thinking, a style that was distilled into the density of the aphorism. 'For the value of a thought is measured by the continuity of the familiar. It is objectively devalued as this distance is reduced; the more it approximates to the pre-existing standard, the further its antithetical function is diminished, and only in this, in its manifest relation to its opposite, not in its isolated existence, are the claims of thought founded.'[13]

In *Minima Moralia* Adorno gives an account whose sensitivity about the loss of language and culture in exile, 'in which one is always astray', is equalled by few of his contemporaries.[14] At the same time, he was well aware of his privileged status as an émigré intellectual who was able to leave first Germany in 1934, and then Europe in 1938, before the outbreak of war. Moreover, these moves were made possible by careful planning, the material assistance of his parents to begin with, of the Academic Assistance Council somewhat later and, finally, of Horkheimer's Institute of Social Research. This good fortune also had its price. 'Even the man spared the ignominy of direct co-ordination bears, as his special mark, this very exemption, an illusory, unreal existence in the life-process of society.'[15] Suspended as he was between security and foreignness, there was another reason why the situation in which Adorno found himself as a 35-year-old in America marked a caesura in his life. His identity as an intellectual was subjected to a stern test. From this time on, he would have to earn his own living if he was to support his wife and himself.[16] Moreover, and this is decisive, he could no longer earn his living either as a music critic or as a philosopher protected by the privileged position of the academic freedom to teach. He now had to survive as a salaried scholar in an environment with specific performance criteria as well as values and forms of cooperation to which he had to adapt. He did so in a professional manner, though in his own way, and without making concessions. He remained the man he was. At the same time, his talent for empathy enabled him to turn to productive use the varied and intensive impressions he received in exile. During his exile years his literary style acquired the contours that turned him into one of the century's most individual writers. During his time in emigration his philosophy acquired the intellectual force and theoretical density that later became manifest in the writings of these fifteen years of exile, writings such as *The Philosophy of Modern Music* (1940–1) and *Dialectic of Enlightenment* (1944–7). During this period in the United States, in which Adorno worked principally in the realm of social research, he laid the foundations for his unique concept of sociology as a science of reflection.[17] While in Britain and the United States he was able to free himself from Kracauer's sociological phenomenology, and also from the utopianism of Bloch's ontological anticipation, as well as Benjamin's re-emphasis on revelation as an integral part of his philosophy of history. Only then did his antithetical way of thinking acquire the weight of an individual dialectical criticism of society. And, finally, his territorial 'non-identity' was also an experience that was channelled into his philosophical *chef d'oeuvre*, *Negative Dialectics* (1966). Adorno was to insert the concept of the non-identical into the very heart of his principal work of philosophy.

11

The 'Coordination' of the National Socialist Nation and Adorno's Reluctant Emigration

Weimar democracy, weighed down by the authoritarian legacy of the German imperial era, was a chronically unstable political system. It had twenty-two different governments between 1918 and 1933, and it was constantly threatened by recurrent economic and political crises until it finally collapsed in the totalitarian system of the National Socialist dictatorship. Inflation, the world economic crisis, unemployment, the crisis of the state finances, political extremism and separatist aspirations all played a role in its undoing. The ultimate demise of the Weimar constitution was brought about towards the end of the 1920s by the growing tension between the political parties on the one hand and the autocratic institution of the presidency of the Reich on the other. The political naivety of Paul von Hindenburg, the anti-republican president and field marshal, was partly a product of the semi-dictatorships of the three cabinets under Brüning, von Papen and Schleicher, the men in charge of the government before Hitler.[1] What was perhaps of greater importance for the progressive destruction of the parliamentary system was the fact that the republic had so few genuinely committed supporters.

Was Adorno fully aware of this absence of commitment to democratic values? He undoubtedly knew that many of his contemporaries hankered after the authoritarian solutions put forward by supporters of a 'conservative revolution', as well as their susceptibility to nationalist and '*völkisch*' ideologies. It would have been impossible to overlook the nationalist and conservative voices in the *haute bourgeoise* circles he frequented, such as the house of Georg von Schnitzler, the sales director of the IG Farben concern. He noted them with irritation, while hoping that the artistic sensibilities of the traditional aristocratic and middle-class elites would help them to resist inhuman political trends. He claimed, for example, that the music of Gustav Mahler was so convincing that anyone able to grasp its import would be immunized against anti-Semitic propaganda. 'Music generates an indestructible minimum of morality that will prove its worth even in these times.'[2] Despite his indifference to, and even ignorance of, political institutions, his lack of interest in the manoeuvrings of the parties, their demagoguery and the fanaticism of their supporters, he was enough of a critic and observer of social developments to become conscious of the anxieties of the petty bourgeoisie. As Kracauer had demonstrated in his sociological study of the white-collar workers, these anxieties encouraged a regression to totalitarian positions. They stood in the way of forming a commitment to defend the achievements of parliamentary democracy. Extremist parties such as the KPD and the NSDAP were hostile to the republic of 1918 from the outset. Moreover, anti-democratic resentments were common currency in the army, the justice system and the civil service. They sought to undermine it at every turn with the declared goal of replacing the 'Weimar system' with different forms of dictatorship. The most visible sign of this hatred of freedom, tolerance and democratic forms of life were the violent confrontations on the street and in the Reichstag in which each side sought to combat and where possible eliminate the other.

Following the inability of the majority parties to sustain their consensus, the Weimar Coalition collapsed, making the rise of the National Socialists irresistible. After the elections of September 1930, this was plain for all to see. In that year the number of Nazi voters leapt from 800,000 to 6.5 million, and on 31 July 1932 the Nazi Party more than doubled its vote, with 37.8 per cent, making it the largest party in the Reichstag.

Scarcely had the Nazis entered the Reichstag than Horkheimer and his closest circle of colleagues in the institute started to reckon with the possibility that emigration might become unavoidable.[3] The first preparations to leave the country had already been made; the institute's assets were transferred to Holland and a branch was set up in Geneva with the title of Société Internationale de Recherches Sociales. Horkheimer was not just responding to the growth in the Nazi vote. His fears that the public might put up with Hitler and even come to support him were confirmed by the results of an empirical study of 1929–30 that had investigated the political attitudes of manual and non-manual workers. This study had been carried out by Erich Fromm with the assistance of Hilde Weiss. It made use of the novel methods of psychoanalytical, in-depth interviews to discover the unconscious psychic dispositions underpinning the opinions, ways of life and attitudes of the blue-collar and white-collar workers studied.[4] The in-depth interviews were carried out on the basis of written questionnaires. Instead of standardized suggested answers, the questionnaires provided a series of questions the answers to which were supposed to make possible a psychoanalytical interpretation. In analysing the interviews attempts were made to explore workers' attitudes towards authority. It turned out that members of the left-wing parties during the Weimar republic were often just as fixated on authority as members of the middle class or Nazi sympathizers. This finding forced Horkheimer and his co-workers to recognize the latent authoritarianism of both manual and non-manual workers before 1933. It was evident that in all likelihood only a minority would resist a victory of the National Socialists. At the time, this explosive finding was kept under lock and key because, as Herbert Marcuse recollected, it was thought to be politically undesirable to give the impression that German workers had always felt attracted to the ideology of National Socialism.[5] However, these findings did give rise to internal institute debates on the future of parliamentary democracy in Germany. What social factors were responsible for the gulf between left-wing political opinions and bourgeois attitudes in everyday life? How was it possible for the objectively oppressed class to fail subjectively to understand its own social situation? The institute gradually came round to the view that, as a political formation corresponding to monopoly capitalism, National Socialism would scarcely be stoppable if the workers submitted to their oppressors instead of resisting them. Once it became clear that sections of the proletariat were willing to join forces with the Nazis, Horkheimer began to lose faith in the key Marxist idea that the working class would emerge as the agents of social change. As early as June 1932, he wrote to Adorno, 'Only one thing is certain: the irrationality of society has reached a point where only the gloomiest predictions have any plausibility.'[6]

Adorno was already publishing in the *Zeitschrift für Sozialforschung*, but he was not yet officially a member of the institute. This meant that he had only sporadically taken part in the discussions about the attitudes of the German working class. He had not been informed about the crucial practical consequence of the empirical study, namely Horkheimer's decision to establish foreign branches of the institute.[7] Löwenthal subsequently emphasized that the results of the research into workers' attitudes had been a major factor in predicting the coming disaster. The institute members had been convinced that the Nazis would come to power and

> that resistance was so poorly developed, particularly in the Liberal Democratic and Social Democratic Parties and in the Christian and Social Democratic trade unions, that they would not be capable of any great resistance against victorious fascism. Moreover, we grew increasingly disappointed and pessimistic, first independently from each other, and then in the political exchange of opinions within our group about the Soviet Union and the international Communist movement. And then developments in the Weimar Republic made us more and more worried and uneasy. Of course there was progressive literature and progressive theatre, but in the final analysis these were only futile fringe-phenomena. No, precisely in cultural matters one could notice, from the middle of the twenties on, that Germany was becoming increasingly conservative, if not reactionary.[8]

At the point in time when the members of the Institute of Social Research started to become conscious of the threat represented by the conservative and reactionary trends of the age, Adorno wrote to Alban Berg, following the dramatic Nazi gains in the election of September 1930, arguing that the Germans 'had succumbed to demonic stupidity'. He explained his recurrent inability to compose music by the absence of future prospects in Germany, something that 'robbed him of all creative energy'.[9] In his letters to Berg in the mid-1920s he had made no secret of his sympathies for the political ideas of the democratic wing of the communist movement, even though he was highly sceptical about the political strategy of the KPD as a whole.[10] The topic of anti-Semitism does arise in Adorno's early letters, but nowhere does he suggest that he had personal experience of it. Not having been confronted personally with the excesses of Nazi behaviour in the first few months after Hitler came to power, he was able to continue his life as normal. Thus in August 1933 he found nothing to prevent him from taking his usual holiday with Gretel Karplus, and they spent several weeks in Binz on the Baltic coast, where they met Paul and Hannah Tillich.[11] And as late as March 1934, when he had taken up his father's contacts in London in order to find out about any future academic prospects, he returned to Germany for a summer holiday in the Alps. He sought to deal with the new situation by continuing to pursue his personal interests as unobtrusively as possible. Nevertheless, the difficulties grew. In spring 1933 he complained about persistent stomach pains and headaches. Anxieties about the future would not go away despite all his whistling in the dark and, together with his habit of constant overwork, they were not without consequences. Kracauer warned him not to overdo things; he should reduce his workload and even consider a spell in a sanatorium.[12] As to the advance of National Socialism, Adorno did not at first believe that this would prove to be a danger to democracy and political freedom in Germany in the long run. He loathed racist nationalism (*das Völkische*) and all the propaganda about 'blood and soil' that went with it. He had first encountered fascism during his various travels in Italy, namely the local petty bourgeois, anti-socialist fascism of the dictatorship of Benito Mussolini, 'Il Duce', and his idea of the '*stato totalitario*'. His response to nationalism and the one-party state had been one of outright rejection.[13]

This dislike did not protect him from making a number of misjudgements concerning the popularity of Hitlerism and the attractions of the leader-and-follower ideology to broad sections of the German people. He was convinced that sooner or later the primitive racial theory, the irrational anti-Semitism, would put many people off, and the same thing applied to the violence of the mob of brownshirts, the wave of arrests after the Reichstag fire on 27 February, the boycott of Jewish businesses on 1 April 1933 and the public book-burnings in May. For a long time he thought it inconceivable that National Socialism could achieve its own stabilization by terrorizing its opponents.

Of course, the idea that the Nazis might fail in the long run, or at least be forced into compromises, was not simply a figment of the imagination at the time. After all, even though they abolished the freedom of speech, the press and assembly after the Reichstag fire in order to shackle rival parties, the NSDAP still did not succeed in gaining an absolute majority in the elections on March 5. Adorno and his family may have taken this to mean the majority of German voters did not support Hitler, and in fact a third of all voters still supported the parties of the Weimar coalition. Nevertheless, Hitler had enough of a mandate to obtain the Reichstag's approval on 23 March 1933 of the 'Enabling Law', which made it possible for him to govern without parliament. The Social Democratic Party and the free trade unions proved too weak to defend the rights of democracy.

Once Hitler had finally put an end to the last vestiges of democracy and the constitutional state, there was no stopping the witch-hunts which had long since been in progress in the universities. After the first intimidatory measures on the part of Nazi student organizations and other right-wing radical groups, a number of universities began to institute purges (e.g., Tübingen and Freiburg). Adorno was one of those affected by these repressive measures, and it was only now that he began to become aware of the danger to himself. The clearest evidence of the threat to his own material existence was the loss of his lectureship at Frankfurt University. He had made use of his right to sabbatical leave during the summer semester 1933, but in an official letter of 8 September 1933 the 'Prussian Minister for Science, Art and Education' wrote to him saying 'On the basis of §3 of the Law for the Restoration of the Professional Civil Service of 7 April 1933, I herewith withdraw your licence to teach at the University of Frankfurt am Main.'[14] Adorno's ironic comment, 'the less *venia legendi*, the better', is only comprehensible against the background that even before this event the purging of the 'Jewish-Marxist university' had long since been started, that the registrar, Kurt Riezler, had also lost his job and that the new rulers had already started to dismiss a number of colleagues on racial and political grounds.[15] These included Max Horkheimer, Paul Tillich, Franz Oppenheimer, Karl Mannheim, Adolf Löwe, Gottfried Salomon and Max Wertheimer.[16]

The work of the Institute of Social Research also came to an untimely end on 13 March. The same day that the swastika was run up on the Römer, the town hall, the institute was searched by a contingent from the Frankfurt criminal police, and temporarily shut down. Thanks to the research on the political consciousness of the workers, the members of the so-called Café Marx had recognized the political dangers even before Hitler had become chancellor of the Reich. Horkheimer had no doubt about the fate that was on the point of overtaking Germany.[17] He had given up his flat in February and gone to live in a hotel near Frankfurt Central Station. This was followed by the illegal occupation by the SA of the house in Kronberg he shared with Pollock, the so-called Schweizerhäuschen. From February they had transferred their research to Geneva, where they continued to work with Löwenthal, Fromm and Marcuse. Other members of the institute had gone underground or had left Germany.

As far as Adorno was concerned, matters did not rest with his dismissal from the university. In July his house in Seeheimer Strasse was subjected to a search. He also had grounds to believe that his post was being spied on. When he took steps to qualify as a music teacher in order to be able to earn his living, he was informed that he could only take on 'non-Aryan' pupils. As if that were not enough, in November 1933 he had found it necessary to apply for membership of the Reich Chamber of Literature. A few months later he was informed by the president of the chamber that his application had been rejected, since membership was restricted to 'reliable members of the *Volk*',[18] i.e., 'persons who belong to the German nation by profound ties of character [*Art*] and blood. As a non-Aryan you are unable to feel and appreciate such an obligation. Signed: Suchenwirth. Certified as correct: Nowotny.'[19] This decision was more than just another act of spite on the part of the Nazi bureaucracy, since it had the effect of suddenly confronting Adorno with the Jewish side of his identity. As a member of the educated middle class, he was made aware by persecution and expulsion that he had a relation to Judaism even though he had always regarded it with scepticism and even mockery.[20]

In retrospect, Adorno frankly admitted that he had completely misjudged the political situation in 1933. During the first months following the political intrigues which culminated in what was after all the legal appointment of Hitler as Reich chancellor, he was under the illusion that the Third Reich would last only a short time because of the economic incompetence of its leaders.[21] This error is all the more significant as Adorno could see plainly what was happening before his very eyes. In 1933 Arnold Schoenberg resigned from his post as professor in the Prussian Academy of Arts because of the Nazis' anti-Semitism, and he was forced to leave Germany. The public performance of avant-garde works such as the compositions of Anton Webern, the operas of Alban Berg, and the music of Kurt Weill and Hanns Eisler was forbidden, and, in general, works by Jewish composers were strictly controlled. Max Horkheimer and Fritz Pollock, Leo Löwenthal, Herbert Marcuse and Erich Fromm had all realized very early on what was about to happen. But they were not alone: people closer to Adorno, such as Siegfried Kracauer, Ernst Bloch, Ernst Schoen and Walter Benjamin, had already turned their backs on their native land in order to escape arrest by the Gestapo. There was nothing unusual about packing one's suitcases as a response to the threats from a state that openly threatened to persecute those who disagreed with it politically and to eliminate both Jews and 'subhumans'. Thousands of intellectuals, writers, journalists and artists went into exile. Those who left were, according to Adorno, the people who counted.

Although he witnessed both this exodus and the increasingly harsh acts of discrimination, his aim was to discover a niche in which he could bide his time until the Hitler dictatorship had found what he hoped would be a speedy end. 'At the time this catastrophic misjudgement was shared even by prominent émigrés who filled the hotels of Paris, Vienna and Prague, sitting there, as it were, without unpacking their suitcases, waiting for a quick return. . . . Not everyone grasped the terrorist nature of the regime from the outset, or saw it as a lethal threat.'[22] Like many of his contemporaries, Adorno regarded Hitler 'as an increasingly poor caricature . . . of himself as well as of a real dictator (Aryan, statesman and general)',[23] a shady figure whose bizarre speech and gestures prevented him from being taken seriously. Adorno might have learnt from Siegfried Kracauer, one of his closest friends, that the National Socialist movement was a real threat, despite the grotesque nature of its '*Führer*'. No later than 1932 Kracauer had drawn attention to some of the signs pointing to the approaching catastrophe. For example, he wrote a highly critical article for the *Frankfurter Zeitung* about the voluntary work service and the work camps that, despite their supposedly unpolitical and purely educational mandate, had turned out to contain 'the nucleus of the political organization, the prototypes of the national community'.

Later, in the same newspaper and while it was still possible, Kracauer attacked the totalitarian nationalism of a writer such as Friedrich Hielscher and the doctrines of his journal *Das Reich*, which he regarded as the advance guard of the ideology of the totalitarian state. As late as the beginning of 1933, Kracauer produced an analysis of the electoral success of the National Socialists and a breakdown of those who had voted for them. However, this article could no longer be published in the *Frankfurter Zeitung*, even though he remained an editor until the spring. Following his clairvoyant study of the white-collar worker (*Die Angestellten*) of 1929, he wrote that the middle-class vote for the Hitler movement resulted from the proletarianization of these social strata. But 'National Socialism had thrived thanks to the financial support of industry.' In the case of industry the hatred of the unions had been the deciding factor, while for its part the upper middle class accepted Hitler's seizure of power from fear of communism. 'Anti-Semitism, which many all too optimistic citizens dismissed as a mere blemish, is in truth at the ideological core of the movement. This is why it is still cultivated. Its true mission is to conceal the facts of class struggle by diverting it into race hatred.'[24]

It is unlikely that Adorno remained in ignorance of this analysis. Even if he did, he had received warning enough in Kracauer's letters. As early as the summer of 1930, Kracauer wrote insistently to Adorno, 'The situation in Germany is worse than serious. . . . This country is facing disaster and I know that it is not just a question of capitalism.

The fact that capitalism can be bestial is not just a matter of economics. . . . In our case a revolution would not . . . stimulate a youthful nation full of energy; nor do I believe in the curative powers of social upheaval.'[25] Adorno's reaction to these forebodings is not known. In general, he refrained from comment on political developments in Germany. An eloquent testimony to Adorno's political naivety can be found in his conversations with Peter von Haselberg in Berlin. In a discussion about the current political situation, he maintained 'that the *purification of the German body politic* would wear itself out in clearing-up operations: after *clearing out* the attics there would doubtless be a propaganda campaign against the rats and then the slogan: *Down with rust*. Moreover, the economy was in too precarious a state for the government to launch any drastic initiatives, if only because of the effect on opinion abroad and the withdrawal of credits. *That is exact imagination*, he concluded.'[26]

Such sarcasm, however, was just one side of Adorno's mood. The other was to be seen in his ties to the culture and language of his native land. These were so powerful that he made every effort to avoid emigration. This included his decision to try and publish in various journals under a pseudonym. The name Hektor Rottweiler seemed to him to be a good piece of camouflage. He explained to Peter von Haselberg that 'the Rottweiler was a typical butcher's dog and was almost always called Hektor. It was a fearsome beast and so no Nazi will ever suspect that it might hide the identity of a non-Aryan writer.'[27]

A later letter to Krenek in October 1934 gives the fullest account of Adorno's attempts to 'go into hibernation' under the Third Reich. Although he experienced the sanctions of the new rulers personally, the decision to emigrate came very hard.

> The events in Germany which I experienced in Unter den Linden in Berlin for the most part, including those of 1 April 1933, first made me go very quiet and threw me back on my own affairs entirely. My work in the university ceased in spring 1933. I had lost the *venia legendi* the previous autumn, on my thirtieth birthday. For the most part, I spent the summer and autumn of 1933 finishing the text of my Tom Sawyer.[28]

Adorno goes on to tell Krenek that he had obtained contacts to the management of the *Vossische Zeitung* and had even succeeded in having some articles published in the first half of 1933. This was thanks to the mediation of a friend of his, Friedrich T. Gubler, who had previously been an editor on the cultural section of the *Frankfurter Zeitung*, and later in the *Vossische Zeitung*. A whole series of articles remained unpublished, however. His expectation of being able to circumvent the press laws and obtain a position as a freelance editor was quickly dashed. The paper itself was forced to close down during the year. This deprived Adorno of a professional opportunity – one of the last straws at which he was clutching in his efforts 'to remain in Germany at any price'.[29]

Despite all the restrictions, he was 'quite able to survive materially in Germany' and – as he explained in a letter – he 'would have had no political difficulties either. The only problem is that I would have had no way of exerting any influence.'[30]

Adorno seemed, then, to have been struck blind politically, and it is in tune with this that he refrained from public criticism of any kind of the Nazis and their 'great power' policies. He undoubtedly rejected their totalitarianism, their anti-Semitism and their militant anti-communism. But even in his private letters, until well into the mid-1930s, we find no more than rather generalized, pessimistic mood-pictures, and no unambiguous statements on the political situation. There was no significant political comment in his correspondence with Benjamin, Berg and Krenek, even though the lives of all three were directly affected by Hitler's politics. It may be that Adorno had the same view of political criticism as he demanded from the musical avant-garde: 'It is not for music to stare in helpless horror at society: it fulfils its social function more precisely when it presents social problems through its own material and according to its own formal laws – problems which music contains within itself in the innermost cells of its technique. The task of music as art thus enters into a parallel relationship to the task of social theory.'[31] Did Adorno become politicized by discovering the vast scope of the barbarism of the dictatorship in Germany and by his insight into its dimensions? Whatever political consciousness he had became evident in his cultural criticism. In this sense his scepticism towards current events was not simply aesthetic. But the political inferences he drew did not lead the philosopher and the musical theorist to a public declaration of his opposition to the totalitarian state.

Hibernating with dignity?

Adorno was not alone in wishing to go into hibernation; in fact he was in the very best of company with many writers who were convinced, as he was, that the regime would soon collapse and who thought of their flight abroad as a sojourn in what Lion Feuchtwanger called Europe's 'waiting-room'. Even major sections of the Jewish population succumbed to the illusion that the regime would not target them but only the orthodox pro-Soviet Bolshevists and communists who had drawn attention to themselves politically or who had been involved in illegal conspiracies. Moreover, despite his declared anti-Semitism, Hitler was keen to create the impression that anti-Jewish acts were the isolated, spontaneous outbursts of the 'national soul' that were approved of only by radicals within the NSDAP. And he showed how extremists should be dealt with on 30 June 1934 when he engineered the so-called Röhm putsch and crushed the SA, which in the eyes of the public had been responsible for the terrorism on the streets. Hitler's success in representing himself as a force for order can be judged not least by the fact that even 'leading figures of the Jewish community were trying to hide their distress behind a façade of confidence. Despite all difficulties, the future of Jewish life in Germany was not being irretrievably endangered.'[32] Such misjudgements on the part of artists were aggravated by, among other factors, the Cultural League of German Jews, with whom, as it happened, Adorno had experience of his own. This organization was one that, although tolerated by the Nazis, was intended to secure autonomous cultural activities for Jews. It had been established in May 1933 by Kurt Singer, who had previously been the deputy director of the Städtische Oper in Berlin. It embraced Jews from all parts of Germany and concentrated on organizing concert and opera performances. These included a performance in Frankfurt of a selection of Schoenberg's works in honour of his sixtieth birthday. When Adorno, who was attracted by this initiative, applied for membership in the Cultural League his application was turned down because 'he was racially a half-Jew' and a Christian by religion.[33]

Just as Adorno kept postponing a decision about his future, so too the relatively well-informed circle around Leo Baeck kept issuing warnings even as late as 1934 about the political risks and material consequences of an over-hasty emigration, particularly in the light of the tax imposed by the Nazis on the export of capital. All these factors played a part in the much commented-on 'seeming lack of enthusiasm for leaving a country where segregation, humiliation and a whole array of persecutory measures were becoming steadily worse. . . . Most of the Jews expected to weather the storm in Germany.'[34] Oscar Wiesengrund, whose family was classified by the Nazis as being 'related to Jews by marriage', belonged to this group. He believed that his military service during the war would protect him.[35] Moreover, he had been awarded the Cross of Honour 'in the name of the Führer and Reich Chancellor', a medal for war veterans that had been established by the Reich president, Paul von Hindenburg, shortly before his death. In the first few years of Nazi rule, Jewish veterans who had been so honoured enjoyed a certain immunity. Since Adorno dismissed racial ideology as insane and could not imagine that the bourgeoisie would allow itself to be governed by what he called 'gang leaders',[36] he daily expected the collapse of the regime whose 'Führer' seemed to him to be 'a mixture of King Kong and a suburban hairdresser'.[37]

As a citizen of Frankfurt, Adorno discovered that a community with a well-developed civic culture and privately run cultural institutions such as the Städel Art Gallery, the Deutscher Hochstift and the Senckenberg Society for Natural Science contained a number of refuges for Jews who were active as scholars or artists. The prominence of Jewish citizens in Frankfurt cultural life as well as a culture that owed so much to private sponsorship provided effective protection, for a time at least, against the all-levelling pressure of the Nazi system.[38]

As late as mid-April 1934 Adorno wrote to Benjamin, who had emigrated to France, expressing his doubts about the stability of the Nazi regime. 'For although I am certainly not optimistic, and expect the future to bring a kind of right-wing anarchy . . . if not a downright military dictatorship or something like the Dollfuss regime, the signs of collapse are nevertheless starting to accumulate so much that one no longer needs to ignore them for fear of the wish proving father to the thought.'[39] He expressed himself similarly in a letter to Leo Löwenthal a few weeks later, in which he wrote that the murders of Röhm and Schleicher had destabilized and compromised the regime 'which was so weakened by the elimination of the SA (which has been reduced to a shadow of its former self) that I do not see how it will be able to cope with the serious difficulties of the winter. I think it will then come to killings and murder with the army as saviour.' In the event of armed conflict, Adorno naively imagined that revolution would break out: 'In general, I think it more likely next year than for the last fifteen years. But will it succeed? I am almost afraid that everything will move too quickly and the dictatorship will disintegrate before the workers can set up an organization to take its place – and then capitalism will emerge the winner.'[40]

In the months preceding and following Hitler's seizure of power down to the time he spent at Merton College, Oxford, as an 'advanced student', Adorno continued with his activities as a writer and composer. Having formally applied for leave during the summer semester 1933, since his licence to teach had been withdrawn as from the start of the winter semester, he was able to use the time to work on his opera project *The Treasure of Indian Joe*. In addition, he wrote a number of reviews of new books on philosophy for the *Frankfurter Zeitung* and for the *Zeitschrift für Sozialforschung*: on Nicolai Hartmann's *The Problem of Spiritual Existence*, a *Festschrift* for Ludwig Klages, and a monograph on Hegel. At the same time as his Kierkegaard book appeared, the *Frankfurter Zeitung* published the surrealist sketches he had written with Carl Dreyfus. Quantitatively, the music articles that appeared in specialist journals stand out; they dealt with such composers as Bach, Schubert, Brahms, and on down to Schoenberg, Webern and Berg.

In number 7 of the *Europäische Revue* edited by Karl Anton Prinz Rohan, Adorno published a review of a performance of Wagner's *Die Meistersinger* which had taken place in the Berlin Festival under the baton of Wilhelm Furtwängler. This 'Note about Wagner' is his first extended discussion of the composer who was being celebrated by the National Socialist regime as the prophet of a new German religion of art. Adorno defended Wagner against Nietzsche's criticism, while distancing himself explicitly from the official eulogies. He emphasized the purely musical dimensions of a work that appears 'both alien and familiar to the contemporary listener, like childhood dreams'. Its secret lies in its use of chromaticism. Whereas Adorno characterized the music of *Meistersinger* as 'the breakthrough of the instincts in the midst of bourgeois order', he noted the innovative technical features of *Tristan*, which enabled Wagner to liberate the music from 'the shell of individual expression'. 'To enable the illumination of the world to rise up from the mineshafts of the unconscious . . . that is the aim of Wagner's music. It has chosen demythologization in the shape of the mythical as the secret of its artistic magic.'[41] In these notes Adorno distinguished between the musical character of the work and its political effect. Ignoring the fact that Wagner and his music were being exploited by the National Socialists, he was able to create a positive picture of the composer. He would produce a more nuanced and critical view of Wagner later in his major study of the composer.

He took a different line in another essay that appeared in the *Europäische Revue*. In number 5, also published in 1933, he provided a gloss on the regulation that had just been issued banning the broadcasting of 'Negro jazz' on German radio. Without directly endorsing the Nazi prohibition of 'un-German [*artfremd*] music', he made the extraordinary assertion that the decree approved retrospectively what had already taken place in music, namely the 'end of jazz music itself'. There was nothing in jazz that could be defended or salvaged, it 'has long been in the process of dissolution, in retreat into military marches and all sorts of folklore.'[42] Jazz was disappearing from the stage of autonomous artistic production thanks to its own 'stupidity'. What is eliminated along with it 'is not the musical influence of the Negro race on the northern one, nor is it cultural Bolshevism. It is a piece of bad commercial art.'[43]

Perhaps Adorno was attempting a sarcastic reaction to the senseless Nazi prohibition. However, his terminology – 'eliminate', 'race', 'cultural Bolshevism' – is not too far from the abuse practised by Goebbels.[44] Adorno showed himself to be culpably careless on one further occasion, in 1934, when he gave a favourable review in *Die Musik*, a journal immediately taken over by the Nazis, of Herbert Müntzel's cycle for male choir on poems by Baldur von Schirach, Hitler's youth leader. To characterize this choral music which 'derived from the more ancient, polyphonic German folksong, especially of the sixteenth century', he made use of Goebbels's term 'romantic realism'.[45]

Years later, in the winter semester of 1963, the Frankfurt student newspaper *Diskus* published this review at the suggestion of a student, Claus Chr. Schroeder,[46] who issued a challenge to Adorno in an open letter: 'As is well known, you have persistently condemned all those people since the war who were guilty in 1934 and after for the way Germany developed. (I refer, for example, to your discussion of

Heidegger.) Why have you remained silent hitherto about your authorship of the accompanying article which appeared in the above-mentioned anti-Semitic and National-Socialist periodical in June 1934?'[47] Adorno published a defence in the very next issue of the paper. He said he had never intended to ingratiate himself with the Nazi rulers; that much was obvious from his defence of the music that the Nazis had slandered as 'decadent'. 'In the situation of 1934, the turns of phrase that I can be reproached with must have appeared to every rational reader as *captationes benevolentiae* [a bid for the readers' goodwill] which allowed me to speak in this way. My true mistake lay in my misjudgement of the situation.'[48]

Haselberg has provided further evidence of Adorno's political myopia. During the Hitler dictatorship, in the isolation of exile in Britain, he began to assemble the personal notes that would form the core of *Minima Moralia*, which was not published until much later. In these notes he attempted to account for the contradictions in his own responses at the time. His unworldliness prevented him from instantly recognizing the barbaric nature of the Hitler regime and this clouded his judgement. However, he had been prepared for Hitler's reign of terror by his 'unconscious fear'. He had a presentiment about the catastrophe brooding at the heart of German society, 'and it often seemed to my foolish terror as if the total state had been invented expressly against me, to inflict on me after all those things from which, in my childhood, its primeval form, I had been temporarily dispensed.'[49]

The unconscious fear of which Adorno speaks saved his life. It encouraged him to take an increasingly realistic view and led to the conviction that in Nazi Germany there could be no future for a left-wing intellectual. He now had no choice but to leave the country. But where should he go? For a brief period he thought about Istanbul. A more obvious choice, given his musical and philosophical connections, was Vienna. Since Paul Karplus, Gretel's uncle, had a chair in neurology at the University of Vienna, he tried to arrange to have his *Habilitation* transferred there. His prospects were not good, however. He received no assistance from his Nazified home university and Vienna was indifferent to both him and his teaching interests. In October 1934, Adorno confessed to Krenek that his efforts had come to naught: 'I should like to add that of course I tried to transfer my *Habilitation* to Vienna, but without success. Herr Gomperz who was charged with the business discovered that the only thing of interest in my Kierkegaard book was the quotations, and that the book could not be judged an above-average achievement. So Vienna shut the door in my face.'[50]

Vienna having shown him the cold shoulder, Adorno began in mid-1934 to think seriously about a British university, and he looked to the Academic Assistance Council for support. Oscar Wiesengrund strongly encouraged his son in this venture. He guaranteed him the financial assistance that would be needed to obtain an academic qualification that would be recognized in Britain. Adorno could see that he would be faced with language difficulties. He had only an elementary grasp of the language and it was only with time that he learned to master it in both speech and writing. Nevertheless, he could leave Berlin 'in a happier mood' now that he had new prospects abroad.[51]

12

Between Academic and Authentic Concerns: From Philosophy Lecturer to Advanced Student in Oxford

Adorno had personal experience of harassment by the Nazis, but this did not lead to his precipitate departure from Germany. His hesitation was in part the result of political misjudgement, but in part arose from a reluctance to leave without at least minimal assurances about his career prospects. If he could not obtain a university post, he wished at least to be able to obtain work as a music critic and pursue his ambitions as a composer. This latter included the possibility of public performances of his work.

Adorno's father urged him to put out feelers in Britain. This advice may have been an effect of his Anglophilia, but more probably the rational calculation that as a wine-merchant he traditionally had close business relationships with his British customers[1] and that his brother Bernhard Wiesengrund had lived there with his wife Helene (*née* Richter) for thirty years.[2] As an electrical engineer, Bernhard Wiesengrund had successfully built up a business, the Power Plant Company, even before the First World War, and acquired a certain reputation as a businessman. He lived in a comfortable house in Finchley with his three children – his daughter, Lina, who was the eldest, and his two sons, Bernhard Theodore and Louis Alexander. He had acquired British citizenship in 1914 and had changed his name to Bernhard Robert Wingfield.[3]

Because the Wiesengrunds had kept in touch with the Wingfields, Adorno's father knew quite early on that there was a private British aid organization devoted to helping émigrés establish contact with Anglo-Saxon universities. This was the Academic Assistance Council (AAC), which had been set up in March 1933 on the initiative of Sir William Beveridge, the director of the London School of Economics. The AAC was renamed in March 1936, after which it became known as the Society for the Protection of Science and Learning.[4] The AAC concentrated on providing an information service, and then on making financial assistance available to émigré scholars, subsidies for travel or university fees and – of particular importance to Adorno – the award of maintenance grants.[5] When Robert Wingfield first heard about the AAC he applied at once to the secretary in order to find out whether his nephew, Fritz Epstein, a lecturer in history who had also been dismissed by the Nazis, had any prospects of finding a job at an English university. Fritz Epstein, who had been born in 1898, was the elder son of Adorno's aunt Alice Betty, who had married Paul Epstein, the mathematician. Fritz Epstein had studied with Richard Salomon in Hamburg, where he had begun his career as a historian in the Institute for East European History.[6] At the time when his uncle approached the AAC, Fritz Epstein had two children of nine and seven to provide for, as well as his non-Jewish wife (*née* Bertelsmann), who was subject to the degrading provisions of a 'mixed marriage'. It is understandable, therefore, that Bernhard Robert Wingfield should have regarded assistance for Fritz, the son of his sister, as a higher priority than concern for his brother's son who was five years younger and as yet unmarried.

Without the help of the AAC it would not have been possible for either Adorno or Epstein to set foot in Britain. A strict asylum policy was in force in the British Isles, thanks to the Aliens Restriction Act. In addition, the Foreign Office pursued a policy of appeasement towards the Third Reich up to the eve of war in September 1939, and this encouraged the British tendency to isolationism. Just as Prime Minister Chamberlain strove to reach an accommodation with Hitler, so too officialdom greeted émigrés from Germany with reserve.[7] The state of the British economy was also a significant factor, in particular, the relatively high rates of unemployment and the fear of the British that jobs would be lost to foreigners. The precondition for immigration in general, and hence also for Adorno, was independent means or the guarantees provided by a private sponsor. Immigrants were also under an obligation to report regularly to the police.

When Adorno established contact with the AAC he was able to benefit from the loose relations his father had cultivated with John Maynard Keynes. Keynes had already been in touch with Sir William Beveridge with regard to the case of the young lecturer from Frankfurt. On 28 September 1939, he wrote to Sir William: 'I do not know Mr T. L. Wiesengrund personally, but I have known his father slightly for some years. It would appear from the papers that he is of rather unusual talent, combining philosophy, primarily the theory of aesthetics, with exceptional musical gifts and qualifications.'[8] Thus Adorno was not entirely unknown when he applied personally by letter to the general secretary of the council in order to give them the names of his referees needed to support his case. He listed Adolf Löwe, the economist, Karl Mannheim, the sociologist, the philosopher Ernst Cassirer, and Edward Dent, president of the International Society for Contemporary Music. With the exception of Dent, they were all immigrants to Britain, and Adorno did not know any of them well. In order to obtain as positive a reference as possible from Dent, Adorno had already written to Berg in November 1933, asking him to put in a good word with Dent. Since Berg knew Dent well, he was happy to do what he could for his former pupil. During the same month he wrote a lengthy letter mentioning Adorno's talents both as a scholar of music and as a composer. Dent's reaction was, to put it mildly, hostile and tainted with anti-Semitism. After this 'unspeakable letter', Adorno made no further attempt to approach Dent.[9]

Aside from that, Adorno was sufficiently self-confident to believe that, if he obtained a qualification that was recognized in Britain, he would soon find an academic position that was the equivalent of his *Privatdozentur* in Frankfurt. How realistic was this expectation? Cassirer, whom the AAC had asked for his opinion, had his doubts about the academic prospects of his young colleague from Frankfurt. He wrote to the general secretary of the AAC: 'if you regard this hope [of obtaining a post] as premature – as I do, at any rate for Oxford, as a result of the enquiries I have made till now – it would perhaps be good for the Academic Assistance Council once again to give him [i.e., Adorno] a clear picture of the situation so that expectations are not deceived.'[10] Adorno's optimism about being able to make at least a modest academic career in Britain was based on a completely mistaken understanding of the university system. An academic career began by working as a tutor to undergraduates until a regular lectureship fell vacant. After the AAC had consulted Professor John Macmurray of University College, Oxford, it was finally suggested to Adorno in a letter that he should acquire a degree at a reputable college in order gradually to position himself in the British academic world.[11] Towards the end of 1934, the general secretary of the AAC, Walter Adams, wrote to Macmurray that Adorno had been recommended to register in Oxford and establish contact with Professor Harold H. Joachim, who would help him to choose a suitable college.[12] Adorno followed the instructions of the AAC to the letter.

Since he now had at least a vague idea of how to proceed, he went to London in April 1934, staying at first with his uncle's family. After a little more than a week he moved to Albermarle Court Hotel in Leinster Gardens, Bayswater, close to Hyde Park. From now on he would always stay there on his frequent visits to Britain. Needless to say, Adorno made a number of visits to the offices of the AAC. The approach favoured by the AAC was to collect data on applicants by making them fill in questionnaires. In his questionnaire Adorno added names to the list of referees that he had given earlier on, and now included Max Horkheimer and Paul Tillich. In response to questions about his financial position, he mentioned, presumably for tactical reasons, only the RM 1200 that he had earned from student fees up to the beginning of 1933. Over and above that, he declared, his costs were covered by his parents in Frankfurt, where he was a resident and registered with the police. Asked about his knowledge of English, he said: 'I am able to read also difficult philosophical writers as Brudley [*sic*].' Speaking, he said, was adequate, but not faultless, while his ability to write was still insufficient. He wished, he said in his application, to study for a doctorate in order to qualify himself to teach philosophy. Adorno had hoped to meet Ernst Cassirer in the London office of the AAC, but nothing came of this. He therefore relied entirely on the suggestions of Harold H. Joachim, a professor of logic at New College, Oxford, who was close to retirement. In May, he had a lengthy talk with Joachim in Oxford, where he went to stay for a few weeks in order to gain an impression of the university. He lived in 47 Banbury Road with a Mrs Ney, 'a very acceptable lodging', as he said, and where he even had the use of a piano.[13]

By mid-June Adorno was in a position to register officially in Merton College as 'an advanced student' in philosophy. The decision to go to Merton may have been influenced by the fact that his older cousin Bernhard T. Wingfield had studied there. Despite this personal success in overcoming the bureaucratic obstacles, there was something absurd about his new status, which was remarkably inappropriate for a man of over thirty who had obtained his doctorate a decade earlier, had been awarded the *Habilitation* a short time before, and had a considerable list of publications to his credit. When dining with the other students in hall, his appearance and manner of speaking made it obvious that he did not fit in. The 'advanced student' told both Horkheimer and Berg that this was his worst 'nightmare' come true, 'to have to go back to school. In short, it is an extension of the Third Reich.'[14] In contrast, he wrote to the general secretary of the AAC: 'Here the June is delightful and I am beginning to feel myself human again; a kind of feeling I had lost in Germany last year.'[15] And he wrote to Berg that Berg absolutely had to come to Oxford; the town could 'only be compared to Venice'.[16] Such diametrically opposed reactions were not unusual for a letter writer who took careful account of the recipients of his letters and what they wanted to hear from him.

The euphoric note in these letters did not last long. During the summer vacation Adorno had returned to Germany. When he arrived in Oxford for the new academic year in autumn 1934, he again felt uncertain about his position in the university and his own future prospects.[17] It seems that it was only now that he began to realize that emigration can mean isolation and loneliness. Some Oxford colleagues rejected him vehemently, others refused to take him seriously. The philosopher Alfred Ayer recalls that Adorno 'seemed to us a comic figure', with his snobbish demeanour, 'his dandified manner and his anxiety' to be accorded recognition. His specific interests in social theory and aesthetics had little resonance in Oxford.[18]

The enduring problems of living abroad included the growing difficulty of transferring funds from Germany to Britain. This problem gained in urgency because he depended on regular payments from his father for his day-to-day living. The difficulty was that the German authorities had outlawed foreign payments. Adorno even needed the permission of the exchange control office to enable him to accept the 'maintenance grant' from the AAC, which went in part to pay the university fees. When finally his solicitor pressed him to obtain official permission, the exchange control office wished to be told the source of his income previously. He was forced to lie and say he had been in receipt of financial support from the AAC prior to that, but had not known that official permission was required. He was then informed that the matter would have to be resolved either by the exchange control office in Frankfurt or before a magistrate's court. This latter possibility could have been the source of further embarrassment. As he explained to Walter Adams in a letter on 14 October, one outcome might have been a custodial sentence. A further problem might arise in connection with renewing his passport, which was due to expire in January 1937. Without a valid German passport he could neither travel nor obtain work. It was vitally important to him to be able to return to Germany at any time to see his parents and Gretel Karplus. After receiving his submission, the official dealing with his case in Frankfurt proposed the imposition of a fine which amounted to 150 *Reichsmark*. Adorno had developed a relationship based on trust with Adams and so was able to ask him to write a letter confirming the award of the maintenance grant for the relevant period and making it clear that these sums went directly to the university and did not represent payment for any work, 'so that they get the impression that I had, if at all, only very little money in my hand.' Adams obliged and sent a very detailed and diplomatically phrased letter, adding unofficially, 'I am willing to say anything that you wish in the circumstances.'[19]

The need for funds was one of the motives leading Adorno to make repeated visits to Germany during his four years in Oxford, for longer stays, as well as short trips. He came to dread these visits: 'The country really has become a hell, down to the smallest detail of everyday life.'[20] On the other hand, he had 'terrible anxieties' about his parents and about Gretel, who was still working in Berlin.[21] Apart from visiting the family in Frankfurt, he accepted the risks associated with the journey in order to spend time between terms with Gretel. As partner in the leather goods factory of Georg Tengler, she was 'relatively unaffected by the anti-Jewish measures', according to Adorno. Nevertheless, he had been working on persuading her to leave Germany since May 1935.[22] This plan shows that Adorno had gradually been forming a more realistic picture of Nazi tyranny and political trends in Germany more generally. The necessity of leaving Germany and his experience of life abroad had evidently helped to politicize him, and this was reflected in the maturing of his opinions in his correspondence during this period. Thus in the winter of 1935, he remarked to Horkheimer that within Germany one was condemned to a 'ghetto life' and that as far as foreign policy was concerned the situation was bleak. 'Concessions are made to Hitler on every front and Russia will probably be handed over to him. . . . I really do not know what keeps people alive apart from the animal fear of suicide. I have stopped having any hopes for Germany.'[23] By the end of 1934 he could see with almost prophetic clarity that the failure of the democracies in dealing with Hitler would make war inevitable, a war 'in which no one knows what would be left and which will be all the worse the later it comes.' Around a year later, he foresaw that Germany would invade Russia, 'France and Britain would take no action because of existing treaties and then nothing will stand in the way of the definitive healing of the world at the hands of Germany. The situation is desperate.'[24]

Adorno's intention of bringing Gretel over from Germany was quite unrealistic in the circumstances. For the 'advanced student' had no secure income of his own and was under pressure to complete his epistemological study of Husserl within a fixed time. This meant regular meetings with his supervisor, who happened to be Gilbert Ryle, the philosophy tutor at Christ Church. Ryle was primarily interested in the philosophy of language, but had also engaged with phenomenology, with Heidegger and Husserl. There was therefore a good objective basis for a productive encounter between the two philosophers despite the fact that they came from two very different traditions. Adorno evidently thought of Ryle as a highly competent interlocutor. For his part, Ryle, who would later achieve fame with *The Concept of Mind*, was able to read the works of classical German philosophy in the original, and hence also Adorno's critique of Husserl. In addition to Ryle, Adorno was in contact with other colleagues, including Alfred Ayer, a representative of logical positivism, Isaiah Berlin, the historian of ideas, the classical philologist Maurice Bowra, and the economist Redvers Opie, who taught at Magdalen College. What Adorno and Ryle had in common was their criticisms of Husserl's phenomenology. Both saw in Husserl's thought an antinomian tension between his systemic and anti-systemic intentions, between the realist and idealist elements of epistemology. They agreed that his programme had to be subjected to a comprehensive critique, starting from the internal contradictions in phenomenology. What would have to be shown would be that Husserl had not succeeded in overcoming idealism and empiricism. Adorno was able to move in the direction of analytical philosophy in that he focused on a conceptual analysis of Husserl, forgoing any additional historical explanations.[25] The working title Adorno chose for his study was 'Phenomenological Antinomies: Prolegomena to a Dialectical Theory of Knowledge'. In short, he was preparing to renew his acquaintance with the philosopher whose work he had studied ten years previously for his doctorate. In his dissertation proposal to the board of the faculty of literae humaniores, he emphasized that his aim was neither 'a reproduction of the substance nor a purely negative criticism of Husserl's philosophy'. Instead, he wanted to lay bare the contradictions of phenomenological thought. In particular, he wished to examine such matters as his conception of 'phenomenological attitude' and 'intuitions of essence' (*Wesensschau*), as well as inconsistencies in his conception of ontology.[26]

This renewed study of Husserl was to be undertaken from the vantage point of dialectical and materialist philosophy, rather than in the context of transcendental idealism. Adorno approached the task with great seriousness, and after initial reservations which he reported to Benjamin – not without coquettishness – he became increasingly enthusiastic about the seemingly arid epistemological subject. He spoke to Horkheimer of the 'exciting task of striking the sparks of historical concreteness at the very point where it appears at its most desiccated.'[27] And he wrote to Krenek in Vienna expressing his satisfaction at his success in establishing himself in Oxford:

> Merton College, the oldest and one of the most exclusive here in Oxford, has accepted me as member and advanced student, and I am now living here in indescribable peace and quiet and with very pleasant external working conditions. As to questions of substance, there are difficulties since it is quite impossible to convey my real philosophical interests to the English, and I have to reduce my work to a childish level in order to make it comprehensible at all – which results in a split between the academic and the authentic sphere for which I really feel too old. But I must simply accept things as they are and be happy to be able to work in peace.[28]

What Adorno says in these letters at the beginning of his first term in Oxford is not something he would have said later on, at least not in this disparaging manner, once he had come to know more about philosophy at Oxford and Cambridge. While he was still in Frankfurt he had made a study of English empiricism and also of the Bradley school. He now took the opportunity created by his stay in Oxford to become better acquainted with modern analytical philosophy, in particular that of G. E. Moore, as well as the history of logic. It is not clear how deep his studies went. He did not come into contact with Wittgenstein, who was a fellow of Trinity College, Cambridge. One link with Anglo-Saxon philosophy was the hostility of both materialist philosophy and analytical philosophy to absolute idealism. Adorno did not retreat into his own philosophical ghetto; on the contrary, he followed where his curiosity led. He attended the talks given at the different philosophy societies – the Jowett Society and the Philosophical Society – and took an active part in the discussions.[29] As early as October 1934 he joined the Oxford University Musical Society, whose vice-president was Redvers Opie, and attended the concerts organized by the society which took place in the Holywell Music Rooms. There he heard chamber concerts with works by Bach, Mozart, Stravinsky and Prokofiev, and even a concert of music for guitar given by Andrés Segovia. In the first half of 1935, as a formal member of the society, he brought guests to three concerts. From the well-equipped library of the society he borrowed scores of music by various composers, including Brahms and Ravel. In addition, he made a number of entries in the book where purchases could be recommended, suggesting a whole series of modern composers, including, of course, Schoenberg and Webern, but also Bartók and Debussy.[30]

In the following term Adorno slowly began to find his feet in Oxford, where he was to remain for the following three years. His cosmopolitan outlook made it easier for him to find his way around London, of which he had no previous experience. His reports to Berg make it clear that he soon felt himself more or less at home in Britain, and that he particularly enjoyed alternating between the idyllic small-town life of Oxford and the metropolitan urbanity of London. In spring 1935 Berg declared his intention of coming to London for a performance of *Wozzeck* (although this finally fell through). Adorno promised to show him all the districts that he by then knew quite well, 'from the Whitechapel streets where Jack the Ripper met Lulu, to the best restaurants in Piccadilly, from the Bloody Tower to Hampstead, London's Hietzing.'[31] Even if Adorno increasingly began to feel comfortable with his situation abroad, his memories of the past in Frankfurt would not leave him in peace:

> In London a precise dream from my childhood came true, too late, and almost painfully. The bus conductor kept all the tickets neatly arranged in all conceivable colours on a box, just as Hauff's grocer kept the magic potions; the cheapest are white, and they rose up to a crescendo of colour. In my home town there were only three colours, white, red and the rare green ones. Nothing can be compared to the bliss of playing with them other than to see the nostalgia they evoked so uncertainly and mockingly fulfilled: faced by these tickets I knew that if I had preserved the three colours of my childhood, instead of sacrificing them to the white printing paper, many disasters would have been averted, and if I had tried out the plenitude of colours everything would have been alright. Today, however, it is no more possible for me to salvage anything than it is possible for the London colours to restore the bliss and nostalgia of childhood.[32]

Sticks and carrots

Adorno had barely begun to enjoy the 'indescribable peace and quiet' that would enable him to advance his philosophical work when at the end of October 1934 his tranquillity was disrupted by a letter from Max Horkheimer. What he read evidently opened old wounds. At any rate, it disrupted his secluded existence. He and Horkheimer had not corresponded for months, and they had last met in March 1933. Given this background, the mere fact of a letter postmarked New York was significant. Horkheimer came straight to the point: he wished to give vent to his growing resentment towards Adorno. He reproached him with having failed to communicate for months and for having left him in the dark about his, Adorno's, concrete plans. He then rapidly switched from complaint to praise. 'If there is such a thing as productive relationships between people working in the realm of theory, then the regular collaboration between yourself and the institute must be included among them. It was simply your duty to remain in contact with us. We could not possibly have advised you to leave Germany and come and join us since this was a decision you had to take yourself. We should soon have worked out a modus vivendi.'[33]

Not entirely without a tinge of jealousy, Horkheimer then rebuked Adorno for behaviour he could only have heard about by rumour – presumably from Tillich – and that by no means corresponded to the facts. The accusation was that Adorno had sought advice about his future from Cassirer instead of the institute. In view of this new alliance, Horkheimer refused to publish in the *Zeitschrift für Sozialforschung* a review Adorno had submitted of an introductory text on gestalt psychology by Walter Ehrenstein, least of all under the pseudonym of Charles de Kloës. Horkheimer's letter ended with an appeal. 'There can be no doubt that the absence of communication causes damage to the institute since you necessarily belong among us. And separation will also have a damaging effect on you. I am very sad about both these things.'[34]

These reproaches came to Adorno in a difficult phase of his life when he was attempting to find his feet again. How did he respond? On the model of someone shouting 'Catch the thief!' he had been accused of something he had not done. Moreover, Horkheimer blithely ignored the fact that objectively Adorno was in the weaker position. After all, it was Horkheimer who had remained silent about his plans for the institute. Dependent on his father's support and having no one to turn to in other respects, Adorno had to make his own arrangements for leaving Germany and settling in Britain.

Having left Germany, Horkheimer had engaged in lengthy consultations with Pollock and other institute members in Geneva about the best place to base the work of the institute. Thanks to his political foresight, he had transferred the assets abroad in good time and had also made preparations to establish branches in Geneva, London and Paris. This secured the survival of the institute during the emigration, which was to last close on two decades. Thanks to these new branches and the contacts with European universities they brought with them, Horkheimer was in the fortunate position of having a number of options for the future. Fritz Pollock's colleague Julian Gumperz, an American, was able to establish personal contact with Columbia University, where he encountered great interest, in particular from its president, Nicholas

Murray Butler, as well as the leading sociologists Robert S. Lund and Robert MacIver. This meant that Horkheimer was able to make a speedy decision in favour of moving to the United States. He had been surprised to find that the members of the institute would be made welcome in New York and given the opportunity to pursue their own work.[35] Horkheimer had a visa enabling him to stay in Switzerland without restriction, but Pollock, Löwenthal and Marcuse only had limited tourist visas. In addition, the position of Jewish émigrés in Switzerland was not without complications. For this reason, and above all because he feared the outbreak of a European war, the decision to leave the Continent in favour of New York was relatively straightforward. There they established themselves in their own building on 429 West 117th Street as the 'International Institute of Social Research affiliated with Columbia University'.[36] In the USA, in the context of diminishing financial resources, the institute strove to support émigrés with commissions, scholarships and research projects. From 1936 on, members of the institute, which was concerned to maintain its independence as a research organization, gave lectures and seminars at Columbia University for the first time.[37]

Adorno took less than a week to respond to Horkheimer. In his letter of 2 November he replied in detail to the allegations and complained that all the institute members, and especially Leo Löwenthal, had failed to keep him informed. 'I had no prior warning of your move to New York. Your scorn about my confiding in Cassirer is wide of the mark. He is a conformist fool, as he always has been, and I never asked his advice. His function was to explain my position to the council. I have seen him only once in Oxford and our conversation was restricted to the exchange of detective novels.'[38]

Because the institute had never made Adorno a firm offer, he had felt unable to take the risk of a precipitate departure from Germany, particularly since this might have involved the additional risk of having his passport confiscated. It was clear, he wrote, that Horkheimer had given preference to other associates of the institute. At the end of his letter, Adorno made a small conciliatory gesture, expressing his enthusiasm about Horkheimer's collection of aphorisms with the title of *Dawn and Decline: Notes 1926–1931*, which had just appeared in Zurich under the pseudonym of Heinrich Regius. And he defended his own choice of pseudonym, Charles de Kloës, for his (unpublished) review of Walter Ehrenstein's *Introduction to Gestalt Psychology* (Leipzig, 1934) by saying that he was a fiction: 'He is mentally subnormal, has a relationship with a child and a herd of gazelles.'[39]

In the correspondence that followed during 1934–5, in which both men sought to clear up any misunderstandings, Adorno addressed one issue of great importance to himself: 'the last point that needs to be clarified between us. It is quite simply the question of the confidence and the honesty of the institute in its dealings with me. . . . In a relationship that presupposes genuine solidarity on both sides, it simply will not do for one side to leave the other in the dark about vital matters of concern.'[40] Adorno had reason to suspect that the institute had something like a 'secret policy' in its dealings with him. He was right to feel disconcerted at having been the only person associated with the institute not to have received an offer of assistance in leaving Germany. He knew, he said, that this grudging attitude came not from Horkheimer, but from other members, particularly Pollock and Löwenthal. He criticized the failure to offer him the directorship of the London branch. In order to preserve the collaboration with himself, Horkheimer should not have hesitated 'to throw others out, no matter who, in order to retain him'.[41]

Confronted with Adorno's unreasonable request to be given a firm position in the European organization, Horkheimer simply declared that he had a mistaken idea of the financial resources of the institute. The London branch, for example, was limited to the relatively unattractive position of an assistant lecturer, which had been given to Jay Rumney, a sociologist who helped out with distributing questionnaires and other minor tasks. Horkheimer went on to explain: 'Much of what you complain about, like your ideas about the London office, seems to go back to your rather exaggerated picture of the scale of the institute's operations. We are a group of people striving with our very limited resources to advance theory. The public face of the organization plays no more than a very minor part. You have always overestimated the question of formal inclusion.'[42] Not unreasonably, Horkheimer reproached Adorno with his political blindness. He had cherished illusions about 'your future life in Germany or an academic career elsewhere and so you expected guarantees from the institute in exchange for giving up those prospects. But we could not possibly give any such guarantee.'[43] Nevertheless, he held the door open for Adorno. He suggested that Adorno should once again start to exchange ideas with the institute so as to be better able to form an idea of its current activities. Furthermore, he invited him to come to New York as soon as possible for detailed discussions on research projects and the future of the journal.

For a variety of reasons, this trip to America was put off from one month to the next and then from year to year. Adorno had to return to Germany to sort out the currency problem, and then he had to undergo a complicated piece of surgery of the urinary tract in Frankfurt. Finally, of course, he had his academic obligations in Oxford to attend to. On the other hand, there was a meeting in London in mid-May 1935 with Fritz Pollock which succeeded in clearing the air. Then, early in December, Adorno met Horkheimer briefly in Paris in the Hotel Lutétia, a famous rendezvous for exiles, and then again in Amsterdam for a whole day, when they finally had a lengthy discussion.[44] The last vestiges of disagreement were removed in the course of their talks, with the consequence that they were followed by a lively correspondence about the affairs of the institute, newspaper articles and potential contributors.

Adorno was convinced that in the long run the offer of a firm position at the institute would be made without the need for 'ruthless dismissals from the institute'. By the time he arrived in New York, he would speak 'perfect English', and his 'book on logic would be available to the institute'. With such prospects he could fulfil his intention of 'marrying Gretel, if only to bring her out of that Hell'. He was 'under an obligation to do this'. The cardinal point for Adorno, however, was the ability to work with Horkheimer once again, the only man with whom he was 'in such broad agreement'.[45] Horkheimer confirmed that Adorno could join the institute, but that this could only be done meaningfully once Adorno had completed his study of English.[46] Even before that, however, he was increasingly drawn into the ambit of the institute. After a vacation spent in Berlin and Frankfurt, he travelled to Paris for a week in autumn 1936 on behalf of the institute. There he busied himself with a proposed publication by Gallimard of a French-language volume of Horkheimer's essays, with the title *Essais de philosophie matérialiste*. He also had conversations with various French intellectuals, as well as intensive discussions with Benjamin about work the latter hoped would appear in the *Zeitschrift für Sozialforschung*. Finally, he met Kracauer, reporting back to Horkheimer that Kracauer was 'a hopelessly difficult case',[47] a comment that was exactly the wrong thing to say to Horkheimer in view of Kracauer's desperate circumstances, but clearly shows how he treated his old friend in such a stressful time, namely maliciously. Back in Oxford after his stay in Paris, he finally felt that he had been initiated into the affairs of the institute and that his opinion carried weight. His following letters to Horkheimer were full of proposals for future prospects. These included an analysis of the concept of decadence as well as a larger study of the 'philosophy of National Socialism'. Its aim was to show that 'the Nazis were incapable of producing an ideology and that a theory disguising the truth had been replaced by the most blatant lies.'[48]

An abiding distaste: jazz as a tolerated excess

Adorno took advantage of the tranquillity of life in an English university not just for his Husserl studies, but for other things too. He produced a series of articles on music theory which he published in the Viennese music journal *23*, which was edited by the musicologist Willi Reich.[49] Reich was in contact with Berg, who had designed the title page of the journal. Reich was very eager to recruit Adorno as a regular contributor since the journal was very committed to the promotion of the avant-garde. For the December issue he contributed a brief essay on 'The Form of the Phonograph Record'. His attitude to this technical innovation was not characterized by elitist, culture-critical reservations. On the contrary, he maintained that the phonograph had opened up novel dimensions of music that were not to be obscured by aesthetic objections about reification. Indeed, it was thanks to reification that 'an age-old, submerged and yet warranted relationship has been re-established; that between music and *writing*.'[50] The phonograph deprives music of its immediacy, but gives it the form of a new script that 'will one day become readable as "the last remaining universal language since the construction of the tower [of Babel]".' Thus music relinquishes its being as 'mere sign'. He ended with the speculative question whether works of art find their true language when the 'appearance of liveliness' has abandoned them.[51] In another article, on the 'Crisis of Music Criticism', published in March 1935, an article he later repudiated, he argues that the poor quality of music criticism springs from the fact that contemporary music critics lack the requisite education which neither the study of music at a university nor a musical training at the conservatory can provide. On the other hand, the crisis of music criticism reflects 'the general fundamental fact of alienation' that ensures that critic and composer stand side by side without anything to bind them together. This absence of a relationship cannot be made good by strenuous efforts to build musical communities.[52]

The critical motifs that surfaced in Adorno's article 'On Jazz' can be traced back to his deep-seated aversion to the formation of groups and cliques among artists and those interested in the arts. He wrote the article in his third year in Oxford, in spring 1936, and it was published in the *Zeitschrift für Sozialforschung* under the pseudonym Hektor Rottweiler – not a bad example in itself of the decline of music criticism as a consequence of the critic's own preconceived opinion.[53] Adorno deserves credit, however, for refusing to dismiss the popularizing forms of jazz, i.e., hits and dance music, merely as harmless entertainment and hence to be ignored. Instead, he insists that jazz must be taken seriously as a *fait social*.

Before Adorno, no one had undertaken a sociological analysis of contemporary popular music; no one had thought that the musical structure of jazz had social significance, that it represented the precipitate of social contradictions.[54] Moreover, Adorno did not presume to judge jazz from an elitist standpoint, i.e., he did not condemn popular music by comparing it unfavourably with classical music. He maintained that turning his attention to 'the dregs of the phenomenal world' was an unavoidable necessity. Popular music reflected a dialectical truth. To regard popular music as of secondary importance was to fall into the same trap as the listener who believes that the hit tune provides harmless pleasure. If we think of popular songs as ephemeral products, as mere entertainment and hence sociologically irrelevant, then we ignore the possibility of discerning in the rubble of a declining culture the truth about a society that manifests itself in all commercial products. Adorno's analysis of jazz places the emphasis on 'its social determinants'. His method was that of immanent analysis. He attempted to show that the societal dimension of popularized jazz did not lie in the fact that it was widely played and highly popular in Europe and the USA. Rather, his analysis focused on tracing the social mechanisms at work in the harmonic, melodic, rhythmic and instrumental qualities of the musical sound. He began with a description of what he thought were striking musical characteristics: the simultaneous presence of individual and stereotypical features. This he related to the historical situation of the people who consume commercial music, and it led him to the notion of the 'compulsive consumer' from a standpoint critical of capitalism. By this he wished to suggest that this type of commercial music was 'pseudo-democratic' 'in the sense that it characterizes the consciousness of the epoch; its attitude of immediacy, which can be defined in terms of a rigid system of tricks, is deceptive when it comes down to class differences. As is the case in the current political sphere, so in the sphere of ideology, reaction is the bedfellow of such a democracy.'[55]

In his investigation of what constituted the deceptive nature of light music, Adorno tried to expose its mechanisms. They amounted to a skilful synthesis of salon music and march music: 'the former represents an individuality which in truth is none at all, but merely the socially produced illusion of it; the latter is an equally fictive community which is formed from nothing other than the alignment of atoms under the force that is exerted upon them.'[56] The jazz fan represents a historically specific social type. By consuming the music he enjoys, the individual seems to gain the feeling of emotional mastery that is suggested to him by the use of improvisation. But the ordered pattern of the music's structure as a whole enforces his subordination: 'to obey the law and yet be different. This type of behaviour is taken over, bound up with the gradual abandonment of the traces of playful superiority and liberal difference, by the "*hot*" subject.'[57] Towards the close of his discussion Adorno proposed the daring idea that jazz has an affinity with fascism: 'In Italy it is especially well liked, as is a commercialized version of cubism. The ban against it in Germany has to do with the surface tendency to reach back to pre-capitalist, feudal forms of immediacy and to call these socialism. But, typically, this ban is a powerless one.'[58]

In 'Farewell to Jazz', an essay that appeared in the *Europäische Revue* in 1933, Adorno had stated that the Nazi decree banning jazz was of no importance because jazz was anyway in decline. So how did he explain the fact, three years later, that Goebbels and his comrades were still agitating against a musical genre that was supposed to be intrinsically close to the Nazi view of art? He attempted to show that the Nazi belief that jazz was 'decadent' was racist in nature, that is to say, that jazz was identified as the original black music. In his new essay written in Oxford Adorno tried to prove that, with the growth in its popularity, jazz had now ceased to be an authentic form of black musical expression. This critique turned racist views of jazz on their head.[59] His assumption was that jazz had now joined the mainstream of dance music and light music, and had accordingly been taken over and lost its significance. It would appear then that he had given his essay the wrong title. His subject was not jazz proper, but what jazz had become now that it had been transformed into dance music and light music, following on in the wake of the popularization of blues and ragtime. He was really talking about so-called ballroom jazz, without making it clear just what he was doing. No wonder, then, that he scarcely refers by name to musicians who might be thought to represent jazz proper. Only Duke Ellington receives a mention, and, apart from him, the Revellers, an American group on whom the Comedian Harmonists, a famous pre-war German ensemble, had modelled themselves.

Even if Adorno did not distinguish sharply enough between jazz and popular music, and constantly referred to them in one breath, it must not be supposed that he did not have his own experience of jazz. Both in Frankfurt and in Berlin, as well as on his different travels, he had plenty of opportunity to hear jazz. And after his emigration to Britain he found himself confronted more directly with the different trends in jazz.[60]

Most of the information he needed for his discussion of jazz came from Mátyás Seiber, whom he knew from Frankfurt. Seiber, a Hungarian by birth and a pupil of Kodály, had been in charge of the famous jazz class at the Hoch Conservatory since 1928. In 1933 the class was disbanded by the Nazis, and Seiber emigrated to Britain. There he frequently met Adorno, not least in order to play him jazz records on the gramophone. In addition, he had compiled some handwritten notes about his personal experience with jazz. He sent them simultaneously to Adorno and Horkheimer under the title of 'Observations on the State of the Jazz Market'. Adorno read them in the summer of 1936 and, taking them as confirmation of his own opinions, he suggested that they should establish a 'sociological jazz archive'.[61] He duly acknowledged the suggestions that Seiber made orally and in writing in a preface to the printed version of 'On Jazz'.

The collaboration between Adorno and Seiber was originally intended to be rather broader and longer term,[62] since at their meeting in Paris Horkheimer had encouraged Adorno to undertake a large-scale empirical sociological study of jazz. Horkheimer was doubtless influenced in this by the links he saw between the major studies on *Authority and the Family* that the Institute of Social Research was just in the process of finishing in New York and Adorno's theories about the jazz fan's authority fixation, an idea that was connected in its turn with Erich Fromm's psychoanalytical interpretation of authoritarianism in the bourgeois family.[63] Adorno was delighted to hear Horkheimer suggesting that a larger collective study of jazz would be a good idea. At the end of 1935, as he spent the Christmas holidays partly in Berlin, partly in Frankfurt, he composed a first draft for a large-scale research project: *Jazz: Exposé of a Sociological Study*.[64] This draft contained the first sketch for ideas that he would formulate more precisely in the planned essay 'On Jazz'.

What characterized jazz, he believed, was the use of vibrato as well as the increasing simplification of structural features such as the elimination of improvisation. Jazz had become very popular among all classes and sections of society, he wrote. This made it a suitable means for obscuring class distinctions in the sphere of culture. Jazz had long since become completely commercialized and in this form was distributed by monopolistic concerns in the entertainment industry which endowed it with the specific image of erotic emancipation and a modern lifestyle in general. The model of the jazz enthusiast was 'the eccentric' who used it to dramatize his nonconformism and whose external distinctiveness served to camouflage his adjustment to society's expectations. Adopting a psychoanalytical standpoint, Adorno ventured the astounding thesis that the jazz band represented a paradoxical synthesis of castration machine and copulation machine.[65] He also interpreted the use of syncopation as the expression of premature ejaculation induced by the fear of impotence.[66]

Adorno sent his draft to Horkheimer and also to Seiber, asking the latter for his comments as an expert on the subject. Seiber obliged and in autumn 1936 responded with cautious but unambiguous criticism of Adorno's arguments.[67] He attempted to correct Adorno's caricature of jazz point by point. He rejected Adorno's assertions about the place of particular instruments in the jazz band, singling out the latter's discussion of saxophone players and their alleged musical amateurishness. Nor did he accept the diagnosis that anarchic rhythms were being sacrificed to the demands that the music be danceable or that improvisation was being sacrificed to the arrangement. Nor was the claim tenable that the commercial success of standardized jazz was something that could be largely planned in advance. Lastly, he criticized Adorno for setting up false analogies between psychoanalytical theories and subjective impressions about jazz. He advised Adorno to listen to the latest products of jazz on the radio or gramophone records.

We do not know how Adorno reacted to this criticism of both his draft plan for the research project and his recently published essay 'On Jazz'. Doubtless, he stood by his own view that jazz was a variant of amateur music-making (*Musikantenmusik*), something he rejected even in the sphere of high culture. A few months after reading Seiber's criticisms Adorno wrote to him with the news that Horkheimer and the institute had decided against supporting the planned project on jazz because all the human and financial resources of the institute were committed to bringing the *Studies on Authority and the Family* to a conclusion. He noted that he had in the meantime made various additions to his theory of jazz, but 'without any intention to publish, mainly for our own archive'.[68] These additions consisted of notes that remained unpublished until 1964, when they appeared in the essay collection *Moments Musicaux* with the title 'Oxford Afterthoughts'. From them we can see that Adorno remained unimpressed by Seiber's objections.

He not only retained his negative judgement on jazz but, if anything, he intensified it. His attitude towards jazz now verged on the vitriolic. Thus he could write, with revealing frankness:

> I remember clearly the shock I felt on hearing the word 'jazz' for the first time. It seemed plausible to think that it was related to the German word 'Hatz' [= the hunt] and evoked images of blood-hounds in pursuit of a slower prey. At any rate, the typographic picture seems to contain the same threat of castration as the jazz orchestra with the piano lid gaping wide.[69]

It was evidently no more than a short step from here to establishing a speculative link between jazz and pogroms. He thought that popular jazz pieces contained a mixture of sentimentality and comedy and inferred that this corresponded to 'the reverse side of the fun that turns to cruelty in a pogrom'.[70]

Adorno's essay 'On Jazz' represented his first return to the pages of the *Zeitschrift für Sozialforschung* after a break of four years. On this occasion, too, it was a musicological study that succeeded, in Adorno's own view, in 'effectively decoding jazz and defining its social function'.[71] He gave this confident assessment of his own work to both Benjamin and Krenek. He regarded Krenek as someone 'who has revealed know-ledge concerning the most recherché aspects of music such as I have hardly ever encountered in anyone before.'[72] Nevertheless, Adorno's various essays on jazz play no part in his correspondence with Krenek. This is very striking because Krenek makes use of the idiom of jazz in his opera *Jonny spielt auf*, and would have been the ideal person with whom to discuss it. Although Adorno won't hear anything said against his essay, he seems to have kept quiet about his ideas about jazz in his dealings with Krenek.

Setbacks ...

As with the earlier essay on 'The Social Situation of Music', in this instance too Adorno had chosen to appear in the *Zeitschrift für Sozialforschung* with a contribution on the sociology of music. He was particularly anxious to avoid being labelled as no more than an expert on music, and so was very concerned to have a critique of Karl Mannheim's sociology of knowledge published, an essay he had revised and improved a number of times during his last two years in Oxford. He had hoped that this essay would establish him as a social theorist. His Husserl studies should help him to obtain an English degree, but over and above that they should demonstrate his qualifications as an academic philosopher. He was therefore bitterly disappointed when Horkheimer declined to print either the essay on Mannheim or a longer piece on

Husserl. To his annoyance the editorial discussions about the two pieces in New York dragged on for months. His incisive and principled critique of Mannheim's 'sociologism' was finally rejected by the institute for what were said to be 'tactical' reasons. The Husserl essay too was rejected, even though Horkheimer described it as 'a huge intellectual achievement'. But he went on to say that it assumed too much knowledge to be comprehensible to the readers of the *Zeitschrift*. He explained the reasons for his rejection in a lengthy letter in October 1936:

> None of your efforts to demonstrate the impossibility of categorial intuition is really compelling. . . . Whether and to what extent you have really done justice to the different strata of phenomenology, both static and dynamic, and to the levels of meaning in Husserl's analyses does not emerge clearly from your essay, if only because it does not begin with an explicit exposition of the theories that you are attacking. . . . Try as I might to immerse myself in your arguments, I find myself unable to confirm your passionate belief that an attack on Husserl's phenomenology as the most advanced form of bourgeois philosophy is also to refute the most important intellectual motifs leading to idealism.[73]

Having failed to deliver proof of his competence as both a sociologist and a philosopher, Adorno fell into a depression, and he reacted with some irritation to the fact of two rejections in such a brief period of time. He reminded Horkheimer that merely from the point of view of 'husbanding his energies' it was scarcely thinkable that he could simply stuff the two essays into a drawer and forget about them. They had after all cost him a huge effort. In terms of their content both essays were important for the institute's sociological programme: the Mannheim article because it had succeeded in providing a definitive account of the limitations of the sociology of knowledge and the Husserl essay because it had 'embarked in earnest on a critique of idealism'.[74] This very confident account of his intentions referred in the first instance to the extended version that Adorno had produced for the *Zeitschrift für Sozialforschung*: a comprehensive treatise over one hundred printed pages in length, and written in a very enigmatic style. Had it been printed it would have had to be serialized over a number of issues of the *Zeitschrift*. Moreover, this essay was the shorter version of what Adorno called his major book on Husserl that had grown over time to over four hundred typewritten pages.[75] This immersion in Husserl's *Formal and Transcendental Logic* and his *Cartesian Meditations* was the means to an end in Adorno's mind. He thought of it as 'a kind of critical, dialectical prelude to a materialist logic'.[76]

Given this specific aim, how did Adorno approach Husserl's phenomenology? He made no attempt to expose logical inconsistencies in Husserl, but discussed his philosophy as measured against the idea of dialectics. His starting-point was Husserl's claim that phenomenology belonged in the tradition of a 'first philosophy', by which was meant a philosophy founded on the premise of a hierarchical 'schema of a first thing which supports everything and from which everything else was derived'.[77] He accused Husserl of attempting to explain the entire universe by positing an originatory principle that was based purely on thought.[78] At the same time, he objected to the legacy of an idealism that placed the subject at the centre of attention. Even if Husserl's idea of an intentional consciousness established a new foundation for the subject–object relation, 'the subject–object remained a subject in disguise.'[79] Adorno went so far as to criticize the entire philosophical tradition since Descartes for having always posited an unalterable ultimate ground. In the process 'the return of subject and object within subjectivity and the duality of the one is detailed in two types of epistemology, each of which lives on the unrealizability of the other. Roughly speaking, these types are those of rationalism and empiricism.'[80]

Husserl's critique is basically a half measure. 'The concept of immanence sets limits to an immanent critique.'[81] In contrast, dialectics not only negates the unity of thing and consciousness, but proves that 'the real life process of society . . . is the core of the contents of logic itself.'[82] Approaching Husserl from a materialist standpoint, this statement is the culmination of Adorno's chief objections to his epistemology. Dialectics is the only possible alternative to phenomenology. Only dialectical thinking is able to lay bare the mediated nature of the phenomenal world and hence to define the ways in which preformed social factors determine contingent individual experience. This conception of dialectics should not be thought of as 'a positive assertion about being', but rather as 'a directive to cognition not to comfort itself with such positivity. It is really the demand to arbitrate dialectic concretely.'[83] Dialectics does not reject epistemology in general, but protests against a monistic view of knowledge that is derived from the principle of identity and that claims to be free from contradiction and therefore true. Knowledge totalized in this way, Adorno claims, is a 'fetishism of knowledge'.[84]

In his critique of Husserl, Adorno constantly referred to the history of philosophy in order to show that phenomenology stands in a tradition and that it clings to ultimate explanations. As far as Husserl's theory of the constitution of consciousness was concerned, he accepted the proposition that the limits of consciousness are revealed *a priori*. But where phenomenology comes to speak of 'the matter itself', its concepts degenerate into 'a fiction' behind which 'the route to facticity is obstructed'.[85] This is also expressed in the language of phenomenology, with its 'metaphorical, *art nouveau*, ornamental' quality. 'The aura of the concrete accrues to the concepts' even though they are no more than 'the labels of pure consciousness'.[86] To illustrate the illusory nature of the 'intuition of essences' (*Wesensschau*), Adorno used the image of the 'old-style photographer . . . who is mysteriously hidden beneath a black cloth and who with the incantatory formula that everyone should keep still produces family pictures of the kind that are found in the collection of examples to be encountered in pure phenomenology.'[87]

With its monadological vision of man, Adorno concludes, Husserl's phenomenology remains trapped within idealism. This conception of the subject as a closed windowless entity 'could only ever be sublated if consciousness could succeed in exercising dominion over being, since hitherto its perennial assertion that being was grounded in consciousness had always been untrue.'[88]

In this critique, as in the Mannheim essay, Adorno wrote from a materialist standpoint in which historical forms of consciousness were analysed in relation to economic modes of production. In a letter to Horkheimer in December 1935 he admitted that, the more he 'burrowed into questions of logic, the more "orthodox" my views become. In principle, I am convinced that the entire subjective philosophy of immanence is really the expression of a property-owning consciousness . . . I can scarcely doubt that our entire logic . . . has been built on the model of legal norms that are designed to protect particular relations of production.'[89]

Even before Adorno had formulated his variously framed criticisms of phenomenology he had started to make notes for a particular book project. Once again, he had the idea from Horkheimer, albeit indirectly. Under the powerful impression made on him by *Dawn and Decline*, Horkheimer's book of aphorisms, he had begun himself to collect fragments of the same type.[90] Horkheimer's aphorisms dealt in an unsystematic way with questions of morality, character, metaphysics and the workers' movement. The title alludes to the demise of the liberal, bourgeois age and the beginning of totalitarianism, the threatened 'night of mankind'.[91] From a social point of view, the book was written in a spirit of a humanist socialism that would hopefully lead to a rational organization of society once economic exploitation had been eliminated and human potential set free. Typical of Horkheimer's outlook is his statement that 'A premium has been placed on vileness'.[92]

Once he had started to become more aware of the implications of being an émigré, Adorno began to make notes about it. He had already experimented with the aphorism in his music reviews. He now set about making use of it to reflect on his own experience. As he remarked in a letter to Horkheimer in February 1935, 'I cannot be accused of mincing my words.' He announced a 'volume of aphorisms that treats the situation in which fascism has *taken over*. The title: The Good Comrade. . . . No one knows of the existence of this volume apart from yourself. It is already very far advanced.'[93] This is the first mention of what was to become his most successful book decades later. He had evidently been considering a collection of aphorisms from the mid-1930s. Ten years later, the volume which he published with the title of *Minima Moralia* had swelled and contained a number of sections. It contained one aphorism, 'The Bad Comrade', that was dated 1935. The title alluded to Ludwig Uhland's poem 'The Good Comrade'. In it he interpreted his experience at the Gymnasium in Frankfurt as an anticipation of the brutality of the totalitarian state. Other fragments referred to his life in Oxford. One, 'Tough Baby', contains the observation that 'the ideal form of human relations is the club, that arena of a respect founded on scrupulous unscrupulousness.' In Oxford, he wrote, 'two sorts of students are distinguished, the tough guys and the intellectuals; the latter, through this contrast alone, are almost automatically equated with the effeminate. There is much reason to believe that the ruling stratum, on its way to dictatorship, becomes polarized towards these two extremes.'[94] Similarly, the fact that intellectuals in emigration found themselves in the position of 'competing petitioners' alludes to situations in which Adorno found himself in Britain. As things turned out, his intention of writing a book of aphorisms could not be carried out while he was still in Oxford. This was not simply because of the burden of his academic duties or his writing commitments. In addition, during his first year in emigration in Britain he had to endure two emotional upsets that could not fail to impinge on his writing plans.

... and personal losses

During the months in which Adorno made his entries in the usual coloured notebooks in order to record his personal experiences of being outlawed from his native country and an outsider abroad, news reached him in Oxford that his 'second mother' had fallen seriously ill with a stroke. He at once returned home to his family in Frankfurt and was able to see his Aunt Agathe, who was sixty-six years old, while she was still alive. He had of course been kept informed about the state of her health. He knew that she had had a mild stroke back in May while she was with the family in Amorbach, and that she had partly lost the power of her speech. After she had suffered subsequent heart failure and further brain damage, Adorno's parents told him about the seriousness of her condition. When he finally arrived in Frankfurt his aunt was 'quite incapacitated and both depressed and confused almost the whole time'. He told Horkheimer that he had stayed with her constantly. 'Her death (on 26 June) was caused by pneumonia, which normally follows the paralysis of the respiratory and swallowing functions.'[95]

The notice of her death that appeared in the *Frankfurter Zeitung* on 1 July 1935 gives some idea of what Agathe Calvelli-Adorno meant to the family. 'Words cannot express what she gave us from the strength and depths of her being in a life full of kindness.' The cremation took place quietly; the Wiesengrund family asked people to refrain from making visits to offer their condolences. For Adorno the death of his aunt meant the painful loss of a person to whom he perhaps had a closer, more trusting relationship than to anyone else. This sense of loss emerges clearly from a letter to Ernst Krenek in response to his letter of condolence. 'I cannot tell you what her loss means to me', he wrote to Krenek, 'not so much the death of a relative as that of the person closest to me, my most faithful friend, a part of nature. Contact with her always brought me new life. I feel utterly stricken and can only gradually begin to contemplate going on with my life. This sounds like a wild overstatement, but you can take it from me that it does not contain a grain of exaggeration or sentimentality.'[96] A few days after the cremation, Adorno went with his mother and Gretel Karplus to spend three weeks in the Hotel Bär, near Hornberg, in the Black Forest, in order to recover from this experience so far as was possible. Reduced to the defective typewriter he found in the hotel, he nevertheless wrote a lengthy letter to Walter Benjamin in which he gave a critical response to the exposé Benjamin had sent him of his planned work on the Paris arcades. In addition, he wrote a short, linguistically diffuse essay on Gustav Mahler which, despite its defects, appeared in May 1936, in the Viennese music journal *23*.[97] In the opening sentence he managed to bring his own highly personal experience of the death of someone he loved to bear on a profound analysis of Mahler's *Kindertotenlieder*. Like every memory, the musical memory of a person who had recently died was said to be 'directed towards the preservation of what was possible, but had not happened'. What marked out Mahler's symphonies was the tendency to smash everything to pieces and at the same time the free constructive use of the theme as musical material. In addition, he stressed the element of reconciliation within a state of hopelessness. For this reason, 'every piece of Mahler's, from the "Wayfarer's Songs" to the "Ninth Symphony" ... was a farewell gesture.'[98] This essay, which deals principally with the *Kindertotenlieder*, shows how keenly Adorno felt the death of his Aunt Agathe and perceived it as a turning point in his life. Six months later, he was confronted by the sudden death of Alban Berg. This was a new catastrophe, all the more painful because it affected his sense of his own identity as a composer and musicologist. He knew from Berg's letters that the latter had spent the summer in his beloved 'forest house' in Auen on the Wörthersee, and that there he had developed an abscess which he had tried to cure himself without consulting a doctor.[99] The need to save money seems to have been the reason for his reluctance to seek professional medical help. For he had found himself in increasingly 'wretched material circumstances', as he explained to Adorno,[100] as a consequence of the discriminatory policies of the Nazis. After the Nazi takeover, Berg's music had been banned as 'degenerate'. It was for this reason that Wilhelm Furtwängler refused to conduct the world premiere of his new opera *Lulu* in Berlin.[101]

Whatever made Berg decide not to consult a doctor, his negligence was to have bitter consequences. According to Soma Morgenstern,

Helene Berg 'sterilized a pair of scissors in boiling water and lanced and drained the abscess herself'.[102] A few days after this reckless action the first symptoms of blood poisoning appeared. During the night of 17 December 1935, Berg had to be admitted to the Rudolf hospital. The blood transfusions he received there were in vain. His superstitious hope that his condition would improve by the 23rd was disappointed.[103] 'About ten minutes after midnight, Helene Berg, her face distorted with grief, came out with her sister, wringing her hands, while her sister stood on the steps and announced [to Berg's many friends who had gathered]: "It is finished".'[104] In the early afternoon of 28 December Alban Berg, whose death mask had already been taken by Anna Mahler, was buried in the cemetery in Hietzing. Only a few months before, he had celebrated his fiftieth birthday. His second great opera, *Lulu*, a musical adaptation of Frank Wedekind's tragedies *Earth-Spirit* and *Pandora's Box* (a subject Adorno and, separately, Morgenstern had drawn his attention to), remained unfinished.[105] Berg had completed the composition, but had left the orchestration unfinished; the third act existed in part only as a short score. In the year of his death Berg had completed the Violin Concerto, a commission from the violinist Louis Krasner which would now become his requiem. According to Adorno, on their walks together, the composer had anticipated his own death with a kind of playful self-irony by imagining different obituaries that remember him as an 'indigent, but significant composer'.

Having returned from Oxford, Adorno was spending the Christmas holidays in Frankfurt when he learned of Berg's tragic death from Ernst Krenek. 'I cannot tell you how this last blow has affected me', he wrote to his friend in Vienna. In view of the grotesque chain of events in which a relatively harmless illness had led to sudden death, he found the thought unbearable that

> material circumstances were to blame for Berg's death. We must think of it in very concrete terms: if he had not wanted to save on doctor's fees, he would certainly have gone to consult one, particularly since he tended to be rather over-anxious by nature. The fact that he did not venture to do so and that he had to weigh up the cost is what resulted in his death. The idea that the life of a productive force like Berg depends on such considerations is enough to drive one to the most radical conclusions about existing society.[106]

The fact that Berg 'succumbed to an illness he misjudged and neglected, that he preferred not to see the danger or considered it exorcized by the date of the 23rd, the fateful number of his eccentric mysticism, that was the final melancholic subterfuge of an existence that for a half-century (as the subterfuge of a desperate man) had been able to maintain itself in music between sleep and death.'[107]

In his letter to Krenek, Adorno referred to their joint knowledge of 'the darkest secret' associated with Berg's death. He recalled the confidential conversations of summer 1935 in Oxford when Krenek was spending some time in Britain.[108] In his reply in January 1936, Krenek responded to Adorno's allusion, relating this secret to *Lulu*. He spoke of the fateful nature of female beauty and its seductive power, the destructive force of the femme fatale. 'She was created', he said by way of summarizing the Prologue of the opera, 'to bring disaster, to entice, to seduce, to poison – and to murder, without its being noticed.'

The secret surrounding Berg's death was the criticism that Morgenstern voiced three decades later, that it was partly Helene Berg's fault that her husband had contracted blood poisoning after her home-made operation with the pair of scissors.[109] The other secret was the long-lasting and passionate love affair between Berg and Hanna Fuchs, a sister of Franz Werfel, who had been married to the Prague industrialist Herbert Fuchs-Robettin since 1917. The affair had been marked by the lovers' self-denial, and this had resulted in great unhappiness. Berg had left his secret mistress a meticulously annotated printed copy of his *Lyric Suite*, dedicated to her. This was a piece of music he had composed for her in 1925–6. In the passionate letters Berg wrote to her between 1925 and 1934 he expressed his growing despair at their being prevented from living their love for each other. In a letter in December 1928, he wrote: 'And I feel ever more clearly, particularly in recent times, how I am going downhill. In every respect! Or at least in all those respects that might make life bearable for the likes of us. It would be unnatural were it otherwise: we know precisely when my life came to an end – to obtain a continuation by force was no more than an experiment.'[110]

According to Krenek, this secret love was already embedded in motifs in *Wozzeck*, but it became much more pronounced in *Lulu*. With Berg's death it stood revealed: it was the impossibility of living a life based on renunciation. Berg had spoken frankly enough in this letter to Hanna of the hopelessness of his situation. He writes, for example, that he is lying 'buried'[111] in his flat in Trauttmannsdorffgasse. Both Adorno and Krenek were familiar with these gloomy moods.[112] Both were convinced that, in addition to the *Lyric Suite*, both the great operas represent in different ways Berg's attempts to express his loneliness and despair. For example, Adorno's first discussion in 1936 of the *Lulu* Symphony in the music journal *23* refers to the retrograde form of the ostinato: 'Time passes and revokes itself and nothing points beyond it but the gesture of those who love without hope.'[113]

When Adorno started to come to terms with his loss of a teacher and a friend, he did so, needless to say, in the form of a written reminiscence of Berg as a man as well as an interpretation of his music. Scarcely had he started this process than he wrote to Krenek with a remarkably aggressive justification of his highly personal obituary of Berg.[114] He addressed himself to Krenek, who was one of those responsible for the special issue of the journal planned by Willi Reich, because in Adorno's eyes he was the fittest judge and one he could respect. Because he felt so secure in his own love for Berg, and because he did not for a second doubt Berg's importance as a composer and music dramatist, he believed he could 'seek out the dead man's flaws'. 'Not', as he observes in the letter, 'in order to defend them, but because there is no love that does not dwell in these flaws, and also because the memory should be so true that one can be conscious of it at every moment without feeling shame, that is to say, in the face of those flaws. To name the flaws of a human being one loves is the last act of love one can perform for him.'[115] This was actually a superfluous justification anticipating the possibility that his obituary might be criticized for its 'lack of enthusiasm and panegyric'. He then referred once again to that 'darkest secret' about which he and Krenek both knew, but which they wished not to disclose. For, apart from the assertion that the composition of musical time in the *Lulu* Symphony was to be deciphered as a 'gesture of those who love without hope', Adorno's two essays in *23* contained only a few obscure allusions to the difficult years Berg had spent torn between despair and the hope of fulfilment. Not until later did he analyse the relationship developed in the opera between Alwa Schön (who bears some resemblance to Berg) and Lulu. Alwa's forbidden love for Lulu, who was married to his father, was the vantage point from which he 'surrenders to that love just as the doomed artist surrenders to the beautiful woman'.[116]

Adorno was much more explicit about Berg's passionate affair in a letter he wrote to Berg's widow, but not until he had allowed over four months to pass. He talked there, in a series of sophistical phrases, about the poetic inspiration that underlay the *Lyric Suite*.[117] As Adorno wrote to Helene Berg, he felt unable to ignore this in his interpretation. The tone of his letter reveals his discomfort. Even so, this does not prevent him from interpreting the Second String Quartet as 'a virtuoso work of despair'. As in the two great operas, *Wozzeck* and *Lulu*, the 'musical protagonist' of the *Lyric Suite* 'cannot master the alien world through love'.[118] To characterize the Allegro misterioso of the third movement, he evokes a poetic association: it is 'a breathless timbral poem', composed for the most part '*sul ponticello* or *col legno*'. 'Those who love poetic associations may be reminded of a desperately passionate scene in suppressed whispers, which erupts but once, only to revert again to feverish whispering.'[119] In the lengthy letter in which Berg confessed to Hanna Fuchs that the *Lyric Suite* was the expression of their love, he explained that the Allegro misterioso depicted 'the mysterious, whispered nature of our meetings, into which the Trio estatico brings the first, short eruption.'[120] There is some evidence that Berg told his pupil about his musical intentions here and that Adorno had made use of this knowledge later on.

In his letter to Helene Berg, Adorno revealed to her that he had been initiated into her late husband's secret from the beginning. Possibly by way of offering consolation, he maintained, against his better knowledge, that Berg had needed unquenchable yearning 'to enable him to compose the *Lyric Suite*, and not that he had composed the *Lyric Suite* for the sake of love.'[121] Finally, he even presumed to claim that the love affair with Hanna was no more than 'a romantic mistake'. Hanna Fuchs (whom he referred to in the letter only as H. F.) 'was a bourgeoise through and through who once in her life was touched by the possibility of being different, without being able to take advantage of it.'[122] At the end of his letter, he even gave Helene Berg a piece of advice; she should resist her inclination to give Hanna the original score of the *Lyric Suite*. The score must not be degraded to the status of a 'museum piece'; it should not be 'sacrificed' for 'the wrong reasons'; it was 'too good to be used to gratify the narcissism of a woman bored to death'.[123] The letter makes it plain that Adorno was very concerned both to maintain a relationship with Helene Berg and to present himself as a person worthy of her trust. He did not do this without an ulterior motive.

What he had in mind at the time was finding a suitable composer to take over the task of completing the orchestration of the missing parts of *Lulu*. He was obviously right to think that its fragmentary nature prevented this masterpiece of a music drama taking its rightful place in the opera houses of the world. And because an opera was no 'sacred text' it must be possible for a composer intimately familiar with Berg's composing style to complete the score in the spirit of its creator. Thus Adorno was preoccupied with the question of how best to proceed. With this in mind, he immersed himself in Berg's works with increasing intensity. 'I am studying with him for the second time', he wrote to Krenek from Oxford.[124] As he said, this was one way of trying to overcome his grief. 'Through work I am slowly coming to terms with Berg's death', he wrote to his friend in Vienna in February 1936.[125] Nevertheless, the sense of loss would not go away. For in May 1936 he had heard the Berg memorial concert broadcast in which the Violin Concerto was performed with Louis Krasner as soloist and Anton Webern conducting. A year later Adorno wrote to Horkheimer with reflections about death and 'Catholic hopes of an afterlife'. In reply to Horkheimer's criticism of Christian teachings, he expressed the view 'that he could not conceive of the death and irretrievable loss of loved ones without hope for those' who suffered an injustice, the greatest of which is death.[126]

The idea of publishing a monograph on Berg with a collection of Berg's own writings was one that came from Willi Reich. It was intended that Adorno and Krenek should contribute analytical essays. Adorno was more than willing to contribute to a book that would champion Berg's oeuvre.[127] Despite his many commitments, he set about this additional task and wrote the major part of the essays that appeared in Vienna in 1937 in the volume edited by Reich.[128] Altogether there were eight analyses of Berg's compositions, and, since his intention was to show the complexity of Berg's works, his contributions were anything but introductory. He had maliciously suggested to Krenek that the book should 'on no account be redolent of that panegyric stable-atmosphere that generally deprives monographs of all their value.'[129] He was more concerned, he said, to render Berg's oeuvre transparent by a variety of methodological approaches that would make the 'reverse tendencies' in Berg's music clear.

If we bear in mind the large number of very different intellectual tasks that Adorno completed up to the middle of 1936, despite the loss of two people who were so important to him, it is difficult to believe that his Underwood typewriter was ever allowed any respite. It is easy to sympathize with his complaint to Horkheimer, 'I am completely exhausted by my efforts of the last three months.'[130] He also complained to Benjamin in a postcard written in January 1936 'from an extremely dark café in the very heart of the city [of London] surrounded by domino-playing characters – a little place that I would love to disclose to you alone.'[131] He had every reason to complain, if only because of the diversity of the texts he had to work on and wanted to or had to complete at more or less the same time. And over and above all this publishing activity, there was an ever-increasing burden of correspondence that claimed his attention, particularly at this point in time.

13

Writing Letters as an Aid to Philosophical Self-Clarification: Debates with Benjamin, Sohn-Rethel and Kracauer

While Adorno was complaining about the excessive burden of work that admittedly he had largely brought upon himself, he did everything in his power to help Walter Benjamin, who was in very difficult material circumstances in exile in Paris. Since 1934 the person Adorno was closest to intellectually had been just surviving at a minimal existence level, forced to live in simple rooms in cheap hotels.[1] Adorno made strenuous efforts to present the facts of Benjamin's case to the director of the Institute of Social Research with a view to ameliorating his material situation. He also enlisted the support of close friends, such as Else Herzberger, a wealthy businesswoman who had been friendly with the Wiesengrund family for many years. She had shown an interest in helping out émigré intellectuals and artists financially. Gretel Karplus, too, did what she could from Berlin.

The regular payments made to Benjamin by the institute from 1934 on were tied to particular research and publication projects. This relationship soon developed into a definite collaboration. One such project, a piece of work Benjamin kept postponing, was a study of Eduard Fuchs, the historian of manners and morals. Of the greatest importance, however, was his study of the Paris arcades,[2] which he had planned as a prehistory of the nineteenth century. Paris was to be the place where Benjamin – bowing to external constraints – intended to bring his Arcades Project to completion.[3] One step in this direction was to produce a detailed exposé of the contents of the study for the Institute of Social Research. The early study that Benjamin had begun in the 1920s together with the Berlin writer Franz Hessel had borne the working title 'A Dialectical Fairyland'. The more recent, sociologically based project was entitled 'Paris: Capital of the Nineteenth Century'. When Adorno learnt in a letter that Benjamin intended the new project on the arcades to be carried out from a historical and sociological perspective, he objected that much more was expected of him, namely a 'philosophical theory' which 'can only find its own dialectic in the polarity between social and theological categories'.[4] Adorno suspected that restricting the Arcades Project to a sociological analysis represented a concession to Horkheimer's expectations and those of the institute, on which Benjamin depended financially. In his letter to Benjamin in May 1935 Adorno had insisted: 'I regard your work on the "arcades" as the centre not merely of your own philosophy, but as the decisive philosophical word which must find utterance today; as a chef d'oeuvre like no other, and as so decisive in every sense . . . that any weakening of the innermost claims of this work, and any consequent repudiation of its own peculiar categories, would strike me as catastrophic.'[5] The categories with which to interpret such social phenomena as the arcade or the department store can be gleaned only from the immanent analysis of the material, not through the adoption of pre-given categories. There was a danger, he maintained, that 'the Marxian concepts would prove to be too abstract and isolated from one another, functioning merely as *dei ex machina*.'[6] Adorno frankly admitted that he had discovered this defect in his own work. Perhaps he was thinking of his early essay 'On the Social Situation of Music', which was grounded in part in the orthodox Marxian scheme of superstructure and base. Now, he said, he was convinced that 'we hold on all the more effectively to the real, the more thoroughly and consistently we remain true to the aesthetic origins, and that we only become merely aesthetic when we deny the latter.'[7]

In the beginning of June, Adorno first obtained the draft of the exposé of the Arcades Project which Benjamin had written at Pollock's instigation. His reaction was somewhat reserved. This exposé contained an overview in six brief sections of the themes and subjects that Benjamin wished to explore in the new book he was planning. This was his first attempt to bring some order into countless quotations and reflective commentaries that he had been collecting for years. As he himself remarked, his point of reference was the Marxian category of the 'fetish character of the commodity'.[8] He now regarded this as the key concept with which to decode the effects of the capitalist economy – 'the enthronement of the commodity'[9] – on traditional culture. Benjamin planned to analyse the commodity regarded as exchange value at the site at which commodities were revered as fetishes: the shop windows in the arcades and the temples of the Parisian department stores. He wished to make clear that in these places the exchange values of the commodity were elevated into cultural goods. The description of the 'phantasmagoria which a person enters in order to be distracted'[10] was what Benjamin wanted to elaborate in his philosophy of history of the collective wish image. In wish images like these the collective sought 'both to overcome and to transfigure the immaturity of the social product and the inadequacies of the social organization of production.'[11] Precisely because they both overcame and transfigured, Benjamin thought of these wish images as dialectical. Ambiguity, which is in general the mark of the epoch, 'is the manifest imaging of dialectic, the law of dialectics at a standstill. This standstill is utopia and the dialectical image, therefore, dream image. Such an image is afforded by the commodity per se: as fetish.'[12]

Once Adorno had worked his way through these and other, occasionally enigmatic, statements in the exposé early in July, he wrote down his criticisms and reservations during August 1935 while he was holidaying in the Black Forest. In this letter, which has become known as the Hornberg letter, his tone remained as friendly as ever, but he nevertheless found fault with the way in which Benjamin had introduced the idea of the dialectical image, namely as the reflection of commodity fetishism in the collective consciousness. Adorno insisted that the fetishism of the commodity, i.e., the phenomenon that social relations between people are experienced as relations between things, is 'not a fact of consciousness', 'but dialectical in character in the eminent sense that it produces consciousness. But, if so, then neither consciousness nor unconsciousness can simply replicate it as a dream.' Even more sharply, he rejected the way in which Benjamin had adapted the concept of the collective consciousness for his own purposes. This 'idea . . . was invented to distract attention from true objectivity, and from alienated subjectivity as its correlate.'[13]

We can see how much store Adorno set by clarifying the concept of the commodity in line with the economic meaning that Marx had given to it from the fact that he had homed in on this sore point in his very first preliminary comment on the exposé on 5 June. The concept of the commodity was 'too generally expressed' by Benjamin 'if it is supposed to disclose something *specific* about the character of the nineteenth century; and it is not really enough to define the category in purely technological terms – in terms of "fabrication", say.'[14] Nor did Adorno spare Benjamin in his explanation of the way in which the old and the new interpenetrate. To link 'the archaic' with 'the classless society' was 'undialectical'. It must be remembered that, 'as illusion and phantasmagoria, the newest is itself the old.' 'Thus the category in which the archaic fuses with the modern seems to me more like a catastrophe than a Golden Age.'[15] Adorno did not share Benjamin's speculative idea that mankind would wake to a future history as soon as the economic foundations of the nineteenth century had been swept away. Thus Adorno did not hold back in his criticism of the exposé which Benjamin had revised several times, but did not publish during his lifetime in either its French or its German-language version.[16]

Adorno was no less blunt in his criticism of another of his friend's essays. This was 'The Work of Art in the Age of Technological Reproducibility', which, together with the studies of Baudelaire, was intended to form part of the future Arcades Project. The essay on 'The Work of Art' was one Benjamin had completed in the course of these last months[17] when Adorno had been working on his jazz essay and on the seven contributions to the book on Alban Berg. This suggests that Benjamin and Adorno may be said to have been asking the same type of question, albeit from different points of view. They were both interested in the changing relations of form and content in the different manifestations of modern art, its production and reception in post-bourgeois society.[18] Whereas Benjamin, in exile in Paris, hoped to 'uncover the hidden structures in contemporary art',[19] the thoughts of Adorno, who was studying in Oxford, were driven by the fear that the aesthetic achievements of the radical avant-garde would fall victim to the integrating mechanisms of mass culture.

At the centre of Benjamin's analysis of the relation between art and technical reproduction stood the concept of aura, the chief characteristic of traditional art.[20] With the mass reproduction of pictures made possible by the invention of photography and film, traditional art loses its original auratic quality.

> What withers in the age of technological reproducibility of the work of art is the latter's aura. This process is symptomatic; its significance extends far beyond the realm of art. It might be stated as a general formula that *the technology of reproduction detaches the reproduced object from the sphere of tradition. By replicating the work many times over, it substitutes a mass existence for a unique existence. And in permitting the reproduction to reach the recipient in his or her own situation, it actualizes that which is reproduced.* These two processes lead to a massive upheaval in the domain of objects handed down from the past – a shattering of tradition which is the reverse side of the present crisis and renewal of mankind.[21]

The point of Benjamin's argument was that it enabled him to perceive a positive benefit in 'the liquidation of the traditional value of the cultural heritage'. He welcomed, therefore, 'the destruction of aura' and the related failure of 'the criterion of authenticity to be applicable to artistic production'.[22] Because the work of art in its transition from the nineteenth to the twentieth century is determined by its 'exhibition value', a change is engineered in the social function of the entire realm of aesthetics. Its theological orientation towards ritual is replaced by the revolutionary task of liberating the suppressed creative potential of the masses. Taking the example of the montage technique used in the avant-garde silent film, Benjamin tried to show that, with the historical change in the production and reception of art, art could become an instrument of political revolution for the first time in history. In the 'simultaneous collective experience' of the film, in its 'collective laughter', the audience organizes and controls itself. Through constant practice it becomes expert. According to Benjamin, the emancipatory effect of a mass art stripped of its aura is a weapon against the fascist 'aestheticization of politics', which he opposed by positing the 'politicization of art'.[23]

Benjamin conceived of these arguments as a kind of pendant to 'Paris: Capital of the Nineteenth Century'.[24] Adorno was far from happy with the result. He had had an original German version and a French translation of the essay on his desk ever since March 1936. He responded in the same month with a long letter containing a fundamental critique. It was unacceptable to transfer the 'magic aura' to 'the autonomous work of art' by way of definition. Instead, the autonomous work of art compounds within itself the magical element with the 'sign of freedom'.[25] The element of freedom in art, however, consists 'in the pursuit of the technical laws of art' from which its character as a construct results. For Adorno, it was a failure of dialectical thinking when Benjamin equated aura and autonomous art 'to which it then flatly assigned a counter-revolutionary function.'[26] Adorno had no time for the assertion that the allegedly emancipatory effect of the film could help the proletariat to become conscious of its position as a potential historical subject and that this would prevent it from becoming bourgeoisified – a process which in his view was long since complete. 'The laughter of the cinema audience', he told Benjamin, 'is anything but salutary and revolutionary; it is full of the worst bourgeois sadism.'[27] The idea that 'a reactionary individual can be transformed into a member of the avant-garde through an intimate acquaintance with the films of Chaplin strikes me as simple romanticization.'[28] Even a film like *Modern Times* was far from being an avant-garde film. On the contrary, its effects were derived from the auratic illusion that is created by mass culture in general. This reference to mass culture points to elements of an argument that Adorno had developed with greater precision in the essay on jazz that he wrote around the same time. In ten years' time, these arguments would blossom into his fully fledged theory of the culture industry.

At a number of points in his letter Adorno warned Benjamin to beware of the dangers of falling too much under the influence of Bertolt Brecht. He was worried both about Brecht's interpretation of Marxism and about the way in which Brecht insisted on the political nature of drama. A dialectical conception of art and mass culture – 'a dialectic between the extremes' – could be arrived at only 'by the elimination of Brechtian motifs'.[29] The way in which Benjamin tried to combine Marx's materialism with a philosophical messianism appeared fundamentally suspect to Adorno. He classified Benjamin's materialism as 'anthropological' and imputed to Benjamin the belief that 'the human body represents the measure of all concreteness'. Adorno felt 'unable to accept' such an undialectical ontology of the body.[30]

The correspondence between 1935 and 1936 testifies to the intensity of the discussions between Adorno and Benjamin. They suggest that the younger man was attempting to define himself against the older one, and to discover his own independent position. This independence was evidently fostered by his prolonged exploration of Husserl's phenomenology, his renewed study of Hegel and, later on, his reading of some of Marx's writings.[31] His critique of some major ideas of Benjamin's, both in conversation and in his letters, had a number of purposes, not least that of preserving his idea of an antithetical dialectic from contamination with theological and political categories or messianic and eschatological motifs of the kind met with in Benjamin. These were the key topics discussed at their meetings in Paris in 1936–7. The two friends met either in Adorno's favourite hotel, the Littré, or in one of the famous cafés in St Germain. Adorno loved Paris, and since Benjamin knew it intimately it was not hard to find congenial meeting places both for their personal conversations and for the culinary delights that Paris had to offer. Apart from that, Adorno enjoyed going to the museums. He especially liked the Jeu de Paume. This is where he learnt to distinguish between the conciliatory German variant of impressionism and the shocks delivered by the French version. He was fascinated both by Sisley's snow landscapes and Monet's and Cézanne's still lifes. He was alert to the impact of van Gogh's paintings, while his dislike of Toulouse-Lautrec was confirmed and even strengthened.[32] Adorno's criticism of Benjamin did not prevent him from responding enthusiastically when he saw *German Men and Women*, the book Benjamin had published under the pseudonym of Detlef Holz in Switzerland in 1936.[33] Nevertheless, his hostility to immediacy of every sort became increasingly clear. His criticism aimed to break down false mediations.[34] The stumbling block was the 'mystificatory element' in Benjamin's thinking.[35] In 1936 this referred above all to his mystificatory view of the workers' movement and the proletarian revolution. Thus Adorno observed in a letter to Horkheimer that Benjamin had a tendency – and here he once again detected the pernicious influence of Brecht – 'to believe in the proletariat as if it were the blind world-spirit'. Such hopes were undialectical. Benjamin had 'some of the qualities of a *Wandervogel* gone mad'.[36] With comments like these Adorno evidently wished to distance himself from some of Benjamin's ideas. At the same time, he was at pains to measure himself against Benjamin's intellectual power and so he sought intellectual confrontation. This ambivalence was doubtless strengthened by the fact that Adorno was well aware how quickly he was able to assimilate original philosophical ideas and that he had constantly to take care that his productive elaboration of other people's ideas did not endanger the independence of his own thought.[37]

This problem presented itself in the case of the highly speculative ideas of Alfred Sohn-Rethel, with whom Adorno was corresponding at the same time. Initially, he was enthralled by the voluminous proposals for a materialist epistemology that Sohn-Rethel had sent him from Switzerland, where he had temporarily emigrated to escape the Gestapo. The fundamental idea of the theoretical study he had written in a period of some eight months was an attempt to explain the abstract forms of knowledge as derivatives of the 'real abstraction' of the 'commodity form'. The commodity form arose, he maintained, as a generalization from the exchange of equivalents as mediated by money. He then tried to demonstrate that the commodity form was associated with a twofold process of abstraction. On the one hand, there was an abstraction from the concrete use of the commodity which was now separated in time and space from the act of exchange. On the other, there was an abstraction from the concrete labour that supplied the foundation of the use value of the commodity.[38]

Adorno and Sohn-Rethel had known one another since 1925, when towards the end of the summer they had engaged in philosophical discussions with Walter Benjamin and Siegfried Kracauer in Naples. There were meetings later on from time to time in Frankfurt and Berlin. In October 1936, a few weeks before Adorno had read the exposés, they had met briefly in Paris, where, together with Benjamin, they had hotly debated Sohn-Rethel's ideas in conversations lasting seven hours at a time.[39] Adorno was not surprised, therefore, to receive a typescript of some 130 pages entitled 'Sociological Theory of Knowledge' that Sohn-Rethel had sent to him from Paris in the autumn of the same year. Sohn-Rethel hoped that this contribution to the origins of abstract thinking would result in a closer collaboration with the Institute of Social Research, or that at the very least they might commission a research project. Then something unusual happened – Adorno capitulated when confronted with the complexity and abstract nature of Sohn-Rethel's argumentation. Nevertheless, he declared his willingness to provide Horkheimer with an expert opinion on Sohn-Rethel's work. For this purpose, he asked Sohn-Rethel to let him have a shorter version of his project,[40] while emphasizing that there was a whole series of similarities between his own epistemological study of Husserl and Sohn-Rethel's attempt to elaborate Marx's analysis of the commodity. What Adorno expected of Sohn-Rethel was nothing less than 'the overcoming of the antinomy of genesis and validity', and he suggested a link-up with 'the dialectical logic planned by Horkheimer and myself'. At the same time, his critical sense warned him of the danger of 'turning a materialist dialectic into a prima philosophia (not to say: an ontology)'.[41]

Sohn-Rethel's response was not long in coming. A few days later he summarized his ideas in a lengthy letter to Adorno. It began with endless explanations of Marxism's true objective. His key concepts were those of 'commodity form' and 'functional socialization' that he had taken from the basic fact of exploitation. The genesis of 'essential forms', and in particular the idea of subjectivity, was mediated by 'the historical dialectic of functional socialization'. It followed that subjectivity must be conceived 'as the inseparable correlative of the development of money as a form of value'.[42]

Having studied the bulky 'Nottingham letter', Adorno wrote to its author enthusiastically, praising Sohn-Rethel's work, 'which had triggered the greatest mental upheaval that I have experienced in philosophy since my first encounter with Benjamin's work – and that was in 1923! This upheaval reflects the magnitude and power of your ideas – but also the depth of an agreement that goes much further than you could have suspected.'[43] On Sunday 22 November, the two men met in Oxford and spent the day in intensive discussions about the problems involved in a 'prehistory of logic'.[44] The next day Adorno wrote to Horkheimer in New York, telling him of his positive view of Sohn-Rethel's planned study. Much along the lines of his own work on Husserl, Sohn-Rethel was attempting, he said, 'to explode idealism from within, on the basis of its own assumptions. . . . His thesis is . . . that the "meaning" of synthesis in a Kantian sense (i.e., a key concept of idealism) is itself social and reducible to the fact of exploitation.'[45] For all his enthusiasm Adorno did suggest that Sohn-Rethel's work was inadequate in its present form. Because it was being written 'in extreme isolation', it 'bore all the stigmata of a monological and even monomaniacal way of thinking'.[46] Nevertheless, he believed that the institute should give it full support. 'In so far as my own assistance as critic is required, I shall gladly make it available. From the end of January, Sohn will be without any means of subsistence . . . And he would undoubtedly manage to survive with a meagre pension.'[47] To Adorno's mind, his work should take precedence over Kracauer's, for example.

Horkheimer reacted much more coolly to Sohn-Rethel's idea that the abstract notion of exchange should be seen as an *a priori* prerequisite of pure rational activity. He raised the objection that 'to return from critical theory to yet another eternal system was highly problematic'.[48] He even went so far as to accuse Adorno 'of having let himself be taken in by Sohn-Rethel's great intelligence'. He took the trouble to expose what seemed to him to be the obvious defects of Sohn-Rethel's manuscript and summarized his objections as follows: 'Sohn-Rethel's constant assurance that proofs would have to be obtained to demonstrate that some "geneses" or other from Being or from history or from the development of mankind or from the deepest roots of the existence of man in his historical being are synonymous with the truth problems of consciousness or the question of when knowledge can be said to be valid or questions of social praxis – all this I find infinitely wearying and boring.'[49] But in addition to this fundamental critique, Horkheimer tried to draw Adorno onto his side. 'You yourself are not particularly sympathetic to such exaggeratedly idealist views. You will recollect those sections of Schelling's identity philosophy that led Hegel to talk about the night in which all cows are grey.'[50] That was evidently a clear enough hint for Adorno. Just as he had been influenced by Horkheimer's criticisms of Walter Benjamin, so too, in this case, he partly came to accept at least some of Horkheimer's objections to Sohn-Rethel's attempts to deduce the transcendental subject from the commodity form. Adorno developed a slightly ironical distance towards 'dear Alfred's' highly abstract and prolix arguments to the point where, in a letter to

Benjamin, he even punned on his name, referring to him as 'So'n-Rätsel' (what a riddle!).[51]

Adorno did not jettison Sohn-Rethel's chief findings,[52] namely that the exchange of commodity values as mediated by money was the precondition of an objective process of abstraction that became in its turn the precondition of the abstract nature of conceptual thought. But he emphasized to Horkheimer that he was well aware of the weaknesses in Sohn-Rethel's argumentation. Nevertheless, he insisted that 'beneath all the rubbish, he could see a very productive idea'. He defended Sohn-Rethel's project against Horkheimer's blanket condemnation, while consoling both Horkheimer and himself with the thought that they simply have to accept 'that we really only have ourselves to rely on to get our work done'.[53] This aside, Adorno repeatedly appealed to the director of the institute to make payments to Sohn-Rethel for the various typescripts he produced in order to help him out in the difficult conditions of exile. Adorno also approached Walter Adams, the general secretary of the Academic Assistance Council. Here too he was successful, for at the end of September 1937, when Sohn-Rethel moved from Paris to London, he received a scholarship from the council to which the Institute of Social Research made a contribution.[54]

In contrast to the closeness of these contacts, both personal and through letters, with both Benjamin and Sohn-Rethel, Adorno confined his relations with Siegfried Kracauer to a minimum. Like them, Kracauer tried to survive in Paris in difficult circumstances. He had been living there with his wife Lili since February 1933, working at first as a correspondent for the *Frankfurter Zeitung*, although he found himself dismissed by the editor-in-chief, Heinrich Simon, after only four weeks. Driven by necessity, he struggled to obtain something more permanent, approaching in turn the Institute of Social Research or the New School for Social Research. At the same time, encouraged by the fact that his first novel, *Ginster*, was published by Gallimard in a translation by Claire Malraux, he tried to complete his next novel, *Georg*, which he had begun in 1929. He also kept himself busy collecting material for a life of the operetta composer Jacques Offenbach.

As one of his numerous initiatives, Adorno had suggested late in 1936 that Kracauer should produce a draft study for the institute on the subject of propaganda and the masses. Horkheimer had no difficulty in agreeing to the proposal, since he already had plans for a large-scale project on fascist systems of rule and the effects of Nazi propaganda.[55]

This was not the first time the institute had approached Kracauer; he had several times been invited to become involved in shaping the policy of the *Zeitschrift* and to take part in various projects. His wife Lili had worked in the institute library in Frankfurt for six years. Despite his current financial difficulties, Kracauer was hesitant about receiving commissions from the institute. He evidently did not wish to become too dependent on Horkheimer, who he knew felt a certain animosity towards him. This hostility presumably went back to 1932, when Kracauer was editor of the arts section of the *Frankfurter Zeitung* and had refused to accede to Horkheimer's request to defend the institute against the accusation that it was in the hands of communists.[56] Kracauer for his part may well have envied Horkheimer, who as director of the institute was able to pursue his sociological interests in conditions of material security, but who – as Kracauer suspected – was abandoning his original Marxist research objectives.

A further factor was that Kracauer wished as far as possible to avoid becoming a recipient of patronage from Adorno, who was in fact responsible for coordinating part of the European research and publication programme of the institute. Relations between the old friends were now rarely free of disputes, and their friendship had reached something of a low point at this time. In general Kracauer was unwilling to make use of Adorno's – by no means always impartial – services in mediating between Horkheimer and himself. As he explicitly stated, he wanted to be approached by the institute and not to have to come to them cap in hand. And he found it intolerable to see Adorno enjoying the role of munificent benefactor. It may be the case that unconsciously he could only see Adorno as the former pupil whose eyes he had attempted to open to the mysteries of Kant's philosophy. In fact their roles had long since undergone a reversal. Adorno may not have felt himself to be intellectually superior to the older man, but he felt growing doubts about his writing activities. In his eyes, Kracauer was increasingly becoming a marginal figure. This went so far that Adorno could even intrigue against Kracauer, writing to Horkheimer that he and Benjamin had agreed that Kracauer ought to be 'declared incapable' in order to save him from himself. Even so, he continued, 'his gifts were so considerable . . . that we ought to be able to do something with him.'[57] He proposed that Kracauer could be asked to write a literary and sociological analysis of the detective novel, as part of a collection of essays which would include Benjamin's 'Work of Art in the Age of Mechanical Reproducibility', a study on architecture to be commissioned from Sigfried Giedion, and Adorno's jazz essay. The book, which would contain an introduction by Horkheimer, would be entitled 'The Art of Mass Consumption'.

Neither this volume nor the essay that Kracauer was supposed to write for it ever saw the light of day. However, Kracauer did write an article on 'Propaganda and the Masses' that the institute both commissioned and paid for. This was a draft text in which Kracauer outlined how he would go about analysing 'the combination of terrorism and intellectual influence', which in his view had become the true core of fascist politics. This study was to form part of a larger future project. His aim was to perform a comparative study of the different forms of propaganda and their different functions in the fascist, soviet and democratic systems.[58] Kracauer produced a 170-page study based on his outline,

with the title 'The Totalitarian Propaganda of Germany and Italy'. When
Adorno was asked by Horkheimer to review it, he not only shortened
it radically, but he also rewrote it so extensively that Kracauer decided
to forbid its publication in the *Zeitschrift für Sozialforschung*. He
informed Adorno of his decision in a letter dated 20 August 1938, and
made it clear that the text as totally revised by Adorno was no longer
his. His original intention, he said, had been to explain the growth of
fascism and its relation to capitalism. Contrary to this, in the version
Adorno had produced, this relationship was 'fixed once and for all . . . the
two things were 100 per cent identical. You identify it [fascism] with
counter-revolution from the outset, claim that its interests are diametrically opposed to those of the majority and simply brush aside the
ambiguities in its relations with capitalism. . . . I must confess that in the
whole of my literary career I have never encountered a revision that so
contradicts every legitimate practice; not to mention that I myself would
never have dreamt of treating someone else's text in like manner.'[59]

Even before this very serious disagreement, Adorno's criticism of
Jacques Offenbach and his Age had led to a considerable cooling of
relations between the two friends. This book, which Kracauer had spent
two years writing, was published in April 1937, and Kracauer hoped
that it would help to alleviate his financial situation. Now, Adorno tore
it to shreds in a review for the *Zeitschrift*. What aroused his disapproval?
Basically, he thought it a mistake to portray the life of a composer
against the background of French history during the Second Empire
without properly taking account of his music. Krenek called it 'the
biography of a musician without his music'.[60] That was the crucial
point, and it was one that Adorno saw too. In addition, he criticized the
exclusion of social theory and also the purely descriptive narrative. Lastly,
he objected to the way in which music was given a social explanation. It
was not good enough for a 'social biography' to be based on 'analogies
and vague parallels' between Offenbach's music and the social conditions of the age. Kracauer understood perfectly well that he was being
accused of superficiality in his analysis of society because of his failure
to make use of materialist categories. He replied by return of post. He
told Adorno that his prejudices prevented him from seeing what he
(Kracauer) had really been doing in the Offenbach book. This was to
describe the collapse of the empire and the subsequent rise of the
bourgeois republic in France. This historical analysis showed 'that the
Second Empire was a farce that had come about as a result of panic
and flight'. The idea that he approved of a society whose problematic
development he had exposed was absurd.[61]

Adorno was unmoved by Kracauer's defence. He repeated his
criticisms in his review of the book in the last issue of the *Zeitschrift
für Sozialforschung* for 1937: 'Distanced from Offenbach's material,
Kracauer's account approaches those found in individualizing biographical novels.' Adorno believed that Kracauer had omitted to explore the

'ephemeral meretriciousness and the stereotypical rigidity' of the operetta and hence its true character as 'the source of kitsch'.[62] In fact, Kracauer had concentrated on portraying the social and cultural manifestations of the Second Empire and Offenbach as the typical artist of the period. His argument was that, because Paris society during the reign of Napoleon III was itself 'operetta-like', it could find its apt expression in Offenbach's music.

This attempt to provide a kind of model of an entire epoch by describing such phenomena as the boulevard, the newspaper, the world exhibitions, etc., seemed quite close to Benjamin's own Arcades Project, especially the study he planned on Charles Baudelaire. Did Benjamin agree with Adorno in rejecting Kracauer's book because it provided competition for his own? Benjamin knew what Kracauer was planning from conversations with him in Paris, and was mistrustful from the outset. His doubts found a ready audience in Adorno, who wrote to Benjamin, who himself needed no convincing: 'No, if Kracauer really does identify with this book, then he has definitely erased himself from the list of writers to be taken at all seriously. And I am myself seriously considering whether or not I should break off relations with him.'[63] Benjamin for his part justified his negative judgement by pointing out that the book was a kind of apologia: 'It is especially flagrant in those passages which touch upon Offenbach's Jewish origins. For Kracauer the Jewish element remains purely a matter of origins. It does not occur to him to recognize it in the work itself.' The theory of operetta was likewise thought to be an apologia: 'The concept of rapture [*Rausch*] which is supposed to support this theory, at least as it appears here, is nothing but a messy box of chocolates.'[64]

For Adorno and Benjamin to agree among themselves to discuss Kracauer's book in such disparaging terms may be understandable as a way of enabling each to have his own negative view confirmed by the other. But greater circumspection than Adorno was able to muster would have been advisable when dealing with Horkheimer. For he also wrote to the latter, damning the book as conformist and regressive. He even went so far as to raise the question whether in the long run a relationship with Kracauer was still possible.[65]

The inability to judge the book of a common friend in a dispassionate way was not just a symptom of the distortions that began to colour communications between the émigrés. After all, this was a book that finally appeared in the United States in 1938 with the title *Orpheus in Paris*, and enjoyed some success. In addition, the tendency grew for what seemed to be minor deviations from a very diffuse group consensus to result in threats of exclusion. Had the conditions under which they laboured in emigration made people forget how to distinguish between personal relations and attitudes on theoretical issues? Whatever the case, the unifying factor of a common hatred of Hitler did not suffice to prevent intellectual disagreements from spilling over into personal rivalries that made life even harder for those concerned than it was anyway. The marginality that should have brought them together, the malaise of exile, was a fertile breeding ground for bitter quarrels. The network of émigré oppositional intellectuals was riven with splits between tactical coalitions and enmities. Under the pressure of the conditions in which they lived, the very art for which intellectuals are known, their ability to judge the consequences of their actions in a spirit of self-criticism, what Horkheimer called their ability to see themselves as 'the subjects of critical behaviour', sometimes failed them.[66]

Although each of them separately was the victim of the tribulations of exile, these were the very difficulties that were ignored. Individual egoisms, made more sensitive by the broken pride of people who had been expelled, were as inflated as were their malice and invective. Later, however, Adorno would account for these undignified reactions by noting that every intellectual is mutilated by emigration.[67] The deformities of emigration are compounded by the fact that the intellectuals form a sort of closed society in which 'they get to know each other in the most shameful and degrading of all situations, that of competing supplicants.' They are thus 'virtually compelled to show each other their most repulsive sides'.[68] This is precisely what Adorno did when succumbing to the disreputable idea of being so outraged by Kracauer's social biography of Offenbach as to contemplate and discuss a common initiative against its author, a conspiracy in which, in addition to Benjamin, Ernst Bloch should also be involved. Fortunately, nothing came of this – but only because they could not agree among themselves. Benjamin, who knew all about the trials of exile, did not wish to attack Kracauer openly for fear of aggravating his already difficult situation. Bloch had a different view anyway and ridiculed Adorno's emphatic rejection of the Offenbach book.

A double relationship: Gretel and Max

In the numerous letters Adorno wrote during his Oxford years, either from Merton or, during his frequent travels, from London, Paris, Frankfurt and Berlin, he talked more and more about the current political situation in Germany. This gave him the opportunity to reflect upon the 'catastrophic course of events'. As early as 1935, he could see the growing danger of war for Britain and France if a National Socialist Germany were to triumph over Russia.[69] With fascism on the march in Europe he advised Horkheimer to mobilize the resources of the institute to produce a theory of its origins and modus operandi. Adorno's increasingly critical view of the global political situation included developments in the Soviet Union which he looked at askance, at least since the Stalin purges, the first death sentences and the cult of personality: 'Has the planet really and truly gone to Hell?', he asked Horkheimer at the end of a letter in October 1936. A little later, he noted in a mood of resignation that

> it looks like a web of delusion from which there is no way out, and one would like simply to sit down and watch in silence, like Wotan in *The Twilight of the Gods*. One of the most important reasons why I am glad to be together with you is that jointly we shall have the strength to look the horrors in the face without losing the vestiges of universal reason that have taken flight and thrown in their lot with us.[70]

In view of the black world situation and the concrete anti-Semitic measures introduced by the reign of terror in Germany, Adorno obviously felt increasingly anxious about Gretel, who was still living in Berlin. As early as the end of 1935, he expressed the fear that she would soon be condemned to a 'ghetto existence' in Germany. This was no idle supposition. He was in an excellent position to be able to assess the changes taking place in the 'Third Reich'. To Horkheimer's horror, he kept returning to Germany at the end of each term in Oxford. When he stayed in Frankfurt and Berlin he could see at first hand both the reality of Nazi despotism and the concessions made by men such as Martin Heidegger and other professors ready to fall into line with the Nazi state.[71] He was also able to witness the success of writers such as Hanns Johst (the author of the famous quotation which Adorno mistakenly attributed to Goebbels: 'When I hear the word "culture", I take out my pistol!'), Ernst Jünger, Ernst Wiechert, Gerhart Hauptmann, Werner Bergengruen, Frank Thiess, Wolfgang Weihrauch and Hans Carossa. Part of the reality of the Third Reich was formed by propaganda campaigns such as the touring exhibition 'Degenerate Art', which was also shown in the Frankfurt Städel. And in the exhibition on 'Degenerate Music', mounted in part on the initiative of artistic director Hans Severus Ziegler, compositions by Adorno occupied what he later called 'a place of honour'.[72]

Of course, in a traditionally left-liberal town like Frankfurt, where Adorno was officially still registered, there were isolated attempts at resistance to the 'coordination' policies of the Nazi mayor, Friedrich Krebs, who called himself an 'old soldier' of the nationalist movement and who wished to coerce everyone into toeing the Nazi line. A few professors publicly protested against the attack on the Jews. They included the botanist Martin Möbius, the microbiologist Max Neisser and the historian Ernst Kantorowicz. Among the students, however, resistance to the policy of regimentation in the university and the refusal to give places to Jewish students was minimal. Adorno reported to Horkheimer about the tragic fate of Liesel Paxmann, a particularly talented student of oppositional views who had studied at the institute. She had been put under pressure by the Gestapo. 'It is not even known whether she killed herself ... or whether she was murdered.' Other former students were also arrested or went into hiding.[73]

The anti-Semitic campaign was growing in ferocity, with only one temporary lull, during the Olympic Games in Berlin in the summer of 1936. At the same time, Germans of Jewish descent found that their lives were being systematically destroyed. Both Adorno's father and his fiancée Gretel were directly affected by the discriminatory legislation, social stigmatization and economic exploitation to which Jews were subjected during the years in which National Socialism consolidated its power. Adorno could scarcely maintain any illusions about the humiliations that awaited him and those closest to him in the immediate future. Once he had begun to assess the situation more realistically, he made efforts to persuade Gretel Karplus to leave Berlin and come to Oxford so that they could marry in Britain.[74] Their relationship had now lasted well over ten years, and it was evident that they both wished to marry. In May 1936 Gretel's father had died in Berlin. Since then she had been trying to sell her stake in Tengler & Co. in order to leave Germany as soon as possible. Her sister Liselotte had been living in America for some time.

However, their wedding plans only began to take concrete shape early in 1937 when the difficult sale of the factory could finally be concluded. In the spring of that year, Adorno and Gretel went on tour through the towns of Franconia. The pressure of fascism seemed to be less marked there than in the big cities. In a letter to Horkheimer, he reported that they had seen the arena for the Nazi party rallies, the place where in September 1935 the 'Nuremberg race laws' had been promulgated.[75] 'There was no one there ... ; the whole thing looks somewhat decayed and wretched, by no means *aere perennius*. Strangely, the buildings all suggest the imago of prison.'[76]

Once a wedding had been decided on, Adorno wrote to Horkheimer that Gretel had begun to learn about housekeeping – a clear indication that there would be a traditional division of labour in their marriage.[77]

And in fact, it did not occur to Adorno to play any part in the organization and conduct of the household or to take any interest in buying furniture, etc. Everyday practical things were left entirely to Gretel. This even included ordering his suits from the tailor. At the same time, he asked Horkheimer to act as a witness at the marriage ceremony in Britain.

This very personal request also had a symbolic meaning. For at the same time as he formalized his relationship with Gretel, his intention now hardened of throwing in his lot with Horkheimer even more decisively than hitherto and hence also with the Institute of Social Research in New York. Adorno's status as the established representative of the institute in Europe had been assured since 1935 and confirmed in writing. In view of this first step towards integration in the institute, he had increasingly made up his mind to seek his professional future in the United States, rather than in Europe. He now had a more realistic view of his career opportunities in Britain than at the start of his Oxford studies.

As late as October 1936, at the time when the currency charges against him were pending, he had still been flirting with the idea of settling in France. Since his grandfather had been a career officer in the French army and his mother was of French origin, he had grounds to hope that, 'as a university teacher expelled by the Nazis, he might achieve an accelerated, or perhaps even immediate, naturalization in France.'[78] Accordingly, he asked Benjamin to make inquiries about his likely prospects. He abandoned the idea once Benjamin had informed him about the actual complications of naturalization. It had anyway only been a possibility he had been playing with, since he was already making initial preparations for an extended visit to Horkheimer in order to gain a better picture of the institute and of what it might be like to live and work in New York.

This intention was strengthened by the fact that early in 1937 Oscar Wiesengrund travelled to the United States on family business, but also to explore the possibility of moving to the New World. He had not been too drastically affected by Nazi measures to eliminate Jews from the economy, but he was enough of a realist to see that, as a Jewish businessman, he would not be able to preserve his independence. He perceived the danger of becoming a defenceless victim of the arbitrary measures of the regime. Accordingly, he considered the gradual sale of property in Frankfurt and Seeheim, as well as of his shares in the Leipzig firm.[79] His son made sure that during his visit to the United States he was to establish contact with Horkheimer. Adorno wrote to the latter: 'One of the principal reasons for his [Oscar Wiesengrund's] journey is to discuss with you questions of concern to Gretel and me, including financial questions. . . . I should like to clarify one point: as you know, my parents still own significant assets in Germany, as does Gretel's mother. It would be not unimportant – and this is something my father has under active consideration – to arrange matters so that, if this inheritance should come down to us, it should not be snapped up from under our noses by the Nazis. He is also looking into placing the assets in a blocked account in the hope that they might somehow be released without too great a loss.'[80] This frankness towards Horkheimer shows clearly that Adorno intended to place himself entirely in his hands as far as his own professional future was concerned. The long-cherished idea of intensive collaboration with him was now finally to become a reality.

Horkheimer evidently took due note of this greater forwardness on the part of Adorno, and adopted a responsible, but in certain respects also an ambivalent, attitude. He declined, politely, but very firmly, to offer Adorno or his father any definite practical advice in financial or inheritance matters. This may have been partly perhaps because he had gained the impression that Oscar Wiesengrund was not yet clear in his own mind about whether and when he might leave Europe for ever. In his letter of February 1937, Horkheimer pointed out to Adorno that both Britain and France would be suitable alternatives to the United States as a base for further collaboration with the institute – however, in both cases he would have to fend for himself as far as a career was concerned. In contrast, once he had the Oxford doctorate, he would be in a good position to obtain a university post in the United States, at Harvard, for example. 'At first sight, the most natural thing would seem to be for you to move here from Britain after a reasonable time has elapsed, unless extremely favourable prospects open up there.'[81]

Because he was well able to picture the anxieties Adorno might be feeling, he expressly mentioned the sums that Adorno could count on if he agreed to sign a contract with the institute. With $350, he concluded, 'the two of you could manage quite comfortably.'[82] Speaking here in the plural, he evidently regarded a marriage (about which he had heard from Adorno's father) as a foregone conclusion. What he wanted above all was to secure Adorno's productivity and creative energy for the benefit of the institute's future research plans and its work on theory. His plan included a renewed invitation to Adorno to visit America, an invitation that Horkheimer would otherwise extend with such generosity only to Benjamin. It is no wonder then that Adorno accepted with some alacrity. He replied to Horkheimer enthusiastically: 'My wish to work with you directly is greater than any other; you may be sure that this wish is not disguised by any academic ambition whatever, however sublimated.'[83] He had already been to Frankfurt to take care of the difficulty that his German passport had expired and had resolved it without any particular complication. Furthermore, to his great relief, and thanks to the assistance of the AAC, his application to the Home Office for permission to stay in Britain indefinitely was granted.[84] In addition, he had received a two-year visa for France. In the four months remaining until June, when he was due to go to New York, he spent a few months away from Oxford in Paris, on institute business. He looked after the French translation of Horkheimer's essays which the latter wished to have published. He spoke to Benjamin, Sohn-Rethel and Kracauer about their different projects. Finally, he just managed to find time to visit an exhibition devoted to the works of Constantin Guys, the watercolour painter and graphic artist, in the Musée des Arts Décoratifs.

Scarcely had he finished dealing with his various appointments, than he travelled from Paris to Germany in order to visit his parents and Gretel. For the summer term he returned to Oxford by car in late April with his English friend Redvers Opie, who had visited him in Frankfurt.[85] Once in London he then tried to organize the ocean crossing. Needless to say, he did not neglect his philosophical and musical projects, which he tried to advance and, where possible, complete before his departure.

Although face-to-face meetings with the permanent members of the institute were likely to take place shortly, this did not stop Adorno from making scathing criticisms of the recent writings of Leo Löwenthal, Herbert Marcuse and Erich Fromm in his letters. Towards Horkheimer, he formulated his objections more diplomatically.[86] But his letters to Benjamin contain outbursts that are as tactless as his judgements on Kracauer had been. He claimed that all these 'camp followers' were 'a real danger. But I know all too painfully from the cases of Sternberger and Haselberg just how difficult it is to defend ourselves against those who imitate us.'[87] To Adorno's mind there was scarcely any doubt that there was little merit in Löwenthal's studies of Strindberg and Ibsen, and later on of Knut Hamsum,[88] all conducted from the point of view of the sociology of literature. The same thing was true of Erich Fromm's socio-psychological work 'The Feeling of Impotence' in the individual, and there was no merit at all in Herbert Marcuse's 'The Affirmative Character of Culture'.[89] All these were recent publications of the *Zeitschrift für Sozialforschung*. By confiding in Benjamin in this way, and reaching an understanding with him about the defects in the publications of other contributors, Adorno was able to express in what high esteem he held him. But even if he thought him superior to the majority of other intellectuals, he still read Benjamin's writings with almost the same critical ferocity as those of Löwenthal, Fromm and Marcuse. Nevertheless, his view of Benjamin was unambiguous. 'I regard Benjamin as one of the most important contributors that we possess', he wrote to Horkheimer a few weeks before embarking for New York, 'and if he is used properly we can expect him to achieve prodigiously. I think, therefore, that it would be very reasonable to express this appreciation in external respects too.'[90] This statement, which is just one of many, shows very clearly that Adorno was very far from wanting to marginalize Benjamin. On the contrary, as long as Benjamin found himself isolated and in need of financial assistance, Adorno constantly and reliably stood by him, and, despite growing differences of opinion on a whole series of social issues, he stuck to him in practical matters.[91]

Adorno had arranged various meetings in Paris before leaving for the United States. In particular, he hoped to see the philosophers Jean Wahl and Pierre Klossowski, and also to visit the Collège de Sociologie, which had been founded by Roger Caillois, Georges Bataille and Michel Leiris. Because of these arrangements, he decided to make the Atlantic crossing on the *Normandie*. The tourist class tickets were paid for by the institute. On 9 June the steamer sailed for New York from Le Havre. Adorno was very anxious to obtain a single cabin, since he was terrified by 'the idea of sea-sickness with a witness'.[92] His intention was to join in the daily work of the institute, meetings, discussions, etc., right after his arrival. He was quite happy about this. 'It is the fulfilment of an old desire of mine, that of "integration" – like Kafka's land-surveyor. And how pleased I am that the institute is not the Castle.'[93]

Adorno's expectations were not disappointed. He lived in comfort in the Barbion Palace Hotel, 1010 West 58th Street, Central Park South, and Horkheimer himself made sure that his needs were catered for. He was very well aware of this. In his thank-you letter to his host, he wrote: 'You have spoiled me like a film star, and my only regret is that I am not a, shall we say, "Dolores del Rio".'[94] He went on to say how happy he had been during the two weeks he had spent there, especially since he had found that, despite his critical attitude and despite his extreme idiosyncrasy in his thinking and writing, he had been made welcome among a group of people in which he was respected and who turned out to be like-minded. Adorno's report of his trip to Benjamin, written during the return journey, while he was still on the *Normandie*, was similarly euphoric. The atmosphere in the institute was 'extremely pleasant'. He also made mention of his new function. He was to take part in the international congress on 'The Unity of Science' from 29 to 31 July and also in the Ninth International Philosophy Congress, which was due to focus on Descartes' *Discours de la méthode*. In both cases he was to attend as an official representative of the institute. He also told Benjamin that he had been able to negotiate an increase in the monthly remittance Benjamin received from the institute.

Adorno and Benjamin went to both congresses and jointly composed two reports for Horkheimer. Adorno's contribution made it clear that he had appropriated Horkheimer's criticism of positivism. In addition, both Benjamin and Adorno had collected material for the latter's newly conceived idea of a 'critical theory' that just at this time was starting to take shape in opposition to what began to be called traditional thought. Concrete pointers for this were to be found in the essay 'The Latest Attack on Metaphysics', with its critique of scientist thinking, as well as the programmatic treatise 'Traditional and Critical Theory'. Both of these texts by Horkheimer appeared in volume 6 of the *Zeitschrift für Sozialforschung*, and Adorno was very familiar with their contents from his correspondence with Horkheimer.[95] While Adorno was in New York these essays had been under discussion. Both essays were to be of signal importance for the whole group's understanding of itself.

The emphasis in the congress reports that Adorno and Benjamin delivered lay on the pleasure they took in depicting the differences of opinion they perceived in the Vienna circle, i.e., between Hans Reichenbach, Carl Gustav Hempel, Rudolf Carnap and Paul Oppenheim. Apart from that, their account of the content of the congress was pretty thin. The discussions of the different theories of truth effectively went unreported. Their account of the Congrès Descartes, which at the time attracted great interest in Paris, was likewise no more than cursory. 'There was a large number of German émigrés with conformist attitudes. . . . The insignificance of their achievement was obvious.'[96] A commitment to existentialism seemed to be a central theme of the congress. Adorno gave a somewhat fuller description of the contributions of the phenomenologists. As an expert on Husserl, he had himself contributed to the debates on this topic. In addition, he spoke approvingly of a lecture given by Martha Wolfenstein, a young scholar from Harvard who had spoken about the position of the painter in industrial society. In a private group outside the official framework of the conference, there was a discussion with Neurath, Carnap, Hempel, Lazarsfeld and Benjamin of Horkheimer's recently published critique of positivism. This gave Adorno the opportunity to improve his acquaintance with the Austrian Paul Lazarsfeld, who was to play an important part in his life a little later on.

After these few days in Paris, where Adorno spent some time in 'chez Routiers' and 'Ramponneau' near the Place d'Alma with a friend from Frankfurt, Gabriele Oppenheim, he hastened to return to Britain. For he was now expecting the arrival of Gretel Karplus, with whom he at long last wanted to set up a household. Gretel was of a practical turn of mind and the first step she took after her arrival, on 20 August 1937, was to rent a small furnished flat with two rooms, in 21 Palace Court, Hyde Park, Bayswater, so that Adorno could give up living in the Albemarle Hotel and henceforth live with her.

Once it became clear that Horkheimer had to spend a few weeks in Europe visiting the different branches of the institute, he promised to travel to London in order to be present at the wedding. On 7 September, he arrived together with his wife. On the very next day, the ceremony took place at the registry office in Paddington. The marriage was registered on 8 September 1937; Redvers Opie and Max Horkheimer acted as witnesses. As Adorno reported to Benjamin, the wedding party was small and on a modest scale, 'in truly total privacy'.[97] Redvers Opie, who was bursar of Magdalen, gave a lunch in the college at which, in addition to the bridal couple and the two Horkheimers, the only people present were Gretel's mother, Emilie, and Oscar and Maria Wiesengrund. Adorno would not be denied the opportunity to play some pieces on the piano, including some Wagner, whose works he was just beginning to explore. He wrote to Löwenthal that a honeymoon was out of the question, 'since we have to fix up our flat, wait for the furniture to arrive and deal with inconveniences of that sort. Incidentally, Gretel is completely occupied with household problems, tasks which I cynically refuse to participate in.'[98]

At this point, when Adorno was coming to terms with the novel experience of marriage and Gretel was starting to deal with the practical problems of daily life, he suggested to the members of the New York institute that they should carry out a study 'of the psychology of the modern bourgeois woman'. This study should focus on the fetishization of appearances, the 'curious transfer of the anal character to consumer goods (shopping, and the entire fixation on life's objects)'. It should go on to examine 'the specific cementing function of women in modern society'.[99] As the author of such a study he proposed Erich Fromm,

surprisingly enough when we consider how much he disliked the psychoanalyst. He expounded his ideas to Fromm in detail: he believed that
women, even more than men, are dominated by commodities and that

> they act as the agents of the commodity in society. . . . It would be
> necessary to analyse the completely irrational attitude of women
> towards commodities, shopping, clothes, the hairdresser, and what
> would emerge, in all probability, is that all these things that seem
> to serve sex-appeal are in reality completely desexualized. . . . What
> would be needed here is a theory of female frigidity. In my view
> frigidity stems from the fact that even during the act of coitus
> women appear to themselves as objects for exchange . . . though
> of course for a non-existent purpose, and that, because of this
> displacement, they never manage to obtain pleasure.[100]

At the time, none of the institute members was willing to take up these
ideas. However, Adorno himself tried to apply them in a variety of
theoretical contexts.[101]

Did these enigmatic reflections on women's sexuality have any
connection with Adorno's newly married status? Up to that point, as a
bachelor, he was able to make his own decisions about the organization
of his life and was under little pressure to consider the needs of his
partner, with whose peculiarities he was now confronted and which
he now had to respect. Another novelty for him was the fact that his
wife wished to make changes in the way he lived and that questions of
style and taste had to be considered. He soon perceived that she wished
to assume the role of housewife, concerned herself with food and meal
times, went shopping in a big way, spent money and put her own ideas
about how to organize their daily routine into practice. He kept his
distance from all these practical tasks – and had to do so, since he was
faced with the task of bringing the Husserl study to a prompt conclusion. Just as he was attempting to concentrate on it, there was yet
another surprising turn of events in his life. Shortly after the wedding,
the opportunity opened up for him and Gretel to move to the United
States. This had been arranged by Horkheimer, who sent him a telegram
on 20 October 1937 and wanted him to come as soon as possible. He
was being offered a position in a research project on the impact of
radio. The couple had scarcely had enough time to make themselves
at home in Palace Court when they found themselves facing the much
greater upheaval of the move to New York.

The fact that Adorno agreed in short order to move to the United
States was by no means a choice without risk. The research project that
he would join under the leadership of Paul Lazarsfeld was a subject
in an area of social research that was completely new to him. A further
factor was that the institute, or rather Horkheimer, was unable to give
him a full-time position as had been the original plan. Instead, he was

being offered a half-post on a reduced salary. This compromise solution was to finance his position on a fifty-fifty basis from the Princeton radio project and the institute's own funds. This in turn was connected with the acute money problems of the institute. Fritz Pollock had invested a part of the institute's capital in the stock market and now, in autumn 1937, found himself forced to sell, incurring serious losses.[102] Horkheimer had not told Adorno about this difficult situation, one which threatened to undermine the institute, until after the latter's wedding: 'Incidentally, you should pray to all the saints that the New York stock market will rise again!'[103]

Against this background, Horkheimer must obviously have been eager to seize the opportunity for long-term cooperation with a different research outfit. Only in that way could he bring Adorno to New York with a good conscience and tie him down contractually without the institute's having to bear the costs of a full position itself. It was agreed that for the first two years the Princeton research group would pay for Adorno.

A few days after Adorno had received Horkheimer's telegram he cabled his agreement in principle back to America and took the opportunity to mention a number of practical difficulties, chief among which was the fact that they had just signed a rental contract for a flat (in 70 Holland Park). Furthermore, they were expecting their furniture, which was being sent over from Germany. In the following letter – addressed to 'Dear Max', a familiar form of address that had been established at the time of the wedding – Adorno acted as if nothing new had happened, and as if this opportunity to live and work in the USA did not exist. He was concentrating on his work on Husserl and Horkheimer's fundamental criticism of his essay on phenomenology to the exclusion of all else. In this sense, this letter is an eloquent testimony to what concerned Adorno most deeply: his own scholarly work. Despite urgent questions about his own life and his future, it was his work that stood at the centre of his being. Hence he explained in detail to Horkheimer how he intended to revise his essay 'On Husserl's Philosophy' – a piece of work of which he remarked: 'I have never been quite so concerned about the fate of one of my writings as I am in this case.'[104] In a letter that almost amounted to a rewriting of his essay in itself, he listed the reasons for dismissing Horkheimer's criticism. His concern was not 'to replace the thesis of the primacy of consciousness with the primacy of being, but to show, first, that the search for an absolute first principle, even it were being itself, necessarily has idealist consequences, i.e., leads back in the last analysis to consciousness. And to show, second, that a philosophy that actually draws these idealist conclusions necessarily becomes entangled in such contradictions that the initial formulation of the question must be seen to be false.'[105] Even if this letter conveys the impression that Adorno was exclusively preoccupied with advancing his work on Husserl and preparing it for publication, the truth is that he was still pursuing other interests as well. He missed his piano, which was indispensable for his current analytical and other writing on music. This included his latest projects: a growing interest in the works of Wagner and also a detailed study of operatic sound; his idea was to explore the way in which revolution and regression are intertwined in opera. Furthermore, Stefan Zweig had suggested to him that he should write a book about Schoenberg, an offer that was not just flattering, but also extremely tempting, since the book on Berg that had been published by Herbert Reichner Verlag had been a success and Zweig, who was actively involved on behalf of the publisher, hoped for a repeat performance. Over and above this, Adorno was busy completing a number of texts that he wished to publish with the title of 'Zweite Nachtmusik', and he also had a text to finish on 'Beethoven's Late Style' for the journal *Der Auftakt: Blätter für die tschechoslowakische Republik*.

At the close of 1937, Adorno must have felt that he was being driven from one improvised situation to the next, and that he was constantly forced to sit between different stools.[106] The reasonably stable residence in London coupled with the prospect of completing his doctorate in Oxford fairly soon had now disappeared. Instead, he was faced with the necessity of starting up again both professionally and privately in New York, where he would have to depend primarily on the institute and on the contacts Horkheimer had made. By the end of 1937, he could no longer count on financial help from his parents. Oscar Wiesengrund had difficulties in Nazi Germany with his wine business, which he was now too old to continue with and had to sell. Furthermore, because of the currency restrictions it was quite impossible for him as a Jew to transfer money abroad. Nevertheless, Adorno was not downcast about his future prospects in the United States. On the contrary, he was looking forward to his collaboration with Horkheimer and attempted to persuade Benjamin of the rightness of this view. This was hinted at in the letter in which he informed him of the latest developments, well aware that his impending move to America would come as a blow to Benjamin because it would increase his sense of intellectual isolation. For this reason, Adorno stressed that in New York – especially there – he would keep an eye on Benjamin's financial situation. He also assured him that, since he was convinced 'that war will be unavoidable in the relatively immediate future', he would do everything in his power 'to bring you over to America as quickly as possible'.[107] He had a personal interest in this of course, since, despite his growing attachment to Horkheimer, he felt that no one was as close to him as Benjamin. Adorno, who had earlier been guilty of mistaken political assessments, could now see the likely course of world events very clearly. With the hegemony of Germany, a catastrophe was now inevitable. That was his message to Benjamin. For this reason it was pointless to 'go on fighting a losing battle in Europe'. 'It might be a source of some ironic consolation that the post we have to defend will prove a lost one everywhere under all circumstances. . . . This catastrophe, dragged out over decades, is the most perfect nightmare of hell which mankind has ever produced up to now.'[108]

Even if Adorno was under no illusions that going to the New World meant that he would be going to a new society, he was already adjusting mentally to the country to which he was about to emigrate. Gretel, who did not feel at home in Britain, was reading books about Harlem and Greenwich Village. Adorno was wondering what the radio research project would mean for him, and whether he would be able to communicate with a pure sociologist like Lazarsfeld. Horkheimer meanwhile attempted to dispel in advance any scruples Adorno might have about his status in the future research group. 'Your role is not to be Lazarsfeld's assistant, but the idea is that you are to be a member of the research project for which Princeton University has awarded Lazarsfeld a largish sum of money. The money will come from the Research Centre of Newark University which, admittedly, is led by Lazarsfeld.'[109] Of greater urgency than the question of cooperating with Lazarsfeld was how to get rid of the flat that had just been rented and the nerve-wracking procedures connected with obtaining an immigration visa from the American consulate. This act set the seal on his and Gretel's emigration from Germany. It was an important caesura in their life history. An appointment at the US consulate in London had been made for mid-December, at which all the relevant documents were to be presented. From these it emerged that Adorno had a firm contract with both Princeton University and the Institute for Social Research. In parallel, he had to submit an application to Horkheimer so that Lazarsfeld could complete the formalities involved in recruiting him officially for the radio research project.

To judge by their complaints, Adorno's and Gretel's nerves were in a bad way. So in the middle of December they travelled to San Remo on the Ligurian coast in order to recuperate. They spent some weeks there in the Villa Verde, a boarding house run by Dora Benjamin, Walter's divorced wife. Benjamin himself came down from Paris, so that they could all spend time together on the Italian Riviera. The fact that the focus was still mainly on scholarly work can be seen from Benjamin's letter to Horkheimer from the Villa Verde. They had discussed both drafts of the article on Charles Baudelaire, with which Benjamin had long been preoccupied, as well as the sketches Adorno had produced on Richard Wagner. Benjamin was unable to restrain his enthusiasm when he heard what Adorno read out to him from his draft essays. 'What was grippingly novel about them for me was the way in which musical facts . . . had been made socially transparent in a way that was completely new to me. From another point of view I was particularly fascinated by *one* facet of this work: to see how the physiognomical realities were directly transposed into a social space, almost without the mediation of psychology.'[110] Benjamin had evidently understood his friend's intentions perfectly. Of course, Horkheimer had long since known all about Adorno's work on Wagner's operas. Ever since Adorno had started his studies of Wagner, Horkheimer had followed them with a very personal interest. As early as the second issue of the *Zeitschrift für Sozialforschung* for 1936, he had expounded his own thoughts about the changes in the 'anthropology of the bourgeois era' in his essay 'Egoism and Freedom Movements'.[111] He had hopes that Adorno's demonstration of the simultaneously authoritarian and rebellious elements in Wagner's character and works would provide confirmation of his own ideas. And Adorno did indeed attempt to pursue this line of thought. 'I believe that the gesture of recoil, of betrayal of revolution, such as becomes most evident in Wotan's treatment of Siegmund, also provides the model for the structure of musical form in Wagner right down to the minutest cells of the music. . . . The intertwining of revolution and regression extends in Wagner right down to the melodic ideas, or rather the way in which these are mutilated by the power of society.'[112]

What Adorno had read out in San Remo were the first drafts of a manuscript that he was able to complete relatively quickly, despite the strains imposed by the imminent move to New York. In 1939, under the title of *Fragments on Wagner*, he published three sections of the much larger study ('Social Character', 'Phantasmagoria', and 'God and Beggar') in the *Zeitschrift für Sozialforschung*.[113] Adorno approached his subject from the point of view of ideological critique,[114] a fundamental tenet of which was the idea that 'progress and reaction in Wagner's music cannot be separated out like sheep and goats'.[115] In the book version,[116] which is subdivided into ten sections, Adorno begins by analysing Wagner's social psychology, 'the configuration of envy, sentimentality and destructiveness', and his anti-Semitism which is located in the no man's land 'between idiosyncrasy and paranoia'.[117] The emphasis of the music analysis in the stricter sense lay on Wagner's use of melody, harmony and orchestration, and finally on the theory of instrumentation that Wagner practised.[118] At the core of his essay, according to Adorno himself, stood what he calls the phantasmagoria, the series of illusory images. He spoke of Wagner's regression 'to the non-temporal medium of sound' which proves to be the source of 'the really productive element' in his music. 'This element, with its two dimensions of harmony and colour, is sonority. . . . It is as expressiveness that the subjective force of production makes its boldest advances at the level of harmony; inventions such as the sleep-motif in *The Ring* resemble magic spells that are capable of enticing all subsequent harmonic discoveries from the twelve-tone continuum. Wagner's anticipation of impressionism in his use of harmony is even more striking than in his tendency to atomization.'[119]

Adorno did not stop there. On the contrary, he emphasized that the sonorities become magic when Wagner transforms them into seemingly natural sound, for in doing so he conceals the way in which the sound effects have been created. 'The occultation of production by the outward appearance of the product – that is the formal law governing the works of Richard Wagner.'[120]

A striking passage of the essay reproduces Adorno's interpretation of 'dominion over nature and subjugation by nature', which he explained with reference to *The Ring*: 'Man emancipates himself from the blind identity with nature from which he springs; he then acquires power over nature only to succumb to it in the long run. . . . The parable of the man who dominates nature only to relapse into a state of natural bondage gains a historical dimension in the action of *The Ring*: with the victory of the bourgeoisie, the idea that society is like a natural process, something "fated", is reaffirmed, despite the conquest of particular aspects of nature.'[121]

The form of music drama as Wagner developed it in the *Gesamt-kunstwerk* was one theme of Adorno's essay; another was the relation of myth and modernity in the subjects Wagner chose for his operas. These ideas led in the final chapter to 'motifs towards a redemption of Wagner'.[122] The composer was 'not simply the willing prophet and assiduous lackey of imperialism and late bourgeois terrorism', he also possesses 'the neurotic's ability to contemplate his own decadence and to transcend it'.[123]

Although Benjamin was greatly taken with Adorno's 'portrait of Wagner', and with 'the precision of his materialist deciphering', he cautiously advanced some reservations. He asked whether Adorno had not made a too undifferentiated use of 'the concepts of the progressive and the regressive'. Adorno's polemical approach ultimately distorts his efforts to provide 'a redemption of Wagner'. Important elements of Adorno's theory of music remain undeveloped. 'Perhaps such a redemption of Wagner might have created a space precisely for one of your earliest themes – that of *décadence* and the Trakl quotation of which you are so fond. For the decisive element in such salvation – am I not right? – is never simply something progressive; it can resemble the regressive as much as it resembles the ultimate goal, which is what Kraus calls the origin.'[124] Adorno accepted his friend's critical remarks, but did not agree that his wish to redeem Wagner was something that could be related to his childhood experience of the composer: 'Wagner never really belonged among the stars above in my childhood, and even today I could not invoke his aura any more effectively than I have already attempted in certain passages.'[125] Adorno was convinced that he had salvaged as much of Wagner as was possible to save. In May 1938 he wrote to Krenek, saying that his sharp debate with Wagner had had as happy an end as was to be found in one of Marlitt's novels. 'The couple are united; nihilism is rescued. In other respects, too, the book is not far behind Marlitt, since it does not lack tension as it shows how Wagner's form develops from the gestures of the conductor.'[126]

These were the ideas with which he had travelled to San Remo for the new year to relax with Gretel and Benjamin. His intention to write a book about Wagner was long since settled. And so, while Benjamin was working away at his study of Baudelaire, Adorno was attempting to give his essay on Wagner a sharper focus.

The return journey from the Italian Riviera took Adorno and Gretel to Brussels, where they said goodbye to his parents. His father was just coming up for his sixty-eighth birthday, while his mother had celebrated her seventieth in September two years previously.

Back in London, Adorno began to prepare himself for his future life and work in New York, while impatiently waiting for their departure. He used what time there was left to bring his different pieces of work to a conclusion, as far as this was possible. In addition, he gave a lecture on 'The Sociology of Art' at the London Institute of Sociology.[127] This did not deter him from indulging his sense of bizarre fantasy, as can be seen from his letter to Horkheimer:

> The rhinoceros king Archibald has a golden crown with a fat pearl and golden layers of skin over his eyes, but stands aloof from active government. He is having an affair with the giraffe 'Gazelle', occasionally wears a silk-grey pair of pyjama trousers, and has published a pamphlet, the pan-humanist manifesto. It has appeared in the publishing house of the united jackals and hyenas. For years he has been working on his magnum opus. It is called 'The Rhinoceros Whip', and is the theoretical groundwork of a human society that includes the animals. In his youth his curly tail was bitten off by his girl-friend at the time, the crocodile Babykroko.[128]

Horkheimer had no wish to spoil his friend's good humour, but he did not leave him entirely to his dreams. He warned him that the initial period in New York would be bound to have its difficulties. He would not be able to work in the institute right from the start since there were no free rooms there. Adorno would have to establish himself by his own efforts as an 'independent theoretician' in academic circles in America. But that was enough cold water. After all, Adorno was not supposed to go to America with the feeling that he was embarking on an uncertain future. 'I am quite convinced', he concluded his letter, 'that you will find opportunity in America to live in a grand bourgeois manner.'[129] This statement tells us not only about Horkheimer, but also about Adorno's wish to live a bourgeois lifestyle, sustained by the expectation, which he rather took for granted, that he would be able to live the life of an anti-bourgeois intellectual on a foundation of material security.

Scarcely four weeks after their return from Italy, on 16 February 1938, the Adornos sailed to New York on the *Champlain*. While they were by no means tormented by the thought that they would be unable to cope with conditions in America, their departure did mean taking leave of Europe, and also of Benjamin and Paris:

> The Eiffel Tower, looked at from below, is a dreadful monster, 'squat', as the English say, standing on four short, monstrously crooked legs, greedily waiting to see if it cannot after all devour the city over which the images of so many disasters have passed, but which has been spared. From a distance, however, the Eiffel Tower is the slender, misty symbol which the indestructible Babylon extends into the sky of modernity.[130]

Adorno and his wife were fully conscious of the privilege of being able to live in New York without money worries, thanks to his work for the radio research project and the contract with the Institute of Social Research. They were well aware that, if they had not taken this step, their lives in Europe would have been in constant danger. Adorno took with him into exile a personal present from his mother, a painting entitled *Die Konfurter Mühle* by Max Rossmann, which he had loved since childhood. Rossmann had painted this view of a farmhouse near Babenhausen in Hessen that was 'unfinished and badly ruined' in his studio in Amorbach, the place that Adorno had described as the only home that remained to him.[131]

This was in the nick of time, Adorno wrote to Horkheimer a day before they sailed: 'The European situation is completely desperate; the prognoses in my last letter seem to have been confirmed in the worst way possible: Austria will fall to Hitler and in a world hypnotized by success this will enable him to stabilize his position indefinitely and on the foundation of the most appalling terror. It can scarcely be doubted any more that the Jews still living in Germany will be wiped out [*ausgerottet*]; for once they have been expropriated, no country in the world will grant them asylum. And once again, nothing will be done: the others fully deserve their Hitler.'[132]

Adorno was just starting to find his feet in New York when the Nazi regime intensified its repressive measures against the Jewish population in the course of 1938. The lethal threat that Hitler represented and his outlandish view of the world were of course well known to Adorno even before the pogroms and the ghettoization of the Jews. He lived in the expectation that the worst was still to come: deportation and genocide. He feared that none of the great powers would take action to save the victims from their executioners.

14

Learning by Doing: Adorno's Path to Social Research

During the last week of February 1938, the steamer belonging to the French Line anchored in New York.[1] For Adorno, the sight of Manhattan was not entirely new, but for Gretel this was the first sight of the Statue of Liberty and the impressive skyline of the city. Both quickly found their way around the American metropolis, the symbol of the American way of life and the epitome of urban modernity.[2] During his three years in Oxford, Adorno had managed to teach himself English to the point where he could survive quite well even in academic discussions.[3] Scarcely had they unpacked than Gretel Adorno announced to Walter Benjamin how well she liked this city of superlatives. It was 'by no means so new and progressive'. She was struck by the contrast of 'the extremely modern and the downright shabby'. 'One does not have to look for surrealist things here, for one stumbles across them all the time. In the early evening the high rise blocks are very imposing, but later on, when the offices are all closed, and the electric lighting is much reduced, they remind me of badly lit European tenements.'[4] Gretel would also have been able to captivate Benjamim by telling him about the cast iron used in the buildings in Lower Manhattan, the *beaux arts* style of the public buildings, with the shopping galleries downtown, the Metropolitan Museum, the Public Library and the bookstores.

Adorno expressed similar views to those of his wife, and declared the city with its seven million inhabitants to be European. Seventh Avenue, where he and Gretel lived during their first few weeks there, reminded him of the Boulevard Montparnasse, and Greenwich Village resembled Mont St Geneviève. On their arrival, the couple occupied an apartment that was temporary, but very agreeable. It was in 45 Christopher Street, from where they had a 'wonderful view' of the city.[5] Later on, from September 1938, Adorno and his wife had a new address, at 290 Riverside Drive, not too far from Columbia University and the Institute of Social Research. There they had rented an apartment on the thirteenth floor with a view of the Hudson River, and were at long last able to unpack the furniture that had arrived from Germany. Adorno even had his piano again. He and Gretel enjoyed receiving guests, who soon arrived in significant numbers. In addition to colleagues and friends from the institute, they included Gershom Scholem, Ernst Bloch and Paul Tillich among the philosophers, musicians such as Ernst Krenek, Eduard Steuermann and Rudolf Kolisch, the art historian Meyer Schapiro, the architect Ferdinand Kramer, a childhood friend, as well as other personal friends, such as Marie Seligmann,[6] Egon Wissing[7] and Liselotte Karplus, Gretel's younger sister. This apartment, with its furniture full of private memories, such as the 'grandfather chair', the 'Biedermeier suite', and the old 'secretaire', was not just 'beautiful and delightful', Adorno wrote to Horkheimer, 'but also a social asset, something that helped to protect us from malice and suspicion, and made it possible for us to invite people without embarrassment.'[8]

The list of visitors included, admittedly not until two years later, Hermann Grab, who had emigrated to Paris from his home town of Prague, and had then succeeded in fleeing via Lisbon to New York. His story 'Wedding in Brooklyn' contained a sensitive account of the reaction of a European to the experience of exile in America. In it he described Adorno's apartment: 'My friend led me to the window. Far below, along the river, you could see the moving car lights, a few lights on the opposite shore were, so I was told, the lights of New Jersey; from the harbour we could hear a foghorn. On that evening, from the height of the apartment on Riverside Drive, New York appeared as a mighty, silent city.'[9] For his part, Adorno had done everything in his power to facilitate Grab's entry into the United States. He hoped that Horkheimer would be able to help and wrote to him on Grab's behalf: 'Grab is a musician, a brilliant pianist; he is a D.Phil. and a Dr. Jur. (a pupil of Scheler, but a renegade); he has written an interesting novel, can recite the whole of Proust by heart and can play all of Strauss's operas without a score – undoubtedly a prodigy of nature, and the fact that he once had God-knows how much money ought in his case to present no obstacle, since he really has turned his back on the world.'[10]

From the outset, the Adornos had no lack of private contacts and relationships in New York City. Despite the extremely hot summer of 1938 in the USA, they soon discovered the attractions of this cultural centre of America. Adorno took the opportunity to go to a 'negro revue in Harlem' with friends. They also gained an impression of the surrounding area during those first summer months. They particularly liked what they saw of New England.[11] In this respect, what Adorno reported in a later reminiscence gives a one-sided view of his experience: 'When you come to America, everywhere looks the same. The standardization, the product of technology and monopoly, is disconcerting.'[12] Things looked different to Adorno on the spot. In August 1938, they spent the holidays in the Hotel de Gregoire in Bar Harbor, 'in an exceptionally pleasant location here, on an island'.[13] Given this background, there can be no truth in the idea that Adorno's experience of the American way of life was nothing but a great shock.

On a different, less immediate level, of course, there were his ideas about the ideological meaning of modern American mass culture and the commercial functionalization of art, about the relations between politics and the economy at the end of the liberal era, about the role of the intellectual in such a society and about expulsion and exile.[14] Adorno was well aware that New York was no more than a refuge, an episode that would have to last as long as Hitler was in power in Germany. He noted an incident that occurred to him late one evening, returning home in the subway, that seemed to him to offer a significant insight into the condition of 'exile in exile'. This concerned a chance encounter with a young woman, obviously a refugee like himself. He smiled at her, but, instead of responding, 'her weary face froze and took on a dismissive expression that she evidently thought ladylike. In Vienna, where she may well have come from, or in Berlin, she would have smiled back. . . . That is Hitler's triumph, I thought. He has not only robbed us of our country, language and money, but has even confiscated a harmless smile. The world he has created will soon make us as evil as him. The girl's rejection and my inconsiderateness are worthy of each other.'[15]

Adorno had little time to familiarize himself with living conditions in Manhattan, since he was compelled to make an almost immediate start with the strenuous work on the radio research project, in other words, he was forced to immerse himself in a completely unknown sphere of activity. To begin with, he was based outside New York City, in Newark, where Lazarsfeld had found space for his project in a disused brewery. 'Whenever I travelled there', he wrote, 'through the tunnel under the Hudson, I felt a little as if I were in Kafka's Nature Theatre in Oklahoma. Indeed, I was attracted by the lack of inhibition in the choice of a locality that would have been hardly imaginable in European academic practices.'[16] He did indeed try to approach his new situation with enthusiasm and an open mind, but he had an outright allergic reaction to the expectation that he would have to adapt to the given realities of the scientific culture of the United States. 'It went without saying that I wanted to maintain intellectual continuity, and this soon became a fully conscious desire in America. I still remember the shock I felt when a woman I met early on in my stay in New York, herself an émigrée, said to me: "People used to go to the philharmonic, now they go to Radio City!"'[17]

No sooner had Adorno moved into his provisional apartment in Greenwich Village, than Paul Lazarsfeld pressed for an early meeting to discuss the future project. In a letter at the end of November 1937, he had already set down in explicit detail exactly what he expected from Adorno when he took over the music section of the project. Adorno was to ensure that the 'research project' would not confine itself to 'fact-finding', but should be embedded in a theoretical framework that embraced both music and society. For his part, Adorno had explained his own view of the matter in a lengthy letter of 24 January 1938, supplementing it with a six-page, closely spaced exposé. In this letter he formulated a series of questions and theses for which he was indebted in part to Ernst Krenek's essay 'Observations on Radio Music', which Krenek had written for the *Zeitschrift für Sozialforschung*.[18] Adorno proceeded from the assumption that the tone colour of music was altered by radio transmission. Broadcasting the music resulted in an artificial sound that contrasted with the natural timbre of music in a concert hall. For this reason, radio music could not be taken seriously: it lost its symphonic qualities and degenerated into a kind of museum piece. The constant background noise led to the phenomenon of the noise band (*Hörstreifen*).[19] Music became part of a more general sound; it lost its depth and, with that, its aura. Since radio music is piped into the house as if it were a public service, it becomes something incidental and dwindles to a kind of background entertainment. Cultural possessions are reduced in this way to domestic objects of no particular significance. Since the listener has no say in the choice of the music that is broadcast into his home, switching off the radio is the last narcissistic pleasure available to the impotent recipient. Because of the constant repetitions of particular popular pieces of music, the programme gives the listener the feeling that there is no alternative. In this way the music becomes affirmative, something you listen to without participating in it actively. Adorno proposed that the letters that were received regularly by the radio stations should be subjected to textual analysis. In addition, he wanted to carry out a number of exemplary textual analyses of hit songs in order to uncover the relation between musical form and the message of the songs.[20]

Following these preliminary written ideas, Adorno met Lazarsfeld on 26 February and Lazarsfeld explained the plan to investigate the impact of broadcast music. The exact title of the overall project was 'The Essential Value of Radio to All Types of Listeners'. Radio was the leading medium at the time, and the original idea of using the methods of empirical social research to explore its effects went back to Hadley Cantrill, a social psychologist at Princeton University, and Frank Stanton.[21] They had received a comparatively large sum of money from the Rockefeller Foundation to enable them to carry out the study. The general aim of the project was to discover the role of the radio in people's everyday life, the motives underlying their listening habits, the types of programmes that were popular and unpopular, and whether groups of listeners could be targeted by broadcasts specifically aimed at them. What stood at the centre of attention was the need to establish data that could be of use to administrators.[22] Lazarsfeld, who had founded an institute of his own at the University of Newark (now part of Rutgers) that was financed primarily by projects researching on mass communications, was entrusted with the implementation of the project on the recommendation of the respected American sociologist Robert S. Lynd.[23]

Paul Lazarsfeld had been born in Vienna into an assimilated Jewish family of left-wing views. Two years Adorno's senior, he had worked in his home town as a social researcher since the late 1920s. He made his name with a study he had undertaken in 1930 with Marie Jahoda and Hans Zeisel, *Marienthal: The Sociography of an Unemployed Community*. In 1933, the Rockefeller Foundation, which had helped to finance this project, offered Lazarsfeld the opportunity of a study trip to the United States in order to learn about the methodology of empirical surveys. Because of political developments in his native country, where the Socialist Party with whom he had personal contacts was banned in 1934, Lazarsfeld decided to apply for American citizenship. Having participated in the *Studies on Authority and the Family*, he was in contact with Horkheimer's Institute of Social Research. Since he had helped with the statistical evaluation of questionnaires, he was listed in the institute prospectus as a 'research associate'.

The radio research project was Lazarsfeld's first major research venture in the USA, one that opened up the prospect of a future university career as a sociologist. For although the nominal conduct of the research was in the School of Public and International Affairs in Princeton, the actual field research took place in Newark, where Lazarsfeld was supposed to carry it out within the space of two years.[24] The pressure he was under is one factor explaining why he was so keen to recruit Adorno for his team. Right from the start, however, the collaboration between the two – the one a social researcher, the other an intellectual – was anything but plain sailing. Adorno admitted later on that he had enormous problems with the kind of empirical social research that predominated in the USA, even though Lazarsfeld thought highly of him as a theoretician and as a stimulating mind, and was anxious to make use of him.[25] Adorno's task in the first instance was to develop further the interpretations of serious and popular music contained or implied in his sociological analyses of music and to reformulate them as a system of hypotheses that could be tested empirically. At the same time, it was proposed that, insofar as these interpretations could be verified empirically, they should be systematically broadened into a theoretical framework for future empirical results. Since Adorno was interested in developing alternatives to the commercial system of a privately run radio network, he wrote to Benjamin at the start of his own project to ask for a brief report on the ideas underlying the so-called listening models that Benjamin had produced and tried out in Germany in the early 1930s.[26]

In March 1938, Adorno began by familiarizing himself with what was being done in Newark in order to consider how best to translate the aims of the project into practice. Looking back on that time, he records that he now heard for the first time of 'words such as "likes and dislikes study", "success or failure of a programme", and so on, of which at first I could understand little. But I understood enough to realize that it concerned the collecting of data. . . . For the first time I saw administrative research before me.'[27] His astonishment at research of this kind focused in the first instance on the fact that the client not only supplied the questions to be investigated, but also determined the analytical framework and the scope of the research. Moreover, Adorno was also surprised to discover that media analysis was restricted to a predetermined set of methods for conducting opinion surveys. The problem with this, he objected, was that such demoscopic methods were capable of eliciting only the subjective reactions of the listeners. In his view, as he emphasized in a lengthy letter to Lazarsfeld on 21 March 1938, it was essential to clarify two questions: first, what were the musical qualities of the content of radio broadcasts, and, second, under what conditions and with what intentions was music broadcast on the radio? In his letter, he stressed:

> The effort to 'quantify' results, to present them in numerical form necessarily leads to a certain simplification. You may well be able to measure in percentage terms how many listeners like preclassical music, how many classical or romantic music and how many prefer verismo opera, and so on. But if you wish to include the *reasons* they give for their preferences, it would most likely turn out to be incapable of quantification. That is to say, these reasons would diverge so utterly that it would be hard to classify more than two under the same head, making it more or less impossible to formulate statistical categories.[28]

Adorno used such objections to resist 'the statement and measurement of effects without relating them to the "stimuli", i.e., the objective realities to which the consumers, . . . in this case the listeners, are reacting.'[29] One concept that struck him as particularly strange was that of the 'programme analyser', an empirical measuring device which enabled the listener to press a button to register what he liked or disliked about a particular piece of music. Adorno refused to measure culture in this way. 'I reflected that culture was simply the condition that precluded a mentality that tried to measure it.'[30]

As for Lazarsfeld, he had succeeded in forming a quite definite impression of Adorno after a few weeks, and he passed it on to the directors of the project: 'He is the very image of what one imagines an absent-minded German professor to look like, and he behaves so oddly that it makes me feel like a member of the Mayflower Society. Admittedly, when you start talking to him, he utters a vast number of interesting ideas. Like every new arrival here, he is determined to turn everything upside down, but when you listen to him most of it sounds quite sensible.'[31]

In fact, Adorno had started his research activity by trying to win Lazarsfeld over to his own views. With his letters, his exposé and also in direct discussions, he tried to convince him that valid results from the research as originally conceived could hardly emerge from a primarily quantitative study.

> My suggestion is simply to ask whether under certain circumstances it would not be more meaningful to keep the questioning of individuals on an individual basis, that is to say, without regard to the quantification of the results – something that plays a decisive role in all the American studies of this subject I have come across up to now. . . . I mean that we should be able to agree readily that truly universal insights are more likely to emerge from the individual himself than from general statements that do not amount to much more than an analytical proposition. Of course, this assumes that we already *possess* in a sense this universality in the form of a 'theory'; but this method is one I think of as dialectical because it attempts to apply the theory to probe individual factuality as deeply as possible, while subsequently using what has been discovered to modify the theory, where necessary. . . . The practical implication of such considerations is to conduct *individual* interviews at the risk that they will not prove representative for the 'average' . . . These interviews should be completely individual, i.e., if possible independent of all questionnaires, and they should try to explore the reactions of each individual as thoroughly and deeply as is at all possible. . . . If only we are able to give an account of the relation of the individual to society, and if only we are able to focus on the individual sharply enough to see him as being socially determined, I believe that the results will have greater significance than if, in our desire to produce quantifiable results, we restrict ourselves to generalities that yield nothing of value for theory.[32]

Against the background of this attempt to win Lazarsfeld round, efforts that Adorno persisted in with scarcely flagging intensity, we can gain a picture of the long-running dispute between a musical theorist and a sociologist. This was evidently a disagreement of principle between Adorno, with his European cultural background and his interpretative view of method, and Lazarsfeld, with his pragmatic approach. But we can see more in it than this. It also provides proof that Adorno was more than ready to involve himself fully in his new tasks. He was very far from willing to take lightly his unaccustomed activity as a social researcher. A mere three months after first meeting Lazarsfeld he produced a memorandum, 'Music in Radio', of no fewer than 160 typewritten pages.[33]

In four meticulously organized chapters, Adorno sketched in the scaffolding for a sociological theory of radio music which he linked with a specific plan for research on the medium. In chapter 1 he asked how subjective listener needs could be uncovered, how communication needs are socially mediated and what role is played in this by the omnipresent medium of mass communications. In chapter 2 Adorno concentrated on the more narrowly musical aspect of radio programmes. He was interested in two problems. On the one hand, he asked how the musical material was affected by its distribution through the medium of radio. On the other, he inquired about the reception given to the different music genres. He focused particularly on the 'Concept of Fetish-Making in Radio Music':

> By musical fetish-making, we mean that, instead of any direct relationship between the listener and the music itself, there exists only a relationship between the listener and some sort of social or economic value which has been attributed either to the music or to its performers.[34]

Following this thesis of the regressive consumption of music by the consumer, Adorno proposed in chapter 3 to turn his attention to the primary emotional effects of radio. His working hypothesis was that listening to the radio was part of a general tendency towards pseudo-activity:

> We believe that most attempts made by radio to 'activate' the listener belong to the sphere of pseudo-activity. Here is one example: the amateur orchestra broadcasts the music and the amateur listeners at home can fit in the noises they make themselves. This is plainly a pseudo-activity insofar as the activized listener actually has no control over the real orchestra because he cannot be heard by it.[35]

Adorno wanted to make use of empirical methods to discover the social situations in which broadcast music is actually listened to:

> The meaning of a Beethoven symphony heard while the listener is walking around or lying in bed is very likely to differ from its effect in a concert-hall where people sit as if they were in church. Do they listen to radio music while sitting, standing, walking around, or lying in bed? Do they listen before meals, during meals, or after meals? ... If music is becoming a sort of daily function then it certainly will be very closely associated with meals. And if people try to break down the distance between themselves and the music by incorporating it, so to speak, within themselves, and if they treat it as a sort of 'culinary' product, all these things could be proved to have a definite relationship with eating.[36]

This extensive memorandum gathered together a number of ideas that Adorno had already worked out, such as his various studies on jazz, his fundamental critique of amateur music-making

(*Musikantenmusik*) and the phenomenon of the 'noise band' peculiar to the radio. Given the scope of his arguments, it was not unreasonable that he should have spoken of it as a 'book' in his letters to Krenek and Benjamin.[37] In fact it was his intention to publish his own reflections on the media together with a number of analyses of specific music programmes on the radio. However, his studies never reached that point. His memorandum, which was written in the alien medium of English, albeit in an ambitious style, ran into some blunt criticism from Lazarsfeld. Lazarsfeld's own copy contains a whole series of scathing marginal comments: 'impertinence', 'idiotic', 'what's the point of this?', 'you never know what he is talking about', 'dialectics as excuse not to have to think in a disciplined way', 'without any feeling for importance'.[38] In particular, he made two criticisms of substance. On the one hand, Adorno was said to have described the radio system from the preconceived standpoint of an elitist bourgeois position that prevented him from envisaging alternative uses of radio that might arise from positions different from his own rejectionist stance. On the other hand, he had a completely mistaken view of social research, and this led him to make statements that were utterly at variance with actual sociological practice. This incompetence undermined the central ideas about music theory contained in the memorandum, although these were of importance for the future work of the project. In the five-page letter that Lazarsfeld sent Adorno, he says, 'You pride yourself in attacking other people because they are neurotic and fetishists, but it doesn't occur to you how open you are yourself to such attacks. . . . Don't you think it is a perfect fetishism the way you use Latin words all through your text? . . . By the way, I implored you repeatedly to use more responsible language and you evidently were psychologically unable to follow my advice.'[39]

Lazarsfeld's criticisms of Adorno's ideas about the social function of radio were in many ways justified. Nevertheless, for all his sometimes unnecessarily polemical tone his letter represented a kind of capitulation: he was evidently in despair at the wild proliferation of speculative ideas that he had conjured up, but which now began to irritate him. Did he really wish to get rid of Adorno, as the latter surmised? Precisely because he was unwilling to draw this conclusion he found himself in the difficult situation of having to feed Adorno's profusion of ideas into an empirical research project that had to be based on the three stages of concept-formation, operationalization and measurement.[40] This was no small task. Adorno evidently perceived that Lazarsfeld was out of his depth and he conjectured that his aggressive tone pointed to an underlying weakness. This made it easy for Adorno simply to turn the tables. On 6 September 1938, he wrote that he had been expected 'to include everything that I could think of in the memorandum, and it was together with you that I conceived the idea of "an experiment in theory".'[41] He also pointed out that he had been too preoccupied with other duties, such as dealing with questionnaires, interviews, content analyses and consultations with experts, to have had enough time to present a fully worked-out memorandum. He had provided sufficient evidence of his ability to produce internally consistent and logically coherent texts in the large number of pieces of music analysis that he had published. This was a reference not just to his older essay on jazz and his articles on light music, but also to pieces he had written during his first few months in New York and had published immediately in volumes 7 and 8 of the *Zeitschrift für Sozialforschung*. These were the essays 'On the Fetish-Character of Music and the Regression of Listening' and the 'Fragments on Wagner'.[42]

In the first article, the first to be written in America, the Marxian and Freudian concepts of fetish-character and regression surface in the German version, just as they had appeared in English in the memorandum.[43] Adorno wished to demonstrate the existence of two phenomena which could simply not be verified by opinion surveys and interview techniques. These were the fetishization of music as the component of a culture that had been commercialized through and through, and, parallel to that, the infantilism of the listening public whose ability to listen had atrophied.[44] According to Adorno, the entire musical culture was drifting towards conformism, trivialization and standardization. This trend went hand in hand with the historical process of the 'liquidation of the individual'.[45] As music gradually lost the sounding-board of a public capable of judgement, it became reduced to entertainment as a form of distraction. Both in this essay and in his discussions in the radio research project, Adorno doubted that the entertainment value of popular music truly delivered enjoyment. But if the entertainment industry does not really entertain, we are left with the paradox of a 'displeasure in pleasure'.[46] Not content with that, Adorno insisted that music is only appreciated for its prestige value as embodied in the star conductor, the prima donna and the current hero of popular music. Furthermore, he maintained that listening to music was confined to picking out pleasurable extracts from a whole composition. 'Ears which are still only able to hear what one demands of them in what is offered, and which register the abstract charm instead of synthesizing the moments of charm, are bad ears.'[47]

Needless to say, these claims, which were set in the context of a general theory of cultural decay,[48] did in fact fall on 'bad', i.e., deaf, ears in Lazarsfeld and his research group. But after their acrimonious exchange of letters, the relationship and hence the prospect of further collaboration was more than fraught. For this reason, nothing came of the next part of the project, the production of a typology of listeners, i.e., a statistical distribution of the different categories of radio listeners on the basis of an opinion survey. An abbreviated version of Adorno's memorandum was discussed by the members of the project, but had little resonance. In the same way, the planned cooperation between Adorno and the young psychologist Gerhard Wiebe, who was supposed to assist him with the practical side of the research, was a disaster. Adorno later recollected that hardly any meaningful communication was possible with Wiebe, who had experience as a jazz musician and was supposed to help Adorno with his study of popular music. Wiebe resented Adorno's socially critical attitude and criticized his European opinions about culture as unwarranted arrogance.[49] For his part, however, Adorno was not at all averse to 'setting out for that famous other side of the fence' [i.e., to study the reactions of listeners].[50] This enabled him to profit from the expertise of other members of the project in the application of empirical methods to social research – both quantitative and qualitative content analysis, case studies and motivation analyses. This led Adorno from his research on subjective attitudes towards music to discover the importance of the category of mediation in the mass-communication process. He perceived the need to show empirically that 'social objectivities also manifest themselves indirectly in subjective opinions and behaviour'.[51]

Adorno benefited greatly from working with the sociologist George Simpson. Simpson had translated Emile Durkheim's book on the division of labour and had interests in sociological theory as well as experience of social research. He was a great help to Adorno when the latter found it necessary to produce papers in English for publication as part of the project. Although Adorno expended much time and effort in the attempt to recast his own ideas in the categories of research,[52] this experience made him only too aware that the link that Lazarsfeld sought to establish between sociological theory and social research amounted to an attempt to square the circle. It was a kind of object lesson in the difference in principle between speculative theorizing and the procedures of a form of social research based on the axiom that 'science is measurement'.[53] Since neither Adorno nor Lazarsfeld could see a way of linking their respective conceptions of scholarship in a productive way, a breach was inevitable in the long run.[54] As late as January 1939, Adorno asked Horkheimer to mediate between him and Lazarsfeld. He did not just want to be pigeonholed as a malcontent and he objected to being dismissed from the project once he had provided it with the requisite theory.[55] Neither the intercession of Horkheimer and Löwenthal nor Adorno's own protest had any effect. At the end of 1939, when Lazarsfeld put in a second application for a grant from the Rockefeller Foundation for two years, the music section of the project was omitted from the programme. Lazarsfeld said subsequently that John Marshall, who was the responsible representative of the foundation, had the feeling that 'the introduction of the Adorno variant of critical research into the study of mass communications' had been a failure.[56] Lazarsfeld undoubtedly perceived the fundamental theoretical differences between Adorno and himself very clearly, but he did not wish to lose him entirely and made efforts to persuade the foundation to maintain its financial support for him until the end of the current project. He suggested to Marshall that Adorno should be asked to produce a publication on music education. 'It seems to me that if all Dr. Adorno's interesting ideas were related to current efforts in mass education, they would find quite a substantial following.'[57]

Lazarsfeld was evidently successful in this proposal. As late as 1940, Adorno developed a scheme for providing highly concrete and illuminating answers to the question of how music could be brought to the interested radio listener without making the mistake of didactic oversimplification. Under the title 'What a Music Appreciation Hour Should Be', he designed twelve units for a New York radio station, four of which were edited into programme format by Paul Kresh and Flora Schreiber. Adorno treated melody using Schubert's B minor symphony as an example; the concept of musical unity was illustrated by the first movement of Haydn's C major symphony; he proposed to explain musical form by discussing the hit song *Avalon*, the form of a song with reference to Schumann, sonata form as exemplified by Mozart and musical style by focusing on Beethoven. These musical illustrations were not to be understood as quotations, however, since one of Adorno's main criticisms of radio music was that 'the quotation . . . was the decadent form of reproduction'.[58] His listening models were preceded by an explanation, and at the heart of this there was the idea of 'right listening', which consisted in 'comprehending the relevant piece directly, spontaneously as a *coherent meaning, a meaningful unity in which all the parts have a function in the totality*. The musical logic of every piece, a logic specific to it, must be spontaneously grasped.'[59] The listener should be brought to the point 'of virtually composing the piece for himself as he listens'. This was what Adorno understood by structural listening, which he contrasted with culinary virtuosity.[60] In fact, Adorno regarded his programme as an alternative to the NBC Music Appreciation Hour conducted by Walter Damrosch, a didactic radio series that was highly popular at the time and was regarded as exemplary. In order to clarify his own programme, Adorno referred polemically to the recommendations in Siegmund Spaeth's *Great Symphonies: How to Recognize and Remember Them*: 'To the beginning of Beethoven's Fifth Symphony, one is told to sing the words: "I am your Fate! Come let me in!"' Advice of this type is contrasted with examples of right listening: 'It is hardly an exaggeration to say that any person who applies the tactics recommended by Mr Spaeth when listening to music, is, to say the least, completely lost to any musical understanding.'[61]

The disagreements with Lazarsfeld did not prevent Adorno from being highly productive during the two years in which he collaborated on the radio research project. Moreover, media research undoubtedly profited from his socially orientated theoretical approach. This can be seen from the texts that he completed in this brief phase. In 'The Radio Symphony', an essay he published in the journal *Radio Research*,

he brought together the results of the study in which he had investigated the claims of the radio organizations to bring classical music to
their listeners. Symphonic music on the radio was questionable, he wrote,
because it delivered only a poor impression of a live performance.[62]
'A Social Critique of Radio Music', the talk given to his fellow members
of the radio project, presented in abbreviated form the sum of Adorno's
general theoretical views on the transmission of music by the mass
media that he described at length in the memorandum.[63] His study
'On Popular Music' appeared in 1941 in the last number of the *Studies
in Philosophy and Social Science*, which also published other contributions that were thematically related to the Princeton project and
to media research. This was an essay he had written with George
Simpson. In it he tried to show that each new hit always contained
a new element, but at the same time it adapted itself to pre-existing
listening habits so as to be able to repeat the success of earlier hits.
The 'Analytical Study of the NBC Music Appreciation Hour' remained
unpublished. In this study he had investigated a series for children
and young people which had attempted to introduce them to serious
music. He concluded that, although the series was widely admired
in America, its design achieved the opposite of what was intended,
and that in reality it promoted the commodity nature of the music and
the consumer habits of the listeners, instead of guiding them towards
informed listening.[64]

Looking back at his work on the project, Adorno acknowledged that
these four essays were no substitute for the social theory of radio he
had aspired to. He had been forced to restrict himself to these 'models'
because 'I did not succeed in making the transition to listener research.
That transition would be absolutely vital, above all else in order to
differentiate and correct the theorems. It is an open question, which in
fact can only be answered empirically, whether, to what extent, and
in what dimensions the societal implications disclosed in musical content analysis are also understood by the listeners and how they react
to them. It would be naive simply to presume an equivalence between
the societal implications of the stimuli and the responses, though no
less naive to regard the two as independent of each other in the absence
of established research on the reactions.'[65] By the end of his work
on radio, Adorno had developed one fundamental conviction about
the media, namely the premise, never subsequently abandoned, that
the stereotypical production mechanisms of popular culture can be
related back to the expectations of consumers. He became convinced
that, in the 'organized' societies of an 'administered world', people's
communicative needs deviate less and less from one another. This
explains why conscious manipulation by radio and the press is basically
superfluous. There is a 'pre-established harmony' that ensures that
media audiences demand the very fare that the newspapers, the radio
and film serve up.

In the Institute of Social Research on Morningside Heights

In view of the wearing conflicts that Adorno was forced to endure in the Office of Radio Research, it was a particular satisfaction to him, and also a genuine relief, to enjoy the support of the Institute of Social Research. Admittedly, despite the solidarity that was shown to him, there were also a few raised eyebrows, particularly on the part of Friedrich Pollock, but also of Leo Löwenthal, neither of whom was willing to rule out the possibility that Adorno had not been flexible enough in his dealings with Lazarsfeld. For his part, Horkheimer treated the entire matter with the maximum of diplomacy. As a proven critic of positivist science,[66] he fully understood Adorno's reservations about a narrowly circumscribed notion of empirical science and could sympathize with Adorno's difficulties with the strategies of empirical media research. But, given the financial straits in which the institute had found itself since the middle of 1937, Horkheimer could not afford to abandon the collaboration with Lazarsfeld and the Office of Radio Research, which had just moved into new accommodation in Union Square and which later became associated with Columbia University (as the Office of Applied Social Research). The losses on the US Stock Exchange that Pollock had incurred by a number of risky transactions forced Horkheimer into cutting back sharply on expenditure. Walter Benjamin, for example, who was living from hand to mouth in Paris, was made aware of 'the very serious economic situation'. 'The major part of our assets are held in property that cannot be sold until the market improves in this sector. . . . The lesser portion is invested in securities and will be exhausted in a foreseeable number of months. . . . I feel obliged to give you this information because despite all our efforts the day may not be too far away when we shall have to tell you that with the best will in the world we shall be unable to extend your research grant.'[67]

Ernst Bloch, who had approached Horkheimer to ask whether there was any prospect of a temporary position in the institute's research programme, was told in a laconic statement in March 1938 that the current state of the institute's finances was deplorable and that it would be irresponsible to take on further commitments. 'We have been forced to discontinue the majority of our grants in America and Europe', Horkheimer wrote, 'and even dismiss permanent employees.' This was the effect, he wrote, of the general economic crisis.[68]

Even Adorno was not immune. The letter Horkheimer wrote to him on his thirty-fifth birthday, on 11 September of the same year, again referred to the 'catastrophic news from the Stock Exchange', even though he had long since known of the severe cutbacks in the institute. Horkheimer did not hesitate to say that the future of the entire institute was at stake since some of the assets had now to be written off completely. 'We shall have to fight for the successful outcome of our work harder than ever since external circumstances are bleaker than ever.'[69]

Adorno took this letter so much to heart that he began to think about how to solve institute's financial problems. With this in view he took up contact with the architect Ferdinand Kramer, a childhood friend from Frankfurt who had arrived in New York as an émigré a few days after him.[70] Adorno's idea was to make use of Kramer's professional expertise. Because of the current shortage of funds, Pollock and Horkheimer had resolved to sell some of the land owned by the institute on Long Island Sound in Port Chester, New York. Kramer was to be entrusted with the sale. The idea was to divide the property up beforehand and build private houses. This plan was in fact carried out successfully. The architect designed two large estates with around thirty-five large houses (in Greyrock Park) and 150 smaller ones. However, this investment only helped to restore the institute's finances in the longer term.[71]

Horkheimer's birthday letter ended with the formula 'Success to our work', which may well have confirmed Adorno's own sentiments. For thanks to his negative experience of American scholarship, he clung increasingly to the hope that he would find comfort among his German friends in the institute on Morningside Heights. Later on, in *Minima Moralia*, he was to use the image of the Bremen town musicians. They welcomed him, and cunningly gave him tasks to perform in the 'robbers' cave' in order to outwit the swindlers there. 'With eyes full of yearning, the frog king, an incorrigible snob, looks up to the princess and cannot leave off hoping that she will set him free.'[72] In fact, Adorno had now served out his time of suffering in the robbers' cave of social research in Newark. And as with the happy end in the fairy tale, he had been rescued, not indeed by the princess, but by Horkheimer, who now procured a permanent post for him in the institute, despite the financial crisis. For reasons of space, he could not yet be given a fixed place to work in 429 West 117th Street on the Upper West Side. According to Alice Maier, one of Horkheimer's secretaries, there was an acute shortage of space in what had formerly been a private house. 'On the ground floor there were no rooms at all. . . . On the first floor, Fritz Pollock occupied the front room, and Leo Löwenthal, who edited the journal, the room at the back. Mr Horkheimer worked in the front room on the fourth floor, and we secretaries worked in the back. Then there were another three or four rooms in the attic, one of which my husband (Joseph Maier) had, and the other Otto Kirchheimer.'[73]

Alice Maier's memoir conveys an accurate picture of the personnel active in the institute at the time. Erich Fromm had already made efforts to make himself independent of the institute because of the growing theoretical disagreements which had arisen following the closer alliance between Adorno and Horkheimer. He had set up a psychoanalytical practice and only made occasional appearances in the institute. Karl Wittfogel and Henryk Grossmann were regular members of the institute, but mainly worked away from it. Their specialized involvement with economic theory and problems of world markets occupied something of a marginal position in Horkheimer's general programme. They were both somewhat older and Adorno never had a closer relationship with either of them.[74]

Pollock was present in the institute chiefly because he took part of the administrative load off Horkheimer's shoulders and was the person principally responsible for financing current expenditure, the projects and the numerous commissions and grants.[75] Löwenthal coordinated the project work and looked after the editorial affairs of the *Zeitschrift für Sozialforschung*, which appeared under the title of *Studies in Philosophy and Social Science* from 1939 on. The two lawyers, Franz Neumann and Otto Kirchheimer, had both found temporary shelter in the London School of Economics. They worked for the institute in New York, but could only be kept on for a few years because of the financial crisis. Alongside a number of administrative tasks, both men pursued the goal of producing a theory of the foundations of the National Socialist system of rule.[76] Marcuse's role was that of the chief philosopher of the institute, together with Horkheimer. In that function he had worked on the new programme that was destined to become the increasingly philosophical conception of a critical theory.[77]

Adorno's duties in the institute included, in conjunction with Löwenthal, editorial work on the *Zeitschrift*, with whose contents and general level he was deeply concerned. Moreover, ever since his time in Oxford, he had been entrusted by Horkheimer with the task of negotiating with Walter Benjamin about the latter's publications in the *Zeitschrift*. Benjamin was undoubtedly one of the prickliest contributors in the inner circle. For this reason, it was left to Adorno to conduct the correspondence once Benjamin had finally submitted the long-awaited essay on Baudelaire. This piece, on which Benjamin had been working, though with interruptions, since 1937, hoping to turn it into a book, had a particular importance. He intended to treat his Baudelaire studies as a model for his larger enterprise, the arcades project. At the same time, the essay was conceived as an independent chapter in the future work.[78] In this preliminary version, Benjamin examines Baudelaire from a social, not a literary, point of view. What he envisaged was a materialist interpretation of the writer in the age of capitalism.[79]

In October 1938, Benjamin wrote to Adorno, saying that he 'had been putting the finishing touches to the second part' of the Baudelaire essay, which was to have three parts in all. This was despite the 'choking anxieties' caused by contemporary events, notably the so-called Munich Agreement of September 1938, which had turned out very much in Hitler's favour, and the heightened risk of war following the entry of the German troops into the Sudetenland on 1 October.[80] A little later on, he forwarded the entire essay to New York. After a close reading of the manuscript, Adorno's reaction was far less euphoric than Benjamin might have hoped. Benjamin had responded to Adorno's study of

Richard Wagner by approving of it in principle, while criticizing a number
of individual passages which in his view were distorted by an interpretation grounded in ideology critique. Adorno, in contrast, was extremely
severe in his judgement of this first version of Benjamin's Baudelaire
essay. Benjamin must have rubbed his eyes in disbelief and re-read the
letter of 10 November 1938 over and over again. Unexpectedly, Adorno
noted that Benjamin operated with a Marxian terminology that seemed
artificial, with the consequence that his analysis, while dialectical in
intention, failed to achieve a proper mediation between Baudelaire's
poetry and the constitution of society. 'You show a prevailing tendency
to relate the pragmatic contents of Baudelaire's work directly and
immediately to adjacent features in the social history and, wherever
possible, the economic features of the time.'[81] Adorno disliked the way
in which Benjamin established causal links between culture and the
economy on the Marxist model of superstructure and base. 'Even though
Baudelaire's wine poems may have been occasioned by the wine duty
or the town gates, the recurrence of these motifs in his oeuvre can only
be explained by the overall social and economic tendencies of the age.'[82]
Adorno even went so far as to reproach Benjamin with having done
violence to himself in order to express what he obviously regarded as
a necessary solidarity with the institute. This had led him 'to pay the
kind of tributes to Marxism which are appropriate neither to Marxism
nor to yourself.'[83] In Benjamin's 'materialist excursions', the reader is
overcome by the apprehension he feels 'for a shivering swimmer who
plunges into cold water'.[84] Instead of such unpleasant leaps, Benjamin
should 'surrender to his own specific insights and conclusions'.[85] Or else
he will have to acquiesce in his own regression to an earlier stage of
historical insight: 'The theological motif of calling things by their names
tends to switch into the wide-eyed presentation of mere facts. If one
wanted to put it rather drastically, one could say that your study is
located at the crossroads of magic and positivism.'[86]

This was, of course, an annihilating judgement, excusable only by
its intention to defend Benjamin against himself, to remind him of his
own theoretical concerns. Benjamin evidently accepted the criticism
in precisely that spirit. For in his first reaction he observed, in a letter to
Scholem: 'The reservations that can be urged against the manuscript
are in part quite reasonable.'[87] The flaws Adorno detected, Benjamin
went on, were connected with the isolation in which he was compelled
to live and work. Furthermore, in the portions of his manuscript that
had been objected to, the 'key importance' of the 'Baudelaire' did not
become sufficiently clear because there, i.e., in the third part of the
planned book, he had failed to lay the theoretical historical foundation
that Adorno had expected. In a letter covering many pages, Benjamin
defended himself by arguing that, when measured against the plan of
the book as a whole, the sections in question were 'essentially composed
of philological material'.[88] And the recourse to dialectical materialism

had nothing to do with a false genuflection to the position of the institute, but arose from 'the experiences which we have all shared during the last fifteen years'.[89]

When Benjamin wrote this letter, he already had before him the galley proofs of Adorno's essay 'On the Fetish-Character of Music and the Regression of Listening'. He announced his own objections to the argument advanced there that, when listening to the music purveyed by the mass media, it is exchange value that is consumed.[90] The fact is that 'one can hardly imagine the "consumption" of exchange value as anything else but an empathy with it.'[91] He also took issue with Adorno's statement that in certain circumstances music can become 'comic'.[92] Adorno had evidently intended to make an indirect criticism of Benjamin's interpretation of Chaplin in the essay on 'The Work of Art'. Such comicalness cannot be seen 'as an entirely negative phenomenon', a sign of decadence.[93] This interplay of criticism and counter-criticism was characteristic of the communication between the two friends; they 'never acted differently' and never practised criticism as a form of one-upmanship.[94]

Although Adorno was much taken up with his various duties both in the institute and outside it, the intensity of his exchanges with Benjamin scarcely suffered. Thus Adorno found time to make suggestions to Benjamin in 1939 when the latter began to revise his Baudelaire essay of the previous autumn and prepare it for publication.[95] Many of Adorno's ideas proved helpful to Benjamin, just as his criticisms had encouraged him to produce a completely reworked essay version.[96] Adorno greeted this new version enthusiastically, describing it as 'the most perfect thing you have done since the book on baroque drama', distinguished by the fact that 'every moment of the work is equally close to the centre'.[97]

After leaving the radio research project, Adorno seemed to enjoy a special status when compared to the core staff in the institute, who also represented the institute in the lecture series of the extension division of Columbia University. He enjoyed the privilege of being a contractually secure employee of the institute. At the same time, he could claim to be Horkheimer's chosen partner in writing the legendary book on 'dialectical logic'. This plan expressed with particular clarity the tendency to 're-philosophize' Horkheimer's programme, which had previously emphasized interdisciplinarity. This trend began with his essay 'Traditional and Critical Theory'.[98] His new philosophical orientation and its accompanying key concept of 'critical theory' fell on fertile soil as far as Adorno was concerned. He hoped that he would soon be able to form a close alliance with Horkheimer. Despite the many other calls on the latter's time, Adorno urged him not to lose sight of this project. His declared enthusiasm was mixed with an undertone of anxiety lest Horkheimer should end up choosing to work full-time on the book on dialectic with Löwenthal or Marcuse instead of him. To his regret, Adorno had to accept the fact that for the time being he had only the administrative machinery of the institute at his disposal. Initially, he could only work there directly part-time, to dictate letters or have memoranda or manuscripts typed up. And even this could only be done by arrangement with Löwenthal or Marcuse. Alternatively, he could use the time when Horkheimer was away, something that happened with growing frequency because he found that the New York climate exacerbated his serious cardiovascular problems.

Unlike Adorno, Horkheimer had few doubts that, if he was to write this fundamental book on 'dialectical logic' at all, it could only be done with Adorno's cooperation. He took the opportunity created by the latter's departure from the radio research project to initiate a series of discussions in spring and autumn 1939, at intervals at first, and then on a regular basis. These discussions focused on topics such as 'criticism in positivism', 'the concept of the individual', 'the concept of myth' and 'knowledge and truth'. These New York discussions, which have been recorded in part by Gretel Adorno, were intended to provide a first draft of the book to be produced jointly.[99]

Even if Adorno frequently worked at home he was far from allowing himself to be seduced by the life of an isolated private scholar. He took an active part in planning and advancing two research projects. His time with Lazarsfeld had taught him how to formulate sociological problems so that the institute could use his detailed plan as a basis for grant applications to the American foundations. One project he had agreed with Horkheimer and worked out partly with Franz Neumann was to look into the causes and functions of anti-Semitism. Typically, he began by establishing a theoretical framework. He also took part in another project on modern German culture. The aim here was to use a wide selection of material with which to analyse the economic, political, social and intellectual development of Germany from 1900 up to the Nazi seizure of power.

In summer 1940, while Horkheimer was travelling on the West Coast on a second, extended trip, Adorno, who was acting as deputy in his absence, took the opportunity to announce 'the birth of the design for our new Jewish project', which had been written at last despite the unbearable New York heatwave (it was 38° Celsius).[100] A short time after that, Adorno wrote to Charles Edward Merriam, the dean of the Department of Political Science at the University of Chicago and a member of the advisory committee of the Institute of Social Research, saying that one aim of this project was 'to trace the psychology and typology of present-day anti-Semitism'.[101] In view of the alarming events that were unfolding, such a topic obviously had urgent significance for the German émigrés. Since 1938 the Nazis had adopted increasingly brutal measures to force Jewish citizens into emigration, and they had also accelerated the process of 'Aryanizing' the German economy. Anti-Jewish repressive measures culminated in the pogroms of 9–10

November throughout the Reich. Previously to this there had been blackmail and boycotts. Now there were open acts of violence and arson attacks on Jewish synagogues and other buildings. The so-called Kristallnacht was the beginning of the Nazi regime's policy of physical violence towards Jews. It would soon lead to the 'Final Solution', the murder of millions of Jews throughout Europe.

Adorno's parents in Frankfurt were not spared the effects of these anti-Jewish measures. His father's offices were ransacked, he himself was injured and finally arrested and forced to spend several weeks in gaol. His wife Maria was also interned for several days and Oscar lost the right to dispose of his own property. Adorno was of course fully informed of these terrible events. Evidently greatly shocked, he described what had happened in Frankfurt in a letter to Benjamin on 1 February 1939. His father was now almost seventy, and following this persecution, with its physical and mental after-effects, he contracted pneumonia, so that the family was prevented initially from making use of its travel permit to Cuba. Not until the spring of 1939 did Adorno's parents succeed in emigrating to the USA, where they arrived safely early in 1940, after a lengthy stay in Cuba.[102] Some of their possessions, including private family papers, were destroyed by fire in a storage warehouse.[103]

Benjamin was to learn from bitter personal experience that even exile in France would not save him from the impact of Nazi rule. Following the November pogroms he had sought French naturalization, but without success. After the Stalin–Hitler Pact of August 1939, the position of the refugees who had fled from the German Reich became increasingly precarious in France. After the German army had invaded Poland on 1 September 1939, and England and France had declared war on Germany, all German-speaking émigrés living in Paris were rounded up and interned in the football stadium Yves du Manoir in Colombes. Among them was Benjamin, who was taken from there directly to a '*camp des travailleurs volontaires*' close to Nevers. He kept the Adornos informed of his fate by the letters he was able to write to Gretel from the camp.[104] Thanks to the efforts of a friend, Adrienne Monnier, the bookseller and publisher famous for her championing of modern writers such as James Joyce, T. S. Eliot and Ernest Hemingway, Benjamin was released from the Château de Vermuche in November 1939, and was able to return to Paris, his health gravely undermined.[105]

The fact that Adorno's parents had become the victims of Nazi terrorism and that Benjamin, with many other émigrés in France, had been interned in contravention of international law undoubtedly helped to sharpen Adorno's assessment of the catastrophic course taken by the Nazi leadership in its pursuit of policies leading to genocide. Bombarded by the news from Europe about Hitler's racial policies, he 'could no longer ignore the fate of the Jews', he wrote to Horkheimer in August 1940. 'It often seems to me as if all the suffering we are accustomed to think of in connection with the proletariat has now been transferred to the Jews in a horrifyingly concentrated form. I wonder whether we should not say . . . the things we are actually planning to say [in the book they were planning jointly] in connection with the Jews who represent the opposite pole of the concentration of power.'[106]

Horkheimer's parents, Moritz and Babette, who were eighty and seventy years old respectively, were similarly affected by the same events, and they had emigrated to Switzerland at the beginning of 1939. Horkheimer too was forced to think about the causes of this horror that had started to assume global proportions. Needless to say, neither man was enough of an optimist to suppose that the insights that might emerge from their research would enable them to prevent or even influence the catastrophic course of events. The only thing they believed they might hope for was articulated in a letter Horkheimer wrote to Salka Viertel, the actress and scriptwriter. What he said there came very close to Adorno's views on the position of the critical intellectual: 'In view of what is now threatening to engulf Europe, . . . our present work is essentially destined to pass things down through the night that is approaching: a kind of message in a bottle.'[107] This image, incidentally, was one that Adorno himself used on occasion.

Given Adorno's intensive working day, the paralysing attitude of resignation was not an option. His time was increasingly filled with the growing number of duties that he had to perform in the institute. In February 1940, he gave a lecture in Columbia University 'On Kierkegaard's Doctrine of Love'.[108] Shortly afterwards, he made his debut on American radio. When Eduard Steuermann and the Kolisch Quartet presented works by Schoenberg, Zemlinsky, Eisler and Krenek, Adorno took part by delivering an introductory talk.

Adorno's frantic activity during these months was accompanied by a growing anxiety about Benjamin, who now found himself in an extremely dangerous situation in Paris. After his return from the internment camp, he soon realized that there was no longer any safe place for him in Europe. Immediately after the German invasion of Poland, Adorno, fiercely supported by his wife, urged Benjamin to start proceedings to emigrate to the USA without delay.[109] However, it was now becoming increasingly difficult to leave. Following Hitler's offensive in the west, over two million refugees – Walter Benjamin among them – fled in panic from Paris in June 1940, hoping to find sanctuary in unoccupied France. The pilgrimage town of Lourdes to the north-west of the Pyrenees was Benjamin's first stopping-place. There he waited for the documents that would permit him to enter the United States. At the urging of Adorno and his wife, Horkheimer had taken out an affidavit, an emergency visa, which had been left with the American consul in Marseilles. In August Benjamin reached Marseilles, which was crammed full with refugees. He hoped to be able to collect the transit visa for Spain and Portugal, and to proceed from there to Lisbon, from where he intended to leave for the USA. In his haste, which was undoubtedly justified, he found he could not wait to obtain an exit visa from France and so he decided on an illegal frontier crossing. Together with a group of refugees that included Henny Gurland and her young son,[110] and guided by Lisa Fittko, a German on the anti-fascist left who helped escaping refugees, Benjamin set out on the taxing journey on foot across the Pyrenees from Banyuls-sur-Mer to Port Bou in Spain.[111] At the frontier town of Port Bou Benjamin learnt that a temporary government decision had rendered his Spanish transit visa invalid. He thus found himself faced with the desperate prospect of being sent back to France, where he would once again be confined in an internment camp. Benjamin, whose heart was troubling him once again and who was now completely at the end of his tether and in despair, decided to end his life with an overdose of morphine tablets. He died late in the evening of 26 September 1940, at the age of forty-eight.[112] The previous evening he had penned a few lines to Adorno, a copy of which Henny Gurland delivered to him in New York in October.[113]

Meanwhile, Adorno and Gretel were firmly expecting their friend to arrive in New York and had already started to look for somewhere for him to live. The news of his desperate last act must have come as a shattering blow to both of them.[114] Adorno wrote to Scholem: 'I cannot express in words what it means to us. Our mental and empirical existence has been transformed through and through. Both Gretel and I have been gripped by an inner torpor that will probably find its limits only just before our own end.'[115] Through Benjamin's death,[116] he wrote, 'philosophy has been deprived of the best . . . that it might ever have hoped for.'[117] In an obituary that appeared in the well-known exile newspaper *Aufbau* on 18 October 1940, he found words that conveyed some sense of the extent to which he saw himself mirrored in the friend he had now lost forever: 'He followed the compulsion of an incomparable talent and did not seek shelter in existing situations, in philosophical schools and recognized habits of thought.'[118]

Adorno's and Gretel's pain was especially acute because they had been convinced that Benjamin 'would have been saved, if he had only held out another twelve hours. . . . It is completely incomprehensible – as if he had been gripped by a stupor and wished to obliterate himself even though he was already rescued.'[119] The statements in Adorno's letters about such shattering events as Benjamin's tragic death show that he felt overcome by despair. Only by doing violence to himself was he able to continue with the daily tasks of research. Adorno reckoned with an 'unending sequence of catastrophes, chaos and horror as far as the eye can see'.[120] He could have few doubts about the realities of political and historical events. Nevertheless, he was as reluctant to think of them as destined by fate as he was to try and protect himself by adopting an attitude of resigned acceptance or by seeking refuge in an ivory tower. Instead, he invested time and energy in the projects undertaken by the institute during the few years remaining until the current research activities in Morningside Heights were gradually wound up with his departure and Horkheimer's to Santa Monica, near Los Angeles.

For his study of 'Cultural Aspects of National Socialism', Adorno designed texts on the topics of 'culture' and 'cultural crises'. Although the institute had made great efforts to enlist the advice and support of recognized American scholars such as Carl Joachim Friedrich, the project was unsuccessful in its application to the Rockefeller Foundation. Unexpectedly, financial assistance was not forthcoming. Similarly, the first attempt to carry out a detailed study on anti-Semitism failed to obtain financial backing from the American Jewish Committee. The institute, and Adorno especially, had done everything in their power to produce a solid methodological and theoretical foundation for this project.[121] Horkheimer conjectured that questions of academic politics must have been at the root of this rejection. 'There is a much larger issue at stake here, the universal law of monopolistic society. In such societies science is controlled by its trusted agents. They constitute an elite that works hand in glove with the economic powers-that-be.' Only those who adjust and adapt have a chance in the American academic system, not those who avoid control and insist on their independence. But this was the precondition of a theory of society in the tradition of Marx.[122] The resigned tone and the rather prolix reflections on the dependence of research on large foundations provoked a succinct reply from Adorno: 'Socially, this is a question of the relation of a cartel to independent small business.'[123] The fact that no American money was forthcoming for the undeniably important anti-Semitism project did not deter Adorno and Horkheimer from trying to construct a theory of anti-Semitism, which now began to preoccupy them more than anything else. As early as 18 September 1940, Adorno sent his first drafts to Horkheimer, who was in California, where he intended to settle down – for preference somewhere near Hollywood. An enclave of affluent German émigrés was already living there.

In his brief exposé Adorno sketched elements of 'a prehistory' of anti-Semitism. He based it on the assumption that, 'at a very early stage of history, the Jews . . . either scorned the transition from a nomadic existence to a settled one, or else clung to the nomadic form or . . . only made an imperfect transition.' They are thus 'the secret gypsies of history'. Adorno connected the fact that the Jews always refused to recognize all particular and local deities with their unwillingness 'to acknowledge any *one*, limited home' as their own. The Jews were the people 'who did not allow themselves to be "civilized" and subjected to the primacy of labour. They have not been forgiven for this and this explains why they are the stumbling block in class society.' This specific Jewish 'extraterritoriality' is what was then being expressed in both anti-Semitism and the Jewish reaction to it.[124] These speculative ideas on the history of anti-Semitism represented Adorno's attempt to link up with Horkheimer's arguments in 'The Jews and Europe', an essay that had appeared in 1939 in the *Zeitschrift für Sozialforschung*, which was renamed the *Studies in Philosophy and Social Science* in that year. Together with Horkheimer's contributions, 'The Authoritarian State' and 'The End of Reason', both written in 1940–1, these texts had emerged from the intensive discussions with Adorno and now constituted a material foundation for the projected book on dialectics. All three essays were underpinned by the same question: what were the causes of the self-destruction of reason as we find it in the different versions of totalitarianism and in anti-Semitism? Horkheimer also thought of his essays as building blocks for a theory of fascism, something which had also been included in the institute's programme since 1940.

The attempts by members of the institute to formulate a theory of fascism or National Socialism led to vigorous in-house controversies. On the one side, there were Franz Neumann, Otto Kirchheimer and A. R. L. Gurland, on the other, Fritz Pollock, Max Horkheimer and Theodor Adorno. The first group defended the somewhat simplistic continuity thesis. According to this, the fascist system sprang from a capitalist system that began by being liberal and then became monopolistic. Thus National Socialism was essentially a form of capitalism, and recurrent economic crises would therefore eventually cause it to founder on its own contradictions. The second group maintained in contrast that fascism was a fundamentally new form of rule. What defined this totalitarian 'state capitalism' was the fact that the economic system was directed by politics, and that the free market operating in liberal epochs was now replaced by a comprehensive planning system. Monopolies, acting as agencies of government, would now replace the market.[125] The controlling apparatus would consist of a cartel of the leading cliques belonging to the party and the state, together with some top managers from major industrial companies. What the two theories had in common was the assumption that National Socialism contained monopolistic elements and command mechanisms alongside one another. But whereas Pollock thought that the market was being replaced by command mechanisms and that state functions disabled the key market functions, Neumann insisted on the crucial importance of crises in the workings of capitalism and on the tensions between the forces and relations of production.[126]

Horkheimer was concerned to bring the two sides together, but he also defended Pollock's 'state-capitalist theory' against Neumann's 'theory of monopoly capitalism'. What was of central importance in his eyes was how to explain the irrationality of racism and of the expulsion and persecution of the European Jews. In his essay of 1939, the most pessimistic he ever wrote, he ascribed the rise of anti-Semitism to the historical end of the liberal phase of capitalism and the simultaneous emergence of the totalitarian form of organized capitalism. In this new

form of capitalism the sphere of circulation, which had been the traditional source of Jewish commercial activity and also the foundation of
bourgeois democracy, ceased to have any meaning. Horkheimer interpreted fascism and anti-Semitism as having arisen from the internal
dynamics of liberal capitalism. 'He who does not wish to speak of capitalism, should also remain silent about fascism.'[127] It follows that, strictly
speaking, any critique of the fate of the Jews should contain a critique
of liberalism and capitalism. Horkheimer sought to deliver some initial
arguments for this. His essay of 1940 on 'The Authoritarian State' pointed
in the same direction. Here too, Horkheimer proceeded on the assumption that the economy was characterized by a growing tendency towards
monopoly and hence by a general dependence on the large trusts.
Competition was being eliminated by the internal logic of capitalism
itself. He perceived the danger that authoritarian states on the model of
the terrorist National Socialist state might be formed elsewhere than in
Germany and the Soviet Union as a complement to the monopolist
tendencies of industry. This meant that a new technocratic power was
on the point of emerging that would lead to an 'integral statism', a state
'that had freed itself of all dependence upon private capital'.[128] Marx's
hope that society could be utterly transformed was not merely an illusion, but utopian in the bad sense. For since reason had placed itself
entirely in the service of domination, the revolutionary will to make
a better humanity can no longer appeal to the forces of production as
the power bases of historical progress. Horkheimer gave added depth
to these ideas in his essay 'Reason and Self-Preservation'. As reason
allows itself to be forced into the service of self-preservation, it is transformed into instrumental rationality. 'The new, fascist order is reason
in which reason is unmasked as unreason.'[129]

Adorno too wished to play his part in ensuring that he and Horkheimer
could finally make a start on their much talked-about book on dialectical
logic. He did not confine himself to verbal and epistolary exchanges
with Horkheimer, but took the trouble to work out his own view of the
debate on totalitarianism. Although he had a number of objections to
Pollock's essays on state capitalism, he nevertheless adopted Pollock's
theory in his own 'Reflections on Class Theory', which he wrote in 1942
in the form of a working paper. However, he did broaden Pollock's
theory, turning it into a general diagnosis of the age: 'The most recent
phase of class society is dominated by monopolies; it is pressing forward
towards fascism, the form of political organization worthy of it. . . . The
total organization of society by big business and its omnipresent technology has taken possession of the world and our minds to the point
where the idea that things could ever be different has become a forlorn
endeavour.'[130] The paper contained a number of judgements on structural
changes in late industrial society that Adorno subsequently probed more
deeply in his sociological analyses of the present. Thus, for example, he
noted that one feature of society was that the proletariat now appeared

as a diffuse mass.[131] Thanks to the concentration of power, domination becomes universal, and thus invisible, so invisible that objective class antagonisms no longer become manifest. The fact that some dependent workers had a higher standard of living at that point arose from their function in contributing to the prosperity of the entire system. The existing distinction between power and impotence is concealed by the 'technological veil' behind which force lies concealed. Adorno thought of these reflections on class theory as well as the other texts he had written up to then as contributions to a second stage which would explore the question of questions, the question of 'Why mankind, instead of entering into a truly human condition, is sinking into a new kind of barbarism.'[132]

Between two stools once again: a long road from New York to Los Angeles

Adorno and his wife were still suffering from the loss of Walter Benjamin when they found themselves having to come to terms with the separation from Max and Maidon Horkheimer, to whom they had grown very close. After some hesitation, Horkheimer had finally decided on the move to the West Coast so as to continue working from there with some organizational changes and with some change of emphasis in the content of his work. Of course, he assumed that the work with Adorno would continue. But for Adorno it was somewhat irritating to learn that the plan – and admittedly the plan could change from one day to the next – was for Pollock, Marcuse and Löwenthal to move too and settle down in Pacific Palisades close to Horkheimer. Even worse, Horkheimer showed himself unwilling to exclude them absolutely from taking part in the great project of a dialectical logic. For Adorno, who was not free from feelings of jealousy, everything hinged on writing the book exclusively with Horkheimer, if possible, without the distraction and the burden of everyday activities on behalf of the institute. In reality, the scene was set for precisely this development. In spring 1941, the Horkheimers had moved into the bungalow that he had had built at 13524 D'Este Drive. Katya and Thomas Mann lived just around the corner, and their house was visible from the Horkheimer house. 'It cannot be denied that he has a certain culture *quand même*',[133] Horkheimer announced to Adorno, who had worshipped the world-famous writer since his youth. Nearby, Lion Feuchtwanger had acquired a magnificent property. In the vicinity of Hollywood and the villas of the suburb of Santa Monica, there was a number of other well-known personalities whom Horkheimer (and later Adorno) knew more or less well. They included Berthold and Salka Viertel, Bertolt Brecht and Helene Weigel, Arnold and Gertrud Schoenberg, Charlotte and Wilhelm Dieterle, and Bruno and Liesel Frank.[134]

Horkheimer was evidently kept busy trying to manage the administrative affairs and questions of personnel from his house in Pacific
Palisades. But, in addition, he took care to make sure that Adorno's
productivity should remain focused on the joint project of philosophical self-clarification. He broached a somewhat arcane topic: that of
questions of the philosophy of language. He wanted to know what
language was appropriate to critical thought in the specific sense of
thought that was both anti-positivistic and anti-idealist.[135] In his first
written response, Adorno argued that the disintegration of language
was unstoppable; it must be understood as the expression of the impotence of the subject in the face of the overwhelming power of social
conditions. 'The power of the facts has become so appalling that all
theory, even true theory, seems ridiculous by the side of it. This has
been burnt into the organ of theory, namely language, and has left its
mark on it.'[136] However, Horkheimer declined to let himself be sucked
into the global critique of linguistic usage. He was interested instead in
clarifying the interplay between language and reason. He asked whether
the universal nature of language was not the precondition of the possibility of reason, and whether 'it might not be possible to ground the
idea of a true society . . . in an interpretation of this universality.' It
would follow that, if language enters into the service of existing society,
it must find itself in constant contradiction to its own nature, and this
would become manifest in individual linguistic structures.'[137] He was
preoccupied by the question of whether language has a transcendental
status, whether it is more than a medium for describing the world
and carrying out actions, and whether all speech presupposes truth and
reason. He had an extremely interesting intuition about language which
he was able to articulate very clearly: 'To speak to someone means
basically to recognize him as a possible member of a future association
of free human beings. To speak presupposes a common relation to the
truth, and hence the innermost affirmation of the alien existence that
is being addressed, and indeed of all existent beings according to their
potential.'[138] Adorno evidently failed to notice Horkheimer's originality, the innovative potential of his reflections on language, for in his
answering letter, which he wrote forthwith, he turned Horkheimer's
tentative ideas on their head. His own view of language was based on
the rather more orthodox idea of its social preformation, its reification.[139]
For this reason, he interpreted Horkheimer's insight into the rational
potential of language as a deciphering of 'the antagonistic character
of all language hitherto. . . . If mankind is not yet mature, that means
literally that up to now human beings have not been able to speak.'[140]
However, in one brief passage an idea surfaces that comes closer to
Horkheimer's speculative notions. He finds it hard to understand,
Adorno writes, 'how a man who speaks can be a rogue or that he
could lie.' The idea contradicts 'the truth claims of language'. 'The statement that a man has said something and it must therefore be true, a

statement that all clever people ridicule – such a statement contains the truth that cleverness betrays.'[141]

At the time, the attempt to arrive at an independent approach to a philosophy of language misfired. Philosophical problems about the course of world history and mankind's role in it moved to centre stage. These were the problems that many intellectuals felt the need to confront.

One specific trigger leading to such a focus was provided by the rescue of a manuscript belonging to Walter Benjamin. This manuscript, which had an electrifying effect at the time, was his set of 'Theses on the Philosophy of History', his last completed work, and one which went missing for some time, before being brought to Adorno in the institute in June 1941. He knew of the existence of the manuscript, since Benjamin had mentioned it in his letters of April and May 1940, and proposed to make its eighteen theses accessible for a first reading and internal discussion, even though 'they open the door to enthusiastic misunderstanding'.[142] Adorno thought of the document as Benjamin's intellectual testament. Nine months after Benjamin's death, Adorno was given a copy of his notes by Hannah Arendt, who had just arrived in New York.[143] She and her husband, Heinrich Blücher, had succeeded where Benjamin had failed and had escaped from Paris via Marseilles. While they were still in Marseilles, Benjamin had entrusted the couple with a collection of manuscripts, among them 'Theses on the Philosophy of History'. Adorno immediately wrote to Horkheimer telling him of the find, which he said came closer to his own way of thinking than anything else. This referred 'above all to the idea of history as a permanent catastrophe, the criticism of progress, the domination of nature and the attitude to culture'.[144] For Adorno, who was contemplating a critique of the entire tradition of Western civilization, Benjamin's ideas about the disruption of historical continuity were a far greater source of inspiration than Horkheimer's ideas about language. Adorno's mind was by no means closed to Horkheimer's suggestions, but he had his own ideas about the shape of the future book. In order to put them forward he wished to go to California as soon as possible so as to continue the discussions that had been broken off.

Nevertheless, it was Marcuse who was the first to follow Horkheimer to the West Coast. Pollock followed soon afterwards. However, both returned a few months later to attend to the increasingly urgent affairs of the institute, and especially to take part in the lecture series at Columbia University. Löwenthal, to his sorrow, was anyway condemned to stick to his post in New York, although he later visited Horkheimer and Adorno in California. Horkheimer's hesitations in making decisions about staffing were not primarily the effect of his own vacillations, but were caused by the fact that since May 1940 the problems of the future organization of the institute were becoming more acute. Among these difficulties was the visit to the institute in the middle of the summer by two detectives who wished to inform themselves in detail about the individual members, their origins, their activities and their attitudes towards the USA. Unlike Pollock, and also Löwenthal, who informed Horkheimer about the visitation in a letter, the latter did not take the matter lightly. He regarded it as the beginning of a changed attitude towards the German immigrants on the part of the American authorities. Horkheimer was alive to the danger represented by Roosevelt's new foreign policy, which was directed against Hitler's expansion plans. Horkheimer approved of the policy, needless to say, but it contained the risk that the immigrants might in general be suspected of being part of a fifth column.[145] In the circumstances, might it not be advisable to dissolve the institute on the grounds that it was an all-too-visible organization of German émigrés? On the other hand, there was the attractive opportunity of becoming more closely integrated in Columbia University or the Department of Sociology there. Such an integration presupposed that the institute could be maintained as a fully functioning and financially secure research organization over the longer term. This meant carrying out empirical research projects and, in the absence of funding of its own, laborious applications to the foundations. Horkheimer clearly understood that such a research programme was very much in tune with the expectations of his colleagues at Columbia University who were protecting him: namely 'solid research and team work in the field of social science'.[146] But, as he put it in a letter to Löwenthal, this 'getting on with the work is destroying us both materially and theoretically. It will be our ruin in every respect.'[147]

The alternative to Horkheimer's bleak view, which was connected in his mind with a research programme on the American model, was to cut back the number of staff and the building space required in order to be able to secure a more or less adequate financial basis for the people who could be regarded as the core members of the institute. Whereas closing the institute meant that Horkheimer and his associates might well lose the extremely valuable protection of Columbia University, further integration meant that the increasing adaptation to the American research model would threaten their own academic identity. According to Horkheimer's view at the time, this identity would find expression in the ability of each individual member to develop his own theory of society in which there would be less emphasis on empirical verifiability than on its philosophical foundations. Despite his negative experience with Lazarsfeld, Adorno was by no means hostile to the idea of empirical research; in fact, he thought it meaningful and necessary in principle. However, his own intentions were naturally closer to Horkheimer's interest in theory. In his frequent letters to Los Angeles, he emphasized his complete agreement with Horkheimer and pleaded 'for the institute to be closed on 31 December, staffing to be reduced to a minimum so that the money will suffice for a few people, unless we really obtain a lot of money in the meantime.'[148] In contrast to Marcuse, Löwenthal and Neumann, Adorno spoke out strongly in favour of reducing his own activities and confining them to giving lectures and seminars within the Social Science Faculty of Columbia University. Pollock played a waiting game. As always, he only gave his true opinion in confidence to Horkheimer: 'It is interesting to observe how our colleagues behave. Marcuse is terrified that after five years he will be running around like Günther Stern [i.e., Günther Anders] and so wants to keep up the links with Columbia at all costs. Teddie has only one interest: to become a small rentier in California as quickly as possible, and he could not care less what happens to the others. Neumann . . . underlines the importance of the link with Columbia. Only Löwenthal . . . is totally loyal.'[149]

Against his own wishes, Adorno had to stay in New York for the time being. However much he may have longed for the West Coast and the great theory project, he and Gretel looked forward to the move with mixed feelings. After all, they had made themselves very much at home in New York, and had a large circle of friends and a daily routine that had become a habit, with fixed working periods in the institute, writing at home in the apartment on Riverside Drive, and the regular vacations in Bar Harbor. 'It is more beautiful here than ever', Adorno wrote at the end of July 1941 to Horkheimer. 'Because of the war and the defence boom, there are only old people here still and we feel very comfortable with them.'[150] The couple had become quite fond of Central Park as well as the zoo in the Bronx. 'The okapi', he wrote to Horkheimer, 'is quite an experience.' 'With a snobbery that would fill fifty pages in Proust, it nevertheless looks quite unassuming; it is housed in the antelope house and hardly anyone comes to see it.'[151]

One further source of pleasure in New York was the fact that Adorno's parents, who were now in their mid-seventies, had been living there since early 1940, after brief sojourns in Cuba and Miami. The proximity to their only son and his wife must have been a great comfort for them. Their inevitable expectations were of course no secret. Adorno and Gretel tried to look after them as much as possible, and where it wasn't they wrote to them, telling them about their lives and letting them share their plans and intentions.

Apart from their personal ties on the Hudson, a further problem was that the move to California seemed to drag on endlessly, and kept being postponed from one month to the next, so that Adorno must have felt that everything was in the balance. The situation did not become clear until summer 1941, when the move was fixed for the end of the year. In September he and Gretel gave up their apartment, put the furniture into store and took a short let in a furnished studio (611 West 113th Street). Now that the die was cast, the irritations that were connected with the projected move all dissolved. Adorno told Horkheimer how happy he was at their being reunited once again. 'Oh, Max, everything is settled now, and we shall manage everything together.'[152] In the same breath he assured Horkheimer that he had made careful preparations for the philosophical labour that awaited them. Thus he had been reading Geoffrey Gorer's new book on the Marquis de Sade,[153] and this had made it clear to him once again that anti-Semitism could be a 'crystalliza-tion point' for the future book. The same letter, on 10 November 1941, contains the first mention of the actual title of the joint work: *Dialectic of Enlightenment*.[154] In his joy about the imminent collaboration, Adorno went so far as to write an 'alphabet in verse', evidently inspired by reading about the Marquis de Sade, with which he hoped to surprise his friend. 'Sodomy comes from need in bed / Sadism makes the cheeks glow red.'[155]

Despite his exuberant high spirits, Adorno did have reservations on one point. Would he not be forced into inferior living conditions in Los Angeles, and would this prevent him from continuing with a life and way of working that had now become a habit? 'You know', he observed in a letter of August 1941, 'how far we are from craving any particular status, but precisely because of that I believe that the protection given by a certain bourgeois solidity cannot be overestimated.' He ended the letter with the question: 'When will we be able to sit in the garden together, dictating, etching, "lammergeiering" together? Soon!'[156] And that is how things turned out. By the middle of November, Adorno and his wife had arrived in Los Angeles.

15

Happiness in Misfortune: Adorno's Years in California

The original plan had been to travel to the West Coast by car, since Gretel had obtained her driver's licence shortly before the move, and had turned out to be an enthusiastic driver. In the event, they went by train in November. In a long letter, Adorno told his parents all about the journey across the continent. From New York, they travelled to Cleveland, where they spent the night. The next stop was Chicago, where they took time to look at the city. The journey was resumed in the evening when they travelled in a sleeping-car through Nebraska, the Rockies and snow-covered Utah. After three nights they were pleasantly surprised by the south, with its palm trees and orange groves. Horkheimer and his wife were there at Los Angeles station early in the morning to welcome them.

Adorno was impressed by the landscape, which reminded him of Tuscany, the sea and the colourful vegetation. A trip to see the ocean at sunset, he wrote to his parents, was one of the most powerful impressions he had ever had in his life. He also liked the style that the houses were built in and, despite the closeness of Hollywood, the landscape was not much spoilt by advertising. Horkheimer had already organized a car for them so that they were mobile from the start and could travel around the neighbourhood. Max's house could be reached in barely more than ten minutes' drive.

Adorno and Gretel were not just enchanted by the scenery; they were also delighted with their new house, which fitted more or less precisely all the criteria Adorno had earlier specified.[1] Immediately on their arrival they had to spend nineteen days in the Brentshire Motel on Wilshire Boulevard, until they were able to move into their own house on 1 December. This was at 316 South Kenter Avenue, Brentwood Heights, an attractively situated house outside Santa Monica, not far from Sunset Boulevard. It was a semi-detached, two-storey house, as he wrote in his second letter to his parents. On the upper ground floor, there was a large, light living room as well as a small dining room with access to the kitchen. On the first floor there were two bedrooms, bathrooms and a study. Even their wish for a small garden had been granted, and the view from there reminded them of Fiesole near Florence. A few weeks after they had moved in, their own furniture arrived, and scarcely had they settled in early in 1942 than they received their first invitations – from Salka Viertel and from the Dieterles. They also met Brecht, Schoenberg and Max Reinhardt.[2] Not only did Adorno find himself accepted into the network of Hollywood society, his material circumstances were also assured thanks to the monthly payments from the Hermann-Weil-Stiftung, so that, financially speaking, he could lead a relatively untroubled life. For his activities at the institute, he drew an annual salary of approximately $3400, which was roughly equivalent to the salary of a professor at an American university at the time. He also received a contribution of $150 towards the cost of the move from New York to Los Angeles. Since Oscar Wiesengrund had been able to salvage at least a portion of his not inconsiderable wealth, Adorno did not have to contribute to the support of his parents in New York.

Now that the long-planned and greatly longed-for collaboration between Horkheimer and Adorno could become reality, both could point to a considerable quantity of preliminary work. This included the records of their discussions in New York in 1939 and Horkheimer's essays. Adorno's contribution amounted to his provisional 'Notes towards a New Anthropology',[3] as well as two essays, one a criticism of Oswald Spengler's two-volume book *The Decline of the West*, or rather the underlying world-view, with its cultural pessimism and its traditionalist view of history and its nature and goals; the other, a discussion of Thorsten Veblen's *Theory of the Leisure Class*.[4] In that book Veblen depicted the conspicuous consumption of the upper class as the expression of its members' exaggerated search for prestige. Adorno decoded Veblen's social critique as a verdict inspired by a cast of mind dominated by the puritan work ethic. It was ineffectual because it went no further than denouncing the external aspect of the consumption of luxury goods. Adorno emphasized his view with an argument that was typical of his way of thinking: 'As the reflection of truth, appearances are dialectical; to reject all appearance is to fall completely under its sway, since truth is abandoned with the rubble without which it cannot appear.'[5]

A very different manuscript had a far greater importance for Adorno than these reflections, partly published and partly only sketched out. On his arrival in Los Angeles this manuscript was already complete and typed out in his suitcase. Horkheimer had already read it. This was the draft of his *Philosophy of Modern Music*, which Adorno explicitly thought of as a kind of preparation for the joint project that would occupy his whole attention over the coming months. In this text, which was written between 1940 and 1941, the composer Adorno criticized the regimenting tendencies of orthodox twelve-tone music. At the same time, he discussed some of the central categories of music theory, such as time, form, material, construction, technique and expression. When

Horkheimer first read the numerous pages of this manuscript, he could not restrain his excitement:

> If I have ever in the whole of my life felt enthusiasm about anything, then I did on this occasion. . . . If there are literary documents today that give any room for hope, then your book must be one of them. The entire work appears to me to provide proof that you do not merely feel the sense of responsibility of which you spoke after Benjamin's death, but that you are able to live up to it in your work. I cannot tell you how pleased and happy I am to know that this document exists. If we succeed in directing the observer's incorruptible gaze . . . away from knowledge of society to society itself, and if we can confront the categories which inform your account, despite your openness to the subject, with reality itself, we shall have achieved what theory expects of us today. . . . This piece of work will go a long way to underpinning our common efforts.[6]

There could have been no better start for the discussions and subsequent writing than Horkheimer's approval of Adorno's philosophy of music. In that spirit, Adorno welcomed his friend's idea that, instead of concentrating on art, he should 'at long last speak of society itself. . . . I myself had the feeling as I wrote about music that I was really taking leave of the theory of art, for a considerable time at least.'[7]

Adorno believed that the philosophy of modern music was basically nothing but 'the attempt . . . to explicate the dialectics of the particular and the general in concrete terms.'[8] Adorno had anticipated topics that he wished subsequently to discuss with Horkheimer at a more general, philosophical level. This applied with particular force to his central thesis that the twelve-tone method begins with a rational technique which is then transformed into an irrational system that stifles the constructive impulses of the composer. Adorno criticized Schoenberg as remorselessly as he defended him, and both criticism and defence occurred in the same breath. He argued that Schoenberg like no one else had succeeded in maintaining the tension between expression and construction. And yet, the perfected twelve-tone system turned out to be a 'system by which music dominates nature' and that runs contrary to the 'musical style of freedom'.[9]

In his discussion of Schoenberg, Adorno drew a distinction between three phases in the composer's works: atonal expressionism, twelve-tone technique, and his late style. In the early period of the Second Viennese School, the revolutionary idea of 'the rational total organization of the total musical material'[10] occupied pride of place. Later on, a common denominator for all the dimensions of music was sought and found in twelve-tone technique. This twelve-tone method, which attempts to bring all the elements of a composition into a relationship of equivalence with one another, thus dissolves the traditional idea of the primacy of one element. It is defined by the desire to suspend 'the fundamental contrast upon which all Western music is built – the contrast between polyphonic fugal structure and homophonic sonata-form.'[11] The accompanying suspension of thematic work and a teleological development of formal constants has its basis in the idea of the twelve-tone method, in which 'every single tone is transparently determined by the construction of the whole work.'[12] The variation, likewise, no longer appears. Variation is relegated to the material, preforming it before the actual composition begins. In order to describe what was novel in the dialectical process of composition, Adorno had recourse to a metaphor he frequently uses: twelve-tone music 'makes the inescapable claim that it is equidistant in all its moments from a central point.'[13] This principle can only be satisfied if every single note is determined by the construction of the entire composition. As in his correspondence with Ernst Krenek in the 1930s, Adorno argued that the highly innovative aspects of Schoenberg's method of composition were squandered by the 'omnipresence' of the row. The multiplicity of relationships which were intended to be dynamic, he went on, inevitably ends in making the music static. 'Once again, music subdues time, but no longer by substituting music in its perfection for time, but by negating time through the inhibition of all musical moments by means of an omnipresent construction.'[14] At this juncture, musical freedom reverses into the composer's unlimited domination of the material. 'Accuracy or correctness, as a mathematical hypothesis, takes the place of that element called "the idea" in traditional art. . . . Structure as such is to be correct rather than meaningful.'[15] If the dodecaphonic principle degenerates into a mathematically predetermined scheme, then the musical material will end up being totally preformed from the outset.

The point of Adorno's argument was to demonstrate the two antinomian sides of the historical stage reached by the musical domination of nature. As he put it, 'The conscious disposition over the material of nature is two-sided: the emancipation of the human being from the musical force of nature and the subjection of nature to human purposes.'[16] He left it in no doubt that the only way for music to develop internally was through the progressive domination of the sound material, through its total construction by means of a system of rules that 'then stands opposed to the subjugated material as an alienated, hostile and dominating power'. This power 'degrades the subject, making of it a slave of the "material", as of the empty quintessence of rules, at that moment in which the subject completely subdues the material, indenturing it to its mathematical logic.'[17] At the same time he maintained, provocatively, that 'the integral work of art . . . is absolutely senseless.'[18] As a way out of this dilemma, Adorno envisaged a new kind of attitude on the part of the composer, one which abandons 'fidelity to the universal domination of the material'.[19] For 'this growing indifference of the material', we must look at Schoenberg's late style. With exemplary logic

Schoenberg drew the conclusion that offers itself to the contemporary artist as a way of expressing the fragmentariness and fractured nature of the work of art. 'Today the only works that really count are those which are no longer works at all.'[20] The twelve-tone composer must not blind himself to this insight. He must remain conscious of the historical significance of dodecaphonic thinking since it made it possible to overcome tradition and open up the horizon. But equally, it may itself be vulnerable, since otherwise it would never be possible to develop a qualitatively new language of music, an emancipated language.

Adorno tried to apply the lessons of his own philosophy of music in his own compositions, which he had taken up again before the move to California.[21] The songs for piano that he wrote no longer stuck dogmatically to the rules of twelve-tone technique. In the six Trakl songs, op. 5, which he completed in 1941, he freely varied the scope of the technique. For example, in *Entlang*, op. 5, no. 4, the row was expanded to ninety-eight notes. The length of the row differed in all six settings.[22]

Adorno's dictum that contemporary composition must prove itself through its reflection on the antinomies it contained within itself was accentuated by his assertion that art in general must be a form of knowledge. But how is it possible for a work of art to become knowledge – and not just any knowledge, but a radical form of knowledge that amounts to a critique of the catastrophic state of the world that also connects up with the state of art? Adorno's answer, one that then became a focal point of his theory of aesthetics, is that the critical insights of a Schoenberg, a Picasso, a Joyce or a Kafka are released in the fragmentary structure of their works.[23] This fragmentation involves not just the loss of aesthetic form, but in modern art it also spells the liquidation of meaning. For music, the 'dissociation of meaning and expression' means that its end links up with its origin. That origin 'is gestural in nature, and closely related to the origin of tears. It is the gesture of release.'[24] The music of the avant-garde resists social constraints and, as oppositional art, represents the gestures of lament about the suffering produced by growing social antagonisms. Authentic music 'has its happiness in the perception of misfortune; all of its beauty is in denying itself the illusion of beauty.' Because its fragmentary nature makes enjoyment difficult, 'no one . . . wishes to become involved with it. . . . It is the surviving message of despair from the shipwrecked.'[25]

This image of messages from the shipwrecked, or messages in a bottle, which appealed to both Adorno and Horkheimer, provided the underlying motif in the texts they worked on intensively from the beginning of 1942, and which were brought together as *Philosophical Fragments* two years later. The manuscript contained a sentence that was programmatic for the whole work and which could well have found a place in the *Philosophy of Modern Music*. The authors spoke of their notes as a 'message' (*Rede*) addressed to an 'imaginary witness' . . . 'to whom we can pass it on – lest it perish with us.'[26] Just as Adorno and

Horkheimer aimed the philosophy they were in the course of formulating at a public that did not yet exist, they were agreed that their theory
of society could not claim to be systematic, nor did it wish to be so.
Instead, it was a critique of existing society: 'Evil rather than good is the
object of theory.'[27] As such it had to be as fragmented as the works of
art of radical modernity. Adorno put the case for this idea very insistently
in a letter to Horkheimer in August 1941. Just as he had already done
in the philosophy of music, he argued the case for the relevance of
gestures in critical theory. Their common philosophical reflections were
'less and less like theories in a traditional sense'. They were rather
'gestures taken from concepts', for which, however, 'the whole labour
of conceptualization' was required.[28] What theory did Adorno have in
mind when he used this metaphor? How did he intend to explain the
relation of language to world once he had rejected the idea of truth as
adequacy, as coherence or correspondence in the course of his critique
of idealism? And what was the metaphysical impulse underlying this
new conception of philosophy that was conceived as a collection of
messages from the shipwrecked – messages that were as shocking in
their content as they were fragmented in form?

Messages in a bottle, or, How to create enlightenment about the Enlightenment

Laugh at logic if it runs counter to the interests of mankind.[29]

'The fully enlightened earth radiates disaster triumphant'[30] – the accusation is directed not at 'the war of all against all' of the world of nature
but at the modern world that lays claim to the fundamental principles of
thought guided by reason and of enlightened action. Because Adorno
and Horkheimer found themselves in a world in which culture and
barbarism lived cheek by jowl, their experience taught them that there
was only one way to go, and this was to undertake a fundamental reconstruction of the rise and fall of Western thought from the standpoint
of a history of philosophy. This reconstruction was linked in their minds
with the wish to pursue the kind of philosophy that would be able to
grasp its epoch in thought. Hegel's dialectical philosophy of contradiction supplied the model for their reconstruction of the history of
civilization in the West, as did Marx with his concept of social labour
and his theories of the historical forms of consciousness. Scarcely less
influential were Nietzsche's *Genealogy of Morals*, with its view of the
emergence of norms and values as a process of overwhelming and dis-
ciplining people, and Freud's late treatise *Civilization and its Discontents*,
according to which an individual's claims to happiness had to be sacrificed
to a social order founded on the compulsion to work and the repression
of the instincts.[31]

Given the objective catastrophe of the age, 'reflection on the destructive aspect of progress'[32] was the decisive imperative guiding their thinking. The ethical impulse leading them towards this undoubtedly gigantic programme of rethinking the process of enlightenment and the principle of rationality by tracing them back to their origins was what they felt to be the urgent need to find the causes of the persistence of suffering in history.

During 1942 their work on this project identified four main themes to be worked on in stages. They wished to show, first, that rationality had a Janus face. The emancipation of the human species from the constraints of nature went hand in hand with the domination of nature both internally and externally. The sovereign subject followed its primary purpose of self-preservation by distinguishing itself resolutely from a reified natural world. But, by doing so, the subject degenerates into a pure means with which to subjugate the whole world without reference to purposes. Adorno and Horkheimer wished to demonstrate the consequences of the high-handedness of the subject by drawing on two unusual examples. On the one hand, they drew on episodes from *The Odyssey*, one of the earliest documents of the human spirit; and, on the other, they explored scenes from the Marquis de Sade's *Story of Juliet*. A second strand of thought focused on the way in which enlightenment becomes transformed into mass deception and a completely commercialized and centrally directed culture attempts systematically to take possession of people's minds. Adorno and Horkheimer went on from there to examine the origins of anti-Semitism, which they treated as a contemporary manifestation of obvious unreason, as the expression of a paranoid behaviour structure. Lastly, the section entitled 'Notes and Drafts' was supposed to contain a number of shorter aphorisms that would shed light on the structure of the entire text, since the authors had renounced the attempt to develop a coherent, logical narrative framework. Instead, the five principal sections of the later book (the concept of reason, the interpretation of *The Odyssey*, the Sade interpretation, analysis of the culture industry and analysis of anti-Semitism) were all conceived as separate essays. Apart from the epistemological reasons[33] that made this approach necessary, their method was also influenced by the working practices that Adorno and Horkheimer had developed over the course of time.

The two men met every afternoon, either in Adorno's or in Horkheimer's house, in order to discuss such central philosophical and sociological problems as the concept of dialectics, the subject–object relation and the domination of nature. These discussions were often quite heated. Their contents were recorded by Gretel Adorno, who then typed them out for further consideration. After many revisions the first drafts for the five sections gradually emerged. The chapters produced by each of them were then discussed line by line. After numerous corrections the texts acquired the status of a provisional version. It was this cooperative work process that they had in mind when in later years they said that they were each responsible for every sentence, since they had dictated their thoughts jointly. They described 'the tension between the two intellectual temperaments' as 'the vital principle' informing their arguments.[34] In reality, the typescripts (and subsequently the pages of the book) do reveal stylistic differences. They show that each author was responsible for specific sections. Thus Adorno later told Rolf Tiedemann that the first chapter on the concept of enlightenment was written jointly, while Adorno wrote the section on *The Odyssey* and Horkheimer that on de Sade. For the chapter on 'Enlightenment as Mass Deception', Adorno wrote drafts that were then revised in detail by Horkheimer. They adopted the reverse procedure for the 'Elements of Anti-Semitism'. Horkheimer wrote the aphoristic texts at the end, to which Adorno appended brief additions.[35]

The book that gradually emerged from 1942 on as the result of the collaboration of these two very distinct temperaments was somewhat different from the book that Horkheimer kept alluding to as a 'dialectical logic'.[36] The reasons for the change were connected with the events of the end of 1941 and early 1942. Horkheimer's already deap-seated pessimism about the course of world history was strengthened further by a number of factors. Chief among these were the expansion of the European crisis into a world war, the news of the massacres of the Jews in the East, the deportations and concentration camps,[37] the appearance of a latent anti-Semitism even in democratic countries, the trend towards the ideological mobilization of the population in the United States, and his sense of horror at the progressive Stalinization of the Soviet Union. For this reason the idea of a negative totality moved to the centre of his thinking about the course of history. It had formed the point of no return of Adorno's thought long before the *Philosophy of Modern Music* and would be expounded more fully in the context of his critique of enlightenment and rationality.

The intellectual harmony between Adorno and Horkheimer was strengthened right from the start by an earlier collaborative effort to prepare the text of *The End of Reason* for publication in the *Studies in Philosophy and Social Science*.[38] This essay, which the two originally intended as a joint venture,[39] already set out to show how the idea of emancipatory reason was turning into a medium of domination. It was a kind of preliminary study for the *Philosophical Fragments*.

The daily work on the comprehensive manuscript on reason and enlightenment had to be interrupted frequently because of the pressure of other commitments. These included such tasks as the rapid production of a report giving the institute's view of method in the social sciences, a programmatic memorandum for the State Department,[40] and various memoranda for the American Jewish Committee, with whom negotiations had been resumed about a number of pending projects.

In addition, Adorno had undertaken the task of finding a publisher for Benjamin's 'Theses on the Philosophy of History'.[41] This manuscript, Walter Benjamin's last, had been in his hands since the summer of 1941. Benjamin's death had made speedy publication a duty. Since the *Zeitschrift* had been suspended for financial reasons (the last issue of the *Studies in Philosophy and Social Science* appeared belatedly in spring 1942),[42] it could not be published there. Adorno decided on a kind of special issue of the journal, which actually appeared in the spring of 1942 in a small mimeographed edition in Los Angeles. It contained the first publication of Benjamin's 'Theses on the Philosophy of History', as well as a 'Bibliographical Note' on his writings.

In one of his last letters to Gretel Adorno, a few months before his death, Benjamin referred to the fact that he had now written down the 'Theses'. He drew her attention, and Adorno's, specifically to the seventeenth thesis, saying that 'it is this thesis that reveals the hidden but conclusive link between these reflections and my previous work, since it contains a concise statement of the method employed in the latter.'[43] The method of materialist historiography delineated there contained ideas that Adorno shared unreservedly. This was true above all of its postulate that 'the lifework is preserved *in* the work . . . ; *in* the life work, the era; and *in* the era, the entire course of history', as well as the idea about 'blasting a specific era out of the era'.[44] The belief that history is a history of catastrophes, that the gaze that the 'angel of history' casts on the ruins of the past (as in the ninth thesis) is a gaze full of horror, was an unconventional view of the age[45] which Adorno hoped to be able to utilize for his own disillusioned balance sheet of a failed epoch.

Alongside Benjamin's posthumous 'Theses', Adorno published in the memorial volume two essays by Horkheimer, 'Reason and Self-Preservation' and 'The Authoritarian State', as well as an essay of his own that Benjamin greatly admired, the essay in which he examined the personal and literary relations between Hugo von Hofmannsthal and Stefan George. Adorno approached the two poets through their correspondence in an attempt to uncover the secret of their lives. In the case of George, he unmasked the stance of the artist hero as the obverse of an underlying coarseness, while the worldly, aristocratic Hofmannsthal is deemed to have failed because he was unable to harmonize his privileged social position with that of the free-floating intellectual. He drew particular attention to the question of the decline of language that is the subject of the so-called Chandos letter. He wrote that the two poets' defiance 'of society includes defiance of its language. Others share the language of men. They are "social". The aesthetes are as far ahead of them as they are asocial. Their works measure themselves against the recognition that the language of men is the language of their degradation.'[46]

Although Adorno and Horkheimer were unable to give the book the continuous attention they would have wished, the *Philosophical*

Fragments gradually assumed concrete shape. In a letter to his mother on 10 February, Adorno wrote: 'The first large section of the book that I am doing with Max and that is supposed to contain our whole philosophy . . . is now ready. In addition, I have an equally large draft in front of me, a historico-philosophical interpretation of Homer, which we shall also plough our way through together.'[47]

The whole manuscript was finally ready in May 1944 and was published in a small mimeographed edition of 500 copies, with a dedication 'For Friedrich Pollock on his Fiftieth Birthday' and an elegant, burgundy-coloured binding.

The *Philosophical Fragments* did not actually appear in book form until 1947, when it was published by the Amsterdam exile publisher Querido Verlag with its definitive title of *Dialectic of Enlightenment*.[48] This publication – Adorno referred to it in a letter to Horkheimer as 'our first legitimate child' – was the living proof that, after barely more than two years of their collaboration, the two authors had succeeded in completing a project that they had been carrying around with them since the mid-1930s. What they had now produced in 310 pages was an act of self-clarification about the premises of a critical theory in the socio-historical circumstances of the day.[49] 'These days are full of sadness', Horkheimer lamented in a letter at the end of 1942. 'The annihilation of the Jewish people has assumed historically unprecedented dimensions. I believe that the night that follows these events will be very long and that it might well consume mankind.'[50] At the same time, he admitted how much it cost him personally to reflect on the philosophical implications of this relapse into barbarism. Sometimes I fear that this enterprise exceeds my powers.'[51] Nevertheless, neither he nor Adorno succumbed to a facile resignation in the face of the horrors of history. 'The possibility that sooner or later we too might fall victim to the concentration camps must not be allowed to justify our abandoning the desperate search for the words that could become deed and liberate us all.'[52] And it was Adorno whose unflagging energy drove him to come up with new ideas and arguments, and it was he who ensured that the book was finally completed. And what the two authors had attempted was no small feat. Their endeavour to settle accounts with a world that had become 'a system of horror' involved nothing less than the uncovering of principles that were inextricably enmeshed with enlightenment and rationality.

Enlightenment is thought of here as something that goes beyond the designation of a particular historical and intellectual epoch. It is treated as the epitome of modern consciousness. For the modern consciousness the subject's striving for complete understanding of the causal relations at work in nature, human actions and society is constitutive. Since enlightenment leads to a constant expansion of freedom in the spheres of pragmatic action, moral duty and emotional desire, it proves to be the guarantor of sustained progress. The concept of reason, the general condition of both the domination of nature and self-determination, is seen to have two aspects.[53] An imbalance has occurred between the instrumental and reflective elements of a rationality that is thought of as a unity. In the view of Horkheimer and Adorno, dialectical thinking is the only way to appropriate the rationality of reason at a more advanced stage of reflection.

Because reason as 'the happiness of insight'[54] has vanished from consciousness, 'men pay for their increase in power with their alienation from that over which they exercise their power.'[55] The fact that people equate reason with self-preservation is a quid pro quo that can even be seen in myth, the prototype of enlightenment. For the narratives about primeval events are themselves early attempts at explanation that serve to secure the human subject's domination over the forces of nature. 'Myth intended report, naming, the narration of the beginning: but also presentation, confirmation, explanation.'[56] And just as myth is already enlightenment, so enlightenment reverts to myth. The mythological or ideological aspect of the modern enlightened consciousness consists in the idea that *Homo sapiens* is able to use his reason to subject the universe to his will. The reason for man's wish to control the world through knowledge, for the merging of enlightenment and domination, lies in his fear of the real overwhelming power of nature. 'Every attempt to break nature's coercive power by breaking nature itself' leads thought 'all the more deeply into enslavement. Hence the course of European civilization.'[57]

This dialectic applies also to the constitution of the subject. By bowing to the need for a methodical conduct of life, the human subject 'is reduced to the nodal point of the conventional responses and modes of operation expected of him.'[58] The progress of individuation in bourgeois society 'took place at the expense of individuality', and at the end nothing was left but 'the resolve to pursue one's own particular purpose'.[59]

In order to persuade the reader of this equivalence of enlightenment and myth in this chapter, perhaps the most impressive chapter of the entire book,[60] Adorno interprets scenes from Homer's *Odyssey* (eighth century BC) as an allegory of the prehistory of subjectivity from which we can read off the conditions and consequences of a rationality in the service of absolute self-preservation. This is the process of liberation from the constraints of nature through self-discipline 'until the self, the identical, purposive and virile nature of mankind was formed'.[61] Odysseus exemplifies the way in which this story of the domestication of man's inner nature was carried out. In Canto 12, when Odysseus and his men risk falling victim to the lethal song of the Sirens,[62] he is warned by Circe that there are 'only two possible ways of escape':

One of them he prescribes for his men. He plugs their ears with wax, and they must row with all their strength. Whoever would survive must not hear the temptation of that which is unrepeatable, and he is able to survive only by being unable to hear it. Society has always made provision for that. The labourers must be fresh and concentrate as they look ahead, and must ignore whatever lies to one side. They must doggedly sublimate in additional effort the drive that impels to diversion. And so they become practical. – The other possibility Odysseus, the seigneur who allows the others to labour for themselves, reserves to himself. He listens, but while bound impotently to the mast; the greater the temptation to listen the more he has his bonds tightened – just as later the burghers would deny themselves happiness all the more doggedly as it drew closer to them with the growth of their own power. What Odysseus hears is without consequence for him; he is able only to nod his head as a sign to be set free from his bonds; but it is too late; his men, who do not listen, know only the song's danger but nothing of its beauty, and leave him at the mast in order to save him and themselves. They reproduce the oppressor's life together with their own, and the oppressor is no longer able to escape his social role. The bonds with which he has irremediably tied himself to practice, also keep the Sirens away from practice: their temptation is neutralized and becomes a mere object of contemplation – becomes art. The prisoner is present at a concert, an inactive eavesdropper like later concertgoers, and his spirited call for liberation fades like applause. Thus the enjoyment of art and manual labour break apart as the world of prehistory is left behind. The epic already contains the appropriate theory. The cultural material is in exact correlation to work done according to command; and both are grounded in the inescapable compulsion to achieve the social domination of nature.[63]

The second excursus focuses on the amorality of de Sade's heroine Juliette. The point of interest here is the depiction of the reverse side of a completely secularized scientistic knowledge that, in its concern with absolute 'do-ability', refuses to acknowledge any moral limits. The authors recognize the achievement of such 'dark' writers of the bourgeois enlightenment as de Sade and Nietzsche for having demonstrated that rational knowledge alone can produce no compelling arguments against murder. These writers have expressed 'the shocking truth' that, if reason is restricted to the tasks of self-preservation, every crime can be justified. 'Freedom from the pangs of conscience is as essential to formal reason as the absence of love or hate.'[64]

A completely different topic is treated in the chapter on the culture industry. What is at issue here is the attempt to show how modern culture turns into its opposite, how creativity becomes consumption, art becomes amusement, culture becomes the condition of being informed. In short, what we are shown is the destruction of culture by its distribution through the mass media. By using the term 'culture industry',

Adorno and Horkheimer wished to show that the mass culture of the present has nothing in common with the spontaneous manifestations of a popular culture, a culture of the people. Instead, it is manufactured and organized from above. The concept refers to the entire network by means of which culture is socially transmitted, in other words, it refers to the cultural goods created by the producers, and distributed by agents, the cultural market and the consumption of culture. The culture industry includes the mass media, i.e., newspapers and newspaper concerns, the publicly and privately owned radio and television organizations, music and film businesses, and also the different organizations concerned with cultivating culture, as well as the different sectors of the entertainment business. All these institutions that make up the system of the culture industry were analysed by Adorno and Horkheimer from the standpoint of one central question: what is the influence of mass culture on the formation of individual consciousness and the ways in which meanings are socially transmitted? A chief function of the culture industry, they maintained, was to produce conformism, i.e., a general approval of the state of the world, through a plethora of consumer goods aimed at different target groups. 'Something is provided for all so that none may escape.'[65] Despite the diversification of what is on offer, 'the bread which the culture industry offers man is the stone of the stereotype.'[66]

The authors' critical fire was drawn in particular to the way in which phenomena of the culture industry were emotionalized and made personal. They explained the social phenomenon of pseudo-education from the way in which the stereotypes of mass culture functioned. This pseudo-education is a result of 'the constant reproduction of the same thing', which of course implies 'the exclusion of the new'.[67] Adorno and Horkheimer constantly stressed that the products of the culture industry function like commodities determined by the market and to that extent they are tailored to the needs of mass consumption. This means that the culture industry does not react to pre-existing demand, but that demand is created by the machinery of the culture industry, which even influences the needs of the recipients. 'The result is the circle of manipulation and retroactive need in which the unity of the system grows ever stronger.'[68]

The 'Elements of Anti-Semitism' represents the attempt to analyse the role of the Jews in the history of Western civilization.[69] Hatred of the Jews is seen as the expression of the hidden self-contempt of the national community. The blind rage of the social collective is directed against minorities who stand out because of their defencelessness. In the case of the Jews, an additional factor is that they form a group that is excluded economically from production, being confined to the sphere of distribution. Their weakness provokes all those who have never been quite able to complete the painful process of repressing their instincts in the interests of civilization, but who deny their anxieties and feel the need to show their strength. The source of anti-Semitism is a collective act of projection: self-hatred transferred to the Jews. The Jews themselves are perceived as a privileged minority who are able to lead a good life without the constant effort of repressive work. 'No matter what the Jews themselves may be like, their image, as that of the defeated people, has the features to which totalitarian domination must be completely hostile: happiness without power, wages without work, a home without frontiers, religion without myth. These characteristics are hated by the rulers because the ruled secretly long to possess them.'[70]

Adorno and Horkheimer conclude that there is no such thing as 'genuine anti-Semitism', and 'certainly no such thing as a born anti-Semite'. On the contrary, 'the victims are interchangeable . . . according to circumstances – gypsies, Jews, Protestants, Catholics' – and today's victim 'may take the place of the murderers tomorrow, with the same blind lust for blood, should they be invested with the title of the norm.'[71] It is a historical accident that the Jews in National Socialist Germany 'are defined as the group which calls down upon itself, both in theory and practice, the will to destroy that has been born of a false social order.'[72] In addition, Adorno and Horkheimer propose religious motives for anti-Semitism. They emphasize the envy felt by Christianity as the religion of the Son reacting to the Jewish religion of the Father. 'The adherents of the religion of the Father are hated by those who support the religion of the Son – hated as those who know better. It is the hostility to spirit of the spirit, grown obdurate in the conviction of its own salvation.'[73] Adorno and Horkheimer do not attempt to evade the question of how the madness of anti-Semitism is to be eliminated. They call for nothing less than the abolition of domination: 'Individual and social emancipation from domination is the counter-movement to false projection, and no longer would Jews seek to appease the evil senselessly visited upon them as upon all persecuted beings, be they animals or men, by trying to placate it, and even identify with it.'[74]

Adorno and Horkheimer thought of their critique of anti-Semitism as containing some of the building blocks of an analysis of fascism[75] in which psychoanalysis played a major part – as can be seen from the heavy reliance on terms such as collective repression, projection and paranoia.

This recourse to Freudian terminology enabled the authors to forge a link with the major project surrounding the studies on anti-Semitism that was just taking shape at around this time and for which the institute did finally manage to get the go-ahead in the course of 1943. The psychoanalytically based discussions about hatred of the Jews would form a frame of reference for what was by far and away the most important segment of this larger project, namely the empirical study of hostility to minorities and ethnic intolerance. To be sure, the psychoanalytical ideas were themselves only to be used 'in the context of an objectively orientated critical theory of society'.[76]

Not that this practical side of a number of arguments in the *Dialectic of Enlightenment* was unimportant in Adorno's eyes. On the contrary.

But these texts always retained a special importance for him, even in their first version of 1944. Unlike Horkheimer, he continued for the whole of his life to remain committed to this book about the self-contradictions of enlightenment, 'the blackest book' of critical theory.[77] Furthermore, in his eyes dialectic had become the critical method, which by means of determinate negation turned the 'Münchhausen trick of pulling himself out of the bog by his own pig-tail into the pattern of all knowledge'.[78] In addition, even if Adorno had not written the whole work, it possessed the unmistakable marks of his style – the dialectical reversals, the contrapuntally arranged clauses – that would become the hallmark of his philosophy. Alongside the allegorical references, incantatory linguistic gestures and consciously chosen exaggerations, the book contained hermetic formulations that were based on huge unspoken assumptions. In fact, the idiosyncratic use of rhetoric,[79] that penetrating linguistic power of the text in images, in the gestural use of language, finds expression in the attempt to give philosophy a literary or aesthetic inflection, while conforming to the rules of discursive logic.

Adorno and Horkheimer thought of their attempt at a demystification of modern rationality as a way of achieving philosophical self-clarification. But more than that, they carried out their radical critique of reason against the background of an Enlightenment whose validity is presupposed. This can be seen from the individual discussions about what they had originally planned as a continuation of their work together. Horkheimer emphasized the need to adhere to the radical impulses of Marxism and the tradition of enlightenment. Like Adorno, who demanded that 'thought must be convicted of its deepest errors through further thought', Horkheimer believed that the reconstruction of the history of reason was the only way to 'rescue enlightenment'.[80] Adorno endorsed this programme wholeheartedly, but gave it a different emphasis. Following Hegel, he wished to 'define the negativity of the negative', because that was the only way to transcend the negativity of the whole. The positive aspect of criticism, its reference point, would then simply be 'the experience of the difference'.[81] Evidently, Adorno already had the outlines of a different book in mind when he entered into these discussions. 'We have to assert what a correct mode of thought would look like, one that is appropriate to the philosophical state of its age and has run through the entire gamut of criticism.'[82] He clearly had an epistemological work in mind, but it was not one he would write together with Horkheimer. Instead, he wrote it alone, more or less precisely twenty years later. This, his *magnum opus*, did not appear until 1966, when he was at the height of his intellectual powers. In the *Dialectic of Enlightenment*, myth and reason appeared as two sides of the same coin. In *Negative Dialectics*, the argument acquired its inner tension from the antinomies of identity and non-identity. Until the book was finished, Adorno had to undergo 'much clattering of roll-top desks' in which 'questionnaires were being stored'.[83]

Merits of social research:
studies in the authoritarian personality

Adorno and Horkheimer worked on their book on dialectics under a certain time pressure, since they hoped to present the finished volume to Friedrich Pollock in spring 1944, in time for his fiftieth birthday. However, in the midst of their labours in Pacific Palisades, they received the surprising piece of news that the American Jewish Committee (AJC) were interested in the research project on anti-Semitism outlined in the *Studies in Philosophy and Social Science*. Moreover, the committee held out the prospect of a significant financial subsidy. This meant that Horkheimer was compelled, rather unwillingly, to spend several weeks in New York in September 1942 in order to negotiate with the AJC.

Adorno took the separation from Horkheimer quite badly. Horkheimer had long since become his closest friend and confidant, the man with whom he could have discussions. For this reason he always waited impatiently for the return of 'Mammoth', as he, the 'Hippopotamus', entitled Horkheimer. To express his joy in Horkheimer's return to their joint labours, he even composed a song for voice and piano, with the title 'Rüsselmammuts Heimkehr'.

Horkheimer's absence meant that for long periods Adorno had to work alone on the manuscript at a time when it was already beginning to take shape.[84] This labour of philosophical self-clarification was now augmented by a huge research project. For thanks to the financial assistance of the AJC, and further grants from the Jewish Labour Committee (JLC), it was now possible to set up a research organization over a period of years.[85] Whereas the Institute of Social Research had sole responsibility for the project on 'Anti-Semitism within American Labour',[86] the second, much larger study, with the title 'The Function of Anti-Semitism within the Personality', was to be carried out in co-operation with other researchers and research organizations. Horkheimer had already become aware of the Public Opinion Study Group, which was directed by the social psychologist R. Nevitt Sanford together with Daniel Levinson and Else Frenkel-Brunswik, all of whom were active at the University of California in Berkeley.[87] After initial contacts, a close cooperation soon developed between Adorno and Horkheimer and the social psychologists. But before Adorno could devote himself wholeheartedly to this collaborative task, he had to complete the manuscript of the *Philosophical Fragments*, which of course themselves contained a historical, sociological and socio-psychological theory of racial prejudice.

By early 1944, when his joint work with Horkheimer was finished, Adorno was in a position to involve himself in the new project on anti-Semitism being carried out under Horkheimer's direction. Adorno had anyway written a whole series of memoranda for Horkheimer on this topic, partly in parallel to the 'Elements of Anti-Semitism' and

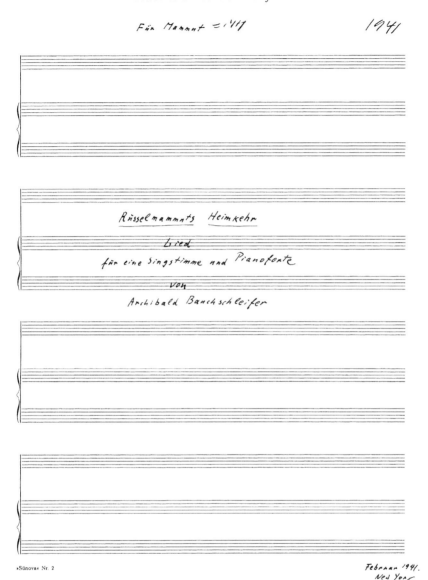

Figure 4 Score of the song 'Rüsselmammuts Heimkehr', for voice and piano, by 'Archibald Bauchschleifer'

Figure 4 (*cont'd*)

Figure 4 (*cont'd*)

partly following it. For example, there was the design of a planned handbook on anti-Semitic clichés and stereotypes, theoretical and methodological proposals for the 'Labour Project' and the 'Child Study',[88] a sketch of the problems to be considered in the 'Research Project on Social Discrimination', a plan for 'Imagery of Subconscious Anti-Semitism', a further plan on 'Totalitarian Anti-Semitism', and a 'Research Project on the Sociological, Political and Economic Mechanisms behind American Anti-Semitism'.[89] The study of racist structures of prejudice that was finally brought to fruition in Berkeley is one that can be said with good reason to have been a continuation of the *Dialectic of Enlightenment* by other means.[90] According to Adorno's recollection, it was 'organized such that Sanford and I served as directors, and Mrs Brunswik and Daniel Levinson as principal colleagues. From the beginning, however, everything occurred in consummate teamwork, without any hierarchical aspects.'[91] Because the research group had its base in Berkeley, Adorno had to travel from Los Angeles to San Francisco every fortnight from the beginning of 1945 so as to take part in the group's meetings.

After a conference of the AJC in New York, there was a symposium in San Francisco in June 1944 attended by psychoanalysts and sociologists and which resulted in important suggestions for research on anti-Semitism. The Freudians Ernst Simmel and Otto Fenichel, with whom Adorno was friendly, gave papers on psychoanalytical aspects of anti-Semitism. Horkheimer concentrated on possible connections between sociological and psychological approaches; Frenkel-Brunswik and Sanford examined the psychodynamics of the anti-Semitic personality. Adorno reported on the results of his content analysis of the speeches of the Californian radio preacher Martin Luther Thomas, the founder of the Christian American Crusade, one of the most dangerous fascist groupings on the West Coast.[92] Adorno's study of the rhetorical patterns of anti-democratic agitators in the USA – 'would-be Hitlers', he called them – was later deepened with the aid of further content analyses, partly in collaboration with Leo Löwenthal.[93] In his analysis of transcripts of the radio speeches of this religious fanatic, Adorno exposed the typical techniques of persuasion used by propagandists. He used 'Thomas's speeches as a kind of key to the psyche of anti-Semitic sectors of the population'. This analysis was supposed also 'to prepare the ground for future field studies', as he noted in connection with the planned collaboration with Berkeley.[94] With his analysis of the psychological techniques of the Californian radio preacher, Adorno established a link with Hitler's propaganda. A common characteristic, he believed, was the tendency to personalize and sentimentalize, as well as the agitator's attempt to gain authority by confessing to his own weakness while at the same time emphasizing his status as one of the chosen. In addition, Adorno pointed to what he termed the '*fait-accompli*' technique, the transformation of feelings of impotence into a feeling of power. He related this psychological mechanism to the widespread phenomenon of declaring the existing state of society to be the best of all possible worlds and hence to identify with the world as it is. The purpose of a limited number of repetitive rhetorical devices is to win over individual sympathizers as a band of followers bound together libidinally. These followers are to be recruited in the name of the leader for purposes that are incompatible with the rational interests of the individuals who make up the group. Because they sacrifice their conscious ability to judge reality, destructive instincts are released. 'As a rebellion against civilization, fascism is not simply the recurrence of the archaic but its re-creation in and by civilization itself.'[95] Speaking in very general terms, Adorno here argues very much along the lines of *Dialectic of Enlightenment* to the effect that the constraints associated with civilization provoke internal and external reactions. He claims that the destructiveness of fascist mass movements has as its obverse the masochistic readiness to submit blindly to leader figures. Such figures are conceived by the individual within the mass as all-powerful, menacing, 'primal fathers'. The mechanism of narcissistic identification functions as long as the leader is both superman and average man: in accordance with the stereotype of the 'great, little man'. 'The agitators disavow any pretence to superiority, implying that the . . . leader is one who is as weak as his brethren, but who is brave enough to confess his weakness without inhibition and is consequently going to be transformed into a strong man.'[96] As a further stereotype, Adorno pointed to the rigid opposition of in-group and out-group which leads to the total identification with one's own group and to enmity towards all deviations from it. A constantly recurring propaganda trick, finally, is the claim that we are all in the same boat. 'A repressive egalitarianism . . . is an essential component of a fascist way of thinking and is expressed in the "if you only knew . . ." technique used by agitators and consists in the promise to reveal as an act of vengeance all the forbidden pleasures that others can afford.'[97]

At the end of his analysis of propaganda, Adorno raised the question of how the agitator manages to enter into the mind of his followers. One reason, he thought, lay in the fundamental similarity between leader and led. So the secret of fascist propaganda was that 'it simply takes people for what they are: genuine children of today's standardized mass culture who have been robbed to a great extent of their autonomy and spontaneity.'[98]

Even though Adorno made use of Freudian theory here, in one of the notebooks that would turn out later on to be a source book of *Minima Moralia*, he nevertheless noted: 'Horror is beyond the reach of psychology.'[99] As a counterpoint to this statement, there is the further assertion on the same page that fascism is 'a dictatorship by persecution-maniacs' that 'realizes all the persecution-fears of its victims'.[100]

Thus Adorno had developed theories with which to explain people's susceptibility to fascism and anti-Semitic prejudice. Now that he had these findings under his belt about the mechanisms at work in extreme right-wing propaganda, with its hatred of minorities, he could move forward, from 1944, to enter into concrete cooperation with the Public Opinion Study Group. The members of this group were all professional psychologists who were primarily interested in socio-psychological explanations of the origins of the structures of prejudice. Nevertheless, he evidently succeeded in persuading the group that the origins and dynamics of authoritarian personalities should be sought in objective social factors. 'To be sure', he observed on a conciliatory note, 'in contrast to a certain economic orthodoxy, we were not dismissive of psychology, but acknowledged its proper place in our outline as an explanatory aspect. . . . We followed what I believe to be the plausible idea that in the present society the objective institutions and developmental tendencies have attained such an overwhelming power over individuals that people . . . are becoming, and evidently in increasing measure, functionaries of the predominant tendencies operating over their heads. Less and less depends on their own particular conscious and unconscious being, their inner life.'[101]

The study he was referring to was the book that appeared in 1950 with the definitive title of *The Authoritarian Personality*.[102] It was published in the framework of the series of *Studies in Prejudice*, of which five volumes appeared. Methodologically it was a pioneering work. It was the first example of the successful integration of quantitative and qualitative methods of collecting and evaluating data, and of the combination of a representative sample and attention to the individual case, while at the same time taking elements of sociological and psychoanalytical theory into account.

Taking their lead from Adorno, the group based their work on an initial, psychoanalytical hypothesis that operated with a distinction between latent and manifest dimensions of personality. The threat to democratic societies arises not just from the attitude and behaviour of a relatively small minority of declared fascists, but from the syndrome of an unexpressed, potential fascism that comes from the hidden layer of the personality. According to a second hypothesis, this potential was traced back to deeper-seated character-structures that predispose people towards authoritarianism. 'We were interested', Adorno explained later, 'in the fascist *potential*. In order to be able to work against that potential, we also incorporated into the investigation, as far as was possible, the genetic dimension, that is, the emerging of the authoritarian personality.'[103] Particular weight was placed on the education and the family background of the 2100 subjects of the study in order to discover the influence of the socialization process and social milieu on the growth of anti-democratic attitudes. In this context, Adorno explored changes in religious ideas on tolerance. With the neutralization of the Christian religions, the religious heritage functioned as a social cement that contributed to the preservation of the status quo and thus ensured social conformity. 'This is by its intrinsic logic tantamount to contempt for the truth *per se*', if 'one selects a *Weltanschauung* after the pattern of choosing a particularly well advertised commodity, rather than for its real quality.'[104] As early as one of the first letters informing Horkheimer of the plans for the project, Adorno made detailed proposals for an empirical approach to understanding potential anti-Semitism: through direct indicators 'that would be both necessary and sufficient conditions of anti-Semitism'. In the same letter he also mooted the idea of including prisoners and prison guards in the study, although this proved to be impossible in the event. Adorno had hoped that by enlarging the scope of the survey in this way it might be possible to have an immediately educative effect: 'If it could be reliably shown that a particularly high percentage of criminals were extreme anti-Semites, the result would in itself be effective propaganda.' In addition, he again spoke out in favour of content analysis. He had the idea of scrutinizing comics and funnies so as to 'work out the underlying stereotyping and link it to the anti-Semitic syndrome'.[105]

Sociological dimensions played an important part because the anti-Semitism arising from authoritarian dispositions could be interpreted as a way of inwardly digesting the socially predominant 'cultural climate'. What was innovative about the research strategy from Adorno's point of view was, on the one hand, the use of standardized methods such as questionnaires and the scales with which to measure attitudes to anti-Semitism, ethnocentrism and conservatism. On the other hand, there were the so-called projective procedures supplemented by qualitative interviews. Adorno described the projective [i.e., open-ended] questions of the attitude scales (e.g., 'obedience and respect for authority are the most important virtues children should learn') as presenting the subject with 'ambiguous and emotionally toned stimulus material. This material is designed to allow a maximum of variation in response from one subject to another and to provide channels through which relatively deep personality processes may be expressed.'[106] The extreme groups of unambiguously authoritarian or anti-authoritarian personalities who emerged from a statistical analysis of the questionnaires were then subjected to clinical interviews, as well as a so-called Thematic Appercep-tion Test, in order to validate the findings of the scale.[107] This innovative combination of methods was as important as the attempt to measure fascist predispositions indirectly in a number of different groups of the population. Adorno himself took great pains with the adequate formu-lation of the scale 'items' (i.e., statements to which subjects could respond affirmatively or negatively), which were particularly revealing about the nine variables (including conventionalism, authoritarian aggression, superstitiousness and stereotyping). In a letter of November 1944 to Horkheimer, who had returned to New York for several months in order to coordinate the nine separate projects and arrange for their financing, he wrote that an enormous number of questions had been worked out for the indirect indices. 'I have distilled a number of questions by means of a kind of translation from the "Elements of Anti-Semitism". It was all a lot of fun.'[108]

The study achieved its fame because of this method for measuring fascist structures of prejudice – the F scale. The method adopted permitted the subjects to make a graduated agreement or disagreement with a number of assertions. These responses were entered on a scale that went from +3 to −3. This meant that in the case of authoritarian statements, for example, the answers could indicate strong, moderate or slight agreement or disagreement. Each degree on the scale was given a score, and hence it was possible simply to add up the score achieved by each respondent. Looking back, Adorno noted:

> In Berkeley then we developed the F scale in a free and relaxed environment deviating considerably from the conception of a pedantic science that must account for its every step. Probably the reason for this was what people liked to call 'the psychoanalytic background' of us four directors of the study, particularly our familiarity with the method of free association. . . . The conjecture is hardly too far-fetched that whatever *The Authoritarian Personality* exhibits in originality, unconventionality, imagination, and interest in important themes is due precisely to that freedom. The element of playfulness that I would like to think is essential to every intellectual productivity was in no way lacking during the development of the F scale. We spent hours thinking up whole dimensions, variables, and syndromes as well as particular questionnaire items of which we were all the prouder the less apparent their relation to the main theme was, whereas theoretical reasons led us to expect correlations with ethnocentrism, anti-Semitism and reactionary political-economic views.[109]

Adorno's own account of the research methods adopted shows the extent to which he was in fact involved in the practical work. It was thanks to him that the research group was able to refine the three scales with which to measure anti-Semitism, ethnocentrism and conservatism and to develop them to the point where specific items could be used as reliable indicators of an all-embracing latent personality type. This was a new way to measure the anti-democratic potential of individuals. Adorno described the underlying authoritarian personality as 'a structural unity'. In other words, 'traits such as conventionality, authoritarian submissiveness and aggressiveness, projectivity, manipulativeness, etc., regularly go together.'[110] In his subsequent evaluation of the qualitative interviews, he presented a broad spectrum of concrete examples of authoritarian and non-authoritarian social characters. He concentrated on analysing the interview material from the standpoint of 'ideological spheres'. In this way he succeeded in opening up a fully differentiated typology which made it possible to understand the authoritarian personality more precisely. By comparing individual cases, he drew up a list of six types, although they had no more than descriptive value:

> *Surface Resentment* can easily be recognized in terms of justified or unjustified social anxieties. . . . With the *Conventional* pattern . . . acceptance of conventional values is outstanding. The superego was never firmly established and the individual is largely under the sway of its external representatives. The most obvious underlying motive is the fear of 'being different'. The *Authoritarian* type is governed by the superego and has continuously to contend with strong and highly ambivalent id tendencies. He is driven by the fear of being weak. In the *Tough Guy* the repressed id tendencies gain the upper hand, but in a stunted and destructive form. Both the *Crank* and the *Manipulative* types seem to have resolved the Oedipus Complex through a narcissistic withdrawal into their inner selves.[111]

Adorno had not only created a typology for the group of people who according to the F Scale had an affinity with authoritarianism. He also produced one for people who are free of prejudice, those who emerged from the tests with low scores. He distinguished here between five types: the *Rigid* low scorers who compulsively cling not to paternal authority, but to socially recognized collectivities; the *Protesting* low scorers whose sublimated hatred of the father idea leads them to become the enemies of every authority; the *Impulsive* low scorers who are threatened by overpowering libidinous energy; the *Easy-Going* low scorers who have sublimated their id into feelings of compassion; and the *Genuine Liberals* who are able to balance the divergent claims of ego, super-ego and id.[112] This last type was exemplary in Adorno's view. He contrasted it with the *Manipulative* type in the group of the prejudiced. Such a person is over-realistic, fixated on self-preservation, and treats everything and everyone as an object to be handled, manipulated. 'The technical aspects of life, and things *qua* tools, are fraught with libido. The emphasis is on "doing things", with far-reaching indifference towards the content of what is going to be done.'[113]

Adorno knew that the Berkeley study was by no means free of the affliction of every empirical sociology: the need to choose 'between the reliability and the profundity of its findings'.[114] Against the background of this dilemma, he summarized the achievement of the study: 'If *The Authoritarian Personality* made a contribution, then it is not to be found in the absolute conclusiveness of its positive insights, let alone in its measurements, but above all in the conception of the problem, which is marked by an essential interest in society and is related to a theory that had not previously been translated into quantitative investigations of this kind.'[115]

Adorno's judgement on the practical side of the study was less optimistic. A piece of sociological enlightenment that confined itself to making visible the danger to democracy from the fascist potential fell short in his view. Instead it was necessary to change the social order, starting with the position of the individual in society. For as long as social pressures continue to bear down on individuals, the risk that half-forgotten prejudices and stereotypes will be revived cannot be ignored. After the conclusion of the study that had lasted several years, Adorno summarized his own personal opinion in the 'Remarks on the Authoritarian Personality'.[116] He wrote: 'But these traces [of prejudices and stereotypes] remain incompatible with the stage of rationality society has reached today. Modern anti-Semitic ideology is the antidote to the sufferings entailed by rational civilization rather than the immediate expression of either this civilization or the kind of irrationality boasted by the anti-Semite. This inconsistency enhances violence instead of mitigating it.'[117]

Moral feelings in immoral times

What would happiness be that was not measured by the immeasurable grief at what is? For the world is deeply ailing. He who cautiously adapts to it by this very act shares in its madness, while the eccentric alone would stand his ground and bid it rave no more.[118]

By abandoning its policy of neutrality at the end of 1940, the American government was reacting to the threat posed to its national interest by the aggressor states Germany, Italy and Japan. On 22 June 1941, the German armed forces opened the attack on the Soviet Union without any declaration of war, deploying a force amounting to 57 per cent of the army and 2000 fighting planes. In December of the same year, in reaction to the American oil embargo, the Japanese attacked the American Pacific fleet anchored at Pearl Harbor, likewise without declaring war. In addition to considerable losses of shipping and airplanes, almost 3000 military personnel lost their lives. This unleashed a wave of patriotism in the USA, which was thenceforth ready for war. 'The liberal left could now mobilize against the fascists, and the xenophobic right against the Japanese, the workers found work, the employers obtained orders, pro-British Southern supporters renewed their military traditions.'[119] When the USA entered the war in December 1941 and renewed its leadership claims in world politics, the European war became a world war.[120]

These dramatic developments on the international stage had direct consequences for the German refugees in America, and hence also for those who had settled in Los Angeles. Since the region around Hollywood had become the second largest centre for émigrés in the

USA, campaigns against foreign takeovers were nothing new. But when refugees were declared 'enemy aliens' and treated accordingly, it became clear that anti-immigrant measures had reached new heights. These measures were government-inspired and led in the long run from anti-Nazism to anti-communism. They were combined with the propagandistic ideological claim that the foundations of the Western democratic tradition were under threat. To this extent, Adorno's fears that the West Coast German immigrants might well be interned, as had happened in France and Britain, and as was the case with the Japanese living in the United States, were not unreasonable. Those who had not yet obtained their naturalization papers found their movements severely restricted by a curfew. A state of emergency had been declared in California, and 'enemy aliens' were forbidden to leave their homes between 8 p.m. and 6 a.m.; they were also prohibited from going more than 5 miles from their houses. Adorno was of course forced to comply with this order, since he received his 'Certificate of Naturalization' only in November 1943, at which point he was formally registered under the name of Theodore Adorno.[121] In his 'Observations on the Curfew', which he published in 1942 in the leading exile newspaper *Aufbau*, Max Horkheimer commented on 'the horror that overcame . . . the isolated émigré' when faced by these restrictions on foreigners.[122] Adorno had occasion to experience such feelings personally in the summer of 1942, when he had a visit from the police in South Kenter Avenue to see whether he and his wife were abiding by the rules and were actually at home during the stipulated times of day. In a letter to his parents, he complained about the situation, which he said was almost like being imprisoned. The car outings that had become a habit for him and Gretel had to be abandoned. And because of the petrol rationing, they would now be immobilized and isolated for an indefinite period. He found it quite incomprehensible that of all people it was the most reliable enemies of Hitler who were being forced to suffer from these restrictions.

Adorno was a frequent blood donor, as a small gesture of solidarity with the American people in its war with Hitler. And, as he told his parents, he was given a small award as a token of recognition of this. But he also had more important news from Santa Monica. Leo Löwenthal, who had introduced his own parents to the Wiesengrunds in New York, warned him to write 'regularly' and to be 'more cheerful' – that was his 'humble advice'.[123] In response to this well-meaning suggestion – which should not have been necessary for a son who was approaching forty – Adorno regularly kept his parents informed about the current state of his work with Horkheimer, about the seminars held by institute members with a changing group of participants, including Bertolt Brecht, Hanns Eisler, Eduard Steuermann, Günther Stern (= Günther Anders), Ludwig Marcuse, Hans Reichenbach, etc. He also talked frequently of the visitors he and his wife received in their attractively situated house. Among these were the 'extremely beautiful violinist' Lisa Minghetti, her husband and her father. They all joined in private concerts together, playing Bach, Beethoven and Debussy. Adorno expressed his regret that he could not make music with his mother, 'the passionate female hippo', as he affectionately called her. In another passage about music, Adorno praised the clarinettist Benny Goodman, who was not just a talented 'swing musician' but had also played good classical music in a chamber ensemble.[124]

Despite the wartime restrictions his letters express contentment with his situation, as can be seen from a letter of September 1942 to Horkheimer, who was in New York. He wrote that, since he could not go to the cinema with him, he and Gretel could at least go with Maidon. In Santa Monica in general, he went on, life was 'very active and lively', 'which we thoroughly enjoy'.[125] He wrote to his parents in the same month, expressing a similar satisfaction. He reported that, although he and Gretel had only been there a short time, they had already become fixtures of Hollywood society.[126] He had already met Thomas Mann, who lived close to Horkheimer. He had met Greta Garbo in the house of Salka and Berthold Viertel. She was 'nice and pretty, even if no great intellectual', as he informed Horkheimer.[127] Did this meeting over afternoon tea inspire Adorno to produce an aphorism? Under the title of 'L'Inutile beauté', itself derived from Maupassant, he wrote: 'Women of exceptional beauty are doomed to unhappiness.'[128] 'Either they shrewdly exchange beauty for success', or else they bind themselves to the first comer, confident that they can choose someone else at any time. 'Just because they were once *hors de concours* they are unsuccessful in competition, for which they now develop a mania. The gesture of irresistibility remains when the reality has passed away; magic perishes the moment it ceases merely to stand for hope and settles for domesticity.'[129]

For their part the Adornos frequently invited guests of their own. They gave a large party in honour of Davidson Taylor, the director of programming at CBS, and another in honour of the actor Alexander Granach, who had worked under Ernst Lubitsch and Fritz Lang[130] and who read from his autobiography on this occasion. Hanns Eisler was a frequent visitor, as were Lotte Lenja, Katia and Thomas Mann, and Charlotte and Wilhelm Dieterle. Adorno was of course under no illusions about the superficiality of social life: 'That this self-fêting in no way enriches life is manifest in the boredom of the cocktail parties, the weekend invitations to the country, the golf, symbolic of the whole sphere, the organization of the social round – privileges giving real enjoyment to none, and serving only to conceal from the privileged how much in the joyless whole they too are without the possibility of pleasure.'[131] He told his parents that he was keeping his distance from 'society', since the social contacts were nothing like as interesting as the philosophical work which was in the forefront of his mind. It follows that the references in his letters to the 'sacred text' on which he was engaged with Horkheimer were very copious, as were those to the studies in anti-Semitism.[132] He even mentioned the little selection of 'Dream Protocols' he had published in the *Aufbau* on 2 October 1942. These, he said, were faithful records of dreams he had had and which he had written down immediately on waking. He had a large collection of such dream protocols.[133] The three published texts are pure descriptions of manifest dream contents, for the most part grotesque scenes, a blend of cultural reminiscences, biographical snippets and daily occurrences. The author made no attempt at interpretation, let alone a psycho-analytical one.

We were walking, my mother, Agathe and I, on a ridge path of a reddish sandstone hue familiar to me from Amorbach. But we were on the West Coast of America. To the left lay the Pacific Ocean. At one point the path seemed to become steeper or peter out altogether. I set about looking for another path off to the right, through rocks and undergrowth. After a few steps I came to a large plateau. I thought I had now found the path. But I soon discovered that the vegetation concealed the dizziest precipices in every direction, and that there was no way to reach the plain that stretched landwards and that I had mistakenly thought to be part of the plateau. There, at frighteningly regular intervals, I saw groups of people with apparatuses, geometers perhaps. I looked for the way back to the first path, and found it too. When I rejoined my mother and Agathe a laughing black couple suddenly stood in our path, he was dressed in bold checked trousers, she in a grey sport-ing costume. We went on. Soon we met a black child. We must be close to a settlement, I said. There were a number of huts or caves of sand or cut into the hillside. A gateway passed through one of them. We went through and stood, overwhelmed with joy, on the square in front of the palace in Bamberg – the 'Chatterhole' in Miltenberg.[134]

Adorno did not conceal from his parents what was for him an exceedingly uncomfortable incident involving Ernst Bloch.[135] Bloch had approached Horkheimer a number of times with the request for research commissions from the institute that would give him some financial assistance and institutional protection.[136] Horkheimer always had his doubts about Bloch, who at the time was the famous author of *The Spirit of Utopia*. These doubts had been reinforced by Bloch's defence of the Stalinist purges. Now, in September 1942, Bloch had turned to Adorno, to whom he had written a heart-rending letter[137] in which he gave a dramatic account of his acute material distress. 'I have lost my job washing up because I couldn't work fast enough. I am now counting and collecting bundles of paper, tying them up and carrying them to a van. Eight hours a day. Counting the journey there and back and an hour for lunch, this makes eleven hours before I get home again. Needless to say, there is no question of doing any work of my own.'

Was it blind naivety or extreme compassion that persuaded Adorno to take this letter literally? The truth is that Bloch had never done any washing up or tying up of parcels. But Adorno was fully convinced that Bloch, with whom both he and Gretel were friendly, had to be helped without delay. After consulting Horkheimer, and independently of the temporary assistance from the institute which he had also endorsed, he published an appeal for Bloch in the *Aufbau*. In his brief explanatory article, he not only gave a summary of the basic ideas of Bloch's philosophy ('the overcoming of the alienation of subject and object'; 'the messianic end of history, the absolutely literal elimination of naturally and socially caused suffering'), but he also wrote: 'The theologian of revolution could not conform and that will not be forgiven him by those who have jobs to hand out, any more than by the intellectuals. . . . His relations to paper have at last become realistic. He bundles it up for eight hours a day, standing in a dark hole. He has escaped the concentration camp, but the fancy ideas will be driven out of his head outside. . . . The emigration owes him a debt. It has treated him like a scapegoat, loading its entire misery onto a man who like few others represents a Germany that has rightly incurred Hitler's deadliest hatred.'[138] Bloch responded to this in an open letter to the journal, saying that he had done nothing to inspire this article. At the same time he wrote to Adorno, objecting to all such initiatives that appealed to 'that false public'. He emphasized that 'I am unable to regard myself as a scapegoat on whom the entire emigration has unloaded its misery. There are many thousands of people who are as badly off as I, or even worse.'[139] This unfortunate incident resulted in a breach between Adorno and Bloch that was to last over twenty years. In a letter to his parents Adorno admitted the damage that his appeal and Bloch's public response had caused him. And he was painfully aware that he had made an enemy of Bloch.

Adorno also told his parents about another problem. This was a love affair that had begun in November and lasted for some months with the actress and filmscript writer Renée Nell. He had composed an album of poetry for Nell, whom he called his 'Baudelairean beloved'.[140] This was a highly erotic relationship, and he confessed as much quite openly in his letters. It had, he said, affected him deeply, shaken him and thrown him off course emotionally. Only his thick-skinned hippopotamus nature had ultimately prevented him from falling victim to the utter misery and suffering that this extravagant love brought him. As the victim of his 'manic-depressive nature', he suffered in quick succession from boundless feelings of happiness followed by violent outbursts of despair. In this sense, and because 'more or less nothing' had actually happened, he was himself 'the scene of this entire novel'.[141] He said of himself that 'I probably would not have the qualities that may enable me to achieve something special in my work, if they were not combined with a boundless capacity for suffering, for letting myself be carried away, and loss of self-control. Since I have to think and react to everything with the subtlest responses of which I am capable, it is easy to understand that these reactions assume a violence that is not compatible either with what common sense expects from a philosopher, or with an ability to preserve the famous sense of proportion.'[142] He had finally succeeded, he went on, in regaining his senses, not least thanks to the 'undeserved understanding' with which Gretel and Max responded to the affair. That Adorno made no secret of his feelings is evident from the fact that he announced that a friend of Renée Nell's would visit his parents in New York. This was the actress Irena Coryan, whose real name was Ira Morgenroth and who was married to the art collector and philosopher Stephan Lackner (i.e., Ernst Gustave Morgenroth), who was friendly with Benjamin and Horkheimer as well as Adorno.

With the affair with Renée Nell happily or unhappily behind him since early in 1943, Adorno started another love affair the following year, on this occasion with a married woman. Whenever he travelled to San Francisco to take part in the discussions on research on anti-Semitism, he stayed over with a friend, Dr Robert P. Alexander, who was also his regular doctor. Alexander was married, but the couple were on the point of separating. Adorno fell in love with Charlotte Alexander. On this occasion, too, he made no secret of it to Gretel, as he in fact reported to his friend Hermann Grab in New York, at the same time confiding that Charlotte resembled him in her outward appearance and in her speech mannerisms. 'We have enjoyed six months of the most unclouded happiness imaginable.'[143] Either she came to Los Angeles for the weekend or else Adorno met her in San Francisco. What fascinated him about her, he said, was her aura. She radiated a kind of magic: 'It was as if the long-forgotten childhood promise of happiness had been unexpectedly, belatedly fulfilled.'[144] When Charlotte Alexander started to flirt with another man and the possibility of another longer-term relationship began to appear, Adorno reacted with jealousy and asked Grab to obtain information about this new rival. He even went so far as to suggest introducing this man to other women from the same circle of acquaintances, since what had to be avoided at all costs was that he should end up thinking he ought to marry Charlotte.[145] Adorno soon realized that his wishes had something 'manic' about them, since he wrote to Grab some six months later that 'he had finally regained his self-control'.[146]

Needless to say, not all of Adorno's relationships with women were complicated and erotically involved. He greatly revered the actress Luli Deste, Countess Goerz, who had been born Baroness Luli von Bodenhausen. He had met her in mid-1943, but the relationship with her was never more than platonic.[147] She was a very attractive, graceful woman with bluish-grey eyes and brown hair. She was two years older

than Adorno, came from Vienna and retained her Viennese accent
even in English, which Adorno evidently found charming. For a time he
looked after the Afghan hounds she had brought with her to the States.
Luli Deste acted in a number of films, including *Thunder in the City*
(1937), *She Married an Artist* (1938), *South of Karanga* (1940) and *Flash
Gordon Conquers the Universe* (1940), until she turned her back on the
film industry early in the 1940s.

Before Adorno had begun to devote his main efforts to the Berkeley
project on social discrimination he published a selection of his dream
protocols and wrote the additional aphorisms in the concluding section
of the *Dialectic of Enlightenment*. As far as the latter were concerned,
he was just resuming the custom of writing aphoristic notes that went
back to his days in Oxford, when he started writing them shortly after
Horkheimer had published his own collection in *Dawn*. It can be assumed
that Adorno had added to those he had written since 1934, so that
he had assembled quite a collection of texts by the time he set about
realizing the plan of producing a substantial manuscript with diary-like
entries for Horkheimer's birthday. In the event, he was able to present
Horkheimer with a collection of fifty aphorisms on 14 February 1945 in
honour of his fiftieth birthday, preceded by a hand-written dedication
'In gratitude and promise'.[148] Unfortunately, Adorno could not present
Horkheimer with the gift in person, since he was in Santa Monica and
working on the anti-Semitism project from California, while Horkheimer
was in New York, attending not entirely with good grace to his obligations in the Department of Scientific Research of the AJC. However,
Adorno was able to present him with the second instalment of the
aphorisms in person for Christmas 1945. On the title page, he had written
'For Max. On your return'. He understood the more than fifty aphorisms
of the third section that he wrote between 1946 and 1947 as part of
'a *dialogue intérieur*: there is not a motif in it that does not belong as
much to Horkheimer as to him who found the time to formulate it.'[149]
This remark was an allusion to the fact that, once the *Dialectic of
Enlightenment* had been completed and the lecture manuscripts arising
from it had been revised for publication by the Oxford University Press
under the title of *Eclipse of Reason*, Horkheimer had been preoccupied
mainly with administrative tasks. Of course, Adorno too had to perform
his share of the 'donkey work' of social research, but he had more
time than Horkheimer to advance his work on the philosophical and
socio-critical ideas on which they had started out in 1942. This can be
seen in those *Reflections from Damaged Life*, which did not appear in
book form with this subtitle until years later, following his return to
Germany. In the letter in which he told his parents about these aphorisms
he emphasized not only their existential significance, but also their fragmentary form, something to which he had been inspired by a renewed
reading of Nietzsche.[150] The leitmotifs of these predominantly brief texts
were emigration and totalitarianism, individuality and psychoanalysis,

the culture industry and the responsibility of intellectuals. But he also treated everyday matters such as dwelling, giving presents, running down the street and, finally, the impossibility of love, the necessity of hope and the hopelessness of lying. In the 'Dedication', which as in Goethe's *Faust* is aimed at the addressees of his reflections, Adorno provided information about his 'melancholy science'. Despite the historical demise of the 'old subject', his starting-point was the experience of individuals: wholly adventitious events, his own observations and perceptions. Even if this 'subjective reflection' has 'something sentimental and anachronistic' about it, the state of society inevitably transmits itself to 'individual experience'. This is why the thinker should trust his own experiences, experiences that derive from 'the narrowest private sphere of the intellectual in emigration', but which may still possess philosophical depth.[151]

Did the shock of being treated as an 'enemy alien' determine the basic tone of these aphorisms? Taken together, the texts of *Minima Moralia* express the melancholy and despair that their author attributed to his own experience of homelessness. It was not for nothing that he took as his motto for Part I of the volume a sentence from the novel *Der Amerika-Müde* (Tired of America) by the Austrian writer Ferdinand Kürnberger: 'Life does not live'. Fatigue with America speaks also from the aphorism 'Protection, Help and Counsel', in which Adorno records that 'the continuity of lived life' has been shattered by expulsion and exile. The émigré 'lives in an environment that must remain incomprehensible to him. . . . He is always astray. . . . His language has been expropriated, and the historical dimension that nourished his knowledge, sapped.' And, as if providing a tacit commentary on his quarrel with Bloch, he goes on: 'Even the man spared the ignominy of direct coordination bears, as his special mark, this very exemption, an illusory, unreal existence in the life-process of society. Relations between outcasts are even more poisoned than between long-standing residents.'[152] Precisely because the domestic sphere has lost its private nature among the émigrés, and because, at the same time, the indiscreet revelation of personal confessions has become respectable, utmost caution is called for, particularly in the choice of private acquaintances. One should beware of seeking out the mighty or their assiduous helpers. But if you obey the maxim of living modestly and minding your own business, you will be threatened by nothing less than 'starvation or madness'.[153]

Apart from his intimate diaries, these aphorisms are the most personal statements Adorno ever made.[154] They make it clear that exile meant above all the feeling of exclusion and homelessness. 'In the recollection of emigration each German venison roast tastes as if it had been felled with the charmed bullets of the *Freischütz*.'[155] On the other hand, the feeling of being uprooted, of release from one's bourgeois traditions, also contained an element of autonomy and freedom. As someone who had been marginalized, Adorno made the acquaintance of the intermediary position of those social critics who both live in society and are yet not quite of it. This state of uncertainty between inside and outside was the ideal observation post from his point of view. Not being tied down in this sense was the ideal experiential background and at the same time the reference point for the formation of moral judgement. Adorno succeeded in training his gaze on society from the standpoint of someone dwelling in no man's land. His privileged personal situation did not prevent him from registering the fact that life had changed into 'a timeless succession of shocks',[156] mediated by the daily newspaper reports and newsreel pictures about the world war and the annihilation of human beings. Neither the relative security of Adorno's material circumstances, of whose advantages he was well aware, nor the view of the enchanting landscape and the Pacific Ocean gleaming in the distance, seduced him into deceiving himself about the element of luck to which he owed his escape.

> Even the blossoming tree tells a lie the moment its bloom is seen without the shadow of terror; even the innocent 'How lovely!' becomes an excuse for an existence outrageously unlovely, and there is no longer beauty or consolation except in the gaze falling on horror, withstanding it, and in unalleviated consciousness of negativity holding fast to the possibility of what is better.[157]

The mood of Adorno's '*dialogue intérieur*' provided a striking contrast with his private utterances in his letters. Although he personally valued the comfort of his life in South Kenter Avenue, his diagnosis in one of his aphorisms was that it 'is part of morality not to be at home in one's home'.[158] As if describing his own situation, he asked 'What does it mean for the subject that there are no more casement windows to open, but only sash windows to shove up and down, no gentle latches, but turnable handles, no forecourt, no doorstep to the street, no wall round the garden?'[159] And while he admired the American landscape in his letters, he complained about it here because the roads 'are always inserted directly in the landscape, and the more impressively smooth and broad they are, the more unrelated and violent their gleaming track appears against its wild, overgrown surroundings.'[160]

Adorno's observations register idiosyncratically the dissolution of the bourgeois world so that the anti-bourgeois intellectuals 'are at once the last enemies of the bourgeois and the last bourgeois'[161] and, paradoxically, they find themselves defending the ruins of the bourgeoisie against its late bourgeois enemies. But for all his criticism of American mass culture, he made no attempt to play off past bourgeois forms of universal education and higher culture against the levelling pressures to conform to the society in which he was living. The good qualities of the bourgeois way of life, such as autonomy and foresight, have revealed their bad side and turn out to be no more than egocentrism and pig-headedness.

'The bourgeois have lost their innocence and have become quite truculent and malevolent in the process.'[162]

A number of aphorisms were evidently highly personal attempts by Adorno to come to terms with his own unhappy love relationships. He gathered them together in Part III of the collection, which he prefaced with a motto taken from a poem by Baudelaire: '*Avalanche veux-tu m'emporter dans ta chute?*'[163] In these aphorisms he reflected on the injustice that is experienced by the man who is rejected, but who may not protest because 'what he desires can only be given in freedom'. When affection is withheld, he who is rebuffed

> is made to feel the untruth of all merely individual fulfilment. But he thereby awakens to the paradoxical consciousness of generality: of the inalienable and unindictable human right to be loved by the beloved. With his plea, founded on no titles or claims, he appeals to an unknown court, which accords to him as grace what is his own and yet not his own. The secret of justice in love is the annulment of all rights, to which love mutely points.[164]

Like Alban Berg's *Lyric Suite*, these aphorisms constitute an interior monologue with the beloved that contains secret messages which are, however, not aimed directly at the addressee; they are messages in a bottle. This includes the description of sleepless nights, those 'tormented hours drawn out without prospect of end or dawn, in the vain effort to forget time's empty passing. But truly terrifying are the sleepless nights when time seems to contract and run fruitlessly through our hands. . . . But what is revealed in such contraction of the hours is the reverse of time fulfilled. If in the latter the power of experience breaks the spell of duration and gathers past and future into the present, in the hasteful sleepless night duration causes unendurable dread.'[165]

Jean Paul's sentence 'All the little flowers [that she gave me]' gave the signal to reflect on memory which is always a blend of past and present. 'He who has loved and who betrays love does harm not only to the image of the past, but to the past itself.'[166] Did Adorno learn from his own, sometimes unhappy, love affairs that the relationship between men and women is entirely based on 'exchange'? Matters could scarcely be clearer when he writes:

> Love is chilled by the value that the ego places upon itself. Loving at all seems to it like loving more, and he who loves more puts himself in the wrong. This arouses his mistress's suspicion, and his emotion, thrown back on itself, grows sick with possessive cruelty and self-destructive imagining.[167]

What Adorno revealed to Grab about Charlotte Alexander is reflected in the aphorism that love falls for the soulless, that it is sustained by 'its desire to save, which can exercise itself only on the lost'.[168] And the fact that Adorno remained committed to his wife Gretel despite all his affairs was undoubtedly in his eyes 'the test of feeling to see whether it goes beyond feeling, through permanence, even though it be as obsession'.[169]

During the month in which Adorno wrote down his aphorisms, he visited his parents in New York, wishing to be close to them in person, rather than just through his letters. Having spent some quiet days with Gretel in San Francisco in July 1943, he left her there in order to be with his parents for a while in the Pocono Mountains to the north of Philadelphia. In February–March 1945 he was back in New York, where he stayed mainly with his parents. Needless to say, there was much talk of the war in Europe following the battle in the Ardennes, the largest land battle involving American troops up to that time and one in which they had lost 19,000 dead and 40,000 wounded. In the USA families who had lost a relative displayed a golden star in their window.

Even before the landing of US forces in Normandy in June 1944, Adorno was well aware that Germany was moving towards catastrophic defeat. He, like Horkheimer, had predicted the future collapse of the 'Greater German Empire' after the inferno of Stalingrad, when General Paulus disobeyed Hitler's orders and surrendered. Around 150,000 German soldiers had fallen, and 90,000 went into Russian prisoner-of-war camps. The fact that this was the turning point of the war was confirmed in 1943, when the German Africa Corps capitulated in the face of superior Anglo-American forces, and when Sicily was invaded two months later. Then came the fall of Mussolini, and in September an armistice was concluded with the new Italian government.

Despite the National Socialist propaganda about 'final victory' and 'miracle weapons', German morale deteriorated sharply, and this was accentuated by the new anti-terrorist regulations, such as those against demoralizing the military or listening to enemy radio. Russian troops conquered Berlin in April 1945, Hitler committed suicide in the same month, and on 8 May the general staff of the German armed forces surrendered unconditionally. In order to end the war in the Pacific, the US leadership deployed the most horrifying weapon at its disposal. In August 1945, two atomic bombs were detonated over Hiroshima and Nagasaki. Almost at the same time as this inhuman act at the close of the Second World War, the world was suddenly confronted with the news of systematic genocide on a scale that defied the human imagination. The foundations of civilization were shaken when the world learnt of the barbaric consequences of the racial policies of the Nazi state. In the German extermination camps and labour camps of Auschwitz, Treblinka, Belzec, Sobibor and Majdanek, the industrial murder of millions of Jews was carried out with great technical efficiency in specially built gas chambers and crematoria.[170]

For Adorno, the meanings that accrued to the metaphor of Auschwitz were to become the starting-point from which it would become necessary to reorientate our thinking about history and to treat it as a history of catastrophe. Auschwitz was 'the infernal machine that is history'.[171] And, confronted with the extermination camps, it is not possible, he thought, to go on thinking as before, and everything that has been thought must now be questioned: 'Auschwitz cannot be brought into analogy with the destruction of the Greek city-states as a mere gradual increase in horror, before which one can preserve tranquillity of mind. Certainly, the unprecedented torture and humiliation of those abducted in cattle-trucks does shed a deathly livid light on the most distant past.'[172] In Part II of *Minima Moralia*, which Adorno was engaged in writing during the months in which he tried to grasp the scale of the collective guilt of the Germans, he noted that their crimes 'seemed to have been committed rather as measures of alienated terrorization'. Their horrific nature passes human understanding. 'Nevertheless, a consciousness that wishes to withstand the unspeakable finds itself again and again thrown back on the attempt to understand, if it is not to succumb subjectively to the madness that prevails objectively.'[173] The total dehumanization of human beings in the extermination camps was the extreme expression of a society that turned all living beings into things. All actual or imagined differences were regarded as 'stigmas' of otherness and to be eradicated. The integral, increasingly societalized society generates a will to destroy from within itself. 'The technique of the concentration camp is to make the prisoners resemble their guards, the murdered, murderers. The racial difference is raised to an absolute so that it can be abolished absolutely, if only in the sense that nothing that is different survives.'[174]

How did Adorno react to the news of Hitler's suicide and the destruction of Germany, which he had heard about over the radio, from the newspapers and on the newsreels? As early as 1 May, he wrote to his parents expressing the hope that the news about the end of the dictatorship was true, and, in words that echoed what he was writing in his 'Reflections from Damaged Life', he added that 'part of the horror of the world is that truth sounds like lying and lying like the truth.'[175] Hitler's death was the occasion for joy since he was the most 'appalling disaster' that had ever occurred in history. The German nation's 'neck had been broken so that, as a subject, it vanishes from history'. In the same letter he also expressed his fear that the elimination of the Nazis did not necessarily imply the disappearance of the Nazi principle from the world. Faced with the tendency of history, his hopes for the future confined themselves to 'pauses for breath and bolt-holes'.[176] In a letter to Horkheimer a few days later, in which he summarized his view of the world situation, he remarked that the Hitler regime that had just come to an end had been 'the direct cause of all external developments in our lives during the last twelve years'. The expectation that 'things would change has been one of the crucial factors that kept us alive, while on the other hand the fact that both our lives have come together in one shared life is something that cannot be separated from fascism.' Over

and above that, Adorno declared not without pride that his thesis 'that
Hitler could not survive has been proved correct, albeit with a certain
time lag that is something of an irony. In other words, the forces of
production of more progressive countries have proved to be the stronger
after all . . . : the war has been won by industry against the military.'[177]
Adorno took up the same theme in *Minima Moralia*:

> Germany's industrial backwardness forced its politicians – anxious
> to regain lost ground and, as have-nots, specially qualified for the
> role – to fall back on their immediate, narrow experience, that of
> the political façade. They saw nothing before them except cheering
> assemblies and frightened negotiators: this blocked their view of
> the objective power of a greater mass of capital. It was immanent
> revenge on Hitler that he, the executioner of liberal society, was
> yet in his own state of consciousness too 'liberal' to perceive how
> industrial potential outside Germany was establishing, under the
> veil of liberalism, its irresistible domination. He, who recognized
> the untruth in liberalism as did no other bourgeois, could yet not
> recognize the power behind it, the social tendency for which Hitler
> was really no more than drummer.[178]

In his letter to Horkheimer, Adorno came to the conclusion that, even
if the historical 'violence of fascism' had only 'changed its domicile',[179]
events had turned out much better than they had always imagined,
since Hitler, that 'most appalling disaster', had now been disposed of.

All in all, then, Adorno now had a more hopeful view of the current
situation, and this may explain why he began to toy with the idea of
returning to Europe. But more than four years would pass before the
idea could become reality. He even had to deny himself a rather shorter
journey to New York. For when his mother celebrated her eightieth
birthday on 30 September 1945, he was unable to travel to the East
Coast, partly for reasons of health, and partly because of his duties
in the Berkeley research project. However, the affectionate tone of the
birthday letter he wrote testifies to the closeness of their relationship.

His next trip to see his mother in New York in September 1946 was
a sad occasion. Oscar Wiesengrund had died on 8 July after a long
illness. He was in his seventy-seventh year. Having been informed by
telegram, Adorno at once wrote to his mother. His sadness at his
father's death, he said, was all the greater as his father had been forced
to die in exile, having been compelled to lead the life of an émigré and
having had to forgo continuity in his lifetime.[180] He was unable to travel
to the East Coast for the funeral, since he had fallen seriously ill. He
was receiving treatment for his blood-sugar levels, a stomach ulcer and
cardiac symptoms. For this reason he asked Leo Löwenthal to give the
oration at his father's funeral. Not until two months later was he in a
position to offer his mother support in her bereavement. For the moment

he could do no more than write. At the end of his letter, he said that, with his father's death, 'his own life seemed like robbery'. This was an idea that appeared here for the first time, but was one he would develop subsequently in *Negative Dialectics*. It was the idea of 'the injustice of continuing to live, as if one were cheating the dead of light and breath. The sense of such guilt is infinitely powerful in me.'[181]

The Privy Councillor: Adorno and Thomas Mann

And at the beginning of October . . . we spent an evening with the Adornos. . . . I read out three pages about the piano that I had recently inserted into my chapter which was becoming worryingly hypertrophic, and our host told us something of his studies and aphorisms about Beethoven. . . . Then Adorno, while I stood next to the piano watching him, played the sonata, op. 111, right through and in a highly instructive way.[182]

What did he talk about? Well, the man was capable of spending a whole hour on the question: Why did Beethoven not write a third movement to the Piano Sonata, Opus 111? . . . And then he sat down at the cottage piano and played us the whole composition out of his head, the first and the incredible second movement, shouting his comments into the midst of his playing. . . . 'Here it comes!' and began the variations movement, the '*adagio molto semplice e cantabile*.' The arietta theme, destined to vicissitudes for which in its idyllic innocence it would seem not to be born, is presented at once and announced in sixteen bars, reducible to a motif which appears at the end of its first half, like a brief soul-cry – only three notes, a quaver, a semiquaver, and a dotted crotchet to be scanned as, say: 'heav-en's blue, lov-ers' pain, fare-thee well, on a-time, mead-ow-land'.[183]

Adorno and his wife valued the dry climate and loved the vegetation of the hilly southern landscape of Los Angeles. Nevertheless, it is striking how often they were unwell. Gretel needed continual treatment for her long-lasting migraines, and her husband visited his doctor, Robert Alexander, with the most varied symptoms – not simply acute psycho-logical crises, depressions and oppressive feelings. In addition, on several occasions he needed treatment for various stomach upsets and also neuralgia.[184] In spring 1946 he had a serious illness of the coronary arteries as a result of which he was bedridden for a lengthy period. Later on, when diabetes was diagnosed, he was forced to keep to a strict diet, and in addition he suffered from stomach ulcers.

All the more vital, then, were the vacations that he and Gretel frequently spent in the mountains, on Lake Tahoe (on the border between California and Nevada) or, during another summer, in Lugana Beach near San Diego, which reminded them of the most beautiful resorts on the French Riviera. Among the attractive sides of American life must be included the close contacts with the other German émigrés as well as Hollywood society, of which Adorno had a somewhat ironic view: 'Usually these blithe spirits are as totally absorbed by everyday practicalities as the petty bourgeoisie. They furnish houses, prepare parties, show virtuosity in booking hotel and airline reservations.'[185] Naturally enough, Adorno wrote to his parents right away to tell them about his impressions of his first encounter with Charlie Chaplin. He thought his 1947 film *Monsieur Verdoux* was a masterpiece.[186] Adorno and his wife were invited by Chaplin to a private showing of the film. After the dinner that followed, Adorno played the piano – a melange of music from operas by Verdi, Wagner and Mozart – while Chaplin accompanied his playing with parodistic enactments. This and other meetings with Chaplin were engraved indelibly on Adorno's memory. An instance occurred in a villa in Malibu at which the actor Harold Russell was also present. He had played the part of a wounded American veteran in the award-winning film *The Best Years of our Life*.

> One of the guests came to say goodbye early while Chaplin was standing next to me. Unlike Chaplin, I extended my hand a little absent-mindedly and then jerked it back violently. The man saying goodbye was one of the main actors in the film *The Best Years of our Life*, a film that had become famous after the war. He had lost one of his hands in the war and wore an artificial claw made of iron, but very effective. When I shook his right hand and it responded to the pressure, I was very taken aback, but realizing at once that I should not let Russell see my reaction under any circumstances, I instantly transformed the shocked expression on my face into a winning grimace which must have looked even more shocking. Scarcely had the actor departed than Chaplin was already mimicking the scene. So close to horror is the laughter that he provoked and only from close up can it acquire its legitimacy and its salutary aspect.[187]

It was not only Chaplin's films that Adorno enjoyed. Thanks to his personal contacts with directors, authors, scriptwriters, actors and producers, he was familiar with the Hollywood productions of those years. No doubt because of his friendship with Fritz Lang and his partner Lily Latté, he would have seen such films as *Fury*, *You and Me*, and presumably also *Jesse James*. His friendship with Alexander Granach, who had died in March 1945, meant that he saw the films Granach had acted in, including, for example, *Hangmen Also Die!*, but also other anti-Nazi films in which people he knew well were involved. As a critic of the culture industry, however, he thought it impossible for the horrors of fascism to be depicted in the cinema, since 'total unfreedom can be recognized, but not depicted'.[188] He ridiculed well-intentioned attempts to transmit correct political opinions through the medium of film. In addition to film, he seems also to have been fascinated by the illustrated episodes 'from the Edgar Bergen/Charlie McCarthy radio programmes, retold by Eleanor Packer'. Even so, he was critical of the underlying pedagogic message whose sole credo was social conformity. He also noted the way language was reduced to hackneyed phrases and catchwords. 'In the all-embracing system conversation becomes ventriloquism. Everyone is his own Charlie McCarthy; hence his popularity. Speech in its entirety is coming to resemble the formulae which used to be reserved for greeting and leave-taking.'[189] Without his knowledge of the internal workings of the film business and without his frequent visits to the cinema and his reading of popular literature, Adorno would scarcely have been able to write the chapter on the culture industry in *Dialectic of Enlightenment*. It follows that it was not true that every visit to the cinema left him 'stupider and worse'.[190] Quite the reverse. He was in a position to form a precise picture of the dream factory and the laws governing its productions. This expert knowledge, to which we may add his experience as former director of the music research project, was soon to bear fruit.

This was connected with the fact that Adorno and Hanns Eisler were near neighbours and had had a close relationship since autumn 1942. Eisler, the composer and musician who was very friendly with Brecht, lived a few streets away from Adorno, and it was his suggestion that they should write a book jointly about film music. He approached Adorno in December 1942 with this idea because, as a former lecturer at the New School for Social Research, he had received a grant from the Rockefeller Foundation for a project analysing film music. However, he was uncertain how to proceed and hoped to profit from the experience Adorno had acquired in the radio research project. Adorno was very ready to take part in a project that sounded interesting for the very good reason that it was envisaged not as a research project but as an artistic experiment. So he and Eisler set to work. Some of the great Hollywood film companies, Twentieth Century-Fox and Paramount among them, provided them with a selection of musical material. In addition, scores were tried out that Eisler had specially composed for the purpose of analysis and which could be deployed in different contexts (scenes with children, nature scenes, feature films, newsreels). What they focused on was the question of how to relate musical forms meaningfully to visual scenes in such a way that something was added to them. Although the two authors based their work on the premise that film was not an art form in its own right, but had to be regarded as a medium of distraction and enjoyment, they put in a plea for its making use of avant-garde music. In particular, the moments of fear which are so common in a traditional type of popular film could be heightened by 'the shocks of modern music'.[191] As an example, Adorno pointed to *King Kong*, in which the musical accompaniment failed to live up to the drama because the shock-effects of modern music had not been used. These would have been especially appropriate in an advanced aesthetics of film because of modern music's use of condensed musical form, sharp contrasts and a 'wealth of dissonances'. Adorno's reflections went well beyond this question of an adequate musical language: following Walter Benjamin's thesis from his essay of 1936, 'The Work of Art in the Age of Technological Reproducibility', Adorno rejected all forms of production that achieved an auraticization of the medium in order to endow it with the false magic of uniqueness. The visual and acoustic techniques were supposed instead to provide a specific material that called for works of art based on the principle of montage. The music was to be one independent element among others. Its gestural power would have the function of bringing movement into the rigidity of the speaking images. 'In its aesthetic effect, therefore, it simulates movement rather than duplicating it.'[192]

The book was written in 1944 and bore the unmistakable signature of the author of the chapter on the culture industry. However, when it was published by Oxford University Press in 1947 Adorno chose that his name should not appear as author on the title page with Eisler's. The reason for this was less the fact of any disagreements with Eisler on matters of substance than the fact that Adorno was afraid to publish a book together with an orthodox supporter of Soviet Marxism who, in that same year, had been summoned to appear before the Committee on Un-American Activities set up by the House of Representatives. Adorno explained his caution by saying that he saw no reason 'to be a martyr to a cause which was and is not my own. In view of the scandal, I withdrew my claims to authorship.'[193] In a letter to his mother, however, Adorno did express his regret that he was mentioned only in the preface to the book and not as official co-author, since he had not only written 90 per cent of the text, but had also put in the intellectual work. It would actually have been more appropriate for Eisler to have renounced his authorship.[194]

Adorno was destined to be the victim of a far more serious case in which use was made of his ideas and writings without acknowledging that he was the author as clearly as he might have expected and had every right to wish for. We are speaking of Adorno's role as music adviser to Thomas Mann when the latter began work early in 1943 on his great novel *Doctor Faustus: The Life of the German Composer Adrian Leverkühn, as Told by a Friend*. This novel described the pact the musical genius had made with the Devil, but in reality it was an intellectual archaeology of German fascism. When it appeared in October 1947, Adorno received a personal copy from Mann with the dedication 'To the real Privy Councillor'.

Ever since his youth, Adorno had felt great admiration for a writer with such a profound understanding of music and culture in general. Many years before, when Adorno was only eighteen, he had seen Mann, who was already a famous novelist, during a vacation in Kampen on the island of Sylt, and had walked behind him, imagining what he might say to him.[195] Twenty-two years later, when the vicissitudes of world history had brought him to Santa Monica, luck would have it that he was able to meet Mann in person, in July 1943, at a large party in the house of Max and Maidon Horkheimer. 'I had the feeling', he wrote shortly after, in a letter on Mann's seventieth birthday, 'that for the first and only time I was able to meet in the flesh the German tradition which had given me everything apart from the strength to resist that tradition.'[196] This first meeting was evidently the occasion of an animated exchange between Adorno and Mann: it was an encounter in which the intellectual culture of the century was refracted as if through a prism. Adorno, who was twenty-eight years younger than Mann, talked about his *Philosophy of Modern Music*; Mann talked about the new novel which he had started to write in May 1943, after intensive preparations.[197] Adorno pricked up his ears when he heard that Thomas Mann's intention was to incorporate the scarcely narratable story of the German tragedy in a novel whose central theme was the history of the tragic life of a composer of modern music. So, shortly after their meeting, he gave Mann a copy of his book analysing the works of Berg.[198] He also showed Mann his hitherto unpublished interpretation of the works of Arnold Schoenberg[199] and his essay on Wagner. This led to an even closer relationship between the two during the next four years. Music was almost always in the foreground when they took turns to invite each other to afternoon tea or dinner.

On 27 September 1943, Thomas Mann invited the Adornos to his beautifully situated home on San Remo Drive and he read them chapter 8 of his manuscript. Adorno spontaneously suggested various objections, additions and corrections and later on put them in writing. For the most part, Mann took Adorno's points into account for the earlier chapters of the novel which he was then writing. And for one of the crucial scenes of the first third of the novel, the talk given by the stuttering music teacher, Wendell Kretzschmar, on Beethoven's last piano sonata, op. 111, Mann was inspired by Adorno's article of 1937 on 'Beethoven's Late Style',[200] as well as by additional written and spoken explanations to do with this work. Was it from gratitude to Adorno that the music teacher explained the motif from the arietta theme in the second movement of op. 111 by referring to 'Wie-sengrund'? In October Adorno and his wife reciprocated and invited the Manns to dinner in their turn. On this occasion philosophical as well as musical topics were discussed. In his thank-you letter for 'yesterday's rich evening', Mann, whose own musical education, as he said, 'scarcely went beyond the late Romantics',[201] expressly acknowledged Adorno's expertise: 'I need musical intimacy and characteristic detail, and can only obtain them from a connoisseur like yourself.'[202]

After Christmas 1945, Mann sent Adorno a detailed letter that had every mark of a document intended for posterity, and in it he set out how he envisaged his hero's *magnum opus*, the 'Apocalipsis cum figuris'. He attempted to cajole Adorno into supporting his project. 'Would you be willing to think through with me how the work – I mean Leverkühn's work – might look; how you would do it if you were in league with the Devil.'[203] On this occasion, too, Adorno did not need to be asked twice; indeed, as someone with an intimate knowledge of avant-garde music, he was excited by the prospect of being able to contribute to the novel. He at once produced a number of ideas. This explains why the majority of the musical works created by Leverkühn are actually inventions of Adorno's.[204] The notes that he had written during the conception of the project were available to Mann to make use of as he saw fit. That is what Adorno wrote to Mann's daughter Erika seven years after her father's death. The truth was that Erika would have preferred it if there had been no musical advice at all. Adorno's recollection was that much was altered, whether because Thomas Mann 'had woven the general themes of the novel much more concretely and vividly into the description of musical detail; whether he had simply changed the emphasis in many instances . . . ; or whether, lastly, and this was perhaps the most important factor, he had just left a lot out. After all, he was writing a novel and not a music guide.'[205]

Thomas Mann's own view of the activities of his 'Privy Councillor' is reproduced in the *Story of a Novel: The Genesis of 'Dr Faustus'*, albeit in a literary form. He describes how at Christmas 1945 he had handed the entire manuscript of *Faustus*, as far as it had been completed, to Adorno to read and had visited him shortly afterwards:

> He and his wife had read the manuscript simultaneously, passing the pages from one to the other, and I, full of doubts as I was, listened eagerly to their report of the involvement, suspense and excitement with which they had read it. The fact that the author of *The Philosophy of Modern Music* put a good face on the way in which with the assistance of his contemporary insights I had let my work-shy Devil 'be ushered into the realm of art', as Adrian expresses it, eased my conscience. Alone with him in his study, I received much good and clever advice from him. . . . He was not much taken with my idea, one which had long since become an irrevocable decision on my part, of basing the oratorio on Dürer's woodcuts of the Apocalypse, and we came to the agreement that the internal space of the work should be expanded into a more generalized eschatology, encompassing, if possible, the entire 'apocalyptic culture' and presenting it as a kind of summation of all proclamations of the end.[206]

In January 1946, in order to convert this plan into a form that would be musically plausible and appropriate as literature, the novelist 'paid a number of visits to Adorno. . . . And in the next few weeks, with pencil and notebook in hand, and over a good home-made fruit liqueur, he "swiftly" recorded keywords, improvements and more precise formulations for earlier musical descriptions and characteristic details that he had thought up for the oratorio. Adorno displayed an intimate knowledge of the intentions of the work as a whole and with this section in particular. His suggestions and proposals consistently went to the heart of the matter.'[207] Mann gave a much more explicit account of Adorno's inventiveness in his diaries. What the 'Magician' writes there gives a more accurate picture since the diaries were not subjected to the censorship of Katia and Erika Mann, neither of whom was keen to see the achievements of the Privy Councillor praised too loudly in public. There he noted the brilliance with which Adorno translated his ideas into novelistic practice. For example, 'the way the choruses developed from whispering, a mixture of speaking and part-singing, to the richest vocal polyphony, and the movement of the orchestra from a primitive, magic sound to music of the most advanced kind. Or the interchange of sound between the vocal and instrumental parts, the shifting of the boundary between man and thing', the idea of '"transferring the part of the Whore of Babylon to an exquisitely graceful coloratura soprano and incorporating her virtuoso runs into the orchestral sound with a flute-like effect", while, on the other hand, conferring on certain instruments the colour of a grotesque vox humana.'[208]

Thomas Mann also sought Adorno's advice for his description of the violin concerto that, after the oratorio, Leverkühn went on to compose for his friend, the violinist Rudolf Schwertfeger. Adorno responded with detailed proposals in a statement entitled 'On the Violin Concerto'.[209] Mann transformed these ideas into his own literary language, but nevertheless in part just adopted them word for word. It comes as no surprise to see how this fictional concert awakened memories of the real concert that Alban Berg had given and of which Adorno had an unrivalled knowledge. Of the three compositions that Leverkühn is credited with following the violin concerto, Adorno invented two. A comparison of Adorno's written proposals and the finished version in the novel shows strikingly how close Mann kept to his draft:[210]

Adorno	Doctor Faustus
This tendency to 'prose' is intensified to an extreme in the string quartet, Adrian's most esoteric work. Where, otherwise, chamber music forms the playground for thematic work, here it is almost provocatively avoided. There are altogether no thematic connections, developments, variations, and	This tendency to musical 'prose' comes to its height in the string quartet, Leverkühn's most esoteric work, perhaps, which followed on the heels of the ensemble piece. Where, otherwise, chamber music forms the playground for thematic work, here it is almost provocatively avoided. There are altogether no

not even repetitions; the new follows unbroken, in an apparently entirely [*ganz*] free way, held together by similarity of tone or colour, or, even more, by contrast.	thematic connections, developments, variations, and no repetitions; unbroken, in an apparently entirely [*völlig*] free way, the new follows, held together by similarity of tone or colour, or, almost more, by contrast.

Shortly before Leverkühn is dragged off by the Devil, he has time for one last composition, the symphonic cantata 'The Lament of Dr Faustus'. Once again Mann appealed to Adorno to help him resolve the problems posed by this difficult task. And in this instance, too, Adorno responded with a detailed proposal[211] which Mann largely adopted.

When *Doctor Faustus* appeared in the USA in the summer of 1947 in an edition published by Knopf, it found a large readership from the start. The first edition of 25,000 copies was soon out of print, once the work had been chosen the 'November Book of the Month' in August and the response of the American critics had been overwhelmingly positive.[212] The impact of the German edition was longer in coming. An analysis by the literary critic Hans Mayer led Adorno to write to Mann the ironist on 6 July 1950, asking whether it was true that he had been portrayed as one of the devil figures in chapter 25: 'horn-rimmed spectacles on his hooked nose.... pale and vaulted the brow, out of which the hair retreats towards the top, yet from there to the sides, thick, standing up black and woolly: a member of the intelligentsia, writer on art, on music for the ordinary press, a theoretician and critic who himself composes, as far as thinking allows him.'[213] Mann's reply, a few days later, was by no means free of the gentle ironic undertone of which he was master. 'And the idea that the Devil in his role as a music scholar was modelled on your appearance is quite absurd. Do you in fact ever wear horn-rimmed spectacles?'[214] Thomas Mann was probably astonished and delighted that of all people the philosopher of music had failed to solve the riddle. For the Devil, who is transformed in the course of the chapter from pimp and professor of theology to music scholar, resembled not Adorno but Gustav Mahler. He had given him horn-rimmed spectacles only 'to disguise him', 'an intentionally misleading model that functioned effectively for decades and prevented commentators from noticing that Adorno might have stood out for all sorts of possible reasons, but not for his magnificent bushy hair.'[215]

Taking all these things together – the conversations, the drafts, the oral and written suggestions for improvements – Adorno might well be thought of 'as co-author.... Our ordinary sense of justice would have deemed it right to award him some financial remuneration if it had occurred to him to demand it. However, Adorno thought of it as a great challenge to be allowed to collaborate on *Faustus*, rather than as a paid service.'[216] In August 1957 Adorno found himself in the position of having to agree to make a statutory declaration in response to a request from Katia Mann, who needed support in defending an accusation of plagiarism against Thomas Mann.[217] In the declaration, he said: 'During the entire work on the novel *Doctor Faustus* I gave friendly advice to Thomas Mann on all musical matters. I was a witness to the writing of the book. At no point was it the writer's intention to give the impression that twelve-tone music was his invention. . . . No less absurd is the insinuation that Thomas Mann made illegitimate use of my "intellectual property", simply because the musical portions of the novel were written with the full agreement of us both. . . . Finally, I wish to state as emphatically as possible that I never received any material remuneration of any kind from Thomas Mann.'[218] This unusual legal step did nothing to prevent further slanders. It was undoubtedly the expression of Adorno's own helplessness and impotence in the face of mud-slinging in which he had no wish to participate. He had, it is true, given a talk on Thomas Mann in March 1962 in connection with an exhibition about the writer.[219] This talk contains one of the most perceptive descriptions of Mann ever to have been written. But he did not carry out his plan of writing a monograph on Mann, something which he had been considering in the 1960s. This was because he felt himself to have 'been slandered from beyond the grave'[220] by the publication of two letters that had been written between 1948 and 1955.[221] Mann had told the literary historian Jonas Lesser that Adorno had been boasting about his work on *Doctor Faustus* now that he, Thomas Mann, had turned the spotlight on to him. The idea that Adorno was making too much fuss about his contribution was evidently the predominant if not the unanimous view within the 'Magician's' family and the immediate circle of his admirers. Katia Mann and her daughter Erika, in particular, later spoke about Adorno in extremely disparaging tones.[222] Adorno was spared the knowledge of this and hence the need to defend his good name. Nevertheless, he did learn of Thomas Mann's own brief utterances, and these were painful enough. It was therefore readily understandable that Adorno should have preferred to keep his own counsel and remain silent instead of publishing further writings on Thomas Mann and his works.

This attempt to keep his distance was the final stage of a cooling-off process that had already begun during Mann's lifetime. For the fact was that the paths taken by these two great figures of the century had already begun gradually to diverge towards the end of 1949.

Despite growing political difficulties in the USA, where he was regarded as a communist,[223] Thomas Mann for a long time resisted the idea of returning to post-fascist Germany, even for a visit. In contrast, no sooner had the war come to an end than Adorno started to think about going back to Europe. He found the idea of his former homeland attractive precisely because a destroyed Germany had a position of only marginal importance on the world stage. For this reason, he was preoccupied by the question of what should be done 'with a defeated Germany'. The two, unsatisfactory, answers in his view were: 'First, under no circumstances would I wish to be an executioner, or provide a licence for executioners. Second, I should not wish to stay the hand . . . of anyone who takes revenge for past misdeeds. This is a thoroughly unsatisfactory, self-contradictory answer, one that makes a mockery of generalization and practice. But perhaps the fault lies with the question and not just in me.'[224]

Adorno's American nationality was anything but a matter of indifference to him, and the decision to leave the USA so as to spend his remaining years in Europe was by no means definitive. But he neither could nor wished to avoid the problem of Germany. It suited his book, therefore, that he soon had an opportunity to transform his wishes into action and to form an impression of the country he had left fifteen years previously. During the last days of October 1949, he made the journey back to Germany. He travelled instead of Horkheimer, who had been unable to accept an invitation from Frankfurt University for reasons of health and was therefore unable to take up his post as professor of philosophy for the beginning of the winter semester 1949–50.[225]

Adorno, the former *Privatdozent*, did not return to Frankfurt empty-handed. The *Dialectic of Enlightenment* was already available in book form. The study on film music had been published in English. Furthermore, he had reached an agreement with the Tübingen publisher Mohr (Paul Siebeck) that they would bring out a greatly expanded version of the *Philosophy of Modern Music*. Moreover, his work over a number of years on the Berkeley project also produced well-deserved success: at the precise moment when Adorno was on his way to Europe, *The Authoritarian Personality* appeared in print as volume 1 of the series *Studies in Prejudice*. He had thus acquired fame as a scholar, and he had also succeeded in completing two compositions: *Four Songs for Voice and Piano from Poems by Stefan George*, op. 7, and *Three Choruses for Female Voices from Poems by Theodor Däubler*, op. 8. Whereas, in Adorno's own words, the first composition 'was based on a twelve-tone row that is employed only in its four basic shapes, without any transposition',[226] the choruses showed that it was possible to organize a musical setting without following the rules of the twelve-tone method.

But what was on Adorno's mind as he returned to Europe on the *Queen Elizabeth* was not the question of how a free musical style would operate in practice. He was now forty-six years old and he was deeply moved by this first contact with European soil after the long years of exile. When he returned to his hotel at 2 a.m., 'walking from the Quai Voltaire through Paris by night', he could tell from the sound of his own steps on the cobbles that 'the difference between Amorbach and Paris . . . is smaller than that between Paris and New York. Even so, as a small child I remember how I thought I could see from a bench halfway up the Wolkmann how the electric light that had just been introduced was switched on in every house. That experience of twilight in Amorbach anticipated the shock that I experienced as a refugee in America. So well had my little town taken care of me that it even prepared me for completely different experiences.'[227] After his arrival in Paris, where he stayed on the Boulevard Raspail in the historical Hotel Lutétia with its traditions of the *belle époque*, he wrote to Horkheimer on 28 October 1949: 'The return to Europe gripped me with such force that words fail me. And the beauty of Paris shines more beautifully than ever through the rags of poverty. . . . What survives here may well be condemned by history and it certainly bears the marks of this clearly enough, but the fact *that it*, the essence of untimeliness, still exists, is part of the historical picture and permits the feeble hope that something humane survives, despite everything.'[228] Adorno's spontaneous joy went so far as to lead him to vary the motto from *Minima Moralia* and to comment that 'life still lives' here. He urged Horkheimer to join him in looking for a life together on this continent – a wish that was to be very shortly fulfilled.

1 Teddie Wiesengrund, around 1910

2 Jean-François Calvelli-Adorno, Adorno's maternal grandfather, around 1860

3 Maria and Oscar Wiesengrund, 1898

4 Elisabeth Calvelli-Adorno, Adorno's maternal grandmother, with her children Louis, Maria and Agathe, around 1878

5 View of the Schöne Aussicht from the Obermainbrücke in Frankfurt am Main, around 1903

6 The Deutschherren Middle School on the banks of the River Main which Adorno attended from 1910 to 1913

7 Agathe Calvelli-Adorno, Adorno's aunt and 'second mother', around 1920

8 One of Teddie's favourite songs that Maria and Agathe Calvelli-Adorno used to sing to him: 'Zwischen Berg und tiefem, tiefem Tal', from the 'Scottish Songbook'

9 Adorno with his 'two mothers' in front of the garden pavilion of the Post Hotel in Amorbach, around 1918

10 View of the Eisengasse in the Ninth District of Vienna; in 1925 Adorno
lived in the Luisenheim, a guest house in this street

11–12 Adorno after 1925

13 Siegfried Kracauer, around 1930

14 Walter Benjamin, Ibiza, 1932

15 Alban Berg, 1925

16 Margarete Karplus, later to become Adorno's wife, around 1925

17 Max Horkheimer (nicknamed 'Mammoth')

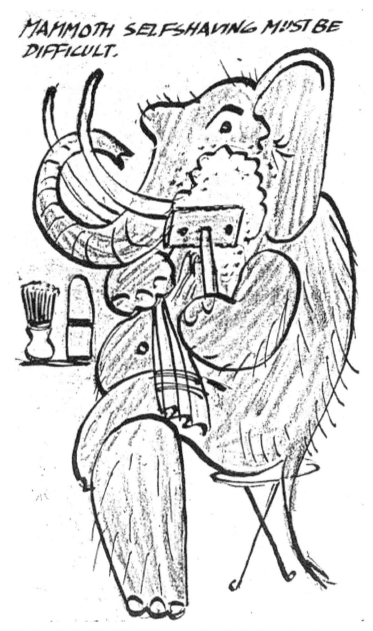

18 A drawing by Max Horkheimer on the front of a postcard

19 Adorno on the beach at Rügen

20 Adorno at his desk in Los Angeles, around 1943

21 The Waldhaus Hotel in Sils Maria

22 Adorno in Sils Maria, around 1963

23 Adorno with his wife, Gretel, around 1967

24 Brenner's Park Hotel in Baden-Baden, around 1955

25 'Himself in a mirror', Frankfurt, 1963 (photograph by Stefan Moses)

26 Adorno playing the piano in his flat in Kettenhofweg, around 1967

27 A recording session for Hessischer Rundfunk, around 1965

28 Adorno introducing Hans Magnus Enzensberger's poetics lectures in the
Johann Wolfgang von Goethe University in Frankfurt (photograph by Abisag
Tüllmann)

29 Adorno, Hans-Jürgen Krahl, Karl-Dietrich Wolff and Jürgen Habermas in a discussion at the Frankfurt Book Fair, 1968 (photograph by Barbara Klemm)

30 Heinrich Böll, Adorno and Siegfried Unseld in the recording studio of Hessischer Rundfunk during a discussion on the emergency laws, 1968

Part IV

Thinking the Unconditional and Enduring the Conditional

The Explosive Power
of Saying No

An indestructible element of the resistance to the world of barter where everything is interchangeable is the resistance of the eye that does not want the colours of the world to fade.[1]

Adorno spent the last twenty years of his life mostly in Germany – he died a few weeks before his sixty-sixth birthday. There he not only enjoyed an incomparably influential life as an academic, but also helped to shape the direction of the Federal Republic in its efforts to discover its own cultural and political identity and to help the post-war generation in its attempts at self-clarification. As a representative of the 'Frankfurt School', he made a significant contribution to 'the intellectual foundations of the Federal Republic'[2] which formed the kernel of the political and cultural self-image of the nation twenty years after the establishment of the institutions of the German state. It may be said, therefore, that he helped to bring about the consistent policy of integration in the West, the process of democratization and, above all, the beginning of a political debate about the German past. Adorno was among those who shaped the political culture of Germany.

As a university teacher, the acclaim he won from his students can be seen in a characteristic photograph of 1964. He is shown standing at the podium of the largest lecture hall in Frankfurt University, surrounded by countless students whom he is facing in an open, attentive manner (see plate 28). That is how he remains in the collective memory: a well-known and admired personality who for all his presence had something of the aura of the isolated intellectual in the midst of frenetic cultural activity. What was admired about his frequent appearances on radio and television and other cultural venues was his instinctive insistence on thinking. On his return to Germany, Adorno was initially by no means free of the anxiety that the horrors of the past might be repeated. Nevertheless, four years after the end of hostilities, he took the decision to return to the land of the 'Horsts' and the 'Jürgens', the 'Bergenroths' and 'Bojungas'.[3]

His decision to return 'was hardly motivated simply by a subjective need, or homesickness, though I do not deny having had such sentiments. An objective factor also made itself felt. It was the language.'[4] As he often pointed out, he was dependent on the German language as a writer because 'it has a special affinity with philosophy' and in particular with its ability 'to express something in the phenomena that is not exhausted in their mere thus-ness, their positivity and givenness.'[5]

A mere year and a half after his return Adorno was already a well-known figure. The reason why he was able to make a name for himself so quickly in the newly founded Federal Republic was the publication of *Minima Moralia*, the completed manuscript of which he had brought with him in his luggage. To his own surprise, the book was an extraordinary success. Difficult as it was to explain this success, Adorno attributed it to the fact that intellectual circles in Germany were gradually tiring of the Heidegger fashion (*Heideggerei*). This assessment was quite accurate. Because Adorno was one of the few alternatives to the neo-conservative climate that he associated with Heidegger, he was able in due course to emerge as the most important figure on the laborious road to intellectual recovery. A crucial turning point was reached with the sentence he wrote in the year after his return and published a little later: 'To write poetry after Auschwitz is barbaric.'[6] With this sentence, which he stood by despite his knowledge of the poetry of Nelly Sachs and Paul Celan, he had taken a stand that would make it more or less impossible for him to retreat into an ivory tower of pure scholarship.

Nevertheless, he had moved to Frankfurt primarily as a scholar. His intention was to take up again the post of *Privatdozent* which had been taken away from him in 1933 and to become a philosophy teacher at his former home university from which he had been expelled. In this he not only succeeded, he also became the representative of another discipline, sociology, which was held to be very advanced in postwar Germany and was therefore treated with some mistrust both inside the university and, more especially, outside it. During his years of exile in America, he had undoubtedly acquired the necessary qualifications for such a post, and he had a number of publications to prove it. It was as a sociologist that he became a key figure in resurrecting the Institute of Social Research. With Horkheimer's withdrawal to Montagnola in Switzerland in 1958 on the grounds of age, Adorno became sole director of the institute. In practice the main burden of directing the institute had rested on his shoulders from its inception.

During his first few years in Germany, Adorno was able to harvest the fruits of his labours on American soil. He had long since completed his first books in draft form – *The Philosophy of Modern Music* (1949), *Minima Moralia* (1951), *In Search of Wagner* (1952) and, finally, the collection of essays in *Prisms* (1955) and *Against Epistemology: A Metacritique* (1956). Some of these books had been partly written in Oxford, but the majority were the products of his stay on the East and

West coasts of America. His scholarly productivity during this time was accompanied by a learning process that was of crucial importance for his specific brand of sociology. His experience of Anglo-American culture led him not only to defend democratic forms of life, but also to learn 'no longer to regard as natural the conditions that had developed historically, like those in Europe: "not to take things for granted". . . . In America I was liberated from a naive belief in culture, and acquired this ability to see culture from the outside.'[7] This and other trends that American scholarship made available to him provided the foundations for his development in the course of the 1950s and 1960s into one of the most important representatives of German sociology. Adorno was one of the chief protagonists in the so-called positivist dispute in German sociology early in the 1960s (alongside Karl Popper, Jürgen Habermas and Hans Albert), and in the period 1963–8 he acted as the president of the Deutsche Gesellschaft für Soziologie (German Sociology Society). In this capacity, he was responsible for the congress devoted to the topic 'Late Capitalism or Industrial Society?'.

At the same time, Adorno made his mark in the musical life of West Germany in the postwar years. His influence was partly as a theoretician whose position had been made clear enough by his *Introduction to the Sociology of Music* (1962) and his monograph of Mahler, *Mahler: A Musical Physiognomy* (1960). But over and above that, he was also influential as a teacher in the International Summer Courses for New Music in Darmstadt.

As far as his position in the current philosophical debates was concerned, his criticism of Martin Heidegger was decisive. His *Jargon of Authenticity* (1964) served notice that he was to be taken seriously as the antipode of the hitherto dominant fundamental ontological school. Further contributions included not only *Negative Dialectics* (1966), the authoritative statement of his own philosophy, but also the *Aesthetic Theory* (1970), which did not appear until after his death.

16

Change of Scene: Surveying the Ruins

Adorno arrived in Paris at the end of October 1949. However, he could not stay there long since he had to be in Frankfurt as soon as possible in order to take up his teaching duties in the Arts Faculty at the start of the winter semester. He had made the journey without Gretel, who wanted to remain in Santa Monica until the questions about her husband's professional future had been resolved, to say nothing of the difficulties of finding somewhere to live in war-torn Frankfurt.

If Adorno had arrived a few weeks earlier, he might have witnessed the ceremonies, radio speeches and debates associated with the foundation of the two German states in May and October of that year. The first elections to the Bundestag had been held shortly before his return and had resulted in the close victory of the conservative parties, which had in turn led to the election of Konrad Adenauer as chancellor of the Federal Republic. The liberal Theodor Heuss, a man with whom Adorno later became acquainted, became the first president.[1] In this early phase of the Federal Republic, the nation's attitude to its own dark past was far from unambiguous. It is true that in 1949 Heuss had spoken of 'the collective shame' of the Germans, and Paul Löbe, the oldest member of the Bundestag, who had been the last democratic president of the Reichstag, had reminded parliament in his inaugural speech of the inherited burden of National Socialism. However, Adenauer, in his first governmental declaration, did not say a word about German guilt in the murder of the Jews and the responsibility arising from that.[2] Even worse, the government had re-employed people who had been active in the administration, justice system and politics under the Nazis. In addition to this continuity in terms of personnel, there had been no break in tradition as far as national values were concerned.[3] This tendency of West German politics to persist in its old ways and to aim at normalization can be seen as having its roots in fear and defiance. It may be linked with the fact that the German Democratic Republic came into existence at the same time with the proclamation of its constitution in the Soviet zone of occupation. This sealed the division of Germany. The delegates of the People's Congress of the GDR, which saw itself as the first 'socialist state on German soil', had been elected from a single list. An integral part of the socialist order of society was the Communist Party's absolute claim to leadership. Because of this, the Western powers and the German Federal Republic refused to recognize the GDR as a state, and this led to increased rivalry between the two and helped to consolidate the formation of hostile blocs.

Adorno obviously was well aware of these political developments, but he was taken up mainly with academic matters and preparations for his own teaching. During his first week in Frankfurt he stayed in the Zeppelin guest house, in Bockenheimer Landstrasse 128, close to the university. He then lived for a short time in a furnished room with a family called Irmer, in Liebigstrasse in the Frankfurt Westend, not far from the ruins of the Opera House. And finally, some months after Gretel had joined him, he moved into his own apartment, likewise in the Westend, in Kettenhofweg 123.

In Adorno's home town in the winter of 1949–50, the devastating effects of the war were still very much in evidence. As a result of the bombing of the 177,000 houses in Frankfurt, only 44,000 were still standing in 1945 and a further 50,000 survived in a damaged state. The Old Town lay in ruins. With one exception all the bridges over the River Main, including the iron footbridge, had been destroyed by German troops in the final days of the war. The theatre, the Opera House and the Stock Exchange, as well as parts of the university, had been badly damaged by the bombing. Most of the patrician houses of the Schöne Aussicht where Adorno had spent his childhood and his father had his business lay in ruins. In addition to witnessing the extent of the destruction, and the increase in the number of inhabitants thanks to the influx of evacuees, refugees and expellees, Adorno also saw the first architectural signs that would come to characterize the reconstruction of the Main metropolis. Although Frankfurt had failed to become capital of the republic, despite widespread expectations, it had re-established itself as a centre for banking, trade and commerce, as well as culture, and during the time in which Adorno took up his new activities it had long since begun to make itself noticed, with the rapid rebuilding of St Paul's Church and the Goethe House, and the revival of the international book fair and a very active publishing industry. Nevertheless, during the so-called years of ruins and of the economic miracle, and well into the late reform phase of the 1960s, the intellectual climate was defined by such slogans as 'loss of the centre', 'existence', 'disaster', and by provincialism, hypocrisy and the repression of the question of guilt.[4] Like Horkheimer, Adorno observed that hardly anyone was interested in asking the former émigrés for advice on political and cultural reconstruction.[5] In spring 1949, Horkheimer was again in Germany. He took steps to regain control of his father's property that had been stolen by the Nazis and reactivated the Society for Social Research. His impressions of Germany barely changed at all. 'Forgetting and cold deceit is the intellectual climate that works best for the heirs of the Nazis.'[6]

A different aspect became clear to Adorno when he reviewed the previous two decades as a former émigré:

> The years of the fascist dictatorship do not fit into the continuity of his [the émigré's] life. What took place in those years scarcely fits into his other life. If he returns, he will have aged and yet remained as young as he was at the time of his banishment, a little like the way in which the dead retain the age they had when you last knew them. He imagines that he can pick up where he left off; the people who are as old as he was in 1933 seem to be the same age as him and yet this gives the lie to his real age, which becomes intertwined with his new age, breaks through it and endows it with a deeper meaning. It is as if fate had transposed those who have this experience and who survive it into a time that is both multi-dimensional and also riddled with holes.[7]

With the assistance of his cousin Franz Wilhelm Calvelli-Adorno, a trained lawyer and *Oberlandesgerichtsrat*, a man with whom he enjoyed playing piano duets, he attempted to obtain the restoration of the former family property. His cousin was officially qualified to deal with compensation cases. As Adorno wrote to Else Herzberger, when he found himself face to face with the son of the present owner of his father's house in Schöne Aussicht, he experienced a 'violent shock. It was the only time that I lost my nerve: I called him a Nazi and a murderer, although I am not at all sure that I had found the guilty party. But that is how things go – it's always the wrong ones who get caught and the villains are always so experienced and able to cope with the real situations that they get by.'[8] The buyer of his father's house in Seeheim Street, which Oscar Wiesengrund had been forced to sell at far below its market price, was evidently no enthusiastic supporter of Hitler. Since the new owners, a family called Wilhelm, paid Adorno a sum of money by way of compensation, he and his wife renounced their claim to the property. They had briefly thought of living in the house, but decided finally not to, partly because of the petty bourgeois character of the old house, but also because it had been damaged by an incendiary bomb. The only comfortable part to survive was the ground-floor room with a parquet floor, on which Adorno could still make out the imprint left by his mother's piano.[9]

Of the significant writings of the period, the *Frankfurter Hefte* was published by Eugen Kogon and Walter Dirks,[10] who followed a strictly democratic, pro-European course. Despite some initial success, they failed to dominate the literary scene. The same may be said of the Gruppe 47, which was to become so much more famous later on.[11]

Instead, the literary climate was still in the hands of writers who had remained in Germany during the Third Reich, writers such as Hans Egon Holthusen, Reinhold Schneider, Ernst Jünger, Werner Bergengruen, Hans Carossa, Frank Thiess and Walter von Molo. This was not Adorno's world.[12] He too noted with the greatest suspicion the turn towards the seemingly unbroken tradition of a 'cultured German nation', and alternatively to the idealized realm of the 'true, the beautiful and the good'. Many of the writers who had remained in Germany laid claim to the title of the 'inner emigration' to describe their conduct in the Third Reich, a stance which in Adorno's view contrasted with 'the attitude of the intransigent avant-garde'.[13] Spokesmen such as Frank Thiess and Walter von Molo mobilized this retreat into inwardness against the émigrés, above all against Thomas Mann, representing it as a respectable alternative to 'fellow-traveller'. A writer such as Marie-Luise Kaschnitz, who paid a visit to Adorno and Gretel in their Frankfurt home early in 1950, had stayed in Germany with her husband, but nevertheless criticized the attempt to whitewash the opportunism implicit in the notion of the 'inner emigration'. 'What was our so-called inner emigration supposed to have consisted in? In our listening to foreign radios, scolding the government and occasionally shaking the hand of a Jew one had met in the street, even if someone was looking? Or did it consist in our having prophesied first the war, then the total war, then the defeat and finally the end of the Party?'[14] Over the years she developed an extremely affectionate relationship with the Adornos. She described her first meeting with them in a letter to her husband, Guido Freiherr Kaschnitz von Weinberg, on 26 May 1950: 'Yesterday, I invited Adorno to coffee. He accepted with pleasure and came with his wife who is very thin, very intelligent and stimulating. Then Gadamer arrived and, instead of half an hour, they stayed a full three hours. Conversation about Joyce and his successors, religion, philosophy and fairy tales. All very lively.'[15]

The hollow pathos so disliked by Kaschnitz, Kogon, Dirks and also Adorno was cultivated by many Germans of the immediate postwar period, who would talk about the dignity of man and the beauty of the soul as a kind of complement to their down-to-earth approach to technical matters. In contrast, Adorno perceived an intellectual restlessness in his students, who were anxiously seeking ideological reorientation after the Year Zero of 1945: a vehement curiosity about intellectual questions which he thought was greater than in the pre-Hitler years.

Adorno had the opportunity to make the direct acquaintance of this 'passionate interest' on the part of the students in his seminar on 'Kant's Transcendental Dialectic', as well as in his lecture course on aesthetics. He continued the aesthetics course in the summer semester of 1951, together with a seminar on Hegel and another on 'Contemporary Problems in the Theory of Knowledge'. Then, in the following semester, he gave a course on 'The Concept of Philosophy'[16] – which he taught in his characteristic method of improvising on the basis of a few handwritten keywords. Even though he told both Horkheimer and Kracauer how excited he was by the interest shown by students, the detailed letters he wrote to Thomas Mann in December 1949 and June 1950 tell a story about the other side of the need to catch up for lost time. This was the students' apolitical focus on the seemingly intact world of pure spirit. Thus he declared over the radio (and published in the May issue of the *Frankfurter Hefte*) his belief that 'Cultural activity in postwar Germany has something of the dangerous and ambiguous consolation of being embedded in a provincial cocoon.'[17] This was reminiscent of Max Frisch's idea of 'culture as an alibi', as an alibi for the absence of political consciousness.

These theses, which Adorno had derived from his own personal experience, were written down during the brief Christmas vacation of 1949–50. In his lengthy letters to both Horkheimer and Thomas Mann he evidently wished to try his ideas out in discussion. For Horkheimer likewise had formed a definite impression of Germany, and so had Thomas Mann, a view that was critical in the extreme. Between May and August 1949 Mann had been engaged on a lecture tour in Europe and had spent twelve days in Germany in order to give the main lecture for the Goethe bicentenary celebrations in both Frankfurt and Weimar.[18] The tenor of what Adorno had to say in his letters to Mann was as negative and critical as the report Mann himself published in October. What emerged with particular clarity from the Nuremberg Trials, Adorno wrote, was that the 'unspeakable guilt' of the Germans was simply 'evaporating'. Hardly any Nazis were to be found in defeated Germany. Not only did no one own up to having been a Nazi, but in addition the Germans were convinced that 'none of them had been. . . . I have noticed that all those who identify with Hitlerism or the newly tinted nationalism claim steadfastly that they had known nothing of the worst things during the entire war – whereas those who were consciously opposed confirm what the meanest intelligence tells us, namely that everything was common knowledge since 1943.'[19] In contrast, in the same letter he praised the level of the students who debated the most difficult philosophical questions with passionate intensity. 'The comparison with a Talmud school suggests itself; sometimes I feel as if the spirit of the murdered Jews had entered the German intellectuals.'[20]

What Adorno had experienced in this first period after his return invited literary treatment. As in reality, so too in fiction: e.g., in the novel *The Old Friend* by Kurt Mautz, Professor Amorelli 'returns to Frankfurt from exile in America'. The hero of the novel learns about this and soon goes to see the philosophy lecturer in his consulting hours. Amorelli

> is delighted to see him, greets him as one of the twelve faithful members of his first seminar and invites him to take part in his

senior seminar on Thursday evenings as a guest. When he could manage it, Ronge [the novel's hero] would be present on these evenings among Amorelli's students and disciples. Of course, there were now more than twelve. They sat in a square at large tables and on folding-chairs pulled up for the purpose, and indeed wherever they could find space. In emigration, Amorelli had become the most important cultural critic of the present; he could write and say what he wanted; whatever he thought was broadcast and printed. These sessions did not take place, as formerly, wherever space could be found – it used to be in the students' library – but in the regular philosophy seminar. Amorelli had changed but little; he had filled out somewhat and had a bald patch surrounded by a light wreath of short, white hair. Behind the horn-rimmed spectacles the large, dark, gleaming eyes were unchanged. The ritual of the sessions too had remained the same. As he had done twenty years before, he began each session with the question: 'Who is going to keep a record?'[21]

In the course of the novel, there is an exchange between Amorelli and Ronge about a highly talented, far-left former student of philosophy and German studies who during the Third Reich had published writings that were full of unambiguously nationalistic and anti-Semitic turns of phrase. Amorelli sought an explanation for this transformation. 'I do not understand', he said finally, 'how a left-wing intellectual who had helped to chase the Nazis out of the university could himself turn into a fanatical Nazi.'[22]

Since Mautz, who had studied with Adorno in the 1930s when he was a young *Privatdozent*, evidently tried to incorporate genuine postwar experiences, what happens to Amorelli may well correspond more or less well to Adorno's own experiences. Adorno was forced to acknowledge that some of his former students had trimmed their sails according to the wind, whether to advance their careers or for reasons of political opportunism. And even though he had plenty of opportunity to point to 'the spurious nature of German democracy',[23] this did not deter him from urging Horkheimer yet again to continue his scholarly work not in the USA but in Frankfurt, 'since the intellectual climate here has something very seductive about it'. But he also saw the danger of being 'pushed into the position of an intellectual confessor who is expected to give disappointed people "something to hang on to" – whereas in a certain sense the disaster lies precisely in that concept of something to hang on to.' Adorno complained about his academic workload and the burdens of teaching: 'I sometimes feel like a worn-out gramophone record, as if I kept expending myself in the wrong way.'[24]

Despite the huge burden of work at the university, he was by no means discontented. Even extra chores were not just things he passively accepted; he entered into them with gusto. One example was his involvement in a new project about topical questions of local-government reform and town planning in which the Institute of Social Research had a hand.[25] As he told Thomas Mann, 'physically' he felt 'exceptionally well, three times as fresh and able to work as on the West Coast and free of headaches – a strange response of a professionally homeless man to his homeland.'[26] A minor counter-initiative to the experience of homeless-ness was his visit with Gretel to Amorbach, where they were able to enjoy a peaceful autumn break. From Amorbach he wrote a birthday letter to his mother, who was now eighty-five and had remained in New York. He told her that they had stayed in the Posthouse and had gone for long walks in the surrounding forests. To his delight he had met the son of the painter Max Rossmann again.[27]

Even if Adorno frequently had the feeling of having to capitulate to the numerous professional claims on his energies, his life had neverthe-less taken a turn for the better. He enjoyed being able to speak his mind and he was happy to have left the travails of emigration behind him. Germany destroyed seemed to him to be the symbol of the era. Even if Adorno was happy to be able to live there once more, that does not mean that his life was free of vexations.[28] For example, he and Horkheimer had to come to terms with the unpleasant fact that *Sinn und Form*, the East German cultural magazine, published extracts from *Dialectic of Enlightenment* without the authors' permission. Shortly afterwards, Max Bense published a critical review of that book as well as *The Philosophy of Modern Music* in the widely circulated West German magazine *Merkur*. The review, entitled 'Hegel and the Californian Emigration', accused the authors of an elitist Hegelian/Marxist orientation.[29] This led Adorno and Horkheimer to consider making a public statement about their relation to Soviet Marxism. In the draft that Adorno wrote and that reflected their political position at the time, he said: 'We are unable to see anything in the practice of the military dictatorships disguised as people's democracies other than a new form of repression and, in what people over there are accustomed to call "ideology", we see only what was originally intended by that word: the lie that justifies an untrue condition of society.'[30] No less irksome for Adorno was the fact that Querido Verlag was making difficulties about the production of *Dialectic of Enlightenment*, which was of course intended for a German readership. Even though it was conceived as a 'message in a bottle', the message was supposed to be found and decoded soon, not just at any old time. In the event, however, people would not have to wait long.

But what most concerned him was his future position in the univer-sity. Initially, he was restricted to an acting professorship. As a former *Privatdozent* he was standing in for Horkheimer as long as the latter was unable to come. But his not unjustified hopes were directed at a chair of his own. In the spring of 1949 Walter Hallstein, in his capacity as rector of Frankfurt University, had made a trip to the United States, including Pacific Palisades, chiefly to contact Thomas Mann, whose name had been discussed as a possible first president of the Federal Republic. Adorno, who was still in Santa Monica, did his best to make a good impression.[31] In Frankfurt he took steps to succeed to Hans-Georg Gadamer's chair, since Gadamer had decided to accept the offer of a chair in Heidelberg.[32] While still in Pacific Palisades, Horkheimer attempted to make use of his already considerable influence. He wrote to Adorno on 9 November, 'If we could acquire this professorial chair, it would be the fulfilment of a dream that only a few years ago would have seemed like a pure mirage. It would bring about a wholly new situation, one in which two people who stand at right-angles to reality and for that reason seem predestined to impotence would suddenly acquire incalculable influence. For if we had two chairs instead of just the one, quantity really would be transformed into quality; we really would be in a position of power.'[33] This letter proved to be prescient as far as the two chairs were concerned, since they brought him and Adorno long-term success, and also with regard to his prediction of influence, which would shortly come true with the emergence of the 'Frankfurt School'.

In 1950, however, there seemed to be no such future in prospect. Adorno was making no headway within the university, even though he was placed third in the competition for the chair. Instead, he was given a supernumerary professorship (*außerplanmäßige Professur*), not least thanks to a reference from Horkheimer. This appointment was the first step to an act of 'reparation' of a sort on the part of the university towards someone who had been hounded out of his post over a decade previously.[34] Adorno's salary was paid from central university funds. For his activities as deputy director of the institute he received compensation for expenses from the foundation Gesellschaft für Sozialforschung.

The outlook for Horkheimer was much more favourable. In the winter semester of 1950–1, he was officially reinstated in his own former chair in social philosophy or philosophy and sociology, and as early as the autumn of 1951 he was elected dean of the Arts Faculty. This was very much a lightning career, since it was not until early 1950 that Horkheimer had set out for Frankfurt from Pacific Palisades in order to take up his new position. Despite the favourable career prospects, he embarked on his journey with mixed feelings – he feared a resurgence of anti-Semitism and nationalism in Germany. Nevertheless, he wrote to Gretel during the journey: 'Teddie is looking forward to our reunion. I am too.'[35] Having arrived in Frankfurt, he put up first of all in the Hotel Carlton, but then moved to his own apartment in Westendstrasse 79, after Maidon and then Gretel had followed on, encouraged by the reports in his letters: 'Life in Germany is European despite everything. Even though the destroyed cities sometimes seem quite spooky, I find it hard to resist the charms of the atmosphere which is horrific politically, but culturally still highly attractive. Whatever has to do with enjoyment – art, poetry, theatre, philosophy, the language and landscape, human intercourse, drinking and eating – it is all of a standard that compels respect.'[36]

In November 1951, with the beginning of his professorial duties and his activity as dean, Horkheimer moved into the newly built Institute of Social Research in Senckenberganlage 26. Thanks to the substantial financial contributions of John McCloy, the American high commissioner, the City of Frankfurt and also private sponsors, the modern, generously proportioned building was completed in a very short time. Those working in it, apart from Adorno, included Pollock and a number of others concerned with empirical social research (such as Ludwig von Friedeburg, Volker von Hagen, Karl Sandemann and Dieter Osmer), who continued the work that had been begun in 1950. The Institute of Social Research was the first academic institute in postwar Germany where sociology could be studied. The reopening of the institute was marked by a ceremony in which the first movement of Schoenberg's F sharp major quartet, op. 10, was performed. Horkheimer gave an address which placed the emphasis on interdisciplinarity and in which he stressed that the institute's particular aim was to combine German sociology together with its theoretical bias with the empirical methods of sociological research that had been developed in the USA. In addition, he argued against the restorative spirit of the age and, quite in harmony with Adorno, he explained that 'in all questions, and indeed in the sociological attitude in general, there is always an intention that transcends society as it is. . . . A certain critical stance towards the world as it is belongs, so to speak, to the profession of the social theorist, and it is this critical dimension that makes sociologists unpopular. To educate students . . . to sustain this tension with existing reality is perhaps the most important and the ultimate goal of education as we understand it.'[37] This speech was given in the presence of the rector, Boris Rajewsky, the mayor, Walter Kolb, and the Hessen minister for education, Ludwig Metzger, as well as the director of the Office of Public Affairs of the US High Commission, Shepard Stone. Its most important programmatic point was the idea which had already figured in his inaugural lecture of 1931, namely the idea of a synthesis of social theory and social research, an interpretative concept of research that was designed to grasp the deeper dimensions of the factors that condition social structures.

To elaborate this conception methodologically and to translate it into research practice was one of the tasks that faced Adorno, who intended to tackle it by building on his practical experience, especially of his work on *The Authoritarian Personality*.

Playing an active role in postwar Germany?

The self lives only through transformation into otherness.[38]

At the end of September and the beginning of October 1951, Adorno was again in the United States for a short, six-week visit made 'in great haste'. He went from New York to Los Angeles, primarily to be present at the opening of the Hacker Psychiatry Foundation in Beverly Hills. Frederick Hacker was a psychiatrist and psychoanalyst with whom the institute had entered into a working relationship. His own intention was to transform his psychiatric clinic into an institute for training and research.[39] He had visited Adorno in Frankfurt in May 1951 and now offered him a position as director of research. Adorno, however, was reluctant to commit himself, not least because Horkheimer had been rector of the university since November 1951 and would therefore have to be ruled out from active involvement in the Hacker Foundation. Once again, Adorno had to substitute for Horkheimer and assume the burden of the journey.

Once in New York, he took the opportunity to visit Leo Löwenthal and Herbert Marcuse, but more significantly his mother, whom he found to be 'barely herself'. He wrote to Thomas Mann about this meeting, which was to be their last, saying that he was conscious of the 'definitive nature' of her condition. 'With someone one loves, one is inclined to regard even their degeneration in old age as something merely provisional, and it can only be hoped that one is not mistaken in this regard.'[40] Needless to say, he knew that such hopes were baseless.

On the return journey, he stopped off in Paris, where he met the famous art dealer and philosopher of art Daniel-Henry Kahnweiler, the writer and ethnologist Michel Leiris, and the conductor, composer and music scholar René Leibowitz. Scarcely was he back in Germany than he had to attend a conference on opinion research. Adorno's introductory lecture 'The Present State of Empirical Social Research in Germany' was a great success. This was his first attempt to define a critical approach to social research, and he sharply distinguished his view of it from that of the German tradition. He declared programmatically:

> Sociology is not one of the humanities. The questions it is concerned with are not primarily and essentially those of the conscious or even the unconscious nature of human beings of which society is composed. Its questions are concerned primarily with the interaction between man and nature and with the objective forms of societalization that cannot be reduced to mind in the sense of the inner constitution of men. The task of empirical social research in Germany is to clarify strictly and without any transfiguration the objective nature of what is socially the case, an objective reality that is largely hidden from individuals and even the collective consciousness.[41]

Thus Adorno championed social research as a corrective to a humanities-based obscurantism in sociology. His primary aim here was to attack the provincialism of postwar German sociology and to lead it back to the international standards that it had lost through its isolation during the years of the Nazi regime. He declared that the methods of collecting precise data and statistical evaluation had a useful democratic thrust for the young republic. Moreover, they were of great practical value in a country destroyed by war. Surveys would make it possible to assemble information needed for reconstruction – information, for example, about housing needs or about the social situation of the refugees. The task of social research is to 'raise the harsh facts to the level of consciousness' so as to be able to refute dogmatic assumptions about social realities. He explained how this might work out in practice with reference to assertions current at the time that farmers were naturally traditionalist in outlook and tended to love their homeland:

> We shall demand compelling proof that these assertions are true. We shall therefore send interviewers familiar with rural life into the countryside and ask them to keep on asking questions when the farmers tell them that they remained on their farms from love of their homeland and loyalty to the ways of their fathers. We shall confront conservatism with economic facts and explore whether technical improvements in agricultural units below a certain size are unprofitable and hence require such a high level of investment as to make technical rationalization irrational in a business of that sort. We shall further inquire whether clinging to landed property even if it does not yield much profit in strictly bookkeeping terms may nevertheless be justified for certain farmers who can achieve a greater financial yield because of the cheap labour costs of their own family than they might achieve in the town.[42]

Eager though Adorno was to defend the use of such research methods, he was equally keen to emphasize that they had only an auxiliary function in sociology. For sociology could not limit itself to the collection of data, but had to lead to the formation of theory. At a conference on problems of method that took place in the institute in March 1952, he made a plea for social research that would seek out the roots of false consciousness in people's heads as well as socio-structural conditioning.

The sociological theory he called for had the purpose of providing critical knowledge about the objects it investigated. This included criticism of quantitative methods in sociology. Such methods tell us something about contemporary society: namely about the 'standardization of human beings' in a technical civilization. Looked at in this light, Adorno defended a particular conception of social research against its champions by clearly defining both its scope and its limits.[43]

In this mission not only was Adorno active as representative of the research projects of the Frankfurt Institute, but contact was also established relatively quickly with the two antipodes of German postwar sociology, especially René König (1906–92), but also Helmut Schelsky

(1912–84). Relations with König, who had emigrated to Switzerland during the Nazi years, were friendly well into the 1960s. With Schelsky, on the other hand, who had been a registered member of the Nazi Party and had acted as adviser on matters of academic policy, relations were rather cooler and tense despite feelings of distanced respect.

In the early 1950s, Adorno's intention was if not to try and coordinate sociological research between the three principal centres of sociological research in West Germany – Frankfurt, Cologne and Hamburg – then at least to achieve agreement on questions of future academic training. In consequence, despite their differing approaches to their subject, he was in constant contact with René König and planned to bring out a joint handbook and instruction manual on the methods of empirical social research.[44] Adorno had hopes of recruiting König as an ally for his conception of a critical approach to social research that would aim to be more than administrative research or market research. König himself was rooted in the Durkheim tradition; politically, he was noted for his uncompromising attitude towards Nazis who were attempting, from 1949 at the latest, to resume their academic careers.[45] He was as critical of the restorative, anti-intellectual tendencies of the Adenauer era as Adorno and Horkheimer, with whom he also shared the experience of exile. For this reason among others, König considered moving from Cologne to Frankfurt so as to strengthen the consolidation and professionalization of sociology as a discipline. Such an alliance would have taken place at the expense of Schelsky and his circle, whose influence was very powerful at the time.[46] The conditions for an alliance between the former émigrés were not unfavourable. Horkheimer took steps to organize the transfer of König from Cologne to Frankfurt. For his part, König approved of *The Authoritarian Personality* as well as the projects recently launched by the institute, such as the local-government study and a further study of the political consciousness of West Germans.

Adorno's relations with Schelsky developed quite differently. Schelsky was part of the Leipzig group whose spokesmen were Arnold Gehlen (1904–76) and Hans Freyer (1887–1969), both of whom sympathized with the idea of a 'conservative revolution' and whom Adorno thought of as belonging to the 'counter-revolution' as late as the 1950s.[47] Schelsky had been teaching since 1949 at the Hamburg Akademie für Gemeinwirtschaft, where he attempted to give the emerging discipline of postwar sociology the stamp of a strictly anti-Marxist science of interpretation. Although his politically conservative conception of sociology was evidently concerned to contribute to the stabilization of social consciousness in West Germany as a consciousness beyond class society,[48] Adorno tried to enlist the support of this former National Socialist. Neither Adorno nor Horkheimer shrank from cultivating professional and to some extent even personal relations with former Nazis. The sociologist Heinz Mauss, during the time he was attached to the institute, announced his intention of publishing a critique of Schelsky and his concept of 'real sociology'. Adorno was not at all happy about this and advised caution: 'Schelsky is a *very* able man, even if this does not always become plain, given the sheer quantity of his publications. Every attack on him that is merely dogmatic in character, in other words, that simply repudiates the tendencies he observes, instead of going beyond him by offering a better explanation, would boomerang.'[49] Günther Anders, who had returned from America in 1951 and settled in Vienna, was not the only one to accuse Adorno of lacking in political instincts. Adorno responded to this accusation in a letter. This arose from an embarrassing situation in which Anders had refused to shake Gehlen's hand while he was talking to Adorno, who wished to introduce them. 'Once people have taken the decision to return, as both you and I have done, it does not seem to me to be possible blithely to adopt an attitude of private intransigence and whenever possible to display one's pride before king's thrones where none exist.'[50] In another letter a few weeks later he explained his attitude even more clearly: 'I avoid contact with people who have done terrible things; someone like Gehlen, undoubtedly one of the most complicated cases, is not in that category. In his case, it is a question of an attitude which is undoubtedly as unacceptable to me as to you, but where mere indignation does not suffice. . . . It is a matter of indifference whose hand I shake as long as nothing remains sticking to the paper on which I am writing . . . I am too accustomed to thinking in social terms to promise myself anything at all today from the spontaneous but isolated actions of the individual. I would much prefer to put a brave face on it and rely on the general effect that my writings will have if I am lucky.'[51]

The *Zeitschrift für Sozialforschung* had been suspended in 1941. Now, Horkheimer and Adorno intended to revive it in parallel to the increasing activities of the institute, and they wished to secure the services of a broad selection of future contributors. Schelsky, meanwhile, had become one of the best-known and most widely read sociologists in the Federal Republic under Adenauer, and such formulae as 'the sceptical generation', 'the levelled-down middle-class society', and 'the technical, scientific civilization' had entered the popular imagination. Adorno invited him to contribute to the *Zeitschrift*. 'I may say that I attach the very greatest conceivable importance to your collaboration.'[52] But he balanced his invitation to Schelsky, as a man of the right, with one to Wolfgang Abendroth, a well-known left-wing intellectual: 'I believe that our journal will provide the solid ground on which our academic relationship can thrive most fruitfully.'[53]

Since the plan to revive the journal came to nothing, and since the gulf between their respective views of society was too wide to ignore, contacts between Adorno and Schelsky were limited to the links between the institute and the Social Research Centre of Münster University, with its seat in Dortmund. This centre was a conservative institute at the time, to judge by its staff, and under Otto Neuloh, its director, it practised applied social research under the heading of 'real sociology'. Schelsky had an association with it dating back to his time in Hamburg. The Institute of Social Research had an interest in collaborating with the centre in the fields of industrial and commercial sociology, where the trade unions also had a connection.[54]

These were years in which Horkheimer was very much taken up with administrative duties: firstly as dean of the Arts Faculty and then as rector of the university. During this time it fell to Adorno both to represent the institute to the outside world and to coordinate the current research projects. He complained in letters to his mother that he was gradually being overwhelmed by the mounting burden of institute work. His lectures which were so important to him had to be made up on the spur of the moment. His multifarious obligations gave him the feeling that he 'came home in the evening feeling like a real pen-pusher'. He was in general too exhausted 'to have time for anything else'.[55]

Nevertheless, he found time for other things. He needed no persuasion to take part in cultural life. As early as January, he accepted an invitation from the music critic Wolfgang Steinecke to give an introductory talk before a concert of the Amsterdam String Quartet at the Kranichsteiner Musikgesellschaft. A little later he gave another talk in connection with the Frankfurt production of Ernst Krenek's opera *Orest*. Nor would he be denied the opportunity to take part in the Fifth International Summer Course for New Music in Kranichstein, which was likewise organized by Steinecke.[56] Schoenberg's *A Survivor from Warsaw*, op. 46, received its first German performance there. For Adorno, Kranichstein was important because after many years it brought him together again with Ernst Krenek and Willi Reich; he met Steuermann and Kolisch there and was introduced to Edgar Varèse. He also conducted five seminars with the title 'Criteria of New Music'.[57] In July 1950 Adorno took part in the *Darmstädter Gespräche* which were devoted to the subject 'The Image of Man in our Time', where the principal topic debated was Hans Sedlmayr's *Loss of the Centre* (1948), a highly controversial book at the time.[58] He defended the thesis that modern art must declare its commitment to radical negativity as the only possible value. The oppositional function of the avant-garde was completely incompatible with the need for harmony through art.

In addition to all these activities, Adorno became increasingly involved in the new publishing house that Peter Suhrkamp had set up in 1950.[59] He had been in touch with both Suhrkamp and his editor Friedrich Podszus even before he met them in person. Thanks to the success of *Minima Moralia*, he came in the course of time to have a certain influence on both men. He persuaded them to agree to the publication of Benjamin's *Berlin Childhood around 1900* as well as the plan for two volumes of his selected writings. He also urged them to publish Siegfried Kracauer's writings and new editions of his novels.[60] In the process, he was able to overcome the 'melancholy scepticism' of Suhrkamp, who looked after 'his firm like an anxious father'. This had the effect of inducing Suhrkamp to publish what seemed to be unsaleable books such as a new edition of Benjamin's *One-Way Street* or Marcel Proust's *A la recherche du temps perdu* in a new German translation.[61] Of especial importance was his success, together with Gretel and Friedrich Podszus, in publishing the two-volume edition of Benjamin's *Writings* (1955), which laid the foundation for the wave of interest in Benjamin's work. He regarded Benjamin's new-found popularity with mixed feelings. As he indicated in a letter to Scholem in March 1951, he felt distinctly uncomfortable in the face of the first reactions to *Berlin Childhood*: 'The idea that the Ernst Jüngers and Max Benses will not only produce the readers of Benjamin, but will even try to monopolize him, is as repugnant to me as to you. But equally, it would not be possible to ban a German publication simply to preserve him from that fate.'[62]

With *Minima Moralia*, his 'Reflections from Damaged Life', Adorno had considerable success as an author, although the tone and his diagnosis of contemporary life were by no means in tune with the age. They derived indeed from the classical tradition, French moralists such as La Rochefoucauld, Schopenhauer's *Aphorisms on the Wisdom of Life* and, finally, Nietzsche's *Human, All Too Human*. One reason for the success of the book, which was published in an edition of 3000 copies, was connected with Suhrkamp's vigorous efforts to arouse interest in it in the media, among potential reviewers and in the book trade.[63] Review copies were sent to the usual papers and magazines, as well as to those who were held to be opinion-formers at the time – Gadamer, Guardini, Heidegger and Jaspers – together with a letter from Suhrkamp, explaining that Adorno's new book was well suited to 'arousing discussion'.[64] In six months the book had received some sixty reviews in the German-speaking media. Moreover, it was generally implied that, as the author of the *Philosophy of Modern Music* and the *Dialectic of Enlightenment*, Adorno was already a well-known and respected writer. However, such fame really lay in the future. The recurring motifs of the reviews stressed five aspects in particular. First, reviewers pointed to the experience of emigration. In order to explain the underlying diagnosis of the age, the Marxist concept of 'alienation' was emphasized; the author's stance was said to be that of a man who enlightens and unmasks. In addition, his pessimistic view of the present was highlighted. Several reviewers raised the question: what are the criteria which will enable us to shape society so that the catastrophe of history, the demise of the individual, can be prevented? Thus a review by the philosopher Hermann Krings summed up his opinion: 'Paradoxical as it may seem when judging a work written in such a carefully constructed and precise language, there is a sense in which this can be called romantic; that is to say, it makes an absolute claim, but does not emerge from the terrain of dialectics.'[65] This was undoubtedly a correct assessment of the contemporary significance of Adorno's book. This was that his position, his intransigent mode of thought and his dissonant way of speaking had created a new type of intellectuality: 'the construction of a critical, oppositional intellectual'.[66]

Did Thomas Mann admire the aphorisms that Adorno had written between 1944 and 1947 because their author had the intellectual courage in a newly conservative age to confront the moral aspirations of a bourgeois liberal society with its reality? 'I have spent days attached to your book as if by a magnet', he wrote to Adorno from America in January 1952. 'Every day brings new fascination . . . concentrated nourishment. It is said that the companion star to Sirius, white in colour, is made of such dense material that a cubic inch of it would weigh a tonne here. This is why it has such an extremely powerful gravitational field; in this respect it is similar to your book.'[67] Since the aphorisms meant so much to Adorno not only as models of a dialectical way of thinking, but because of their particular prose form, he may well have cherished Thomas Mann's judgement more than Kracauer's: 'Really, Teddie, I was completely fascinated by your ability to enter mentally into the material of existence, and what most impressed me, and often convinced me, was that, when an interpretation seemed one-sided or otherwise unsatisfactory, it was soon followed by another one that revised or supplemented the first one so that it ended up with the entire phenomenon having been drawn into the dialectical process. Many of the objections that occurred to me as I read were anticipated by you as you developed the idea.'[68]

Kracauer nevertheless criticized the book on the grounds that Adorno left the reader in the dark about 'the criteria by which the author had judged "mere existence"'. In fact, Adorno did proceed *ex negativo*, without a fixed position, as indeed we can see from the section entitled 'On the Morality of Thinking': 'what is asked of the thinker today is that he should be at every moment both within things and outside them – Münchhausen pulling himself out of the bog by his own pig-tail becomes the pattern of knowledge which wishes to be more than either verification or speculation. And then the salaried philosophers come along and reproach us with having no definite point of view.'[69]

Thus Adorno did not claim to know the only tune that would make society dance. The only thing that was clear was that, in so far as the total fabric of morality had become torn and bourgeois consciousness had turned cynical, the maxims of what an Aristotelian ethical code thought of as a 'magna moralia' had lost their credibility. If 'the whole is the false',[70] the substance of morality must shrink to an infinitesimal quantum. At the same time, the moral philosopher must become a social critic whose paradoxical interventions shock us into perceiving the conditions that make a binding moral code impossible. This means that the question of how it can be possible for 'a rightly lived life to be lived within the wrong one'[71] is no mere piece of rhetoric, but strictly a matter of sociology: it is a question of the social presuppositions of a responsible life.

Adorno conceived his aphorisms as model analyses of the contemporary world by a meticulous observer; they are microcosmic case studies that disclose the overwhelming power of social structures, the superficial nature of both human relations and the practices of daily living. Knowledge was supposed to flow from the contradictory form of the argument. The aphoristic mode of reflection did not keep to any truth criterion of adequacy, nor did Adorno accept the law of non-contradiction. Instead, what is 'essential to his way of thinking is an element of exaggeration, of over-shooting the objects, of freeing itself from the deadweight of the factual, so that instead of merely reproducing being, thought can, at once rigorous and free, determine it.'[72] By formulating antitheses Adorno wished to convict the extremes of their one-sidedness. 'Dialectical thinking . . . advances by way of extremes . . . , driving thoughts with the utmost consequentiality to the point where they turn back on themselves.'[73] By shedding light on both sides not just of one coin, but of all the coins in play, reading the book generated a kind of provocative surplus of meanings that compels the reader to take stock. As Kracauer suggested in his enthusiastic letter, what the reader understands at first glance is subsequently questioned. This is why he remarks in part III, in the section entitled 'Monograms', that 'True thoughts are those alone which do not understand themselves.'[74]

Minima Moralia is a major work precisely from an epistemological standpoint, as Jürgen Habermas observed in an article in the *Frankfurter Allgemeine Zeitung* on the occasion of Adorno's sixtieth birthday in 1963.[75] And in fact, Adorno's social criticism often took the form of reflections in miniature, triggered by a kind of linguistic analysis.

The phrase '*Kommt überhaupt gar nicht in Frage*' ['It's completely and utterly out of the question'], which probably came into use in Berlin in the 1920s, is already potentially Hitler's seizure of power. For it pretends that private will, founded sometimes on real rights but usually on mere effrontery, directly represents an objective necessity that admits of no disagreement. At bottom, it is the refusal of a bankrupt negotiator to pay the other a farthing, in the proud awareness that there is nothing more to be got out of him. The crooked lawyer's dodge is brazenly inflated to heroic steadfastness: the linguistic formula for usurpation. This bluff defines equally the success and the collapse of National Socialism.[76]

His polished style enabled him to articulate what the age of total communication had done to culture and language. It explains, too, why even Thomas Mann could be fascinated by these ingenious aphorisms, a collection of vivid scenes taken from such apparently unassuming or remote subjects as the fate of Snow White, the sadness of the frog prince, the happiness of the three hares, scenes that for the most part treated motifs drawn from Adorno's visual memory, furnished in part with the coloured pictures from the song book illustrated by Ludwig von Zumbusch that had accompanied him through childhood.[77]

> As long as I have been able to think, I have derived happiness from the song: 'between the mountain and the deep, deep vale': about two rabbits who, regaling themselves on the grass, were shot down by the hunter, and, on realizing they were still alive, made off in haste. But only later did I understand the moral of this: sense can only endure in despair and extremity; it needs absurdity in order not to fall victim to objective madness. One ought to follow the example of the two rabbits; when the shot comes, fall down giddily, half-dead with fright, collect one's wits and then, if one still has breath, show a clean pair of heels. . . . He alone could pause to think on the illusoriness of disaster, the 'unreality of despair', and realize not merely that he is still alive but that there is still life. The ruse of the dazed rabbits redeems, with them, even the hunter, whose guilt they purloin.[78]

These aphorisms and brief texts, with their peculiar combination of philosophical reflection and literary form, constituted an unusual commentary on contemporary issues. Autobiographical experience went hand in hand with subtle observation, the interpretation of everyday phenomena and, not least, philosophical aperçus. Perhaps this can help to explain the book's success. Fifty years after its first appearance, the German edition had sold over 100,000 copies. Deservedly so, since a critique of 'damaged life' that avoided 'arbitrary sententiousness' was one of the factors enabling Adorno, so Albrecht Wellmer believed, to speak to a postwar generation that was unsure of its own identity and insecure in its sense of values. Amidst a German culture poisoned by reactionary values and beliefs, he liberated something of an authentic tradition.[79] By making the horrors explicit, Adorno made it possible to formulate questions about the preconditions of a true life: 'as the mirror-image' of the false one.[80] 'Perhaps the true society will grow tired of development and, out of freedom, leave possibilities unused, instead of storming under a confused compulsion to the conquest of strange stars.'[81] In the light of this utopian hope even disasters in everyday life of which one does not become aware acquire their contours, as in the case of the careless slamming of doors or running down the street: 'The victim's fall is already mimed in his attempt to escape it. The position of the head, trying to hold itself up, is that of a drowning man, and the straining face grimaces as if under torture.'[82]

The success of Adorno's books and his growing reputation in Suhrkamp was such that he felt able to intervene publicly in a seemingly trivial matter. The publisher Rowohlt had issued Heinrich Mann's novel *Professor Unrat* with the title of the film version of the book, *The Blue Angel*. Adorno objected to this at the end of January 1952 in the *Neue Zeitung*.[83] According to him, 'The publisher had submitted yet again to the dictates of conformism.' For the film had removed the critical sting from the novel. It was 'one of those revoltingly false, and also – apart from the famous legs [of Marlene Dietrich] – fairly boring films that make the excursion into full human life only to ensnare customers and carefully filter their view of the subject through the distortions that the rulers ascribe to the viewers in order to force them on the latter more effectively.'[84] Adorno called for the restoration of the original title. Thomas Mann wrote to him with approval: 'What you wrote about "Unrat" was good and apposite. . . . I also wrote a barbed letter to Rowohlt about the title, and received an apologetic and sheepish reply.'[85] Rowohlt denied responsibility, and in fact it proved impossible to find out who had authorized the change. A few weeks later, Adorno wrote in the same paper, 'Earlier, it was reserved to potentates and statesmen to say "I did not wish for this" when they had instigated a war. Today, every scriptwriter and camp warder appeals to that statement and no longer needs to lie. Everybody is his own alibi. Lack of responsibility is no longer a privilege.'[86]

No less typical of Adorno's vehemence and his readiness to enter the public arena was his declaration of sympathy for the campaign conducted by Bernhard Grzimek, the director of Frankfurt Zoo, against the 'scandal of big-game hunting'. His support for this cause had nothing to do with the Institute of Social Research, 'but all the more to do with the deeper impulses that such an institute obeys if it wishes to do justice to the human tasks facing it.'[87] He suggested writing a short essay on the topic and went on to say that when he returned from emigration he had found copies of the *Deutsche Jägerzeitung* (German Hunting News) in the seminar. He made a rule that his magazine would only be permitted there 'if the German Butcher's News were also made available'.[88] It was no mere accident that Adorno should have corresponded with Grzimek, whose TV broadcasts had made him a popular figure. He had loved the zoo from childhood on. This passion may explain why he suggested buying a pair of wombats for Frankfurt Zoo. 'I have fond memories of these little round friendly animals . . . and would be delighted to see them again. . . . Then I would like to remind you of the babirusa pig, which was also one of my favourites in my childhood . . . And finally, what happened to the dwarf hippos they used to have in Berlin?'[89]

Preoccupied with all these academic duties and cultural activities, how did the Adornos fare in private life? They continued the tradition begun in America of inviting guests to the Kettenhofweg for conversation and informal gatherings. Monika Plessner recalls an evening she spent there with her husband. She met Peter Suhrkamp there with his wife, and Gershom Scholem was also expected. Gretel Adorno made a favourable impression on her, 'although she radiated a certain coolness. She adopted a waiting stance. . . . Evidently, she was too proud to put on a front and too clever to provoke others to do so.'[90] The Adornos' apartment was 'aesthetically unpretentious, but functional.... The furniture was modern and not particularly comfortable; it seemed to be arranged in a provisional way. The only item that did not fit in was the piano, which was surrounded by a large, shiny, polished parquet floor and looked as if it were in a different country.'[91] Evidently, the Adornos did not want luxurious furnishings. One feature, however, was a reproduction of Paul Klee's famous watercolour *Angelus Novus*, the original of which had belonged to Walter Benjamin, who had interpreted it in the ninth thesis of his 'Theses on the Philosophy of History'.[92] Adorno also owned a painting by Fritz Wotruba with a dedication by the Viennese artist, a print by the painter Bernhard Schultze and graphics by Picasso and Hans Hartung. Monika Plessner recalls that, on the evening she was there, there was boiled fillet of beef (*Tafelspitz*) for dinner.

Adorno served wines from the Rheingau, which were particularly enjoyed by Helmuth Plessner and Peter Suhrkamp. The latter's wife, however, hastily swigged one glass after the other. The conversation was dominated by the men, 'by the tall Frisian [Suhrkamp], whose earnest features lay in the shadows, and Helmuth and Adorno, so that the ideas flew back and forth like ping-pong balls.' During a tense moment during the evening Mrs Suhrkamp's wine glass fell over and she burst into tears. Adorno 'leapt over to the piano and hammered on the keys. What music! Utter anarchy ... and finished up, as if order had been restored, with a plagal cadence.' Later on, they were joined by Gershom Scholem. 'It grew very late. I just sat still and listened.'[93]

After his return to Frankfurt, Adorno soon acquired a large circle of friends and acquaintances. Apart from Max and Maidon Horkheimer, they included the architect Ferdinand Kramer and his wife, two university colleagues, Willy Harfner and the professor of English, Helmut Viebrock, the education expert Hellmut Becker, the conductor Georg Solti, Adolf Frisé and Horst Krüger, who were both writers, and the lyric poet and story-writer Marie Luise Kaschnitz. He also re-established links with members of the family. He learnt of the deterioration in his mother's health from his uncle, Louis Calvelli, his mother's younger brother. Of course, he had known from his visit to New York in October 1951 that she was not well. She had been in hospital for some time, suffering from a fractured thigh. In the last days of February 1952, when he had only been back four months from his hectic trip to the USA, he received the news of her death, on 23 February. Presumably the news had been telegraphed to Frankfurt by Julia Rautenberg, who had accompanied his parents to New York and looked after them for many years.[94] Adorno was so shocked by his mother's death that he felt unable to travel to New York for the funeral.[95] One of the reasons for his inability to talk about her death can be guessed at from a sentence from *Negative Dialectics*: 'Attempts to express death in language are futile ... ; for who is the subject of whom we are saying that it is dead, here and now?'[96]

Back to America: horoscope analysis and TV research

Max, let's go home![97]

Adorno had so much work he did not know where to turn: teaching obligations in the university, the day-to-day management of the institute, advising on and implementing the research projects and, finally, the publication of articles and books, contributions to radio programmes and other cultural bodies. All of this testified to the need for him to stay in Frankfurt. Nevertheless, despite these activities he felt unable to commit himself definitively to settling in Germany. For the middle of 1952 was the deadline beyond which he could not stay outside the USA without forfeiting his American citizenship. In addition, he could scarcely reject the offer of director of research at the Hacker Foundation without at least looking at the prospects there on the spot. It seems that his journey was not entirely voluntary, but rather half-hearted from the outset. He travelled there on behalf of Horkheimer, since the institute's financial future was opaque at the time. Moreover, Adorno's own pro- spects of an academic post in the Arts Faculty were still uncertain. So he and Gretel temporarily decamped from the apartment in Kettenhofweg in order to return to the old apartment in 803 Yale Street in Santa Monica for ten months. On the way, he spent a few days in Paris in the Hotel Régina, in the Place des Pyramides. Despite this luxury he wrote a mournful letter to the then rector of Frankfurt University: 'I am travelling with an infinitely heavy heart.'[98]

His ill humour was increased when a few days later he learnt about his future tasks and conditions of work from discussions with Friedrich Hacker.[99] He realized that he would be isolated in his planned research activities, and would have to run research as a 'one-man show'. In these circumstances, he was only able to initiate and complete smaller pieces of work. One was a content analysis of horoscopes in the daily papers, which he did by taking a random sample from the astrology column of the *Los Angeles Times*. He completed this in a period of two months. 'The method I followed was that of putting myself in the position of the popular astrologer, who by what he writes must immediately furnish his readers with a sort of gratification. . . . The result was the reinforcing of conformist views through the commercial and standardized astrology as well as the appearance in the technique of the column writer . . . of certain contradictions in the consciousness of his audience.'[100] By count- ing and analysing certain constantly recurring 'basic tricks', Adorno concluded that in many respects the ideology of the astrologers resembles that of political demagogues and agitators.[101]

The second project he undertook while he was in Beverly Hills was a media study. Adorno was among the first to analyse the impact of television 'in the system of the culture industry'. Once again his approach was to analyse contents, that is to say, he examined the scripts of thirty-four of the current, highly popular television dramas and concluded that 'Even the modest development of action and character . . . is prohibited; everything must be fixed from the outset; the stereotyped approach and the ideological rigidity profits from the alleged technological necessity, which itself stems from the commercial system.'[102] Adorno's study of television went beyond genre analysis inasmuch as he also examined its cultural effects in the context of a media theory based on systematic observation. Thus he arrived at the conclusion that media drama cannot really be taken seriously by its audiences. 'The little men and women who are delivered into one's home become playthings for unconscious perception. There is much in this that may give the viewer pleasure; they are, as it were, his property, at his disposal, and he feels superior to them.'[103] Adorno reflected on the question of the role played by the mass media in the individual psyche. He came to the conclusion that the contents of television function as a kind of regulator of the desires and needs of the audience. This leads to the increase in images and plots that are aimed directly at internal psychological experiences, unsatisfied desires. He concluded that 'this Sisyphean labour of every individual's psychic economy appears to be "socialized" today, brought into direct control by the institutions of the culture industry.'[104] He expressed this idea more pointedly in the thesis that viewers wished to be deceived by the beautiful appearance (*den schönen Schein*) of popular culture, even though they saw through the deception. 'In a kind of self-contempt, they affirmed what was being done to them'.[105] On the other hand, Adorno saw clearly that the audiences of television shows were perfectly well able to distinguish between their real experiences and the staged experiences of the media. It followed that 'the real interests of individuals . . . are still strong enough to resist, within certain limits, total inclusion.'[106]

Adorno gave greater depth to the multiplicity of his individual insights into the effects of American popular culture and the changes in intellectual interests in his 'Theory of Pseudo-Culture', which he first presented to the German Sociology Congress in May 1959 in Berlin and subsequently published in *Der Monat.*[107] The distribution of fragments of cultural knowledge in the mass media leads to the phenomenon of pseudo-culture. This includes showing off one's knowledge to prove one is educated. The element of prestige, of being in the picture, is decisive in the consumption of culture, not the active engagement with its contents. Pseudo-culture bears 'the physiognomy of the lower middle class. Culture has not simply disappeared from this class; it drags on by dint of the interests even of those who do not participate in the privilege of culture.'[108] He summed up the specific decay of education, which he regarded as a world-wide phenomenon, with the statement: 'Whoever still knows what a poem is will have difficulty finding a well-paid position as a copy-writer.'[109]

It was above all this essay on pseudo-culture that not only incorporated his own experience but expressed the discomfort that he felt when contemplating the American way of life.

> In the US – the most advanced bourgeois country, behind which all others hobble along – the imageless nature of existence can be observed in its most extreme form as the social precondition of universal pseudo-culture. Religious imagery, which endows what exists with the colours of something greater than bare existence, has faded; the irrational *imagines* of feudalism, which developed with those of religion, are gone. Elements of non-synthetic folk-lore that have managed to survive can no longer compete. But existence simply liberated did not thereby become meaningful; deprived of its magic it remained prosaic in the negative sense of the word; a life modelled in accordance with the principle of equivalence down to its fingertips can do no more than simply reproduce itself, repeating its actions mechanically.[110]

Evidently, the old circle of friends and acquaintances in Santa Monica had evaporated by 1952–3. Adorno had been corresponding with Thomas Mann, and he hoped to the last moment that he would still find him there in his house, but this was doomed to disappointment. As early as 1949 Mann had begun to think that he would leave the USA and return to Europe. This was after Henry Wallace, the presidential candidate of the Progressive Party and Mann's preferred candidate, had lost to the Democratic Party nominee, Harry S. Truman, the vice-president who with his 'policy of strength' pursued intellectuals and alleged communists even inside America. Mann told Adorno of his intentions in January 1952 in the course of a description of an extended visit to Europe.[111] Having been denounced during his absence as a 'fellow traveller of Moscow', Mann did not return to Pacific Palisades but went instead to Switzerland, where the family rented a house in Erlenbach, near Zurich.

In his novel *The Holy Sinner*, which he was writing at this time and which Adorno had devoured 'like cake',[112] Mann penned a sentence that Adorno might well have written: 'For all of us have the wish to return to what was and to repeat it, so that if it was ill-starred, it should now be made good.'[113]

Adorno had no doubt that this second stay in America was purely transitional, and behaved accordingly, since he wanted to return 'to where I had my childhood'.[114] This desire to return determined the character of his entire correspondence with Horkheimer, which was not confined to the reports he was sending him on his work in the Hacker Foundation. In his letter of 12 November 1952, he described the problems he encountered as a result of Horkheimer's decision to stay in Frankfurt to attend to his duties there as rector. 'The entire situation is as repulsive as you predicted, although I did not demur at the time; I only left because of *force majeure* and in order not to miss anything.' His letter culminated in the appeal to concentrate his efforts on Frankfurt in the future. 'The risk of going to rack and ruin in every respect is very real here, and I cannot stop thinking about it for a moment.' He ended the letter with a heartfelt plea: 'Max, in the past, in hard times, – and since 1933 I have never been so down[115] as I am now – Gretel and I used to console each other by saying, "Go and see Mammoth". Now I really am coming to see Mammoth. If we did not have each other I would not want to go on living.'[116] And in a further letter to Horkheimer, written some four months later, Adorno urged him to plan his life so that they would be able to work together in Germany on the crucial philosophical questions. 'If the world permits us to reach that point, then let it be where we both belong.'[117] With his fiftieth birthday approaching in September, and in the light of the fact that both he and Horkheimer were childless, the task that faced them was to achieve what they had set out to do as philosophers, to achieve what Adorno in that early letter from Paris had called 'the unconditional'. 'There is nothing else.'[118] In his letter of March 1953, Adorno reminds Horkheimer of the wisdom of 'the old rule that the refugee returns to see what he can do'. Alluding to a pub near the university, and evidently a favourite habit, he went on to say 'Every glass of kirsch at the Schlagbaum has more to do with our philosophy than Riesman's collected works. I do not know how far I can speak for us both in what is literally a matter of life and death . . . but I would rather run the risk of being beaten to death over there than "build something up" somewhere else or even retreat into private life.' He ended the letter with the need to 'create time to think and to live', and 'the two are one and the same thing'.[119]

This exhortation did not fall on deaf ears. Since the collaboration with Hacker and his colleagues became more and more difficult,[120] since the two projects he had started could be finished quite quickly, and because the shortage of staff at the institute was causing productivity to suffer, the decision to return finally came in March 1953. In fulfilment of his innermost wishes, Adorno was able to return to the Arts Faculty in Frankfurt and to resume his work as co-director at the institute.

During Adorno's last months in California, Horkheimer had kept him informed in detail about plans for the institute and about current problems on the research front. Above all, he had urged him to take steps to establish a journal to be published by the institute. Adorno had

already started to do this while he was still in Frankfurt in order to have
an organ with which to reinforce the type of philosophy and sociology
that he and Horkheimer wished to promote. 'I shall adopt the plan with
enthusiasm. I guarantee that there will be no lack of material.'[121] This
was his optimistic assertion from afar. Since he was urgently needed in
Frankfurt, on this occasion he and Gretel travelled from San Francisco
to New York by plane. He recorded his impressions on this trip, his first
by plane, in a short essay, 'Caught in Flight'. He was struck first of all
by the evidently genuine indifference of the passengers to the adventure of flying across the American continent. The passengers were not
interested in looking out of the window, not even the children. Their
dependence on the gigantic machine was very striking. 'One makes no
contribution at all, one is nothing but an object, whether of an apparatus entirely independent of one's will, or of the ministrations of the
crew.' So even people who have long hesitated about flying do so without fear.[122] From New York, the Adornos continued their journey back
to Europe on 19 August, on the *Queen Elizabeth*.

During their ten months' absence, Adorno's academic duties had
been taken over by Helmuth Plessner, while institute business had been
conducted in conjunction with Horkheimer and two young sociologists,
Dietrich Osmer and Egon Becker. Plessner had a chair at Göttingen
University. As a Jew, he had emigrated to the Netherlands, where he
had taught at the University of Groningen until the German invasion.
In Göttingen, Plessner had his own teaching duties, his publications
on philosophical anthropology and, in addition, his own sociological
research work. This meant that he was unable to invest as much time
and energy in the work of the institute as would have been necessary.[123]
Nevertheless, with his young wife, who after the war had been involved
in adult education, he was active in the institute, where Friedrich
Tenbruck and Richard Wolff, as well as Heinz Mauss and Ludwig von
Friedeburg, had already started on different projects. Monika Plessner
recalls that Gretel Adorno enjoyed great respect at the institute. 'She
was evidently everybody's mother confessor.'[124] For his part, Horkheimer
was serving a second term as university rector, and this made huge
demands on his time, but he nevertheless made great efforts to supervise the orderly progress of the current empirical study of the political
consciousness of the Germans and the presentation of the study's conclusions. He was very relieved when Adorno returned to Frankfurt in
the summer of 1953 and instantly plunged into work at the institute.
Since Horkheimer wanted him to produce attractive publications and
also a journal for the institute, it was necessary to bring the current
projects to a successful conclusion as briskly as possible. It was important to produce valid results that would then make publication worthwhile. Adorno thought his most pressing task was to work out his own
approach to research and to distil his findings into a social theory so as
to give his ideas the shape of a paradigm.

Letting the cat out of the bag: Kafka, Beckett, Hölderlin

> ... to think dangerously; to spur on thought, to shrink from nothing in the experience of the matter, not to be intimidated by any convention of received thought.[125]

Although Adorno was now fully occupied with his academic duties, both in the university and in the institute, he was very much concerned to maintain his flow of publications on literary and cultural topics, so as to give the German reading public a first impression of this Frankfurt *homme de lettres*. 'The cat can't leave off catching mice and the critic can't stop writing' – a self-ironizing sentiment he often repeated when talking about his intellectual obsessions. Between 1952 and 1953 he had written a bulky treatise on Kafka, which he at once placed in the cultural magazine *Die neue Rundschau* and republished a short while later in *Prisms*, a collection of essays.

Kafka's stories and novels had fascinated Adorno since the mid-1920s. His discussions and correspondence with Benjamin often focused on *The Country Doctor*, *In the Penal Colony*, *The Trial* and *The Castle*, and during the 1930s Benjamin had published his own notes on Kafka in two essays entitled *Potemkin* and *The Little Hunchback*.[126] Having read these notes in December 1934, Adorno wrote to Benjamin expressing, not for the first time, his complete 'agreement in philosophical fundamentals'. This referred to both Benjamin's idea of Kafka's 'inverse theology' and 'the category of ambiguous and alienated thinghood'. He also emphasizes the idea that 'it is only to a life that is perverted in thingly form that an escape from the overall context of nature is promised.' Adorno's lengthy letter of December 1934 contains in essence the programme of his own Kafka interpretation, which in his own words 'would have to begin with the relationship between prehistory and modernity'.[127] This programme now lay twenty years in the past, but even so Adorno now tried to put it into practice in his 'Notes on Kafka', undoubtedly a work of central importance in his oeuvre and one he dedicated to Gretel. The extent to which he was disturbed by his early encounter with Kafka can be gauged from his suggestion that there can be no distanced, contemplative view of the Prague writer. Instead, 'the narrative will shoot towards him like a locomotive in a three-dimensional film.'[128]

At the very start of his 1953 essay, Adorno refers to Benjamin and in particular his definition of Kafka's prose as 'parable. It expresses itself not through expression but by its repudiation, by breaking off. . . . Each sentence says "interpret me", and none will permit it. Each compels the reaction, "that's the way it is", and with it the question, "where have I seen that before"?'[129] So it is all the more important not to approach Kafka's seemingly philosophical or metaphysical novels with ready-made interpretative tools, but instead to start from the literal meaning of the text. 'The gesture is the "that's the way it is"; language, the configuration of which should be truth, is, as a broken one, untruth.'[130] Adorno insisted that the scenes and events in Kafka's writings did not suggest the need for a psychoanalytical interpretation, but that they were themselves literal applications of, i.e., transformed, psychoanalysis. Kafka derived his materials from the ruins of reality. This explains why they are the reflexes of social untruth which, however, must be read as 'the negatives of truth'. To elucidate the Kafkaesque experience of the abnormal that defines normality, Adorno referred to an incident that had taken place when he was twenty-five. He wrote that 'One must have experienced an accident in a large city; countless witnesses come forward, proclaiming themselves acquaintances, as though the entire community had gathered to observe the moment when the powerful bus smashed into the flimsy taxicab.'[131] Adorno placed Kafka, 'the parabolist of impenetrability',[132] in a literary context in which he included Robert Walser, Edgar Allan Poe and Ferdinand Kürnberger, claiming that they had invented a specific sub-genre of 'the detective novels in which the criminals fail to be exposed'.[133]

Adorno interpreted the figures in Kafka's stories as embodiments of the labour it must have cost the human race to achieve the process of civilizing the individual, a process that each person must undergo in childhood without his ever succeeding in becoming certain of his identity. This is why Kafka focuses on the instability of the self, since it is constantly exposed to the danger of lapsing into an instinctual, animal condition. The individual is torn hither and thither between utter conformism and rebellion. 'Kafka's hermetic memoranda contain the social genesis of schizophrenia.'[134]

It often seems, quite rightly, that in such stories as *The Metamorphosis* or *In the Penal Colony* Kafka anticipated certain aspects of National Socialism. Nevertheless, Adorno believes that he also went beyond this unique catastrophe. For, as Adorno put it, following Benjamin, in Kafka's works the entirety of previous history has become a hell. This inferno was created by the late bourgeoisie in a far more real fashion than Kafka could ever have imagined. 'In the concentration camps, the boundary between life and death was eradicated . . . As in Kafka's twisted epics what perished there was what provided the criterion of experience – life lived out to its end.'[135]

Adorno's discussion of Kafka contains numerous echoes of *Dialectic of Enlightenment*. One example is his claim that 'Kafka reacts in the spirit of enlightenment to the latter's reversion to mythology.'[136] Just as the deceptions of myth are once more brought to account, so too his novel 'The Trial is itself the trial of a trial.'[137] Kafka proposes the use of cunning as an antidote to the mythic powers: 'Kafka's humour hopes to reconcile myth through a kind of mimicry.'[138] Thus myth must show itself for what it is. 'Myth is to succumb to its own reflected image. The heroes of *The Trial* and *The Castle* become guilty not through their guilt

– they have none – but because they try to get justice on their side.'[139]

In July, when Adorno offered his Kafka essay to Rudolf Hirsch,[140] the editor of the *Neue Rundschau*, he wrote to him saying that he had a special relationship with it. And later, in the letter accompanying the finished text, he added: 'To be honest, it is the first time in my life that I have the feeling that I have written something that more or less corresponds to what I must expect of myself.'[141] Even if some of Adorno's readers were familiar with his prose, they may have found it as hard to read these 'Notes on Kafka' as some of his other contributions to the magazine, notably his essay 'Valéry Proust Museum' of the same year and the essay on Schoenberg written in 1952, shortly after the composer's death. Adorno admitted to Scholem in a letter in January 1954 that he did not exactly go out of his way to make his readers' job easy. He explained that, although his own basic position was made explicit in the 'Notes on Kafka', he 'had operated on the "*Landjäger*" principle', by which he meant that it was like a '*Landjäger*' sausage, tightly stuffed and hence very compact.[142] Kracauer seems not to have been disturbed by the density of the prose. He wrote to Adorno at the end of August 1954, saying that it was one of his best pieces. He had greatly approved of Adorno's insisting on the need to take Kafka literally and, in particular, 'Your leitmotif that Kafka understands the "system" from its own waste . . . , his consistent intuition that power has to be allowed to declare itself.'[143]

His essay collection *Prisms* was published by Suhrkamp in 1955 in an edition of 2000 copies. However, the particular importance of the Kafka essay in his own eyes was obscured by the presence of the other essays. As a whole, the book was given a predominantly positive reception from a series of prominent critics such as Peter Merseburger, Thilo Koch, Rudolf Hartung, Ivo Frenzel, Hans Kudszus and Walther Friedländer.[144] Even if the volume did not arouse the same interest as *Minima Moralia*, it was still a success. Eight years later, it was reissued as one of the 200 initial volumes of the Deutscher Taschenbuchverlag, but now in an edition of 40,000 copies. Adorno announced the publication of *Prisms* to Baroness Dora von Bodenhausen, to whom he explained the meaning of the title: *Prisms* 'means that the world is perceived through a medium, namely the various objectifications treated in it, which are then brought to the point of transparency.'[145] Adorno was now becoming known as 'a thinker who helps to define the scope of legitimate intellectual discourse'.[146] No less a figure than Thomas Mann noted that Adorno had become established in Germany and had been able to gain acceptance for 'his critical style'. 'I have not only read your fantasy about Kafka . . . It is only now becoming clear that when you were in America you were half-mute, and that Europe has vastly increased your productivity by opening up quite different opportunities for it. There really does seem to be something like a "motus animi continuus" at work.'[147]

Thomas Mann had occasion to experience Adorno's energy at first hand when the latter wrote him a long letter in January 1954 on the subject of Mann's *The Black Swan*, which had been published shortly before. He spoke with enthusiasm of the 'scandalous parable' about the ageing Rosalie von Tümmler who lets herself be captivated by the young American Ken Keaton. What impressed Adorno was precisely the metaphoric nature of the story, 'the excess of idea over material . . . This time even I could not help thinking of the musical technique of variation, so that I flatter myself with the notion that you had provided variations on your insistent fundamental theme . . . : it is not, then, life greedy for death that speaks here but death greedy for life.'[148] At the suggestion of Walter Höllerer,[149] the co-editor of the literary journal *Akzente*, this letter was published in full in a special Thomas Mann issue in July 1955. Mann had given his agreement to the publication.[150]

From the time Adorno started to write for *Akzente* he did not cease to be in demand. The clearest evidence of this was the series of texts he produced in 1958 with the title *Notes to Literature*. The programmatic lecture 'On Lyric Poetry and Society' contains a clear indication of Adorno's reasons for seeing in music and literature, and more generally in the arts as such, an ultimate refuge of the anticipatory glimpse (*Vor-Schein*) of the utopian as a possible state of otherness: 'In industrial society the lyric idea of a self-restoring immediacy becomes – where it does not impotently evoke a romantic past – more and more something that flashes out abruptly, something in which what is possible transcends its own impossibility.'[151] Just as sentimentality seemed out of place in the reified world, so too Adorno had an aversion towards the auratic gesture, the lofty tone, for example, in the poetry of Rainer Maria Rilke, whose secret gesture he thought betrayed 'its blending of religion with arts and crafts'.[152] He thought of art and poetry as refuges in which the antagonism between individual and society can be expressed, 'the cleft between what human beings are meant to be and what the order of the world has made of them.'[153]

For this reason, the poetry of Eichendorff, Hölderlin, Heine and Borchardt was not only 'the subjective expression of a social antagonism', but also the aesthetic test of a core theme of dialectical philosophy, namely that 'subject and object are not rigid and isolated poles but can be defined only in the process in which they distinguished themselves from one another and change.'[154]

Adorno's fundamental conviction that literature is 'a protest against a social situation that every individual experiences as hostile, alien, cold, oppressive', and that these historical circumstances leave a negative imprint on works of art,[155] led him, a philosopher and sociologist, to champion the literary works of one of the most important avant-garde writers of the twentieth century: the prose and drama of Samuel Beckett. Adorno made efforts in 1958 to use the good offices of Peter Suhrkamp to obtain an introduction to Beckett in Paris. At this time, a number of

Beckett's major works had already appeared – *Molloy* (1951), *Malone Dies* (1951), *The Unnameable* (1953). Suhrkamp Verlag had wished early on to publish German translations of Beckett's works, so that Adorno was undoubtedly familiar with them before Beckett's great theatrical successes with *Waiting for Godot* (1953), *Endgame* (1958) and *Krapp's Last Tape* (1958). Adorno evidently first saw a performance of *Endgame* in April 1958 when spending a week in Vienna shortly after Easter.[156] In a letter to Horkheimer, he told him about the magnificent production of *Endgame*, observing that the author had certain intentions that 'coincide with our own'.[157] Horkheimer seems not to have shared Adorno's enthusiasm wholeheartedly. In conversation with Fritz Pollock, he expressed his reservations about Beckett and linked them with criticism of Adorno: 'Beckett is concerned with the same phenomenon as critical theory: to depict the meaninglessness of our society and to protest about it, while preserving the idea of better things in that protest. For each one of his analyses, Adorno also says the opposite. But despite a dialectics carried to extremes, what he says remains untrue. For the truth cannot be spoken. And personally he remains detached. But what has to be done is to make real whatever truth one happens to possess.'[158]

At the end of the year, Adorno flew from Frankfurt to Paris in order to give some lectures on philosophical topics at the invitation of the Faculté des lettres et sciences humaines. He stayed at the Hotel Lutétia, which is where the first meeting between him and Beckett took place, on 28 November.[159] It appears from Adorno's diary[160] that their conversations lasted well into the night in the Coupole, and were continued in Les Isles Marquises, the restaurant in the rue de la Gaité that Beckett favoured.[161] After this first meeting, Adorno began to make notes for an essay on *Endgame*. His intention was to finish it between the summer of 1960 and early in 1961. He spent the holiday week in the Waldhaus, the hotel in Sils Maria in the Upper Engadine, reading the play thoroughly and writing down what seemed important for his own interpretation.[162] The completed essay, together with essays on Proust, Balzac and Valéry, formed the central text in volume 2 of the *Notes to Literature* (1961).[163] He dedicated 'Trying to understand *Endgame*' to Beckett in memory of their first meeting in Paris.

On 27 February, Adorno read large extracts from the essay to an audience in Frankfurt at a party given by Suhrkamp Verlag in honour of Beckett. The party took place in the Cantate Hall, next to the Goethe House. This 'Hommage à Samuel Beckett' event aroused great interest, though there was little on offer except for the somewhat hermetic lecture given by Adorno, who was of course already a familiar figure in intellectual circles in Frankfurt. Adorno stood on the podium and read his talk out with immense concentration, giving a little bow at the end as if he had been giving a piano recital rather than a lecture. Before the event, Siegfried Unseld, who had taken Suhrkamp's place after the latter's death in March 1959, had invited the Adornos to a luncheon with Beckett at which Adorno took the opportunity to try out some of the arguments he was going to present in the evening. Unseld recalls that Adorno maintained that Hamm, the name of the anti-hero, was derived from Hamlet.[164] Although Beckett flatly denied even having thought about Shakespeare's hero in connection with his own play, Adorno persisted in his view, adhering strictly to his thesis that there is an objective surplus of meaning that has greater weight than authorial intentions.[165] It is evident that Beckett's almost completely static play, with its pantomime-like elements, held a great fascination for Adorno, and this arose from his own stylistic ideal. How great that fascination was becomes clear from the fact that he chose Thomas Mann of all people, who thought little of Beckett, to be the recipient of his postulate of 'an asceticism with regard to the direct statement of the positive; a genuine asceticism, believe me, for by nature I am more inclined to the opposite, namely the unfettered expression of hope.'[166] However, in his interpretation of the play with the slave Clove and the master Hamm, the lame and the blind, with their parents vegetating in the ashbins, there is no sign of this.

Adorno placed Beckett in the tradition of James Joyce and especially of Franz Kafka: 'For Beckett absurdity is no longer an "existential situation" diluted to an idea and then illustrated. In him literary method surrenders to absurdity without preconceived intentions.'[167] What Adorno found really convincing about *Endgame* was the 'act of omission', since 'in the act of omission, what is left out survives as something that is avoided, the way consonance survives in atonal harmony. The apathy of the endgame is registered and sounded out with great subtlety. An unprotesting depiction of ubiquitous regression is a protest against a state of the world that so accommodates the law of regression that it no longer has anything to hold up against it.'[168] The shocking desolation of the dramatic scenes in Beckett in which everything has dwindled to the point of being mere gesture has its counterpart in the debacle of social theory. 'The irrationality of bourgeois society in its late phase rebels at letting itself be understood; those were the good old days, when a critique of the political economy of this society could be written that judged it in terms of its own *ratio*. For since then the society has thrown its *ratio* on the scrap heap and replaced it with virtually unmediated control. Hence interpretation inevitably lags behind Beckett.'[169] It is precisely the affront to 'the cultural spokespersons of authentic expression',[170] Beckett's absolute refusal to provide either political accusation or metaphysical hope, that makes *Endgame* the contemporary play par excellence; it reveals more 'than would taking a stand with an intent to expose, as exemplified by Bertolt Brecht or Rolf Hochhuth.'[171] As a dramatic elegy about the state of the world, it is conscious of its own impossibility. 'No weeping melts the armour; the only face left is the one whose tears have dried up.'[172]

Just as Adorno had referred to his own experience of a car accident in 1928 by way of illustrating the grotesque in Kafka, so here he recalled an episode from childhood: playing in no man's land. The absence of a 'position' in Beckett's drama, as well as its ambivalence towards the historical demise of the subject, its reduction to itself, is a sort of 'fun', 'the way it might have been fun to hang around the border markers between Baden and Bavaria in old Germany as though they encompassed the realm of freedom. *Endgame* takes place in a neutral zone between the inner and the outer, between the materials without which no subjectivity could express itself or even exist.'[173] Adorno's interest in Beckett went well beyond his plays, as can be seen from his half-implemented decision to write about *The Unnameable*, the novel that is concerned with the dissolution of the identity of a man who lives in a flowerpot, reduced to his own language: 'That's . . . all words, there's nothing else, you must go on, that's all I know, they're going to stop, I know that well, I can feel it, they're going to abandon me, it will be the silence, for a moment, a good few moments.'[174] In a letter of May 1952 to the poet Werner Kraft, a friend of Benjamin's in his youth,[175] he wrote that he 'had read the novel almost feverishly. . . . I sketched out an interpretation while I was still reading it . . . You absolutely must read it, although you need good nerves for it – in comparison, Kafka's *Penal Colony* reads like *The Indian Summer*.'[176] He evidently possessed good nerves himself, since he noted down his own impressions and ideas on the seven preliminary leaves of the German edition of 1959.[177] On page 3, for example, he noted that 'criticism of Beckett amounts to the statement that that's really terrible, things can't be like that. Reply: It is terrible.' Or, ' "drop out". It would be important to know when the word first appeared; an index of Beckett's historical significance. What Beckett does is to compose variations on this word [*auskomponieren*].'[178]

An important contribution to the debate on Beckett in Germany was provided by the television discussion of the film version of a French production of two of his plays – *Comédie* and *Film* – with Buster Keaton and directed by Alan Schneider. Shortly before it, Adorno had met Beckett in Paris and went from there on 17 January 1968 to the studio in Cologne. In the course of this extremely lively live discussion Adorno was able to articulate some of the elements of his view that had already appeared in print:

> These human stumps, that is to say, these people who have actually lost their selves, really are the products of the world we live in. It is not Beckett who has reduced them to what they are for speculative reasons of his own, but he is, to put it pointedly, realistic in the sense that, in these figures who are *both* just stumps *and* also something universal, he is the accurate interpreter of what individual people are capable of as the mere functions of a universal social totality. He is the photographer of a society in

which everything has become a function, and he depicts it from its shabby side since he shows what happens to these people in this functional world.[179]

Adorno had great reservations about television and what he saw as its infantilizing effects, but in this case he wrote to Hans-Geert Falkenberg, the moderator of the programme, on 5 April 1968, saying: 'On Wednesday evening, I saw our Beckett discussion on the Third Programme of Hessen Television, and would like to tell you that I was extraordinarily impressed by it, even though I am perhaps not the right person to say so. The atmosphere was human and, above all, the completely informal nature of the discussion and the fact that there were no time constraints made possible a kind of spontaneity, an alternation of demanding and undemanding moments that is normally not available on television. I have also heard very favourable reactions from other viewers.'[180]

If in Adorno's view Kafka was emblematic of the approaching age of barbarism, then Beckett's plays were the definitive expression of the epoch's experience of catastrophe. Whereas Kafka destroys the apparently meaningful by its plurality of meanings, Beckett even more radically destroys meaning to the point of meaninglessness. 'Just as after an intensive reading of Kafka alert experience thinks it sees situations from his novels everywhere, so Beckett's language effects a healing disease in the sick person; the person who listens to himself talk starts to worry that he sounds the same way.'[181]

These two major essays demonstrate that Adorno could feel sufficiently confident to take part in literary discourse. He even ventured into the illustrious circle of the Hölderlin Society in June 1963 in order to give a talk on the poet at its annual conference in Berlin. Kracauer expressed his admiration for the fact that Adorno intended to deal with this difficult material in the presence of an audience of specialists, and inquired what the secret was of Adorno's amazing productivity – a question that went unanswered. Adorno's lecture was given to an exclusive circle of literary scholars and Germanists – as speaker he followed lectures by Emil Staiger and the classical philologist Uvo Hölscher. His talk unleashed vehement responses, and during it one woman left the hall in agitation. She wished to protest against his criticism of Heidegger. Adorno later gave a report on this incident to Marcuse: 'The only reaction to the Hölderlin in Berlin was that of a Heideggerian megaera. She reproached me with having formerly been called Wiesengrund, and backed up this reproof by pointing out that she was half-Jewish and that her father had been gassed in Auschwitz.'[182] The lecture was followed by an animated discussion in the foyer of the Academy of Arts in which Adorno was unable to participate, since he had to leave early.[183]

This essay, which appeared in the *Neue Rundschau* early in 1964, opens with an account of Adorno's particular approach to literary interpretation and derived from ideas he had previously stated in his important essay 'The Essay as Form'.[184] His view was that the adventitious causes, particular intentions and individual goals of the authorial personality could only be reconstructed if they had been objectified in the text. With Hölderlin especially, the critic's task was to focus entirely on the 'objective linguistic shape'. Rather than the poetic work complying with the author's intentions, the author obeyed the 'compulsion of the work itself. The more completely the artist's intention is taken up into what he makes and disappears in it without a trace, the more successful the work is.'[185] This view, which is in harmony with Adorno's theory of musical reproduction,[186] is repeated with particular emphasis in this lecture.[187] 'What unfolds and becomes visible in the works, the source of their authority, is nothing other than the truth manifested objectively in them, the truth that consumes the subjective intention and leaves it behind as irrelevant.'[188] How can the objective truth content of Hölderlin's poetry be made accessible? Adorno appealed to immanent analysis, which he distinguished from both the genetic and the biographical methods. The immanent method strives to grasp the poetic structure that is made up of a multiplicity of individual moments. It then proceeds to penetrate 'the configuration of moments that taken together signify more than the structure intends.'[189]

When Adorno said of music, and indeed art in general, that it needs the assistance of philosophy to interpret it, this was intended to apply also to Hölderlin's poetry, which, however, he was concerned to snatch from the jaws of Heidegger's fundamental ontology. His own philosophical access to the riddle of Hölderlin's poems was gained in the relations between intellectual content and lyrical form. 'What philosophy can hope for in poetry is constituted only in this relationship; only here can it be grasped without violence.'[190] The propositional content of the poems is made available through a particular expressive method, through 'the parataxes . . . artificial disturbances that evade the logical hierarchy of a subordinating syntax.'[191] Paratactic language is the attempt to suspend the logic of syntax. This enabled the poems to draw their dignity from the artistic aspect of language formation. What Hölderlin wanted, according to Adorno, was 'to allow language itself to speak'.[192] This primacy of expression made it possible to elevate language above the human subject through the free action of the subject. 'In this process the illusion that the language would be consonant with the subject or that the truth manifested in language would be identical with a subjectivity manifesting itself disintegrates.'[193] From a historico-philosophical perspective, Adorno interpreted the content of his poems as a lament about the domination of nature. Even though Hölderlin was aware that the appropriation of nature was a condition of humanity, he was not blind to the oppression that resulted from the principle of self-assertion. 'The immanent dialectic of the late Hölderlin . . . is a critique of the subject as much as a critique of the rigidified world. . . . For the late hymns, subjectivity is neither the absolute nor the ultimate. Subjectivity commits a violation in setting itself up as absolute, when it is in fact immanently compelled to self-positing.'[194] Adorno's lecture culminated in the recommendation to read Hölderlin's poetry as an aspect of de-mythologization because it protests against the myth of the 'self-deification of man'. With this, however, the poet has distanced himself from classicism and identity philosophy: his poetics is one of non-identity and non-conceptuality.

With this conclusion, Adorno had let the cat out of the bag, since a philosophy of non-identity was to become his principal concern during the coming years, and it had already been a topic frequently mentioned in his letters. His demonstration of the paratactical structure of Hölderlin's poetry was also the attempt to put his own cards on the table without revealing the secret of his game. For Adorno Hölderlin's treatment of language was as important as the affinity he detected between his view of the world and those of Kafka and Beckett. This explains why he regarded the essays on these writers as key texts. He made this clear to Jürgen Habermas in a letter of July 1963. He approached Habermas having heard that Habermas intended to write an essay for the *Frankfurter Allgemeine Zeitung* that would appear on 11 September 1963, Adorno's sixtieth birthday.[195] Habermas utterly failed to take the hint, and focused instead on a different text in his appreciation, which turned out to be one of the most penetrating contributions to be written at that time. The essay he chose bore the succinct title 'Progress', a talk that Adorno had given on 22 October 1962 at the Philosophers' Conference in Münster. Habermas instantly grasped the meaning of the situation in which Adorno, the outsider, addressed the assembled guild of philosophers: 'A writer among bureaucrats'.[196] Adorno's shrewd reflections on the concept of progress were a masterpiece of the essay form that he himself had discussed elsewhere. He had emphasized there that in the essay what counted was not just the way in which ideas were expressed, but that they should transform their object into a 'force field' and 'move in so close to the hic et nunc of the object that the object becomes dissociated into the moments in which it has its life.'[197]

The theme of his lecture was his analysis of progress in contemporary society from the standpoint of the philosophy of history. Adorno took up an older idea that he had referred to in a letter to Horkheimer of February 1957. There he had pointed to the anachronistic element in the idea of improving the world. 'The measure of what is yearned for is always to a certain degree happiness that has been lost thanks to the progress of history. Whoever finds himself up with events and in tune with his age is always entirely in conformity with it and does not wish things to be otherwise.'[198] Horkheimer agreed with what Adorno had termed his 'little idea' and emphasized for his part the irrational form in which progress currently took place. 'However advanced we are technologically, historically we are on the way down. At the same time, we need to distinguish history from natural history. I suspect that, from the point of view of natural history, mankind's forward march continues undaunted, and what we call history . . . will be no more than an episode.'[199] Adorno now took up this idea of Horkheimer's. The 'force field' he had mentioned in his lecture on 'Progress' was formed by two poles: first, by reflection which decoded the validity claims of the concept of progress, the antinomy of concept and thing; and, second, by the critique of the progress that human beings have actually achieved socially. What progress has been achieved in man's relations with nature? Can we speak of progress in the way in which people live together or in people's relationships with one another? Over and above the discussion of such questions, Adorno proposed a conception of progress that would attempt to discover the conditions of its own possibility: 'the idea of reconciliation – the transcendent *telos* of all progress'.[200] As the author of *Dialectic of Enlightenment*, and intimately familiar with Benjamin's 'Theses on the Philosophy of History', Adorno took good care not to impute to history surreptitiously any automatic development in the direction of growing freedom or growing oppression. 'Progress should be no more ontologized, unreflectedly ascribed to Being, than should decline, though indeed the latter seems to be the preference of recent philosophy. Too little of what is good has power in the world for progress to be expressed in a predicative judgement about the world, but there can be no good, not a trace of it, without progress.'[201] As a way out from the blind alley of optimism and pessimism, Adorno made it clear that progress in living conditions has created the precondition for breaking with the history of progress hitherto: 'Progress means to step out of the magic spell, even out of the spell of progress . . . In this way it could be said that progress occurs where it ends.'[202] Adorno's starting-point, his normative point of reference, is the secular idea of mature subjects living together in harmony. He thus criticized the notion that progress could be reduced to the domination of nature. He objected also to the way such an idea developed analogously to the dynamics of a natural process. To equate progress with the control of nature is a blind faith like that of the ancient myth that ought really to have been superseded by knowledge of the laws of nature. This quid pro quo according to which the subjugation of nature ensures that natural coercion is maintained is an idea he illustrated with the image of a giant of whom we are reminded by the image of human progress: 'For this giant, after sleeping from time immemorial, slowly bestirs himself, and then storms forth and tramples everything that gets in his way. Nonetheless his unwieldy awakening is the sole potential for attaining political maturity – [the assurance] that nature's tenacity, into which even progress integrates itself, will not have the final word.'[203] The only way to salvage progress, in Adorno's view, is to mediate between the extremes, to confront the differing aspects of rationality that unfold in the course of progress:[204]

rationality as self-reflection is the corrective to ends–means rationality. This is what Adorno had in mind when he proposed that 'the devastation wrought by progress can be made good again, if at all, only by its own forces.'[205] For this reason he warned against Ludditism. On the one hand, he pointed out that the critique of progress is not to be confused with the critique of technology. On the other, not every technical innovation can claim to be advanced or progressive. He illustrated this with reference to the mastery of materials in art. While 'a quartet by Mozart is not simply better made than a symphony of the Mannheim school . . . it also ranks higher in an emphatic sense', it is questionable 'whether thanks to the development of perspective the painting of the High Renaissance truly surpassed so-called primitive painting.'[206] And in philosophy the idea of constant improvement is dubious in the extreme: 'To assume there has been progress from Hegel to the logical positivists . . . is no more than a joke.'[207]

Adorno formulated his own idea of intellectual progress seemingly by the way, but emphatically. 'Good is what wrenches itself free, finds a language, opens its eyes. As it struggles to free itself, it is interwoven in history which, without being organized unequivocally so as to lead to reconciliation, in the course of its movement allows the possibility of redemption to appear in a flash.'[208] What did Adorno wish to say with this cryptic statement about 'what finds a language' and 'what wrenches itself free'? Two ideas became increasingly important for his thinking at around this time. On the one hand, he wanted as a social theorist to emphasize the basic social and cultural conditions of progress. This consists in the ability of individuals to recognize one another mutually in their difference and to have the capacity to develop: the degree of progress attained can be discerned not from the unity and coherence of society or from the extent of social integration, but from the possibility of experienced difference and human individuation. On the other hand, Adorno wished to be as specific as possible and to name the sphere in which individuation could take place and flourish: the sphere of language. Language for him was not just a means of communication and as such a language deformed by commerce.[209] Rather, language had an outstanding significance because Adorno assigned it a dual characteristic: through language human subjects become part of the universal, and at the same time they can assure themselves of their own individuality; language is 'the collective force that produces spiritual individualization in the first place.'[210]

If Adorno was able to develop this emphatic concept of language as opposed to communication, he did so by appealing to a concept that he had tried to develop in his discussions of Kafka, Beckett and Hölderlin. He envisaged a language that was not restricted to its instrumental function but that would enable the particular, the non-identical, to express itself. In the book he planned on aesthetics he intended to explain how it would be possible to achieve with art something that was denied to discursive knowledge: to say what cannot be said, to make the non-conceptual manifest. How this could be explained through the medium of philosophical concepts still awaited clarification. These two great plans – they would turn into books – were described by Adorno as 'my real concerns'. As late as the end of the 1960s he still had the feeling that these real concerns still lay in the future; everything he had written up to then was nothing but preliminary studies that would, he hoped, lead to something greater.

17

Gaining Recognition for Critical Theory: Adorno's Activities in the Late 1950s and Early 1960s

Late in August 1953, Adorno returned to Germany for the second time. He was quickly able to settle in at his old flat in Kettenhofweg. From this point on, it was clear to him that he wanted, if at all possible, to remain in Germany and to work as a philosopher and sociologist. Following an application from the dean of the Arts Faculty, his professorial post was upgraded to that of a permanent extraordinary professor. The granting of status as a civil servant was justified by the need to make 'reparations'. He resumed his teaching for the winter semester on his customary two afternoons per week. The topics were all within the discipline of philosophy. Thus in the winter semester 1953–4, he offered a two-part lecture course on 'The Problem of Idealism'. In the first part the focus was on Plato's theory of ideas, in the second, epistemological issues arising in connection with the *Critique of Pure Reason*.[1] In the summer semester of the following year, 1955, he lectured on 'Kant's Transcendental Logic'. In the winter semester of 1957–8 he again lectured on the theory of knowledge; in the following semester he offered a course on 'Introduction to Dialectics' (1958) and also on 'Aesthetics' (1958–9), returning to Kant's *Critique of Pure Reason* the following year.

Simultaneously with the lectures, Adorno conducted a seminar on Thursday afternoons. In the first few years, he often did this jointly with Horkheimer. Here, discussions focused on individual texts, mainly by Kant and Hegel. 'The Hegel seminars generally dealt with very little text in the course of a semester: never more than a few pages from the Doctrine of Essence from the *Logic*. The strategy was . . . to begin by accepting Hegel's critique of Kant, but then to use Marx's critique of Hegel. However, in this critique of Hegel elements of Kant recurred. We always remained within this triangle.' The general atmosphere, as the philosopher Herbert Schnädelbach recalls, was one of 'deep feeling'. This was connected with the fact that 'Adorno was always fully committed. . . . This meant that the seminar never got bogged down in a welter of detail, though on the other hand it was all extremely demanding for the students.'[2] Jürgen Habermas recollects a further ritual that formed a standing feature of the Kant and Hegel seminars: Horkheimer's attempt to upstage Adorno. He frequently came half an hour late to the seminar, sat down next to Adorno and got him to give an account of the discussion up to that point. Horkheimer then as a rule felt it incumbent on himself to put forward a counter-thesis to Adorno's difficult dialectic interpretation. Although this was often much simpler, Adorno would instantly adopt it: 'Exactly, that's just what I think, Max.' Those present found it hard to accept Adorno's opportunistic behaviour, but many, especially among the younger members of the institute, disapproved much more of Horkheimer's superior attitude. Adorno was regarded as much the more original thinker and also as the person who was responsible for dealing with institute business and the research projects. Oskar Negt, for example, who came to Frankfurt in the mid-1950s, took note of 'the play-acting element in Horkheimer's thinking', while Adorno was a man 'who thought while he talked'.[3]

In his lectures, there were only two occasions when Adorno turned his attention to sociological questions. In the summer semester of 1960, he gave a course of lectures on 'Philosophy and Sociology' which in a number of respects anticipated arguments that appeared later in 'The Positivist Dispute' and also his criticism of Émile Durkheim's *Essays on Sociology and Philosophy*.[4] His last course of lectures, in the summer semester 1968, bore the title 'Introduction to Sociology'.[5]

Even though lectures on sociological topics were something of an exception, Adorno did in fact teach sociology from the mid-1950s on. This took the form of weekly seminars for sociology students, and the atmosphere there was felt to be far less elitist and tense than in the philosophy seminars. Adorno was always at pains to transmit a sociological way of thinking by analysing specific social phenomena and by endeavouring to make them comprehensible in a lively manner. A knowledge of the history of sociological thought was presupposed. The emphasis was placed on the analysis of contemporary society, its classes and stratification, and its social conflicts. Alongside the 'classics' of sociology, such as Claude Henri de Saint-Simon, Auguste Comte, Émile Durkheim, Herbert Spencer, Karl Marx, Max Weber, etc., there was an ongoing preoccupation with the logic of the social sciences and the relationship between social theory and social research. But, as Adorno emphasized in his seminars from the outset, what sociology is cannot be laid down by any precise conceptual definition, nor can it be reduced to a single scientific methodology, but can only be learnt 'by doing it'.[6]

Adorno's open-mindedness and the broad spectrum of his interests encouraged his contact with Arnold Hauser, the sociologist of art and culture of Hungarian origin who had been teaching art history at the University of Leeds since 1951. He was invited to give a talk at the institute in January 1954. This talk led to a friendship between him and Adorno. Hauser's first letter was full of enthusiasm: 'If I say that knowing you personally confirmed everything that I could have promised myself after coming to know your writings, you will be able to judge my feelings by the enthusiasm you know I feel for your achievements as a writer.'[7] For his part, Adorno did what he could to find an appropriate position for him at a German university. He used his contacts in Frankfurt, but also appealed to Karl Löwith in Heidelberg, Helmuth Plessner in Göttingen and Wilhelm Weischedel in Berlin. Wilhelm Weischedel, who had been born in 1905, had already asked Adorno in the summer of 1954 whether he would be willing to accept an offer for the second chair in philosophy at the Free University of Berlin. This was very flattering for Adorno and he told Hauser about it in a letter on 18 July 1954, trying at the same time to encourage him with the thought that this inquiry proved that 'people like us have not been completely forgotten in the world'.[8] This episode is of some importance, since the biographical literature about Adorno is unanimous in its belief that the Frankfurt outsider never in his entire life received an offer of a post at another German university. This is quite true, but there were informal inquiries like this one.[9] Adorno's respect for Hauser was not confined to his efforts to find him a job, as is evident from his comments on the German version of his *Social History of Art.* 'I was completely immersed in your book . . . I felt so enthusiastic that I can scarcely find words for it, and I shall try to express that fact. That such a book is still possible in the present situation is almost miraculous and you have set a standard here that no responsible thinker with a respect for truth will be able to ignore.'[10]

Adorno also attempted to help Jean Gebser, an unconventional philosopher ignored by the academic establishment. He assured him in a number of letters that he and Horkheimer would do everything in their power to procure an honorary doctorate for him.[11]

Adorno's dual activity as sociologist and philosopher resulted from the fact that as from July 1957 he had been made a full professor for the two disciplines.[12] This definitive material settlement and the formal recognition of his academic achievement in Frankfurt was a great satisfaction to Adorno. As he wrote to Friedrich Hacker: 'You will know that I have in the meantime become a full professor. These things remind me of Anatole France's wonderful comment about Bergeret. He despised the cross of the Legion of Honour, but it would have been even better to receive it and then to despise it.'[13] This change of status was anything but smooth, however. In a lengthy report the education expert Heinrich Weinstock pointed out that Adorno's appointment was essentially just a doubling of the chair occupied by Horkheimer. Even taking the 'reparations' aspect into account, such an increase conflicted with all university procedures. The historian and orientalist Helmut Ritter was even more scathing in discussion of the appointment in the meeting of the faculty. He said that this was an instance of favouritism. To make a career in Frankfurt, you had only to be a Jew and a protégé of Horkheimer. Horkheimer was present at the meeting. He accused Ritter of anti-Semitism and left the room, slamming the door. He then applied to the ministry in Wiesbaden for early retirement. Following this outburst, the faculty passed a resolution expressing its regrets that such an incident could take place, and 'that any utterances against Jewry and specifically against our Jewish colleagues could occur in our meetings. We condemn this statement as incompatible with the spirit that has guided and informed our faculty and university, and repudiate it as a stain on our academic community.'[14] Ritter was called upon by the faculty to apologize formally, and Horkheimer was asked not to send off his application for retirement, since the faculty 'placed decisive value on his continued activity in our faculty . . . towards the reconstruction of which Mr Horkheimer has devoted a major part of his life's work.'[15] For Adorno himself, the whole affair was gravely embarrassing. He was very conscious of the problematic nature of the reparations regulations in the universities. He was very keen to obtain an appointment to a chair in his home university independently of the third set of amendments to the Law for Reparations for National Socialist Injustice, an appointment based purely on his qualifications and his actual functions in the disciplines of philosophy and sociology.

As things turned out, Horkheimer's early retirement did go through in 1958 and Adorno took over the direction of the institute completely. This meant a significant strengthening of his position despite the debate that had been triggered by the uproar over his chair. As institute director his duties increased considerably and occupied most of his time. His plan to revive the old journal proved unviable, but ever since his return he had worked on the idea of publishing a book series, the *Frankfurter Beiträge zur Soziologie*. The first volume was the collection of essays entitled *Sociologica* (1955), which was dedicated to Horkheimer on his sixtieth birthday. Then came the *Gruppenexperiment*, edited by Pollock. A further volume was the study of work satisfaction among the blue-collar and white-collar workers in Mannesmann; this appeared with the title *Betriebsklima*. Volume 4 of what was to become a celebrated series of texts was edited by Adorno and Walter Dirks. This was the *Soziologische Exkurse*. This textbook-like anthology was intended as an introduction to the fundamental concepts of 'sociology', 'society', the 'individual', the 'group', the 'family', etc. At the same time, the book was designed to build a bridge to empirical social research and its methods, whose applications were explained in the fields of research on prejudice, sociology of the community, and research on ideology. In his teaching Adorno constantly resisted the canonization of the twelve thematic fields of sociology contained in the book and urged that they should not be regarded as the be-all and end-all of sociology. Students duly noted his efforts to play down the *Exkurse*, but the chapters in this slim volume soon came to be regarded as, if not a sufficient foundation for an understanding of what students began to identify as the 'Frankfurt School', then at least a necessary one. For whole generations of Frankfurt sociology students, the *Soziologische Exkurse* came to be the first point of access to the way of thinking that incorporated the 'spirit of the house'. The *Exkurse* were distinguished from the few other sociological textbooks available then by their philosophical grounding, their interdisciplinary perspective and the critical thrust of the individual contributions. A typical example can be found at the end of the article on 'Sociology': 'But only in the spirit of criticism can science be more than the mere duplication of reality by thought, while explaining reality always means breaking the spell of duplication. Such criticism, however, . . . means confronting the object with its own concept. Data yield only to the gaze that examines them from the standpoint of a genuine interest, the standpoint of a free society.'[16] Did Adorno have an insight into the plight of growing numbers of students at the time who wished to study social theory but who regarded statistics and the study of methodology as a necessary evil?

Frankfurt, 12 November 1955
I dreamt I had to take the diploma examination in sociology. My performance in empirical social research was very poor. I was asked how many columns there are in a punched card. I put down twenty at random. That was quite wrong of course. The position with regard to concepts was even worse. I was presented with a series of terms in English and I was supposed to give their precise meaning in empirical sociology. One was 'supportive'. I boldly translated this as '*stützend*', helpful. But in statistics it turned out to be the exact opposite, something completely negative. Out of pity for my ignorance, the examiner now decided to test my knowledge of cultural history. . . . Here he was impressed by my profound knowledge and I was told I had passed.[17]

There can be no doubt that social research with Hollerith tabulating machines did not come easily to a philosopher and music critic like Adorno. Nevertheless, he developed an impressive productivity in this area. As institute director, he did not indeed undertake any field studies himself, nor did he become involved in the evaluation of data. However, there were regular meetings of the different research projects in which he intervened and proved able to impress the other participants, both by his innovative suggestions on points of methodology and by his interpretative imagination.[18] 'Adorno's relation to empirical social research was highly ambitious.' This was Ludwig von Friedeburg's judgement on the collaborative work done during the 1950s. 'Adorno's requirements were determined not just by his theoretical ambitions but also by his quite extraordinary ability to detect the general in the particular.'[19] Adorno was in strong demand in the institute soon after his return to Germany, and this comes as no surprise since it was because of the current research projects that he had been asked to return. In addition, a number of ideas for future projects and specific commissions were appearing on the horizon. Together with the continuation or completion of the existing large empirical studies, Adorno had had the plan since 1950 of a study of the German resistance movement. At the same time, he wanted to adapt the F scale from *The Authoritarian Personality* to German conditions. He wished to investigate how the originally authoritarian disposition of the Germans had been transformed into democratic attitudes. This project was probably conceived in January 1952 at a meeting in the institute attended by sociologists, social psychologists and political scientists (in addition to Horkheimer and Adorno, those present included Alexander Mitscherlich, Helmuth Plessner, Ernest Bornemann and Friedrich Tenbruck, etc.).[20] The institute had also taken other projects under its wing. One of them was a smaller study for the Office of the Federal Chancellor. This was a highly controversial project in the institute because its aim was to provide a selection method for the officers of the future German army. The institute had even agreed to a cooperative venture with the Federal Office for the Protection of the Constitution because in August 1952 Adorno had gained the impression during a meeting in Cologne that he might expect financial assistance from this source for his plan to reconstruct the history of the German resistance to the Nazi regime.

As representative of Frankfurt sociology, Adorno gave a lecture on the theory of ideology at the Twelfth Conference of German Sociologists in Heidelberg in October 1954, and at the end of December he presented a radio talk with the title 'Sociology as Science'. He used this lecture to give an account of the theoretical and methodological foundations of this the most modern of the social sciences and he took the opportunity to introduce the research and teaching programme of the Institute of Social Research. Shortly afterwards, in January 1955, he and Horkheimer organized a small conference on the problems of the sociology of the family. This was attended by members of the institute such as Walter Dirks and Ludwig von Friedeburg, as well as René König and Helmut Schelsky as guests. Soon after, Adorno took part in an internal institute conference on industrial sociology which was attended by the acknowledged specialists of the day: Heinrich Popitz, Hans-Paul Bahrdt and Theo Pirker. The last was active in the field of industrial and factory sociology and had strong links with the trade unions. He recalls the meeting in the building of the institute. 'We saw very little of Horkheimer; he sat in his room like Zeus above the clouds. . . . Adorno regarded me as someone who by rights ought not to exist at all. In his eyes the workers' movement was dead, finished historically. It was entirely inexplicable how a person like myself could not only have academic qualifications and be reasonably intelligent, but could also be active in a trade union, an organization. It simply did not fit into his image of the world.'[21]

At this time, Adorno gave his support to a plan to publish a second series of books with S. Fischer Verlag, alongside the *Frankfurter Beiträge zur Soziologie*. This new series would be devoted to important writings of American sociologists in German translation. Among them would be texts by William Graham Sumner, Thorsten Veblen, Robert Lynd, John Dewey and Robert K. Merton, as well as extracts from the *Studies in Prejudice*. But nothing came of this any more than of the idea of publishing Enlightenment texts from the eighteenth and nineteenth centuries, together with commentaries, by writers 'who were swimming against the tide'.[22]

In the mid-1950s, given the varied nature of the institute's research projects, it was very difficult to come by a sufficient number of qualified sociologists who could also satisfy the theoretical ambitions of the two directors. The hopes that Adorno and Horkheimer placed in the appointment of the young Ralf Dahrendorf in July 1954 were correspondingly great. Their intention was that he should take over a survey of the political attitudes of students as well as their attitudes towards their studies, their own education and their future careers. This study had been started as early as 1951–2 and had been further developed by Helmuth Plessner. Dahrendorf recalled twenty-five years later how Adorno had welcomed him in the institute.

> He gave me a detailed account of the work of the institute, all of which seemed to me to come within the normal scope of social research. The institute had initiated a number of surveys of the attitudes of German students to university and society. Now there would be a meeting of the Conference of Rectors at which a report had to be given. This was of great importance for the institute and he expected me to submit a report on this research (which was entirely unknown to me at the time) within three weeks.[23]

Having received the offer of a chair in Saarbrücken, Dahrendorf resigned his post in the institute in the same year. Adorno wrote about it to Horkheimer, who was in Chicago at the time as guest professor. Adorno felt some regret at Dahrendorf's departure: although he was 'a very talented man, when it comes down to it, he hates everything we stand for.' The fact that 'our work together failed' was proof of the thesis 'that after us, strictly speaking, there will be nothing.'[24] In his reply, which he sent to Locarno where Adorno was spending the summer with his wife in the Hotel Reber au Lac, Horkheimer sought to cheer him up: 'everything you tell me about the institute makes it clear that everything is going well. That is a great comfort to me. We need shed no tears over Dahrendorf. If he runs after a better offer we will not have lost anything of great importance. We have not grasped just how high our reputation stands here.'[25] This referred to the USA, where Horkheimer had made his name with the *Studies in Prejudice* and Adorno had done the same as co-author of *The Authoritarian Personality*. In Germany, Horkheimer's reputation was that of the public face of Frankfurt University where, as rector, he had received the likes of Thomas Mann, Theodor Heuss and Konrad Adenauer. By the end of the 1950s Adorno too was no longer an unknown, and this was connected with the fact that, in addition to his books and articles, he had become a public figure through his activities in the media, particularly the radio.

There were regular broadcasts – talks, interviews, round-table discussions – on Hessen Radio, South-West Radio and Radio Bremen, mainly thanks to his personal contact with people such as Alfred Andersch, Adolf Frisé, Gerd Kadelbach, Volker von Hagen, Horst Krüger and Helmut Lamprecht.[26] The topics treated included 'The Administered World' (September 1950), 'Philosophy and Music' (January 1952), 'Mythology and Enlightenment' (September 1952), 'Lyric Poetry and Society' (April 1956), 'What is the Meaning of "Working through the Past"?' (February 1960), 'Society between Education and Pseudo-Culture' (April 1961), 'Why Still Philosophy?' (January 1962), 'The Jargon of Authenticity' (April 1963) and 'The Teaching Profession and its Taboos' (August 1965).

Adorno had also suggested to the poet Gottfried Benn, somewhat surprisingly, that they should join in a radio talk show on the subject of 'The Loss of the Centre'. He wrote to Alfred Andersch, the director of the Evening Studio on South-West Radio, saying that he 'was extremely interested' in strengthening his ties with Benn.[27] This proposal came to nothing even though Benn and Adorno met at a conference in Bad Wildungen in the summer of 1955. Benn was an essayist and lyric poet who had once been part of the expressionist movement and after that was for a time sympathetic towards National Socialism. His meeting with Adorno impressed him sufficiently for him to give a detailed account of it in a letter to his close friend, the Bremen businessman F. W. Oelze. 'I made the acquaintance of Mr Adorno who also gave a talk; a *very* intelligent, not very good-looking Jew, but with such an *intelligence* as really only Jews have, good Jews. We flew into each other's arms, only he is very egotistical, vain and in need of recognition, to be sure in a very legitimate way.'[28] Adorno admired Benn's linguistic artistry and regarded him as the consistent representative of a modern literature, without however deluding himself about the nature of his political errors. As he wrote to Peter Rühmkorf, 'Politically, Benn has committed atrocities, but in a higher political sense he is still closer to us than are many others.'[29]

In addition to his work for radio, Adorno produced contributions for the two major daily newspapers in Frankfurt. He had access to the *Frankfurter Allgemeine Zeitung* through Karl Korn, and to the *Frankfurter Rundschau* through Karl Gerold. He also wrote increasingly for the weekly *Die Zeit*.[30] And, from the start, he was active in the greatly respected debating forum of the *Darmstädter Gespräche*, in which he had already taken part as early as summer 1950 when they focused on modern art, and he was a contributor once again in September 1953 when the topic under discussion was 'The Individual and Organization'. Parts of the *Darmstädter Gespräche* were broadcast, and the lectures and discussions also appeared in book form.[31] The reason why Adorno became such a ubiquitous presence in the media was connected with the fact that he could claim to be an authority not just in one field, but in equal measure in philosophy, sociology, music theory and literary criticism. He frequently proposed the subjects of discussion himself and had a great flair for knowing what would be of interest. His commentaries were distinguished by his ability to tackle them in an interdisciplinary way and then to debate them in a controversial and even explosive form. He had a particular affinity for the radio, the dominant medium at the time. He consciously wished to make use of it to gain a wider audience for his critical mode of thinking. Moreover, what was expressed in this desire for media coverage was his sense that, as an intellectual, he had a particular responsibility. He saw himself not only as a specialized scientist but also as a committed, critical intellectual, trying to develop a lecturing style on the radio and later on in television that would be as comprehensible as possible. He was skilled in expressing his complex ideas while speaking off the cuff, well aware that he could not speak to the media 'as he would have to if he were to give an authoritative written account of a subject . . . ; however, nothing that he says can do justice to what he would demand from a text'.[32]

In the stream, but swimming against the tide

The power of thought not to swim with its own current is the power of resistance to what has previously been thought. Emphatic thought calls for the courage to stand by one's convictions.[33]

In many respects Adorno led a double life. As an academic teacher and researcher he transcended the traditional boundaries separating philosophy, sociology, and the study of literature and music. But, in addition, he regularly combined the role of the social researcher and social theorist with that of the intellectual. He was well aware that this 'suspension of the division of labour' was held to be particularly disreputable 'since it betrayed a disinclination to sanction the activities approved of by society, and domineering competence permits no such idiosyncrasies. The compartmentalization of mind is a means of abolishing mind where it is not exercised *ex officio*, under contract. It performs this task all the more reliably since anyone who repudiates the division

of labour . . . makes himself vulnerable by its standards in ways inseparable from elements of his superiority.'[34]

Adorno may well have thought of his wide-ranging discussions of a
variety of current topics as a practical contribution to political education. This was a field with which he was preoccupied throughout the
1950s. He believed that there was a great need for reform both there
and also in the methods of teacher training.[35] The German Sociology
Society had formed a sub-committee in 1958 to address the question of
the sociology of education and culture, and he had been involved in this
from its inception. The conference in the Akademie für Unterricht und
Erziehung in Calw in 1954 focused on the problems of the sociology of
education. Adorno had received an invitation to the conference at the
suggestion of Hellmut Becker. Alongside such topics as the structure
of authority in German schools or education and social stratification,
he was particularly interested in the deterioration and even crisis in
education, a subject he also discussed in his 'Theory of Pseudo-Culture'
at the Fourteenth Conference of German Sociologists in Berlin in 1959.[36]
He had previously tackled the question of university education, some
time before his interlude with the Hacker Foundation, when he had
written drafts that Horkheimer used as the basis for addresses that he
gave at the matriculation ceremonies as rector of the university in both
the summer semester 1952 and the winter semester 1952–3. On the one
hand, Adorno criticized the predominant demand for experts and the
resulting growth of specialization and purely specialist education. He
put in a plea for students to seize the opportunity offered by university
education to cultivate their capacity for unregimented thinking. On the
other hand, he questioned the idealist conception of education that
contributed, so he maintained, to the barbarizing of mankind. In the
theses he wrote on 'The Democratization of the German Universities'
he welcomed the dismantling of authoritarian structures and hierarchies
because this was a precondition for the emergence in the university realm
of 'the type of the free human being' who would be capable of free self-
determination. At the same time, he called for academics to tackle tasks
in the public arena and not 'to privatize', i.e., not to devote their energies to the accumulation of expert, professional knowledge and the promotion of their own careers. For 'the retreat from politics negates the
democratic principle even allowing for its validity as contemplation. It is
the Achilles heel of the democratization of the German universities.'[37]

Adorno's various ideas and initiatives in the sociology of education
were closely related to the research work being done at the time in the
institute.[38] One project was concerned with 'The Political Consciousness
of Students' (Ludwig von Friedeburg, Jürgen Habermas, Christoph
Oehler and Friedrich Welz), another with 'The Effectiveness of Political
Education' (Egon Becker, Joachim Bergmann, Sebastian Herkommer,
Michael Schumann and Manfred Teschner). Both were commissioned
projects that Adorno followed throughout their development. The survey

of student opinion was one of the projects carried out by Adorno together with the young philosopher Jürgen Habermas, whom he had brought to the institute in 1956 and who he hoped would not immediately resign as Dahrendorf had. His fears were groundless, to begin with at least, since Habermas was attracted by the very sort of theoretical thinking about society that was pursued by Adorno in the institute. Habermas had obtained his doctorate in Bonn in 1954 with a dissertation on Schelling.[39] He had come to Adorno's notice with a review he had written in the *Frankfurter Allgemeine Zeitung* in July 1953 following the publication of Heidegger's notorious lecture of 1935. The passage the lecture contained about the 'greatness and inner truth of National Socialism' had appeared without change.[40] The essay that Habermas wrote with the title 'Dialectics of Rationalization' and which appeared in the cultural magazine *Merkur* in August 1954 also pointed to the affinity between his way of thinking and Adorno's. The two men had met through Adolf Frisé, the culture editor of the *Handelsblatt* who had moved from there to Hessen Radio. Habermas had already read *Dialectic of Enlightenment* and *Prisms*, and was familiar with the idiosyncrasies of Adorno's philosophical thought. Habermas has a clear recollection of his first few months in the institute: 'When I arrived in Frankfurt, it struck me that Horkheimer and Adorno did not refer much to contemporary philosophy. . . . Nor was I ever convinced that Adorno had read Heidegger closely. . . . There was something exotic about this selectivity. . . . Subjectively, when faced with this very narrow selection of "permitted" texts, so narrow as to run the risk of being dogmatic, I felt that I was less constrained in my absorption of philosophical and scientific traditions.'[41] When Habermas came to Frankfurt, he soon realized that Adorno's extreme sensitivity was a sign of his vulnerability. He sat in his institute as if it were a fortress besieged by his enemies. It was only later on that Habermas's own contribution to the defence of critical theory took on the character of philosophical or epistemological back-up. Initially, he had to set about familiarizing himself with the methods of empirical social research so as to be able to help complete the university study that was already under way. This empirical project, an in-depth survey of 171 Frankfurt students, sought to find out about their political activities, their attitudes towards democracy and their view of society. It was Habermas who was really in charge of bringing the project to a successful conclusion. However, the study did not appear in the institute's own series because Horkheimer had raised objections to it.[42] His criticisms were directed chiefly at Habermas's prefatory theoretical remarks 'On the Concept of Political Participation'. In these comments Habermas had argued that the changes in the function of the university had arisen directly from the way in which late capitalist society had become permeated by science. The consequence was that the economy had a direct impact on the system of knowledge. According to Habermas, this growth in the power of private economic interests had to be countered by 'the political control of the functions of private capital'.[43] In order to achieve this it was necessary to work to reduce the depoliticization of the masses and to strengthen the participatory elements of democracy.

By way of underpinning the notion of political activity with theory, Habermas drew on the Marxist-inspired model of social democracy that had been developed by the left-wing political scientist Wolfgang Abendroth, not least in lectures that he had delivered at Adorno's invitation in the institute in 1955 and 1957.[44] In his theoretical introduction, Habermas defined democracy as a form of life that went hand in hand with a free society and the maturity of its members. This understanding of democracy was identical with the ideas that Adorno had developed in his essays on politics and education at the end of the 1950s. The same could be said of the observation arising from the students' responses in the survey that their political attitudes were characterized by a resigned 'adaptation to what was the case'. This too coincided with Adorno's own interpretation of the present. 'The totality no longer appears in view, let alone in conceptual form.'[45] This agreement, which Adorno himself perceived between his views and those of Habermas,[46] undoubtedly helps to explain why he defended his assistant against Horkheimer's vehement criticism.[47] He singled out Habermas's introduction to *Student und Politik* for particular praise as 'a bravura piece', and insisted to Horkheimer that 'it should remain in the book at all costs'.[48] Nevertheless, because of Horkheimer's objections publication was delayed, and the book finally appeared outside the institute series. Having seen the warning signs, once the study of student political attitudes was finished, Habermas took advantage of the material independence given him by a scholarship with which to study for his *Habilitation*, and left the institute in October 1959. He moved in 1961 to Marburg, where he wrote *The Structural Transformation of the Public Sphere* (1962) for his second doctoral thesis. This book, which would make him famous, was written under the supervision of Wolfgang Abendroth. Habermas maintained his close relations with Adorno while he was professor of philosophy in Heidelberg, where he remained until 1964. He then returned to the University of Frankfurt where, by an irony of history, he became Horkheimer's successor as professor of philosophy and sociology at the age of thirty-four.[49]

One of Adorno's tasks as director of the institute was to gain a place for the institute within the scientific community and to cultivate contacts with colleagues in many different areas of research. This meant that he was active not just in the German Sociology Society and the General Philosophical Association, at both of which he gave lectures,[50] but also that he tried to establish relations with a whole series of figures in academic life. He was well aware that such people wished above all to promote their own academic interests, but he still thought it important to cultivate many different contacts. He corresponded with René

König just as he did with Arnold Gehlen in the 1960s. He took part in a radio discussion with Elias Canetti, and also with Karl Kerényi, Lotte Lenya, Daniel-Henry Kahnweiler and Hellmut Becker. The people he invited to give lectures at the institute included Wolfgang Abendroth, Hans-Georg Gadamer and Herbert Marcuse.

With all these efforts, whose tactical side he despised, Adorno was nevertheless quite unwilling to compromise his own views. This can be seen from his attitude to the proposed appointment of Arnold Gehlen, the right-wing intellectual, to a chair in Heidelberg. In 1958, when this was on the agenda, Adorno and Horkheimer both objected to the appointment of Gehlen, who had been a Nazi sympathizer. In April of that year, they wrote a report[51] in which they pointed out that, even though Gehlen was no doubt extraordinarily talented, there was a certain continuity in his thinking. On the one hand, they objected to the way in which he deduced the necessity of an authoritarian society from human nature, from certain anthropological constants. On the other hand, he endorsed a conception of power that closely resembled the interpretation of Nietzsche favoured by the Nazis. Gehlen was unaware of the existence of this report so that as far as he was concerned there was no obstacle to the personal relationship between him and Adorno that did not begin until the early 1960s. Although Adorno found Gehlen's conservative theory of institutions unacceptable, and although he made no secret of that fact, he valued him as a debating partner and made efforts to keep on good terms with him personally. The position was very different with Golo Mann, who had applied for a chair in political science at Frankfurt in 1963. Horkheimer had objected to a lecture that Mann had given to the Rhein-Ruhr-Klub in summer 1960 and subsequently published. In it he warned Germans not simply to exchange anti-Semitism for philo-Semitism. He went so far as to inquire into the historical truth of anti-Semitic cliches. Furthermore, he gave it as his view that the hostility of Weimar intellectuals towards politics had been a contributory factor in the demise of the republic and Hitler's victory.[52] For his part, Adorno had been aware since his time in Pacific Palisades that Golo Mann had been critical of him: Mann disliked his style of writing and rejected *Minima Moralia* because of what he saw as its clever-clever manner. This made it easy for Adorno to endorse Horkheimer's opposition to Mann. In the crucial faculty meeting he voted against Mann, who was the favourite for the post, and this helped to ensure that instead of the famous historian the position would be offered to Iring Fetscher, the young political scientist who enjoyed the support of both Adorno and Horkheimer.[53] Adorno's sympathies were never determined simply by the extent of his political or ideological agreement with someone, even though he never failed to make a precise assessment of the people with whom he chose to become more closely acquainted. His relations with Arnold Gehlen were significant in this respect. Gehlen had first been invited by Horkheimer to give a lecture at the institute in the winter of 1953. Gehlen was one of the conservative intellectuals from whom Adorno did not recoil; indeed, ever since their joint participation in the debates about art in Baden-Baden in October 1959, their initial politeness had given way to a more personal warmth. The correspondence between them, which lasted from 1960 to 1969, is proof of this. Adorno always sent Gehlen his own publications and offprints; he read Gehlen's book *Zeit-Bilder* (1960) and was able to tell him that he had unexpectedly found himself in agreement with what Gehlen had written about modern art. What he particularly liked was Gehlen's defence of modern art 'without lapsing into apologetics or denying the element of negativity that is an essential part of it.' In addition, he emphasized:

When it comes to the analysis of the contemporary situation, including the socially prescribed dumbing-down and mystification, we are not likely to differ greatly. I would not be able to marshall anything by way of opposition to this other than what you call 'the a priori of experience', something that is very much in tune with my own way of thinking: I believe I am unable to give up the possibility and the idea of the possibility of this. I believe that without this idea it would not be possible to think at all, or even, strictly speaking, to say a single word.[54]

Adorno evidently regarded Gehlen as the ideal opposite number in radio or television debates, and they encountered each other in this way on four occasions. They also met privately with their respective wives, in January 1961 in Kettenhofweg and in October in Gehlen's home, from where they made an excursion to the Weinstraße and the cathedral in Speyer.[55] Because both men were well aware of their political differences,[56] the subject was excluded from their letters and their public discussions. Each man expressed opinions that were critical of the other's views on society. In this sense, the relation between the two intellectuals was based on mutual respect and on common philosophical interests, but not on genuine friendship.[57]

As critical theory began to take shape at the end of the 1950s and the early 1960s, it was associated topographically with Frankfurt am Main, the seat of the Institute of Social Research, and, at a personal level, it focused increasingly on the figure of Adorno. In a review that Thilo Koch wrote on *Sociologica*, the *Festschrift* in honour of Horkheimer, he claimed that Adorno 'was one of the best minds at work in Germany today . . . the range of his knowledge and his interests is extraordinary, subtle and extremely diverse . . . You need only read a few pages of Adorno to realize that these Frankfurt academics are the vanguard for the most modern of all forms of humanism conceivable today.'[58] Adorno embodied the synthesis of distinct, often incompatible forms of thought. These included Karl Marx's theories of capitalism and reification which were somehow combined with Sigmund Freud's theories about human drives and the nature of the human subject, Émile Durkheim's theory of the coercive character of social conditions which was synthesized with Max Weber's theory of progressive rationalization and bureaucratization, and the categories of Kant's epistemology which were amalgamated with Hegel's dialectical philosophy of history. From this time on (together with Horkheimer at first, then, later, with Herbert Marcuse and Jürgen Habermas), Adorno came to be regarded as the outstanding speculative mind of critical theory, known for his ability to track down the symptoms of reification in an increasingly integrated society. As director of the institute, he initiated important projects in social research and social theory; as a cultural critic, he intervened in the current public debates on music and literature. And, finally, he was known as the representative of an independent philosophy, a philosophy of negativity which attempted 'to bear up under the suffering of alienation by exceeding it on the horizon of undiminished and thus no longer violent rationality.'[59]

Speaking of the rope while in the country of the hangman

> What the Nazis did to the Jews was unspeakable. The language had no words for it. . . . Despite everything, an expression had to be found if the victims, who were anyway too numerous for them all to be remembered by name, were to be spared the obloquy of being consigned to oblivion.[60]

Adorno's plea for a critical sociology that must be conscious of its own scope and limitations was no mere abstract programmatic desideratum. On the contrary, what he had said on the subject in his Weinheim lecture, 'On the Contemporary Situation of Empirical Social Research in Germany', was closely linked to the concrete research the institute had carried out since early 1951 with the title of 'Group Experiment'. Initially, the directors and their colleagues were still housed in the ruins of the original building, and this lasted until they could move into the new buildings in October 1951. The new project was concerned with uncovering both the manifest opinions and latent attitudes of the members of individual social strata towards ideological and political issues. The research team employed what was at the time a novel technique of data gathering in their efforts to understand the dynamics of the processes involved in opinion-formation in small-group discussions. It was the use of this technique that led them to give the study its title, 'Group Experiment'. In this case, the method was to be used in order to ascertain what were assumed to be the characteristic strategies employed by Germans to deny their own past – doubtless a challenging task. To research this 121 group discussions were conducted, involving over 1800 people of different social backgrounds. These groups were relatively homogeneous social units of between eight and sixteen participants (e.g., teachers, graduates, refugees, farmers, members of clubs) and their spontaneous statements were recorded onto tape and then transcribed – at the time, a laborious and costly procedure. The qualitative evaluation of the data took the form of a descriptive text analysis based on the records of the 121 group discussions amounting to 6000 typewritten pages. To motivate the various group discussions a 'basic stimulus' was used, the so-called Colburn letter. This letter contained the fictitious description of Germany in the postwar years by a sergeant in the occupation forces. It said, among other things, 'Only very few people admit openly that they were Nazis and the ones who admit it are often by no means the worst. Only a small minority are said to be guilty. In a sense that is true, but today there are only a few among the majority who unequivocally distance themselves from the past.'[61]

This novel method involving group discussion arose from suggestions by Max Horkheimer, who wanted to convey the realistic and direct expression of opinion as it emerges in such situations as in conversations between passengers in a train.[62] The train situation was to be re-created artificially in an experimental framework. The idea was that, thanks to the stimulus of the Colburn letter and the skilful guidance of the group leader, the discussion would more or less spontaneously bring to the surface the true underlying attitudes and thought patterns of the participants.

Adorno was responsible for the most important part of the study, the investigation of the complex of *guilt and defensiveness*. He could have used a sentence from *Minima Moralia* as the motto for the entire study: 'The obviousness of disaster becomes an asset to its apologists: what everyone knows no one need say – and under cover of silence is allowed to proceed unopposed.'[63] This thesis about the reasons for silence was connected with the reflection entitled *Pseudomenos* (The Liar), which alludes to a morbid defect of memory. Adorno surmised that the National Socialists were protected from the exposure of their misdeeds 'the more wildly the horror increased. The implausibility of their actions made it easy to disbelieve what nobody, for the sake of precious peace, wanted to believe, while at the same time capitulating to it.'[64] Adorno wished to get to the bottom of this complex relationship between what the German population must have known about the daily acts of discrimination against the Jews during the Nazi regime, the burning down of the synagogues, the acts of violence towards their property and their ultimate deportation, and what they denied, presumably because the horror was too great to acknowledge. As in the case of *The Authoritarian Personality*, his study of the interaction of guilt and defensiveness was based on psychoanalysis. In his introduction to the interpretative section of the study, he wrote that the research group 'constantly came up against subjective opinions and opinion formation that, because they conflicted so sharply with objective reality', were scarcely capable of explanation without recourse to psychoanalysis as a theory of the origins of a collective psychopathology.[65] In the course of analysing the data on the transcripts Adorno came across a specific mechanism of repression. People developed defensive reactions in proportion to the degree of their moral consciousness of the crimes that had been committed. The internal function of these reactions was to create an equilibrium between their bad conscience and their need to identify with Germany as a collective entity despite the Nazi past. Those Germans who reacted defensively in this way 'would not sympathize with the repetition of the past. Their defensiveness is itself a sign of the shock they had experienced, and to that extent it offers some hope.'[66]

As far as the first dimension of his analysis was concerned, it confirmed Adorno's hypothesis in *Minima Moralia* that the enormity of the crimes produced 'its own veil'.[67] The second dimension focused on the question of guilt. Here Adorno pursued the justifications put forward by those who inclined towards National Socialist views and hence were openly unapologetic about it. Although the total denial of guilt was relatively rare, Adorno's analysis came across attempts to convert the guilt problem into a private, internal matter. Furthermore, the admission of guilt could be dismissed as a contemptible form of self-pity and worldly innocence. There was a particular tactic that Adorno decoded as the expression of an authoritarian disposition. This was the tendency to claim that 'the people at the top', the ruling clique of Nazis, should bear the entire guilt. Since people who made use of these justifications did not reach the point of having a bad conscience, 'it was all the easier for them to remain loyal to the advantages that the regime had offered them.'[68] This went together with the rationalization that, since the individual was helpless and impotent, it would be wrong to impute guilt to him.

A further dimension of the analysis concerned the self-image of Germans in the years after the war. Adorno thought that this was notable for a certain self-stylization. According to this interpretation it was claimed that a sick nation could not help but incur guilt precisely because it was sick. Adorno spoke here of the 'magical transformation' of guilt into a neurosis that then became the alibi for one's own political failure as well as for a certain need to be protected. This was contrasted with an 'ideology of minding your own business' that asserted that what had happened in Germany was an internal German matter. At the verbal level, the repudiation of guilt made use of certain claims in mitigation. For example, the effectiveness of Nazi propaganda and its repressive measures was frequently cited. Rationalizations such as the threat of Soviet communism and the maltreatment of German prisoners of war were especially prominent in the attempt to deflect guilt.

What was particularly explosive was what emerged about the survival of elements of National Socialist ideology. Not only did some participants mention the allegedly good sides of Nazism, its idealism and noble intentions, but the transcripts also contained clear evidence of racist, nationalist and anti-Semitic attitudes. As far as anti-Semitism was concerned, however, Adorno's interpretation revealed the powerful feelings of ambivalence that came together to form a specific syndrome:

> Ambivalent people do not combine anti-Semitism and anti-democratic attitudes, but appeal to democracy in order to argue against the Jews without asking whether their principle of excluding the Jews from the universe of citizens does not constitute a fundamental breach of the democratic principle to which they appeal. Their reaction is: we have nothing against the Jews, we have no wish to persecute them, but they should not do things that conflict with an interest – wholly undefined and arbitrarily selected – of the nation. In particular, they should not have an over-representative share of highly paid and influential jobs. This kind of thinking . . . provides a way out for people caught in a conflict between bad conscience and defensiveness. They can appear to themselves as human, open-minded and unprejudiced, and at the same time they can in practice reconcile any anti-Semitic measure with their own convictions by treating it as an act of compensatory justice, as long as legality is more or less preserved.[69]

At the end of his content analysis, Adorno discussed a group of more open-minded people who were in a position to deal with guilt because they were not the prisoners of stereotyped thinking. 'It is the people who do not repress their consciousness of guilt and have no desperate need to adopt defensive attitudes who are free to speak the truth that not all Germans are anti-Semites.'[70]

A brief glance at the quantitative distribution with which Adorno ended his monograph shows very clearly that, on the guilt question in particular, the number of the open-minded was very much smaller than those who were ambivalent or who made outright negative statements. Roughly one half of the people who spoke up in the discussions rejected any question of their own guilt in the crimes committed during the Hitler dictatorship. This corresponded to their predominantly negative view of the West and their ambivalent attitude towards the young German democracy, which at the time was accepted wholeheartedly only by a minority – a finding that gave few grounds for optimism about the future of a democratic society in Germany.

Even if people were shocked to learn about the atrocities committed in the concentration camps, it was to be hoped that the Germans would recognize their guilt for the murder of six million Jews and realize the dangers of totalitarianism and anti-Semitism. However, Adorno's general diagnosis about the state of public opinion and the mentality of his fellow citizens was more than sceptical. What he diagnosed, in addition to the persistence of authoritarian attitudes, was a loss of autonomy and a general tendency to conform. The *Group Experiment* finally appeared in book form in 1955. Adorno hoped that its findings would have positive effects and he believed that the future of German democracy depended on the nation's willingness to face up to its past. All the greater was his disappointment, indeed indignation, when a negative review appeared in René König's journal, the *Kölner Zeitschrift für Soziologie und Sozialpsychologie*. The review was written by the Hamburg social psychologist Peter R. Hofstätter, and he accused the author of 'Guilt and Defensiveness' of having interpretated the records of the group discussion in a tendentious fashion. Adorno discussed his review in a letter to Franz Böhm, the former rector of Frankfurt University, in January 1957: 'It goes without saying that the entire Hofstätter question has to be seen in a much larger context. . . . It would be necessary to write something about the regressive tendency in the social sciences in Germany. This consists in the way that so-called factual research is increasingly being used as a pretext not to recognize or to talk about the things that hurt. There seems to be a tacit agreement about this among people like Hofstätter, Schelsky, Wurzbacher and a whole host of others, and attacks like the one by Hofstätter are the symptom of a renewed wish to take science in hand once again under the pretext of greater scientific precision.'[71] In his review, Hofstätter had objected that the true aim of the analysis was not to establish the facts but to 'unmask' and 'accuse'. What the Frankfurt authors wanted was to accuse an entire nation and force it 'to repent'. 'But how far can we assume that the majority of the members of a "nation" can be capable of collective self-accusation for years on end? I see scarcely any possibility of a single individual being able to assume the responsibility for the horrors of Auschwitz.'[72] Adorno was given the option of publishing a reply to Hofstätter in the same issue of the journal. René König had invited him to do so having taken a positive view of the *Group Experiment* and having told Adorno as early as May 1954 that he was impressed by both the method and the contents of the study.[73] In his response Adorno did not mince words. To identify defects in society that are also to be found in people's heads and that need to be changed by enlightenment was not a matter of making accusations. Hofstätter's allegation of one-sidedness, in contrast, was nothing but 'an appeal to collective narcissism'. As for his claim that it is too much to expect one individual to come to terms with the entire guilt of the past, Adorno countered with the argument that 'it was the victims who were forced to bear the burden of the horrors of Auschwitz, not the people who did not want to know about it, to their own cost and to the cost of their nation. "The question of guilt was a matter of desperation" for the victims, not for the survivors. It takes some nerve to drown this distinction in a general sea of despair and it is not for nothing that this concept has become so popular. But in the house of the hangman you should not speak of the rope; otherwise, you will open yourself to the suspicion that you are a rancorous person.'[74]

Precisely this was Adorno's own practice, however. Thus in late autumn 1959, he gave a lecture at a conference of the Coordinating Council for Christian–Jewish Cooperation that was devoted to the question: 'The Meaning of Working Through the Past'. The ideas put forward in this talk were subsequently extended in his public lectures on 'Fighting Anti-Semitism Today'[75] and then, in 1966, 'Education after Auschwitz'. By this time, he stood in the spotlight of public affairs. This was a moment when people were once again calling for the restoration of sovereignty for the Federal Republic and when the democratic state and the rule of law were having to prove that they could provide a stable foundation for the new society. It was at this point that the Frankfurt sociologist put his reputation on the line to warn against the danger of the survival of National Socialism. 'I consider the survival of National Socialism *within* democracy to be potentially more menacing than the survival of fascist tendencies *against* democracy.'[76]

What had induced Adorno to sound the alarm about the imminent threat of a relapse into authoritarian modes of reaction was an outbreak of swastika daubing in Cologne during Christmas 1959. This had led to a public debate about the stability or instability of West German democracy.[77] What was striking was the muted nature of the protests against these outrages,[78] while in the press it was the negative impact on foreign opinion that was stressed. The self-image of the homeland of the economic miracle had been tarnished.[79] Given this background, Adorno asked provocatively whether democracy in Germany was any more than a foreign import or a political formation imposed by the victorious Western powers that was accepted in Germany only because it seemed to work and had brought economic prosperity. This economic prosperity supplied the secondary reason for accepting the demands made by democracy, an arrangement that also represented compensation for the damage done to the collective narcissism of the nation. He finally ventured to speculate whether parliamentary democracy might not be regarded as a manifestation of power, a feature that would endear it to a nation traditionally bound to authority. Adorno interpreted this opportunistic attitude towards democracy as a sign that 'democracy has not become naturalized to the point where people truly experience it as their own and see themselves as subjects of the political process. Democracy is perceived as one system among others, as though one could choose from a menu between communism, democracy, fascism and monarchy: but democracy is not identified with the people themselves as the expression of their political maturity. It is appraised according to its success or setbacks, whereby special interests also play a role, rather than as a union of the individual and the collective interests.' The view current at the time that democracy was a political formation that citizens still had to learn was rejected by Adorno as the expression of false consciousness. It was the view of 'people who play up their own naivety and political immaturity in a disingenuous manner'[80] so as not to have to confess their inability to override the limits imposed on their actions by rigid social structures.

Adorno's starting-point in public speeches, in his many radio talks, but also in his seminars and lectures, was the contradiction he diagnosed between a social structure that had frozen into objectivity, on the one hand, and a democracy that was based on self-determination, on the other. It was social circumstances that were the real reason why individual human subjects felt themselves to be dependent and determined by others. A further negative burden was the fact that 'the oft invoked working through of the past . . . was unsuccessful and has degenerated into its own caricature, an empty and cold forgetting.'[81] This explained why democracy in Germany was built upon sand.[82] Burdened by a history they have repressed and by a growing compulsion to adapt, people are forced to 'negate precisely that autonomous subjectivity to which the idea of democracy appeals; they can preserve themselves only if they renounce their self. . . . The necessity of such an adaptation with the given, the status quo, with power as such, creates the potential for totalitarianism.'[83]

This social diagnosis of the lethal interaction between historical blindness, the compulsion to adapt to existing social conditions and the heteronomy of the subject was a theme on which Adorno played many variations. At the same time, he was well aware that his interpretation consciously overemphasized the sombre side. Thus in the first half of the 1960s, at a time when in Germany the whole process of working through the past slowly and hesitantly began to gather momentum with the Eichmann trial in Israel and the Auschwitz trials in Frankfurt, he practised sociology as a mode of enlightenment directed at individuals and groups. 'A working through of the past understood as enlightenment is essentially . . . a turn towards the subject, the reinforcement of a person's self-consciousness and hence also of his self.'[84] This 'turn towards the subject' was the practical goal for Adorno's conception of a critical sociology. But he stressed that this subjective enlightenment had its limits since the politically dangerous potential of fascism had its roots in social conditions, social pressure and its 'objective force'. It is certain, Adorno concluded, that the real consequences of the catastrophic policies of fascism were still present. 'Despite all the psychological repression, Stalingrad and the night bombings are not so forgotten that everyone cannot be made to understand the connection between the revival of a politics that led to them and the prospect of a third Punic war. Even if this succeeds, the danger will still exist. The past will have been worked through only when the causes of what happened then have been eliminated.'[85]

By attempting to keep alive an awareness of 'the causes of past events', both in the university and as a public intellectual, Adorno made a significant contribution to raising consciousness about the function of a democracy. His efforts prepared the way for the idea that a democratic system was a form of political rule that is based on many assumptions that call for the autonomous involvement of mature adults. Linked with this was the question of the social conditions in which democracy in West Germany might be expected to achieve stability and continuity. At the same time, his criticism of the apolitical attitudes of the German population helped launch a public discussion of the importance of the values implicit in a democratic constitution. He emphasized the idea of political criticism since, in Adorno's understanding of democracy, the intellectual practice of criticism was a defining element. Criticism was an essential component of all democracy; democracy was in fact to be defined by criticism. Freedom as self-determining action and the recognition of a plurality of views are the preconditions for a criticism that is effective in practice.[86] Adorno belonged to that stratum of West German intellectuals consisting of scientists, artists, writers and politicians who had unleashed a process of moral reflection and sustained it with their arguments. In this way they contributed to what might be called a 'second', 'intellectual' founding of the republic.[87] The commitment that Adorno displayed in public had an impact on his exposed position as a cultural and social critic: he came to be perceived as a moral authority. As a former émigré and an independent Jewish intellectual, he acquired a credibility that was vouchsafed to very few other personalities in cultural life. When he commented on topical issues he tended to exaggerate for polemical purposes, just as he was ready to pick a quarrel when the occasion presented itself. In this way, by what he himself called a process of *Interventions*, he became an influential factor in stimulating the formation of public opinion.[88]

The crisis of the subject: self-preservation without a self

> Today self-consciousness no longer means anything but reflection on the ego as embarrassment, as realization of impotence: knowing that one is nothing.[89]

A central feature of bourgeois self-understanding is the idea of man as an autonomous subject. From Adorno's sociological perspective the relation between individual and society, and hence between the disciplines of psychology and sociology, had necessarily to become the focus of attention. The fact, therefore, that in spring 1956 the Institute of Social Research took the lead in a number of activities arising from the centenary of Sigmund Freud was very much in tune with his own inclinations. A commemorative ceremony followed by a lecture series provided the opportunity to clarify the scientific status of psychoanalysis. In particular, Adorno believed that the concept of the individual was in need of fundamental revision. He thought this necessary because the concept of the individual formed the outer limit of his own theory of society. He understood individuality, on the one hand, in the sense of self-determining active subjects. On the other hand, he used the concept descriptively, in order to describe changes in social character. The lectures took place over a period of two months in Frankfurt and Heidelberg, but even though the topic was close to his heart, he was not one of the speakers. He will not have been too disappointed, however, since he was still on his travels. A month before the ceremony he spent a week in Vienna where, among others, he met Helene Berg. He had wanted also to go to Oldenburg to see the much praised production of Berg's *Wozzeck*, but this too proved impossible.

As for the lecture series on Freud, Adorno made way on this occasion for Herbert Marcuse. Marcuse gave two lectures, on 'The Theory of the Instincts and Freedom' and 'The Idea of Freedom in the Light of Psychoanalysis', and it was through these lectures that he first made a name for himself in postwar Germany. Adorno took a back seat on this occasion in part because he had already published his essay 'On the Relationship between Sociology and Psychology' in *Sociologica*, the Horkheimer *Festschrift*. So he confined his efforts to working on the volume in which the lectures were published, *Freud in der Gegenwart*, which appeared in the *Frankfurter Beiträge zur Soziologie*. Nevertheless, he remained one of the initiators of the lecture series and also of the centennial ceremony in the main lecture theatre of Frankfurt University, which was attended by the federal president, Theodor Heuss, and also the prime minister of Hessen, Georg-August Zinn. In addition to Horkheimer, the participants in the lecture series included Alexander Mitscherlich and Erik Erikson, who talked about psychoanalysis as a form of therapy and the theory of the unconscious. Adorno described the event to Friedrich Hacker, who had tormented him in Beverly Hills, but with whom he still kept in touch. He reported that the lecture series organized by the institute had been a huge success. 'The impact was very great and, without boasting too much, I believe that we have finally succeeded in breaking through the mechanism of repression that has surrounded Freud in Germany and Austria and has lasted well beyond the demise of Hitler.'[90] Adorno had no need to fear that his assessment of psychoanalysis as a critical theory of the subject or his legitimately claimed competence in these matters would fail him. The preface to the collected lectures, *Freud in der Gegenwart*, clearly bore his imprint, insisting on the need to bring socio-psychological research up to date. 'If, twenty-five years ago, the aim of research was to investigate the manner in which social coercion extended into the most subtle ramifications of the individual human psyche which had hitherto imagined that it existed for itself alone and belonged to itself alone, then, today, reflections on psycho-social mechanisms are frequently used to deflect attention from the power of society. Difficulties and conflicts of the present are played down once they are reduced directly to individual human beings, to merely internal processes. This explains why a synthesis of sociology and psychology seems less appropriate to us at the moment than sustained, independent work in both disciplines.'[91] Adorno had already advanced this argument in his essay 'On the Relationship between Sociology and Psychology', although this was one of the texts he was not entirely happy with after publication. In October, he confessed to Alfred Andersch, to whom he nevertheless sent a copy, that he was not satisfied with the piece; it was one of his 'failed efforts'.[92]

The theme of this failed effort was his assertion of the end of individuality in modern society.[93] This assertion was linked to an older essay on 'Psychoanalysis Revised' that he had given as a paper to the Psychoanalytical Society in San Francisco.[94] His – admittedly fitful – preoccupation with the topic of the transformations of the self under the growing social pressure to conform in fact dates from that early period.

At around this time, Adorno collected a number of reflections under the heading 'Notes on the New Anthropology'.[95] Some of these were now incorporated into the aphorisms in *Minima Moralia*.[96] He returned to these in the early 1950s when he was framing his objections to revisionist tendencies in psychoanalysis and was himself proposing changes in socio-psychological research: 'Our descriptions of early childhood behaviour must inevitably become much more precise and discriminating than hitherto if we are to gain access from the inside to the substratum at which psychoanalytical anamnesis is aimed.'[97] Adorno's general diagnosis of the subject without a self went far beyond his disagreement with the ego-psychology of Erich Fromm and Karen Horney. His observations dated from the last years of his stay in America. At that time, he had doubts about the reduction of psychoanalysis to a therapeutic procedure. But he also went far beyond this. From the vantage point of sociology, he noted the elimination of the internal imagos of the father and mother and their replacement by direct social power. There no longer was an unconscious, and repression too had become superfluous. The Freudian censor was now replaced by defiance and universal hostility. The Oedipus complex had become redundant in the new anthropology and, in the absence of an ego, the category of egoism lost all meaning as well. The image of the body had become desexualized, 'either because of the cult of functioning . . . as such or because of the way in which sexuality had been liberated, which meant that the withdrawal of resistance had led to the loss of pleasure.'[98]

Adorno's critical reflections on the subject are to be found in many places in his cultural criticism and his sociological writings. They must be regarded as a central feature of his analysis of the age. For he proceeded from the assumption that you can read off the state of society as a whole from what you can discover about individual living beings. From this vantage point, Adorno reconstructed the individual as a historical form of the subject that owed its existence to the process of emancipation of bourgeois society. The individual, he explained in September 1953 in the *Darmstädter Gespräche* on 'Individual and Organization', 'scarcely extends back beyond Montaigne or Hamlet, certainly no further than the early Italian Renaissance'.[99] This view of the historical origins of autonomous subjectivity supplied Adorno with a normative reference point for his critique of the impotence of the individual in the administered world, but he did not confine himself to a confrontation between the abstract idea and the sobering reality.[100] Instead, he constructed his critique of the subject as a critique of society that started out from the predominance of social conditions, the network of social functions, over human beings. The relationship between individual and society was like the negative identity of universal and particular. In his famous radio debate with Arnold Gehlen in 1965 he argued that this was neither an anthropological constant nor a historical necessity, but the product of a historical and social development. Since 'man is shaped by history, and that means by society, down to the innermost depths of his psyche', it follows that the divergence of individual and society must be capable of an explanation in social terms.'[101] And this explanation must also hold good for the paradox that modern industrial societies have witnessed a process of growing individualization that leaves less and less room for individualism, difference and alterity. Here he takes up an idea he had already proposed in the *Minima Moralia*: 'In the midst of standardized, organized human units the individual persists. He is even protected and gaining monopoly value. But he is in reality no more than the mere function of his own uniqueness, an exhibition piece.'[102] Adorno now gave this critical perspective a radical turn by arguing that the dominant social mechanisms of integration had undermined the individual. He maintained that the socially prescribed maxim of the confident, well-integrated person was unacceptable because 'it requires of the individual that balancing of forces that does not exist in society as it is at present constituted.'[103] At the end of this essay, 'On the Relations between Sociology and Psychology', Adorno summed up his thesis of the demise of the individual in a hazardous conclusion. He not only claimed that man had been perverted into a 'hideous caricature',[104] but surmised that a kind of alliance had been formed between the objectively repressive society and the psychological system of the unconscious. As he put it, 'the victory of the id over the ego' is in tune with 'the triumph of society over the individual'.[105]

This extreme critique of social change did not prevent him from postulating as the end point of his theory that 'the trace of humanity seems to persist only in the individual in his decline'.[106] This utopian streak was the background for his emphatic rejoinder to Arnold Gehlen's pessimistic anthropology. In their radio debate in 1965, Adorno stated bluntly: 'I have a conception of objective happiness and objective despair, and I would say that, as long as ... people are not required to assume complete responsibility and self-determination, their entire well-being and happiness in this world is an illusion. A bubble that at some point will burst. And when it bursts this will have terrible consequences.'[107] Gehlen immediately accused Adorno of reverting to an irresponsible idealism, while for his part Adorno insisted materialistically on the horizon of possibilities that would open up once human beings no longer had to suffer from 'the overpowering organization of the world'. For what would drive people to the relief from institutional burdens postulated by Gehlen was 'precisely the strains ... imposed on them by institutions'.[108] In this way Adorno was able to hold fast to his belief in the subject's capacity for autonomous action even at the point where his critique of society was at its most stringent. It followed from this that reification must have its limits. For only if Adorno believed that there were limits to the process by which difference was brought into line with eternal sameness, could non-identity, the central concept of *Negative Dialectics*, have a proper foundation.[109] Thus he did not doubt that the subject 'resisted the societal spell with forces mobilized from the stratum in which the principle of individuality which enabled civilization to prevail, was able to assert itself against the process of civilization that was liquidating it.'[110] The thesis that 'societalization finds its limits in the subject'[111] was one Adorno defended explicitly at the end of a lively debate with Alexander Mitscherlich in early November 1965 in an internal conference of the German Sociology Society. Adorno took the opportunity to clarify his diagnosis of the total impotence of the individual by placing the emphasis on the latter's potential for freedom. This meant that human subjects were by no means condemned to utter impotence by the constraints of society. He put it succinctly: 'Critique of the individual does not mean the abolition of the individual.'[112] A few years later, he would point to the example of the student movement as proof that the forces of resistance can in fact be mobilized within individuals.[113] And as far as the masses of the population were concerned, he diagnosed 'a double, self-contradictory consciousness'.[114]

At the end of May 1969, in one of the last lectures before his death, Adorno stressed that, 'apparently, the integration of consciousness and free time has not yet wholly succeeded.' He refers to 'the real interests of individuals' as the disruptive factor. They are still 'strong enough to resist, up to a point, their total appropriation. This would accord with the societal prognosis that a society whose fundamental contradictions persist undiminished cannot be totally integrated into consciousness.'[115] For this reason, the complexity of the social system appears as no more than a veil. 'In many respects ... society has become more transparent than ever before. If insight depended on nothing but the functional state of society, then it would be possible for the proverbial man on the Clapham omnibus to understand how it works today.'[116]

The purpose of life: understanding the language of music

Musicians are usually truants from maths classes; it would be a terrible fate for them to end up in the hands of the maths teacher after all.[117]

Even apart from his activities as a philosopher and sociologist, Adorno's influence in the late 1950s was not confined to a literary public. He also had a growing impact on musical life in West Germany. The year after his second return to Frankfurt, he had again taken part in the Summer Courses for New Music in Kranichstein near Darmstadt, thus continuing the work he had done there in 1950 and 1951.[118] In 1951 he had the opportunity to make the acquaintance of the Dutchman Karel Goeyvaerts, the pioneering exponent of serial music at the time. This was an aspect of the musical avant-garde that was soon to become the subject of passionate controversy. In July of the same year, the premiere took place of Adorno's *Four Songs to Poems by Stefan George for Voice and Piano*, op. 7. The composer accompanied the soprano Ilona Steingruber on the piano.

At the invitation of Wolfgang Steinecke, he then conducted six seminars on the topic of 'New Music and Interpretation', jointly with Eduard Steuermann and Rudolf Kolisch, the 'honorary old gentlemen'.[119] Adorno began with an introductory lecture in which he explained the relation of modern music to the musical tradition and that in his view its performance should be determined by its objective content. These ideas were directly linked to his theory of musical reproduction.[120] In the course of discussions with Kolisch about the seminar on music theory, he stated that what was crucial was 'to make clear to students what a structurally meaningful interpretation is. I imagined that I could make a kind of introductory talk out of my extremely numerous notes on the theory of musical reproduction which we could follow up with Kolisch and Steuermann giving practical illustrations.'[121]

Kranichstein was the forum for modern music that had existed since 1946. Adorno had supported it energetically in public since 1952 and he had defended it against attack.[122] There he saw himself not just as a theoretician, but also as a practical, active composer. Indeed, as the singer Carla Henius reported, he felt he was a 'legitimate musician'.[123] In fact, if the summer courses became the focal point of new music, this was in great measure his doing. He was particularly keen to be invited by Steinecke in his capacity as a composer and as the author of *The Philosophy of Modern Music*, and Steinecke did in fact invite him regularly up to 1958. Adorno had a talent for defending the cause of musical truth with passion. He was a powerful advocate both of free atonality as the climax of Western music and of the Second Viennese School as opposed to other trends. This led to controversy between the Viennese school and the Darmstadt school, which consisted of the younger generation of composers such as Pierre Boulez, Karlheinz Stockhausen,

Karel Goeyvaerts, Luciano Berio, and Gottfried Michael König. An initial confrontation was unleashed by Adorno's lecture that he gave on 'The Ageing of the New Music' in April 1954 during a festival for new music, and which was later broadcast on the radio. It created something of a sensation among members of the musical avant-garde. In May he published the lecture in the cultural magazine *Der Monat* and then included it in the volume of essays *Dissonances: Music in the Administered World*, that was published a year later. He argued there that the achievements of freedom in music that were owed primarily to atonality were being restricted by serialism much as they had been earlier on by twelve-tone music. Furthermore, he retained his belief in the creative power of composers and on the idea of music as determined by time and process, reproving 'the imitators of modernity' for having 'forgotten what the whole thing was supposed to be about'. Their actions would lead to a growing neutralization and levelling down of the material, and to a decrease in the 'quality, the authoritative nature of musical works'.[124]

Adorno was not unaware that this lecture brought him applause from the wrong camp. In the first edition of *Dissonances*, he commented: 'The author feels no need to defend himself from the misuse of his reflections for restorative purposes. No aspect of dialectical thought is safe from such misuse. It can only be met . . . by the force with which one puts one's case.'[125] He developed his critique of serialism – 'Webern on the Wurlitzer Organ'[126] – in his contribution to the summer course in 1955. There Adorno gave three lectures with the title 'The Young Schoenberg', which he used in order to attack serial and electronic music.[127] This he thought was necessary in order to counter the opposition in Kranichstein and the danger of sectarianism on the part of the group he described in a letter to Kolisch as 'twelve-tone hotheads', who 'really would like to follow Boulez's lead and . . . abolish music in favour of stubborn rationalization.'[128] The high point of this debate came with an essay by the music theorist Heinz-Klaus Metzger,[129] which he had published in *Die Reihe* in 1958 with the title 'The Ageing of the Philosophy of New Music'. Over twenty years later, Metzger admitted that Adorno had been in the right. 'He had recognized the ageing process in the new music much sooner than I, at a time when the symptoms were not even visible. With hindsight, Adorno's view turned out to be prophetic.'[130]

In musical matters, Adorno was close not only to Kolisch, but also to Eduard Steuermann, his former piano teacher, with whom he had enjoyed a close friendship since 1925. From the beginning of the 1960s, Steuermann had distanced himself from the Darmstadt summer courses, partly for health reasons and partly from disagreement on musical matters. When Adorno, who had been caught up in a whirlwind of lectures, learnt that his old friend had died in New York on 11 November 1964, the news came as 'an indescribable blow'. It had affected him, he wrote to Carla Henius, as deeply as Benjamin's suicide.[131]

Adorno's importance as a philosopher of music showed itself in the fact that he analysed not just the works of the avant-garde and their implications, but also the works of composers of the classical and late romantic tradition, such as Beethoven and Mahler. Admittedly, as far as Beethoven was concerned, he did not get further than a large number of handwritten sketches in a variety of notebooks.[132] But taken together, these fragments provided sufficient material for a fairly bulky volume that appeared posthumously, dealing with Beethoven as the composer of the bourgeoisie as it emancipated itself and achieved hegemony. In the dynamics of Beethoven's music could be seen, in Adorno's view, the productive energies of this bourgeois society, with its utopian hopes for a new world. At the same time, it is informed by 'the conviction that the self-reproduction of society as a self-identical entity is not enough, indeed that it is false.'[133] With Beethoven's ascetic restraint towards spontaneous inspiration, 'this music is precisely the way to elude reification. Beethoven, the master of positive negation: discard, that you may acquire.'[134]

Elsewhere in his anthology of provisional notes, in his comments on the *Eroica*, Adorno notes:

> An expression of *pride*, in that one is allowed to be present at such an event, to be its witness; for example, in the first movements of the E flat major Piano Concerto and of the *Eroica*. 'Exaltation.' How far this is the *effect* of the composition – a joy which rivets the listener's attention to the dialectical logic – and how far the *expression* creates an illusion of such joy, rests on a knife's edge. Expression is a prefiguration of mass culture, which celebrates its own triumphs. This is the negative moment of Beethoven's 'mastery of the material', his ostentation. This is one of the points which criticism can engage.[135]

As with the Beethoven fragments, whose philosophical contents derived from a host of analyses of individual compositions, the book on Gustav Mahler was a study of the composer's work. When it appeared in 1960 as volume 61 in the Bibliothek Suhrkamp, Adorno made clear from the outset what he aimed at: not to portray the composer's life, his personality and the innermost motives behind his music, but to approach the works through the 'constellation of . . . individual analyses' of his compositions.[136] To probe Mahler's subjective intentions was a matter of secondary importance since intentions could rarely be elicited. Instead, the artist should be regarded as 'the executive organ' of 'the objective logic of the art-work'.[137]

Apart from this approach, a central pillar of Adorno's view of art, the Mahler book showed once again that Adorno thought of his texts as literature even when they consisted at least in part of technical analyses. What he said of 'decent prose' in general was to be true of this book, which was particularly rich in metaphors, for example, his statement that such prose resembles the candle 'that is lit at both ends. Where the two flames meet, the title must flare up.'[138] In this case: *Mahler: A Musical Physiognomy.*[139]

Adorno called his Mahler monograph his 'jungle book'; never before had he 'known so little' about what he had created through his writing.[140] This statement referred less to the fact that he had written it under great time pressure – he had retreated in spring to the Bad Hotel in Überlingen on Lake Constance – than that this was a highly personal piece of work in tone and in the vividness of his style.[141] He told Arnold Gehlen that this book was far less sociological than others of his.[142] His aesthetic approach became apparent in his linguistic inventiveness, as for example when he remarks that the epic nature of Mahler's symphonies reminds him of 'the long gaze of yearning' of Proust's *A la recherche*: 'In both, unfettered joy and unfettered melancholy perform their charade; in the prohibition of the images of hope, hope has its last dwelling-place. This place is in both, however, the strength to name the forgotten that is concealed in the stuff of experience. Like Proust, Mahler rescued his idea from childhood.'[143] This interpretation reveals the closeness of Adorno's childhood memories to those of Proust, but also of Mahler, since his memories of music-making in childhood were a determining factor that reverberated even in his theoretical texts.[144]

Adorno confined his discussion chiefly to the nine great symphonies and some of the songs. Tracing out 'the mimetic gesture of the music', he analysed in particular the use of variation, the popular tone, and the Chinese element in *Das Lied von der Erde*. It was this work above all that attracted Adorno's physiognomical gaze. This work, and the Ninth Symphony even more, inspired the comment that on this music 'lies beauty as the reflection of past hope, which fills the dying eye until it is frozen below the flakes of unbound space. The moment of delight before such beauty dares to withstand its abandonment to disenchanted nature. That metaphysics is no longer possible becomes the ultimate metaphysics.'[145] What Adorno highlighted as the chief characteristic of Mahler's musical idiom was his use of familiar musical materials whose traditional meaning was then fractured. 'Each Mahlerian symphony asks how, from the ruins of the musical objective world, a living totality can arise.'[146] At the same time, the composer did not create the illusion of reconciliation, preferring instead to dismiss the principle of 'coherence or rightness' (*Stimmigkeit*), and thus to end up indicting the course of the world. Collapse appears as 'negative fulfilment', as truth. Mahler's 'music is a plea for peasant cunning against the overlords, for those who desert their marriages, for outsiders, the persecuted and incarcerated, starving children, forlorn hopes. The term socialist realism would fit only Mahler if it were not so depraved by domination. . . . Berg is the legitimate heir of this spirit.'[147] The element of expression in Mahler's music is true in its moments of rupture. It draws its force from unconscious experiences 'that come into the music from its remotest past, before the phase of rationality and unambiguous significance.'[148] Adorno describes this as the expression of negativity that in Mahler 'has become a purely compositional category: through the banal that declares itself banal; through a lachrymose sentimentality that tears the mask from its own wretchedness.'[149]

By way of illustrating Mahler's polyvalent parody and ambiguity, Adorno referred to the bells at the start of the Fourth Symphony, which he interpreted as 'fool's bells' which, 'without saying it, say: None of what you now hear is true.'[150] Even if he had reservations about the Rondo finale in the Seventh Symphony because it appeared over-theatrical, and the Fourth Symphony which he condemned as a largely unsuccessful revival of the cultic, his discussions as a whole sought to prove that the new music of the Second Viennese School emerged from Mahler's music in a process of dialectical reversal. Mahler, he claimed, had shaped his tonal chords as the 'cryptograms of modernity', as the 'guardians of absolute dissonance'.[151]

Following his controversies with the serialists and post-serialists, Adorno attempted to formulate his definitive attitude towards the musical avant-garde. This was around a year after the appearance of his successful book on Mahler and the well-received centenary address. He now gave a lecture on the subject at the Kranichstein Summer Course for New Music, from which he had been absent since his lecture in 1957. He had been invited once again by Wolfgang Steinecke and took the opportunity in September 1961 to give a programmatic talk that was constructive in the best sense of the word. In it he gave a detailed account of the project of an informal music that he understood as the logical development of free atonality. Adorno did not shrink from criticizing his own past statements, his earlier response to electronic experiments:

In Kranichstein, I once accused a composition, which in intention at least had managed to unify all possible parameters, of vague-ness in its musical language. Where, I asked, was the antecedent, and where the consequent? This criticism has now to be modified. Contemporary music cannot be forced into such apparently uni-versal categories as 'antecedent' and 'consequent', as if they were unalterable. It is nowhere laid down that modern music must *a priori* contain such elements of the tradition as tension and resolu-tion, continuation, development, contrast and reassertion; all the less since memories of all that are the frequent cause of crude inconsistencies in the new material and the need to correct these is itself a motive force in modern music.[152]

Following this act of self-criticism as well as a revision of the concept of the composing subject, on the one hand, and the musical material, on the other, Adorno (in agreement with Metzger's 'aserial music') called for what for the first time he termed *musique informelle*. By this he understood a further step towards musical emancipation.[153] He conceived of a future in which the avant-garde would be overtaken by a more precisely defined practice of absolute freedom. He wished to liberate composers from traditional forms, and aimed at the autonomous shaping of all musical parameters. He called for a mode of composition at the most advanced level of current musical material, an absolutely autonomous art, distinguished by its ability 'really and truly to be what it is, without the ideological pretence of being something else. Or rather, to admit frankly the fact of non-identity and to follow through its logic to the end.'[154]

Adorno wished for musical freedom instead of a flight into the adventitious, which appeared to him, as to György Ligeti, as absolute determination. In contrast, an aleatory approach to music freed from the constraints of musical form leads to a static cul de sac. Adorno issued an explicit warning in his Kranichstein lecture: 'I am unable to discern any guarantee of truth in this eternal recurrence of the need for an order based on known systems; on the contrary, they seem rather to be the symptom of perennial weakness.'[155] The composer must free himself from the fear that freedom will lead to chaos by placing his trust in the reflective impulses of an informal music.

By testing out his own musical ideal in the Kranichstein lecture, and by attempting to make his own conception of future composition sound plausible, Adorno opened the door to a highly relevant post-avant-garde form of music, one that would avoid the usual pitfalls of affirmation and escapism. 'In a *musique informelle* the deformation of rationalism which exists today would be abolished and converted to a true rationality. . . . *Musique informelle* would be music in which the ear can hear live from the material what has become of it. . . . The musicality which a *musique informelle* would require for this would both carry the constituents of the old music in itself, but would also recoil from the demands of the conventions.'[156] Adorno's programme contains the call for composers to give shape to difference, for example the difference between construction and expression, between repetition and variation, in order to achieve mediation between the extremes. If in the course of his lecture he kept returning to the freedom to shape the composition, he did so not with the 'emphasis of the aesthetician of expression',[157] but so as to procure for the artist the breathing space he needs if he is to liberate himself from the preforming authority of a reified material and the internalized tendency to revert to conventional values. Admittedly, this freedom should also imply the integration of tradition by sublating it, as Adorno had shown in his analysis of Mahler. Elsewhere, he argued that the traditional tools of music should not be restored but that instead 'equivalents should be developed to suit the new materials. . . . The secret of composition is the energy which moulds the material in a process of progressively greater appropriateness.'[158]

Adorno had attempted to provide examples of how this mystery of integrating tradition by sublating it is to be solved, apart from in his book on Mahler. His book on *Alban Berg: Master of the Smallest Link*, which he wrote barely a year before his death, contained a further illustration of how a composer can 'elevate what was at one time incidental and conventional to fundamental significance and, through consistent use, transform it into the means by which – with inexorable tenderness – convention is destroyed.'[159]

Right living? Places, people, friendships

Adorno made no secret of the fact that certain places held a special importance for him. This included the little Bavarian town of Amorbach, barely two hours distant from Frankfurt by train. As a child, he had gone there regularly with his family. They always stayed in the same room, number 3, in the Posthouse Inn, which had been in the possession of the Spoerer family since 1772. The Wiesengrund family had long since developed ties of friendship with the Spoerers.[160] Oscar Wiesengrund supplied the hotel with his own wines from the Palatinate and the Rheingau. The hotel itself had a kitchen that tried to satisfy the elevated culinary demands of an urban clientele like the Wiesengrunds. Here Adorno was first introduced to what would become favourite dishes, such as Odenwald trout fried in butter or roast venison with cranberries. On his walks in the nearby forests, he would come face to face with the 'primeval world of Siegfried', who 'was said to have been killed there'. And the sound of the ferry over the Main 'that you have to take in order to reach . . . Engelberg Monastery' conveys the feeling of a history thousands of years old. Hiking from Amorbach via Reuenthal and Monbrunn to Miltenberg, he imagined himself retracing the footsteps of Neidhard, who is said to have had his home there.[161]

And lastly, he recalls the strikingly eccentric figure of the man in the Posthouse Inn, 'drinking his pint, with a beard and strange attire . . . as if he had come straight from the Peasants' War about which I knew from the memoirs of Gottfried von Berlichingen that I had acquired in the little Reclam edition from the automatic vending machine in Miltenberg Station.'[162] Amorbach was his 'Combray' from Proust's *A la recherche du temps perdu*, the book which according to Adorno was 'the autobiography of every individual'.[163] Like Proust, he knew about the happiness felt by an adult when he hears someone mention the names of the villages of his childhood. 'One thinks that going there would bring fulfilment, as if there were such a thing. Being really there makes the promise recede like a rainbow.' And yet, as Adorno continues in *Negative Dialectics*, 'to the child it is self-evident that what delights him in his favourite village is found only there and nowhere else. He is mistaken; but his mistake creates the model of experience of a concept that will end up as the concept of the thing itself, not as a poor abstraction from things.'[164]

Adorno did not fail to introduce people he loved to his 'favourite little town' and its surroundings. At the end of the 1920s he was there with Gretel, and also with Kracauer, Löwenthal and Hermann Grab. In the 1950s he would often spend Sundays or holidays in the Odenwald, sometimes travelling in his own car, accompanied by the architect Ferdinand Kramer and the latter's second wife, Lore.[165]

As late as the beginning of 1968 Adorno made vigorous representations to the town council, who had plans to build in Amorbach and modernize it, urging them to preserve its unique squares and streets. He kept in contact with the family who owned the Posthouse as well as with Berthold Bührer, the town's director of church music, whom he had known since childhood from playing in the family sawmill. In a letter of January 1968 he told Berthold Bührer how pleased he was that Bührer was now in charge of the organ in the church and hoped that he would play Bach for him when he next came to Amorbach.[166]

Vienna was another city of which he had happy memories. It reminded him of Alban Berg and the stimulating months they had spent together. Adorno had lived in the Austrian metropolis with its splendid feudal buildings in 1925, his first lengthy separation from his family in Frankfurt, the first time he had to make his own way. It was here that he met Arnold Schoenberg and Anton Webern, attended the public readings of Karl Kraus, was introduced to Alma Mahler, made friends with Soma Morgenstern and met Hermann Grab. It is no wonder that, after his return from emigration, Adorno visited Vienna almost every year, attempting to combine private and professional interests. He tried to cultivate relations with Helene Berg, so far as was possible, strengthened his relationship with Lotte Tobisch, the Burgtheater actress, and became friendly with Andreas Razumovsky, who was later to become the music critic of the *Frankfurter Allgemeine Zeitung*. Razumovsky was a direct descendant of the Russian ambassador in Vienna who had been Beethoven's patron.[167] Even in the 1950s and 1960s Adorno remained fascinated by the easy-going Viennese manner, as well as by the Viennese love of the macabre. 'Anyone who does not take grave matters too much to heart will be happy to give grave matters a free rein. In this respect the spirit of the city is inexhaustibly creative. A few years ago a man stabbed a ballet student to death in the labyrinth passages of the Opera House. His name was Weinwurm' (Weeping worm).[168]

For Adorno, Vienna was in the first place the city of great music and the city with the famous Opera House that he liked so much to patronize during his visits. 'When you enter the Opera House . . . you still have something of the feeling of a child longing for Christmas. This Opera House radiates a suggestive power that despite everything promises something extreme. . . . Added to this is its unimpaired international prestige, but also the fact that even the city's own inhabitants still revere its nimbus. . . . Even the notorious gossip that is rife in Viennese music-ality is not completely unproductive.'[169] He liked the realistic setting for the production of *The Bartered Bride* with the much-admired soprano Irmgard Seefried even though it crossed the boundary to kitsch. 'The images of the village had discovered the secret of stage scenery as a form: the ability through yearning to bring things that are far distant right up close, as if one were inside them, without diminishing the aura of distance.'[170] He also liked Caspar Neher's set for a production of *Wozzeck* and he noted with pleasure that the Viennese audience was now prepared to applaud Berg's music.

Adorno was in contact with Egon Hilbert, the director of the Opera. Hilbert was opposed to the so-called Karajan clique and Adorno was able to put to him his proposals for the reform of the Opera. At a panel debate in May 1966 in the Palais Palffy he developed his ideas on 'Stagione or Ensemble Opera', filling them out two years later in a lecture. His ideas on reform amounted to liberating opera both from the standard repertoire and the pomp of the star cult, the famous con-ductors and soloists. 'The stuffy, sloppy nature of the repertoire opera which Gustav Mahler desperately battled to change has become in-creasingly prevalent in the meantime. You only have to attend a normal performance anywhere in the world . . . to see how dreary and god-forsaken it all looks.'[171] In contrast, he lambasted the stagione opera because of its fixation with top performances, because of its mistaken ambition to present 'only the most beautiful voices in the world', and because its ideology of 'markets' and 'customers' made it put 'pre-artistic, culinary, sensuous aspects of opera before everything else'.[172] The town and its surroundings which reminded Adorno of 'the South Germany of my childhood'[173] not only had an incomparable cultural aura, but for Adorno it also had its culinary attractions, either in the various coffeehouses or in such restaurants as the Hotel Sacher, one of the best addresses for Austrian boiled fillet of beef (*Tafelspitz*) with potatoes and horseradish. There, 'among the habitués and their acquaintances you find that easy communication that otherwise seems natural only on the stage. . . . It is seldom that you dine there without meeting someone you know or you see people meeting up with each other, say, after the opera.'[174] One of the delightful aspects of the city was the ease with which one could associate with the nobility, particu-larly for Adorno, who had a foible for the aristocracy: 'What is attract-ive about the aristocracy and what attracts some of them to intellectuals is almost tautologically simple: the fact that they are not bourgeois. The conduct of their lives is not in thrall to the principle of exchange, and the more discriminating of them maintain a freedom from the coercion of purposes and practical advantage that is achieved by few others.'[175]

From Vienna Adorno sometimes travelled on towards the south, beyond the Alps, where there were places and landscapes in which he felt happy. These included Tuscany, with its vineyards and cypresses, pines and olive trees, and cities, especially Lucca and Florence with their churches and palaces, but also Rome. In these southerly regions, to which Adorno regularly travelled from the mid-1950s, he liked the fact that life took place in the streets and that the streets had become interiors. 'The shop windows . . . seem to contain treasures. They are at the disposal of whoever passes by.'[176] And even the autostrada, lined by countless advertisements, cannot spoil the beauty of the Tuscan landscape.

Lastly, Adorno was enchanted by the bizarre mountain landscape and the lakes of the Upper Engadine. Adorno and his wife were particularly fond of the small resort of Sils Maria, situated between the fashionable St Moritz and the Maloja Pass, with the Waldhaus and its grand hotel style. Sils Maria had become especially well known among intellectuals because of Friedrich Nietzsche. He had spent his summers between 1881 and 1888 in this 'loveliest corner of the earth', where he relaxed, went on long walks, and wrote parts of *Thus Spoke Zarathustra*.[177]

The village lies at a height of around 1800 metres with extensive views over a huge plain to the south. It contains barely more than forty houses, but its previous visitors include Marcel Proust, Hermann Hesse, Rainer Maria Rilke, Karl Kraus and Ernst Robert Curtius. And when Adorno and his wife entered their names in the register of the unostentatiously elegant Hotel Waldhaus, they would have seen a whole host of well-known names of musicians, writers and other intellectuals, including Thomas Mann, Georg Solti, Otto Klemperer, Bruno Walter, Wilhelm Backhaus, Wilhelm Kempff, Alexander Mitscherlich and Siegfried Unseld. During the four-week-long summer vacations in Sils Maria the Adornos met literary scholars such as Peter Szondi and Hans Mayer, philosophers such as Helmuth Plessner, Karl Löwith and Herbert Marcuse or the Burgtheater actress Lotte Tobisch. So there were plenty of opportunities for evening conversations over a bottle of Veltliner. Adorno, particularly at times when he was not under excessive work pressure, was capable of displaying a 'carefree lightheartedness', as Lotte Tobisch and others have testified.[178] The conversations about music, literature and philosophy were continued during the walks through Val Fex to the Chasté peninsula, to the hamlet of Isloa situated directly on Lake Sils and on to the Laret Heights: 'From the heights the villages look as if they had been deposited from above by light fingers, as if they were moveable and without firm foundations. This makes them look like toys that promise happiness to those with giant imaginations: it is as if one could do with them as one wished. Our hotel, however, with its disproportionate dimensions, is one of the tiny buildings crowned with battlements like those in childhood that used to adorn the tunnels through which the toy railway roared. Now, at long last, one has the chance to enter them and see what is inside.'[179]

Of course, Adorno also tried to find traces of Nietzsche in the old visitors' book. His name was listed in the Pensiun Privata. When Adorno finally learnt that Christian Zuan, the senior manager of the local grocer's shop, had as a child known Nietzsche, he went with Herbert Marcuse to visit Zuan, who was by then, the early 1960s, into his nineties. 'We were given a warm welcome in a kind of private office. In fact Mr Zuan had a good memory. When we pressed him he told us that Nietzsche used to carry a red parasol, regardless of whether it was raining or sunny – presumably to provide some protection for his headaches. A gang of children, including Zuan, amused themselves smuggling stones into the closed parasol so that they all fell on his head when he opened it up. He would then chase after them, waving the parasol and uttering threats, but he never caught them. What a terrible situation for the suffering man, we thought, vainly pursuing his tormentors and perhaps even thinking they were in the right after all, because they represented life as opposed to mind.'[180]

In August 1959, Adorno should have met the poet Paul Celan in Sils Maria. The meeting had been arranged by Peter Szondi, who knew both men well and was aware of the intellectual affinity between the philosopher of determinate negation and the Jewish poet who had been born in 1920 and who wrote in the language of the murderers, despite his traumatic experience of the Shoah from which he had barely escaped with his life. There was potentially a mutual interest, then, as a basis for a personal acquaintance, but in the event nothing came of the promised encounter. Celan left the Engadine with his wife Gisèle and his son Eric and returned to Paris before the Adornos had even arrived.[181] Once there, he wrote his prose piece 'Conversation in the Mountains' and then entered into correspondence with Adorno.[182] Ever since his poem *Todesfuge*,[183] Celan had been looking for a poetic expression for the unending suffering of the Jews in the death camps. He did not share Adorno's consciously provocative verdict of 1951 about the impossibility of poetry after Auschwitz. Nevertheless his attitude towards Adorno and his philosophy was one of fundamental sympathy.[184] The hidden theme of this fictitious 'Conversation in the Mountains', an extremely idiosyncratic text linguistically, unlike any other in the poet's work as a whole, was Jewish identity or non-identity, the possibility or impossibility of art after Auschwitz. At the point when the meeting in Sils Maria was supposed to take place, Celan was still convinced that Adorno was a Jew like him. Hence the dialogue between the 'Jew Big' and the 'Jew Little':

> One evening, when the sun had gone down, and not only the sun, there went, stepped out of his house, and there went the Jew, the Jew and the son of a Jew, and with him went his name, the ineffable one, went and came . . .
> Big came up to Little, and Little, the Jew, told his stick to be silent in the presence of the stick of Jew Big . . .
> and I know, I know, cousin, I know I met you here, and that we talked, a lot, . . . the Jews who came, like Lenz, through the moun-

tains, you Big and me Little, you the prattler and me the prattler, both of us with our walking-sticks, with our names, the ineffable ones, we with our shadows, our own and the strange ones, you here and me here.[185]

In this 'Conversation in the Mountains', Celan hoped to discover himself through the imagined counterpart of the other. He sent it to Adorno after learning from Hermann Kasack, the president of the German Academy for Language and Literature, that he was to receive the renowned Büchner Prize for that year. In his letter to Adorno, Celan wrote: 'Here . . . comes the little prose piece of which I told you in Frankfurt, ogling its way up to you in Sils Maria. . . . Even the title is "Jewish German" . . . I would really like to know whether you like it.'[186] Shortly before he wrote this letter, he and Adorno had finally met in person in Frankfurt. Celan may have come to Frankfurt in order to hear the poetics lectures that were being given that year by Marie Luise Kaschnitz, with whom he had been friendly for years.[187] This was an annual course of lectures initiated in part by Helmut Viebrock. Kaschnitz was giving the second series in the summer of 1960, after Ingeborg Bachmann had given the first set in the previous winter semester. That Adorno's philosophy meant a lot to Celan can be seen from the fact that his literary response to the 'failed meeting in the Engadine' formed part of his speech of thanks for the award of the Büchner Prize on 22 October. Here he defended the view that poetry must become a 'calling into question', it must tend towards a 'falling silent', and a poem must assert itself 'at its own margins'.[188] All these ideas fitted in with similar ones in the essays in Adorno's *Notes to Literature*. Months before Celan's speech of thanks Adorno had responded positively to Celan's prose text. He quoted from his interpretation of Mahler's Ninth Symphony in the last chapter of his monograph. In doing so, he wished to indicate that the dialogical structure of the controversial exchange in 'Conversation in the Mountains' had not escaped his notice: 'It seems to me that a musical element really has made its way into poetry.' At the same time, he congratulated Celan on winning the Büchner Prize: 'Of all the German literature prizes, it is more or less the only one that really means anything.'[189]

When Adorno gave three lectures at the Collège de France in spring 1961, he arranged for Celan to be given a personal invitation. Celan was in fact present at the first lecture on 15 March on the subject of 'Le Besoin d'une ontologie'. During his week's stay in Paris, Adorno also tried to introduce Celan to Beckett, but without success, and undoubtedly to his disappointment. For these were the two artists he undoubtedly had in mind when he wrote in an essay that he published in the *Merkur* in 1962:

The concept of a cultural resurrection after Auschwitz is illusory and absurd, and every work created since then has to pay the bitter price for this. But because the world has outlived its own downfall, it nevertheless needs art to write its unconscious history. The authentic artists of the present are those in whose works the uttermost horror still quivers.[190]

During the so-called Goll affair[191] in the early 1960s, in which Celan stood accused of plagiarism, Adorno held back, although he had heard from Marie Luise Kaschnitz and Ingeborg Bachmann of Celan's intense mortification. Adorno decided to show his solidarity with an essay on the *Sprachgitter* collection of poems. He was particularly influenced in this by the anti-Semitic flavour of the critical reception of Celan by such critics as Hans Egon Holthusen, but also Günter Blöcker, and the tendency to marginalize him as a 'foreigner' in West German literature. He had made some notes on the subject following 'an improvised paper on hermetic poetry' that he had given in summer 1967 in Peter Szondi's seminar in Berlin. But in the end he proved unable to write the essay because he was trying to concentrate on his new book, the *Aesthetic Theory*.[192] Celan doubtless regretted Adorno's failure to write the essay on *Sprachgitter*. But his disappointment did not prevent him from declaring his unreserved approbation of *Negative Dialectics*, praise which gave Adorno great satisfaction. For here, in the 'Meditations on Metaphysics', he arrived at the definitive formulation of his dictum on poetry after Auschwitz: 'Perennial suffering has as much right to expression as a tortured man has to scream; hence it may have been wrong to say that after Auschwitz you could no longer write poems.'[193]

Adorno's repeatedly revised reflections on 'culture after Auschwitz', which 'including the urgent critique of it, is garbage',[194] was a challenge and not just for Paul Celan. During the 1950s, there was a long line of writers[195] who made clear their objections to Adorno's verdict, not least Alfred Andersch, Hans Magnus Enzensberger and Wolfgang Hildesheimer.[196] They interpreted Adorno's provocative assertion as a call for the abolition of art and literature altogether – a conclusion they would not have come to had they read the aphorism on the 'baby with the bath-water' from the *Minima Moralia*: 'That culture has so far failed is no justification for furthering its failure, by strewing the store of good flour on the spilt beer like the girl in the fairy-tale.'[197] It is true that the voluminous correspondence between Adorno and Andersch[198] made no mention of the question of poetry after Auschwitz. They were concerned rather with other matters, such as the significance of Arno Schmidt, the critical response to Benjamin, the mediation of modern music, and dates for discussion programmes in the Evening Studio. But in November 1959, Andersch gave a speech at a reception at the publisher Arnoldo Mondadori, at which he pointed to the absurdity of writing in Germany following the catastrophe.[199] In seeming contrast to Adorno, he called for a literature that consciously faced up to the horror, a literature after the end of literature.[200]

It fell to Enzensberger in 1959 to give an example of this literature: Nelly Sachs. 'The redemption of language and its enchantment is the province of those who were *In the dwellings of death*.'[201] Hildesheimer, in his poetics lectures of 1967, went a step further by designating poetry as the only possible literary option after Auschwitz, pointing to Paul Celan's *Todesfuge* and Ingeborg Bachmann's *Früher Mittag*, among other poems. 'So it's not just horror, then, but flight and flashes of insight into the terrifying instability of the world, the absurd.'[202]

Adorno was of course well aware of the debate that had been triggered by his dictum. He responded with his own contribution, 'Commitment', a talk given first on Radio Bremen in 1962 and published shortly thereafter in the *Neue Rundschau*: 'I have no wish to soften the saying that to write lyric poetry after Auschwitz is barbaric; it expresses in negative form the impulse which inspires committed literature. . . . But Enzensberger's retort also remains true, that literature must resist this verdict, in other words, be such that its mere existence after Auschwitz is not a surrender to cynicism. Its own situation is one of paradox, not merely the problem of how to react to it. The abundance of real suffering tolerates no forgetting.'[203]

Four years later, in his philosophical *magnum opus*, Adorno proposed the new 'categorical imperative', 'to arrange one's thoughts and actions so that Auschwitz will not be repeated.'[204]

During these years it became common in Germany to argue that a line should be drawn under the past. Marie Luise Kaschnitz and Ingeborg Bachmann were among the writers who felt that Adorno's call to remember the past was a moral imperative. Ever since their return to Frankfurt, the Adornos had had a close friendship with Kaschnitz. Their contact with the younger Austrian poetess, Ingeborg Bachmann, a woman with a 'very wayward and shy' disposition,[205] did not develop until she gave the poetics lectures in Frankfurt in mid-November 1959. Relations with Adorno then quickly became friendly. Adorno began his letters with 'Dear Ingeborg', and her essay 'Music and Poetry' of 1959 was obviously a subject after his own heart.

Kaschnitz and Bachmann, who were themselves good friends, were preoccupied with the question of the meaning of poetry and, over and above that, the problem of whether 'in these desolate times' every poem was senseless and the poet would do best to remain silent.[206] The closeness Adorno felt to the literary works of these two writers could be traced back to their self-doubts, and their search for new forms of expression and new stylistic methods. 'In a society whose totality has sealed itself up as ideology, only what does not resemble the façade can be true.'[207] For their part, the two poets were attracted by Adorno's critical radicality, by his intellectual ambitiousness, and his profound knowledge of literature, music and philosophy. The short texts that Kaschnitz assembled in her book *Steht noch dahin* of 1969 contained definite signs that she had been grappling with Adorno's social theory. 'Whether we shall escape without being tortured, whether we shall die a natural death . . . , whether we shall be driven in herds, we have seen these things. . . . Whether we shall slip away at the right time, to a white bed, or whether we shall perish in a hundredfold nuclear flash, whether we shall succeed in dying filled with hope, remains to be seen, all that remains to be seen.'[208]

Adorno used to take long walks with Kaschnitz in the Palmengarten in Frankfurt, which was not far from where they both lived. Kaschnitz had lived for a long time in Rome, both before the war and in the 1950s. In May 1961, when she was a guest of honour in the Villa Massimo, Adorno and Gretel took the opportunity to visit her.[209] Kaschnitz was a frequent visitor in Kettenhofweg. She was there, for example, for New Year's Eve 1962–3:

> With Adornos before midnight. Listened to *Ariadne* (with Karajan with the London Symphony Orchestra and singers from Vienna and Salzburg), as well as Act II of *Tristan*. Adorno: '*Tristan* and Manet are the two great spiders sitting in the nineteenth century.' He was very pleased with the *Tristan* performance by Solti, and played his own interpretation on the piano. A few words from the director of the radio station . . . then the countdown of the last ten seconds of the old year, like a rocket being launched, ten – nine – eight, etc. . . . After that, we looked out of the windows onto the snow-covered roofs, behind which rockets, palm fronds and stars rose up in pillars of light surrounded by smoke.[210]

When Ingeborg Bachmann gave her lectures on poetics, she talked about literature's falling silent and about ways to overcome the silence, a topic that Adorno was certain to approve. She was conversant with Adorno's *Notes to Literature* and with a number of his writings on the philosophy of music.[211] Bachmann knew Paul Celan well and had made an intensive study of the Jewish tradition. Adorno introduced her to Gershom Scholem, who visited her in 1967 in Rome, where they went to the former ghetto together.[212] This had been preceded by a visit to Rome in November of the previous year, when Adorno and Scholem's wife called on Bachmann. Rome was one of the Italian cities that Adorno enjoyed staying in precisely because he had good friends there – in this instance, Franco Lombardi, Bachmann, Kaschnitz and her daughter Iris, who subsequently married the composer Dieter Schnebel, whom Adorno had met during the Darmstadt Summer Courses for New Music and who was very close to him.

Adorno knew Paris even better than Rome. Throughout his entire life Paris had had mythic qualities.[213] He had frequently visited it from Frankfurt before his emigration and also from London in order to see Benjamin and to carry out various tasks for the Institute of Social Research. As professor at Frankfurt University, he had been in touch with Daniel-Henry Kahnweiler, the patron and connoisseur of the arts. Kahnweiler later presented him with a folder of graphics by Picasso. Other acquaintances included Frederick Goldbeck, the conductor, music critic and author, whom he had known since the 1920s, René Leibowitz, the conductor and music writer,[214] as well as Lucien Goldmann, the Marxist literary sociologist. As early as November 1956, he gave three lectures at the Sorbonne and the Faculté des lettres et sciences humaines, one on the experiential contents of Hegelian philosophy, the second on the sociology of music and the third on the relations between sociological theory and social research. Three years later, on the initiative of the French Germanist Robert Minder, he was invited to speak at the Collège de France. He gave three late afternoon lectures, using material from the course he had been giving on 'Ontology and Dialectics' in Frankfurt during the winter semester of 1960–1.[215] Adorno's lectures, which he gave in French, were evidently well attended. Among others, Maurice Merleau-Ponty and Jean Wahl were present, as was Robert Minder, of course, as well as other acquaintances from the French metropolis,[216] including Roger Caillois, George Friedemann and Frederick Goldbeck.

Adorno's friendships with writers and artists were strikingly numerous. One instance in 1957 was his friendship with Hans Günter Helms, the composer and musicologist born in 1932 who worked with Heinz-Klaus Metzger, Dieter Schnebel and Gottfried Michael König, and later with John Cage. Adorno was more interested in his experiments in the realm of 'language music' than in his sociological attempts at a critique of the ideology of West German society.[217] Adorno was receptive to Helms's musical and literary work because he perceived it as a set of aesthetic experiments with the similarities of music to language. Above all, he regarded it as proof of something that ever since his pioneering lecture at the Berlin Academy of Arts in July 1966 he had described as the 'erosion, fraying [*Verfransung*] of the arts'.[218] In 1960, when Helms gave a public reading of his literary production 'FA: M'AHNIESGWOW' in Cologne,[219] Adorno was one of the few who were in a position to provide an introduction to the artist's work. The expectation that one should be able to understand avant-garde art like a foreign language turns out, according to Adorno, to be an illusion.[220] What is decisive is 'the co-execution [*Mitvollzug*, i.e., by the reader/listener as well as the author] of the tensions sedimented in the work of art'.[221] This is connected with the contingent, improvised elements of the modern work of art that exploits such features to create free space for itself.[222] Our task as consumers of art is to use our ears to compose a piece of music again, to use our eyes to paint a picture for the second time, to use our linguistic sense to re-create a poem. At the same time, he again put forward the argument that the modern work of art tells the truth about society 'all the more accurately, the less it takes society as its subject'. In the modern work of art, the tension between expression and meaning is not resolved in favour of one side or the other, but 'is respected as an antinomy'.[223] Confronted with the experimental lyric poetry of H. G. Helms, Adorno pointed out that the recent avant-garde was striving to surpass both Proust and Kafka, and even Joyce, although the affinity between Helms's poem and *Finnegans Wake* was as self-evident as the links with Karlheinz Stockhausen. The most advanced literary works take 'the same steps in literature that contemporary music has taken in music . . . The construction no longer conceives itself as an achievement of spontaneous subjectivity . . . The whole is composed in structures, put together in each case from a series of dimensions, or in the terminology of serial music, parameters, that appear autonomously, or combined, or ordered hierarchically.'[224]

Thus Adorno took the works of the artistic avant-garde very seriously and made them the object of his philosophical reflections – Stockhausen and Cage in music, the novels and plays of Beckett and the works of Helms in literature. In the same way, he responded to Alexander Kluge, a film-maker and writer who had previously studied law as well as history and church music. Kluge was also a qualified lawyer who succeeded Hellmut Becker in advising the Institute of Social Research on legal matters and who sat on the board of trustees. Adorno had been on friendly terms with him since the 1950s. With a side glance at the age of Kluge's mother, he had even jokingly referred to Kluge, who had been born in 1932, as the nonconformist child he had always wanted. He even recommended him to the legendary Fritz Lang, with whom Kluge then worked for some time as an assistant. Kluge was one of the moving spirits behind the Oberhausen Manifesto and was in Adorno's eyes the chief representative of ambitious developments in the medium of film. Adorno saw the films that Kluge made during this period: *Yesterday Girl* (1966) and *Artistes at the Top of the Big Top: Disorientated* (1967). However, this did not mean that Adorno was ready to abandon his contempt for film as a genre, even though under Kluge's influence he did show himself willing to allow the validity of exceptional films like Antonioni's *La Notte*. Nevertheless, we can find this statement in *Negative Dialectics*: 'Demythologization, the intention of thought to bring enlightenment, destroys the image character of consciousness.'[225] Kluge believed that what Adorno really liked about his films was his use of music, the sound track. Adorno was also familiar with Kluge's literary works, *Lebensläufe* (Curricula Vitae), first published in 1962, and his Stalingrad novel, *Schlachtbeschreibung* (Description of a Battle), of 1964. In addition the two shared an interest in music, a passion for the opera, the opera as 'a power house of the feelings'. The kind of question they discussed in their conversations in Adorno's flat or during the evening visits to a restaurant or wine bar near the Frankfurt Opera was whether the making of a film resembled the composition of a piece of music, or how the visual dimensions of the musical and linguistic side of films could be exploited to achieve a three-fold harmony of image, words and music. When Adorno wished for information about the modern film, Kluge was the man he consulted. He explained his own idea of a good film, vague though it was, with reference to the colourful images of the landscape that the inner eye of a sleeper might glimpse in a state of relaxation: 'images of an interior monologue' that come to resemble writing when they stop moving. 'As the objectifying re-creation of this type of experience, film may become art.'[226]

Although in general Adorno despised film as a medium and dismissed it as phantasmagoria, Kluge could not help but be impressed by Adorno's criticism, though not to the point where he stopped making films. Nevertheless, he was less impressed by Adorno's theses on the aesthetics of film than by his interpretation of Bizet's opera *Carmen*, the 'Fantasia sopra *Carmen*' which he published in the *Neue Rundschau* with a dedication to Thomas Mann. In that essay, Adorno described *Carmen* as the prototype of 'those operas of exogamy which begin with *La Juive* and *L'Africaine* and proceed via *Aida*, *Lakmé*, and *Butterfly* to Berg's *Lulu*. All of them celebrate eruptions from civilization into the unknown.'[227] And the exotic woman who turns men's heads must die of such love, a lethal conclusion on which opera insists – that is how Kluge saw the genre in his 'Imaginary Guide to Opera'.[228] This project of an 'imaginary guide to opera' is undoubtedly one that could have counted on Adorno's sympathy since opera was one of his own private passions, one 'he surrendered to unconditionally'.[229]

Another friendship was with Hans Magnus Enzensberger, the writer, whom Adorno had known since the 1950s. He had met him through Alfred Andersch in the Evening Studio of South-West German Radio. In a letter of July 1962, Adorno acknowledged that they shared 'similar intellectual temperaments' and, years before, he had not only sent Enzensberger little commentaries on his own philosophical writings, but also made no secret of his horror at the state of postwar German philosophy. Remarkably, he felt it necessary to justify his own willingness to work for the radio: 'It would just be pig-headed, and a piece of the cultural conservatism that only benefits the culture industry, to reject the mass media in favour of handmade paper. . . . if anywhere, it is here that the Brechtian concept of "changing functions" [*Umfunktionieren*] has its place. . . . I think of myself as anything but defeatist.'[230] The contact between them increased when Enzensberger came to live in Frankfurt for a time, working as an editor for Suhrkamp along with Karl Markus Michel and Walter Boehlich. In fact, he lived opposite Adorno and could see over to the latter's apartment from his kitchen balcony. One day, when Kluge was visiting him, Adorno told him that Enzensberger was living opposite, adding that 'he was the only one able to write poetry. He did not think that any of the other poets in the *Gruppe 47* were worthy of mention.'[231] Adorno particularly liked the two volumes of verse *Verteidigung der Wölfe* (In Defence of the Wolves) (1957) and *Landessprache* (The Language of the Country) (1960), as well as the anthology of modern poetry *Museum der modernen Poesie*

(1960). For his part, Enzensberger was evidently attracted to some of Adorno's ideas. As he said, they 'belonged to the hand luggage of every intellectual at the time'.[232] His reading of Adorno had an impact on the essays he wrote on culture and the media in 1962. The concept of the 'consciousness industry' was clearly influenced by the criticism of the media in the *Dialectic of Enlightenment*. In the winter semester of 1964, when Enzensberger gave the poetics lectures in Frankfurt University, they took place in the largest lecture hall, which was full to bursting. He was introduced by Adorno as a friend whose thinking was close to his own. This referred both to Enzensberger's criticism of *Der Spiegel*, the *Frankfurter Allgemeine Zeitung* and the *Wochenschau* (the weekly newsreel), and to his poetry. A new volume, *Blindenschrift* (Braille), had appeared in time for the poetics lectures. The social criticism in the collection was very striking:

> massacre for a handful of rice
> I can hear it, for everyone every day
> a handful of rice. a barrage of bullets
> beating down on flimsy huts,
> I can hear it
> at dinner.

When Enzensberger wrote in his poem 'doubt', 'Are we allowed to doubt?', this was very much in tune with Adorno's self-reflexive dialectical way of thinking. Enzensberger's contribution to the *Festschrift* volume *Zeugnisse*, which Horkheimer organized for Adorno's sixtieth birthday, was one of the most sensitive portraits to have appeared on Adorno and his impact as a critic and champion of enlightenment.

> hard labour   for theodor w. adorno
>
> in the name of the others
> patiently
> in the name of the others who know nothing about it
> patiently
> in the name of the others who wish to know nothing about it
> patiently
> holding fast to the pain of negation
>
> mindful of the drowned in the suburban trains at 5 am
> patiently
> unfolding the sudarium of theory
>
> in the face of those running amok in the shopping malls at 5 pm
> patiently
> turning over every idea that conceals its backside

eye to eye with the death wishers at every hour of the day
patiently
pointing to the barricaded future

door to door with the counter-espionage service at every hour of
   the night
patiently
exposing the vibrant collapse

impatiently
despairing
in the name of the satisfied

patiently
doubting despair
in the name of the desperate

impatiently patiently
teaching
in the name of the unteachable.[233]

18

Eating Bread: A Theory
Devoured by Thought

The philosophical ideal would be to obviate the need to account for the
deed by doing it.[1]

In January 1955 Adorno's American passport expired. He ought to
have returned to the United States so as to avoid losing the US citizenship he had acquired in 1943.[2] Despite his fear of radical right-wing
nationalism and forms of 'crypto-anti-Semitism',[3] Adorno, who was
now fifty-one years old, decided to renew his German citizenship. What
led him to make this decision? It seems he was influenced by the role he
played in German cultural life, by the recognition he enjoyed as a university professor in Frankfurt and by the positions he occupied in the
Institute of Social Research. His many publications in cultural journals
and his activities on behalf of the new music had given him prominence
and the reputation of being a respected and feared intellectual with
a sharp tongue.[4] Despite his high profile both in print and on the radio,
he was not overwhelmed with public honours. Nevertheless, as early as
1954 he was awarded the Arnold-Schoenberg-Medaille, and five years
later, the Deutscher Kritikerpreis für Literatur; in 1963, he was even
given the Goetheplakette of the City of Frankfurt.

Adorno believed that 'he would be able to do some good to counter
the hardening and the repetition of the catastrophe [in Germany].'[5]
How realistic was this expectation in a country in which the prevailing
trend in the first decade after the war was one of restoration? Neither
domestically nor from a foreign-policy point of view was it realistic to
believe in German neutrality as a long-term contribution to security and
disarmament in Europe. Nor was it possible to prevent the remilitarization of Germany. In view of the growing East–West tensions, the members of NATO abandoned their opposition to rearming West Germany,
which in May 1955 had once again become a sovereign state. In reaction
to this, the Warsaw Pact was set up under Soviet leadership in the same
month and the GDR became a member on terms of equality. As the
ideological rift between the Great Powers grew deeper, the opposing
military alliances became increasingly important.

On 14 February 1955, Max Horkheimer celebrated his seventieth birthday. His position had become more or less impregnable by that time since he was one of the most highly respected and best-known scholars in the Federal Republic. This was an appropriate occasion for his friend and co-director to publish an appreciation in the *Frankfurter Allgemeine Zeitung*. This provided a kind of speeded-up overview of Horkheimer's contributions to the *Zeitschrift für Sozialforschung* and the *Studies in Philosophy and Social Science*, his activities as director of the institute and his books, the *Studies in Prejudice*, the *Critique of Instrumental Reason* and the *Dialectic of Enlightenment*. But what Horkheimer actually stood for 'went far beyond his objective works. For he mistrusted such things as works at a historical moment in which scarcely any idea has a right to exist unless its innermost meaning strives to be put into effect. . . . He never abandoned his hope that things would turn out well, and he acted responsibly in that conviction.'[6] This maxim is one Adorno might have chosen for himself.

In the same year, 1955, Thomas Mann died at the age of eighty in Kilchberg on Lake Zurich. Adorno heard the news in the Hotel Waldhaus in Sils Maria, where he was spending the summer vacation. He at once wrote to Mann's widow: 'I do not know what to say – the blow is paralysing. Only this, which perhaps can only be said in such a moment: I loved him very, very dearly.'[7]

Adorno was an acute observer of current events, and he watched them with great scepticism and reserve. His comments on German and international politics are highly critical, in so far as they have been recorded. For example, he was afraid that official West German politicians were reluctant for the most part to take energetic measures to prevent the spread of fascist groups.[8] Towards the end of 1956, when France and Britain launched a military assault on Egypt and an article in *Der Spiegel* attacked the way the United Nations had condemned their invasion, Adorno and Horkheimer wrote to the writer Julius Ebbinghaus, agreeing with *Der Spiegel*.[9]

The fact that people have discovered humanity when faced by a fascist chieftain like Nasser who conspires with Moscow; that, as in Hitler's time, they show greater concern about breaking treaties than about the treaties themselves and their sanctity; and that no one even ventures to point out that these Arab robber states have been on the lookout for years for an opportunity to fall upon Israel and to slaughter the Jews who have found refuge there – all this is a symptom of public consciousness that has to be taken very seriously indeed. The hypocrisy . . . in almost every camp is proof of a confusion of thought that bodes ill for the future.[10]

Against the background of a widespread anti-communist climate in West German society, the conservative CDU/CSU was highly successful with its programme based on freedom, security and German sovereignty, so much so that Konrad Adenauer was elected federal chancellor four times in succession from 1949. As early as 1953, the CDU/CSU had emerged the winner from the elections, thanks to the impact of the violent crushing of the uprising against the GDR government in Berlin. And in September 1957, the year of the establishment of the European Economic Community, Adenauer, who had campaigned with the slogan 'No experiments', obtained an absolute majority of votes as well as parliamentary seats. The Paris treaties of 1955 provided for the creation of a new Federal German army, and during this same period there was a growing political debate in Germany about whether this army should be equipped with tactical nuclear weapons. As a warning against underestimating the lethal capacities of such weapons, eighteen leading scientists declared their opposition to arming the Bundeswehr with a nuclear capability. In their protest, the 'Göttingen Eighteen' pointed out that each of the nuclear weapons in question would have the destructive force of the Hiroshima bomb, and they called for a general renunciation of nuclear weapons. A group of well-known intellectuals came out in support of them. Like Horkheimer, Adorno tended to hold back from making political statements in public – as far as was possible. Neither director of the institute signed the German Manifesto of January 1955 against rearmament and in favour of reunification that was decided on in St Paul's Church by the assembled protesters. Adorno commented on this issue in a note he planned to include in a second volume of aphorisms with the title *Graeculus*.[11] In answer to the question whether one ought ever to make one's political opinions known publicly by signing manifestos, he wrote: 'It is difficult even to sign appeals with which one sympathizes, because in their inevitable desire to have a political impact, they always contain an element of untruth or presuppose a knowledge of specific circumstances. . . . The absence of commitment is not necessarily a moral defect; it can itself be moral, since it means insisting on the autonomy of one's own point of view.'[12]

Nevertheless, on balance both Adorno and Horkheimer were opposed to the dynamics of the arms race that followed from the creation of hostile blocs.[13] But they did not share the fear that was widespread in intellectual circles of the risks posed by a new German army. Hence they had no scruples about carrying out a study in conjunction with the German Defence Ministry. The aim of the study was to discover how to select volunteers for the future German army on the basis of their democratic attitudes.[14] Younger institute members were opposed to this project, and in much the same way they were not enthusiastic about the 'political attitudes' of the directors towards such matters as the war in Algeria or the rearmament question. Jürgen Habermas recollects, for example, that Horkheimer's rather timorous reserve was much criticized: 'His public demeanour and his policy for the institute too seemed to us to be almost the expression of an opportunist conformity which was at odds with the critical tradition which, after all, he embodied.'[15] The same thing applied to Adorno, who at the time adopted the same 'us and them' attitudes that Horkheimer displayed for public consumption, such as when he observed to Adorno that 'it was almost self-evident that pluralist societies were not equal to the challenge of the savage barbarism of the East with all its pomp and circumstance.'[16] Adorno and Horkheimer were in agreement in their assessment of the so-called Eastern bloc, i.e., the Soviet Union, but also communist China. Thus they objected to Khrushchev on the grounds of the cult of personality, his destruction of human beings, and his treachery. Against this background, they constantly emphasized their fundamental disagreement with the 'dialectical materialism' of the Eastern bloc parties. As critics of society, 'they would long since have been killed', they remark in a letter to Herbert Marcuse, who had referred to them as 'the taskmasters of the East'. 'Whereas', they continue, 'in the West there is at the moment a freedom of thought which in comparison can only be described as paradisal. That this has material grounds is no news to us. It is well known that freedom of every kind depends on them.'[17]

This fundamental attitude also determined Adorno's cautious reaction when Alfred Sohn-Rethel wrote to him after a gap of fourteen years, announcing his return to Frankfurt and proposing a meeting. He intended to combine this trip with a visit to East Berlin, where he had been invited to give a lecture at the Humboldt University. For Adorno, this latter fact was enough to prevent him from issuing an invitation to Sohn-Rethel to speak at the institute. He warned him that his lecture would be used by the GDR 'for propaganda purposes', 'while every idea that you wish to express will be condemned to total impotence in the face of the ineffably servile vulgar materialism of the secretarial mind that prevails there. Here, for the time being, one can tell a great deal of the truth, at least in individual work of one's own. Over there, that is quite impossible.'[18]

Even if Adorno was generally reluctant to become involved in political pronouncements and demonstrations, he continued to follow political developments in Germany and the world very attentively. As he wrote to Horkheimer, who between 1954 and 1959 had a guest professorship at the University of Chicago and hence lived there for longer periods, 'It is frightening to see how everything is becoming gloomier. I expect you will have picked up something of what is going on here. The fact that we predicted it does not make it any better. Moreover, these new developments are not just a matter of domestic German politics, but very much what the new German term calls "global"; and I have the feeling that it really does not matter any more where one happens to be, so that at least one has a good rationalization to hand to justify staying wherever one feels most at home.'[19] The news that was supposed to have reached Horkheimer concerned the growing tensions between the opposing military blocs following the crushing of the uprising in

Hungary and the suppression of democratic stirrings in Poland. Then there was the quickening pace of the nuclear arms race and, especially, the speech in which Adenauer tried to play down 'tactical nuclear weapons' as no more than an extension of the artillery. As public opinion became increasingly politicized, there was a growing wave of protest against agreeing to remilitarization and the acquisition of nuclear weapons as the price for achieving the integration of the Federal Republic in the West.[20] As the only opposition party, the SPD launched the anti-nuclear campaign 'Fight against Nuclear Death', which attracted not just prominent figures in politics, the church and the trade unions, but also scholars and writers such as the journalist Axel Eggebrecht, political scientists such as Eugen Kogon, sociologists such as Alfred Weber, and writers such as Heinrich Böll, Hans Henny Jahnn and Erich Kästner. But in this instance, too, Horkheimer and Adorno gave their signatures neither to the Frankfurt declaration of March 1958, nor to the subsequent poster campaign.

However, one young member of the Institute of Social Research did play an active part in the Frankfurt protest of May 1958. The 28-year-old Jürgen Habermas addressed thousands of protesters in front of the Römer and criticized the logic of a 'politics of strength' as well as a notion of democracy which restricted the power of the people to acclaiming the decisions taken by the government. His speech was printed in the student newspaper *Diskus* with the title 'Unrest is the Citizen's First Duty'.[21] With his call for 'civic courage', Adorno's assistant put into practice what his teacher had earlier said about the task of contemporary philosophy, namely that it 'has its lifeblood in resistance', in the criticism of 'the common practices of the day'.[22] Adorno had originally put forward his theses about the aim and purpose of philosophy in 1955, in the Frankfurt Student Union, in the context of a student study group.[23] But his past commitment to a practical philosophy of negation was not the real or only reason why Adorno was prepared to defend Habermas against Horkheimer's criticism, some of it very sarcastic. Horkheimer had his suspicions about both Habermas's political activities and his publications on the grounds that Habermas refused to give up 'the expectations of the pre-1848ers' about 'the sublation of philosophy in revolution'.[24] In this instance, however, Adorno refused to allow himself to be intimidated. According to Habermas, he said that 'he had never shared Horkheimer's prejudice against me, and he kept me in the institute in defiance of Horkheimer's pressure.'[25] Moreover, Adorno could see that, given the explosive situation and the passionate debates that were going on, it would not be possible for the institute to abstain from comment on political issues in the long run. It was this conviction that inspired him to take the initiative and propose that Horkheimer should mount a series of lectures in the institute on the highly topical subject of 'Politics and Society'. He suggested that these lectures would show, on the one hand, 'that politics is a façade, an ideology, and society the supporting reality, while, on the other hand, it would become clear that a changing social practice would assume political form: politics for the elimination of politics.'[26] Horkheimer, too, believed that politics was a second-order phenomenon, namely 'the immediate function of the economy. Even the fear of atom bombs is nothing compared to the concern for the good conduct of business.'[27] Horkheimer was evidently tormented by this concern when he warned Adorno that, as the 'propagandist of the anti-nuclear movement', Habermas might gain undue influence in the institute. After all, 'the institute was dependent, in part at least, on industry for research commissions.' 'But we must not let the institute be ruined by what is probably the heedless attitude of this one *Assistent.*'[28] This anxiety would soon be shown to be wholly without foundation.

In the initial phase of the Federal Republic, the Social Democratic Party had rejected a market economy based on tax concessions for business and low wages. But in the light of the sustained success of the governing conservative party, it was forced to review its position. With the aim of winning votes from sectors of the electorate that went beyond its traditional supporters, the party convened an extraordinary congress in Bad Godesberg in November 1959. There it produced a new fundamental programme in which it committed itself firmly to a policy of integration in the West and also to a market-based economy. This new policy was the brainchild of Carlo Schmid and Herbert Wehner, with some support from Willy Brandt. It alienated a number of more strongly left-wing delegates, who regarded it as a capitulation and the complete abandonment of Marxism. This triggered a lengthy debate about the programme of the SPD, which was further exacerbated in 1966 by the formation of the Grand Coalition in which a government was formed from an alliance of the CDU/CSU with the SPD.[29] Seven years after the publication of the Godesberg Programme, Adorno wrote to Enzensberger that he wanted to write a fundamental critique of the Godesberg Programme, modelled on Marx's famous critique of the Gotha Programme of 1875. His idea was that Enzensberger would publish this critique in *Kursbuch*, a magazine edited by him and published by Suhrkamp.[30] Even if Adorno was not fully in agreement with the cultural revolution propagated by the magazine and its general renunciation of bourgeois literature, he was attracted by the idea of writing and publishing such a critique in the tradition of Karl Marx. He had in fact already begun to make notes in the margins of a copy of the Godesberg Programme. It is evident from these that he was highly critical of the new programme. Where its authors had written of the danger that man had 'unleashed the primal power of the atom', he noted, 'regression to "man"'; furthermore, he observed, 'they point to contradictions, not the contradiction'. At the point where the programme discusses the justice of the material distribution of goods, he wrote in the margin: 'ambiguous, i.e., formulated as if it could be achieved

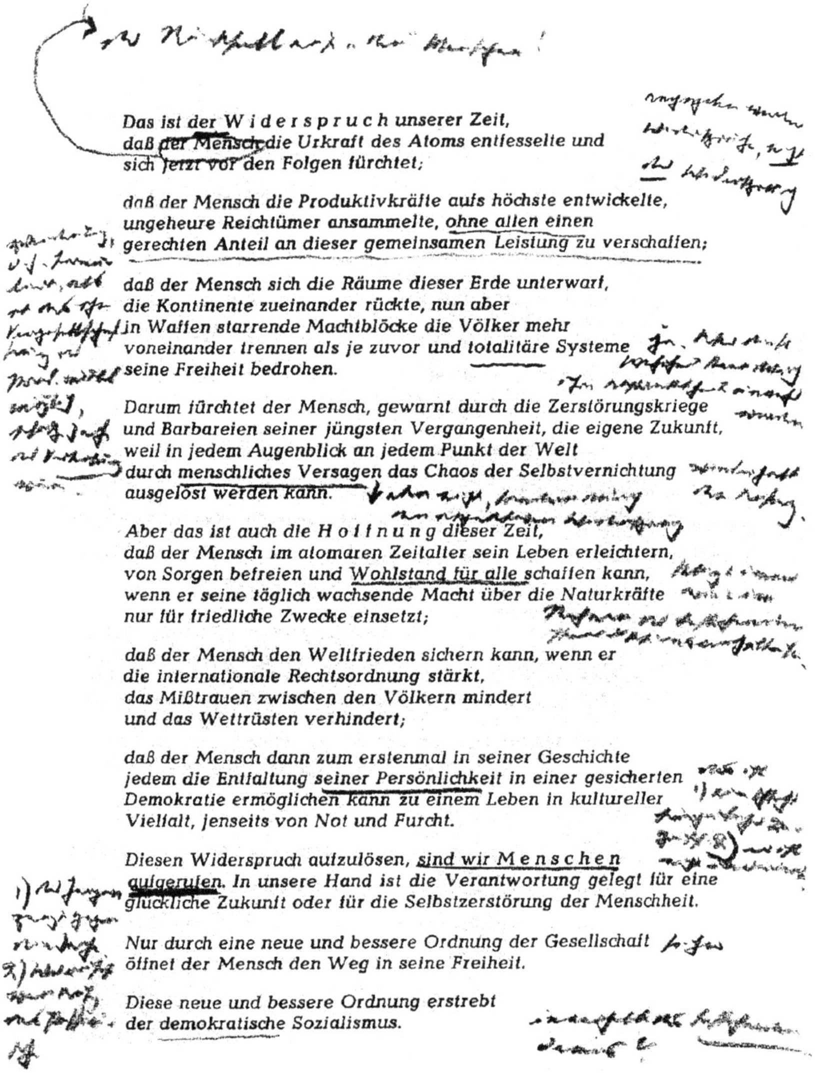

Das ist der W i d e r s p r u c h unserer Zeit,
daß der Mensch die Urkraft des Atoms entfesselte und
sich jetzt vor den Folgen fürchtet;

daß der Mensch die Produktivkräfte aufs höchste entwickelte,
ungeheure Reichtümer ansammelte, ohne allen einen
gerechten Anteil an dieser gemeinsamen Leistung zu verschaffen;

daß der Mensch sich die Räume dieser Erde unterwarf,
die Kontinente zueinander rückte, nun aber
in Waffen starrende Machtblöcke die Völker mehr
voneinander trennen als je zuvor und totalitäre Systeme
seine Freiheit bedrohen.

Darum fürchtet der Mensch, gewarnt durch die Zerstörungskriege
und Barbareien seiner jüngsten Vergangenheit, die eigene Zukunft,
weil in jedem Augenblick an jedem Punkt der Welt
durch menschliches Versagen das Chaos der Selbstvernichtung
ausgelöst werden kann.

Aber das ist auch die H o f f n u n g dieser Zeit,
daß der Mensch im atomaren Zeitalter sein Leben erleichtern,
von Sorgen befreien und Wohlstand für alle schaffen kann,
wenn er seine täglich wachsende Macht über die Naturkräfte
nur für friedliche Zwecke einsetzt;

daß der Mensch den Weltfrieden sichern kann, wenn er
die internationale Rechtsordnung stärkt,
das Mißtrauen zwischen den Völkern mindert
und das Wettrüsten verhindert;

daß der Mensch dann zum erstenmal in seiner Geschichte
jedem die Entfaltung seiner Persönlichkeit in einer gesicherten
Demokratie ermöglichen kann zu einem Leben in kultureller
Vielfalt, jenseits von Not und Furcht.

Diesen Widerspruch aufzulösen, sind wir M e n s c h e n
aufgerufen. In unsere Hand ist die Verantwortung gelegt für eine
glückliche Zukunft oder für die Selbstzerstörung der Menschheit.

Nur durch eine neue und bessere Ordnung der Gesellschaft
öffnet der Mensch den Weg in seine Freiheit.

Diese neue und bessere Ordnung erstrebt
der demokratische Sozialismus.

Figure 5 A page of the Godesberger Programme of the SPD with Adorno's annotations without the socialization of the means of production, as if it were merely a matter for negotiation.'

Where the programme called for the development of the personality, he wrote, 'that is 1) a bad bourgeois concept; 2) it is not a constant.'[31] However, the article was never written. If it never progressed beyond the note stage, this is probably because the matter was delicate enough for Adorno to think it prudent to consult Horkheimer. Doubtless he was mindful of Horkheimer's strictures on Habermas's foray into politics. A few days after the formation of the Grand Coalition, he wrote to Horkheimer that he was having second thoughts: 'If anyone attacks the SPD today – and that is what it would amount to, however one formulated one's comments – that would be grist to the mill of everyone who wants to shake the already frail pillars of democracy.... I would not wish to contribute to the same sort of disaster that people brought about in an earlier age when they coined the slogan of social fascism.' Adorno declared that he agreed with intellectuals who were close to him and Horkheimer who believed that, in view of the possible threat to democracy from the Grand Coalition, it was time to speak out in public. 'Only an extremely acute, critical process of self-reflection can help the SPD not to wear itself out in this alliance.' Somewhat self-critically, Adorno confessed to his friend in Montagnola that he was unsure of his own political judgement in this situation. On the one hand, he saw the risk that the SPD would simply be co-opted into a conservative agenda. 'On the other hand, I regard the Grand Coalition as a real opportunity for a transition to a two-party system of the kind that you envisage, and this in turn would lead to the elimination of the NPD which despite all reassurances I take as seriously as you.'[32] Adorno decided to give Horkheimer a casting vote, and, when Horkheimer advised against it, he abandoned the plan for the *Kursbuch* article.

Nevertheless, two years later he saw no reason to revise his principled critique of the SPD programme. In November 1968, he wrote to Günter Grass that with their new programme the Social Democrats were in the process 'of forswearing all the theoretical ideas that had ever inspired them'. However, it was not possible, he thought, to criticize them because politically there was no alternative. To the left of the SPD there were only anarchist activists or groups subservient to Moscow 'who were even prepared to defend the ghastly invasion of Czechoslovakia'.[33]

Adorno's decision not to proceed with the article resulted only partly from deference to Horkheimer's opinion. In addition, Adorno found himself increasingly under pressure from left-wing groups, and he feared that he might end up being used for the political purposes of others.[34] In his letter to Enzensberger, saying he could not write the piece, Adorno blames the lack of time. He was busy working on *Negative Dialectics* and a variety of other publications. 'I was completely exhausted and have not picked up a pen in the entire five weeks of vacation in the

Waldhaus, nor have I read anything, and yet I still do not feel as fresh as I should be if I am to finish writing *Negative Dialectics* soon.' At the same time, Adorno expressed his liking for the *Kursbuch* and suggested that it should in future be willing to deal with musical topics. As early as 1965, he had written to Enzensberger from Sils Maria: 'I think that it would be necessary, as a matter of urgency, to write a really incisive account of logical positivism, or analytical philosophy, as they call it, as the current form of stupidity.'[35] Two weeks later, Adorno again confirmed his withdrawal. 'The fact is that I am a slow worker and cannot produce a critique of the Godesberg Programme at the drop of a hat. It calls for reflection on the writer's situation . . . as well as the historical context.'[36]

Precisely that, the historical context, was the theme of a discussion that Adorno took part in with Peter von Haselberg for the literary magazine *Akzente* in the summer of 1965: 'On the Historical Appropriateness of Consciousness'.[37] Admittedly, current political issues figured only on the margins of the discussion, when they talked about regressive tendencies in the present and the emergence of fascist movements, which Adorno described as 'the ghost of a ghost'.[38] What he focused on instead were fashionable phenomena, such as the Beatles, since he was keen to distinguish them from advanced modernity, whose condition could be measured by the progress of avant-garde art. 'What can be urged against the Beatles . . . is simply that what these people have to offer is . . . something that is retarded in terms of its own objective content. It can be shown that the means of expression that are employed and preserved here are in reality no more than traditional techniques in a degraded form.'[39] He argued that it was necessary to develop a sense of what was appropriate to the age, both in art and in social theory, in the light of the current stage of development. Simply to stick to what was given in a positivistic frame of mind, however, was 'to sabotage thought'.[40] This was identical with the line of thought with which Adorno took part in the dispute about positivism. However, positivism was only one of the opponents to attract his criticism during these years. The other main opponent was Heidegger, the 'Master from Germany',[41] who lived in the south German Black Forest and whom he found it absolutely necessary to attack more or less at the same time.

Early in the 1960s there was a somewhat cautious rapprochement with Ernst Bloch. They had avoided each other for years, and an initial meeting took place at a Hegel conference in Frankfurt in 1958 at an evening reception organized by Suhrkamp. According to a letter Adorno wrote to Horkheimer, the encounter was 'somewhat disappointing'. There were points of contact and Bloch was likeable enough personally. 'But that is not enough. The truest insights are of no use if they are all bluster and nothing is thought out.'[42] Nevertheless, Adorno wrote a detailed review when Suhrkamp published a new edition of Bloch's volume of aphorisms, *Spuren* (Traces). And Bloch belatedly congratulated Adorno on his sixtieth birthday. 'What has "actually" happened for us no longer to be what we once were to each other now that we have grown older? It is true that when we meet we are what we were, but not at all with regard to whatever the history of philosophy may preserve.'[43] On Bloch's eightieth birthday, Adorno returned the compliment and wrote an article in a Festschrift for Bloch published by Siegfried Unseld. Adorno's birthday telegram was quite emphatic: 'Ernst, old friend since very early on, philosophy chieftain, we wish you the undiminished power of dreams, and are with you in spirit. Gretel and Teddie.'[44] Later on, Adorno put forward the idea of a discussion on Beckett, on the assumption that they shared a common evaluation of the writer. Adorno wished to make use of Beckett to throw into focus the relations between utopia and negativity, that is to say, his and Bloch's fundamental philosophical positions. This was in essence the continuation of an earlier debate. In 1964, in Baden-Baden, there had been a radio debate with the title 'Something Missing . . . On the Contradictions of Utopian Yearning'. The two discussants were eager to keep things on a friendly footing, referred to each other as 'my friend' and took care to keep the debate within the bounds of genuine dialogue. Both were concerned to prevent the devaluation of utopian thinking. While Bloch attempted to demonstrate the attractions of utopia by displaying its contents, Adorno insisted that there could be no substantively definable utopia; for utopia's own sake we must resist 'making an image of utopia'. For 'utopia is to be found essentially in the determinate negation . . . of what is, since, by demonstrating that what is takes concrete form as something false, it always at the same time points to what should exist.'[45]

The dispute about positivism: Via discourse to the Frankfurt School

The scientistic adult mockery of 'mind music' simply drowns the creaking of the cupboard drawers in which the questionnaires are deposited – the sound of the enterprise of pure literalness.[46]

In the course of the 1960s, Adorno had consolidated his position in West German sociology to such a point that in November 1963 he was elected to the post of chairman of the German Sociological Society. He succeeded Otto Stammer, who had a chair in Berlin and belonged to his own generation. He was followed in 1968 by Ralf Dahrendorf, who had been born in 1929. At Adorno's own suggestion, Ludwig von Friedeburg was chosen as his vice-chairman. His period of office witnessed two of the most important sociology conferences of the postwar era. The first took place in Heidelberg in 1964 and was devoted to the topic of 'Max Weber and Sociology'; the second, in Frankfurt am Main in 1968, was concerned with the topical subject 'Late Capitalism or Industrial Society?'.[47]

How are we to explain Adorno's relatively powerful position in the academic community of sociologists? The reasons are not to be sought so much in the influence he wielded among the German Sociological Society as director of the Frankfurt Institute of Social Research, or in his prominence as a speaker at the sociology conferences from the very outset, or even in the large number of significant publications and research projects that he could claim to his credit. It was rather that, following Horkheimer's retirement in 1959 and consequent withdrawal to Montagnola in the Ticino,[48] Adorno became the most prominent and most important representative of critical theory.[49] He was well aware of the responsibility implicit in the role of chairman of the German Sociological Society, since it meant that he could rely not just on the support of the members of the Institute of Social Research, but also on recognition by a small but weighty number of colleagues in the discipline, despite self-evident differences of opinion.[50]

Adorno was one of the major co-organizers of the Heidelberg Sociology Conference in 1964. It attracted a large number of professional participants. The tone of the conference was set by Herbert Marcuse, who gave a paper on 'Industrialization and Capitalism in the Work of Max Weber'.[51] Adorno had written a detailed letter to Marcuse in September 1963, making a number of concrete suggestions as to the content. He advised him

> to examine Weber's concept of rationality . . . and to show that his idea of *ratio* as a means–ends relation, as opposed to the full concept of reason, in itself represented such a crippling of the concept that not much could be gleaned from it. In this connection, I would introduce a critique of his bureaucratization thesis which is what his entire book [*Economy and Society*] amounts to if you set aside all the waffle about value-freedom . . . As a person, I find Weber just as disagreeable as you do, but compared to the Lazarsfelds, he was still the very thing for which he is wrongly taken.[52]

The aim of this sociology conference was to commemorate the centenary of Weber's birth. In addition to Marcuse, Adorno had invited the leading American sociologist Talcott Parsons to give the other plenary session, and also Raymond Aron. Horkheimer chaired the plenary debate on Parsons's paper 'Value Freedom and Objectivity'. Habermas gave a presentation on the interpretations offered by Marcuse and Parsons. Strikingly, the greatest applause was reserved for Marcuse, with his thesis that Weber's central category of formal rationality helps to promote the authoritarian form of rule in capitalist economy and the plebiscitary state. 'In Max Weber's sociology, formal rationality turns into *capitalist* rationality. Thus it appears as the methodical taming of the irrational "acquisitive drive", the taming that finds its typical expression in "innerworldly asceticism".'[53] Marcuse's success among the German sociologists was partly blighted in the following discussion thanks to the mauling he received at the hands of such experts on Weber as Reinhard Bendix and Benjamin Nelson.[54]

The conflicting interpretations of Max Weber undoubtedly contributed to the polarization of schools and intellectual trends in sociology. Adorno remained unperturbed by this. Following the Heidelberg conference, he wrote to René König, saying that 'the divergent tendencies in German sociology . . . cannot be eliminated by administrative fiat, and no rational person would have an interest in doing so.'[55] Adorno's self-confident assertion that his own sociological publications as well those of the institute amounted to a paradigm was based on the reputation he had built up from the early 1960s of taking a prominent role in the slowly emerging dispute on the logic of the social sciences and the relations between social research and social theory. Unlike the American sociologist Talcott Parsons, he never claimed to have developed a systematic sociological theory. But he did try to explain his own specific approach to sociology in epistemological terms and to ground it methodologically. He has given a number of accounts of the principal obstacles standing in the way of a systematic theory of society. As early as summer 1939, he recorded in one of his notebooks that 'there were prohibitive difficulties for such a theory' and they showed themselves in the nature of language. 'Language no longer permits us to say things as they have been experienced. . . . Language denies itself to the object; it has succumbed to a dreadful disease . . . The fact that the power of facts has become so horrifying, that all theory, even true theory, reads like a mockery of this, – this has been burned into language, the organ of theory, like a stigma.'[56]

A further explanation for the problems of a critical theory of society can be found in a longer text that Adorno had written for a collection of fourteen philosophical and sociological essays that appeared in 1962. This volume, *Sociologica II*, contains eight essays by Horkheimer and six by Adorno. It is claimed in the introduction that, taken together, these essays should not be thought to aspire to the status of a 'theory'.[57] None of the essays provides any explanation for this defensive stance, though the original introduction itself goes some way towards this. It had been preceded by an (unpublished) correspondence between Adorno and Horkheimer on the status of their own theory of society. The theme of these letters had been the question of what obstacles might present themselves to a comprehensive theory of society. Adorno rejected Horkheimer's argument that a unanimous theory was ruled out by the divergence of interests as to how a future social order might be constituted. Horkheimer had long since jettisoned the hope that society might of itself generate a social movement that would represent the universal interest and with it the abolition of systems of domination that had become obsolete. In contrast, Adorno emphasized in the draft sketch of the introduction that the authors were conscious of the claim they had made to a coherent theory of society ever since the *Dialectic of Enlightenment*. However, in the light of the systematic state of total societalization, it would be wrong to entertain a theory that merely duplicated this coherence. Furthermore, even though society appeared to be so unified and so utterly organized, it was really riddled with contradictions. This irrationality of the whole could not be grasped in a rational theory, but only in fragmentary form.[58]

Even if Adorno passionately advocated the use of the methods of social research, he made no attempt to conceal their merely auxiliary function in sociology, which as the science of society could not confine itself to 'mere findings', but which had to advance further to the formation of theory. If there were any danger that sociology would come to be dominated by techniques derived from the natural sciences such as the statistical quantification of social phenomena, then this would tell us something about the standardization of human beings in contemporary mass society. Thus he believed that social research that was adapted to commercial and administrative purposes would be appropriate to a society in which human beings have become primarily the objects of administrative acts. This critical approach is not directed at defects within science itself, but at a society in which the principle that 'science is measurement' could prevail. Thus Adorno defended research methods based on the model of formulating hypotheses from which deductions could be made, while at the same time criticizing their predominance in sociology. This was an approach he retained in his later writings as well. He insisted on the methods adopted by empirical social researchers as the tool of an incorruptible process of sociological enlightenment because it contributed to 'the demystification of sociological constructs that have lost all contact with the reality that supported them'.[59] At the same time, however, he insisted that the limited value of these methods was to be clarified.[60] 'Legitimate though method is as an antidote to uncritical intuition, it becomes perverted as soon as it abandons the process of interacting with its object and insists inflexibly on its own criteria instead of reflecting on what it is being applied to.'[61]

At the beginning of the 1960s, Adorno broadened his critique of methodology by engaging in a comprehensive debate with positivism.[62] His aim was to make use of the critical scrutiny of the positivist model of science in order to elucidate the validity criteria governing the critical theory of society. The combination of reflection on method, criticism of positivism, and epistemological self-clarification created the impression that Adorno – somewhat in contradiction to his own practice as a social scientist – was setting up an opposition in principle between two types of sociology, one empirical and based on experience, the other speculative and theoretical. In fact, he wanted to define the scope and limits of the divergent approaches, both of which aimed to understand and explain social reality.[63] The methods appropriate to grasping the different dimensions of social reality formed the subject of a debate launched in 1961 by Adorno and Karl Popper.[64] The background to this confrontation was a set of disagreements that had emerged in 1959 during the Fourteenth German Sociology Conference in Berlin. The West German sociologists were celebrating the fiftieth anniversary of the Sociological Society. The occasion had generated a quarrel about the National Socialist past and also the future of the discipline.[65] One group, around Helmut Schelsky, wished to establish a general situating of German sociology, while others, such as René König and Ralf Dahrendorf, were also concerned to draw a line under the past, separating modern sociology from National Socialist transgressions in the years 1933–45, so as to liberate the new discipline from the ballast of the past and enable it to join forces with American sociology, which led the field internationally. It was disputes of this kind about the best approach to take that led to a workshop in Tübingen on 'The Logic of Scientific Discovery'. This was initiated by Ralf Dahrendorf, who was entrusted with the task of choosing the speakers: Popper, and Adorno. He knew both of them personally. Popper, who was teaching at the London School of Economics, had made his name with the *Logik der Forschung*, which had appeared in the early 1930s and which set out to develop a theory of scientific knowledge arising from his disputes with the logical positivists. For his part, Adorno had made his name as a social researcher not least with *The Authoritarian Personality*, and in addition he had become known for his theories about the relation between social theory and social research through two articles that had become standard.

The starting-point for the discussions within the discipline was Popper's paper, which consisted of twenty-seven theses setting out his programme for a critical rationalism. The question he was concerned to ask was how to construct empirically sustainable theories and how to distinguish them from theoretical speculations.[66]

In his presentation, Adorno used Popper's theses to show that critical theory was an independent paradigm in its own right. He began by defining the specific nature of the social sciences; he went on to explain the concept of society as a totality and, finally, he discussed the methodological status of criticism. In contrast to the scientific ideal of his adversary, Adorno emphasized that sociology, unlike the natural sciences, did not deal in unqualified data, but only in data that have emerged from the socio-cultural context and that bear its stamp. The available facts are social in origin right down to their linguistic formulation.[67] Adorno began by clarifying the concept of the social because his starting-point was 'the priority of society as that of something all-encompassing and consolidated above its individual manifestations'.[68] The totality of the social manifests itself in every individual phenomenon, and yet is more than the sum of individual phenomena. Society is not just omnipresent but also internally self-contradictory. The consequence of this for the social sciences is that they must represent this contradictoriness at the level of theory. In the same way that the facts do not obey logical precepts, so too knowledge of society cannot claim to be free of contradiction, in other words, consistent with formal logic. Where sociology goes beyond the observation and description of facts, it becomes criticism, which, according to Adorno and in conflict with Popper, necessarily contains a speculative element. Furthermore, 'the critical path is not merely formal but also material'.[69] The critical element of sociology results from the experience that society is antagonistic, conflict-ridden. Adorno described this experience of social contradictions as the historical starting-point of sociological thought, as the 'motive which first constitutes the possibility of sociology as such'.[70]

The discussion of Popper's and Adorno's presentations during the Tübingen workshop was less heated than had been expected. One reason was that the two opponents confined themselves to introducing their basic positions, without attempting to differentiate between them. A sharper tone made its appearance in the second round of the discussions where the two sides were represented by Jürgen Habermas and Hans Albert. Habermas published his criticism of critical rationalism in the Festschrift *Zeugnisse* that was produced by the institute for Adorno's sixtieth birthday. Adorno evidently regarded this essay, 'Analytical Theory of Science and Dialectics', as confirmation of his own position. For when, later on, he was asked by Frank Benseler, the editor of Luchterhand Verlag, to write an introduction to the volume containing all the significant talks and essays on the positivist dispute, he produced a scathing criticism of everything that he understood by positivism.[71] As an explanation for this renewed attempt to define his own position, he argued that 'the amiable tolerance towards two different coexisting types of sociology would amount to the neutralization of the emphatic claim to truth.'[72] He now brought the truth claims of his own approach to sociology to bear in an attack on critical rationalism.[73]

On the whole, Adorno simply identified critical rationalism with logical positivism, which in turn he regarded as forming part of the 'nominalist, sceptical tradition'.[74] The thrust of his attack emerged clearly in his comments on Popper's postulate of scientific objectivity, which Popper thought was guaranteed by competition among scientists, mutual criticism and free discussion.[75] Adorno, who on this occasion saw no reason to pull his punches, objected that the questionable nature of these categories was very striking. 'For instance, the category of competition contains the entire mechanism of competition ... Success in the market place has primacy over the qualities of the object, even of intellectual formations. The tradition upon which Popper relies has apparently developed within the universities into a fetter on productive forces. In Germany, a critical tradition is completely lacking.'[76]

Adorno began to write his introduction to the collection of essays that made up the dispute on positivism under great external pressure in mid-1968. The subject matter was loosely related to that of a lecture course he was giving during that summer semester.[77] His introduction contained a number of references to the 'Frankfurt School'. This suggests that he may well have thought of his renewed criticism of positivism together with his lectures on the *Introduction to Sociology* as a step towards a definitive attempt to establish the epistemological foundations of his own approach to sociology. This venture was based on a *contradictio in adjecto* that he was concerned to resolve. The contradiction consisted of the attempt to demonstrate its paradigmatic status as a critical theory of society so that its characteristic way of thinking would emerge clearly without its acquiring the dogmatic character of a doctrine. This explains why he defined sociology as a mode of reflection. It was said to burst the bounds of the individual disciplines; it was 'a piece of intellectual compensation for the division of labour, and should not, in turn, be unconditionally fixed in accordance with the division of labour. But it is no more true to claim that sociology simply brings the contents of these areas of study into . . . contact. What is called interdisciplinary cooperation cannot be equated with sociology. It is the task of the latter to reveal the mediations of the object categories. . . . Sociology is orientated towards the immanent interplay of the elements dealt with in a relatively independent manner by economics, history, psychology and anthropology. It attempts to restore scientifically the unity which they form.'[78] His objection to positivism, as he saw it, was its failure to acknowledge the collapse of subjective reason, its hypostatization of the knowing subject and its forms of thought, and its conversion of science into a technology. It was this that explained its orientation towards the primacy of functioning techniques and the emphasis on deductive, defining theorems, as well as the primacy of formal logic. Its instrumentalization of science was so comprehensive that the knowing subject was itself caught up in it and thus converted itself into an object, a development that ultimately led to the loss of spontaneity. This reification of consciousness took place at the expense of the immediate ability to experience. For his part, Adorno thought it essential for the knowledge of society to remain open to pre-scientific experience so that knowledge could keep in touch with life as it is lived. This relation between knowledge and life, however, must be critical, and it must be based on the 'legitimation of the reality recognized'[79] rather than confining itself to ensuring that propositions are free of contradictions.

'To perceive something in the features of totality's social givenness',[80] in other words, to track down the structure of society in the individual phenomenon, was something that in Adorno's view could only be achieved by unregimented experience. Such experience was for him the first condition of the theoretical knowledge of society to which he aspired. 'Only an experience that succeeds in perceiving changes in the physiognomy of society without reaching prematurely for ready-made theories . . . is capable of serving as a starting-point for a relevant

theory.'[81] The process of unregimented experience should be continued
in the form of interpretation, for interpretation is able to penetrate
the façade of appearances by means of conceptual reflection. It is 'the
attempt to make experience, the process of wanting to express something . . . , binding, to give it objectivity.'[82] To make something binding
means the formation of a theory which represents the culmination of
the unity of concept and thing.

Elsewhere, Adorno had defined the relation of theory to experience
as comparable to that of a person to the bread he eats: theory lives on
experience as an eater lives on bread: 'Theory is consumed by thought,
thought lives on theory and theory vanishes into thought at the same
time.'[83] Adorno was convinced that the tools of methodology point our
attention in a fixed direction from the outset and thus lead us to a
specific but distorting point of view. This was the dilemma that Adorno
hoped to resolve through his own approach. Its point lay in 'passively
and without fear trusting oneself to one's own experience'.[84] This trust
in our own experience does not absolve us from intellectual exertion.
'But this intellectual exertion is predominantly the destruction of its
usual exertion, of its using violence towards the object.'[85] Truth, according to Adorno, does not lie 'in fitting propositions . . . to data that
happen to be given', but in the element of expression, that is, in saying
what 'the world reveals to us'. The validity of what the world so reveals
is to be gauged by the criterion of the evidence. Given the objective
nature of reality, the process of cognition can only be painful since it is
a matter of accounting for the absurdity of the world while remaining
conscious of the possibility of a life lived rightly.[86] He did not succeed
in formulating this idea satisfactorily until his philosophical *magnum
opus*, the *Negative Dialectics*: 'The need to lend suffering a voice is
a condition of all truth. For suffering is objectivity that weighs upon
the subject; its most subjective experience, its expression, is objectively
conveyed.'[87]

Because society is both rational in its means and irrational in its ends,
the criterion of non-contradiction cannot be maintained for the objects
of sociological knowledge. The science of society must live with the
paradox that the object of its gaze is both comprehensible and incomprehensible at the same time. It is comprehensible because it deals
with human beings who enter into relations with one another; incomprehensible because these human beings are subject to the abstract rule
of the universal laws of exchange. This, Adorno believes, is what gives
rise to the dual character of sociology. Its field of investigation is both
subjective and objective. It is subjective inasmuch as social relations
are reducible to relations between human subjects. Society is objective,
however, as a structured entity, a systemic totality in which human
subjects are perforce integrated.

When Adorno undertook to refine this conception of a critical sociology within the framework of his introduction and his lecture course, he

was able to fall back on the explanations he had offered in 1966 in *Negative Dialectics*. There, it was possible to discover in detail what he had meant when he described sociology as an interpretative procedure that he called 'micrological'. His method envisaged the individual analyses of different types of data which could be concentrated in different explanatory models that could then be synthesized in a constellation. 'Becoming aware of the constellation in which a thing stands is tantamount to deciphering the constellation which ... it bears within it.'[88] What Adorno formulated as a constellation was supposed to culminate in theoretical knowledge that would not be confined to classification or schematization: 'As a constellation, theoretical thought circles the concept it would like to unseal, hoping that it might fly open like the lock of a well-guarded safe-deposit box: in response, not to a single key or a single number, but to a combination of numbers.'[89]

By way of illustrating such combinations of numbers, Adorno referred in *Negative Dialectics* to Max Weber's 'ideal types' as aids to understanding. Weber thought of ideal types as heuristically useful constructs that are utopian in character because as 'composed' entities they have no reality. However, ideal types have nothing in common with an ideal state to be striven for. It is rather the case that 'the idea of what ought to be, the paradigmatic, should be kept at a distance from what are in a logical sense "ideal images of thought".'[90] As a music theorist, Adorno regarded this method of creating ideal types as a form of composition at the level of abstract theory. Since Weber himself spoke of 'composing' in connection with ideal types, it was all the easier for Adorno to take up this idea. In analogous fashion to these ideal types, whose purpose is to make the process-like nature of social developments comprehensible, objects have to be encircled by the constellation of intellectual models, instead of being subsumed under concepts. Thinking in constellations is itself neither associative nor non-conceptual, since 'Concepts alone can achieve what the concept prevents.'[91]

Alongside this way of thinking in terms of sociological models, Adorno tried to clarify the concept of social totality. He defined totality as the assemblage of the relations formed by individuals which have their own weight over and against him. The 'totality' is society as a 'thing in itself', as a system. Without the previous experience of society as a totality, it is scarcely possible to comprehend the individual facts elicited in the course of research. To elucidate this idea of the need to use the objectivity of society as a whole as a starting-point, Adorno produced an instructive illustration: 'In order to know what a worker is one must know what capitalist society is; conversely, the latter is surely no more "basic" than are the workers.'[92]

At the conclusion of his introduction, and on a number of occasions in his lecture course, Adorno commented on Max Weber's postulate of value freedom, a concept to which Popper's critical rationalism adhered strictly.[93] Adorno maintained in contrast that sociology was a normative science in that its discoveries made sense only if they envisaged an improvement in social living conditions. A further consideration was that to make science value neutral could lead to its manipulation for political ends. 'Just as a strictly apolitical stance becomes a political fact, a capitulation in the face of might . . . , so value neutrality generally subordinates itself . . . to what . . . are known as value systems.'[94] This implies an explicit commitment to the value of critique.[95] As he remarks in his lecture course, thanks to this link with the concept of value, critical theory is identifiable '*tant bien que mal*' as 'the Frankfurt School'.[96] This value-laden commitment to critique laid the Frankfurt conception of sociology open to the accusation of backwardness. But, according to Adorno, the prediction that the philosophy of the Frankfurt School was becoming old-fashioned reminded him of 'the question asked by the little girl upon seeing a large dog – how long can such a dog live?'[97]

Against German stuffiness

Fundamental ontology behaves towards existence a little bit like the wicked stepmother in the fairy tale of 'Snow White'. She is 'the fairest in the land', which is immeasurably large, but somewhere far away, 'beyond the hills, with the Seven Dwarfs', lives Snow White, who is fairer far than she. Fundamental ontology cannot bear there to be even a small exception, and so it is . . . continually spurred on to eliminate every trace of the memory of existing things, to obliterate them even at the risk of finally becoming so abstract that nothing at all remains of itself.[98]

In the 1950s, when Adorno first began to respond to the dominant climate in post-Nazi Germany, he discovered that in public lectures and speeches, newspaper articles and monographs, in Protestant academies and writings on education, as well as in a large part of the prose and poetry that was fashionable at the time – wherever he looked, in fact – there were symptoms of what he called 'Heideggerism' (*Heideggerei*). He had already started compiling some initial notes for a subsequent critique of Heidegger's theory of being,[99] elements of which went back to his inaugural lecture of 1931 and were then picked up again in his lecture course on 'The Concept of Philosophy' in 1951–2. Thus we can read in the transcript of the lecture of 6 December 1951 that Heidegger's authoritarian language 'created a theological aura'. He went on to say that Heidegger gave the impression that his language was 'the language of being itself. It is reminiscent of the way in which the Kabbalists derived objective structures from the divinely revealed Hebrew language. Heidegger is nothing but a kind of Kabbalist. Since this language lacks history, history becomes mythologized. There is a connection between this philosophy and the fascists.'[100]

But he did not produce his detailed, fundamental criticism of Heidegger's ontology until his own lecture course on 'Ontology and

Dialectics' in the winter semester of 1960–1. This criticism remained true to his original intention of using dialectics to interrogate a philosophy of origins. Adorno attempted to implement a programme of 'smashing Heidegger' that Benjamin had conceived as early as 1930.[101] This intention also underlay Adorno's Frankfurt lectures and the lectures he gave at the Collège de France that were in part derived from them. In June 1959, Adorno wrote to Robert Minder, the French Germanist who had invited him to Paris, 'that it would be a good idea to tackle the entire phenomenon of "Heideggerism" for once in a very principled way. In order not to do him an honour that in my view he does not deserve, such a critique should not focus on him and his personality, but it should be formulated more as a matter of principle.'[102] This means that Adorno must have distinguished between Heidegger's philosophy and what he understood by Heideggerism.

Shortly after his letter to Minder, he started to work on a voluminous draft for the lecture. He begins his outline with the statement: 'Chief motif: that ontology cannot be found to be free of history, and is not free of history.'[103] Adorno's intention was to attack Heidegger's definition of ontological difference, in other words, his definition of the relation of being to things that exist. Whereas, according to Heidegger, existing things can only be experienced by thinking of being, Adorno tried to derive the question of being from things that exist. Only by taking the historicity of existing things as the starting-point does it become possible to interpret the tendency to reification, which Heidegger also diagnoses, in social rather than ontological terms.[104] In his lectures, Adorno made no attempt to provide a 'true' dialectic with which to refute a 'false' ontology – that would be 'standpoint' philosophy which he rejected as a type of thinking that had degenerated to the level of mere 'world views'. Instead, he was concerned to mediate between opposites. 'I wish to show you', he said in the first lecture, 'that the antagonism between these two philosophies is not unmediated; it is not like choosing between two different brands, much as you can choose between the CDU and the SPD. The approach I propose to you is rationally motivated. It is based not on the arbitrariness of a so-called decision, but has grown out of the subject matter itself.'[105]

Adorno's criticism developed in the first instance from his study of *Being and Time* (1927) and then in connection with Heidegger's later volume of essays *Holzwege* (False Trails) of 1950. His general objection was that Heidegger constantly regresses to the unhistorical and the archaic because he has rejected the reduction of primordial being to existing things. Heidegger's trick is to ontologize what actually exists. 'For example', he explains in the eighth lecture, 'the celebrated formula of man as "the shepherd of being" is an ontic turn of phrase; that is to say, the attempt to grasp a primordial metaphysical reality goes back to the primitive, pre-agrarian conditions of a pastoral society and thus to something very existing, very time-bound – as is well known, shepherds have now died out and are only rarely encountered even in the Black Forest.'[106] Adorno thus attacks a linguistic practice 'that surrounds itself with a halo', so as to give itself 'the appearance of something loftier, more metaphysical'.[107] Immediately following his lectures in Frankfurt and Paris, Adorno wrote *The Jargon of Authenticity* in order to explain even more clearly the nature of the counter-enlightenment against which we ought to be on our guard. This book, which he wrote between 1962 and 1964, was not concerned to deploy dialectics in order to undermine Heidegger's ontology, even though it might have given that impression, since the term 'authenticity' was in fact a key concept of *Being and Time*. His criticism was directed exclusively at the lofty tone that predominated in postwar Germany until well into the 1960s, the inflated pathos that was the essence of the Heideggerism that was mechanically imitated by 'the mass of authentics'.[108] Adorno was undoubtedly able to distinguish between Heidegger's substantive philosophy and his apologists and imitators who made use of his 'existential' language. According to Adorno, Heidegger was 'not the matador of such political strategies of the jargon and in fact takes care to avoid their crassness.'[109] The situation was otherwise with the writings of Karl Jaspers and Otto Friedrich Bollnow, who had become fashionable exponents of existentialism. It was mainly their writings from which Adorno quoted in order to demolish the wide-spread jargon of authenticity – which he described as 'the Wurlitzer organ of the spirit'.[110] This polemic was evidently not without its effect. In a letter to Herbert Marcuse on 15 December 1964, he wrote: 'Ernst Bloch phoned to say that because of the "Jargon" Bollnow is having a nervous breakdown. Let him.'[111]

At least one element of Heidegger's thought was not alien to Adorno – this was his condemnation of the modern will to power. But even so, if you take the first part of *Negative Dialectics* into account (the 'Relation to Ontology'), he does not have a good word to say about him. Heidegger, who was fourteen years older than Adorno, appears to have simply ignored this attack from Frankfurt.[112] At any rate, there is no known public comment on Adorno by Heidegger; nor did the two ever have a proper meeting in postwar Germany,[113] although they had once been introduced to each other, in January 1929, in the house of Kurt Riezler, the university registrar.[114]

Adorno provided a first foretaste of his polemic in November 1964, when he gave a reading at an evening event organized by Suhrkamp Verlag. This consisted of extracts that then appeared in advance in the *Neue Rundschau*. The same month saw the publication of *The Jargon of Authenticity*, with a dedication 'For Fred Pollock for 22 May 1964' and a motto from Samuel Beckett's *The Unnameable*: 'Il est plus facile d'élever un temple que d'y faire descendre l'objet du culte.'[115] The Cantate Hall in which the Suhrkamp readings were traditionally held was full, with every seat taken. On this occasion, Adorno's reading was frequently punctuated by laughter and applause.[116] At the centre of his linguistic analysis were those highly marketable exclusive terms and phrases such as 'in the decision', 'commission', 'appeal', 'encounter', 'genuine dialogue', 'statement', 'concern', 'commitment', but also lines of poetry such as Rilke's famous verse about 'poverty as the great inward gleam of the spirit'.[117] Since this jargon amounts to a German ideology that has somehow infiltrated language, it must be analysed linguistically. 'The fact that such language has become an ideology unto itself, socially necessary illusion, can be demonstrated by the contradiction between what it says and how it says it.'[118]

This was the programme that Adorno implemented in detail. In the first sections he unmasked the jargon as a rhetorical technique that stood in the way of a critical scrutiny of content because the words were said to be what mattered, the things that could not be interrogated existentially. The jargon that arose hand in hand with a resurrected metaphysics of origins presented itself as a form of compensation for the real losses of meaning to which the individual was forced to submit in the administered world. It is suggested that, by turning the language of the depths into the language of higher realms, by immersing oneself in an archaic language, it would be possible to conjure up the spirit of a truly human existence. In fact, the jargon fills the breach created by the disintegration of language,[119] and as such it is the complement to the positivist view of language that permits language only as an instrument of meaningful signs. Adorno also used Heidegger's own texts to illustrate the nature of the jargon, showing that in his case it was a style 'that aimed, synthetically, to create a primal sense for pure words'.[120] Thus Heidegger was said to have packed commonplace turns of phrase into the universal concepts of his philosophy in order to create the impression of magical participation in the absolute. At the same time, however, the nullity of human existence was raised to the level of an essential category so that the destinies of individual human beings appear worthless.

It is these passages on Heidegger that exemplify Adorno's original intention. This linguistic criticism was intended as merely the first step in a comprehensive critique of Heidegger for which *The Jargon of Authenticity* was to be no more than 'a kind of propaedeutic'.[121] But since these sections had become so voluminous, and since they had a different character from the as yet uncompleted *Negative Dialectics*, Adorno decided to publish them on their own.[122]

The fat child

Greyness could not fill us with despair if our minds did not harbour the concept of different colours, scattered traces of which are not absent from the negative whole.[123]

Adorno's lecture at the Collège de France in March 1961 led to close contact with a number of French colleagues over the years.[124] At the same time, he began work on the long-cherished plan of writing a book on dialectics. At first, he 'just plunged straight into it . . . and later on this created huge difficulties of organization.'[125] The book was conceived as the sum of his philosophical thinking and would have therefore to satisfy the highest expectations. Towards the end of 1965, it seemed to be taking shape, but as Adorno wrote to Marcuse with some self-irony, 'It was like the dialectical logic of Buff the Master Tailor: what he sewed up one day, he unpicked the next.' It is not surprising that ten days later he added, 'I am working very hard and am so exhausted that I am looking forward to the few miserable days at Christmas.'[126]

He had been working on *Negative Dialectics* for seven years, he reflected, when he finally held the book in his hands. It appeared with its elegant grey binding in November 1966, in an edition of 4000 copies. When he announced the forthcoming publication to Helene Berg he described it as 'my chief philosophical work, if I may call it that. . . . Henceforth, my work will be concentrated, far more strongly than for years now, on artistic matters.'[127] Many of his letters contain comments in which he stresses the huge effort that it cost him to bring this book of all his books to fruition.

Having begun to write this large-scale formulation of his philosophy, he used his preparatory work to produce three lecture courses which he then gave between 1964 and 1966. In the winter semester of 1964–5, he lectured on 'The Doctrine of History and Freedom', in the following semester the subject was 'Metaphysics', while in the winter semester 1965–6 the lecture course bore the title of the book: 'Negative Dialectics'. These lectures provided him with the ideal forum to present his ideas and test their plausibility before an audience. Adorno referred to some of his listeners as 'my pupils'. He did so not just from a sense of pride, but because it meant that he thought of them as his equals in discussion, people who could act as a kind of control over what he was saying and whom he did not need to fob off with the history of philosophy, let alone with formulae taken from *Weltanschauungen* or 'standpoint' thinking.[128] The three courses[129] corresponded to the three main sections of *Negative Dialectics*: 'The Introduction expounds the concept of philosophical experience. . . . Part Two proceeds from the results of the introduction to the idea of a negative dialectics. . . . Part Three elaborates models of negative dialectics.'[130]

Adorno himself thought of *Negative Dialectics*, with its paradoxical and antinomian structure, as one of his most complex and stylistically ambitious books. Despite the density of its subject matter, its transparent structure is remarkable. The book sets its face against a type of dialectical thinking that goes back to Plato and is characterized by its affirmative streak. Thus even in Hegel, the principle of negation ultimately takes a positive turn. Adorno, in contrast, wished to deny negation the chance to turn into positivity. His intention was to present a form of self-reflection that could apprehend the truth in an unconventional way. This approach would question the validation of data by reference to their genesis, i.e., their origins, and at the same time the illusion of an identity of thought and existence would be abandoned. 'No object is wholly known.'[131] This breach with the past was to open the way to a material philosophy that constitutes the constructive goal of *Negative Dialectics*.[132]

The core of the lengthy introduction consisted of the exposition of a conception of philosophical experience that Adorno contrasted with scientific knowledge. The criticism of Bergson, Husserl and especially Heidegger in part I was the starting-point from which to develop his own concept of truth. 'What is true in the subject unfolds in relation to that which it is not, but by no means in a boastful affirmation of the way it is.'[133] The ontological need (Husserl's 'Let's get back to things') was something Adorno took seriously in the sense that he interpreted it as the desire for philosophical experience.

In part II, Adorno explicated the central concepts of non-identity and non-conceptuality, as well as the idea of thinking in constellations. In the course of his discussion of Kant's epistemology, with its emphasis on the primacy of the subject, he formulated a critique of idealism in the light of specific materialist insights. His aim was to pave the way for the thesis of the primacy of the object, a thesis he defended in a variety of ways. As opposed to identity philosophy, with its separation of subject and object, Adorno emphasized the tension between the universal and the particular, a tension which in Adorno's view should not be resolved in favour of the universal. In order to escape the reductiveness of purely conceptual understanding, the abstract nature of classification, he appealed to 'the cognitive utopia' that consisted in 'using concepts to open up the non-conceptual, without making it their equal.'[134] For whatever lacks a concept he introduced the term 'non-identity'.[135] He did not think of non-identity as a superior alternative to identificatory thought, but as a corrective to a conceptualizing procedure. When philosophy surrenders the autarky of the concept, 'it strips the blindfold from our eyes'.[136] It then realizes that 'in truth the subject is never quite the subject, and the object never quite the object.'[137]

In part III Adorno tested his own principles on three models: the philosophies of Kant and Hegel and also metaphysics. Thus he discussed the question of free will in relation to the idea of morality as this was elaborated in Kant's theory of morality. Adorno made freedom dependent upon a future world order in which 'human beings would no longer need to be evil. Evil, therefore, is the world's own unfreedom. Whatever evil is done comes from the world.'[138] As opposed to an idea of free will based on the *principium individuationis*, Adorno formulated his criticism of 'the fallacy of constitutive subjectivity',[139] that is to say, of the privileging of the subject that posits its individual self-preservation as an absolute.

Kant's expectation that freedom would be realized in the transcendental subject and Hegel's that reason would become real in the world spirit were unacceptable in Adorno's view. He opposed to them the historical fact of the failure of culture that has been 'demonstrated irrefutably' by Auschwitz.[140] The twelve 'Meditations on Metaphysics' dwell on the extreme margins of what philosophical reflection is capable of. Adorno inquired whether the idea of the humanity of mankind can possibly be salvaged in the face of the realities of the death camps. Is there no alternative to Nietzsche's nihilism?

With this work the author passed through the 'icy wastes of abstraction'. It is by this book that the substance of his philosophy should be measured. Its scope and weight may well explain why privately he thought of it as 'his fat child'. This was the phrase he used in a number of letters, although in fact the epithet derives from one of the fascinating, autobiographically tinged short stories by Marie Luise Kaschnitz.[141] So as to be able to finish writing *Negative Dialectics* Adorno had obtained leave from all his teaching commitments for two semesters. He was able to finish the manuscript by the end of July 1966 and then travelled to Sils Maria for a six-week vacation. He left Frankfurt in a 'state of extreme exhaustion', accompanied by insomnia and after a painful operation on his elbow. These discomforts did not prevent him from contemplating his next projects. In a letter to his old friend Carl Dreyfus, he wrote: 'I simply have the feeling that I need to get all my crucial things safely gathered in, if I am to get them done at all while I am still in full possession of my powers.'[142] All the more important to him were the weeks in which he could recuperate in the Waldhaus in the Upper Engadine. This vacation was followed by an extended trip to Italy, where he went without Gretel. The journey took him to Rome, Naples and Palermo. Having arrived in Sicily, he visited Segesta in the north-west of the island with its archaic ruins and its Doric temple from the fifth century BC, as well as the ancient ruins of Selinus. This stimulated him to ask 'what the current relation of consciousness to traditional art might look like'. During this trip he met Jutta Burger, and went on with her to visit Paestum and Ravello. They also went to Naples and Rome, where Adorno met Iris von Kaschnitz and Ingeborg Bachmann.[143]

Shortly after returning to Frankfurt, Adorno learnt of the death of Siegfried Kracauer. Kracauer had died of the effects of pneumonia in New York on 26 November 1966. In October, Adorno had written to him from the Hotel Quirinale and reported on the different stages of his Italian journey. In his letter of condolence to his widow, he emphasized the important part Kracauer had played in his development and how he had been someone he was close to and could exchange ideas with easily. When he and Horkheimer exchanged the news about Kracauer's death, it became clear how shocked Adorno was. It had reminded him, he said, that it was Kracauer who had introduced him to philosophy in the 1920s.[144]

After his extended period of recuperation in Switzerland and Italy, Adorno wrote to Gershom Scholem with a particularly detailed account of the content of *Negative Dialectics*, a book which, against his normal practice, was addressed to professional colleagues.[145] He wrote to him in March 1967: 'In the immanent epistemological debate, once one has escaped from the clutches of idealism, what I call the primacy of the object . . . seems to me an attempt to do justice to the concept of materialism. The telling arguments that I believe I have advanced against idealism present themselves as materialist. But the materialism involved here is no conclusive, fixed thing, it is not a world-view. This path to materialism is totally different from dogma, and it is this fact that seems to me to guarantee an affinity with metaphysics, I might almost have said, theology.'[146] Adorno went into greater detail about metaphysics itself, the subject of part III of *Negative Dialectics*: 'The wish to salvage metaphysics is in fact central in *Negative Dialectics*.'[147] Scholem had gained the same impression from his own reading of the book: 'If you would permit me to sum up my opinion in a few sentences, I would say that I have never read a purer, more restrained defence of metaphysics. Starting from a standpoint from which its defence must appear so hopeless and quixotic . . . you have undertaken a breakout whose energy and resoluteness I find admirable. . . . If one takes your materialist thesis into account, the battle you have waged on behalf of metaphysics is admirable.'[148] Adorno responded to this praise: 'I am delighted that this has come out so clearly and that you sympathize with it.'[149]

Despite Scholem's general approval of *Negative Dialectics*, he nevertheless questioned whether Adorno could rely on materialist theory if Marx's ideas on the historical subject had proved illusory. Scholem put his finger on the crucial question when he asked whether critical theory meant anything more than the attempt to retain Marx's analysis of capitalism while abandoning the theory of class struggle. He put forward the cautious suggestion that 'the thesis of mediation by the totality of the social process . . . plays the part of a deus ex machina.'[150]

Nor was Scholem won over by Adorno's attempt to make use of Sohn-Rethel's assertion that a compelling link could be established between the universal process of exchange and 'the processes of abstraction in consciousness'. 'I do not wish to rule out *a priori* the proposition that ideas and categories can have a social content. What I cannot understand is the claim that there really is a method for strictly inferring them.'[151] How did Adorno react to this criticism? Not only did he accept the differences of opinion between himself and Scholem as they emerged in this letter, he even admitted 'that of course they lay in their respective attitudes to materialism. I lack the naivety to deceive myself about this and to adjust the weight of the arguments in your letter in my favour.'[152]

While Scholem advanced a number of weighty objections to *Negative Dialectics*, Sohn-Rethel's enthusiasm was boundless. 'Your book has just arrived! Wonderful! What a Xmas gift!' Admittedly, he did have queries about it, and since they came from the point of view of the Marxist theory of revolution they naturally differed from those put by Scholem, a professor of Jewish mysticism. Did '*Negative Dialectics* have nothing to say about changing the world? Is all that [namely the Cultural Revolution of the Red Guard in China] part of the "affirmative tradition" from which "the book wishes to liberate the dialectic"? Or is it the case that you do not think changing the world is impossible, but only question that it means "putting philosophy into practice"? In that event, then, the forms of thought would *not* be determined by social being and would have reverted to a dialectical idealism.'[153] In his reply, a few days later, Adorno advised Sohn-Rethel, in a slightly schoolmasterly tone, that he should read the book right through, since it was 'highly structured' and one could only gain a complete impression 'by following the argument through to its end'.[154] On the questions about putting philosophy into practice, Adorno replied that he rejected 'the moral pressure coming from official Marxism, which amounts to a specific type of positivity'. He agreed with Grabbe's statement that 'nothing but despair can save us. . . . I am unable to believe that what is happening in China can be any cause for hope. I would have to deny everything I have thought my whole life long if I were to admit to feeling anything but horror at the sight of it.' What they had believed in their youth and had discussed with Kracauer and Benjamin in the 1920s was something that had been bypassed by 'the world spirit, or whatever it may be called'. 'We should truly strive to learn from our mistakes without being untrue to our motives.'[155]

To what motives did Adorno remain true? For one thing, he remained true to the idea of a materialist dialectics that Scholem had found fault with but that he had pursued since his inaugural lecture of 1931. According to that dialectics, the social world was to be understood in principle as an open-ended, historically changing space produced and shaped by human hand. The underlying theme of *Negative Dialectics* was in fact its author's conviction that, even though the world appears as a given, it must be held to be contingent and with an open-ended future. If in his book Adorno constantly insists on the primacy of the object over the subject, he was nevertheless concerned to criticize the thing-like nature of social relations and the blind coercion exercised over human beings by material conditions. The book aimed to be a philosophical denunciation of the social causes of suffering and want. It is for this reason that Adorno speaks of 'the convergence of specific materialism with criticism, with social change in practice'.[156]

Proceeding from this starting-point, Adorno deepened his criticism of philosophical systems in *Negative Dialectics*; this too was a theme to which he remained true. He had challenged their claim to validity in Husserl and later in Hegel and had then expanded this line of thought in the *Dialectic of Enlightenment* with a deconstruction of reason and of logocentrism. Likewise, his concern with the history of nature was a renewal of arguments he had developed earlier on in his lecture of 1932 on 'The Idea of Natural History'. In the current book, he defined the thinking subject as well as existing objectivity from the dual perspective of a dependence upon both nature and history.

Finally, Adorno attempted in *Negative Dialectics* to redeem the ambitious pledge of providing a complete rethink of metaphysics in order to express 'solidarity with it at the moment of its fall'.[157] Since he had no wish to surrender the idea of a metaphysical knowledge that 'had taken refuge in profanity', he held on to an emphatic conception of truth: namely to the unconditional necessity of a knowledge that is more than thought in the sense of identification. Adorno reckoned with a capacity for suffering and a need for sensuous happiness that resisted the 'world of barter where everything is interchangeable' and that 'does not want the colours of the world to fade'.[158]

This reference to the world of barter where everything is interchangeable reminds us that *Negative Dialectics* was conceived as a contribution to a critical theory of society which is realized 'when things in being are read as a text of their becoming'.[159] Nevertheless, Adorno had the feeling that this aspect of the book had been sold short. He told Horkheimer of his fears that critics might well raise this objection to the book. Does this mean that if the book focused on the theory of knowledge rather than the theory of society, Adorno must have conceived it as the last great attempt at a subject–object philosophy? Or did he think he had succeeded in overcoming the aporias of a philosophy of consciousness? Whatever the case, his hope for *Negative Dialectics* was that the intransigent nature of his philosophy of contradiction, his insistence that 'dialectics is the consistent consciousness of non-identity',[160] would have a liberating effect in principle, particularly since he believed that he had succeeded in dismantling the supposed validity of existing reality and its transcendent self-justifications. 'The means employed in negative dialectics for the penetration of its hardened objects is possibility – the possibility of which their reality has cheated the objects and which is nonetheless visible in each one.'[161]

Despite its technical philosophical content and its high degree of abstractness, the book found a relatively large number of readers in a short space of time. A year after its first publication a second reprint of 5000 to 7000 appeared. This was followed by translations into French, Italian and English. The publisher's blurb referred to it as an anti-system, by analogy with anti-drama and anti-hero. It was evident that it would not achieve the same popularity as his essay volumes. Nevertheless, there was great interest in it, especially among young intellectuals.

In a review in the *Süddeutsche Zeitung* of 2 October 1967, Ivo Frenzel described the book as 'an extraordinary achievement that stands out in the hardly glorious landscape of German philosophy of the present as a pinnacle with unmistakable contours.'[162] The Munich philosopher Dieter Henrich was cautiously critical, pointing out that 'what could be called theory here is not developed from within itself and the critique of particular theorems, like the entire book, is aimed at a critique of reality.' Adorno may well have read this with approval, and the same may be said of the comment that 'the author writes lucidly'.[163]

The majority of reviews were not really in a position to do justice to the actual content of the book, even less than usual, in fact. This was even the case where reviewers delivered a positive judgement. In order to avoid having to comment on the philosophical substance of the book, many writers concentrated on criticizing the author's use of language. Ludwig Marcuse was particularly scathing in a review that appeared in *Die Zeit* in October 1967 with the title 'The Beautiful Tongue', a reference to a poem about Adorno by Günter Grass. Marcuse, who had known Adorno personally in exile in California, was one of many who objected to his use of language, something with which Adorno was increasingly confronted during this period. According to Marcuse, he wrote a jargon that aimed 'to drive the harmlessness out of harmless souls'.[164] A little later Adorno referred to this polemic as 'a tit-for-tat response, moreover one from which I have been left out. . . . The so-called jargon . . . I am reproached with, if its distinguishing feature is that it is not easily understood, then that comes from the fact that I have been striving to express myself very precisely in order to escape from the general sloppiness of communication.'[165]

In order to provide an adequate forum for a truly substantive discussion of *Negative Dialectics*, Adorno offered two regular philosophy seminars in the summer semester 1967 and the winter semester 1967–8 so as to create an opportunity for the book to be examined in detail. The high level of the seminar was guaranteed by the fact that it was attended not only by Horkheimer on occasion, but also by a whole series of assistants and colleagues of Adorno's from both philosophy and sociology. These included Werner Becker, Herbert Schnädelbach, Arend Kulenkampff and Karl-Heinz Haag. Among the students, of whom there were very many, despite the need to register officially, were Americans such as Angela Davis and Irving Wohlfahrt, as well as a number of people who were later to make their mark in university teaching as the younger representatives of critical theory.

The seminars dealt with the book chapter by chapter and involved proper seminar papers that were followed by discussion. Adorno took the discussions very seriously. The controversies generated by the seminars focused on the historicity of dialectical logic and the principles of reason and criticism, as well as the question of internal inconsistencies and contradictions in Adorno's own philosophy. One objection arising from the political climate of the day was that all consciously critical thought must adopt the standpoint of the socially oppressed. Adorno responded to this with the very characteristic comment that his dialectics was concerned 'with the dissolution of standpoint-thinking itself'. This is to be achieved 'by means of a procedure in which the phenomena under investigation are not scrutinized from any outside perspective, but are judged in accordance with their own concept.'[166] Nevertheless, the question of the impartiality of critical theory had now been raised; it forced itself on Adorno's attention and would preoccupy him in the near future more than almost any other.

What kind of a society do we live in?
Adorno's analysis of the present

'All theory is grey,' Goethe has Mephistopheles preach to the student he is leading around by the nose; the sentence is already ideology from the very beginning, fraud about the fact that the tree of life the practical people planted and the devil in the same breath compares to gold is hardly green at all; the greyness of theory is for its part a function of the life that has been stripped bare of qualities.[167]

As a philosopher who had passed his sixtieth year, what Adorno had to show was chiefly the *Negative Dialectics*, but there was also the *Aesthetic Theory*, although this book, which remained a fragment, was not published until shortly after his death. In sociology he had published a considerable number of essays on a great variety of subjects, demonstrating that his unorthodox social theory was eager to overcome the separation between pure philosophy and pure sociology that was currently practised by both disciplines. But even more importantly, the micrological form of sociological theory formation fitted his conception of the subject. As he explains in *Negative Dialectics*, his first concern was to make use of models in his work on sociology, in other words, 'to *interpret* phenomena, not to ascertain, organize and classify facts, let alone to make them available as information.'[168] In his epistemology, Adorno insists on 'binding statements without a system'.[169] As a sociologist, too, he had little interest in creating a consistent theory of society. What he wanted above all was to clarify the way in which we acquire knowledge of society. He wanted to show in practical terms how social knowledge is to be understood as a specific form of reality, to discover 'how matters have developed thus far and where they are going'.[170] Adorno approached sociology by a process of immersion in the particular nature of specific social phenomena, such as quarrels or situations of spontaneous laughter,[171] so as to decipher them as expressions of the universal. He did not analyse the universal, that is contemporary society, from the perspective of an observer contemplating it from outside, but from within. This internal perspective revealed 'what secretly holds the machinery together',[172] namely the way in which modern society functions.

As early as the lecture course on 'Philosophy and Sociology' of 1960,[173] Adorno had stressed repeatedly that sociology was dependent on philosophy if it aspired to be anything more than mere technique. On the other hand, even though philosophy is opposed to sociology by nature, it needs the spur of the empirical. Since sociology essentially refers to the object world, a mode of thought that fails to penetrate the objects is a mere copy. Enlightenment, which formerly belonged to philosophy, has now gone over to sociology, which discloses what exists as something that has become what it is. In contrast, philosophy is nothing but a theory of science, and Adorno criticized it as being pre-scientific since it accepts science without question, even though the interrogation of science is its true task.[174] In order not to succumb to the power of an object arising simply from too close a proximity, distance must be guaranteed by the use of concepts, concepts that are in constant motion.

In these lectures, Adorno compared the situation of social science researchers with that of a cameraman who constantly changes his vantage point, looking at things at first from close to and then in a larger context, seeing them as a whole from a distance.[175] Although the discursive rationality of concepts has its validity in sociology, science begins at the moment when you enter the open spaces and surrender to your own unregimented experience. Dialectics is nothing but the attempt to experience things without methodological and conceptual restrictions.[176] Theory in the social sciences must take its cue from this. If sociology claims to be the theory of society, it must confront social conditions with the reason that is inherent in them. We must constantly inquire whether society lives up to the claims of its own rationality. A theory of society must be able to come to terms with the fact that its object is determined by an amalgam of rationality and irrationality. As for Adorno's own concrete analysis of contemporary society, he was concerned about three main features: the socially integrating effects of the culture industry, the individual's loss of autonomy and identity and, finally, the anonymous mechanism regulating a society based on exchange.

Adorno had thought of his introduction to *The Positivist Dispute in German Sociology* as a key text for his conception of sociology. In the same way, he regarded the paper with which he opened the Conference of the German Sociologists in Frankfurt in April 1968 as crucial for the diagnostic content of his social theory. The link with the present came directly from the question in his title: 'Late Capitalism or Industrial Society?'. As president of the German sociologists, he had chosen this theme for the conference not least because it was the 150th anniversary of the birth of Karl Marx. The topic was of burning interest to professional sociologists, and also to the growing number of students in this discipline. For this was a year of radical change both politically and socially, and people were agitated by such questions as whether contemporary society was still a capitalist society in its basic economic structure, whether the conceptual apparatus of Marx's *Critique of Political Economy* was still viable as a description of modern society, and how far modifications were needed in Marx's theories about the world of work and his theory of classes and the state.[177]

These were indeed topical issues. The contemporary relevance of Marx's theory of capitalism was the subject of heated discussion among the students in Adorno's sociology seminars. He never resisted this interest in theory; on the contrary, discussions were encouraged with the help of his assistant, the economist Ernst Theodor Mohl. They went into great detail about the concepts with which to grasp the meaning of economic crises, the 'laws of motion' of organized capitalism.[178] The political assumption underlying these discussions was that democratic societies above all others should not be thought of as static, but are capable of being changed by political action. This possibility of change is what Dahrendorf must have had in mind when he commented in his welcoming address to the Frankfurt Sociologists' Conference that they found themselves in a situation in which 'those who had sown the wind might well find themselves unexpectedly reaping the whirlwind.'[179] This statement, at the opening of a conference that attracted considerable attention far beyond the conference hall, was a clear pointer to the controversies that had been unleashed by the extra-parliamentary opposition and student demonstrations. These were the years that witnessed a process of politicization that proceeded at a furious pace and which involved an increasingly militant protest against authoritarian structures and traditional values of the establishment. At the time, the reforms that began slowly to emerge in the early 1970s were not yet in sight and the political demands of the 'New Left' provoked the hostility of the majority of the population, while moral protests against the war in Vietnam, dictatorships and the emergency laws were met by incomprehension. All the more striking, then, was Adorno's initial sympathy for the protesters.[180]

In the first weeks of April, a few days before the conference was due to begin, there were two explosions in Frankfurt, where it was due to convene. These explosions in two department stores started fires that caused major damage. A little later, two men and two women were arrested who declared at their trial that they wanted to burn the department stores down 'in order to protest against society's indifference towards the murders in Vietnam'. At the same time, leaflets were distributed that were full of the inhumanity of capitalism, exploitation and consumer terrorism, and revolution and militant attitudes.[181] This was evidently the unexpected whirlwind which, according to Dahrendorf, had been sown by the critical theory of the Frankfurt School.

Adorno's opening address at least alluded to these contemporary events in passing. He interpreted the student movement as a resistance to the pressures to conform. Student protest was motivated by 'revulsion from the world as swindle and idea'.[182] It expressed, he said, the wish for freedom and change.

Adorno's theses on the question of 'Late Capitalism or Industrial Society?' were intended as a concrete contribution to the diagnosis of the current social situation. Right at the start, he made it clear that he was not concerned with the clarification of terminology: 'Experts might be thought to be tormented by the vain anxiety that the present phase was one thing or the other and hence deserved to be called by one name rather than the other. In reality, however, there is a crucial matter of substance at issue. What is at stake is whether the capitalist system still predominates according to its model, however modified, or whether the development of industry has rendered the concept of capitalism obsolete.'[183] Adorno's argument was based on the premise that rational analysis of contemporary society by social theory was ruled out by the irrationality of the totality. This irrationality was manifested, he thought, in the mechanisms by means of which individuals were directly integrated into society. He noted the atrophy of social spheres that enabled individuals to familiarize themselves with the social values, the recognized norms and the traditions of society.

Since Adorno made use of Marx's terminology to describe the basic structures of modern society, it was logical to begin with the question whether capitalism could still be used as a structural concept. In doing so, he started from the premise that what was really social about a society was its structure, which in this instance he defined as antagonistic. This meant that society as a whole consisted of institutions, norms, dominant interests, etc., which have become autonomous as a real sphere of antagonistic forces opposed to the intentions of individual actors. Admittedly, this antagonism no longer takes the form of class distinctions as we have known them historically, since class consciousness in its traditional sense can no longer be established empirically. In the same way the practical experience of exploitation has ceased to determine the actions of workers who themselves have been subject to a process of social integration. 'No longer does the employer confront workers as the physical incarnation of the interests of capital.'[184] The subjects of domination are without distinction and in equal measure the agents of functions that the production apparatus dictates. Domination thus assumes an impersonal character; it manifests itself as the coercion exercised by the system.

The decisive modification of the classical model of capitalism that justified the prefix 'late'[185] was that the state control of the economy had largely eliminated the dynamic of the marketplace. What, then, justifies us in describing contemporary society as late capitalist rather than industrial society? Adorno suggested three reasons. First, within the system of social labour, people's lives are dependent upon fundamental economic factors. Second, class antagonisms have been transformed on the international plane into the opposition between rich and poor countries. And third, social cohesion is indirectly created now as it always was by relations of exchange. The universal reach of the laws of exchange is the cause of the abstract nature of social relations. Following this clarification of the structural elements in society, Adorno argued in favour of a definition that would avoid the need to choose between late capitalism or industrial society. Present-day society is an industrial society as judged by the state of its productive forces, for the pattern of industrial labour has stamped itself on every aspect of society. In contrast to this, 'society is capitalist in its *relations* of production.'[186] For on the one hand, people living in contemporary society are forced to adjust completely to the apparatus of production; on the other hand, production takes place for the maximization of profit. This has the consequence that commodities are produced merely as exchange values; they are the expression of needs created in the first instance by the profit motive. The predominance of the interest in exploiting capital is maintained at the expense of the objective needs of consumers. 'Even where there are goods aplenty, this abundance seems cursed. Since need tends towards illusion, it infects the commodities with its own illusory character.'[187] The irrationality of social relations is accepted as a necessary price for preserving this state of affairs, even though the short-term benefits that the system seems to guarantee the individual are of dubious value. The expression of social irrationality is the fact that poverty persists even in the affluent society. The fact that extremes of wealth and poverty can exist side by side is manifest proof of the absurdity of society as a whole.

Adorno refused to accept a technocratic justification according to which social domination is merely the product of material circumstances. Domination is rather a means by which to ensure that certain definite social interests prevail: 'It is not technology that is at fault, but its entanglement with the social relations which hold it in their grip.'[188] The control of technology by economic interests so that those interests remain invisible is referred to by Adorno as 'the technological veil' behind which real relations of power and domination lie concealed. 'It is not for nothing that the invention of weapons of destruction should have been the prototype of the new technology.'[189] The dynamics of technical rationality do not lead to the dissolution of outdated relations of domination, as Marx had predicted in his philosophy of history. 'The signature of the age is the dominance established by the relations of production over the forces of production which have long since made a mockery of those relations. The fact that the extended arm of mankind can reach out to remote, empty planets, but is unable to establish eternal peace on its own planet, is a striking proof of the absurd direction in which the social dialectic is moving.'[190] This is the high point of Adorno's diagnosis of his age. He understood society as a coherent system whose stability arises from rising productivity which itself stems from society's increasing success in subduing nature.[191] The domination of nature continues as a systemic relationship that in the meantime has become a 'second nature'. It appears to be a natural, irrevocable given. Adorno summed up the tendency for the whole of the social life process to be enveloped in a comprehensive administrative organization with the concept of 'the administered world'. This tendency was expressed in the different forms of intervention in a state-regulated capitalism, on the one hand, and the control exercised by the welfare state, on the other. The precautionary measures taken by the welfare state seemed to be alien to the system, but actually served to sustain it. This was Adorno's interpretation of the fact that, while the social system was becoming increasingly integrated and independent, that independence had long since become marginal and was really a symptom of its growing disintegration.

The isolated possibilities for resistance that developed within the social system were taken in hand by the culture industry, thanks to which 'even the ability to imagine in concrete terms that the world might be different' was largely paralysed.[192]

At the end of his analysis of the present situation, Adorno admitted pessimistically that 'there was no vantage point outside the machine'.[193] This raises the question whether we are left with any scope at all for a project of social enlightenment. Against this background, he pointed at the end of his diagnosis to the 'free-floating anxiety' that arises from the overwhelming power of the things that confront us. This anxiety liberates impulses that might give rise to recognizable potentials for resistance.

Dahrendorf was the second principal speaker at the conference, and he took the opportunity to formulate a fundamental criticism of the Frankfurt School's theoretical base as well as its relation to practice. His main objection was directed at the degree of conceptual abstraction and the generality of Adorno's diagnosis of the age. According to Dahrendorf, 'an all too confident analysis of the totality of our social development' was itself part of 'an ossified world; it duplicates this ossified world'.[194] With its turn to the level of principle, it casts doubt on the possibility of a practical politics that might achieve concrete social reforms that could lead to improved living conditions. Furthermore, the predictive value of theories of social totality was small; theories of this type were limited to producing 'a neo-pessimistic picture of historical inevitabilities'. Finally, Dahrendorf proposed that the potential for development in the advanced industrial nations made a future state of affairs free from domination quite conceivable. He went on to ask, not without a polemical side-swipe at Adorno: 'Are there identifiable conditions and identifiable groups where we can find this idea of doing away with the domination of human beings by other human beings? What sociological factors can we point to with which to explain the return of this dream of anarchy?'[195]

Adorno took his time to reply impromptu and at length in a speech that was frequently interrupted by applause from the hall. Partly as a response to Dahrendorf, but also with one eye on the political actionism of the student movement, he said that he was fully aware that 'the call for the unity of theory and practice can easily lead to a kind of censorship of theory by practice.' To demand of thought that it give proof of its utility was itself the mark of instrumental rationality. He insisted, much as he had done before in *Negative Dialectics*, that theoretical reflection was the basis of practice. At the same time, he had no doubt that 'the actual life of individual human beings' stood in need of change.[196] But if we set aside the nature of the social totality as incomprehensible because it is too general, then effective intervention is an illusion. Adorno declared that the priority to be given to the criticism of domination was to be explained by the progressive advance of authoritarian structures in every aspect of society. The objection that his views were too utopian was not new. He countered it here by pointing out that the regulative idea of a society that was better organized meant nothing more or less than a society 'in which the many could live in security and peace with one another'.[197]

19

With his Back to the Wall

We literally have no one but ourselves.[1]

Together with composing music, writing books had always been an essential part of Adorno's life, and had become even more important now. But even though writing was an inner necessity and the expression of his greatest ambitions, his growing teaching commitments and his responsibilities as director of the institute meant that his writing was purchased at ever greater internal cost. 'It is all more than I can manage, physically', he wrote to his old friend Dreyfus.[2] And when he made similar complaints to Alfred Andersch at around the same time, he mentioned his wishes for a future life: if he were to be given a second chance on earth, he would like next time round to be a playboy.[3]

Despite his feeling overworked, he continued to accept invitations to lecture, including the labour-intensive Paris lectures that he gave in March 1965 in the Deutsches Haus and the Cité internationale and later on in the Amphithéâtre Descartes of the Sorbonne. Even though he keenly felt the honour it was to give these lectures, it nevertheless cost him a great deal to speak in French. Despite this, a few months later, he was in Berlin lecturing in the biggest lecture hall to an over-capacity crowd on 'The Concept of Society'.[4] Shortly afterwards, he was in Brussels, where he gave four guest lectures on an 'Introduction to the Sociology of Music'. These appeared in book form three years later in the celebrated series *rowohlts deutsche enzyklopädie*. They were in fact a revised version of a text that had been published by Suhrkamp in 1962: 'Twelve Theoretical Lectures', with a dedication to the members of the Institute of Social Research.

In the light of all these activities, it was perhaps inevitable that Adorno's health would suffer. His letters contain constant references to insomnia, headaches, a sore throat and the like. And it goes without saying that he would never have been able to cope with all these activities and demands without Gretel's constant support. In the year in which *Negative Dialectics* appeared, an aggravating factor was his growing concern about political developments in Germany. A glance at the newspapers, which were full of such topics as emergency laws and the Grand Coalition, was cause enough to reflect on the stability of the political system. This was particularly true in the light of a study published by the institute in 1967 which gave plenty of reasons to question the future of parliamentary democracy in Germany. The institute study had conducted surveys of public opinion after such events as the *Spiegel* affair of 1962, the metal workers' strike in Baden-Württemberg in 1963 and the Eichmann trial of 1961.[5] All three studies pointed to education and the level of information as being significant factors in promoting politically conscious action and democratic attitudes. Strikingly, the research groups working under Adorno's direction found a frighteningly high degree of political indifference. In crisis situations in particular, such as strikes following disputes about wages, there was the danger that the widespread tendency to political apathy would slip into authoritarian attitudes. The sociologists Egon Becker and Regina Schmidt, who had conducted the study based on a model devised by Adorno, linked this authoritarian disposition to the absence of real power in society. It was this absence of power that led in their view to a strong sense of resignation on political issues.[6] The reactions to the sentencing of Adolf Eichmann by an Israeli court were interpreted as indicating a reluctance to confront the events from the National Socialist past. Taken together, the results from these studies seemed to show that in a large majority of the population the predominant feeling was one of hostility to politics, an attitude that might well have fatal consequences for democracy. Egon Becker and Regina Schmidt drew pessimistic conclusions from these studies which Adorno shared and had already formulated in his 1959 essay 'The Meaning of Working Through the Past'. They agreed with Adorno that the public's identification with West German democracy was superficial, that democracy was 'not seen from the standpoint of political self-determination, but primarily from the point of view of the consumer and de-politicized private person who wishes to see the status quo guaranteed.'[7]

It was not simply the half-hearted attitude of many Germans towards the democratic state that gave Adorno cause for anxiety, but also his observation of official government policy. He was highly critical of the behaviour of the Christian Democrats and Free Democrats who formed the government coalition. In September 1965, just before the general elections in October, he wrote to Marcuse, who was working at the University of California in San Diego: 'Politics are hopeless. I shall indeed vote for the Social Democrats *faute de mieux*, but have refused to lend my signature to any appeal on the part of intellectuals in support of Mr Wehner's party [i.e., the SPD]. Anyway, I am pretty certain that the CDU will obtain an absolute majority. . . . It really is a joy to be alive.'[8] However, Adorno's prognosis was only partly right. The Christian Democrats gained a clear victory and emerged as the largest party, with 47.6 per cent of the votes. Despite the Godesberg Programme, which Adorno had judged to be conformist through and through, the SPD were only able to improve their position slightly by taking votes from the Free Democrats. Perhaps this explains why the Social Democrats thought their best chances lay in the Grand Coalition with the CDU.

Horkheimer and Adorno had always been extremely wary of national-conservative tendencies in Germany. They believed that the government was not energetic enough in combating the right-wing parties and the resurgence of anti-Semitism. And until the Auschwitz trials in Frankfurt (1963–5) there had also been a lack of urgency in prosecuting those guilty of the mass crimes of the Nazi period. Lawyers such as Richard Schmid, Fritz Bauer and Martin Hirsch, all of whom urged that the criminals should be investigated and punished, including the desk murderers, were few and far between.

Politically the year in which *Negative Dialectics* appeared was undoubtedly something of a watershed. The collapse of the cabinet under Ludwig Erhard, with his authoritarian programme of a 'fully-formed society',[9] had led at the end of 1966 to the establishment of the Grand Coalition of Christian Democrats and Social Democrats. Their declared goal was to introduce change into ossified policies both at home and abroad, but they were perceived at the start as the promoters of the long-planned emergency laws. Many people, Adorno included, saw these laws as a threat to democracy, particularly since, as the alliance of the two largest parties, the Grand Coalition implied the loss of a strong parliamentary opposition. This democratic deficit, of which Adorno was very conscious, was ultimately one of the chief causes for the establishment of the extra-parliamentary opposition (APO), which turned out to be a crucial critical force against the emergency laws. In addition to these domestic targets, further factors included the American war in Vietnam, to which the West German government gave its support; the monopolistic trends in the media, and especially the Springer Press; the visit in 1967 of the dictatorial shah of Persia; and, lastly, the educational crisis in German universities. In November 1967 a ceremony in honour of the university rector was disrupted by the action of the increasingly politicized students. Two student representatives brought what became a celebrated banner into the largest lecture hall in the presence of the body of academic staff. It bore the motto: 'Beneath their robes: the mustiness of two thousand years'.

The student groups who came out in favour of reforms in the universities were identical with those who formed the core of the growing anti-Vietnam protesters as well as with those who sympathized with liberation movements in the Third World. They received backing from younger members of the institute such as Oskar Negt, but also from Herbert Marcuse and Jürgen Habermas, both of whom spoke in the first large German anti-Vietnam protest gatherings in Frankfurt am Main and Berlin, the most notable of which was the student congress entitled

'Vietnam: Analysis of an Example'. Jürgen Habermas also took part as the leader of a discussion group in the mass meeting against the emergency laws that took place at the end of October 1966. The event organized in May 1968, 'Democracy in a State of Emergency', took place in the large auditorium of Hessen Radio. Adorno, who had helped to organize it, was present and made a short speech. It is not necessary, he said, 'to be filled with political hysteria in order to be afraid of what is appearing on the horizon'. He recalled the arrest of the editor in chief of the weekly magazine *Der Spiegel* on an unwarranted charge of high treason, as well as the cynical attitude of leading politicians towards the Basic Law. Given the background of a still unstable democratic order in Germany, it was necessary to protest as vigorously as possible against the emergency laws on the grounds that they were a legal device to undermine democracy.[10]

Adorno left no one in any doubt about his solidarity with the opposition as far as the emergency laws were concerned. But it was a different story when it came to the anti-Americanism that had begun to spread in Germany among the growing number of opponents of the war in Vietnam from the time of the assassination of John F. Kennedy, the suppression of the race riots and the subsequent murder of Martin Luther King. Adorno felt in sympathy with Horkheimer, who had demonstratively proclaimed his pro-American views during the German-American Week in Frankfurt in May 1967.[11] In speeches and discussions, Horkheimer stressed that he had close ties to American democracy. It was a land in which those persecuted by the National Socialist regime had once found refuge. He could accept the critical attitude of intellectuals towards US policy in Vietnam, but he believed that the American war was also a defence of the democratic constitution. To that extent, the Americans deserved our gratitude, not least because they had liberated Germany and Europe from the most terrible totalitarian terrorism.[12] In contrast, in his lectures on *Metaphysics* in summer 1965, Adorno had described the war in Vietnam as proof of the continued existence of the 'world of torture' that had begun in Auschwitz.[13]

A final test of the state of West German democracy was provided by the extraordinary security measures taken by the German authorities. These included closing the motorways and the Rhine and the surveillance of the Iranians living in the Federal Republic before the state visit of the shah of Persia in summer 1967. The shah's regime had totalitarian features such as the use of the secret service to spy on Iranian students and his use of torture against members of the opposition. It was politically committed students who took the lead in the protests. In a number of large towns, thousands of students and schoolchildren followed their call to take part in the demonstrations. In Berlin the demonstration took place on 2 June in front of the Schoeneberger Town Hall and the Deutsche Oper. In the following scuffles with the police, who violently pursued the fleeing demonstrators, a student, Benno

Ohnesorg, was shot in the back by a policeman. The Berlin Senate responded by banning future demonstrations, and this was condemned in its turn by the APO as 'a non-declared emergency'. It formed the chief topic of debate in many student meetings in the universities.[14]

The events leading to the death of a fellow student as well as the campaign of the populist Springer Press against the demonstrating students persuaded Adorno to raise the matter in one of his sociology seminars. He remarked that 'the students have taken on something of the role of the Jews.'[15] A little later on he spoke of the death of Benno Ohnesorg, but also about the so-called Six-Day War between Egypt and Israel. He began his aesthetics lecture on 6 June with the words:

I find it impossible to begin my lecture today without saying something about the events in Berlin, overshadowed though they are by the terrible threat to Israel, the refuge of countless Jews who have fled a horrifying fate. I am conscious of how difficult it is to form a just and responsible opinion about even the simplest fact because all the news that reaches us is so slanted. But that cannot prevent me from expressing my sympathy for the student whose fate, whatever the reports, is so disproportionate to his participation in a political demonstration. . . . It is not merely the urge to ensure that the victims receive justice, but also the fear that the democratic spirit which is only just developing in Germany might be stifled by authoritarian practices that make it necessary to demand that the authorities who will be carrying out the investigations in Berlin should not be connected with those who wielded the cosh and did the shooting. Moreover, they should be free of the suspicion that they might have an interest in the direction taken by the investigation. The desire that the inquiry should be carried out in complete freedom, uninfluenced by authoritarian wishes and in accordance with the spirit of democracy, is one that I do not think of as only my own private wish, but as one that arises from the objective situation. I presume that you share it. I now invite you to stand in memory of our dead colleague Benno Ohnesorg.[16]

Two days after Adorno's statement the funeral of Benno Ohnesorg took place. There were a large number of expressions of condolence, including a convoy of vehicles from Berlin to Hanover. Hanover was to be the setting for a major congress on the subject of 'Democracy and the University – the Conditions and Organization of Resistance'. In the midst of heated debate about the legitimacy of political forms of resistance, Jürgen Habermas warned of the dangers of actionism in the student movement. He described the task facing the APO as 'if not to rectify, at least to proclaim the absence of a policy that is enlightened in its intentions, honest in its methods, and progressive in its interpretations and actions.'[17] However, the idea of a programme of political resistance with the aim of directly provoking the power of the state belonged to 'a voluntaristic ideology' that could easily turn into 'left-wing fascism'.[18] Did Adorno's great sympathy for his Frankfurt colleague include agreement with this formula which undeniably contained a criticism of the student opposition? What is known is that Adorno did use the same epithet of 'left-wing fascism', not at the time, admittedly, but a year or so later, particularly in private conversations, but also in interviews in which he referred to Habermas. Habermas himself admitted that his contribution to the debate was not unproblematic, even though events were to show that the dangerous experiment of militant attacks on the state monopoly of violence could degenerate into terrorism.[19] Adorno shared with the oppositional students the idea of emancipation as well as their belief that there was a significant need for educational reforms. He agreed also that changes in obsolete authoritarian and hierarchical structures were overdue and that the norms that obtained in the penal code on sexual matters were repressive. His reaction at the time was characteristic. Karl-Heinz Kurras, the policeman who had shot the fleeing student, was acquitted of the charge of culpably negligent homicide by the Landesgericht in Moabit in Berlin. Adorno took this astonishing news as the occasion for a further statement during his aesthetics lecture on 23 November 1967.

> If the police officer cannot be condemned because it has not been possible to find him guilty in accordance with the law, the guilt of his superiors is all the greater. The fact that the police went armed to a student demonstration gives rise to the temptation to take action that the police officer concerned would like to justify with the term 'orders' [*Auftrag*]. In Frankfurt it has been shown time and again that the police have no need of such methods. This makes it all the more important to discover urgently why they were used in Berlin, who the people responsible are and what sort of orders were involved. Beyond all that, however, there is the impression that I have of Mr Kurras when he appeared on television. I heard him utter a sentence to the effect that 'I am sorry that a student lost his life.' There was an unmistakable reluctance in his tone, as if Mr Kurras had forced himself to utter those few meagre words, but had somehow not taken in the full seriousness of what he had done.[20]

The nature of the disagreements and the shared opinions between the left-wing students and Horkheimer and Adorno encouraged both groups to discover just where their views diverged. Adorno in particular was keen to reach an understanding. So he arranged a meeting for a discussion between the two heads of the institute on the one hand and the Sozialistischer Deutscher Studentenbund (SDS) on the other.[21] Such a discussion in fact took place in the Walter Kolb student residence in the middle of June and focused initially on the question of the relevance of critical theory for a political practice that envisaged changing the social order. Shortly before the discussion took place, Horkheimer had written an open letter, questioning the one-sided political commitment of the left-wing movement. He asked whether 'the claim made by Asiatic potentates to base themselves on the doctrines of communism had not degenerated into a macabre farce when these doctrines were compared to the ideas of their founders.'[22] He warned against the unquestioning acceptance of the socialist model on the grounds that it blinded people to the totalitarian potential of communist systems. In the subsequent discussion, Adorno kept his sense of proportion. On the one hand, he interpreted the increasingly defamatory strategies marshalled against the political demands and actions of the students as the expression of a repressive society. On the other hand, he objected vehemently to the idea of making immediate practical use of critical theory. It was an illusion to speak of a revolutionary situation and, for that reason, the students' provocations 'resembled the actions of caged animals seeking a way out'.[23]

On this occasion, Adorno was able to defend his position unhindered. It was different a little later on in a talk he gave at the Free University in Berlin. His reactions were correspondingly helpless. What had happened? Having received an invitation to lecture from Peter Szondi, he had planned, in this highly explosive situation, to give a talk on Goethe's *Iphigenie in Tauris*. He had provisionally entitled his lecture 'Against Barbarism' and had worked on it during his summer vacation in the Engadine in 1966 and into the new year, finally finishing it in January 1967. He had then given the talk in Hamburg and also in Brunswick.[24]

On this occasion, a group of left-wing students marched up to the lectern, unfurling a banner. It bore an inscription: 'Berlin's left-wing fascists greet Teddy the Classicist'. The trouble-makers, whose banner was seized by another group of students in the lecture hall and torn to pieces,[25] publicly called on Adorno to act as witness in a trial that had just begun against a prominent activist. In the SDS leaflet which they circulated, it said: 'Herr Professor Adorno – this indispensable theatre prop of cultural events who purveys critical impotence at festivals, and in Third Programmes, academies, etc., would like to assist us this evening in creating a solemn occasion. . . . Herr Prof. Adorno is ready at all times to certify that the Federal Republic has a latent tendency towards inhumanity. Confronted with the inhumanity contained in the accusation against Fritz Teufel, however, he declines to make a statement. He prefers to endure in silence the contradictions whose existence he has previously drawn to our attention.'[26]

After Adorno refused to abandon the talk he had planned in favour of a discussion of his attitude to this situation, a number of those present left the hall under protest. The talk that he next gave contained statements that may well have been meant as criticism of the behaviour of the protesters. He refers there to 'the dark secret of a revolution and an allegedly emancipated consciousness' and also to the fact that 'humanity can become repression', thus preventing the emergence of 'full humanness'.[27] In this sense, Peter Szondi, who in his welcoming speech had described himself as a pupil of Adorno, was right in claiming that Adorno would have less of a 'classical' nature to say about Goethe's *Iphigenie* than 'those people wished to hear who go around quoting Mao's sayings in much the same way that their grandfathers quoted the sayings of the Weimar "Greats". But if *I* could choose a saying from Adorno's *Minima Moralia* it would be this one: "You can't scare me. And that's how things should remain." '[28]

It was then widely reported in the media how, at the end of the lecture, a student in a green mini-skirt tried to present Adorno with a red teddy bear. This happening was one of the topics of conversation in the house of the philosopher Wilhelm Weischedel, who had invited Adorno and some other colleagues after the lecture. Adorno later described what he called this 'abusive behaviour' as 'exhausting'.[29] Nevertheless, outwardly at least, he tried to react calmly to the affront. 'I have survived the entire nuisance without coming to any harm. *Au fond*, it was not so bad as is claimed by the reactionaries who hope to draw me over into their camp.'[30]

Shortly after this incident, there was a meeting with representatives of the Berlin SDS in the Republican Club, the centre of the APO in Berlin. Adorno reported that the discussion was productive and the atmosphere friendly.[31] A few weeks later there was a discussion between Adorno and Szondi on 'Student Unrest' in the studio of West German Radio. Here he explained that there were good reasons for the protest movement as an international phenomenon extending from Frankfurt, Berlin, Paris, Rome and Prague to San Francisco. He 'accepted the student movement's criticism of our university system'. It was rightly claimed that the strict separation of individual disciplines led to the neglect of specific subjects, for example, 'the way in which the basic structures of the economy and their dynamics determine the basic structures of society.' With regard to the students' proposals for reform, he suspected that often they just wanted to make studying easier. Such a desire could not form a basis for reform. He himself would gladly 'help anything that contributed to strengthening the intellectual energy of the university'. He took the view that, on the one hand, 'certain archaic practices should be done away with, . . . on the other hand, other archaic practices should be defended as refuges of the humane, of what could not be fully absorbed by the machine. . . . I believe that there is no possibility of using the university as a base from which to change society. On the contrary, isolated attempts to introduce radical change in the university . . . will only fuel the dominant resentment towards intellectuals and thus pave the way for the reaction.'[32]

Adorno went back to some of the ideas put forward in this radio talk when he agreed to a discussion with the students attending his lectures on aesthetics at the end of November. The question at issue was whether the provocative disruption of lectures could be regarded as a legitimate method of debate in the universities. Adorno expressed his support for the idea of student co-determination on university committees, even on the committees for appointing professors. He also defended the students against the accusations of fascist behaviour. On the other hand, he argued that, instead of constantly breaking rules, the students should try to take advantage of the opportunity to bring about university reform by means of open discussion. He also reminded them that it was important to respect the personal rights of the university teaching staff. The formalized statutes had a positive aspect for anyone who has discovered 'what it means when the doorbell rings at 6 a.m. and you do not know whether it is the Gestapo or the baker'.[33] At the end of what was a lively discussion, Adorno made it clear that, whatever the current threats to democracy in West Germany might be, the Federal Republic could not be regarded as a fascist state. To ignore the differences was a sign of fanaticism. He warned the students not to make the mistake of 'attacking what was a democracy, however much in need of improvement, rather than tackling its enemy, which was already starting to stir ominously.'[34]

Adorno was astonishingly open in his efforts to enter into dialogue with the political students and in his sympathy for their motives, while at the same time he did not hesitate to explain his reservations about their strategy of a targeted breaking of the rules, of violence towards things and provocation of people. His doubts about the political consequences of direct action were expressed even more frankly in his letters. In summer 1967, for example, he wrote to Marcuse, the theoretician and 'sacred cow' of the student movement,[35] that many of their representatives tended 'to synthesize their practice with a non-existent theory, and this expresses a decisionism that evokes horrific memories.'[36]

Adorno wished to spend the vacation weeks in July and August with Gretel somewhere where they could put the requisite distance between themselves and the agitating events in Frankfurt. For years they had found the rest they needed in the Waldhaus Hotel in Sils Maria. On this occasion, however, they chose to spend the summer in the Hôtel L'Etrier in Crans sur Sierre in the Valais. Gretel was fed up with the food in the Waldhaus, and he was fed up with the company there. He hoped to meet up with Marcuse, who was staying in Zermatt, which was not far away. Adorno hoped that they would discuss their political disagreements and hopefully come to an understanding about the relation of critical theory to practical politics.

Patricide deferred

The feeling of suddenly being attacked as a reactionary at least has the virtue of being a surprise.[37]

In the course of 1968, Adorno's statements on student demands, as well as the go-ins, teach-ins, happenings and provocations, tended to become sharper in tone. 'The only thing to say otherwise is that I am gradually becoming sick and tired of student affairs. Especially here because here – and the same thing holds good for Habermas and Friedeburg – we are all coming to the conclusion that the students are just manipulating us – it's a case of patricide deferred.'[38] He wrote in a similar vein to Elisabeth Lenk a few days later. The long-drawn-out debates with the students had something paradoxical about them. 'Habermas, Friedeburg, Mitscherlich and I, as well as one or two others, constitute an increasingly small oppositional minority, but find ourselves attacked by the students . . . with their calls for direct action. We have nothing standing behind us, but on the other hand, this seems to be the way it has to be.'[39]

Patricide of a different sort was how Adorno regarded the initiative launched principally by the magazine *alternative*. Adorno was far more deeply hurt by this than by the spectacular events at the university. For, very much to his surprise, he found himself accused of having subjected Benjamin to pressure during his years in exile in Paris and of having proceeded selectively in compiling the two-volume edition of *Writings* in 1955 and the *Letters* in 1966[40] in order to suppress Benjamin's turning to Marxism.[41] After Hannah Arendt[42] and Helmut Heißenbüttel had given a critical account of Adorno's practice as editor and of his relations with Benjamin in the *Merkur*,[43] Wolfram Schütte publicized the controversy once again in the *Frankfurter Rundschau* on 19 January. He reiterated the criticism of Adorno and called for a response from the editor of the *Writings* as well as from Suhrkamp Verlag. For it appeared that Adorno's personal integrity and his integrity as a scholar were now in question.[44] Adorno made no attempt to avoid controversy but met it head-on in *alternative*, not indeed as an open letter, but in the form of an article, the fee for which he proposed to donate to the Berlin Republican Club as a contribution to its legal fighting fund. In this 'Interim Judgement'[45] he explained the criteria that had determined his choice of texts for this anthology of Benjamin's writings. Furthermore, he rejected outright the assertion that he and Benjamin had ever been at loggerheads, and he attempted to demonstrate that the letters showed that the discussions they had had were always comradely. He also rejected the allegation that he was monopolizing the Benjamin Archive, which was located in the Institute of Social Research:[46] 'I have done nothing apart from making sure that the material was all kept together.' He finished by saying that 'The slanderous nature of the accusations levelled against me lies in the insinuation that there is a connection between theoretical discussions and Benjamin's financial position. There is no truth in this. . . . It did not occur to anyone to make use [of financial subsidies from the institute] to exert pressure on him or to censor him.'[47] Adorno did not leave matters there. At the end of March 1968, he brought together some notes for an essay he planned on 'Interpreting Benjamin'. This collection of jottings was supplemented by a list of questions: 'Is it so terrible if Benjamin from whom I have learnt so much is supposed also to have learnt something from me? Arendt's monolithic ideas. . . . Point out the way in which Hannah Arendt and Helmut Heißenbüttel contradict each other. . . . The false priority given to biographical information and historical circumstances, which incidentally did not destroy other people despite their identity. . . . She would really like to turn us into his murderers, even though it was we who kept him above water for seven years.'[48] Adorno had planned to provide a detailed rebuttal in the *Neue Rundschau* but, in view of his many commitments and the effect on his nerves, he decided against doing so.[49]

Even though these accusations soon proved to be without foundations, Adorno nevertheless found them deeply painful. How painful could be seen from his letters to Gershom Scholem. He asked him, as Benjamin's closest friend, to intervene on his behalf. 'The crucial thing would be not so much the formalities and correcting the lies, . . . but that you, as the man best qualified to do so, should emphatically confirm my objective philosophical qualifications as far as Benjamin is concerned.'[50]

Scholem's replies were both sympathetic and diplomatic. He wrote that the malice of his critics and their wish to attack him personally and wound him were evident. He counselled composure in the face of such rancour. In his view, Adorno had no need of 'philosophical legitimation as an interpreter of Benjamin'.[51] That aside, 'it was perfectly possible for people to differ in good faith about Benjamin's writings and ideas . . . and the same thing applied to opinions about his biography.' No one had the right to an official reading of Benjamin. 'The vileness lies in other assertions and as far as these are concerned the philosophical issue is important only where it is claimed, grotesquely enough, that you are an anti-Marxist who disapproved of Benjamin's Marxism, rather than a Marxist for whom Benjamin's Marxism had not been fully thought through.'[52] Scholem also contacted Hans Paeschke, the editor of *Merkur*, to express his disapproval of the 'in part, shameful, not to say disgraceful' remarks by Hannah Arendt.[53] Adorno evidently took Scholem's lengthy reply as proof of his support. In a further letter he wrote in a calmer mood to say that the quarrels were lacking in objectivity and had become 'sensationalist'.[54] This was also the tenor of other letters in which Adorno complained about the 'witch-hunt' that he was being subjected to. He was having to endure 'the crassest possible injustice'.[55]

He made similar complaints to Benjamin's son, Stefan, who was living in London and who at once identified with Adorno.[56] Adorno gave the matter a slightly different interpretation in a letter to Gabriele Henkel, a member of the family of the Düsseldorf industrialist. He believed that the campaign against him expressed an ambivalence towards a father figure. People were disappointed by him as a theoretician because he refused to involve himself in practical politics.[57] This comment referred of course to his disagreements with the student movement, and on that front relations were going to deteriorate sharply.

In spring 1968, there had been an assassination attempt on the life of Rudi Dutschke, the best known of the spokesmen of the SDS. This attempt had been made the day after the end of the sociologists' conference in Frankfurt. Dutschke, who had become a public figure thanks to his appearances in the media, had been gunned down on the street in broad daylight in Berlin and critically injured by Josef Bachmann, a man who had fallen under the influence of neo-Nazi ideas. This led to a large number of demonstrations in the Easter holidays in various West German cities. These demonstrations were directed in particular against the Springer Press because the APO claimed there was a link between the attempt on Dutschke's life and the witch-hunt of the Springer newspapers against the politically active students. Mass demonstrations tried to prevent the distribution of Springer papers, especially the main tabloid paper *Das Bild*. In Munich there were sustained confrontations between around 50,000 demonstrators and 21,000 police, some of them mounted, who fought them for days on end with truncheons and water cannon. These battles resulted in the deaths of one student and a photographer. At a special session of the Bundestag the minister of the interior described the SDS as an organization hostile to the constitution.

A few days later, Adorno signed an open appeal that was published in the weekly newspaper *Die Zeit* and which called for an inquiry into the social reasons underlying the attempted assassination of Dutschke, and in particular the manipulation of public opinion by the Springer Press. On the other hand, he was unwilling to join in the programme of the anti-authoritarian movement to increase the politicization of academic scholarship, and also refused to allow his two-hour weekly sociology seminar to be used for a discussion about how to block the emergency laws. He insisted on his right to academic freedom and to use the teaching time available to him exclusively for the topics that had been announced, in other words, social theory. At the same time, he criticized the custom of disrupting teaching and in his own sociology lectures, which always attracted a huge audience, he went so far as to ask the activist students directly to put a stop to their violent struggle for university reform and social change.[58] Adorno made this criticism at the end of his last lecture in July 1968, quite unaware that this was the last lecture course he was destined to complete without disruption.

The futility of defending a theory as practice

Theory, precisely because it is looked at in isolation, is something like a substitute for happiness. The happiness that should be created by practical action finds no other reflex than the behaviour of the man who sits on a chair and thinks.[59]

In Frankfurt Adorno witnessed the escalation of the student movement, which saw itself as the avant-garde of a global revolutionary movement. After the May revolt in Paris, the street fighting in Berkeley, after the great march on Bonn in protest against the emergency laws, the conviction grew that an objective revolutionary situation had arisen. In the universities the activists introduced strikes so as to set an example to the working class whom they thought of as their allies. Thus there were strikes in Frankfurt University at the end of May 1968, complete with pickets, the blockade of the entrances to the main building, the violent occupation of the rector's office, the renaming of the Johann Wolfgang Goethe University as Karl Marx University, and so forth. Adorno continued to refuse the students' request that, as the leading representative of critical theory, he should declare his solidarity with their political goals. It was clear to him that he ran the risk of being used, and he made desperate efforts to preserve his independence as a theoretician. In a letter to Gabriele Henkel on 17 May, he wrote that he was 'really very taken up with student affairs, particularly since the children are rebelling against authority but then come running to me in a way that is almost touching. The responsibility is great if you are as aware as I am of the contradictions between the students' movement and their actual situation.'[60]

Having more or less survived the excitements of the sociology conference in April 1968 on 'Late Capitalism or Industrial Society?', and the summer semester with its recurrent strikes, Adorno found that he was still held in respect by the responsible part of the student movement as the man who stood for the public criticism of society and a left-wing intellectual opposition. At the end of September, following the Frankfurt Book Fair and the disturbances occasioned by the award of the Peace Prize of the German book trade to the Senegalese president, Léopold Sédar Senghor, he found himself in a public discussion on the topic 'Authority and Revolution'. This discussion had been organized by Luchterhand Verlag in order to provide a forum for a debate between the leading figures of the student movement, such as Hans-Jürgen Krahl, and prominent left-wing intellectuals, including Jürgen Habermas, Ludwig von Friedeburg and Günter Grass. On this occasion, too, attention was focused on people's expectations of the representatives of critical theory: 'Six months ago', Krahl said, 'when we were besieging the council of Frankfurt University, the only professor who came to the students' sit-in was Professor Adorno. He was overwhelmed with ovations. He made straight for the microphone, and just as he reached it, he ducked past and shot into the philosophy seminar. In short, once again, on the threshold of practice, he retreated into theory.'[61] In the course of further discussions, the student leaders complained because Adorno had not joined in the march on Bonn to protest against the emergency laws. He replied, *inter alia*, that 'I do not know if elderly gentlemen with a paunch are the right people to take part in a demonstration.'[62] Adorno found the whole event and its consequences somewhat depressing. He regretted the waste of time that he could have used much more profitably in other activities. He felt, he wrote to Szondi, as if he no longer had his feet on the ground, a 'state of mind such as occurs with normal people only under the influence of drugs. I am only thankful that I have no need of them.'[63]

The day following the discussion Günter Grass accused Adorno, first in a talk and then in a letter, of being far too opportunistic. Grass thought that Adorno was obviously afraid of the rebels even though some of them were his own students.[64] Adorno sent Grass a polite but firm letter in reply, denying that he lacked courage. He was firmly resolved, he said, 'not to let himself be browbeaten into what for years now I have called the principle of unilateral solidarity.' At the same time, Adorno tried to clarify his political stance more precisely. It was determined by the wish to avoid becoming a renegade. 'To distance myself publicly from the APO . . . would make me look like a renegade even though everything I have written makes clear that I have nothing in common with the students' narrow-minded direct action strategies which are already degenerating into an abominable irrationalism. In truth, it is they who have changed their position rather than I mine.' He went on to tell Grass, whose own commitment was to the SPD, that he hesitated to issue a statement attacking the SDS, which 'had become the victim of its own publicity', because he did not wish to join 'the platform of the German reactionaries' in their witch-hunt of the New Left. His letter concluded, 'I increasingly see it as my task simply to say what I think without taking anyone else into consideration. This goes together with a mounting aversion to practical politics of whatever kind, an aversion in which my natural disposition and the objective futility of practical action at this moment of history coincide.'[65]

These very decided comments in his letter to Grass were not the product of ideas that simply occurred to him on the spot. They were based on detailed notes that served to help him give a principled account of the relations of theory and practice.

His declared aim was 'to produce a consciousness of theory and practice that neither divides the two such that theory becomes powerless and practice becomes arbitrary',[66] nor posits either as a 'simple identity'. In particular, he opposed the student postulate of the unity of theory and practice by postulating a dialectical interaction of theoretical reflection and practical commitment. This seemed to him to be absolutely inescapable, since he was outraged by some of the things that had come to his ears. 'When a student's room was trashed because he preferred to work rather than join in actions, on the wall was scrawled: "Whoever occupies himself with theory without acting practically is a traitor to socialism." He is not the only one to have practice used against him as an ideological pretext for exercising moral blackmail. The thinking denigrated by actionists apparently demands of them too much effort: it requires too much work, is too practical.'[67]

Adorno's starting-point was the assumption that 'practice is the source of energy of theory', but no path leads from the latter to the former. Theory is 'not only a means of the totality but also a moment of it; otherwise it could not resist to any degree the captivating spell of that totality.'[68] If, on the other hand, the distinction between theory and practice is negated and the idea of an indistinguishable unity is promulgated, this leads to the primacy of practice. Mind then finds itself committed to a concretism that is entirely in harmony with 'the technocratic-positivistic tendency it believes itself to be opposing'.[69] Adorno clarified the dangers of an unreflecting call for practice by referring not only to this attack on the student who took an interest in theory, but also to the discussions in political groups in which free dialogue is submerged by the 'privilege accorded to tactics over everything else'. 'Every argument, untroubled by the question of whether it is sound, is geared to a purpose. Whatever the opponent says is hardly perceived and then only so that formulaic clichés can be served up in retort. No one wants to learn.'[70] Adorno also discerned this tendency to authoritarian thinking in the mechanisms involved when 'someone demands to see your papers'. 'More implicit and therefore all the more powerful, is the commandment: you must sign. The individual must yield to the collective; as recompense for his jumping into the melting pot, he is promised the grace of being chosen, of belonging.'[71]

Adorno was not opposed to people organizing themselves for political purposes. He wished rather to draw attention to the Archimedean point at which 'a non-repressive practice might be possible, and one might steer a path between the alternatives of spontaneity and organization.' 'This point, if it exists at all, can only be found through theory.'[72] With these reflections, Adorno sought to steer his way between a practicism devoid of concepts and a conception of doctrinaire theory uncoupled from practical action. His own sympathy for theory arose from a political judgement that was based in turn on a sober 'analysis of the situation'. He made this clear in his controversy with Marcuse. At issue was not any disagreement about how to conceptualize the relation of theory and practice. It was rather their differing interpretation of the political situation which led the two men to different conclusions. 'You believe', Adorno says in a letter to Marcuse, 'that practice in an emphatic sense is not prohibited today; I see the matter differently.'[73] Given the actual power relations, he was convinced that the student protest was condemned to failure from the outset. In the essay on 'Marginalia to Theory and Praxis', which reads like a post-script to the correspondence with Marcuse, he writes that the building of barricades is 'ridiculous against those who administer the bomb'.[74] A practice that refuses to acknowledge its own weakness when confronted by 'real power which hardly feels a tickle' is 'deluded', 'regressive' or, at best, 'pseudo-activity'.

Does this mean that a theory that aspired to 'becoming practical', in the sense of introducing real social change, has become resigned to failure? Adorno turns this accusation on its head. In reality, it was the 'uncompromisingly critical thinker' who initiated the political practice that could lead to changes in society.[75]

Following this discussion at the Frankfurt Book Fair in September 1968, which focused on what was in his eyes the false question of re-volutionary practice, Adorno was able to pause for breath. He went to Vienna on 22 October for the publication of his book *Alban Berg: Master of the Smallest Link*. Two days later, he was the guest of the Institute for Evaluation Research in Graz, which had been established by the culture editor of the Graz daily *Neue Zeit*. Adorno gave a talk in the auditorium of the Music Academy in the Nicolaigasse on a burning cultural topic of the day: the crisis in Vienna, where they had been unable to fill the post of director of the Vienna State Opera. His talk was entitled 'Conception of a Vienna Operatic Theatre'.[76] This was followed the next day by a three-hour discussion of his talk in the Institute for Evaluation Research. For once the topic was not theory and practice, but true and false needs in the world of opera. The press reports on his lecture were extraordinarily enthusiastic. Harald Kaufmann wrote to Adorno, saying, 'I cannot remember ever having read such detailed and for the most part serious reactions to any lecture in the Austrian papers. The whole event was a huge success and it looks as if it will have genuine consequences. For the Viennese papers won't let the matter rest and will keep coming back to your proposals.'[77] There was a further event in Graz in November to celebrate the appearance of Adorno's book. This was a reading from the chapter entitled 'Reminis-cences', and it was accompanied by a performance of songs by Gustav Mahler.

Having returned to Frankfurt, Adorno found himself committed to a whole series of talks. What he wanted, however, was to spend his time writing up his book on aesthetics which he had constantly been forced to postpone. Given the political excitements of the time, however, he was able to devote only part of his energies to this. There was no ques-tion of simply retreating to his desk, one of his favourite places. He was constantly being called away from writing. He was shocked to hear that Herbert Marcuse had received actual physical threats and was forced to keep his whereabouts temporarily hidden.[78] Adorno at once wrote to him expressing his sympathy, and in the middle of December, when

Marcuse had reappeared, he wrote: 'Everything is topsy-turvy here at the moment. Quite a few of the lecture rooms are occupied. Many seminars cannot take place, including some of the most progressive ones. Valid student claims and dubious actions are all so mixed up together that all productive work and even sensible thought are scarcely possible any more.'[79]

When Adorno reported to Marcuse about the occupation of university rooms, he was writing under the influence of the sense of shock he undoubtedly felt. At the beginning of December a largish group of students had 'refunctioned' the sociology seminar, as they then termed it, in order to discuss the reform of their course of studies and the examination system, as well as broader political activities. Day and night, ever-changing strike committees occupied the seminar rooms that Frankfurt University had rented. Moreover, the words 'Spartakus Seminar' had been painted on the façade of the building in large letters. 'Critical theory has been organized in such an authoritarian manner', it said in the leaflet that had been distributed in connection with the occupation, 'that its approach to sociology allows no space for the students to organize their own studies. . . . We are fed up with letting ourselves be trained in Frankfurt to become dubious [*halbseiden*] members of the political left who, once their studies are finished, can serve as the integrated alibis of the authoritarian state.'[80] A few days after the distribution of this pamphlet, and following the occupation, there was an open discussion with the professors, including Adorno and Habermas. In the presence of the majority of the students studying sociology, the professors were called upon to renounce their institutional rights while continuing to carry out their professorial duties. The discussion culminated in the proclamation of the slogan about smashing the bourgeois academic machine, and Adorno and Habermas were subjected to a good deal of verbal pressure, whereupon the two men left the hall without a word. Shortly afterwards, they distributed a statement of their own saying that cooperation with groups who had inscribed 'smash science' on their banners was quite out of the question. Nevertheless, the professors sought to continue the dialogue with the striking students and were willing to accept publicly demands that were concerned with specific concrete reforms in the university, such as the equal representation of professors, lecturers and students (*Drittelparität*) and the recognition of working parties as an institutionalized part of the activities of the academic departments.

Adorno wrote to Marcuse after these events, scarcely able to disguise his doubts and anxieties about this escalation of the protest movement. Irrationalism was on the increase, the university of the future was in danger of losing the freedom without which speculative thought was impossible. In the hope that Marcuse might command the attention of the students and could contribute to a rapprochement between hostile and increasingly irreconcilable fronts, he once again tried to persuade him to come to Frankfurt. Apart from this invitation, Adorno and Habermas did everything in their power to mediate between the two opposing sides. Agreement was prevented, however, by the intransigence of the student leaders. Matters came to a head after a renewed occupation of the sociology seminar rooms, when the strike committee threatened in a leaflet to strip the seminar of all its furnishings and equipment ('its means of production').[81] In response, the professors responsible for the seminar brought the police in to close the buildings. In the days that followed, on 31 January 1969, a group of striking students under the leadership of Hans-Jürgen Krahl set off for the Institute of Social Research in order to discuss further political initiatives. The directors of the institute, with Adorno at their head, declared that this occupation was trespass and called for police protection. A note for the files, written by Adorno or at his behest, stated baldly: 'The institute's directors ... had no choice, if only for legal reasons, but to accept the confrontation that had been forced on them. They decided to ask for police assistance in clearing the institute of intruders and to request them to bring charges for trespass against Herr Krahl and others who had forced an entry into the building.'[82] In justification of their action, the directors of the institute noted in the same memorandum: 'It is vital that precisely those who believe that university reform is overdue and who wish to bring about a democratic and social institution in harmony with the Basic Law, it is vital precisely for those who identify wholeheartedly with this aim of the extraparliamentary opposition, that they should feel obligated to resist their own criminalization: they should resist all authoritarian tendencies and equally all pseudo-anarchistic acts of violence on the part of ostensibly left-wing activists as well as crypto-fascist actions from groups on the extreme right.'[83]

He also wrote to Marcuse: 'I am quite unable to explain why I feel so calm and with what infinite astonishment I register all these things. Whether it is age or intensive repression so that I can bring my own work to completion, I am unable to say.'[84] Despite this attempt to raise his own spirits, Adorno was not quite able to master his own fears. Looking forward with some anxiety to the end of his sabbatical semester and the return to teaching, he wrote: 'God knows what will happen in the coming term when I shall be teaching once again.'[85]

Moments of happiness, despite everything

The collusion of children with clowns is a collusion with art, which adults drive out of them just as they drive out their collusion with animals. Human beings have not succeeded in so thoroughly repressing their likeness to animals that they are unable in an instant to recapture it and be flooded with joy.[86]

Despite the disruptions caused by the student unrest, and despite all the unforeseen extra burden of duties arising from the conflicts in the university and the constant discussions about reforming university studies, Adorno tried as far as possible to stick to his accustomed way of life. On the one hand, there were his academic duties, his lectures and seminars, as well as a large number of examinations in both philosophy and sociology. On the other hand, there was a growing pressure of work connected with his public lecturing and his publishing activities. In addition, there were the meetings in the Institute of Social Research and the flood of correspondence that this brought in its train. More than ever, he wrote letters on a daily basis to people dear to him or important, or to those with whom he felt he had to remain in contact.

Apart from all that, Adorno's life was given a structure by the four- to six-week vacation that he spent in the Swiss mountains every year in July and August, for many years in the Engadine and later on in the Valais. In early spring he and Gretel preferred to take a break in the spa of Baden-Baden, where they stayed in the luxurious Brenner's Park Hotel, with its rich traditions and a clientele drawn from the fashionable world, with prominent representatives of the aristocracy and the worlds of business, politics and culture. He liked to spend the periods free of teaching in September and October travelling to Paris, Vienna or Rome. Since recovering his German citizenship he had had no opportunity of travelling to Britain or the USA; his effective radius was confined to Central Europe. In the many letters he wrote while on vacation he claimed that he did no reading at all, apart from thrillers, and that he never picked up a pen. But such statements should be taken with a pinch of salt. In reality he used the holidays as an opportunity to plan lectures, to take notes in his various notebooks or at least to jot down key ideas for essays he planned to write. Nevertheless, he was no workaholic, not a man unable to do anything but carry out his obligations in a kind of blind rage.

The times when he could retreat to his desk to write were rare and all the more precious for that reason, as were the hours he would spend at the piano playing either his own compositions or those of others. In an essay on 'Free Time', he wrote, evidently referring to himself:

I take the activities with which I occupy myself beyond the bounds of my official profession, without exception, so seriously that I would be shocked by the idea that they had anything to do with hobbies – that is, activities I'm mindlessly infatuated with only in order to kill time – if my experience had not toughened me against manifestations of barbarism that have become self-evident and acceptable. Making music, listening to music, reading with concentration, constitute an integral element of my existence; the word hobby would be a mockery of them. And conversely my work, the production of philosophical and sociological studies and university teaching, so far has been so pleasant to me that I am unable to conceive of it within that opposition to free time that the current razor-sharp classification demands from people.[87]

As always, the Adornos were generous with their hospitality. There was always a kind of *jour fixe* for acquaintances and friends to gather, mainly intellectuals and artists. After the sociology seminars on Tuesday evenings the Adornos frequently invited a small circle of guests to dinner. Visits to the theatre and concerts were taken for granted, and the same thing was true of important exhibitions. They regularly visited the Documenta, the great international exhibition of the contemporary visual arts in Kassel. Adorno was always present at the Frankfurt Book Fair in the autumn, despite his loathing for the 'circus', and he regularly attended receptions given by his publishers, Suhrkamp.[88] Readings in bookshops, sometimes even in galleries, were a matter of course; he enjoyed receiving invitations from the chief editors of the culture studios of the German radio stations, most of whom he knew well personally. His above-average income enabled him and Gretel to lead a carefree life financially. The fashionable hotels aside, they were relatively uninterested in luxury, but they liked the material security guaranteed both by his professorial chair in Frankfurt[89] and by the fees he received from various radio stations and other cultural bodies. In addition, there were the royalties he received twice a year from his book publications, although it was not until the late 1960s that these amounted to significant sums. As for his publications, by 1969 he had over twenty book titles to his credit.

Adorno enjoyed the rare, carefree hours he could spend in the Palmengarten in Frankfurt, and also in Frankfurt Zoo. Despite his reservations about the new medium, he and Gretel enjoyed watching different series on German television. Visitors in the know were careful not to disturb the Adornos when ZDF was screening *Daktari*, an American wild-life series with Judy the chimpanzee and Clarence the cross-eyed lion.

Adorno had evidently succeeded in achieving a certain balance in his life. His music, especially his love of playing duets, and conversations with people he knew well were compensation for the onerous duties at work and the gruelling disputes with the students and the militant spokesmen of the student movement. When he accepted invitations, as he frequently did, or when he acted as host, he displayed his talent for entertaining his guests, while Gretel served the cocktails.

Some instances of his wit can be seen in the half-playful, half-grotesque dialogues that he wrote, evidently without a particular aim but just for his own amusement. These dialogues always had the same two figures, Maman and Luiche. The latter name was an allusion to his uncle, Louis Calvelli-Adorno (1866–1960). The name itself was a parodic diminutive form of the name Louis in Frankfurt dialect.[90] Adorno would make Luiche ask questions in Hessen dialect to which Maman always finds witty replies:

LUICHE: Maman, when I have been crucified and am all bent over double – do you think I shall look like a genuine Riemenschneider?

MAMAN: Not really, my love, – but you will certainly make an excellent copy.[91]

In another fantastic scene Luiche had swallowed a miniature time-bomb: 'One minute before it was due to explode, he says: "Yes – Nietzsche is quite right. You have to have chaos inside you if you wish to give birth to a dancing star".'[92] As far as Luiche's career prospects were concerned, Adorno thought of making him a bullfighter so as to give the bulls a chance.

These *jeux d'esprit* may have been diversions for Adorno from his intensive labours. He would even indulge in them on occasion during faculty meetings, a standing horror punctuating the semesters. He decorated the notifications of the meetings with their accompanying agendas with funny drawings, teddy bears with a dummy or a dancer called Marlene. He would also play around with the text of the agenda, for example changing 'the establishment' (*Einrichtung*) of an office called dean of studies into 'the execution' (*Hinrichtung*) of the dean of studies.

This foible for playful irony is also in evidence in the loving letters Adorno wrote with great regularity to his parents. He rightly sought to conceal this side of himself from the gaze of a public whose cynicism he was frequently made to feel during this year. But many people whom he thought of as his intimate friends became aware of his personal difficulties, if only because he took no trouble to conceal them.

Anyone who heard his radio talk 'Resignation', which was broadcast in February 1969 by the Sender Freies Berlin, and who has read the little essay 'Critique', which had appeared in the weekly newspaper *Die Zeit* a few weeks before his death, would obtain a fairly accurate picture of Adorno's state of mind at the time. He felt himself to have been pilloried by the public attacks and expressions of hostility from both right and left. He was particularly hurt by the fact that these reproofs came not just from conservatives, but also from the New Left. Nevertheless, he was determined not to be deflected from a life of contemplation, since meditation was in his eyes a chief goal of living. 'The happiness that dawns in the eye of the thinking person is the happiness of humanity.'[93] He admired the cunning of the two rabbits who, when the hunter's shot came, fell down half-dead with fright, but then, having realized they were still alive, jumped up again and made their escape.[94]

Among the things that saved him and gave him pleasure was the publication of a collection of poems by Rudolf Borchardt. The plan for this edition went back to 1967 when Adorno exchanged letters with

Marie-Luise Borchardt, the second wife of the poet and scholar who had died in 1945.[95] In his letter to her he stressed several times over that for him it was 'both a pleasure and a matter of responsibility' to make a selection of Borchardt's poems and to write an introduction for the volume that Suhrkamp intended to publish. He was, he said, fascinated by Borchardt's language; there was 'a remarkable meeting of what might be called Borchardt's radical conservatism with avant-gardist positions'.[96] The book publication was linked to a talk entitled 'Charmed Language' that Adorno was to give in Zurich. He intended to combine the talk with a reading from the anthology: 'I believe I have some idea of what I can and cannot do; and reading is one of the things I can do.'[97]

After some strenuous days in January 1968 in Paris, where he gave a talk on aesthetics at a conference and met Samuel Beckett, he gave the lecture on Borchardt's poetry in Zurich in the Theater am Hechtplatz. Adorno's pupil Dieter Schnebel remembers the occasion. He arrived late and was not allowed in so that he could only hear the lecture and the reading from behind the closed doors:

His soft voice was not able to make itself heard beyond the hermetically sealed door. Only by holding my ear to the door could I understand the text as he read it out. By just standing in front of it . . . I could only hear the cadence of his speech. This meant that I could hear how musical it was. There were strong main subjects, melodic secondary subjects of great tenderness, passages of elaboration in which the characters quickly changed. Recapitulations stirred memories of earlier statements, and, finally, the entire piece faded away in an extended coda which nevertheless ended with a clear point.[98]

In April 1968 Adorno was to give the opening address at the sociology conference in Frankfurt. By then he had already completed the introduction for the anthology of Borchardt's poems. In this text Adorno situates the poet within the tradition of writers who had experienced the decay of language. But also, through 'the educated, cultured element in his poetry', he established his affinity 'with Eliot and Pound, Joyce and Beckett'.[99] His poetry 'speaks into a darkness. . . . The heroic gesture of Borchardt's speech is a despairing response to absolute solitude. This is the way a child speaks to himself in the darkness, interminably, in order to exorcize the anxiety darkness causes him.'[100] At the end of his talk Adorno pointed to Borchardt's musical side, illustrating it with reference to an early poem: 'Do not look into my windows, day. / My ship wants storm and not a star. / The final thing the heart can do / Is to be ready to die gladly.' Adorno concludes: 'No purer voice of Saturnian melancholy has sounded since Verlaine.'[101]

A source of pleasure for the 65-year-old Adorno, despite his distance from official recognition, was to receive the accolades that greeted him on his birthday. His friend Count Andreas Razumovsky wrote an affectionate congratulatory article in the *Frankfurter Allgemeine Zeitung* with the title 'Schöne Aussicht'. In it he emphasized that Adorno could not only recite the Frankfurt-dialect poems of Friedrich Stolze for hours on end in the original accent and knew all of Beethoven's compositions by heart, but that 'his intellectual productivity was simply incredible. At its heart was language, something that can be said of few people who occupy the chairs in our universities today.'[102] He also received a cordial birthday letter from Horkheimer: 'All your efforts to educate an enlightened, nonconformist youth that will act to bring about a better world . . . belong to the highest achievements of an intellectual resistance to the course of the administered world.' Horkheimer described the influence Adorno had had upon him and stressed the great impact of his writings. He ended by speaking of the important role Gretel had played in his life: 'Without her everything might have been quite different.'[103]

The divided nature of art

Art that forswears the happy brilliance that reality withholds from men and women and thus refuses every sensual trace of meaning, is spiritualized art; it is, in its unrelenting renunciation of childish happiness, the allegory of the illusionless actuality of happiness while bearing the fatal proviso of the chimerical: that this happiness does not exist.[104]

The hours that Adorno spent labouring at his *Aesthetic Theory* were hours of maximum strenuous concentration, but also of fulfilment. This was a book he had begun work on intensively in October 1966.[105] He gave two sets of lectures on the topic in the summer semester of that year as well as in the winter semester 1967–8.[106] Lengthier typescripts that he had dictated were already in existence and he edited and supplemented these, though with long interruptions thanks to deadlines on other sociological work.

In summer 1968, he told Hans G. Helms that his aesthetics book was ready in draft form. He also kept Elisabeth Lenk informed of his progress in editing the text. He was busy introducing detailed annotations into the text and was treating himself 'like an untalented pupil. Perhaps he will learn something, after all.'[107] And months later he was still saying, in a letter to Marcuse, 'I am desperately burying myself in my aesthetics book, and am making so much progress in my so-called research semester that I have every hope that when it is at an end I shall only have to concern myself with the "fine cut" and the difficult questions of organization (elimination of overlaps and the like).' He added that he had never tried to write a book in which 'the arrangement of the material presented such difficulties. Obviously, as a consequence of the critique of *prima philosophia* it is no longer possible to write in the traditional style of "only after", but in a certain sense I can only write paratactically. This extends right into the microstructure of language.'[108] This was one reason why Adorno thought he might not be able to publish the book with Suhrkamp in 1969, although Suhrkamp was very keen to take it. Instead, as he wrote to Elisabeth Lenk, 'I shall hurl something else, something shorter, into Unseld's jaws.'[109] What he had in mind was the volume of *Stichworte: Kritische Modelle* (Catchwords: Critical Models), which he completed in June 1969.

Adorno was still working on the *Aesthetic Theory* a few weeks before his death and had again revised the book, which had now grown to far more than 300 pages. The final publication, without any division into chapters, was undertaken by Gretel Adorno and Rolf Tiedemann and appeared a year after his death. It remained a fragment. Adorno himself would scarcely have approved the text in the form in which we possess it, even though, with its blend of metaphorical power and conceptual structure, it is a masterpiece of dialectical writing, one that he had never thought of as a definitive philosophical statement.[110] The fragmented form of the book is in complete harmony with the discontinuous development of central themes such as the music of Beethoven and Schoenberg, the painting of Klee and Picasso and the writings of Beckett and Celan. This work, in which he inquires into the truth content and exceptional status of the work of art, is one of his most important.[111] Its subject was closer to his heart than any other. This may explain the apodictic style that characterizes many passages in the book.

The argument of the *Aesthetic Theory* circles round the question of the possibility of autonomous works of art in the present. Adorno's approach is to go back to the traditional aesthetic theories of Kant and Hegel while attempting to bring them up to date by confronting them with the art of the avant-garde. He concentrated entirely on the aesthetics of the works themselves. This led him to posit 'the primacy of the object' as opposed to the subject, in other words, the artistic subject seemed to him to be of a second order. This led him in turn to ignore the public reception of art. Adorno understood the priority of the object not only as a plea for the intrinsic (*werkimmanent*) analysis of the text, but also committed art to being an implicit writing of history.[112] As such, it is tied to the reality it finds before it. And yet, by a paradox, it is also supposed to be the plenipotentiary of a utopia for which, in line with its riddle-like character, it can never find positive expression.

As a composer of free atonality and a theoretician of the New Music, as well as a subtle interpreter of modern literature, Adorno treated the theoretical discussion of aesthetics as a constant in his work. Given that in this politicized age many people wished to liquidate art in the cause of revolution, his own desire was to salvage art. In his language, he aimed at 'the redemption of semblance' (*Schein*). For 'the emphatic right of art, the legitimation of its truth, depends on this act of salvaging',[113] which was needed because only the great work of art is free from lies. This redemption, however, must fail, or so Adorno argued in many passages, if art, which is neither solace nor ecstasy, conforms, or even adapts itself, to the taste of the recipient and thus enters into collusion with the sphere of communication. Instead, art is the anticipatory manifestation (*Vorschein*) of something non-existent and thus the expression of what might be possible objectively, in the realm of freedom. Art is part of the world and yet its other. 'Artworks have no truth without determinate negation.'[114] This is the source of their irreconcilable nature. Admittedly, all art is a *fait social*, part of the historical process, but it is valid only as a strict repudiation of an antagonistic society. 'Art keeps itself alive only through its social force of resistance. . . . Its contribution to it is not communication with it but . . . resistance. . . . Radical modernity preserves art's immanence by admitting society only in an obscured form, as in dreams.'[115]

An art that left social reality unscathed is nothing but commercial art. Only those works of art that adopt an antithetical stance towards society contain truth. This element of truth, however, can turn into its opposite if works of art are themselves so successful that they suggest the possibility of 'reconciliation' in our society. On its own art itself is not in a position to sublate a world situation moving towards catastrophe. The 'promise of happiness' that arises from the utopian moments of art is one that is always 'broken'.[116] This applies even to the most radical expression of art, such as Beckett's anti-dramas, which are not free of deception because, even though they may call for the abolition of the bad, antagonistic side of reality whose absurdity is manifest, they cannot achieve this themselves. 'Artworks draw credit from a praxis that has yet to begin and no one knows whether anything backs their letters of credit.'[117]

In so far as art has powers of resistance at its command, it shares with philosophy the impulse to salvage the non-identical. While philosophy, despite its utopian goal of cognition ('striving by way of the concept to transcend the concept'),[118] nevertheless continues to dwell in the medium of concepts, art, as the sphere of the expressive, inhabits a non-conceptual realm. For it makes use of mimetic means, rather than discursive ones. Adorno saw art as the site of a particular rationality, one which neither appropriates objects for instrumental purposes nor tries to 'slay' them analytically in a cognitive discourse, but one that can be defined by empathy and imitation as a different form of cognition.[119] In the *Aesthetic Theory* the term to which Adorno has recourse is that of mimesis, or the mimetic faculty or impulse.

In the successful work of art mimesis and reason are not irreconcilable opposites; on the contrary, art arises from these opposite poles. 'Art is mimetic comportment that for the purpose of its objectivation disposes over the most advanced rationality.'[120] However, this element of rationality consists in the complete domination and shaping of the artistic material, in obedience to the laws of form in the process of aesthetic construction. The mimetic aspect of art should not be misconstrued as the mere imitation of pre-given objectivities. Instead, mimesis assists the expression of things that elude objective representation. 'The survival of mimesis, the non-conceptual affinity of the subjectively produced with its unposited other, defines art as a form of knowledge and to that extent as "rational". For that to which the mimetic comportment responds is the telos of knowledge, which art simultaneously blocks with its own categories. Art completes knowledge with what is excluded from knowledge.'[121] But art should not be confined to the realm of knowledge. Adorno uses the concept of mimesis to underline art's expressive function. This can only be understood as the expression of 'suffering – joy has proven inimical to expression, perhaps because it has yet to exist.'[122] For this reason, the 'primary colour' of the authentic art of the present 'is black'.[123] In another, central passage of the *Aesthetic Theory*, Adorno remarks that, in a world that is out of joint, the utopia of art 'is draped in black'. But in its dissonance it is 'recollection of the possible in opposition to the actual . . . something like the imaginary reparation of the catastrophe of world history'.[124] Reparation is possible in art if music, literature and painting express what does not yet exist. In this context Adorno made a connection with Kant's category of natural beauty. But as 'the trace of the non-identical in things', natural beauty is quite uncertain.[125] It can be equated neither with mere nature, nor with what has been shaped by human hand. Instead, Adorno saw natural beauty as the cipher of how nature could be. 'What is beautiful in nature is what appears to be more than what is literally there. . . . As true as the fact that every object in nature can be considered beautiful is the judgement that the landscape of Tuscany is more beautiful than the surroundings of Gelsenkirchen.'[126] The task of art is to remind us of this potential: 'What nature strives for in vain, artworks fulfil: They open their eyes.'[127]

With his *Aesthetic Theory*, Adorno succeeded in a highly complex balancing act. He wished to show the work of art as a contradictory unity: it both denounced and anticipated. On the one hand, it could only preserve its authenticity by negating the catastrophic course of the world; on the other, it was supposed to be the 'plenipotentiary of a better practice'.[128] As far as the work of art articulates the negative nature of existing reality, its ruthless accusation can change that reality for something better. The break with the principle of representation, the concrete, and in general with what is already known was in Adorno's eyes the signature of modernity. In this respect he appealed to Baudelaire's notion of the '*inconnu*'. The mark of the avant-garde was the 'fraying' of the genres of art that went hand in hand with the decay of traditional aesthetic norms.[129] What interested Adorno here was, as he formulated it in a talk he gave to the Berlin Academy of Art, the erosion of the traditional boundaries of the forms of art, the way in which the individual arts were growing together. This showed itself, for example, in the way in which quasi-musical structures found their way into pictures, or even into literary texts, especially lyrical texts. By drawing attention to the fact that 'the individual arts were aspiring to their concrete generalization',[130] Adorno inaugurated a new conception of avant-garde art, while at the same time revising the concepts specific to each of the arts.

Adorno did not live to see the publication of the book and its reception. He thought of it as an instance of his idea of thinking in constellations. In this late text he achieved what he had posited as a crucial task in *Negative Dialectics*: a philosophy that did not exhaust itself in categories, but was to be a composition. For 'the crux is what happens in it, not a thesis or a position; the texture . . . not the course of one-track minds.'[131]

Death

The woods are lovely dark and deep,
But I have promises to keep,
And miles to go before I sleep,
And miles to go before I sleep.
Robert Frost, *Stopping by Woods on a Snowy Evening*

While on Sabbatical leave in the winter semester 1968–9, Adorno was able to limit his duties to the not exactly simple business of institute director, and otherwise to devote himself entirely to finishing the *Aesthetic Theory*. Although he tried to put as great a distance as possible between himself and the conflicts that were raging in the university, he could not fail to be affected by the increasingly militant attacks, partly aimed at him. In March, when he learnt that one of his doctoral students, who had been working on Hegel's philosophy, had committed suicide by jumping to his death from the Goethe Tower in the City Forest in Frankfurt, he made this note: 'Once again Rolland Pelzer. He had bequeathed his body to the anatomical institute in order to spare his extremely impoverished family the costs of the funeral but the institute rejected it because it was so damaged that it could no longer be of use. – And then the students who think themselves revolutionary hold discussions on equal representation [*Drittelparität*] in the committees.'[132]

Another death in this year affected Adorno particularly keenly. He learnt in March of the death of Carl Dreyfus, whom he had known well since the 1920s. Dreyfus had emigrated to Argentina, but had returned to Germany with his wife Tilly in 1962 and had been living in Munich. Adorno wrote to his widow: 'Carl was one of the people who played a central role in my life, and today I incline to the view that his life was better than my own. But where is the authority who can decide such things?'[133]

The vacation in April, which he spent this year in Brenner's Park Hotel in Baden-Baden, was barely sufficient to give him the relaxation and recuperation he needed so badly after the physical and psychological stresses that had preceded it. In addition, there were private problems arising from his sometimes stormy love relationships, which frequently ended with painful separations. A lover of great importance in his life had broken off with him in autumn 1968 when he was visiting her in Munich because she intended to marry. That was an escape into a golden cage, he remarked later with some bitterness. Such events 'are the saddest things that can happen and they are a sign of age.' He wrote this in a state of depression to a close friend, the singer Carla Henius.[134]

For the approaching summer semester, Adorno had announced a course of lectures entitled 'An Introduction to Dialectical Thinking', as well as an advanced seminar on the dialectics of subject and object. Following his sabbatical term, the audience for his lectures in which he intended to discuss the relation of social theory and practice was larger than usual; the auditorium was filled with up to one thousand people. Despite these unfavourable conditions, Adorno wished to alter the traditional shape of the academic lecture and invited his students to put questions to him at any time so as to create a forum for open discussion. This attempt to change the nature of a lecture course was not only doomed from the outset, but was evidently taken as an invitation to disrupt the proceedings – to the point, indeed, where they turned effectively into a regular tribunal. At the very first lecture on 22 April, there was an incident, evidently organized by the direct-action wing of the SDS, the so-called leather-jacket party. The trouble-makers, two tall men, went up to Adorno on the platform and demanded in Stalinist style that he perform an act of self-criticism for having recently called in the police to clear the institute and for the legal proceedings against Hans-Jürgen Krahl.[135] This was accompanied by shouts of 'Down with the informer!'. At the same time, a student wrote on the blackboard: 'If Adorno is left in peace, capitalism will never cease.' A large part of the audience expressed their anger about the interruption, but without intervening to quell those responsible for it. Adorno proposed that he would give everyone five minutes in which to decide whether or not they wished the lecture to proceed. Scarcely had he finished speaking than he was surrounded on the platform by three women students who scattered rose and tulip petals over him. They then bared their breasts and tried to approach him while performing an erotic pantomime. Adorno, whose desperate anxiety was plain to see, snatched up his hat and coat and, waving his briefcase in self-defence, made his escape from the hall.[136]

After a moment of shock, the majority of those present reacted with indignation to this almost physical attack on the lecturer. Following inconclusive discussions between the few supporters of this disruption and their critics, the lecture hall emptied. The Grassroots Sociology Group distributed leaflets with the title 'Adorno as an Institution is Dead'.

Adorno himself was unable to believe that of all lectures his should have been singled out for 'this propaganda of deeds', this spectacular happening. 'To have picked on me of all people, I who have always spoken out against every type of erotic repression and sexual taboo! To ridicule me and set three girls dressed up as hippies against me in this way! I found that repulsive. The laughter that was aimed at me was basically the reaction of the philistine who giggles when he sees girls with naked breasts. Needless, to say, this idiocy was planned.'[137]

Adorno was well aware that 'the idiotic brutality of the left-wing fascists' would trigger 'the malicious joy of all reactionaries'.[138] For this reason, in his public comments on the brutal disruption of his lecture, he took care not to play into the hands of the 'reactionaries' or to lend them arguments that would help to blacken the anti-authoritarian movement and their motives in attacking the defects of the education system. For example, in an interview with the *Süddeutsche Zeitung* at the end of April, he spoke out clearly against the widespread view that ideas he had defended were now being turned against him as people tried to put them into practice. According to Adorno, this particularly popular thesis was probably invented by people 'eager to say "I told you so" in the hope of paralysing critical thinking. I am no more tempted to succumb to this gesture than I am to cave in to the enforced solidarity of the supporters of direct action.' Merely because he had been attacked in this way was no reason to behave like a broken man full of remorse. In the interview, he emphasized that his own attitude was not one of resignation, even if he could see that what the students were looking for by resorting to practical demonstrations was a blind alley. Blind action was obviously not the way out of the dilemma. To 'absorb this objective contradiction into his thinking and not try to remove it by force' was in his view a sign of strength. His relation to the students, moreover, 'was no more impaired than relations generally in the present climate of conflict in the universities'.[139]

The same picture emerged in a further interview shortly afterwards, in May, on this occasion for the weekly magazine *Der Spiegel*. Adorno refused to allow himself to be lured into a wholesale condemnation of the protest movement.

SPIEGEL: Herr Professor, two weeks ago all was well with the world . . .
ADORNO: Not for me.[140]

He made use of this interview with *Der Spiegel* to modify a statement he had made earlier. In a previous interview on television, he had let drop the remark that he had never imagined that people might exploit his ideas to justify using Molotov cocktails. On this occasion, he denied that his writings 'had ever supplied the model for any acts or political actions whatever'. Nevertheless, it was indisputable that, 'if you teach and publish for twenty years with the intensity I have shown, something will certainly enter into public consciousness.'[141] He noted that 'the mismatch between theory and practice today consists in the circumstance that theory is subject to censorship exercised in the name of practice. For example, people want to forbid me to say quite simple things that would expose the illusory nature of many of the political aims of certain students.' Adorno emphasized that, despite all the necessary critical debate with the catastrophic philosophy of direct action, a philosophy to be ascribed to the 'despair' at the fact 'that people feel how little power they have', the urgently needed university reform would never have got off the ground but for the student protest. 'I believe that the general attention now being paid to the dumbing-down processes that prevail in present-day society would never have emerged without the student movement.'[142] On 12 June, some seven weeks after the happening, Adorno resumed his lectures. However, there were further disruptions, and he decided to cancel his lectures for the rest of the semester while persevering only with his philosophy seminar. He wrote to the dean to say that his lectures had been disrupted by Hans Imhoff and Arno Widmann, students familiar in the Frankfurt 'scene' at the time. Given the situation, it had not been possible, he said, to discover from the majority of students whether they wished the lectures to continue.[143]

Adorno made no secret of the bitter disappointment he felt as a result of this new assault aimed at him personally. He also felt oppressed by the additional burden of having to appear at the magistrates' court as a witness against Hans-Jürgen Krahl, one of his doctoral students. Adorno stressed once again that he had perceived the group of students as occupiers. This produced a scornful reaction on the part of many of the students who followed the proceedings and he was well aware of this.

A few days after he decided to abandon his lectures he admitted in a letter to Marcuse that he was 'in a phase of extreme depression'. One of the many reasons for this was that Marcuse made a point of refusing to sit down and discuss the situation privately with his Frankfurt friends, Adorno, Horkheimer and Habermas.[144] In particular he blamed Adorno for the fact that the institute as it was then was not the institute as it had been. 'You know as well as I the essential difference between the work the institute did in the 1930s and the work it is doing in present-day Germany. The qualitative difference is not one that arises from the development of theory. . . . But our (old) theory had an inner political content, an inner political dynamic that calls more urgently today than ever before for a concrete political position.'[145] Adorno rejected this criticism and rather helplessly attempted to show by drawing up a list of successful research projects that the critical tradition was still alive and well in the institute and that its concrete work was not being swayed by the influence of its financial sponsors. 'I believe that, if one is mindful of the difficulties with which the institute has had to contend our whole life long as much as it does today, the end result is not unworthy.' In response to Marcuse's accusation that the political dimension of critical theory had faded out, Adorno stressed almost desperately that the current social situation ruled out revolutionary action and it would therefore be wrong to imagine 'that the student protest movement had even the slightest chance of having any impact on society.'[146] And because it could not have any such impact, its influence 'is doubly' damaging; it arouses 'a fascist potential'[147] and, at the same time, there is a danger that authoritarian attitudes may come to prevail within the militant groups. These were the fears from which Adorno increasingly suffered after he became the victim of acts of aggression that were, he said, 'collective insanity'. 'Here in Frankfurt', he went on in his letter to Marcuse, 'the word "professor" is used to dismiss people, to "demolish" [*fertigmachen*] them, as they put it so nicely, much as the Nazis used the word "Jew". . . . I take the risk that the student movement may turn to fascism much more to heart than you.'[148] He took many things to heart at the time: his work on the *Aesthetic Theory*, his private problems, and the realization of his publication plans, which was the most important thing of all to him.

The state Adorno found himself in during the early summer of 1969 was one he himself described as desolate. Exhausted as he was, he undertook more than he could cope with. In addition to being 'completely overworked' as usual, there was the never-ending torment of the discussions and disputes with the radical students that just kept going round in circles. And these were the very students who had sought him out as the star of critical theory, not least for publicity reasons. Adorno was not only forced to endure hostility and even open hatred, which he remained convinced was aimed at him as a theoretician, but he was also pursued by the nightmare that the general political situation might easily slip overnight into totalitarianism. In his last, handwritten letter to Marcuse on 26 July – the typed version did not reach Marcuse until 6 August – he referred to himself as 'a badly battered Teddie'.

In this depressed state of mind Adorno and Gretel travelled to Switzerland, where the extended walks normally succeeded in restoring his equanimity. He now needed the break more than ever. On Tuesday 22 July the couple drove to Zermatt in order to spend the vacation in the Hotel Bristol in the well-known resort, 1600 metres high at the foot of the Matterhorn. A few days after their arrival, they went for an excursion to a mountain peak of some 3000 metres that could be reached by cable car.[149] This was in spite of urgent warnings from Dr Sprado, his family doctor and a heart specialist, to avoid all strenuous physical activity. At the top of the mountain, he started to have pains in his chest. This made him go back to the resort. The same day, they went down the valley to the town of Visp, about 30 kilometres away. Adorno's mountain boots had a hole that he wanted to have repaired. In the shoeshop the pains came back again. As a precaution he was taken to the local hospital. Towards the evening, Gretel Adorno went back to the hotel. The following day, 6 August, she set out to visit her husband in the St Maria Hospital and to provide him with reading material, only to learn that he had suddenly had a heart attack at around 11.20 a.m. and died. He would have turned sixty-six on 11 September.

The news of his death was reported in the most important media the same day. Radio and television produced appreciations of the life and work of the Frankfurt scholar. The death notice in the *Frankfurter Allgemeine Zeitung* was so decorous that, like a similar notice he had once read, it avoided 'the spirit of a communicative language which by diminishing all distances even manages to do violence to the respect due to death.'[150]

THEODOR W. ADORNO
Born 11 September 1903
died peacefully on 6 August 1969

In deepest sorrow
Margarete Adorno
née Karplus
Frankfurt/Main, Kettenhofweg 123, 9 August 1969

The funeral will take place on 13 August 1969
at 11 a.m. in Frankfurt Central Cemetery.
We hope you will understand the family's
wish for privacy at this time.

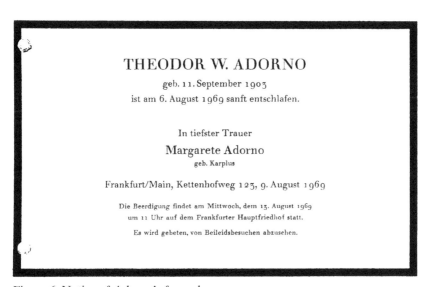

Figure 6 Notice of Adorno's funeral

On 13 August, a week after his death, the funeral took place at the Frankfurt Central Cemetery, where he was laid to rest in the family tomb. The funeral, which took place without religious rites, was held in the presence of two thousand mourners. Afterwards, many of the mourners met in the house of the publisher Siegfried Unseld.

The ceremony was broadcast on Hessen Radio. The prime minister of Hessen spoke about Adorno's achievements as a public intellectual and as professor of sociology and philosophy. Ralf Dahrendorf, as chairman of the German Sociology Society, spoke about Adorno's relations with the student movement and Ludwig von Friedeburg discussed his importance for the development of the Institute of Social Research. Max Horkheimer made a very personal statement about his collaboration with Adorno over the decades:

> Adorno's works, whose depth and historical relevance arose from his unique energy as a writer and a dedication that is difficult to comprehend, are a testimony to critical theory. . . . However intensively he sought reform, he refused to commit himself without reservation to collectives that appealed to his theories instead of reflecting on their implications for their own actions. . . . His attitude was both productive and anti-conformist. . . . Today, we mourn the passing of one of the greatest minds of this age of transition.[151]

Epilogue: Thinking Against Oneself

> But it is evidently my fate to have to coax my entire production from my life by a gradual process, and that may well be far from the worst way to work. I could imagine that this is connected with another peculiarity that I have observed in what I cobble together – that in truth every text of mine is a kind of leave-taking.[1]

Fifteen years before his death, Adorno wrote to Thomas Mann that 'death was a human scandal', that there was no cause 'to celebrate it in the name of tragedy', and that it 'should be abolished'.[2] The provocative aspect of death and the aspect that unleashes resistance, Adorno once remarked in a conversation with Ernst Bloch, lay in the utopian desire to abolish it. All utopias were at heart a desire for eternal life, and thus arise from the provocation of death. 'Where the threshold of death is not implied in the idea, there really is no utopia.'[3] This is why utopia cannot be depicted; indeed, for its own sake we must not form an image of it.

Adorno also devotes an entire section of *Negative Dialectics*, the 'Meditations on Metaphysics', to 'Dying Today'. The solemn rituals with whose assistance human beings do not so much commemorate the dead as attempt to overcome their own impotence serve to resist the existential experience of death. Adorno perceived the decisive reason for repressing death as consisting in the fear of being robbed of one's own possessions. He registered this idea in an unpublished note in a quite unmetaphysical style: 'Banknotes can hardly be transferred to hell, and it may be hoped that anyone who presents himself there as a VIP will be greeted with the customary derision. . . . Of course, we cannot know even that with certainty. . . . Even so, the metaphysics of death nowadays includes the idea that death reminds men just how frail the order is that they have erected so solidly on earth that they imagine it is absolute.'[4] Associating with death is all the more intolerable for mankind, the more an autonomous, happy life is rendered impossible by the social conditions of their lives. It follows that the relation to death is not a constant but is preformed by society. Adorno interpreted the physical and psychological decay of human beings with increasing age and as a prelude to the definitive end as the reason why it was impossible to conceive of any hereafter. Nevertheless, the thought that death is 'the last thing pure and simple'[5] cannot be accepted because it would make every idea of truth meaningless. 'For it is a feature of truth that it will last, along with its temporal core. Without any duration at all there would be no truth, and the last trace of it would be engulfed in death, the absolute.'[6]

Adorno's wish to be judged by his substantial achievements as a philosopher may well have inspired him to make a rare emotional diary entry, as he did while speaking of Beethoven's *Missa Solemnis*: 'Thank heaven I was spared to complete this.'[7] At the age of sixty-five, Adorno still wished to place more in the scales than he had already done. He had wanted to write a book about Beethoven for years and had made notes for it in over forty notebooks. As early as 11 June 1940 he had written to his parents, saying that 'the next major piece of work I shall undertake will be the book on Beethoven.'[8] He had repeatedly tried to bring the book 'home and dry', as he put it, but he ended up just adding it to the list of tasks to be undertaken once he had finished the *Aesthetic Theory*.[9] For Adorno the completion of this great music project on Beethoven was a perpetual challenge, and it appears that it was less the difficulties of substance that were the problem, than those of organizing the heterogeneous materials. A further music project that had preoccupied him ever since he had studied with Berg in Vienna was the *Theory of Musical Reproduction*. His notes on this subject assumed a definite shape in the years in Los Angeles. But in this instance, too, the plethora of notes he had taken in his so-called Black Book could not be published until thirty years after his death: a theory of true musical interpretation, one that adhered closely to the music's objective substance, its structure.[10]

These two great projects did not prevent him from conceiving a plan for yet another book, this time on moral philosophy, for which he could draw on extensive materials for a lecture course he had given in 1963.[11] Judging by these lectures it is reasonable to assume that his thesis was the impossibility of a moral philosophy as a binding doctrine, a thesis already contained in his celebrated formula 'There can be no good life within the bad one.'[12] Adorno would no doubt have linked his argument to the ethical premises he had referred to in *Negative Dialectics* as the 'new categorical imperative': that human beings should 'arrange their thoughts and actions so that Auschwitz will not be repeated, so that nothing similar will happen again'. Admittedly, Adorno makes explicit in the same passage that this imperative 'is as resistant to justification as the one given by Kant was in its day.'[13] It would have been interesting to know how Adorno would have resolved this difficulty.

The same may be said of the book he had planned on social theory. In it he aimed to collect his current analyses of society together with an essay with the highly topical title 'Integration and Disintegration in Contemporary Society'.[14] This book was not his last project by any means. Incidentally, despite his writing ambitions, he did not plan to retire early to devote himself to them because, even with the conflict with the students, he found academic teaching an inspiration. Moreover he had no desire to withdraw from his responsibilities for his numerous doctoral students.[15] He had the intention of following up his first book of aphorisms with a second one, which he entitled *Graeculus*. Here, too, he had made a preparatory collection of notes. As in *Minima Moralia*, he wished to produce an anthology of epigrammatic texts on a variety of topics, with observations on musical, cultural and socio-critical subjects.[16] The aphorisms in existence included comments on smoking as a habit of men and women, on good and bad prose, and on politics and death. Some of the aphorisms were short and pithy: 'Education equals the ability to wait';[17] or, again, 'I find it easier to believe in the Christ child than in Jesus Christ';[18] or, 'Is there a transcendence of yearning? Without the wish there is no truth, but the wish cannot guarantee it.'[19]

In the same category are his 'Dream protocols' which he recorded throughout his life. When he had to spend the night in Stuttgart on one occasion, he dreamt that 'the most painful form of execution – evidently intended for me – would be to have to stand up to my head in water while being roasted at the same time. Because of the extinguishing effect of the water this would last especially long.'[20] Another dream recurred frequently. He dreamt he was in a concentration camp where he heard a group of Jewish children singing a song. At the end of the narrative he wrote: 'Awoke with an unspeakable sense of horror.'[21]

Adorno's writing plans were on the one hand intentions that took their toll of his energies – in his letters he speaks frequently of exhaustion – while on the other hand they were a concrete future from which he derived his creative energy. All these projects were the tasks that awaited him and needed to be written up responsibly. After all, writing was the essence of his life. Before leaving for Zermatt, he viewed the approaching years with some optimism, despite his 'battered' condition. A little while previously, together with the educationalist Hellmut Becker, he had recorded what would become a famous conversation about 'educating people to maturity'. The discussion was broadcast on the day of his funeral. He had been planning further broadcasts. He and Gretel had also intended a trip in September to Venice, where he had been invited to give a paper at a congress on critical theory and art.[22] Rooms had already been booked in the Hotel Regina.[23] He had also had discussions with Gershom Scholem about a lecture tour in Israel.[24] Even if the conflicts of the past term were very much present in his mind, Adorno still looked forward with some confidence to the coming semester. At the last meeting of his class in the philosophy seminar he had taken his leave with the words: 'If you are all looking forward to the next semester as keenly as I am, we shall be able to do some very good work.'[25]

All these statements certainly amounted to something more than whistling in the dark. Nevertheless, with hindsight there were good reasons to put a different complexion on the situation. Dr Paul Lüth wrote in his 'Letter from a Country Practice', which appeared in the volume with reminiscences of Adorno: 'Adorno, ground down, overworked . . . left on the planned vacation. . . . As we doctors know, heart attacks do not come out of the blue. They build up carefully, collecting all the frustrations and exhaustions on the way, and then strike suddenly.'[26] Marie Luise Kaschnitz dedicated a poem to her friend after his death:

> Th. W. A.
> Something opened up
> Something fluid and yet firm
> Crept down the meadows
> Then the street
> And finally reached his chest.
> He died of himself
> Of no longer being at one
> With his youth
> And all youth
> His experience taught him
> To hate violence
> And so he was called a turncoat
> No one needed
> To push him into his grave
> In this radiant summer.
> He had long been sad
> He fell.[27]

The view of Adorno's condition expressed in this poem seems to correspond to the picture Gretel had formed of her husband's physical and mental condition a few days before his death. When close friends offered to come to see her right after his unexpected death in the hospital in Visp, she refused, not indeed brusquely, but quite firmly. She had already arranged to have Adorno's body taken back to Frankfurt.

Gretel Adorno had been a direct witness of the impact of the student attacks on her husband, and how he had been prevented from continuing what he saw as his true task in life. As widow, she did what she had done for her decades-long life with him; she placed herself at the service of his work. She herself had talked of their relationship as a symbiosis. In her heart of hearts, she was convinced that he was committed to her despite his passionate love affair with the 'beautiful child', the actress from Munich, which had ended so painfully for Adorno at the end of the previous year.[28] After the death of her husband, Gretel Adorno continued to live in the Kettenhofweg. She sought to overcome her grief by continuing with the task of working on the unfinished manuscript of the *Aesthetic Theory* together with Rolf Tiedemann and bringing it to the point of publication. When, two days after Adorno's death, Elisabeth Lenk wrote to Gretel that she was 'still stupefied' by the news, Gretel sent her a hand-written reply: 'Dear Elisabeth, the time may come when I need your help with the *Aesthetics*. I shall certainly call on you then.'[29]

She knew like no one else just how much this book had meant to him. And not content with just taking over this task, she also involved herself in the edition of the *Gesammelte Schriften* and arranged personally for his artistic and scholarly papers to be deposited in the Theodor W. Adorno Archive. Having dealt with her husband's literary estate, she saw no reason to survive him further.[30] Shortly after the publication of the *Aesthetic Theory*, she attempted to kill herself by taking an overdose of sleeping pills.[31] She survived, but was in permanent need of nursing during the remaining twenty-three years of her life. For as long as was possible, she was looked after round the clock by friends and some of Adorno's former students; later she was moved to a sanatorium in the Taunus.

A day before Adorno's funeral an interview with Horkheimer appeared in *Der Spiegel* with the title 'Heaven, Eternity and Beauty', in which he defended his friend against the charge that he had become disillusioned.[32] Horkheimer emphasized something that had already become apparent at the funeral with the presence of many of his students, namely that many of them 'had retained their love for him'. Drawing on theological motifs, he emphasized that Adorno's 'negativism implied the affirmation of something "other"', which, however, is not susceptible to definition. This was not a negative theology 'in the sense that there is no God, but in the sense that God cannot be represented.'[33] Horkheimer was evidently attempting to identify the legacy of Jewish thought in Adorno. The notion of truth as temporal knowledge that is always gradually unfolding could be combined with the prohibition on graven images, as could the concept of being mindful of the messianic aspect of redemption or reconciliation: hope for the sake of those who are without hope.

A very different tone was to be heard from over thirty students of Adorno's from the younger generation. They had produced a statement that appeared in the *Frankfurter Rundschau* a few days after the funeral with the title 'Continuing Critical Theory'.[34] Alluding to Horkheimer's funeral oration and his obituary, which had included a reference to Adorno's genius, the authors wrote: 'The more monumental the gravestone built from effusive reverence and piled on top of the no-sayer, the more surely his explosive power will be buried for ever.' There is a danger that 'argument will be supplanted by rapt wonder at the sight of the genius who confronts us like a natural force.' The authors of the statement expressed their fears that the inflation of Adorno into a hero of the intellect would turn critical theory into a museum piece.[35] The same newspaper contained an obituary of Adorno by Hans-Jürgen Krahl, his doctoral student whom he had testified against a few weeks before in a trial for trespass. The student leader now reproved Adorno by alleging that, despite his critique of the bourgeois individual, he was 'irresistibly imprisoned within the ruins of the bourgeois subject' and accusing him of having proved unable 'to translate the organized partisanship of theory into the emancipation of the oppressed'. Thus Adorno's 'negation of late capitalist society remained abstract.'[36] Both the students' statement and Krahl's obituary were deeply indebted to Adorno's thinking, right down to their turns of phrase. The validity of his ideas seemed to be beyond question. The students, of course, had no idea how Adorno's philosophy might be developed substantively following his death. The same may be said of Marcuse, who gave his first public reaction in a magazine programme on German television. He confined his comments to calling on people 'to think radically and impart this radicality to others'. He also remarked that he thought the future would bring a debate about the substance of Adorno's important work.[37] Thus Horkheimer's pessimistic review of a past beyond recall was counterbalanced by Marcuse's hope that Adorno's death would not mean the extinction of the revolutionary spark that he saw glowing at the heart of his ruthless critique.

In contrast, the obituary penned by Jürgen Habermas in *Die Zeit* was one of the few that attempted to provide a proper assessment of both Adorno's history of philosophy and his highly individual form of thinking. His portrait of the philosopher captured a number of crucial features: his spontaneity and his refusal to identify fully with the role of 'the fully fledged adult'.[38] But Habermas was also the only person to raise the question of Adorno's 'philosophical legacy'. He foregrounded in particular the concept of self-reflection.[39] He emphasized that Adorno had defined the concept of reflection as the movement of critical thought, a 'finite energy' that drew its strength from what was false in its object. And in fact, in the last essay he wrote before his death, Adorno stressed the importance of the way in which reality is interpreted, both for philosophy and sociology, defining this critical reflection as 'resistance to . . . everything that is merely posited and that regards its own mere existence as justification enough'.[40] Criticism as determinate negation is tied to the historical conditions of the negativity of existence. Critical reflection calls for the contrary reality of a society in which human beings experience real suffering. Habermas, who tried to follow on from Adorno with the 'negative idea of abolishing discrimination and suffering',[41] nevertheless posed the central question 'How can critical thinking be justified?'.[42] The problem then was to provide a rationale of criticism against the background of the total web of delusion. The task was not to avoid this problem but to accept it as something that belonged to the essential legacy of Adorno's critical theory and one of his most productive ideas.[43] It is a legacy that arises from consistently following critical theory through to its logical conclusion, in particular the idea that it 'must also be a thinking against itself'.[44]

Dialectic, then, is conceived as immanent critique, as a method with which to expose the internal contradictions in society and in thought itself. Whether this key to his thought is sufficient to unlock all the treasures it contains must remain an open question. The intention in reconstructing Adorno's life and work was not to provide a secret key for treasure hunters, although it was hoped that it would stimulate their curiosity. It would be rewarding, however, to hold fast to his visible legacy[45] and to build on it: the critique of the coercion implicit in the act of identification (*Identifikationszwang*) and of the restrictive concept of rationality, the micrological method of interpretion of the analysis of music and literature, the theory of the avant-garde and the criticism of the media. Then there is the thread running through his writings of the internal tension between negativity and messianism, between (a bad) reality and (a better) possibility, between identity and non-identity, ratio and mimesis, and especially between truth content and the desire for expression that runs through the late writings. These extremes are all characteristic of Adorno's thinking. He wanted to be both an artist and a scientist, a composer and a writer, a philosopher and a sociologist. He had no ambition to be 'a mediator between extremes', in thought any more than in his personality and his life. Instead, 'mediation takes place in and through the extremes, in the extremes themselves.'[46] In his eyes a no man's land was the symbol of the place where you can be different without fear and where conflicts can be resolved without having to take sides in advance.

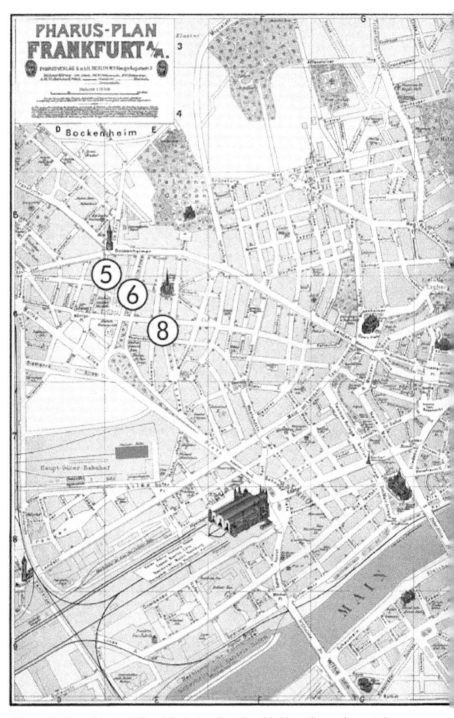

Figure 7 Map of central Frankfurt showing the chief locations where Adorno
lived and worked

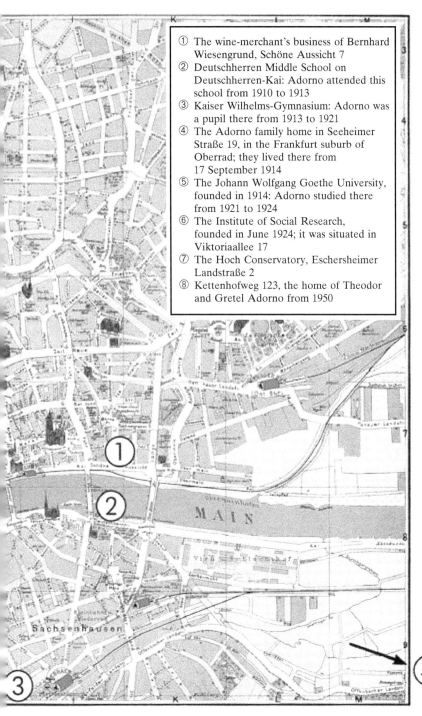

① The wine-merchant's business of Bernhard Wiesengrund, Schöne Aussicht 7

② Deutschherren Middle School on Deutschherren-Kai: Adorno attended this school from 1910 to 1913

③ Kaiser Wilhelms-Gymnasium: Adorno was a pupil there from 1913 to 1921

④ The Adorno family home in Seeheimer Straße 19, in the Frankfurt suburb of Oberrad; they lived there from 17 September 1914

⑤ The Johann Wolfgang Goethe University, founded in 1914: Adorno studied there from 1921 to 1924

⑥ The Institute of Social Research, founded in June 1924; it was situated in Viktoriaallee 17

⑦ The Hoch Conservatory, Eschersheimer Landstraße 2

⑧ Kettenhofweg 123, the home of Theodor and Gretel Adorno from 1950

The Wiesengrund-Adorno

Theodor Ludwig Wiesengrund-Adorno
* 11.9.1903 Frankfurt am Main
÷ 6.8.1969 Visp, Switzerland

Married
in

Married

Mathilde C.
Wiesengrund
* 5.11.1876
Frankfurt am Main
÷ 11.3.1878
Frankfurt am Main

Paul Friedrich
Wiesengrund
* 30.5.1869
Frankfurt am Main
÷ 7.9.1886
Frankfurt am Main

Alice Betty
Wiesengrund
* 2.9.1873
Frankfurt am Main
÷ 14.11.1935
Frankfurt am Main

Jenny L.
Wiesengrund
* 22.9.1874
Frankfurt am Main
÷ 22.1.1963
Hamburg

Bernhard Robert
Wiesengrund
* 13.11.1871
Frankfurt am Main
÷ 2.3.1935
London

Oscar Alexander
Wiesengrund
* 30.7.1870
Frankfurt am Main
÷ 8.7.1946
New York

Married
22.5.1868

David Theodor Wiesengrund
* 3.7.1838 Dettelbach
÷ 7.3.1920 Frankfurt am Main

Caroline Mayer
* 30.9.1846 Worms
÷ 28.1.1894 Frankfurt am Main

Family

8.9.1937
London

Gretel Adorno
* 10.6.1902 Berlin
† 16.7.1993 Frankfurt am Main

July 1898

Maria Barbara
Calvelli-Adorno
* 30.9.1865
Bockenheim, Frankfurt am Main
† 23.2.1952
New York

Agathe
Calvelli-Adorno
* 27.9.1868
Frankfurt am Main
† 26.6.1935
Frankfurt am Main

Louis Prosper
Calvelli-Adorno
* 26.11.1866
Auerbach
† 22.2.1960
Frankfurt am Main

Married
February 1862

Jean François Calvelli-Adorno
* 14.4.1820 Corsica
† 3.5.1879 Frankfurt am Main

Elisabeth Henning
* 23.2.1835 Offenbach
† 28.11.1897 Frankfurt am Main

Notes

Preface

1 Adorno, 'The Essay as Form', *Notes to Literature*, vol. 1, p. 21.
2 Institute of Social Research, *Soziologische Exkurse: Nach Vorträgen und Diskussionen*, p. 43.
3 T. W. Adorno, *Minima Moralia*, p. 112.

Part I Family Inheritance

1 Walter Benjamin, 'Theses on the Philosophy of History'. In *Illuminations*, ed. Hannah Arendt, trans. Harry Zohn. London: Jonathan Cape, 1970, p. 255f.

Chapter 1 Adorno's Corsican Grandfather

1 The historian François Guizot, who was prime minister under Louis Philippe, gave what was perhaps the most succinct description of the political programme of the Restoration and the spirit of the age: 'Strengthen your institutions, inform yourselves, enrich yourselves, improve the moral and material condition of France' (André Jardin and André-Jean Tudesq, *La France des notables*, p. 161). In his biography of the literary critic Sainte-Beuve, Wolf Lepenies provides an apt summary of 'bonapartisme industriel': 'This society was interested exclusively in itself, its own development, its own advancement, its own expansion in every conceivable sense, and its own prosperity' (W. Lepenies, *Sainte-Beuve*, p. 128).
2 Prosper Mérimée, *Colomba*, p. 28.
3 The following information comes from an interview with Mrs Elisabeth Reinhuber-Adorno on 15 January 1999. Adorno was a cousin of her father and hence she is his first cousin once removed. Franz Wilhelm Calvelli-Adorno, the father of Elisabeth, was a Frenchman by birth and a *Landgerichtsrat* by profession; his mother, Martha Katz, was Jewish in origin. After being dismissed from the civil service when the Nazis came to power, he struggled to earn a living as a music teacher, though of course he was

allowed to teach only Jewish children. Following a brief period in the army, he survived the war as assistant to a lawyer, partly in hiding. He sent his children to Britain in 1939 as part of the so-called *Kindertransport* programme that was set up after the pogroms of November 1938. They were aged twelve and thirteen at the time. After the war, Elisabeth Adorno studied economics and sociology in Britain. In the 1950s she married and went to live in the German Federal Republic, settling finally in Oberstedten and Oberursel on the outskirts of Frankfurt am Main. Mrs Reinhuber-Adorno and her husband conducted quite extensive research on the life of her grandfather Jean François, and made notes on their findings which she has generously made available to the present writer.

4 Taken from documents supplied by Elisabeth Reinhuber-Adorno.

5 Heinrich Heine, *Schriften über Deutschland*, p. 20f.

6 The country estate of Della Piana is situated above Bocognano, close to the River Gravona.

7 I have obtained a copy of the two letters to M. Conti and Napoleon III from Elisabeth Reinhuber-Adorno. It is an open question whether either reached its destination. Whether they did or not, they are illuminating since they shed light on the precarious economic situation of Adorno's grandfather, as well as giving us an idea of the importance that the committed Bonapartist attached to his family origins.

8 His letter ends with the words: 'I have followed the example of my parents [that is to say, I have never asked for reimbursement of the advances and loans provided by my family], but because of my marriage in a foreign country, the persistent and costly illness of my wife and child and the unemployment in which I find myself, I see myself obliged in this painful situation to call to mind the services rendered by my family. I do so mindful of your gracious benevolence and your sense of justice, and in the hope that you will be pleased to listen to my request and grant me compensation in the light of that wise judgement that guides all your actions. This compensation, the need for which arises above all from those loans, would do much to alleviate the unfortunate situation of a family whose descendants will be as devoted to Your Majesty as were their forefathers. In this hope, I remain Your Majesty's most respectful, obedient and loyal subject.'

9 W. Benjamin and T. W. Adorno, *The Complete Correspondence 1928–1940*, p. 150.

Chapter 2 Wiesengrund: The Jewish Heritage

1 Konrad Reinfelder has significantly enlarged our knowledge of the history of the Wiesengrund family through his research on the history of the Jews of Dettelbach. I am indebted to his work here. See K. Reinfelder, 'Zur Geschichte der Juden in Dettelbach'.

2 A list drawn up by the government of the electoral prince in 1803 includes the entry: 'Beritz David, 39, his wife, 36. Children: 2 sons, 6 and 2, 1 daughter, 1; house number 230 . . . cattle-dealer.' Ibid.

3 See Günther Vogt, *Frankfurter Bürgerhäuser des 19. Jahrhunderts*, p. 124.

4 Johann Jakob Hässlin (ed.), *Frankfurt*, p. 186. The street name 'Schöne Aussicht' means 'lovely view' [trans.].

5　See Günther Vogt, *Frankfurter Bürgerhäuser des 19. Jahrhunderts*, p. 126.
6　See Evelyn Wilcock, 'Adorno's Uncle', p. 335ff.
7　Information from the Saxon State Archive in Leipzig, July 2002.
8　Information from the borough of Seeheim-Jugenheim, 13 June 2002.
9　The present writer has learnt from Elisabeth Reinhuber-Adorno that the Calvelli-Adorno family rarely made use of the name 'della Piana'. However, envelopes are said to have existed on which the additional name 'della Piana' is to be found. With the emigration of the Wiesengrund family from Nazi Germany in the spring of 1939, their papers were put into storage and were all lost in a fire. It has therefore not been possible to confirm the facts about their name.
10　The documents relating to the Wiesengrund family in the city archives include the entry: 'Stillborn child, 21 October 1900.' The present author is indebted to Reinhard Pabst for this information, which has been confirmed by the Frankfurt am Main Institute for the History of the City.
11　Under the heading 'Regressions', Adorno wrote in *Minima Moralia*: 'The sleepy child has already half forgotten the expulsion of the stranger, who in Schott's *Song-Book* looks like a Jew, and in the line "to the gate the beggar flees" he glimpses peace without the wretchedness of others. So long as there is still a single beggar, Benjamin writes in a fragment, there is still myth; only with the last beggar's disappearance would myth be appeased.' *Minima Moralia*, p. 199.
12　In the biographical literature about Adorno it is sometimes claimed that Oscar Alexander Wiesengrund was an assimilated Jew who had converted to Protestantism, and that his son was baptized into the Protestant Church. No evidence has been forthcoming hitherto to support either claim. Adorno was introduced to Catholic teachings by his 'two mothers'. During his time at school he evidently attended either interdenominational or Protestant religious teaching. The questionnaire of the Academic Assistance Council which Adorno filled in before his move to Oxford in 1934 contained the question 'Do you agree that we should approach any religious organizations on your behalf?'. He replied: 'Please *no*, I am without any touch with "positiv" religions' [*sic*]. Bodleian Library, Wiesengrund-Adorno MS SPSL 322/2, no. 49.
13　Peter von Haselberg, 'Wiesengrund-Adorno', p. 16.
14　Frankfurt am Main dialect for 'south of the river' [trans.].
15　Max Horkheimer, 'Jenseits der Fachwissenschaft', *GS*, vol. 7, p. 261.
16　In 1910, when Adorno was seven, his father announced his departure from the Frankfurt am Main Israelite community.
17　See Adorno, 'Im Gedächtnis an Alban Berg', *GS*, vol. 18, p. 501. Adorno confesses there, as a grown man after the Second World War, that it was only through his friendship with Alban Berg and Soma Morgenstern that he began to abandon his prejudice against the East European Jews. Admittedly, this was at a time when he had just reached the ripe old age of twenty-two.
18　Siegfried Kracauer, *Ginster*. In *Schriften*, vol. 7, p. 58.
19　Peter von Haselberg, 'Wiesengrund-Adorno', p. 16.
20　In a letter to Ernst Krenek on 7 October 1934, Adorno recalls that in his later years at school he had toyed with the idea of converting to Catholicism, but had dismissed this step as 'incurably romantic'. See Adorno and Krenek,

Briefwechsel, p. 46. What he writes on this occasion is: 'I once imagined that the Catholic *ordo* might make it possible to put to rights the world which was so out of joint, and at that . . . time I was on the point of converting, an action that seemed natural since my mother was Catholic.' Since Adorno had been baptized a Catholic, this talk of a conversion seems strange at first sight. In the baptism book of the Catholic parish of St Bartholomäus, there is nothing to show that Adorno ever left the church.

21 'The *Lehrhaus* was a kind of Jewish centre for adult education; its spiritual fathers were Franz Rosenzweig and Martin Buber. The *Lehrhaus* also saw itself as a secularized form of Jewish Talmudic study. The concept of "study" was supposed to remind us that it represented a secularized, modern version of Jewish teachings' (Leo Löwenthal, *An Unmastered Past*, p. 21); see also Wolfgang Schivelbusch, *Intellektuellendämmerung*, p. 27ff.

22 [The 'religious Tyrolean' suggests a crass backwoodsman; trans.] See Peter von Haselberg, 'Wiesengrund-Adorno', p. 12. These stories have evidently not survived, or at least are not referred to in the Adorno Archive.

23 The festival newspaper of the *XVII. Deutschen Bundes- und goldenen Jubiläums-Schießen*, no. 6, 3 August 1912.

24 This information, which derives ultimately from Adorno himself, can be found in Andreas Razumovsky, 'Schöne Aussicht', *Frankfurter Allgemeine Zeitung*, 11 September 1968. [The English-speaking reader may wish to know that the Sachsenhausen referred to in this chapter is not the infamous concentration camp (which is near Berlin), but a district of Frankfurt just south of the Main. It is known for its popular pubs, famous for their local cider, and for its up-market restaurants. It can be regarded roughly as the Frankfurt equivalent of London's Soho (trans.).]

25 This was how Mrs Reinhuber-Adorno's mother remembered it. She was Helene Calvelli-Adorno, *née* Mommsen, who told her daughter that she had been a frequent visitor to the house in Seeheimer Straße. Like Adorno, she had studied piano at the Hoch Conservatory and had later married Franz Wilhelm Calvelli, the offspring of the first marriage of Louis Prosper Calvelli-Adorno and Martha Katz. He was said to have been a first-rate violinist.

26 See 'Graeculus (1)', *Frankfurter Adorno Blätter* VII, pp. 22 and 34.

27 Marie Luise Kaschnitz, *Tagebücher aus den Jahren 1936–1966*, p. 602.

28 Adorno, *Mahler*, *GS*, vol. 13, p. 288.

29 Adorno, 'Zum Problem der Familie', *GS*, vol. 20, p. 307.

Chapter 3 Between Oberrad and Amorbach

1 Adorno, *Mahler: A Musical Physiognomy*, p. 152.

2 Adorno, *Minima Moralia*, p. 110. It is likely that the wrong subjunctive was 'kreechste', from 'kriegen', to get [trans.].

3 Max Horkheimer, *GS*, vol. 3, p. 404.

4 Adorno, 'Auf die Frage: warum sind Sie zurückgekehrt?', *GS*, vol. 20.1, p. 395.

5 As an active politician concerned with social questions – he had connections with Paul Göhre and Max Weber – Friedrich Naumann had founded a Protestant Workers' Association as early as 1890. Later he founded the

Nationalsozialer Verein. From 1910 on he was the leader of the left wing of the Fortschrittliche Volkspartei, with its Christian socialist leanings. By the beginning of the Weimar Republic, Naumann had shed his dogmatic religious allegiance. He now became a member of the Reichstag and of the National Assembly set up to frame a constitution. He was also chairman of the Democratic Party.

6   See Ralf Roth, *Stadt und Bürgertum in Frankfurt am Main*, p. 539ff.
7   Siegfried Kracauer, *Ginster. Schriften*, vol. 7, p. 20.
8   See Ingomar Bog, 'Die Industrialisierung in Hessen', p. 192.
9   The Römer is the old town hall. It is all part of the same central complex of (formerly) medieval buildings as the cathedral and the 'Schirn', which is now a museum [trans.].
10 A vivid description of the age is to be found in Mile Braach, *Rückblende: Erinnerungen einer Neunzigjährigen*, memoirs written when the author was ninety years old. See also Ralf Roth, *Stadt und Bürgertum in Frankfurt am Main*, p. 600ff.
11 See Siegfried Kracauer, *Schriften*, vol. 5.1, p. 347.
12 Adorno, *Alban Berg*, p. 1.
13 Adorno and Berg, *Briefwechsel 1925–35*, p. 9.
14 Adorno, *Erziehung zur Mündigkeit: Vorträge und Gespräche mit Hellmut Becker 1959–1969*, p. 117f.
15 Adorno, 'Vierhändig, noch einmal', *GS*, vol. 17, p. 303ff.
16 Amorbach is about 60 miles south-east of Frankfurt [trans.].
17 Adorno, 'Amorbach', *GS*, vol. 10.1, p. 306.
18 Ibid.
19 Ibid., p. 303ff. The building that Rossmann lived in had previously been the home of the Amorbach Court Theatre. Drawings by Rossmann, including designs for the Bayreuth stage, can be seen in the museum in Amorbach.
20 Adorno, *Minima Moralia*, p. 177.
21 Ibid., p. 190.
22 Leo Löwenthal, *An Unmastered Past*, p. 203.
23 Adorno, 'The Curious Realist', *Notes to Literature*, vol. 2, p. 75.
24 Adorno, 'Words from Abroad', *Notes to Literature*, vol. 1, p. 186.
25 Adorno, 'Offener Brief an Max Horkheimer', *GS*, vol. 20.1, p. 155.
26 Adorno, *Minima Moralia*, p. 161.
27 Adorno, 'Zur Psychologie des Verhältnisses von Lehrer und Schüler', *GS*, vol. 20.2, p. 720.
28 Ibid., p. 718f.
29 Adorno, 'Reinhold Zickel', *GS*, vol. 20.2, p. 759.
30 Leo Löwenthal, *An Unmastered Past*, p. 44.
31 Adorno, *Minima Moralia*, p. 192f.
32 Erich Pfeiffer-Belli was later to become editor of the *Frankfurter Zeitung* and an author. He kept in contact with Adorno.
33 E. Pfeiffer-Belli, *Junge Jahre im alten Frankfurt*, p. 51.
34 Adorno, 'Zur Psychologie des Verhältnisses von Lehrer und Schüler', *GS*, vol. 20.2, p. 727.
35 Ibid.
36 This dog features not just in this photo, but also in the so-called dream protocols. In an unpublished piece Adorno recounts a dream sequence that takes place at a school dance at a previous school. He was dancing 'with a

giant brownish-yellow Great Dane (the Great Dane of my childhood). This dog stood on her hind legs and wore evening dress. I accepted her completely and had the feeling for the first time in my life that I knew how to dance. We kissed several times, the dog and I. Woke up very satisfied.' Adorno, *Traumprotokolle*, mid-September 1958, Theodor W. Adorno Archive, Frankfurt am Main, TS 51772.

37 Adorno, *Musikalische Aphorismen*, *GS*, vol. 18, p. 35.

38 The award took place on 13 June 1935, as can be seen from a document in the Theodor W. Adorno Archive, according to which, 'in the name of the Führer and Reichskanzler, the . . . Cross of Honour for War Service has been awarded to the businessman Oscar Wiesengrund . . . in memory of the World War 1914–1918.'

39 Georg Voigt was mayor of Frankfurt from 1912 to 1924. 'Unlike his predecessors (Johann Franz von Miquel and Franz Adickes) he belonged on the left rather than in the National Liberal camp, and in this respect he reflected more adequately the political complexion of the city.' Wilfried Forstmann, 'Frankfurt am Main in wilhelminischer Zeit 1866–1914', p. 375ff.

40 'Only the firm alliance of the SPD with the Centre Party and the left-liberal Democrats, as the pillars of the so-called Weimar Coalition, could enable the city to function.' Dieter Rebentisch, 'Frankfurt am Main in der Weimarer Republik und im Dritten Reich 1918–1945', p. 438ff.

41 St Paul's Church had been the location for the Constituent Assembly in the short-lived revolution of 1848–9 and has traditionally been regarded as the standard-bearer of German liberalism [trans.].

42 In Adorno's critique of Lukács in 1958, he defended the latter's early writings – *Soul and Form*, *The Theory of the Novel* and *History and Class Consciousness* – against his later writings in which Lukács had sought to adapt himself to the dreary level of Soviet thought. Adorno focused on Lukács's *The Meaning of Contemporary Realism*, which appeared in German in 1956. Here he comments: 'The core of his theory remains dogmatic. The whole of modern literature is dismissed except where it can be classified as either critical or socialist realism, and the odium of decadence is heaped on it without a qualm, even though such abuse brings with it all the horrors of persecution and extermination, and not only in Russia' (Adorno, 'Reconciliation under duress', in Ernst Bloch et al., *Aesthetics and Politics*, p. 154). In its incisiveness and its pointed emphasis, Adorno's critique in the year of the publication of Lukács's book left nothing to be desired. At a conference ten years later, he met Agnes Heller, Lukács's most prominent student, who had repudiated her teacher's orthodoxy in her own way. He used the occasion to ask her to mediate between him and Lukács. 'Up to then, he said, they had only abused and slandered each other, but now he would like to get on speaking terms once again.' See Agnes Heller, *Der Affe auf dem Fahrrad*, p. 239.

43 Ernst Bloch (1885–1977) finished his course in philosophy after only six semesters with a dissertation on epistemological problems. Disillusioned by academic philosophy, he worked as an independent writer, partly for the *Frankfurter Zeitung*. He moved in the intellectual circles that had formed around Georg Simmel in Berlin and Max Weber in Heidelberg. Towards the end of the 1920s Adorno, who was eighteen years younger than Bloch, met him in Berlin for the first time, thanks to introductions from Siegfried

Kracauer and Walter Benjamin. Bloch wrote his chief works during his years of emigration in the United States, though they could only be published much later. They include *Hope, the Principle* (1954 and 1959) and *Natural Law and Human Dignity* (1961). After his return to Germany, Bloch was appointed to a chair at Leipzig University. Because of his political differences with the communist leadership of the German Democratic Republic he took the opportunity created by a conference in Tübingen not to return to Leipzig and instead to accept a guest professorship at Tübingen. Bloch and Adorno had a lot in common, including their 'precocious intellectuality', their 'anti-academic style of writing', their intellectual nonconformism and their passionate interest in music and art. Adorno frankly admitted his admiration for the older man, asserting that 'he had never written anything either explicit or implicit without reference to it [*The Spirit of Utopia*]' (Adorno, 'The Handle, the Pot, and Early Experience', *Notes to Literature*, vol. 2, p. 212). See Peter Zudeick, *Der Hintern des Teufels: Ernst Bloch – Leben und Werk*; Gunzelin Schmid Noerr, 'Bloch und Adorno: Bildhafte und bilderlose Utopie', p. 25ff.

44 Adorno, 'The Handle, the Pot and Early Experience', *Notes to Literature*, vol. 2, p. 212.

45 Siegfried Kracauer, *Georg. Schriften*, vol. 7, p. 256.

46 Adorno, 'The Curious Realist', *Notes to Literature*, vol. 2, p. 58.

47 Adorno, 'Vierhändig, noch einmal', *GS*, vol. 17, p. 303.

48 Cf. Peter Cahn, *Das Hoch'sche Konservatorium in Frankfurt am Main*, p. 59ff. and p. 106ff.

49 Bernhard Sekles was born in 1872, the son of a Frankfurt businessman. At the time when Adorno was a student, Sekles was the director of the High School for Music. He was regarded as 'a composer of quality and above all as an excellent teacher of composition, a versatile and sensitive human being and a capable organizer' (Peter Cahn, *Das Hoch'sche Konservatorium in Frankfurt am Main*, p. 246ff. and 257ff.). Sekles's pupils included Rudi Stephan, Paul Hindemith and Ottmar Gerster. It was partly owing to his energy that by the middle of 1923 the conservatory enjoyed a recovery. He improved the quality of the orchestra to the point where conductors such as Wilhelm Furtwängler and Erich Kleiber were pleased to be invited to conduct concerts for the benefit of the conservatory. He triggered a minor scandal in 1928 when he introduced a jazz class taught by Matyás Seiber. Does this explain why Adorno, who was no friend of jazz, adopts a rather critical note in his reminiscences of his first composition teacher? He suggests that Sekles was concerned to cure him of his 'atonal whims' by taking advantage of what he regarded as his weak point, namely his desire to be up to date. 'The ultramodern, his argument ran, was no longer modern. The stimulations I sought were already numb, the expressive figures that excited me belonged to an outdated sentimentality, and the new youth had, as he liked to put it, more red blood corpuscles. His own pieces, in which oriental themes were regularly elaborated with the chromatic scale, betrayed the ultra-subtle deliberations to be expected of a conservatory director with a bad conscience' (Adorno, *Minima Moralia*, p. 218). Cahn disputes the validity of this negative description of Sekles by his former pupil, and conjectures that Paul Hindemith, whom Adorno always criticized, was the true target of his comments. 'This may explain the venom of that

passage. Sekles himself was and remained a representative of late romantic expressive art' (Cahn, *Das Hoch'sche Konservatorium*, p. 297).

50 Rudolf M. Heilbrunn, 'Erinnerungen an das Frankfurt Max Beckmanns', p. 17.

51 Adorno, 'Expressionism and Artistic Truthfulness', *Notes to Literature*, vol. 2, p. 258.

52 Adorno, 'Platz', *Notes to Literature*, vol. 2, p. 264f.

53 Ibid., p. 265f.

54 During the 'new era' of Mayor Landmann (1924–33) culture was constantly supported despite the city's financial problems. In particular, under the direction of Arthur Hellmer, the New Theatre witnessed the performance of the modern, socially critical plays of Walter Hasenclever, Georg Kaiser and Bertolt Brecht in productions by Max Ophüls. Richard Weichert had overall responsibility for the municipal theatres. As both producer and artistic director, he was likewise committed to modern drama with an emphasis on contemporary expressionist plays. In the Frankfurt Opera House, in addition to a Wagner cycle, there were premieres of works by Béla Bartók, Paul Hindemith and Alban Berg. With the appointment of the talented young Clemens Krauss as director of the Opera House in 1924, there were productions of modern works by Sekles, Busoni, Krenek and Weill on the programme, alongside classical operas such as Mozart's *Don Giovanni*. Adorno missed hardly any of them.

55 Adorno, 'Kammermusikwoche in Frankfurt am Main', *GS*, vol. 20.2, p. 771.

56 The *Rentenmark* which was introduced in November 1923 by the government of Gustav Stresemann put an end to the spiralling inflation that had destroyed the old currency. That inflation had been triggered by the German refusal to pay reparations and the consequent French occupation of the Rhineland. Now, the old currency was withdrawn and exchanged for the new *Rentenmark* at the rate of one billion to one. Together with the resumption of negotiations on reparations leading to the Dawes Plan of 1924, the *Rentenmark* inaugurated a five-year period of stability, lasting until the Wall Street crash of 1929 [trans.].

57 Rudolf M. Heilbrunn, 'Erinnerungen an das Frankfurt Max Beckmanns', p. 17.

58 Peter von Haselberg, 'Wiesengrund-Adorno', p. 17. Dapsul von Zabelthau features in Hoffmann's story 'The King's Bride' [trans.].

59 Adorno, 'The Curious Realist', *Notes to Literature*, vol. 2, p. 58.

60 Siegfried Kracauer, 'Gedanken über Freundschaft', *Schriften*, vol. 5.1, p. 143.

61 Ibid.

62 Adorno, 'The Curious Realist', *Notes to Literature*, vol. 2, p. 58f.

63 Ibid., p. 59.

64 Siegfried Kracauer, 'Das zeugende Gespräch', *Schriften*, vol. 5.1, p. 225f.

65 See Leo Löwenthal, *An Unmastered Past*, p. 203.

66 Ibid.

67 Ibid., p. 21.

68 Siegfried Kracauer, *Soziologie als Wissenschaft. Schriften*, vol. 1, p. 79.

69 Ibid., p. 82.

70 Adorno, *Musikalische Schriften VI*, *GS*, vol. 19, p. 24.

71 Ibid., p. 20.

72 Ibid., p. 14.

73   Ibid., p. 70.
74   Ibid., p. 24.
75   Ibid., p. 28. *Zivilisationsliteratur* was frequently contrasted with 'Kultur' in the debates of the day, e.g., in the quarrel between Heinrich Mann and Thomas Mann in which the latter, who identified with 'Kultur' and its deep authentic spiritual roots in the nation, criticized 'Zivilisationsliteratur' as cosmopolitan, rationalistic, enlightened and superficial' [trans.].
76   Adorno, *Musikalische Schriften* VI, *GS*, vol. 19, p. 43.
77   Ibid., p. 59.
78   Ibid., p. 23.
79   Siegfried Kracauer, *The Mass Ornament*, p. 138.
80   Ibid., p. 131 (translation altered).
81   Ibid., p. 138f.
82   Siegfried Kracauer, 'Empfindsame Suite von der Bergstraße', *Schriften*, vol. 5.1, p. 229.
83   Ibid.
84   Siegfried Kracauer, *Der Detektiv-Roman. Schriften*, vol. 1, p. 116.
85   Ibid., p. 120.
86   Ibid., p. 201.
87   Adorno, 'Schlageranalysen', *GS*, vol. 18, p. 781.
88   Ibid., p. 782.
89   Ibid., p. 785f.

Chapter 4 Éducation sentimentale

1   Adorno and Horkheimer, *Briefwechsel*, vol. 1, p. 112.
2   Städelsches Kunstinstitut, *Max Beckmann: Eisgang*, p. 5.
3   Ibid., p. 23.
4   Quoted from the *Marbacher Magazin*, 47 (1988), p. 39.
5   Siegfried Kracauer, *Georg. Schriften*, vol. 7, p. 403.
6   Ibid., p. 339.
7   I owe important information to my conversations both with Elfriede Olbrich, Adorno's secretary after his return from the United States, and with Stasi von Boeckmann, who has researched the life of Gretel Karplus in the context of work on women's biographies.
8   The tannins left over from processing grapes in the production of wine were converted into tannic acid. This was indispensable in the leather industry. In 1911, Karplus & Herzberger had taken out a patent for a new chemical process for tanning leather.
9   The friendship included Else's brother Alfons and also Gretel Herzberger, who became mentally ill early in the 1920s. In fact she took her own life in the summer of 1921, an event that evidently affected Adorno deeply. It had been his intention to visit the two women while holidaying in the south, close to Bad Aussee. Some four years later he chanced to meet a girl in Vienna who had witnessed Gretel's suicide.
      After the Nazi seizure of power, Theodor and Gretel Adorno repeatedly begged Else Herzberger in conversations and letters to give financial support to Walter Benjamin, who was living in Paris in very straitened material circumstances. Her nephew Arnold Levy was living in Paris at the

time and was in contact with Benjamin. For a time Benjamin had a room in Else Herzberger's Paris flat. This room was separate from the main flat, but was otherwise not very comfortable. Else Herzberger did help Benjamin out with sums of money for a time. Apart from Adorno's dedication of his early songs to Else, his closeness to her is expressed in the aphorism entitled 'Heliotrope', in *Minima Moralia*, p. 177.

10 Adorno, *Minima Moralia*, p. 172.

11 I am indebted here to Rudolf zur Lippe, who was in close contact with Adorno in the late 1960s and remained close to Gretel Adorno for years after her husband's death.

12 Egon Wissing was a doctor and the son of Benjamin's much-loved aunt Clara Wissing, *née* Schoenflies. In emigration in the United States, Theodor and Gretel Adorno were in frequent contact with Wissing, who held a post at the Massachusetts Memorial Hospital in Boston. In 1938, for example, they spent their summer holiday with Egon and Lotte in the Hotel Gregoire in Maine.

13 'Felicitas' is the name of the principal woman character of Wilhelm Speyer's play *Ein Mantel, ein Hut, ein Handschuh* (Coat, Hat and Glove), in which Benjamin had had a hand. Gretel Adorno addressed him by his 'Aryan' pseudonym Detlef Holz. See Benjamin and Adorno, *The Complete Correspondence 1928–1940*, pp. 17 and 26f.

14 See W. Benjamin, *Briefe*, vol. 4, pp. 205ff., 216ff., 229ff., and 249.

15 Adorno, *Minima Moralia*, p. 212.

16 Ibid.

17 'From 1937 on, the first versions of all Adorno's writings were taken down in shorthand and the transcribed text was then revised by hand.' See Rolf Tiedemann, 'Editorisches Nachwort'. Adorno, *GS*, vol. 20.2, p. 823. See also Tiedemann, 'Gretel Adorno zum Abschied', p. 150.

18 Adorno, *Minima Moralia*, p. 172.

19 Adorno, 'Worte ohne Lieder', *GS*, vol. 20.2, p. 537.

20 Ibid., p. 539.

21 See Adorno and Horkheimer, *Briefwechsel*, vol. 1, pp. 112 and 405.

22 Adorno, *Minima Moralia*, p. 192.

23 Adorno to Horkheimer, 8 February 1938. Horkheimer, *GS*, vol. 16, p. 386.

24 Gretel Karplus to Walter Benjamin, 17 June 1932. Luhr, '*Was noch begraben lag*', p. 85.

25 Adorno to Bloch, 2 October 1937. Adorno and Horkheimer, *Briefwechsel*, p. 536ff.

26 Adorno to Horkheimer, 12 March 1953. Horkheimer, *GS*, vol. 18, p. 247.

27 Adorno, *Minima Moralia*, p. 31.

28 Ibid., p. 30.

29 Ibid., p. 96.

30 Ibid., p. 167.

31 Ibid., p. 168.

32 Ibid., p. 169.

33 Regina Becker-Schmidt, 'Wenn die Frauen erst einmal Frauen sein könnten', p. 210.

34 Adorno, *Aus dem Poesiealbum für Renée Nell*, 20 May 1943, Theodor W. Adorno Archive, Frankfurt am Main, TS 51835.

35 Adorno, *Minima Moralia*, p. 31.

36 Adorno to Robert and Anita Alexander, 3 January 1948, Theodor W. Adorno Archive, Frankfurt am Main, Br 13/2.
37 Adorno to Hermann Grab, 27 October 1945, Theodor W. Adorno Archive, Frankfurt am Main, Br 497/39–40.
38 Adorno to Hermann Grab, 2 May 1946, Theodor W. Adorno Archive, Frankfurt am Main, Br 497/41–42.
39 Adorno, *Aufzeichnungen zum neunzackigen Krönchen*, Theodor W. Adorno Archive, Frankfurt am Main, TS 51902.
40 This magnanimity on Gretel Adorno's part has been confirmed by Elisabeth Lenk and Rudolf zur Lippe, both of whom were close friends of the couple.
41 See Adorno, *Im Gedächtnis an Alban Berg*, GS, vol. 18, p. 480f., and also Constantin Floros, *Alban Berg und Hanna Fuchs: Die Geschichte einer Liebe in Briefen*. The allusion is to the traditional comparison between Prussia and Austria, according to which in Prussia conditions were said to be serious, but not desperate, while in Austria it was the other way round [trans.].
42 Adorno, *Traumprotokolle*, 16 March 1969, Theodor W. Adorno Archive, Frankfurt am Main, TS 51810.
43 Adorno, *Traumprotokolle*, 16 June 1960, Theodor W. Adorno Archive, Frankfurt am Main, TS 51779; see also Rolf Tiedemann, 'Gretel Adorno zum Abschied', p. 151.
44 Adorno, *Minima Moralia*, p. 192.

Part II Commuting between Philosophy and Music

1 Adorno, *Minima Moralia*, p. 150.

Chapter 5 The City of Frankfurt and its University

1 See Wilfried Forstmann,'Frankfurt am Main in Wilhelminischer Zeit 1866–1918', p. 415ff.; Andreas Hansert, *Bürgerkultur und Kulturpolitik in Frankfurt am Main*, p. 122ff.
2 No less a person than Max Weber had spoken out in favour of such an unconventional institution in 1910, when he was in Frankfurt am Main for the Sociology Congress. A little later, he underlined his support for such an autonomous institution in an official report to the Prussian Ministry of Education – this was undoubtedly a challenge to official Prussian policy on the universities. Weber's recommendation stood four-square with the tradition of a civic cultural life based on its own resources and independent of a centralist state policy. And this was what the commercial and cultured Frankfurt middle class envisaged for its university. It was to be autonomous, and thus independent of pressures from both the state and private interests. 'This led to the creation, unique in Germany, of a state university without the state funding that would have been subject to parliamentary scrutiny. It was to be an endowed, civic university, authorized by royal decree, supported by the city of Frankfurt's desire for reform and its financial resources as well as the resources of its mainly

Jewish benefactors' (Ludwig von Friedeburg, 'Frankfurt – die Stadt und ihre Soziologie', p. 157). The history of Frankfurt University has been recorded in two comprehensive studies: Paul Kluke, *Die Stiftungsuniversität Frankfurt am Main* (1972); and Notker Hammerstein, *Die Johann Wolfgang Goethe-Universität* (1989).

3 Hammerstein, p. 37.
4 Jürgen Habermas, 'Soziologie in der Weimarer Republik', p. 187.
5 See Karl Korn, *Lange Lehrzeit: Ein deutsches Leben*, p. 112ff.; Andreas Hansert, *Bürgerkultur und Kulturpolitik in Frankfurt am Main*, p. 107ff.; Wolfgang Schivelbusch, *Intellektuellendämmerung*.
6 In view of the muted resonance of Cornelius's writings, it is all the more remarkable that Lenin should have 'done him the honour' of referring to him in his anti-positivist tract of 1909, *Materialism and Empirio-Criticism*, where he describes him as an 'agnostic semi-solipsist' as well as a 'flea crusher' (see H. Scheible, *Theodor W. Adorno*, p. 22ff.). In reaction to this, Max Horkheimer, whom Cornelius had supervised for his doctoral dissertation, wrote a review of Lenin's book, which, although never published, expressly defends the positivists against speculative, metaphysical tendencies. On Cornelius's sixtieth birthday, Horkheimer penned an appreciation that appeared in the *Frankfurter Zeitung* in 1923 (Horkheimer, 'Hans Cornelius', *GS*, vol. 2, p. 149ff.). See also Michael Korthals, 'Die kritische Gesellschaftstheorie des frühen Horkheimer', p. 317; Hans-Joachim Dahms, *Positivismusstreit*, p. 27f.
7 The fact that Adorno really did profit from the discussion of this version of transcendental idealism can be seen from the increasing frequency with which in later years, as an ever more popular professor of philosophy, he would refer to Cornelius's interpretations of Kant in the seminars and lecture courses in which he dealt with this topic. This applies, for example, to the lectures on Kant's *Critique of Pure Reason* that he gave in the summer term of 1959. In his discussion of the distinction between synthetic and analytic propositions, he follows the arguments Cornelius had set out in his own *Commentary on the Critique of Pure Reason* in 1926. He singles out an example that Cornelius himself particularly liked with which to illustrate the idea of synthetic *a priori* judgements. According to Cornelius, '"Orange comes between red and yellow on the colour scale." As long as you are familiar with red and yellow, this statement has an absolutely compelling truth; it remains valid for all future experience. This means that it is a synthetic *a priori* judgement according to this definition of the term. However, it unquestionably arises from experience and not from pure thought.' And in a subsequent lecture, too, when discussing the concepts of the self, causality and the thing, Adorno refers repeatedly to Cornelius. See Adorno, *Kant's Critique of Pure Reason*, p. 28. See also ibid., pp. 240–1, n. 2; 244–5, n. 8; 253, n. 15; 254, n. 1.
   The same can be said of his lectures on the problems of moral philosophy which he gave in the summer term of 1963. In these lectures he discusses Kant's doctrine of the antinomies, and once again quotes freely from Cornelius's *Commentary*. See Adorno, *Problems of Moral Philosophy*, pp. 29 and 188, n. 10.
8 Hans Cornelius, 'Leben und Lehre', in *Die Philosophie der Gegenwart in Selbstdarstellungen*, Leipzig, 1923. This volume, edited by Raymund Schmidt,

contains accounts by sixteen contemporary philosophers, including Paul Barth, Hans Driesch, Paul Natorp, Ernst Troeltsch and Hans Faihing, in addition to Cornelius himself.

9   Ibid., p. 8.
10 Ibid., p. 9.
11 In an essay on Cornelius, Horkheimer attempts to define what he regards as a chief merit of his philosophy. It consists in 'his having demonstrated that immediate data possess qualities, so-called gestalt qualities . . . that are lost . . . if we examine and pass judgement on individual experiences in isolation.' We owe to this insight the radical transformation of psychology at the hands of Max Wertheimer and Wolfgang Köhler, whose work is based on 'the view of consciousness centred on the concept of gestalt or shape' (M. Horkheimer, 'Cornelius', *GS*, vol. 2, p. 151f.).
12 Hans Cornelius, 'Leben und Lehre', p. 17.
13 Ibid., p. 19.
14 Adorno, *Minima Moralia*, p. 148f.
15 Salomon-Delatour finally made something of a name for himself as the editor of the writings of Giambattista Vico and also of Lorenz von Stein. In addition, he wrote about the early French socialists, such as Saint-Simon and Proudhon, as well as translating works by René Worms into German.
16 Adorno's Prague friend, Hermann Grab, had better luck. He was able to obtain his doctorate under Salomon-Delatour's supervision with a study of Max Weber's concept of rationality. This was published in 1927 with the title *Beitrag zu dem Problem der philosophischen Grundlegung der Sozialwissenschaft.*
17 Franz Schulz was a literary historian who had had a chair in Frankfurt since 1921–2. He was thought to have liberal views and to be in sympathy with the circle around Stefan George, but he was hardly an outstanding representative of the discipline. Nevertheless, scholars of the calibre of Hermann August Korff and Wilhelm Pfeiffer-Belli were able to qualify for the *Habilitation* under his supervision.
18 'He wanted to free capitalism from the power of the monopolies and the embargo on land sales. In the society of free and equal human beings that he envisaged, with open access for all to the ownership of land, it would "no more be necessary to sacrifice freedom for the sake of equality, than to sacrifice equality for the sake of freedom"' (Ludwig von Friedeburg, 'Frankfurt – die Stadt und ihre Soziologie', p. 158). See also Dieter Haselbach, 'Franz Oppenheimer', p. 55ff.
    Oppenheimer's chief work was the *System der Soziologie*, which appeared in eight volumes between 1923 and 1935. It was a long-winded account of the origins and growth of the new discipline, as well as its conceptual foundations. According to Oppenheimer, sociology was a basic science in its own right, to be distinguished from both philosophy and economics. Its object was society regarded as a totality that had its origins in history and that was constantly changing. The social dynamics that informed it were a function of the class struggles or power struggles between social groups. The hegemony of a given group manifested itself in the state and the legal system.
19 Horkheimer, *Briefwechsel*, *GS*, vol. 15, p. 77.

20 Ibid.

21 Adhémar Gelb worked with Max Wertheimer at the Psychology Institute, which had been founded by Friedrich Schumann and which enjoyed a good reputation at the time. Horkheimer had begun his studies there and, later on, spoke in positive terms of the experimental research that went on there. See Notker Hammerstein, *Die Johann Wolfgang Goethe-Universität*, p. 122.

22 Adorno, 'Offener Brief an Horkheimer', *GS*, vol. 20.1, p. 156.

23 Ibid.

24 Adorno to Leo Löwenthal, 16 July 1924, in Löwenthal, *Mitmachen wollte ich nie*, p. 247. The 'Schumann' referred to is the gestalt psychologist with whom Adorno had studied and who acted as the second examiner on his dissertation. Adorno's impression of Horkheimer and Pollock's political views has given rise to misunderstandings. It is true that they had both concerned themselves with Marx's economic theories and his philosophy of history, and that they were both interested in a revival of Marxism. However, neither was ever a member of a Communist Party.

25 Horkheimer, 'Das Schlimmste erwarten und doch das Gute verstehen', *GS*, vol. 7, p. 448.

26 The concept of gestalt is based on the idea that the multiplicity of psychic experiences is subsumed into a unity. As a totality, the gestalt is more than the parts that it organizes into a whole. The qualities of a gestalt are based on objective data.

27 Horkheimer, *Einführung in die Philosophie der Gegenwart*, *GS*, vol. 10, p. 264.

28 See Michael Korthals, 'Die kritische Gesellschaftstheorie des frühen Horkheimer', p. 319ff.; Hans-Joachim Dahms, *Positivismusstreit*, p. 21ff.

29 Adorno, *Der Begriff des Unbewußten in der transzendentalen Seelenlehre*, *GS*, vol. 1, p. 81. It should be pointed out that Adorno's later philosophy expressly rejected any kind of 'perspectival', standpoint philosophy.

30 Leo Löwenthal, *Mitmachen wollte ich nie*, p. 247.

31 Ibid., p. 248.

32 Adorno, 'Résumé der Dissertation', *GS*, vol. 1, p. 376.

33 Adorno, *Die Transzendenz des Dinglichen und Noematischen in Husserls Phänomenologie*, *GS*, vol. 1, p. 71.

34 Ibid., p. 66.

35 Ibid., p. 76.

36 Horkheimer, 'Die Sehnsucht nach dem ganz Anderen', *GS*, vol. 7, p. 385; see also 'Das Schlimmste erwarten und doch das Gute versuchen', ibid., p. 442.

37 See his letter to Berg of 30 March 1926. There Adorno gives an account of the changes in his philosophical outlook following his discussions with Walter Benjamin in the summer of 1925 in Naples. Adorno and Berg, *Briefwechsel 1925–1935*, p. 75.

38 Walter Benjamin, 'The Storyteller', in *Illuminations*, p. 84; cf. G. Lukács, *Die Theorie des Romans*, p. 32.

39 Adorno, 'Frank Wedekind and his Genre Painting', *Notes to Literature*, vol. 2, p. 268.

40 Adorno, 'Expressionism and Artistic Truthfulness', *Notes to Literature*, vol. 2, p. 259.

Chapter 6 The Danube Metropolis

1 Walter Gerlach, who was head of the Board of Trustees, also deserves a mention for his part in overcoming the crisis at the university. But even he was forced into crisis management for a while. For even after the introduction of the stable new currency, the *Rentenmark*, the Finance Ministry still kept public expenditure on a very tight rein.

2 Adorno, *Minima Moralia*, p. 66f.

3 See Benjamin and Adorno, *The Complete Correspondence 1928–1940*, p. 120. Berg was particularly pleased by the production in Oldenburg in north Germany in March 1929 under Johannes Schüler. For the first time he had given an introductory talk about the work for this production. At a production of *Wozzeck* in Prague in the Czech National Theatre, protests by right-wing radicals and anti-Semitic groups led to a scandal. See Adorno and Berg, *Briefwechsel 1925–1935*, pp. 121ff. and 197f.

4 Ibid., p. 74.

5 See Ibid., p. 42ff.; Heinz Steinert, in his *Adorno in Wien*, p. 127, has an illuminating explanation for this slightly obsequious form of address. He claims that it was directed against the sobriquet of the 'Schoenberg school', and its aim was to stress Berg's independence. For this it was necessary for Berg to abandon his status as Schoenberg's pupil, which he had essentially been up to 1908, and instead to become a 'master' in his own right. He had long since earned this right as a composer, and in Adorno's eyes he had also deserved it as a personality since the 1920s.

6 Adorno, 'Alban Berg', in *Sound Figures*, p. 70.

7 In a portrait of the conductor published in 1926, Adorno praised him for his ability 'to free the works from the rottenness of individual psychology. He was inspired by the idea of shedding light on the work's structure' (Adorno, 'Drei Dirigenten', *GS*, vol. 19, p. 455f.).

8 Adorno, *Alban Berg: Master of the Smallest Link*, p. 13.

9 Adorno attempted to accede to this request, but how could he do so, given that he had his own 'secret agenda': 'namely to write the essay in the same style that you [Berg] employ in composing such pieces as your quartet' (Adorno and Berg, *Briefwechsel 1925–1935*, p. 44).

10 Adorno, 'Alban Berg: Zur Uraufführung des "Wozzeck"', *GS*, vol. 18, p. 462f.

11 Adorno, 'Schoenberg: Serenade, op. 24', *GS*, vol. 18, p. 335.

12 Adorno, 'Der dialektische Komponist', *GS*, vol. 17, p. 201. According to Adorno, Schoenberg's musical development proceeds from the free tonal compositions, notable both for their melodic qualities and for their wealth of dissonance (e.g., *Pelleas und Melisande* and the *Gurrelieder*), to the chamber-music period. Here he develops a polyphonic form carried by a four-part string movement, a form of counterpoint in which the harmony merges completely with the overall progression of the music (e.g., the First Chamber Symphony, the Second Quartet). The third period is the phase of free atonality (e.g., the *George Songs*, *Pierrot lunaire*), in which the twelve-note technique appears in its full form (the Piano Suite, op. 25, the Wind Quintet, op. 26, the Variations for Orchestra, op. 31). This is an integrated form of composition in which all the components are related to one another. 'The twelve-note technique that is supposed to make such

works possible consists of managing the process of thematic work in every direction, without any remnant and without treating any note in an arbitrary way. Every twelve-note composition is based on a particular arrangement of all twelve notes of a "basic row". An example is C$\sharp$ – A – B$\flat$ – G – A$\flat$ – F$\sharp$ – B$\flat$ – D – E – E$\flat$ – C – F, as in Schoenberg's first twelve-tone publication, a waltz' (Adorno, 'Arnold Schoenberg', *GS*, vol. 18, p. 317).

13 Adorno, *Alban Berg: Master of the Smallest Link*, p. 13. Adorno's memory seems to have misled him here, since at this time, January 1925, he was still in Frankfurt am Main, from where he wrote to Berg in order to ask in writing whether Berg would take him on as a pupil. Adorno finally moved to Vienna in the first week in March. Cf. also 'Im Gedächtnis an Alban Berg', *GS*, vol. 18, p. 487ff.

14 Adorno and Berg, *Briefwechsel 1925–1935*, p. 9f.

15 See Heinz Steinert, *Adorno in Wien*, p. 13f.

16 Arthur Koestler, *Arrow in the Blue*, p. 92.

17 Adorno, 'Im Gedächtnis an Alban Berg', *GS*, vol. 18, p. 496.

18 Heinz Steinert, *Adorno in Wien*, p. 17 and also p. 74ff.

19 Ibid., p. 52ff.

20 Adorno, 'Vienna', in *Quasi una fantasia*, pp. 201 and 204.

21 Adorno, *Alban Berg: Master of the Smallest Link*, p. 13f.

22 Ibid., p. 32.

23 Ibid., p. 27. Apart from Adorno, Berg had almost no other pupils. He gave lessons only to Julius Schloß, who had also studied at the Hoch Conservatory. Adorno had no more time for Schloß than did Berg.

24 Adorno, 'Nach Steuermanns Tod', *GS*, vol. 17, p. 312.

25 Ibid., p. 314f.

26 See Adorno, *Zu einer Theorie der musikalischen Reproduktion*, *NaS*, vol. 2.

27 See Adorno, 'Zum Problem der Reproduktion', *GS*, vol. 19, p. 440ff.

28 A year after the death of his first wife, Schoenberg married Rudolf Kolisch's sister.

29 A glance at the index of his writings on music yields a list of around 200 composers whose works he analysed. In some cases, such as Gustav Mahler or Alban Berg, he discussed the entire oeuvre, in others, such as Beethoven, Mozart, Schubert, Hindemith, Krenek, Debussy, Ravel and Wagner, he focused on major compositions.

30 Quoted in Rolf Wiggershaus, *The Frankfurt School*, p. 73.

31 A year before Adorno arrived in Vienna, and following the death of his first wife, Mathilde, the sister of his teacher Zemlinsky, Schoenberg had remarried. His second wife, Gertrud Kolisch, the sister of Rudolf, was significantly younger than him. To Adorno it seemed as if this second marriage had caused Schoenberg to lead a more private life, and this resulted in a loosening of the previously firm and continuous ties binding the circle of his pupils and followers. See Adorno, *Alban Berg: Master of the Smallest Link*, p. 29; and also Heinz Steinert, *Adorno in Wien*, pp. 22ff. and 60ff.

32 Adorno, *Alban Berg: Master of the Smallest Link*, p. 16, alternative translation [trans.].

33 See Adorno and Berg, *Briefwechsel 1925–1935*, p. 17.

34 Ellen Delp belonged to the circle around Lou Andreas-Salomé, Rainer Maria Rilke and Max Reinhardt. See R. M. Rilke, *Briefwechsel mit Regina Ullmann und Ellen Delp*, p. 449.
35 See Constantin Floros, 'Alban Berg und Hanna Fuchs: Briefe und Studien', p. 30ff.; see also Floros, *Alban Berg und Hanna Fuchs: Die Geschichte einer Liebe in Briefen.*
36 Adorno, *Berg: Master of the Smallest Link*, p. 10.
37 Ibid., p. 30.
38 Soma Morgenstern, *Alban Berg und seine Idole*, p. 161f. [Presumably from 'daigen', to worry. 'Bellyaching' might be nearer the mark; trans.]
39 Benjamin and Adorno, *The Complete Correspondence 1928–1940*, p. 332.
40 Soma Morgenstern, *Alban Berg und seine Idole*, p. 118f.
41 Ibid., p. 123.
42 Adorno and Berg, *Briefwechsel 1925–1935*, p. 17f.
43 Lukács had made his name with these books. Before the First World War, he belonged to the so-called Max Weber circle in Heidelberg, along with such very different people as Ernst Bloch and Stefan George, Emil Lask and Friedrich Gundolf. Despite approval and support, he failed to obtain the *Habilitation* in Heidelberg. In particular, he was formally disqualified because he was not a German national. In 1918, he joined the Hungarian Communist Party and served as the People's Commissar for Education during the brief rule of the Hungarian Soviet republic. After the fall of the republic, he settled in Vienna for the next ten years.
44 Adorno and Berg, *Briefwechsel 1925–1935*, p. 20.

Chapter 7 In Search of a Career

1 Adorno and Berg, *Briefwechsel 1925–1935*, p. 24. By 'fascism' Adorno meant the movement led by Benito Mussolini in Italy after the First World War. Espousing a policy of extreme nationalism, it replaced parliamentary democracy with a one-party state after taking over the government in 1922.
2 Siegfried Kracauer, 'Felsenwahn in Positano', *Schriften*, vol. 5.1, p. 335.
3 Adorno and Berg, *Briefwechsel 1925–1935*, p. 33.
4 Alfred Sohn-Rethel was born in Neuilly-sur-Seine, near Paris, and came from a wealthy family of art collectors. As a student of economics and sociology in Heidelberg and Berlin, he made a thorough study of Marx's *Capital*, and this became a lifetime's obsession. His dissertation, for which he studied with the Austro-Marxist Emil Lederer, was concerned with marginal utility theory. In 1936 he emigrated to Switzerland for a brief period. From that point on, he focused on epistemological problems based on the materialist theory of society. His own thinking was grounded on the assumption that all theoretical knowledge was characterized by structures that arose from the conditions of 'intellectual labour'. These achievements of mental abstraction were in his view not merely conscious acts, as in Kant, but were based on the social process of 'real abstraction'. The precondition of this real abstraction was the exchange of goods as mediated by money. As soon as exchange value had assumed sensuous form in the shape of money, the real or exchange abstraction could be transformed

into a 'mental abstraction'. See Alfred Sohn-Rethel, *Warenform und Denkform*, and also Adorno and Sohn-Rethel, *Briefwechsel 1936–1969*.
5 See the worklist in Heinz Klaus Metzger and Rainer Riehn, 'Theodor W. Adorno: Der Komponist', p. 144.
6 See Martin Hufner, *Adorno und die Zwölftontechnik*, p. 71.
7 See Siegfried Mauser, 'Adornos Klavierlieder', p. 46ff. We can place Adorno's compositions at this period somewhere between Schoenberg, Berg and Webern. 'We are reminded of Schoenberg by their explosive express-iveness, of Berg by their tone values and of Webern by his work with minuscule motifs.' See Dieter Schnebel, 'Einführung in Adornos Musik'.
8 Adorno and Berg, *Briefwechsel 1925–1935*, p. 134.
9 Hans Heinz Stuckenschmidt, Adorno's rival as a music critic, quotes Schoenberg as saying, 'He [i.e., Adorno] knows all about twelve-tone music, but has absolutely no idea about the creative process' (H. H. Stuckenschmidt, *Schönberg: Leben – Umwelt – Werk*, p. 462).
10 Adorno and Berg, *Briefwechsel 1925–1935*, p. 131.
11 Soma Morgenstern, *Alban Berg und seine Idole*, p. 171.
12 Adorno and Berg, *Briefwechsel 1925–1935*, p. 130.
13 Soma Morgenstern, *Alban Berg und seine Idole*, p. 171.
14 Adorno and Berg, *Briefwechsel 1925–1935*, p. 57.
15 Ibid., p. 65.
16 Ibid., p. 66.
17 Ibid., p. 47.
18 Ibid, p. 102f.
19 Ibid., p. 130.
20 Elisabeth Lenk notes in her edition of her correspondence with Adorno that this pseudonym emphasizes the dual authorship: '"Castor" refers to Pollux, from whom he is inseparable, while "Zwieback" [biscuit or rusk] alludes to the "twice-baked" origin of these texts' (Adorno and Lenk, *Briefwechsel 1962–1969*, p. 44).
21 Adorno and Dreyfus, 'Lesestücke', *GS*, vol. 20.2, p. 591. At the time, only four of the eighteen pieces appeared in the *Frankfurter Zeitung*.
22 Not until thirty years later could the majority of these texts appear in full. They were published in the literary magazine *Akzente*, once again under a pseudonym. The occasion may have been provided by Dreyfus's return from exile in Argentina. Despite the fact that these pieces were over thirty years old and Adorno had meanwhile become critical of surrealism, it was important to him to see the majority of them in print. They were examples of literary experimentation that were new territory for him, comparable to his writings on music. See *Akzente*, vol. 10, 1963. Adorno wrote about them to the editor, Walter Höllerer, on 10 April 1963: 'These pieces amount to what may be a not uninteresting experiment which I do not want to disown even though I did not pursue it further subsequently; certain developments over the last thirty years have shown that my intention here was not outlandish, or rather that what is outlandish is not as outlandish as all that. . . . I would ask you to understand why I want to see these pieces published. I feel particularly attached to things that crystallize a possible development in me that never came to fruition. . . . This is connected with my distrust of the concept of maturity and the so-called logic of development.'

23 I had an extended conversation with Marianne Hoppe in her Berlin flat in the summer of 1999. See also Petra Kohse, *Marianne Hoppe: Eine Biografie*, p. 76ff., and Carl Zuckmayer, *Geheimreport*, pp. 339 and 396.

24 Her relationship with Dreyfus lasted until his emigration to Argentina via Britain. After the Nazi takeover, Dreyfus, who as a Jew and a Marxist was in constant danger, continued to live in Berlin, initially in Marianne Hoppe's flat. In the early 1960s, protracted legal proceedings for compensation were finally resolved in his favour and he returned to Germany. Both Adorno and Hoppe made efforts to find him a job in the film industry. Since Adorno had been on friendly terms with Hoppe, he also resumed contact with her on his return to Germany, partly in order to produce a radio programme jointly with her. In this programme Marianne Hoppe read passages from Proust's *A la recherche du temps perdu*. Adorno contributed an introduction and provided a commentary on the readings.

25 Adorno and Berg, *Briefwechsel 1925–1935*, p. 276.

26 Andreas Hansert, *Bürgerkultur und Kulturpolitik*, pp. 137 and 141ff.

27 Adorno, 'Kultur und Verwaltung', *GS*, vol. 8, p. 134. For an alternative English translation, see Adorno, *The Culture Industry*, p. 103 [trans].

28 See Wolfgang Schivelbusch, *Intellektuellendämmerung*, pp. 42ff. and 62ff.

29 Adorno, 'Frankfurter Opern- und Konzertkritiken', *GS*, vol. 19, p. 113.

30 Ibid., p. 99.

31 Adorno, 'Drei Dirigenten', ibid., p. 456. Because at this time music had absolute priority for Adorno, he neglected the plastic arts despite his interest in them. He must have come across Max Beckmann in the salon of Lilly and Georg von Schnitzler, and been familiar with his paintings. But he never made any comment on his art, perhaps because he did not trust his judgement. In his retrospective discussion of the 1920s, he attempted to argue that this period did not really succeed in producing the revolutionary innovations that were later claimed for it: 'The heroic age of the new art was actually around 1910: synthetic cubism, early German expressionism, and the free atonalism of Schoenberg and his school' (Adorno, 'Those Twenties', in *Critical Models*, p. 41).

32 See Adorno and Berg, *Briefwechsel 1925–1935*, p. 98f. Henri Lonitz, the editor of the correspondence, points out that there is no sign of either the third movement of the Quartet or the Piano Pieces in Adorno's literary estate. Ibid., p. 99.

33 See Adorno, 'Musikalische Aphorismen', *GS*, vol. 18, p. 13f.

34 Adorno and Berg, *Briefwechsel 1925–1935*, p. 170.

35 M. Horkheimer, *Über Kants 'Kritik der Urteilskraft'*, *GS*, vol. 2, p. 146.

36 Adorno, *Der Begriff des Unbewußten in der transzendentalen Seelenlehre*, *GS*, vol. 1, p. 96.

37 Ibid., p. 230f.

38 Ibid., p. 232.

39 Ibid., p. 320.

40 Ibid.

41 Decades later, when the question arose of publishing this dissertation in the *Complete Writings*, Adorno criticized the Freud chapter. He said that he had focused too narrowly on epistemological questions at the expense of 'the materialist dimension that was evident in the fundamental concept of organ-pleasure' (Rolf Tiedemann, 'Editorische Nachbemerkung', in

Adorno, *GS*, vol. 1, p. 381f.). Against this, it could be argued that in fact the epistemological interpretation of Freud was its truly innovative aspect. This question was not pursued until it was taken up again later by Jürgen Habermas in *Knowledge and Human Interests* (1968). See Stefan Müller-Doohm, *Das Interesse der Vernunft: Rückblicke auf das Werk von Jürgen Habermas seit 'Erkenntnis und Interesse'*.

42 Adorno, 'Berliner Memorial', *GS*, vol. 19, p. 265.
43 Adorno and Berg, *Briefwechsel 1925–1935*, p. 169.
44 Ibid., p. 170.
45 Ibid., p. 171.
46 Adorno, 'Motifs', in *Quasi una fantasia*, p. 13.
47 Ibid., p. 16.
48 See, e.g., ibid., p. 14f. At around this time, Adorno described Chopin's method of developing his themes in a style bordering on the lyrical: 'With eyes averted, like a bride, the objective theme is safely guided through the dark forest of the self, through the torrential river of the passions' (ibid., p. 17). Referring to the task of the music critic, he notes that he must decode it from within as well as observe and describe it from a distance. 'To think about twelve-tone technique at the same time as remembering that childhood experience of *Madame Butterfly* on the gramophone – that is the task facing every serious attempt to understand music today' (ibid., p. 20).
49 See Heinz Steinert, *Adorno in Wien*, p. 136ff.
50 Adorno, 'Zum "Anbruch"', *GS*, vol. 19, p. 602.
51 See Notker Hammerstein, *Die Johann Wolfgang Goethe-Universität*, p. 114f.

Chapter 8 Music Criticism and Compositional Practice

1 See Erwin Stein, 'Neue Formprinzipien', p. 286ff. In addition to free atonality, Stein discusses the elimination of keynote dependency, the intensivized use of counterpoint and the importance of dissonance.
2 Adorno, 'Schoenberg: Suite', *GS*, vol. 18, p. 362.
3 Later on, Adorno made the criticism that in Schoenberg's twelve-tone works there was a tautologous relation between twelve-tone technique and formal shape. See Giselher Schubert, 'Adornos Auseinandersetzung mit der Zwölftontechnik Schoenbergs', p. 238ff.
4 Adorno, 'Nachtmusik', *GS*, vol. 17, p. 55ff.
5 Adorno, 'Zur Zwölftontechnik', *GS*, vol. 18, p. 367.
6 See Reinhard Kager, 'Einheit in der Zersplitterung: Überlegungen zu Adornos Begriff des "musikalischen Materials"', p. 94ff.; see also Max Paddison, *Adorno's Aesthetics of Music*, p. 65ff.
7 Adorno, 'Reaktion und Fortschritt', *GS*, vol. 17, p. 134f.
8 Ibid., p. 135.
9 Ibid., p. 138.
10 Adorno, 'Kontroverse über die Heiterkeit', *GS*, vol. 19, p. 452.
11 Adorno, 'Die stabilisierte Musik', *GS*, vol. 18, p. 721ff.
12 See the following accounts: Wolfgang Fink, '". . . in jener richtigen, höheren Art einfach": Anmerkungen zu Adornos kurzen Orchesterstücken, op. 4', p. 100ff.; Martin Hufner, *Adorno und die Zwölftontechnik*, p. 34ff.

13   In September 1988 an evening concert devoted to Adorno's compositions
      was given in the Alte Oper in Frankfurt am Main. In addition to the *Six
      Short Orchestral Pieces*, op. 4, the programme included the *Two Pieces
      for String Quartet*, op. 2, the *Three Poems by Theodor Däubler* arranged
      for four-part women's choir *a cappella*, *Two Songs with Orchestra from the
      Singspiel 'The Treasure of Indian Joe'*, and also *Kinderjahr*, six pieces from
      Robert Schumann's op. 68, arranged for small orchestra. The music was
      performed by the Buchberger Quartet and the Frankfurt Opera and
      Museum Orchestra, conducted by Gary Bertini. The concert was recorded
      and a CD has been issued (Wergo 6173–2).

14   In a letter of 8 April 1929 to Berg, he remarked that the flop of the pre-
      miere of his song-cycle in Berlin almost robbed him of the courage to finish
      his orchestral pieces. However, encouraged by Kurt Weill and the con-
      ductor Walter Herbert, he finally completed the score in Berne in February
      1929. He dedicated the work to Herbert, who conducted the premiere in
      Berlin. On this occasion, the performance was a success. See Adorno and
      Berg, *Briefwechsel 1925–1935*, p. 200.

15   See Walter Levin, 'Adornos Zwei Stücke für Streichquartett, op. 2', p. 83.

16   See Martin Hufner, *Adorno und die Zwölftontechnik*, p. 38; Martin
      Blumentritt, 'Adorno, der Komponist als Philosoph', p. 16f.

17   Adorno discussed this concept in theoretical terms in the essay 'Zweite
      Nachtmusik' (*GS*, vol. 18, p. 50), published in 1937. The principle of com-
      plementary harmony states that the antagonism between consonance and
      dissonance is not absolute. There is a complementary relationship between
      the tension and resolution of harmonic functions.

18   Adorno defended the *George Lieder* against criticism after the failure of
      the Berlin premiere in a concert given by the International Society for
      New Music. Moreover, he continued to think well of them, placing them
      higher than his instrumental works. In the mid-1930s, two songs from
      the cycle were performed – successfully, incidentally – in a programme
      devoted to contemporary music. On that occasion, Adorno put in a plea
      for the work to be performed in its entirety since he thought of it as a unity,
      'in the choice of texts, a kind of lyrical requiem, motivically through the
      head motif of the first song, admittedly subjected to countless transforma-
      tions, or, rather, through the basic shape consisting of seconds and thirds
      (or vice versa); and as a form, since this amounts to a sonata for voice
      and piano; the first movement appears to me to be clearly sonata-
      like, the second an intermezzo with trio, the third an adagio, the fourth a
      rondo. Of course, I would be delighted if the songs could be performed
      altogether, just as they were conceived' (Adorno and Krenek, *Briefwechsel*,
      p. 60).

19   Hufner writes of the 'compositional anarchy' of Adorno's songs for piano,
      and goes on to say that 'the continuous formation of variations on the
      minutest musical ideas . . . and the absence of large thematic complexes
      erodes the distinctions between free atonality and purely technical atonality'
      (Martin Hufner, *Adorno und die Zwölftontechnik*, p. 78).

20   On this point, Adorno wrote later, 'Musicians are usually truants from
      maths classes; it would be a terrible fate for them to end up in the hands
      of the maths teacher after all' ('Vers une musique informelle', *Quasi una
      fantasia*, p. 269).

21 Hans-Klaus Jungheinrich, 'Wie kompositorische Praxis in Sprachkunst übergeht', p. 139; Martin Hufner, *Adorno und die Zwölftontechnik*, p. 53ff.
22 See Lucia Sziborsky, *Adornos Musikphilosophie*, p. 91ff.
23 This rationalization thesis is in tune with a major finding of the failed *Habilitation* dissertation. Its aim had been to make a contribution to 'demystifying the unconscious'. Adorno's criticism here is in harmony with that goal. Its target was the idea (defended above all by Ernst Krenek) of representing atonality as a 'fact of nature', or even as 'primal meaning'. In opposition to this, Adorno insisted that twelve-tone technique, as a method of composition consisting of twelve interrelated notes, rendered possible the rationalization and hence the demythologization of all irrational elements in music.
24 Adorno, 'Zur Zwölftontechnik musikalischer Aphorismen', *GS*, vol. 18, pp. 16 and 364.
25 Adorno and Krenek, *Briefwechsel*, p. 8.; see also Ernst Krenek, *Im Atem der Zeit: Erinnerungen an die Moderne*, pp. 474 and 728ff. In his autobiography in diary form, Krenek observes that during his first meetings with Adorno he 'was struck by his frequent praise of surrealism'. 'In general, his discourse was full of melancholic allusions pointing to the crumbling of all traditional values. One of his favourite expressions was "crumbling substance", and he used it so often that we ended up joking about it' (ibid., p. 729).
26 See Adorno, *Frankfurter Opern- und Konzertkritiken, GS*, vol. 19, p. 117ff.
27 See Krenek and Adorno, 'Arbeitsprobleme des Komponisten', Adorno, *GS*, vol. 19, p. 437.
28 Ibid., p. 438.
29 Adorno and Krenek, *Briefwechsel*, p. 12f.
30 Ibid., p. 13f.
31 Ibid., pp. 53 and 55.

Chapter 9 Towards a Theory of Aesthetics

1 Krenek's articles were 'Freiheit und Technik' and 'Fortschritt und Reaktion'; Adorno's were entitled 'Zur Zwölftontechnik' and 'Reaktion und Fortschritt'.
2 See the letters from Oscar Alexander Wiesengrund to Adorno on 3 and 13 May 1929, Theodor W. Adorno Archive, Frankfurt am Main.
3 Adorno and Berg, *Briefwechsel 1925–1935*, pp. 209f. and 214.
4 Ibid., p. 351ff.
5 Ibid., p. 229.
6 Ibid., p. 239f.
7 Asja Lacis (1891–1979) studied theatre and film in Moscow, where she was also an active member of the Communist Party. She had met Benjamin in Capri early in 1924. It was because of her influence that Benjamin came to concern himself with the writings of Marx and with historical materialism. See *Marbacher Magazin*, 'Walter Benjamin 1892–1940', p. 161ff.
8 Adorno, *Erinnerungen, GS*, vol. 20.1, p. 175. Adorno had first met Benjamin in Frankfurt and then, in 1925, in Naples. They did not have a deeper exchange of ideas until February 1928, when Adorno spent some weeks in Berlin. It was during this time that Benjamin first met Gretel Karplus.

9 W. Benjamin, *The Arcades Project*, p. 864; see also Rolf Tiedemann, 'Einleitung des Herausgebers', ibid., p. 24; Susan Buck-Morss, *The Dialectics of Seeing*, p. 59ff.

10 Adorno and Berg, *Briefwechsel 1925–1935*, p. 88.

11 Kracauer to Löwenthal, 8 December 1923, Löwenthal's Literary Estate, Universitätsbibliothek, Frankfurt am Main.

12 Adorno, *The Jargon of Authenticity*, p. 105.

13 See Adorno, *Negative Dialectics*, p. 62, for a different translation.

14 It has not been possible to clarify the extent to which, when writing his Kierkegaard book, Adorno was already fully conversant with Benjamin's essay on Goethe's novel *Elective Affinities* (see Benjamin, *Selected Writings*, vol. 1, pp. 297–360), which the latter wrote in 1921–2 but did not publish until 1925. However, there are obvious parallels between the two works.

15 Georg Lukács, *History and Class Consciousness*, p. 83.

16 Adorno to Kracauer, 6 August 1930, quoted in Rolf Wiggershaus, *The Frankfurt School*, p. 92.

17 Adorno and Berg, *Briefwechsel 1925–1935*, p. 250.

18 Ernst Schoen (1894–1960) was a musician and a poet. Since 1929, he had been in charge of programming in the South-West German Radio in Frankfurt am Main, in succession to Ernst Flesch. He and Benjamin had been friends since their schooldays. Early in the 1920s, he had a brief affair with Benjamin's wife Dora. As the programme director, he pursued a policy of encouraging modern music as well as using radio for experimental art forms. Adorno recalled Schoen's 'indescribable distinction and exquisite sensibility'. See Adorno, 'Benjamin, der Briefschreiber', *GS*, vol. 11, p. 588; see also *Marbacher Magazin*, 'Walter Benjamin, 1892–1940', p. 77; Wolfgang Schivelbusch, *Intellektuellendämmerung*, p. 62ff.

19 See Adorno, *GS*, vol. 20.2, p. 555ff.

20 This is not the place to decide whether Adorno's critique of what he calls the 'logic of the spheres' does justice to Kierkegaard. Kierkegaard distinguishes between three modes of existence or attitudes to life which Adorno calls 'spheres'. The aesthetic stage consists of pleasure, the pure enjoyment of the senses. The ethical stage is characterized by a sense of responsibility. This stage stands in opposition to the aesthetic stage. The religious mode of existence envisages a self that relates to itself through the relationship with God. This stage in its turn negates the preceding two. In order to reach the religious stage, the 'existential leap of faith' is needed. See S. Kierkegaard, *Either/Or*; Michael Theunissen and Wilfried Greve, *Materialien zur Philosophie Sören Kierkegaards*; Hermann Deuser, *Dialektische Theologie: Studien zu Adornos Metaphysik und zum Spätwerk Kierkegaards*.

21 Adorno, *Kierkegaard: Construction of the Aesthetic*, p. 3.

22 Ibid., p. 13.

23 Ibid., p. 29.

24 This dismissal of identity philosophy is important for Adorno's own thinking because it is the starting-point for his own concept of the non-identical. See Adorno, *Negative Dialectics*, p. 135ff.

25 Adorno, *Kierkegaard: Construction of the Aesthetic*, p. 32.

26 Ibid., p. 33.

27 Ibid., p. 39.

28 Ibid., p. 75.
29 Ibid., p. 133.
30 Ibid., p. 132.
31 Ibid., p. 126. There are similar ideas towards the end of an essay on Schubert that Adorno had written as early as 1928. He goes in search there of the decayed images in Schubert's music that make 'the tears flow from our eyes': 'We weep without knowing why; because we have not yet become what that music promises, and in the indescribable happiness that the music needs only to be what it is in order to assure us that we will one day become like that. We cannot read them, but the music holds out to our fading eyes, brimful of tears, the ciphers of ultimate reconciliation' (Adorno, *'Can One Live After Auschwitz?'*, p. 313).
32 Adorno, *Kierkegaard: Construction of the Aesthetic*, p. 125.
33 Adorno discussed the idea of 'exact fantasy', to which we have already alluded, in his inaugural lecture on 'The Current Relevance of Philosophy'; see *GS*, vol. 1, p. 342.
34 Adorno, *Kierkegaard: Construction of the Aesthetic*, p. 125.
35 Paul Tillich, 'Gutachten über die Arbeit von Dr. Wiesengrund: Die Konstruktion des Ästhetischen bei Kierkegaard', File on Theodor W. Adorno, Archive of the Dean of the Faculty of Arts of the Johann Wolfgang Goethe University, Frankfurt am Main (Section 134, Number 4, Sheets 17–24).
36 Max Horkheimer, 'Bemerkungen in Sachen der Habilitation Dr. Wiesengrund', File on Theodor W. Adorno, Archive of the Dean of the Faculty of Arts of the Johann Wolfgang Goethe University, Frankfurt am Main (Section 134, Number 4, Sheets 25–31).
37 Benjamin and Adorno, *The Complete Correspondence 1928–1940*, p. 20. See also Benjamin, *GS*, vol. III, pp. 380ff. and 660ff.
38 Benjamin and Adorno, *The Complete Correspondence 1928–1940*, p. 20f.
39 Adorno, *Kierkegaard*, *GS*, vol. 2, p. 261.
40 See *Marbacher Magazin*, 'Siegfried Kracauer', p. 74ff.
41 See Bloch's letter to Kracauer in January 1931, in E. Bloch, *Briefe 1903–1975*, p. 351.
42 Benjamin, *Selected Writings*, vol. 2, p. 705.
43 Adorno, 'Kierkegaard noch einmal', *GS*, vol. 2, p. 247.
44 Ibid., p. 250.
45 Ibid., p. 258.
46 S. Kracauer, *Der enthüllte Kierkegaard*, *Schriften*, vol. 5.3, p. 263.

Chapter 10 The Institute of Social Research

1 Hermann Weil was born in 1868 into a family of Jewish businessmen. Together with his brother, he had established a grain-trading firm in Buenos Aires and, later on, a wholesale importer's in Rotterdam. These businesses had made him extremely wealthy. Having returned to Germany in 1908 for reasons of health, he settled in Frankfurt and emerged as benefactor to a number of institutes in the new university. During the First World War, he had connections with the Institute for Marine Transport and World Trade in Kiel, and, because of his expert knowledge

of world markets, he served as adviser to the German General Staff on food supplies and military policy more generally.

2 Felix Weil obtained his doctorate in 1920 after studying with the social economist Adolf Weber. 'He was one of those young people who had been politicized by the war and the November Revolution, who were convinced of the practicality and superiority of socialism as a more advanced form of economic organization, and who devoted themselves to the study of socialist theories so that they could take up leading positions in the workers' movement or in a new socialist order as soon as possible. But he kept himself at a certain distance while devoting himself to this goal as a patron of the left and a part-time scholar' (Rolf Wiggershaus, *The Frankfurt School*, p. 13).

3 According to §2 of the Statute of January 1923, the two principal tasks of the institute are described as follows: 'First, it aims to cultivate and promote the scientific research and description of social conditions and movements of both past and present. This research should be comprehensive and should not be confined to one particular country. Second, the institute shall focus particularly on the training of young researchers in the fields of the social and economic sciences, and enable them to pursue their own independent work.' See Ulrike Migdal, *Die Frühgeschichte des Frankfurter Instituts für Sozialforschung*, p. 51.

4 Apart from those already named, the group included Eduard Ludwig Alexander, the lawyer and co-founder of the Spartacus League; the economist Julian Gumperz; Kuzuo Fukumoto, who had links with the Japanese communist movement; the historian Karl Wittfogel; the economist Richard Sorge (who was an assistant to the director designate of the institute, Kurt Albert Gerlach); the Hungarian philosopher Béla Fogarasi; Konstantin Zetkin, the youngest son of Clara Zetkin; as well as Rose Wittfogel, Christiane Sorge, Hedda Korsch, Käte Weil and Hede Massing.

5 See Michael Buckmiller, 'Die "Marxistische Arbeitswoche" 1923 und die Gründung des Instituts für Sozialforschung', p. 158ff.

6 Felix Weil, too, had scholarly ambitions in the sense that he wished to exert a controlling influence on the development of the institute. In his memorandum of 1 November 1929, he announced quite openly: 'I regard the work of the institute and my participation in it as my life's task.' He evidently had no wish to confine his role to that of financial benefactor. The first memorandum produced by Kurt Gerlach, the Aachen economics professor, formulated the programmatic research goals of the new institute in even vaguer terms than the statute. He says, for example, 'that the knowledge of social deprivation in all its implications is indispensable; as is an understanding of that vast tangle of interacting economic foundations, of political and legal factors right up to and including the final ramifications of intellectual and spiritual life in the community and in society. We need only remind ourselves of international trade unions, strikes, sabotage, revolution as a wages movement, anti-Semitism as a sociological problem . . .'

Weil's interventions had led to tensions with Gustav Mayer, the biographer of Engels. Weil had at first thought of Mayer as a possible director of the institute, but Mayer rejected the idea that the benefactor should be in a position to influence the scientific direction of the institute.

See Ulrike Migdal, *Die Frühgeschichte des Frankfurter Instituts für Sozialforschung*, pp. 54 and 52ff.

7 As already mentioned, the reason was Weil's wish as benefactor to influence the academic direction of the institute.

8 Grünberg had been born in Romania in 1861 and had studied with both Lorenz von Stein and Anton Menger. His *Habilitation* thesis was concerned with agrarian reform in Bohemia. In his book *Socialism and Communism*, which appeared in 1907, he subjected aspects of Marx's analysis of capitalism to a critical revision.

9 See Ulrike Migdal, *Die Frühgeschichte des Frankfurter Instituts für Sozialforschung*, p. 76ff.

10 Ibid., p. 98ff.

11 Max Horkheimer, 'Beginnings of the Bourgeois Philosophy of History', in *Between Philosophy and Social Science*, p. 373 (translation slightly altered).

12 M. Horkheimer, 'The Present Situation of Social Philosophy', in *Between Philosophy and Social Sciences*, p. 11.

13 Ibid., p. 9.

14 Ibid., p. 14.

15 Löwenthal (1900–1993) had worked at the institute since 1921, part-time to begin with and then, four years later, as a senior assistant.

16 Erich Fromm (1900–1980), who had been born into a Jewish family in Frankfurt, trained as a psychoanalyst after finishing his university studies. As an expert on psychoanalysis, he was a member of the Institute of Social Research from 1930 to 1939 where he strove to establish connections between Marx and Freud. This applies particularly to his early writings, which were republished in 1970 with the title *Analytische Sozialpsychologie und Gesellschaftstheorie*.

17 Herbert Marcuse (1898–1979) was the son of an assimilated Jewish businessman from Berlin. He came relatively late to the circle around Horkheimer and the Institute of Social Research via a recommendation from Edmund Husserl. He was in charge of the Geneva branch of the institute from 1932. Following his studies with Husserl, which he concluded with a dissertation on the artist novel, he tried to forge a link between Heidegger's existential philosophy and Marx's materialist philosophy of history. He had planned a *Habilitation* dissertation on 'Hegel's Ontology and the Theory of Historicity' (1932), but because of his political differences with Heidegger, who had embraced National Socialism, the thesis was never submitted. Adorno reviewed the book version of the thesis in the second issue of the *Zeitschrift für Sozialforschung*. What brought Marcuse close to the Horkheimer circle was his interest in Marx's theory of revolution on the basis of the latter's *Economic and Philosophical Manuscripts of 1844*, which were first published in 1932.

18 We can describe his programme as that of an *interdisciplinary materialism*. On this notion, see W. Bonß, *Die Einübung des Tatsachenblicks*; H. Dubiel, *Wissenschaftsorganisation und politische Erfahrung*. For the differences between Horkheimer's and Adorno's philosophical programmes, see Susan Buck-Morss, *The Origin of Negative Dialectics*; Martin Jay, 'Positive und negative Totalität', p. 67ff.

19 Adorno, 'Die Aktualität der Philosophie', *GS*, vol. 1, p. 340.

20 Ibid., p. 334.
21 Ibid., p. 335.
22 Ibid.
23 Ibid., p. 340.
24 Ibid., p. 342.
25 M. Horkheimer, 'The Present Situation of Social Philosophy', in *Between Philosophy and Social Science*, p. 9.
26 M. Horkheimer, Preface to the first year's issues of the *Zeitschrift für Sozialforschung*, GS, vol. 3, p. 30ff.
27 He did make the attempt to clarify his thoughts on this subject in the ten 'Theses on the Language of the Philosopher'. He dedicated the typescript to Gretel Karplus. In the ninth thesis, which contains a summation of the preceding argument, he asserts that philosophical criticism should take the form of linguistic criticism. Such linguistic criticism is to make use of a configurative language mindful of 'the *aesthetic* dignity of words'. Adorno inferred this truth criterion from the 'convergence of art and knowledge', a phenomenon with two aspects. On the one hand, true propositions can only be expressed in linguistic form; on the other, the element of expression, and art in general, 'conveys knowledge'. The language of art 'is only aesthetically consistent if it is "true", that is to say, if its statements correspond to the objective stage reached by history.' In the light of this truth criterion, Adorno rejected the claim that philosophical language should aspire to comprehensibility, i.e., communication. Instead, following the downfall of metaphysics and the disintegration of language, the philosopher has the opportunity to make use of 'the ruins of language', and to reassemble its fragments into a novel configuration. This language will then 'disclose the historical stage reached by truth in faithful agreement with the objects referred to and with a faithful application of words' (Adorno, 'Thesen über die Sprache des Philosophen', *GS*, vol. 1, p. 368ff.).
28 W. Strzelewicz, 'Diskurse im Institut für Sozialforschung um 1930', p. 164.
29 Kracauer to Adorno, 7 June 1931, Kracauer's Literary Estate, Deutsches Literaturarchiv, Marbach.
30 Ibid.
31 Peter von Haselberg, 'Wiesengrund-Adorno', p. 9.
32 Adorno, 'The Curious Realist', *Notes to Literature*, vol. 2, p. 60.
33 Peter von Haselberg, 'Wiesengrund-Adorno', p. 10.
34 See Adorno, 'Aufzeichnungen zur Ästhetik-Vorlesung von 1931/32', *Frankfurter Adorno Blätter* I, 1992, p. 35ff.
35 Ibid., p. 38.
36 Ibid., p. 77.
37 Ibid., p. 83.
38 Ibid., p. 87.
39 Peter von Haselberg, 'Wiesengrund-Adorno', p. 11.
40 Kurt Mautz, *Der Urfreund*, p. 43f. Kurt Mautz later became a literary scholar and a novelist. Before his death in November 2000, I was able to have a number of telephone conversations with him in which we talked about his memories of Adorno, during his early period as a *Privatdozent*, and then again since the 1950s. After Mautz's death, his son Rolf gave me permission to look through his papers, which included the records of those

seminars in 1932 as well as the notes he had taken on the lectures Adorno had given during his years in Frankfurt.
41 Wilhelm Emrich, 'Ladenhüter', p. 213.
42 E. E. Noth, *Erinnerungen eines Deutschen*, p. 194.
43 See Notker Hammerstein, *Die Johann Wolfgang Goethe-Universität*, p. 37ff.
44 See Karl Korn, *Lange Lehrzeit: Ein deutsches Leben*, p. 142.
45 Adorno, 'Erinnerungen an Paul Tillich', p. 29.
46 Peter von Haselberg, 'Wiesengrund-Adorno', p. 13.
47 See Max Horkheimer, *GS*, vol. 12, p. 351ff.
48 Ibid., p. 346.
49 See 'Adornos Seminar vom Sommersemester 1932', *Frankfurter Adorno Blätter*, IV, 1995, p. 52ff.
50 W. Benjamin, *The Origin of German Tragic Drama*, p. 29f.
51 Ibid., p. 30.
52 Ibid., p. 36.
53 Ibid., p. 28ff.
54 See Adorno, *Negative Dialectics*, p. 185ff.
55 Ibid., pp. 127 and 365.
56 'Adornos Seminar vom Sommersemester 1932', *Frankfurter Adorno Blätter*, IV, 1995, p. 74.
57 W. Benjamin, *Gesammelte Briefe*, vol. IV, pp. 128 and 156f.
58 Benjamin and Adorno, *The Complete Correspondence 1928–1940*, p. 9f.
59 After reading the Kierkegaard book, Benjamin's closest friend, Gershom Scholem, told Benjamin frankly that it was 'a sublime piece of plagiarism of your writings, written with unusual chuzpah'. 'At many points I could not help thinking *utinam Walter ipse scripsisset!*' (Benjamin and Scholem, *Briefwechsel 1933–1940*, p. 109).
60 When he republished this essay in 1958 in the *Neue Deutsche Hefte*, he added the dedication 'In memory of my mother, Maria Calvelli-Adorno'. She had died in New York in 1952, at the age of eighty-seven. [This essay, 'The Natural History of the Theatre', can be found in English in *Quasi una Fantasia*, pp. 65–78; trans.]
61 Benjamin and Adorno, *The Complete Correspondence 1928–1940*, p. 15.
62 Adorno, 'Die Idee der Naturgeschichte', *GS*, vol. 1, p. 345.
63 Ibid., p. 364.
64 Ibid., p. 365. This idea might well have served as motto for a book that Adorno was to write more than a decade later with Max Horkheimer. This was the *Philosophical Fragments*, which were published in 1947 with the title *Dialectic of Enlightenment*. Some of the ideas about the complex intertwining of history and myth in this pioneering study were already to be found in this early essay. In later years, Adorno gave his own view of this anticipation of his subsequent philosophical ideas. 'Much of what I wrote in my youth reads like a dreamlike anticipation, and it was only with a certain moment of shock, one that coincided with the emergence of the Hitlerian Reich, that I began properly to do what I have done.' Letter to Bloch, 26 July 1962, Frankfurt Adorno Archive; see also Rolf Tiedemann, 'Editorische Nachbemerkung', *GS*, vol. 1, p. 384.
65 There is now a bibliophile version of the *Berlin Childhood*, with an Afterword by Rolf Tiedemann: W. Benjamin, *Berliner Kindheit um Neunzehnhundert*.

66 Leo Löwenthal, *An Unmastered Past*, p. 68f. See also Martin Jay, *The Dialectical Imagination*, pp. 26–7; Alfred Schmidt, *Die Zeitschrift für Sozialforschung*, p. 5ff.
67 Max Horkheimer, 'Preface', *ZfS*, III, *GS*, vol. 3, p. 36ff.
68 Horkheimer's diagnosis was based on the following ideas: modern science is inextricably intertwined with the dominant society. This intertwining can be seen in the fact that science is not just a means of production, but functions as the most important productive force contributing to the creation of social wealth, admittedly only in accordance with the power available to particular social interests. These have a restrictive effect on the development of the sciences. 'Their application is sharply disproportionate to their high level of development and to the real needs of mankind.' The political control of the sciences is accompanied by an ideological control, that is to say, a tendency to disguise 'the true nature of a society built on antagonisms'. 'As an existing society is increasingly endangered by its internal tensions, the energies spent in maintaining an ideology grow greater and finally the weapons are readied for supporting it with violence.' The task of a science dedicated to truth and enlightenment is to expose these abuses. How can science go about making itself transparent? Only by means of the critique of ideology which is a precondition of a correct theory of the present situation. Max Horkheimer, 'Notes on Science and The Crisis', *Critical Theory and Society*, pp. 53 and 55.
69 Adorno, *Essays on Music*, p. 412.
70 Ibid., p. 414.
71 Ibid., p. 397f.
72 Ibid., pp. 410 and 416.
73 Ibid., p. 429.
74 Ibid., p. 430.
75 Adorno and Krenek, *Briefwechsel*, p. 29.
76 Ibid., p. 36f.
77 Ibid., p. 37.
78 Ibid., p. 38.
79 Adorno, *Essays on Music*, p. 401.
80 Adorno, 'Die Aktualität der Philosophie', *GS*, vol. 1, p. 341.
81 Adorno to Horkheimer, 2 November 1934, Horkheimer, *GS*, vol. 15, p. 201f; Adorno and Horkheimer, *Briefwechsel*, vol. 1, p. 22ff.; Adorno, 'Neue wertfreie Soziologie', *GS*, vol. 20.1, p. 13ff.
82 M. Horkheimer, *Between Philosophy and Social Science*, pp. 129–49.
83 Ibid., p. 145.
84 See Adorno, *Essays on Music*, pp. 404 and 407.
85 Karl Mannheim, *Die Gegenwartsaufgaben der Soziologie*, p. 41; see also Wolf Lepenies, *Die drei Kulturen*, p. 388ff.
86 Karl Mannheim, *Ideology and Utopia*, p. 38.
87 Benjamin and Adorno, *The Complete Correspondence 1928–1940*, p. 55.
88 Adorno to Horkheimer, 24 November 1934, Adorno and Horkheimer, *Briefwechsel*, vol. 1, p. 40.
89 Adorno, 'The Sociology of Knowledge and its Consciousness', *Prisms*, p. 43. This essay of 1953 is a revised version of a lecture given in 1950 with the title 'Über Mannheims Wissenssoziologie', which is based in its turn on his original critique of Mannheim. Adorno had written that

critique in 1937 for the *Zeitschrift für Sozialforschung*, but it was not published out of consideration for the plight of the émigrés, even though the article was already typeset. For the first version of his criticism of Mannheim, see Adorno, 'Neue wertfreie Soziologie: Aus Anlaß von Karl Mannheims *Mensch und Gesellschaft im Zeitalter des Umbaus'*, GS, vol. 20.1, p. 13ff.

90 Karl Mannheim, 'Heidelberger Briefe', p. 75.
91 See Benjamin and Adorno, *The Complete Correspondence 1928–1940*, p. 55f.
92 Adorno to Horkheimer, 19 February 1937, Adorno and Horkheimer, *Briefwechsel*, vol. 1, p. 288ff.
93 Adorno to Horkheimer, 28 February 1937, ibid., p. 301f.; see also Horkheimer, *Briefwechsel*, GS, vol. 16, p. 69f.
94 A letter from Adolf Löwe, an economist who had been on the faculty at Frankfurt University and who, having emigrated to Britain in 1933, worked as a lecturer in Manchester and London, makes it clear that Horkheimer was not averse to a rapprochement: 'I was in London last week and discussed the matter with Mannheim, putting your point of view. Although Mannheim had no objection to the publication of the critical article [by Adorno], and would even welcome the publication of a dispassionate discussion, he understands your formal reservations entirely. He especially appreciates the friendly feelings which led you to embargo the article, even though he would welcome the opportunity to discuss the issues of substance in some form or other. Perhaps you could find the time to write to him directly about the matter. I myself think it highly desirable to keep talking, particularly when there are serious disagreements. Otherwise, there is a danger that our family quarrels will make us forget the common front that we have been placed in by inclination and fate.' Horkheimer, *GS*, vol. 16, p. 387.
95 Ibid., p. 370f.
96 Adorno, 'Neue wertfreie Soziologie', *GS*, vol. 20.1, p. 31.
97 Adorno, 'The George–Hofmannsthal Correspondence, 1891–1906', *Prisms*, p. 204.
98 Rolf Tiedemann reports that forty-five notebooks have survived among his unpublished works. The earliest is dated 1932, the others were written between 1938 and 1939. These exercise books constitute a kind of philosophical diary, even though they also contain addresses, telephone numbers and appointments, as well as observations and ideas. According to Tiedemann, these notes 'appear shapeless, but in fact possess a form which is not unlike that of the fragments written by Novalis and Friedrich Schlegel. They might also be compared to the notes found in Nietzsche's posthumous papers.' *Frankfurter Adorno Blätter* VII, 2001, p. 9.
99 Adorno and Berg, *Briefwechsel 1925–1935*, p. 263.
100 Ibid., p. 263f.
101 See Adorno, *Kompositionen*, vol. 2, pp. 63–72.
102 In a letter to his closest friend, Gershom Scholem, on 28 February 1933, Benjamin wrote that, since 'the new regime' had seized power, 'it was scarcely possible to breathe any more; admittedly, this was a circumstance of diminished significance now that they had their hands round your throat.' Benjamin, *Gesammelte Briefe*, vol. IV, p. 162f.

103 Margarete Karplus to Benjamin, 24 September 1933, in Geret Luhr, '*Was noch begraben lag*': *Zu Walter Benjamins Exil: Briefe und Dokumente*, p. 87f.
104 Benjamin and Adorno, *The Complete Correspondence 1928–1940*, p. 24.
105 Adorno, *Der Schatz des Indianer-Joe*, p. 28f.
106 Ibid., p. 33. Cf. Adorno, *Minima Moralia*, p. 199f.
107 See Benjamin and Adorno, *The Complete Correspondence 1928–1940*, p. 10 and p. 12n. Adorno planned a theory of beggars but never wrote it. The beginnings of one can be seen in chapter 9 of the *Versuch über Wagner* of 1939: 'The threatening image of the beggar contains that of the rebel: by adopting the stance of the petitioner he has found himself a bourgeois home in Bohemian circles.' According to Adorno, the image of the beggar merges with that of God, because, like God, the beggar who has been dispossessed 'once had the opportunity to change the world and lost it. In the second place, . . . the rebel who appears as God goes over to the side of authority, and acts as the representative of the world that he ought to have changed' (*In Search of Wagner*, p. 135f).
108 Adorno, *Der Schatz des Indianer-Joe*, p. 58.
109 Ibid., p. 57.
110 Benjamin and Adorno, *The Complete Correspondence 1928–1940*, p. 26.
111 This novel deals with a group of seven children growing up in great freedom in Jamaica. On their journey home to England they are captured by pirates. During the long, adventurous journey on the pirates' schooner, a mutual respect gradually develops between the children and the pirates. After their rescue, the children smoothly adjust to being back to ordinary life in London, where they are feted, while the pirates are captured, put on trial and sentenced. What seems to have fascinated Adorno, apart from the unusual and exciting events of the story, are comments by Hughes: 'Of course, it is not really so cut and dried as all this; but often the only way of attempting to express the truth is to build it up, like a card house, of a pack of lies' (Richard Hughes, *A High Wind in Jamaica*, Leipzig, 1931, p. 155). The book originally appeared in 1929, followed by a German translation in 1931.
112 Adorno and Krenek, *Briefwechsel*, p. 56f.
113 The manuscript, in Adorno's own hand, is preserved in the Theodor W. Adorno Archive, Frankfurt am Main, KO, 213–4. For the printed version of the score, see *Kompositionen*, vol. 2, p. 69ff.
114 For a description and comment on the serial form, see Martin Hufner, *Adorno und die Zwölftontechnik*, p. 91. The two completed songs were performed in 1988 in the Alte Oper in Frankfurt, where they were recorded (Wergo 6173–2).

Part III A Twofold Exile

1 Adorno, 'Heine the Wound', *Notes to Literature*, vol. 1, p. 85.
2 The concentration camps harshly highlighted the criminal nature of the regime. The first camps were established in March and April 1933, as, for example, in Oranienburg near Berlin and Dachau near Munich. In the following months around seventy camps were set up. With the SA or SS

installed as guards, a brutal reign of terror began. See Wolfgang Benz, Hermann Graml and Hermann Weiß, *Enzyklopädie des Nationalsozialismus*, p. 284ff.

3 Adorno, *Minima Moralia*, p. 104.
4 Ibid., p. 33.
5 Ibid. Cf. also Adorno, 'Frage an die intellektuelle Emigration' (1945), *GS*, vol. 20.1, p. 352ff.
6 Adorno and Mann, *Briefwechsel 1943–1955*, p. 49.
7 Adorno, *Minima Moralia*, p. 26.
8 Adorno and Mann, *Briefwechsel 1943–1955*, p. 82.
9 Adorno, *Minima Moralia*, p. 87.
10 'Existential outsiders . . . are those who have been destined from birth to be outsiders.' The intentional outsiders are deliberate outsiders, 'transgressors. Anyone who crosses a frontier stands on the outside' (Hans Mayer, *Wir Außenseiter*, p. 16f.). Cf. also Hans Mayer, *Außenseiter*.
11 Adorno, *Minima Moralia*, pp. 27–8.
12 See Dirk Auer, 'Paria wider Willen: Adornos und Arendts Reflexionen auf den Ort des Intellektuellen'.
13 Adorno, *Minima Moralia*, p. 80.
14 Ibid., p. 33.
15 Ibid.
16 The family's finances had been exhausted by the economic difficulties experienced by Oscar Wiesengrund in managing his wine-merchant's business in National Socialist Germany. Wiesengrund had evidently succeeded in moving part of his assets to bank accounts abroad before his own emigration. When he left Germany, he was also able to take with him a small proportion of the sums he had raised by selling real estate. At an advanced age Adorno's parents emigrated via Cuba to the United States, where they were obliged to live from what remained of their assets.
17 See Stefan Müller-Doohm, *Die Soziologie Theodor W. Adornos*, as well as Stefan Müller-Doohm, 'Theodor W. Adorno', pp. 51–71.

Chapter 11 Adorno's Reluctant Emigration

1 See Detlev Peukert, *Die Weimarer Republik*; cf. Michael Burleigh, *The Third Reich*, p. 178ff.
2 Peter von Haselberg, 'Wiesengrund-Adorno', pp. 15 and 20.
3 Hans Mayer, who was in close touch with Horkheimer, comments on his clear-sightedness on political matters. According to Mayer he asked the right questions at the right time about the crisis of Weimar democracy. He was not satisfied with the simplistic interpretations of the left-wing parties: 'Horkheimer wanted to know the score. He and his associates were dispossessed by the Aryan legislation. The Jewish and obviously Marxist professor for social philosophy was instantly relieved of his post. Later, in Montagnola, he would talk about those days in March 1933. At the time, Adorno wanted them to remain in Germany to provide intellectual contraband with the help of the so-called slave language and with constant friends. Horkheimer's response was that they had to leave the country as quickly as possible! He was the son of an industrialist and, as a practical

man, knew what had to be done' (Hans Mayer, *Ein Deutscher auf Widerruf*, p. 182f.).

4 Erich Fromm, *Arbeiter und Angestellte am Vorabend des Dritten Reiches*, p. 52; cf. Wolfgang Bonß and Norbert Schindler, 'Kritische Theorie als interdisziplinärer Materialismus', p. 61; Bonß, *Die Einübung des Tatsachenblicks*.

5 See Fromm, *Arbeiter und Angestellte*, p. 42, n. 56.

6 Horkheimer, *Briefwechsel, GS*, vol. 15, p. 97.

7 Indeed, Adorno later complained to Horkheimer that 'in matters specifically affecting the institute he had frequently been confronted by a fait accompli . . . without any real involvement on his part.' Adorno to Horkheimer, 24 November 1934, ibid., p. 271.

8 Leo Löwenthal, *An Unmastered Past*, pp. 29–30.

9 Adorno and Berg, *Briefwechsel 1925–1935*, pp. 253 and 263f.

10 Ibid., p. 75.

11 See Adorno, 'Erinnerungen an Paul Tillich', p. 31.

12 Kracauer to Adorno, 26 April 1933, Kracauer's Literary Estate, Deutsches Literaturarchiv, Marbach.

13 This rejection also characterized his response as a 23-year-old when nationalist and clerical groups protested publicly against the Prague production of Berg's *Wozzeck*. Adorno hated every kind of irrationalism and reactionary thinking, and had a deep loathing for the mythologizing notions of the *Volk* at the heart of Nazi ideology.

14 The Archive of the Dean's Office of the Philosophical Faculty of the Johann Wolfgang Goethe University, Frankfurt, Adorno's personal file.

15 When Ludwig Landmann, Frankfurt's left-liberal mayor, was forced to resign in March 1933, the university lost one of its most important patrons and protectors. Friedrich Krebs, his Nazi successor, together with the Berlin state commissar, as well as August Wisser, the new registrar, and Ernst Krieck, the rector, completed the purge of the university in a few months.

16 More than a hundred members of staff responsible for teaching and research, i.e., over 30 per cent of the professors, were stripped of their chairs and their livelihoods. 'That was a significant loss of substance for the university and moreover a breach with an important tradition of scholarly effort unparalleled elsewhere in this way. The liberal, in some ways even left-wing, open-minded Frankfurt approach to science, which had consciously ventured on a number of innovations, could . . . no longer be sustained' (Notker Hammerstein, *Die Johann Wolfgang Goethe-Universität*, p. 221).

17 On 3 April 1933 Horkheimer wrote to Benjamin that 'prospects are not very favourable for Europe as a whole.' 'There is the risk of war, and in addition apathy is spreading rapidly, as is the hostility towards independent scientific research' (Horkheimer, *Briefwechsel, GS*, vol. 15, p. 99).

18 Adorno's occasional naivety in his dealings with the Hitler dictatorship went so far that, in two letters to Benjamin, who was in Paris, he advised him that he too should apply for membership of the Reich Chamber of Literature. Benjamin and Adorno, *The Complete Correspondence 1928–1940*, pp. 37 and 43.

19 The document is in the Theodor W. Adorno Archive, Frankfurt am Main.

20 See Micha Brumlik, 'Theologie und Messianismus im Denken Adornos', p. 36ff.; Joachim Perels, 'Verteidigung der Erinnerung im Angesicht ihrer Zerstörung – Theodor W. Adorno', p. 271ff.

21 Adorno, letter of January 1963 to the Frankfurt student newspaper *Diskus*, *GS*, vol. 19, p. 637.
22 Ernst Erich Noth, *Erinnerungen eines Deutschen*, p. 202.
23 Ibid.
24 Siegfried Kracauer, *Schriften*, vol. 5.3, p. 233; cf. also pp. 223ff., 186ff. and 107ff.
25 Kracauer to Adorno, 28 August 1930, Kracauer's Literary Estate, Deutsches Literaturarchiv, Marbach.
26 Peter von Haselberg, 'Wiesengrund-Adorno', p. 18.
27 Ibid., p. 20. The reader will recollect that Adorno had a Great Dane in his childhood.
28 Adorno and Krenek, *Briefwechsel*, p. 43.
29 Ibid.
30 Ibid., p. 44.
31 Adorno, 'On the Social Situation of Music', *Essays on Music*, p. 393.
32 Saul Friedländer, *Nazi Germany and the Jews: The Years of Persecution 1933–1939*, p. 60. 'Thirty-seven thousand of the approximately 525,000 Jews in Germany left the country in 1933; the majority tried to emigrate to the countries of Western Europe. In addition, there were the refugees who had left the land legally or illegally for political reasons. By the summer of 1933, fifty thousand people had been arrested in Germany, hundreds lost their lives.' Ibid., pp. 29 and 35 of the German edition.
33 See Adorno and Berg, *Briefwechsel 1925–1935*, p. 287; see also Friedländer, who points out that 'the Kulturbund played another role, unseen but no less real, which points to the future: as the first Jewish organization under the direct supervision of a Nazi overlord, it foreshadowed the Nazi ghetto, in which a pretence of internal autonomy camouflaged the total subordination of an appointed Jewish leadership to the dictates of its masters.' Saul Friedländer, *Nazi Germany and the Jews*, p. 66.
34 Ibid., p. 62.
35 During the First World War about 100,000 Jews served in the armed forces, 80,000 of them at the front out of a total population of 550,000 Jews in the Reich. See Ulrich Sieg, *Jüdische Intellektuelle im Ersten Weltkrieg*.
36 See Leo Löwenthal, *Mitmachen wollte ich nie*, p. 255.
37 Adorno, 'Die Freudsche Theorie und die Struktur der faschistischen Propaganda', p. 49.
38 See Andreas Hansert, *Bürgerpolitik und Kulturpolitik in Frankfurt am Main*, p. 188ff.
39 Benjamin and Adorno, *The Complete Correspondence 1928–1940*, p. 46.
40 Adorno to Löwenthal, 6 July 1934. See Löwenthal, *Mitmachen wollte ich nie*, p. 250ff.
41 Adorno, 'Notiz über Wagner', *GS*, vol. 18, p. 209.
42 Adorno, 'Farewell to Jazz', *Essays on Music*, p. 496. The thesis that jazz was in a process of dissolution was false despite the restrictions in Nazi Germany, where jazz was held to be a form of sabotage against German culture but showed no signs of disappearing. For example, the swing band of the Swiss Teddy Stauffer, the Original Teddys, kept on having engagements and enjoying commercial success. Moreover, the most important recordings of musicians such as Louis Armstrong, Count Basie, Tommy Dorsey, Duke Ellington and Coleman Hawkins appeared despite all the

propaganda against 'Negro jazz'. The distribution of records by Benny Goodman's popular band was not finally prohibited until 1937, when Goodman's Jewish origins became known. See Hans Dieter Schäfer, *Das gespaltene Bewußtsein: Deutsche Kultur- und Lebenswirklichkeit 1933–1945*, p. 171ff. Cf. Susanne Keval, *Widerstand und Selbstbehauptung in Frankfurt am Main*, p. 65ff.

43 Adorno, 'Farewell to Jazz', *Essays on Music*, p. 497.
44 From among Adorno's posthumous papers Rolf Tiedemann has unearthed an essay by Adorno called 'Radio Authority and the Broadcasting of Hit Music' (1933), which has not been included in the *Gesammelte Schriften*. In this short text, which the author may have intended for publication in the *Vossische Zeitung* but which in the event remained unpublished, Adorno suggested that the state ownership of radio should be used to improve the quality of the programmes. His line of argument is bizarre. He begins with the statement that, 'as an instrument of the state', the radio, which had been centralized by the Nazis, 'had . . . demonstrated a public, political force that no one had expected of the blaring accompaniment to domestic life' (*Frankfurter Adorno Blätter* VII, 2001, p. 90). It was only logical for 'alienated musical commodities' like jazz, hits and folk music 'to be given short shrift by the radio'. He came out in favour of a kind of music propaganda to improve the taste of listeners. If there was not enough demanding music, intermissions should be introduced. This would enable the listener to discover silence. 'And just think of the effect of a late Beethoven quartet, coming right after such a silence!' (p. 92). Adorno went even further. He proposed a decree banning the broadcasting of hit songs overnight and at the same time 'exposing' this trivial music 'to public *ridicule* . . . in short, the hit song will be *outlawed* with the aid of the irresistible methods available to a modern centralized system of propaganda' (p. 93). Even if we were charitably to suppose that Adorno had himself decided not to proceed with publication, it is hard to disagree with Rolf Tiedemann when he observes that these embarrassing comments are by no means 'free from the opportunism that is prepared to use the enemy's weapons for one's own purposes' (ibid., p. 95).
45 See 'Adorno's Kompositionskritik zu Herbert Müntzel', *GS*, vol. 19, p. 331f.
46 Out of interest in the personal motives and possible political intentions behind the open letter to Adorno, I traced the author and exchanged letters with him. Today he is a lecturer in psychology in the Fachhochschule in Munich, and he wrote to me in some detail about the exchange with Adorno and his own motives. He had learnt of Adorno's dubious review from Adorno's colleague in philosophy Wolfgang Cramer (who seems to have heard about it from Golo Mann). He wished to learn what Adorno had been thinking about 'when he tried to ingratiate himself, . . . presumably in the hope of being allowed to stay in Germany. In my opinion at the time, . . . since he was attempting to immunize a whole generation against the return of fascism, he should have . . . spoken out frankly about any conflicts he had had at the time, and perhaps have given some thought to how he might have acted if he had not been the son of a Jewish wine-merchant. It did not occur to me to try and prove that Adorno had any skeletons in the cupboard, to say nothing of anti-Semitic motives. . . . The

decision to ask Adorno publicly about his authorship, and to ask why he had been silent at the time, was one I took entirely on my own early in December 1962. On the other hand, it is true that I showed Cramer the draft of my open letter, Adorno's reply and my reply to his.' Schroeder indicated that a further reason for his public inquiry was his fear 'that the *political right* might have exploited the situation if Adorno had maintained his silence.' In retrospect, Schroeder thought it was obvious that he had made mistakes. He knew too little about Adorno's writings and had been naive about the unintended effects of his public letter. Furthermore, there were elements of projection in his attack on Adorno. The original letter of 3 January 1963 which Adorno wrote to Schroeder contains a passage that Adorno omitted from the published version after Schroeder in his reply of 8 January 1963 had objected to Adorno's 'implicit criticism' that he had allowed himself 'to be manipulated by reactionary circles'. The original text of Adorno's letter contained the lines: 'Dear Herr Schroeder, You say in your open letter that every effort must be made "to prevent people who would not scruple to make use of this information for their own disreputable purposes from getting hold of it". You probably do not know who has gone to the trouble of disinterring this business. As far as I know, it was an arch-reactionary and mortal enemy of modern music who wanted to "shoot me down". . . . The campaign was further orchestrated by another man who attributes the collapse of the Weimar Republic to supposedly subversive intellectuals, among whom he includes me. It is perhaps not unimportant to know this.' In his letter on this subject to Schroeder on 11 January 1963, Adorno wrote, 'I have always taken care not to keep reminding people of statements they made during the Hitler period, unless they were guilty of any real nastiness. When I attacked them . . . I was concerned about current tendencies, the potential for further damage.' Concurrently with this debate, *Diskus* was conducting a campaign against the Germanist Heinz Otto Burger, since incriminating documents about his activities in the Nazi period had been discovered. Following their campaign Burger resigned from his post as rector of the university.

47 Wolfgang Kraushaar (ed.), *Frankfurter Schule und Studentenbewegung*, vol. 2, p. 166. See also Heinz Steinert, *Die Entdeckung der Kulturindustrie*, p. 35ff.

48 Adorno, 'Editorisches Nachwort', *GS*, vol. 19, p. 638. Hannah Arendt, who had a lifelong antipathy towards the representatives of critical theory, and especially Horkheimer and Adorno, reacted very critically to Adorno's reply in *Diskus* in a letter she wrote to Karl Jaspers. 'Before I forget, I owe you a reply to your question about Adorno. His failed effort to fall into line [*Gleichschaltungsversuch*] in 1933 has been discovered by the Frankfurt student newspaper *Diskus*. He responded with an unspeakably wretched letter which deeply impressed the Germans' (Arendt and Jaspers, *Briefwechsel*, 1993, p. 679). A cynical and defamatory reaction to Adorno's open letter also appeared in the radical right-wing *Deutscher Studenten-Anzeiger* (4 May 1963).

49 Adorno, *Minima Moralia*, p. 192.

50 Adorno and Krenek, *Briefwechsel*, p. 44. Heinrich Gomperz, to whom Adorno refers here, was the professor of philosophy at the University of

Vienna and was in contact with Karl Popper. See Heinz Steinert, *Adorno in Wien*, pp. 30 and 150ff.

51   Benjamin and Adorno, *The Complete Correspondence 1928–1940*, p. 37.

Chapter 12 From Philosophy Lecturer to Advanced Student

1   The materials in the Bodleian Library reveal that Oscar Wiesengrund had established a wine-merchant's business in London for which he was looking for a partner in 1936. He had approached Walter Adams, who had recommended Hermann Hirsch for the post (in a letter of 5 February 1936). MS SPSL, 322/2, No. 138.

2   Evelyn Wilcock has researched the British connections of Oscar Wiesengrund and Adorno's Oxford years with great meticulousness over a number of years. Her publications based on the primary sources have been a great help in reconstructing Adorno's activities during this phase of his life. See Evelyn Wilcock, 'Adorno's Uncle' and 'Adorno in Oxford', and Andreas Kramer and Evelyn Wilcock, 'A Preserve for Professional Philosophers'.

3   At the end of the First World War political constraints forced Robert Wingfield to sell his shares in the business. The company manufactured parts for ships' screws without which the British navy would not have been able to match the speed of German ships. Since the company products were vital for the war effort, and because of the risk that property belonging to native Germans might be confiscated owing to the prevailing war hysteria, Wingfield finally gave in to the pressure and withdrew from this branch of production. Henceforth his business activities were confined to the Steam Fitting Company, specializing in measuring devices, thermostats, etc.

4   See Gerhard Hirschfeld, ' "The Defence of Learning and Science": Der Academic Assistance Council in Großbritannien und die wissenschaftliche Emigration aus Nazi-Deutschland', p. 28ff.

5   Adorno's entire correspondence with the AAC is preserved in the Bodleian Library in Oxford, where it can be inspected.

6   His younger brother, Peter Epstein, who had been born in 1901, was a musicologist married to a pianist. He had died as early as 1932.

7   See John P. Fox, 'Das nationalsozialistische Deutschland und die Emigration nach Großbritannien', p. 14ff.

8   Bodleian Library, MS SPSL, 322/2, No. 51.

9   Adorno and Berg, *Briefwechsel 1925–1935*, p. 297; Evelyn Wilcock, 'Alban Berg's Appeal to Edward Dent on behalf of Theodor Adorno', p. 365ff.

10 Letter of 12 March 1934, Bodleian Library, MS SPSL, 322/2, No. 65.

11 This was precisely what Professor Macmurray had recommended in his letter of 12 December 1933: 'With regard to Dr. Wiesengrund-Adorno I should judge from the papers you have sent me that his unusual combination of musical and philosophical ability should make him an acceptable member of academic society, particularly in Oxford or Cambridge, where philosophical specialization is possible. Since no financial obligation is incurred, I should think it possible that he might find an opportunity to

take part in University life in either place. A great deal would depend on the attractions of his own personality – of which I have no knowledge. He should I think come over to England as he suggests and be provided with introductions to proper persons, and left to find or create a place for himself. Professor Cassirer might be willing to introduce him to Oxford.' Bodleian Library, MS SPSL, 322/2, No. 56.

12 Bodleian Library, MS SPSL, 322/2, No. 81.
13 Adorno to Horkheimer, 24 November 1934. Horkheimer, *Briefwechsel, GS*, vol. 15, p. 272; Adorno and Berg, *Briefwechsel 1925–1935*, p. 297.
14 Adorno to Horkheimer, 2 November 1934. Horkheimer, *GS*, vol. 15, p. 262.
15 Bodleian Library, MS SPSL, 322/2, No. 94.
16 Adorno and Berg, *Briefwechsel 1925–1935*, p. 295.
17 His correspondence gives some indication of the constraints that he experienced. He frequently mentions that, like ordinary undergraduates, he had to 'keep terms', a concept unfamiliar to his correspondents in Germany. Similarly, the Oxford practice of ejecting students at the end of term meant that he, like them, had to return home for the vacations, and this was a financial necessity for him too. See Andreas Kramer and Evelyn Wilcock, 'A Preserve for Professional Philosophers', p. 127.
18 Alfred J. Ayer, *Part of my Life*, p. 153.
19 Bodleian Library, MS SPSL, 322/2, No. 153/155.
20 Adorno and Horkheimer, *Briefwechsel*, vol. 1, p. 85.
21 Ibid., p. 92.
22 Ibid., p. 66f.
23 Ibid., p. 92.
24 Adorno to Horkheimer, 24 November 1934 and also 21 March 1936. Horkheimer, *Briefwechsel, GS*, vol. 15, pp. 276 and 496.
25 It is true that his Husserl critique still contains 'Hegelian overtones. But over the next two-and-half years, Adorno largely frees himself from this even though this exposes him to some sharp criticism from Horkheimer.' Despite a certain amount of common ground in their criticism of Husserl, major differences separate Ryle and Adorno. While Ryle develops his arguments epistemologically, the critique of ideology stands at the forefront of Adorno's analysis. See Kramer and Wilcock, 'A Preserve for Professional Philosophers', pp. 154 and 160.
26 Oxford University Archive, Board of the Faculty of Literae Humaniores, File 'Wiesengrund-Adorno'.
27 Adorno to Horkheimer, 24 November 1934. Horkheimer, *GS*, vol. 15, p. 274. See also Adorno to Benjamin, 6 November 1934. Benjamin and Adorno, *The Complete Correspondence 1928–1940*, p. 55. He writes there: 'As far as my work on Husserl is concerned, I have simply marched on with my eyes blindfolded as if to the place of execution, which is perhaps not so entirely inappropriate for a logical contribution of this kind.'
28 Adorno and Krenek, *Briefwechsel*, p. 44.
29 See Andreas Kramer and Evelyn Wilcock, 'A Preserve for Professional Philosophers', p. 136ff.
30 See Evelyn Wilcock, 'Adorno in Oxford 1: Oxford University Musical Club', p. 11f.
31 Adorno and Berg, *Briefwechsel 1925–1935*, p. 296.

32 Adorno, 'Aus dem grünen Buch', West Drayton, 27 April 1934, *Frankfurter Adorno-Blätter* II, 1992, p. 7.
33 Adorno and Horkheimer, *Briefwechsel*, vol. 1, p. 18.
34 Ibid., p. 19.
35 'The Horkheimer circle arrived during a period in which the government was sympathetic towards intellectuals and prepared to entrust them with important tasks. It was a government which, by American standards, was left-wing, but at the same time successful and popular. The group arrived with a great deal of money, and at a moment when the numbers emigrating to the USA to escape the Nazis were still small.' Rolf Wiggershaus, *The Frankfurt School*, p. 148.
36 Even so, the Geneva branch was maintained, initially under Andries Sternheim and later under Juliette Favez. There was also a London branch under Jay Rumney, which had a small office in Le Play House belonging to the Institute of Sociology, as well as the Paris branch under Paul Honigsheim and Hans Klaus Brill, which was situated in the Centre de Documentation at the Ecole Normale Supérieure. The *Zeitschrift für Sozialforschung* appeared in the Librairie Félix Alcan in Paris until the outbreak of war.
37 See Martin Jay, *The Dialectical Imagination*, p. 115ff.; Wiggershaus, *The Frankfurt School*, pp. 133ff. and 149ff.
38 Adorno and Horkheimer, *Briefwechsel*, vol. 1, p. 25.
39 Ibid., p. 26.
40 Ibid., p. 36f.
41 Ibid., p. 64f.
42 Ibid., p. 49.
43 Ibid., p. 50.
44 See Adorno to Benjamin, 29 December 1935, and Benjamin's letter to Adorno of 7 February 1936. Benjamin and Adorno, *The Complete Correspondence 1928–1940*, pp. 120f. and 123f.
45 Adorno and Horkheimer, *Briefwechsel*, vol. 1, pp. 64 and 66.
46 Ibid., pp. 122 and 128ff.
47 Ibid., p. 185.
48 Ibid., p. 149.
49 Willi Reich was born in Vienna in 1895 and he died there in 1960. He studied composition and music theory with Alban Berg and Anton Webern. He published the journal *23: Eine Wiener Musikzeitschrift*. In 1935 he emigrated to Switzerland, where he worked first as a music critic for the *Neue Züricher Zeitung* and afterwards as lecturer and then professor at the polytechnic in Zurich.
50 Adorno, 'The Form of the Phonograph Record', *Essays on Music*, p. 279.
51 Ibid., p. 279f.
52 See Adorno, 'Zur Krisis der Musikkritik', *GS*, vol. 20.2, p. 746ff.
53 Martin Jay remarks, not unreasonably, that Adorno's essay on jazz contains 'occasionally outrageous assertions, made in an uncompromising manner designed less to persuade than to overwhelm. . . . Still, what must be remembered is that the jazz he was most concerned with was the commercial variety churned out by Tin Pan Alley, not the less popular variety rooted in black culture itself.' See Martin Jay, *The Dialectical Imagination*, p. 186f. See also Michael Kausch, *Kulturindustrie und*

Populärkultur, pp. 34ff. and 248; Heinz Steinert, *Die Entdeckung der Kulturindustrie*, p. 93ff.

54 Horkheimer emphasized this aspect in his praise of the jazz study. 'In your rigorous analysis of this seemingly insignificant phenomenon, you have made visible the whole of society with its contradictions. Your work . . . also has the merit of forestalling the erroneous belief that our method can only be applied to so-called major problems and all-embracing historical epochs.' Adorno and Horkheimer, *Briefwechsel*, vol. 1, p. 199.

55 Hektor Rottweiler, 'On Jazz', *Essays on Music*, p. 475.

56 Ibid., p. 485.

57 Ibid., p. 489.

58 Ibid., p. 485. In fact, despite Nazi propaganda against 'Jewish or nigger music', and despite the decrees of the Reich Culture Chamber banning it, there were opportunities to play jazz in Germany and to hear it privately. The young people who were enthusiastic about jazz were anti-Nazi for the most part, and this was expressed in their casual Anglophile lifestyle. See Susanne Keval, *Widerstand und Selbstbehauptung in Frankfurt am Main 1933–1945*, p. 66ff.

59 See Evelyn Wilcock, 'Adorno, Jazz and Racism: "Über Jazz" and the 1934–7 British Jazz Debate', pp. 63ff.

60 Evelyn Wilcock has shown that during his Oxford years Adorno had ample opportunity to become acquainted with the jazz of the day. Jazz was an integral part of the student culture with which Adorno was in contact when he participated in the social life of the university city, which in fact he did. He would even have been able to hear black jazz musicians live in one or other of the London clubs, as well as the greats of American jazz, such as Louis Armstrong, Coleman Hawkins and Duke Ellington, all of whom gave performances in Britain. See ibid., p. 63ff.

61 See Nick Chadwick, 'Mátyás Seiber's Collaboration in Adorno's Jazz Project', pp. 275 and 268.

62 See Heinz Steinert, *Die Entdeckung der Kunstindustrie*, pp. 63ff. and 94ff; see also Nick Chadwick, 'Mátyás Seiber's Collaboration in Adorno's Jazz Project', p. 259ff.

63 With the findings about the latent authoritarian attitudes of manual and non-manual workers, Horkheimer, together with Erich Fromm, had launched a major psychoanalytically orientated study about the origins and impact of authoritarianism. This was the product of the last phase of the institute's activity in Frankfurt. On the one hand, the aim was to investigate authority as a socially integrating factor, a factor for social bonding. On the other, the family was to be studied as the social institution in which specific (sado-masochistic) character-structures supplied the foundations for an authoritarian disposition. This was an ambitious empirical project, and its results appeared in 1936 in Paris with the title *Studies on Authority and the Family* in the series put out by the Institute of Social Research. Attempts were made to tackle the subject with a variety of analytical techniques. A report was compiled on the literature on authority and the family. At the same time, a series of specialized studies was initiated in a number of countries, examining the economic, legal and political situation of the family. Furthermore, surveys were

undertaken on the relations between the stability or instability of the family and the authoritarian views of its members. On the basis of the data collected by these methods, a generalized sociological account was drawn up of the problem of authority from a historical point of view. See Wolfgang Bonß, *Die Einübung des Tatsachenblicks*, p. 175; Rolf Wiggershaus, *The Frankfurt School*, p. 149ff.; Martin Jay, *The Dialectical Imagination*, p. 124ff.

64 The typescript is in the Theodor W. Adorno Archive in Frankfurt (Ts 22300–22322). Nick Chadwick was the first person to explore the collaboration between Adorno and Seiber on this subject. He has examined Seiber's papers, which were housed in the British Library following Seiber's death in 1960. In the course of his research he came across unpublished letters of Adorno's. See Nick Chadwick, 'Mátyás Seiber's Collaboration in Adorno's Jazz Project', p. 259ff.; see also Evelyn Wilcock, 'The Dating of Seiber', p. 264ff.

65 The idea that the jazz orchestra was a copulation machine had also been used in the article for the *Zeitschrift für Sozialforschung*, but this passage had been deleted by the editors. See Adorno and Horkheimer, *Briefwechsel*, vol. 1, p. 199.

66 Steinert has criticized Adorno's idea that 'syncopation represents premature ejaculation'. Jazz embodies something much deeper, namely 'the shift of emphasis on the beat from the European norm. In addition, you find a number of overlapping rhythms so that the different emphases interfere with one another and cancel one another out.' This is not adequately encapsulated either in the simplistic formula of 'premature ejaculation', or by 'analogies taken from the theory of instinctual drives in general'. Heinz Steinert, *Die Entdeckung der Kulturindustrie*, p. 108f.

67 See Nick Chadwick, 'Mátyás Seiber's Collaboration in Adorno's Jazz Project', p. 275.

68 Ibid., p. 285.

69 See Adorno, *Moments Musicaux: Impromptus*, GS, vol. 17, p. 100ff.

70 Ibid., p. 102.

71 Benjamin and Adorno, *The Complete Correspondence 1928–1940*, p. 132. He gave Horkheimer a rather more modest description of his essay: 'Needless to say, the whole thing is mainly important as a methodological model of a materialist analysis of a conveniently observable superstructural phenomenon.' Adorno and Horkheimer, *Briefwechsel*, vol. 1, p. 220.

72 Benjamin and Adorno, *The Complete Correspondence 1928–1940*, p. 62.

73 Adorno and Horkheimer, *Briefwechsel*, vol. 1, pp. 427 and 429.

74 Ibid., p. 456.

75 Theodor W. Adorno Archive, Frankfurt am Main (Ts 3221). He published the texts that arose from his three-year-long preoccupation with Husserl in Oxford in revised form in 1956 with the title *Against Epistemology: A Metacritique – Studies in Husserl and the Phenomenological Antinomies*. In the same context we should mention the essay version 'Zur Philosophie Husserls' and the later, shorter text 'Husserl and the Problem of Idealism', which was published in the *Journal of Philosophy* in the United States in 1940. See Adorno, *Against Epistemology*; 'Zur Philosophie Husserls', *GS*, vol. 20.1, p. 46ff; 'Husserl and the Problem of Idealism', ibid., p. 119ff.

76 Adorno and Horkheimer, *Briefwechsel*, vol. 1, p. 41.
77 Adorno, *Against Epistemology: A Metacritique – Studies in Husserl and the Phenomenological Antinomies*, p. 6 [translation amended].
78 Adorno's criticism of the philosophy of origins, namely that 'the reduction of one thing to the other is not possible without giving rise to a paradox', also contains the germ of a critique of essentialism. For, according to Bonacker, 'the idea of a dialectics that sets out with an intrinsic analysis and advances by a process of negation . . . aims at dissolving entities that seem to be clearly delimited and immediately given' (Thorsten Bonacker, *Die normative Kraft der Kontingenz: Nichtessentialistische Gesellschaftskritik nach Weber und Adorno*, p. 145ff.).
79 Adorno, *Against Epistemology*, p. 20 [translation altered].
80 Ibid., p. 23. Bonacker points out that Adorno links rationalism with idealism and empiricism with ontology and realism. Thorsten Bonacker, *Die normative Kraft der Kontingenz*, p. 142.
81 Adorno, *Against Epistemology*, p. 25.
82 Ibid., p. 26.
83 Ibid., p. 24. On the concept of 'dialectics without dialectics', see Alexander García Duttmann, *Das Gedächtnis des Denkens: Versuch über Heidegger und Adorno*, p. 90f.
84 Adorno, *Against Epistemology*, p. 27.
85 Ibid., p. 123.
86 Ibid., p. 36f.
87 Adorno, 'Zur Philosophie Husserls', *GS*, vol. 20.1, p. 62.
88 Adorno, *Against Epistemology*, p. 234 [translation altered].
89 Adorno and Horkheimer, *Briefwechsel*, vol. 1, p. 101.
90 Horkheimer's book had appeared in Switzerland under the pseudonym Heinrich Regius. It contained notes from the last years of the Weimar Republic. In 1934 Adorno wrote to Löwenthal, 'I have now read this book a number of times with close attention, and have been greatly impressed by it. . . . I find myself identifying almost completely with it, so much so that I would be hard put to put my finger on points of difference. What was especially new and important to me is what I would describe as his interpretation of the problem of personal contingency as opposed to the thesis of radical justice, and in general his critique of static anthropology in every respect. One ought perhaps at some point to speak generally about our relation to enlightenment.' Adorno to Löwenthal, 6 July 1934. See Löwenthal, *Mitmachen wollte ich nie*, p. 253f.
91 Horkheimer's title, 'Dämmerung' ('Twilight'), conveys this sense of pessimism rather better, perhaps, than 'Dawn and Decline', the actual title of the English translation [trans.].
92 'The capitalist system in its present phase is organized exploitation on a world-wide scale. Its preservation creates boundless suffering. . . . Things are so complicated that English textile workers profit from the hunger of the Indian pariah and the drudgery of Chinese coolies, and that work in Bacon's and Galilei's science serves the interests of today's armaments industry. . . . Every thought, every show of sympathy, every relationship, every minor or major act *against* the ruling class involves the risk of personal disadvantage. Every thought, every show of sympathy, every relationship and every act *on its behalf*, i.e., on behalf of the world-wide

apparatus of exploitation, means an opportunity. People who want to get somewhere must early acquire beliefs which enable them to have a good conscience as they do what reality demands, for if they do it *contre coeur*, it will be noticed by others and they will perform badly. The system affects everything, down to the most delicate tendrils of the individual's soul. It has placed a premium on vileness' (M. Horkheimer, *Dawn and Decline*, p. 30f.).

93 Adorno to Horkheimer, 25 February 1935. Horkheimer, *GS*, vol. 15, p. 131; Adorno and Horkheimer, *Briefwechsel*, vol. 1, p. 57.

94 Adorno, *Minima Moralia*, p. 46.

95 Adorno and Horkheimer, *Briefwechsel*, vol. 1, p. 81f.

96 Adorno and Krenek, *Briefwechsel*, p. 91.

97 Linguistically, this essay is very different from an older one with the title 'Mahler Today' that appeared in *Anbruch* in 1930. There, in opposition to a premature classification of Mahler's works as romantic, he described them as 'salvaging the formal cosmos of Western music . . . by combining the ruins of its basest elements with its supreme truths.' In this first analysis of Mahler's music Adorno tried to establish a link with Arnold Schoenberg. Both composers were said to use different methods to protest 'against the bourgeois symmetry of form'. Both shared the technique of variation. Adorno, 'Mahler heute', *GS*, vol. 18, pp. 228 and 232.

98 Adorno, 'Marginalien zu Mahler', *GS*, vol. 18, pp. 235 and 238.

99 See Adorno, *Alban Berg: Master of the Smallest Link*, pp. 32–3.

100 Adorno and Berg, *Briefwechsel 1925–1935*, p. 324.

101 Only the *Symphonic Pieces* from *Lulu* were played in Berlin in November 1934, in a performance conducted by Erich Kleiber.

102 Soma Morgenstern, *Alban Berg und seine Idole*, p. 368.

103 Alban Berg was superstitious about numbers. He thought 23 was a lucky number. When he survived the 23rd of December in hospital, even though he had a high fever, he had every hope that he would recover, despite the worsening of his condition. See Willi Reich, *Alban Berg*, 1963, p. 95ff.

104 Soma Morgenstern, *Alban Berg und seine Idole*, p. 371.

105 Adorno was uncertain later on who had been the first to mention Wedekind's plays to Berg. 'I cannot say with certainty whether it was I who first pointed him towards *Lulu*, as it now seems to me upon reflection; in such cases it is easy to err out of narcissism. In any case I brought all my arguments to bear on behalf of the Wedekind opera' (Adorno, *Berg: The Master of the Smallest Link*, p. 26). Morgenstern wrote to Berg as early as 28 August 1928: 'I feel . . . as responsible for *Lulu* as if I had seduced her for you and would soon have to be shot by her' (Soma Morgenstern, *Alban Berg und seine Idole*, p. 215).

106 Ibid., p. 112f.

107 Adorno, *Berg: The Master of the Smallest Link*, p. 11.

108 Adorno and Krenek, *Briefwechsel*, p. 105.

109 Soma Morgenstern, *Alban Berg und seine Idole*, p. 376.

110 Constantin Floros, *Alban Berg und Hanna Fuchs*, p. 77.

111 Ibid.

112 Adorno was in fact one of the few people Berg had initiated into his secret. Even when he was still studying with Berg in Vienna he knew of

Berg's feelings for a married woman, feelings he attempted to conceal from his wife.

113 Adorno, *Berg: Master of the Smallest Link*, p. 124.
114 We are speaking here of two texts, *Erinnerung an den Lebenden* and 'The *Lulu* Symphony', which was first published in *23: Eine Wiener Musikzeitschrift*, nos. 24–5, 1936. This issue bore the subtitle 'In Memory of Alban Berg'. See Adorno, *Berg: Master of the Smallest Link*, pp. 9–34 and 120–5.
115 Adorno and Krenek, *Briefwechsel*, p. 108f.
116 Adorno, *Berg: The Master of the Smallest Link*, p. 130.
117 As early as February 1925, a few weeks after meeting Hanna Fuchs, Berg wrote to her: 'Will I be allowed to find the peace of mind to express in music what I have experienced in and since those days in Prague-Bubeníč? . . . What I would like best, would be to compose songs. But how can I? The words of the text would betray me. So it will have to be songs without words which only the person in the know – only you – will be able to read. Perhaps it will turn out to be a string quartet! These four movements will contain everything I have felt from the moment I entered your house. From (1) the first hours, and days and evenings spent among you in the faint, noble gleam of contemplation, (2) through the silently and ever more sweetly burgeoning love I have felt for you, (3) through the bliss of that half hour and the entire eternity of that morning, (4) to the torpid, icy night of separation, of being alone, of utter hopelessness, renunciation and desolation.' Constantin Floros, *Alban Berg und Hanna Fuchs*, p. 32.
118 Adorno, *Berg: Master of the Smallest Link*, p. 104.
119 Ibid., p. 109f.
120 Constantin Floros, *Alban Berg und Hanna Fuchs*, p. 45; see also p. 126f.
121 Adorno and Berg, *Briefwechsel 1925–1935*, p. 332. Elsewhere Adorno wrote that Berg's love affairs 'were a part of his "production apparatus" from the very outset' (Adorno, 'Im Gedächtnis an Alban Berg', *GS*, vol. 18, p. 490).
122 Adorno and Berg, *Briefwechsel*, p. 333.
123 Ibid., p. 334.
124 Adorno and Krenek, *Briefwechsel*, p. 112.
125 Ibid.
126 Adorno and Horkheimer, *Briefwechsel*, vol. 1, p. 280f.
127 Adorno thought highly of Willi Reich as Berg's secretary and former pupil. He was 'a delightful man', as he wrote to Benjamin, 'like a sort of travel junction' with a great many contacts in Vienna. See Benjamin and Adorno, *The Complete Correspondence 1928–1940*, p. 160.
128 These were his analyses of the Piano Sonata, op. 1, the *Four Songs*, op. 2, the *Seven Early Songs*, the String Quartet, op. 3, the *Four Pieces for Clarinet and Piano*, op. 5, the *Lyric Suite* arranged for string quartet, and the concert aria '*Der Wein*'. See Willi Reich, *Alban Berg*.
129 Adorno and Krenek, *Briefwechsel*, p. 111f.
130 Adorno and Horkheimer, *Briefwechsel*, vol. 1, p. 132.
131 Benjamin and Adorno, *The Complete Correspondence 1928–1940*, p. 122.

Chapter 13 Debates with Benjamin, Sohn-Rethel and Kracauer

1 'Initially, until the middle of 1935, Benjamin lived in a series of hotels in the 16th, 6th and 14th arrondissements. For a short time he was a guest in homes of his sister Dora, who had also emigrated to Paris. From August or September 1935 to June 1937, he had a furnished room in Montparnasse, at 23 rue Bénard. . . . In September 1937, on his return from a stay in San Remo, he found the room had been rented to someone else and had to move out to the suburb of Boulogne for four months, where an acquaintance let him have a servant's room for the time being. The room looked out onto a main road which was too loud for him to concentrate on work. Not until January 1938 did Benjamin succeed in finding somewhere to live on his own; a studio in 10 rue Dombasle in the 15th arrondissement' (Rolf Tiedemann, 'Zeugnisse der Entstehungsgeschichte', in Benjamin, *Das Passagen-Werk*, *GS*, vol. V.2, p. 1144.

2 The New York Institute of Social Research declared the arcades project to be an integral part of its research plans from 1936 on, and included it in the report on its activities under the heading of *Études sur l'histoire de la culture française*. Benjamin was listed there among the 'research associates'. See Rolf Wiggershaus, *The Frankfurt School*, p. 163f.

3 'The covered shopping arcades of the nineteenth century were Benjamin's central image because they were the precise material replica of the internal consciousness, or rather the *un*conscious of the dreaming collective. All the errors of bourgeois consciousness could be found there (commodity fetishism, reification, the world as "inwardness"), as well as (in fashion, prostitution, gambling) all of its utopian dreams. Moreover, the arcades were the first international style of modern architecture, hence part of the lived experience of a worldwide, metropolitan generation' (Susan Buck-Morss, *The Dialectics of Seeing*, p. 39).

4 Benjamin and Adorno, *The Complete Correspondence 1928–1940*, p. 84.

5 Ibid.

6 Ibid., p. 85.

7 Ibid.

8 W. Benjamin, *Das Passagen-Werk*, *GS*, vol. V.2, p. 1112.

9 W. Benjamin, *The Arcades Project*, p. 7.

10 Ibid.

11 Ibid., p. 4f.

12 Ibid., p. 10.

13 Benjamin and Adorno, *The Complete Correspondence 1928–1940*, pp. 105 and 107.

14 Ibid., p. 92.

15 Ibid., p. 106.

16 See Rolf Tiedemann, 'Zeugnisse zur Entstehungsgeschichte', in Benjamin, *Das Passagen-Werk*, *GS*, vol. V.2, pp. 1206ff., and especially pp. 1237ff. and 1255ff.

17 Benjamin had started work on it in autumn 1935 and had produced several versions subsequently. See ibid., p. 1145.

18 On 30 June 1936 Benjamin wrote to Adorno that their 'respective investigations, like two different headlamps trained upon the same object from

opposite directions, have served to reveal the outline and character of contemporary art in a more thoroughly original and much more significant manner than anything hitherto attempted.' Benjamin and Adorno, *The Complete Correspondence 1928–1940*, p. 144.

19 Benjamin to Gretel Adorno, 9 October 1935, in Benjamin, *Das Passagen-Werk*, *GS*, vol. V.2, p. 1148.

20 Benjamin defined aura as 'the unique phenomenon of a distance, however close it may be. If, while resting on a summer afternoon, you follow with your eyes a mountain range on the horizon or a branch which casts its shadow over you, you experience the aura of these mountains, of that branch' (Benjamin, *Illuminations*, p. 224f.).

21 Walter Benjamin, *Selected Writings*, vol. 3, p. 104.

22 Ibid., pp. 223 and 226.

23 Ibid., p. 244.

24 See Benjamin's letter of 9 November 1935 to Horkheimer, cited in Rolf Tiedemann, 'Zeugnisse zur Entstehungsgeschichte', Benjamin, *Das Passagen-Werk*, *GS*, vol. V.2, p. 1151.

25 Benjamin and Adorno, *The Complete Correspondence 1928–1940*, p. 128.

26 Ibid., p. 129.

27 Ibid., p. 130.

28 Ibid.

29 Ibid., p. 131. It should be noted that Brecht, too, reacted sceptically to Benjamin's essay on 'The Work of Art'. He bluntly rejected the concept of aura entirely. In the *Journals*, he observes that 'the aura . . . is supposed to be in decline of late, along with the cult element in life. b[enjamin] has discovered this while analysing films, where the aura is decomposed by the reproducibility of the art-work. a load of mysticism, although his attitude is against mysticism. this is the way the materialist understanding of history is adapted. it is abominable' (Brecht, *Journals 1934–1955*, p. 10). Benjamin was friendly with Brecht, whom he knew from Berlin, just as he knew Adorno. Benjamin spent several weeks in Brecht's house in Svendborg in the summer of both 1936 and 1938. See Gershom Scholem, *Walter Benjamin: Die Geschichte einer Freundschaft*, p. 198ff.

30 Benjamin and Adorno, *The Complete Correspondence 1928–1940*, p. 146f.

31 Ibid., pp. 194 and 331.

32 Adorno, 'Im Jeu de Paume gekritzelt', *GS*, vol. 10, p. 321ff.

33 This was a collection of letters by German scholars between the years 1783 and 1883. See Benjamin, *Selected Writings*, vol. 3, pp. 167–235.

34 See Benjamin and Adorno, *The Complete Correspondence 1928–1940*, p. 146.

35 Ibid., p. 193. See also Adorno's 'Einleitung zu Benjamins "Schriften"', *GS*, vol. 11, p. 574ff.

36 Adorno and Horkheimer, *Briefwechsel*, vol. 1, p. 131f. [A *Wandervogel* was a hiker or rambler. It referred to the youth movement of the early twentieth century. Benjamin was an enthusiastic member before the First World War; trans.]

37 See Michael Pauen, 'Der Protest ist Schweigen', p. 1428ff.

38 See Alfred Sohn-Rethel, *Warenform und Denkform: Aufsätze*.

39 Adorno and Horkheimer, *Briefwechsel*, vol. 1, p. 225.

40 Ibid., p. 187. In 1970 Sohn-Rethel recollected that Adorno had asked Horkheimer to give this task to Benjamin. That was not so easy, according

to Sohn-Rethel: 'It is difficult to imagine today just how hard it was to overcome Benjamin's mistrust of and resistance to other people's ideas. Adorno warned me when we first met in Paris to discuss ideas with Benjamin that "you have to force-feed him with them; it is worse than feeding a Strasbourg goose." Benjamin could only gradually be induced to abandon his resistance and be brought round to a more sympathetic response' (Alfred Sohn-Rethel, *Warenform und Denkform: Aufsätze*, p. 87f.).

41 Adorno and Sohn-Rethel, *Briefwechsel*, p. 10f.
42 Ibid., pp. 21 and 24. Cf. also Alfred Sohn-Rethel, *Geistige und körperliche Arbeit: Zur Epistemologie der abendländischen Geschichte*, p. 131ff.
43 Adorno and Sohn-Rethel, *Briefwechsel*, p. 32.
44 Ibid., p. 23. See also Adorno and Horkheimer, *Briefwechsel*, vol. 1, p. 225.
45 Ibid., p. 226.
46 Ibid., p. 227.
47 Ibid.
48 Horkheimer to Sohn-Rethel, 25 November 1936. Horkheimer, *Briefwechsel, GS*, vol. 15, p. 746.
49 Adorno and Horkheimer, *Briefwechsel*, vol. 1, p. 249.
50 Ibid.
51 Benjamin and Adorno, *The Complete Correspondence 1928–1940*, p. 235.
52 Sohn-Rethel regarded Adorno, along with George Thompson and John D. Bernal, as a great supporter of his claim that the transcendental subject was to be discovered in the commodity form. In an interview, he said that 'Adorno's death was a terrible blow for me since he was my main supporter in Germany. When he died [on 6 August 1969] I flew to Frankfurt and was present at the funeral' (Sohn-Rethel, 'Einige Unterbrechungen waren wirklich unnötig', pp. 280ff. and 283ff.). Adorno noted in his magnum opus: 'Not only the pure I is ontically transmitted by the empirical I, the unmistakably pellucid model of the first version of the deduction of purely rational concepts; the transcendental principle itself, the supposed "first principle" of philosophy as against existing reality, is so transmitted. Alfred Sohn-Rethel was the first to point out that hidden in this principle, in the general and necessary activity of the mind, lies work of an inalienably social nature' (Adorno, *Negative Dialectics*, p. 177; translation altered).
53 Adorno and Horkheimer, *Briefwechsel*, vol. 1, p. 272; cf. also pp. 327f. and 357f.
54 See Adorno and Sohn-Rethel, *Briefwechsel*, p. 37 and p. 67f.
55 Adorno and Horkheimer, *Briefwechsel*, vol. 1, p. 222.
56 Martin Jay, 'Massenkultur und deutsche intellektuelle Emigration: Der Fall Max Horkheimer und Siegfried Kracauer', p. 230.
57 Adorno and Horkheimer, *Briefwechsel*, vol. 1, pp. 185 and 294.
58 See *Marbacher Magazin*, 47, 1988, p. 85; cf. Momme Brodersen, *Siegfried Kracauer*, p. 98ff.
59 Kracauer to Adorno, 20 August 1938. Kracauer's Literary Estate, Deutsches Literaturarchiv, Marbach.
60 *Wiener Zeitung*, 18 May 1937.
61 Kracauer to Adorno, 25 May 1937. Kracauer's Literary Estate, Deutsches Literaturarchiv, Marbach.

62 Adorno, 'Siegfried Kracauer, *Jacques Offenbach und das Paris seiner Zeit'*, *GS*, vol. 19, p. 363ff.
63 Benjamin and Adorno, *The Complete Correspondence 1928–1940*, p. 184.
64 Ibid., p. 186 (translation slightly amended).
65 Adorno and Horkheimer, *Briefwechsel*, vol. 1, p. 354.
66 Max Horkheimer, 'Traditionelle und kritische Theorie', *ZfS*, VI, 2, 1937, p. 245ff.; *GS*, vol. 4, p. 162.
67 Adorno, *Minima Moralia*, p. 33.
68 Ibid., p. 28.
69 Adorno and Horkheimer, *Briefwechsel*, vol. 1, pp. 43 and 228.
70 Ibid., p. 478.
71 An excellent account of Heidegger's role in the Third Reich has been provided by Rüdiger Safranski in *Martin Heidegger*, p. 228ff.; see also Victor Farías, *Heidegger und der Nationalsozialismus*. Among the professors in Frankfurt University resistance to Nazi rule and the 'purging' of the university was minimal. Instead, 'the professors mainly kept their heads down and tried to maintain their status in a politics-free existence so as to continue their research' (Notker Hammerstein, *Die Johann Wolfgang Goethe-Universität*, pp. 186, 188ff. and 320ff.). In reality the situation in the Arts Faculty had changed completely. With Tillich's chair now vacant, it was filled temporarily by Arnold Gehlen and Gerhard Krüger. Then, in 1935, with Heidegger's assistance, the opportunistic Hans Lipps was appointed. He was followed as *Privatdozent* by Karl Schlechta, who for a time was also cultural adviser on the city council. The chair for philosophy and education was given to the Nazi Josef Nelis. See ibid., p. 361ff.
72 Adorno to Willy Hartner, 29 December 1961, *Frankfurter Adorno Blätter*, VII, 2003, p. 95. Hartner, who was two years Adorno's junior, had been a close friend since their youth. He had studied 'astronomy, chemistry and mathematics, as well as oriental and Far Eastern languages at the universities of Frankfurt, Oslo and Paris'. He was guest professor at Harvard between 1935 and 1937. 'Hartner never joined the Party or any of its organizations. Inwardly, he felt no sympathy towards it. Nevertheless, he was appointed lecturer and acted as deputy director at the China Institute in 1940.' After the war, he was appointed to a chair in the history of science. Adorno often sought his advice, as an experienced and influential friend, on academic matters, when he himself was professor in Frankfurt. See Notker Hammerstein, *Die Johann Wolfgang Goethe-Universität*, p. 518ff.
73 Adorno and Horkheimer, *Briefwechsel*, vol. 1, p. 85.
74 Ibid., p. 66. In his letter of 13 May 1935, he wrote to Horkheimer, 'Nor can I deny that I feel under an obligation to marry Gretel, if only to save her from this hell.'
75 These laws decreed that 'persons with three or four Jewish grandparents were full-Jews; those with two "Aryan" and two Jewish grandparents were "half-Jews"'. Michael Burleigh, *The Third Reich*, p. 295f.
76 Adorno and Horkeimer, *Briefwechsel*, vol. 1, p. 341.
77 Ibid.
78 Benjamin and Adorno, *The Complete Correspondence 1928–1940*, pp. 150–1.

79 In 1936 Oscar Wiesengrund resigned from his post as manager of the Daehne company in Leipzig; two years later he sold his property in Seeheim, as can be seen from the documents of the Municipal Archives of Seeheim/Jugenheim.

80 Adorno and Horkheimer, *Briefwechsel*, vol. 1, p. 272.

81 Ibid., p. 292f.

82 Ibid., p. 292.

83 Ibid., p. 308.

84 Home Office File No. SPSL 44/2, 190–224, No. 219.

85 Opie was an economist and had translated Joseph Schumpeter's *The Theory of Economic Development* into English. He was among the Englishmen with whom Adorno had managed to develop a closer relationship in Oxford. As so often, the foundation of their friendship was music, which Opie, who taught at Magdalen, tried to promote in the university.

86 See Adorno and Horkheimer, *Briefwechsel*, vol. 1, p. 324ff.

87 Benjamin and Adorno, *The Complete Correspondence 1928–1940*, p. 180.

88 In a letter to Horkheimer, Adorno argued that 'the fundamental error in my view lies in his inexperience in the things in question; he [Löwenthal] applies ready-made categories to them, instead of entering into a genuine interaction with the subject in hand. At any rate, I would recommend the greatest possible caution in dealing with such an enormously difficult case as Hamsun. It is childishly easy to show that Hamsun is a fascist, but just as hard to make this insight productive, and what is hardest of all is to save Hamsun from himself' (Adorno and Horkheimer, *Briefwechsel*, vol. 1, p. 346).

89 He summed up his objections to Marcuse's concept of culture as follows: 'The image of art appears in all essentials to be that of Weimar classicism; I would like to know how he would cope with the *Liaisons dangereuses* or with Baudelaire, to say nothing of Kafka or Schoenberg. It appears to me that art has an entire stratum – the crucial one, in fact – that he ignores completely. That is the stratum of *knowledge* in the sense of what cannot be acquired by bourgeois science. The roses strewn through life – that will really only do for the sixth form; and the dialectical counter-motif that the art of a bad reality provides a contrast to the ideal is much too tenuous to approach the decisive products of art' (ibid., p. 355).

90 Ibid., p. 344.

91 The reproaches of Hannah Arendt that Adorno and Horkheimer had failed to give Benjamin adequate support in exile in Paris, and had only ever exploited him for the purposes of the institute (cf. Elizabeth Young-Brühl, *Hannah Arendt*, p. 241), are untenable in the light of the correspondence published up to now. Jürgen Habermas rightly pointed out after the publication of the Adorno–Benjamin letters that this correspondence 'provided a convincing refutation of the accusations advanced by Hannah Arendt' (Jürgen Habermas, 'Das Falsche im Eigenen: Der Briefwechsel zwischen Theodor W. Adorno und Walter Benjamin', p. 77).

92 Adorno and Horkheimer, *Briefwechsel*, vol. 1, p. 367.

93 Ibid.

94 Ibid., p. 374.

95 See Horkheimer, 'Der neueste Angriff auf die Metaphysik', *ZfS*, VI, 1, p. 4ff, and 'Traditionelle und kritische Theorie', *ZfS*, VI, 2, p. 245ff., and also *GS*, vol. 4, pp. 108ff. and 162ff.

96   Adorno and Horkheimer, *Briefwechsel*, vol. 1, p. 571f.
97   Benjamin and Adorno, *The Complete Correspondence 1928–1940*, p. 208.
98   Adorno to Löwenthal, 15 September 1937. Löwenthal Archive, Stadt-
     und Universitätsbibliothek, Frankfurt am Main.
99   Adorno to Löwenthal, 1 October 1937. Ibid.
100 Adorno to Fromm, 16 November 1937. Adorno and Horkheimer,
     Briefwechsel, vol. 1, p. 541ff.
101 See Adorno, *Minima Moralia*, p. 95f. Three decades later, in the context
     of his diagnosis of late capitalist society, Herbert Marcuse produced sim-
     ilar ideas under the heading of a theory of 'repressive tolerance'. See
     Marcuse, *One-Dimensional Man*; 'Repressive Tolerance', in H. Marcuse,
     R. P. Wolff and Barrington Moore Jr., *A Critique of Pure Tolerance*.
102 Between 1937 and 1938 the Dow Jones lost 49 per cent of its value. The
     bear market lasted twelve months and twenty-two days. In March 1938
     the economy was revived by a spending programme. One cause of the
     recession was a wave of strikes and labour disputes which involved almost
     two million people by the end of 1937. This had led President Roosevelt,
     who had been re-elected in 1936, to come out in favour of a law regulating
     wages and working hours. See David M. Kennedy, *Freedom from Fear:
     The American People in Depression and War 1929–1945*, p. 286ff.
103 Adorno and Horkheimer, *Briefwechsel*, vol. 1, pp. 416 and 422f.
104 Benjamin and Adorno, *The Complete Correspondence 1928–1940*, p. 213.
105 Adorno and Horkheimer, *Briefwechsel*, vol. 1, p. 448.
106 See ibid., p. 472; Benjamin and Adorno, *The Complete Correspondence
     1928–1940*, p. 229.
107 Ibid., p. 228.
108 Ibid., p. 229.
109 Adorno and Horkheimer, *Briefwechsel*, vol. 1, p. 480.
110 Benjamin to Horkheimer, 6 January 1938. Horkheimer, *Briefwechsel, GS*,
     vol. 16, p. 360.
111 In this essay he explored the reasons why the struggle for social justice
     was always linked in the history of bourgeois emancipation with the
     suppression of the individual's search for happiness. In the process he
     reconstructed the outlines of an optimistic and a pessimistic anthropology
     whose common denominator was the condemnation of egoism. 'The
     tabooing of "common" pleasure has succeeded so well that the average
     citizen who allows himself any becomes shabby instead of free, crude
     instead of grateful, stupid instead of clever' (Horkheimer, 'Egoismus und
     Freiheitsbewegung', *ZfS*, V, 1936, p. 172; *GS*, vol. 6, p. 9ff.). Adorno was
     'deeply moved and gripped' by this essay of Horkheimer's. 'I would like
     especially to emphasize our agreement in our view of those revolutionar-
     ies who take over bourgeois morality in a positive spirit. . . . The language
     you use is a particular confirmation of your essay for me. . . . It is as if in
     your hands even the tactic of keeping silent is transformed into a means of
     expression: the entire essay throbs with what has not been said. It seems
     to me that our stylistic ideals are no longer so far removed from each
     other' (Adorno and Horkheimer, *Briefwechsel*, vol. 1, p. 174f.).
112 Ibid., p. 438f.; cf. p. 492ff.
113 Adorno, *Fragmente über Wagner*, *ZfS*, I, 2, 1939, p. 1ff. The complete
     manuscript was not published for another thirteen years. It appeared in

1952 with the title *Versuch über Wagner* (*GS*, vol. 13, p. 11ff. [Eng. trans.: *In Search of Wagner*, 1981.]) The text that Adorno himself called an essay was integrated by Rolf Tiedemann into the *Gesammelte Schriften* in vol. 13, *The Music Monographs*. This corresponded to Adorno's own express wish. Cf. also Adorno's letter of 8 February 1938 to Horkheimer, *Briefwechsel*, *GS*, vol. 16, p. 383. On the book's reception, see Richard Klein, *Der Kampf mit dem Höllenfürst*, p. 167ff.; on Wagner, see Martin Gregor-Dellin, *Richard Wagner*, and Barry Millington, *The Wagner Compendium*.

114 Ideological critique (*Ideologiekritik*), as Adorno understands it, attempts to reveal the way in which mental artefacts are mediated by their historical and social conditions. He defines ideological critique as the attempt to uncover the social content of phenomena by means of an immanent mode of analysis in which concept and object are related to each other. The task is 'by analysing a form and its meaning to comprehend the contradiction between its objective idea and what it pretends to, and to name whatever the consistency or inconsistency of artefacts tells us about the nature of existence' (Adorno, 'Kulturkritik und Gesellschaft', *GS*, vol. 10.1, p. 27; see also *Prisms*, p. 32).

115 Adorno, *In Search of Wagner*, p. 47.

116 Adorno dedicated the Wagner book to Gretel. The dedication also had an epigraph: 'Horses are the survivors of the age of heroes.' When speaking to Horkheimer and also his parents, Adorno often referred to Gretel and himself as 'horses'.

117 Ibid., pp. 17 and 25.

118 Klein points out that, 'in his analysis of the relation between individual instruments and the ways in which they merge in the orchestra, . . . Adorno attempted the first systematic description of the basic problems of orchestration in the nineteenth century.' Adorno was able to show 'how Wagner's technique of continuously blended sound was developed by combining a radical de-individualization of the individual colours simultaneously with an extreme individualization of the total sound' (Klein, *Der Kampf mit dem Höllenfürst*, p. 183f.).

119 Adorno, *In Search of Wagner*, p. 63.

120 Ibid., p. 85.

121 Ibid., p. 136f.

122 Ibid., p. 154f.; see also 'Selbstanzeige des Essaybuchs "Versuch über Wagner"', *GS*, vol. 13, p. 506.

123 Ibid.

124 Benjamin evidently knew that while Adorno was in Oxford he had intended to write an essay about decadence; as a motto he had envisaged a line from Trakl's *Heiterer Frühling*, which he often quoted: '*Wie scheint doch alles Werdende so krank*' ('How everything that grows seems struck with sickness'). Benjamin and Adorno, *The Complete Correspondence 1928–1940*, p. 259.

125 Ibid., p. 265.

126 Adorno and Krenek, *Briefwechsel*, p. 128. [Eugenie Marlitt (1825–87) was a highly popular writer of what are usually regarded as sub-literary novels. Her novels are now forgotten; trans.]

127 On the occasion of this lecture, Horkheimer, the author of *Traditional and Critical Theory*, warned Adorno urgently 'to speak in a highly scientistic

manner and not to say a word that could be given a political interpretation. Expressions such as "materialist" should be avoided like the plague. . . . Your lecture should avoid . . . giving the impression that accusations about the materialism of the institute are in any way justified. Make every effort to talk as simply as possible. Complexity is always suspect' (Adorno and Horkheimer, *Briefwechsel*, vol. 1, p. 513).

128 Ibid., p. 498.
129 Ibid., p. 515.
130 Adorno, 'Im Jeu de Paume gekritzelt', *GS*, vol. 10, p. 325.
131 Adorno to his mother, 24 September 1950, Theodor W. Adorno Archive, Frankfurt am Main; Adorno, 'Amorbach', *GS*, vol. 10, p. 304.
132 Horkheimer, *Briefwechsel*, *GS*, vol. 16, p. 392.

Chapter 14 Adorno's Path to Social Research

1 Adorno and his wife had made the ocean crossing on the *Champlain*, a steamer of 28,094 tonnes and a capacity of 1086 passengers. The boat struck a German mine and sank off La Pallice in 1940.
2 At this time, compared with other countries, the USA had relatively liberal immigration laws. Furthermore, America was 'younger, less constrained by rigid traditions, and had a more open social structure which enabled different nationalities to co-exist . . . It was elastic enough to enable it to absorb alien elements' (Helge Pross, *Die deutsche akademische Emigration nach den Vereinigten Staaten 1933–1941*, p. 33). Up to the outbreak of the Second World War around 100,000 people fled from Germany and Austria to the USA, 7.3 per cent of whom were members of the academic professions. New York was the centre for immigrant intellectuals. Cf. Klaus Mann, *Der Wendepunkt*, p. 377, and also Joachim Radkau, *Die deutsche Emigration in den USA*, p. 23ff.
3 See Adorno, 'Scientific Experiences of a European Scholar in America', in *Critical Models*, p. 216f.
4 Benjamin and Adorno, *The Complete Correspondence 1928–1940*, p. 241.
5 Adorno to Horkheimer, 28 June 1938, Horkheimer–Pollock Archive, Stadt- und Universitätsbibliothek, Frankfurt am Main.
6 A sister of Rudolf Kolisch and Gertrud Schoenberg.
7 Egon Wissing was a doctor, a cousin of Walter Benjamin, who had married Liselotte Karplus, a dentist.
8 Adorno to Horkheimer, 10 August 1941; also Gretel Adorno to Horkheimer, 19 August 1941, Horkheimer–Pollock Archive, Stadt- und Universitätsbibliothek, Frankfurt am Main.
9 The volume with Grab's stories was reissued in 1995; one story, 'The Attorney's Office', is dedicated to Theodor and Gretel Adorno. Hermann Grab, *Hochzeit in Brooklyn*, p. 115.
10 Adorno to Horkheimer, 18 August 1940, Horkheimer–Pollock Archive, Stadt- und Universitätsbibliothek, Frankfurt am Main.
11 See Adorno and Krenek, *Briefwechsel*, p. 129f.
12 Adorno, 'Amorbach', *GS*, vol. 10, p. 304ff.
13 Benjamin and Adorno, *The Complete Correspondence 1928–1940*, p. 265.

14　See Helmut Dubiel, *Wissenschaftsorganisation und politische Erfahrung*, p. 87ff.

15　Adorno, 'Kein Abenteuer', *GS*, vol. 20.2, p. 585f. Material for an 'iconography of exile' can be found in the memoirs of Hans Sahl, *Das Exil im Exil*, p. 130ff.

16　Adorno, 'Scientific Experiences of a European Scholar in America', in *Critical Models*, pp. 218–19.

17　Ibid., p. 215.

18　See Ernst Krenek, 'Bemerkungen zur Rundfunkmusik', *ZfS*, VII, 1/2, 1938, p. 148ff. Adorno was familiar with the manuscript version of this essay; he hoped to be able to use it to help Krenek find a position in the radio research project.

19　In his essay 'The Radio Symphony', which Adorno wrote in English, he translated *Hörstreifen* literally as 'hear-stripe'. I felt that 'noise band' conveys his intention more felicitously [trans.].

20　Adorno to Lazarsfeld, 24 January 1938, Horkheimer–Pollock Archive, Stadt- und Universitätsbibliothek, Frankfurt am Main; cf. Paul Lazarsfeld, 'Eine Episode in der Geschichte der empirischen Sozialforschung', p. 179ff.; see also Adorno, 'Über die musikalische Verwendung des Radios', *GS*, vol. 15, p. 369ff; David E. Morrison, 'Kultur and Culture: The Case of Theodor W. Adorno and Paul F. Lazarsfeld', p. 339ff.

21　Hadley Cantrill, together with Gordon Allport, had published a book with the title *The Psychology of Radio* (New York and London, 1935). Frank Stanton was research director of the Columbia Broadcasting System.

22　This project laid the foundations for modern media research. In addition to Lazarsfeld, this is associated with such names as Herta Herzog, Joseph Klapper, Bernard Berelson, Charles Osgood and Samuel Stouffer. See Wilbur Schramm, *Grundfragen der Kommunikationsforschung*.

23　On what follows, see Martin Jay, *The Dialectical Imagination*, p. 235ff.; Rolf Wiggershaus, *The Frankfurt School*, p. 248ff.; Michael Kausch, *Kulturindustrie und Populärkultur*, p. 34ff.

24　In later years, Lazarsfeld had a brilliant career as the founder and director of the Bureau of Applied Social Research, as well as being an expert in the field of empirical social research whose methods of standardized surveys and attitude measurement enjoyed widespread success in the USA of the 1930s. The scientific products of his advanced quantitative sociological studies, making use of panels and multidimensional measurements, can be seen in *The People's Choice* and *The American Soldier*, studies which Lazarsfeld designed and carried out with a variety of researchers.

25　See Paul Lazarsfeld, 'Eine Episode in der Geschichte der Sozialforschung', p. 179ff.

26　Walter Benjamin had developed the 'listening models' for the South-West German Radio in Frankfurt and for the Berlin *Funkstunde*. In addition to the discussion of recent literary publications, he produced the listening models on the analogy of Brecht's Epic Theatre. His intentions were didactic and aimed to oppose consumerist attitudes towards the new medium. 'A form of radio transformed into a dialogical medium should abolish the *separation between performers and audience* and in this way become the model for a new people's art.' Bernd Witte, *Walter Benjamin*, p. 88; Benjamin, *Drei Hörmodelle*.

27 Adorno, 'Scientific Experiences of a European Scholar in America', in *Critical Models*, p. 219.
28 Adorno to Lazarsfeld, 21 March 1938, Löwenthal Archive, Stadt- und Universitätsbibliothek, Frankfurt am Main. The texts arising from the radio research project can be found in the Theodor W. Adorno Archive, Frankfurt am Main (Ts 51320ff.).
29 Adorno, 'Scientific Experiences of a European Scholar in America', in *Critical Models*, p. 219.
30 Ibid., p. 223.
31 Paul Lazarsfeld, 'Eine Episode in der Geschichte der empirischen Sozialforschung', p. 176.
32 Adorno to Lazarsfeld, 21 March 1938, Löwenthal Archive, Stadt- und Universitätsbibliothek, Frankfurt am Main. Both of Adorno's exposés 'Fragen und Thesen' of January and February 1938 have been published in the *Frankfurter Adorno Blätter*, VII, 2003, pp. 97ff. and 114ff.
33 A photocopy of the original with Lazarsfeld's notes is in the archive of Columbia University (Butler Library). I have examined the typescript in the archive and excerpted essential portions of it. The texts that Adorno wrote arising from the radio research project and collected for publication in 1940 (Theodor W. Adorno Archive, Frankfurt am Main, Ts 49565) under the title of *Current of Music: Elements of a Radio Theory* are due to appear in 2005 as volume 3 of the *Nachgelassene Schriften*. They are being edited by Robert Hullot-Kentor. The Theodor W. Adorno Archive is general editor of the *Nachgelassene Schriften*.
34 Adorno, 'Music in Radio', Archive of Columbia University (Butler Library), 1938, p. 93f.
35 Ibid., p. 123.
36 Ibid., p. 132.
37 Adorno and Krenek, *Briefwechsel*, p. 130; Benjamin and Adorno, *Briefwechsel*, p. 326.
38 Archive of Columbia University (Butler Library).
39 Undated letter from Lazarsfeld [in his English], Löwenthal Archive, Stadt- und Universitätsbibliothek, Frankfurt am Main. See also Martin Jay, *The Dialectical Imagination*, pp. 222–3.
40 Wolfgang Bonß, *Die Einübung des Tatsachenblicks*, p. 194ff.
41 Adorno to Lazarsfeld, 6 September 1938, Horkheimer Archive, Stadt- und Universitätsbibliothek, Frankfurt am Main.
42 'Über den Fetischcharakter in der Musik und die Regression des Hörens', *ZfS*, VII, 3, p. 222ff. (*GS*, vol. 14, p. 14ff.); 'Versuch über Wagner', *ZfS*, VIII, 8, p. 1ff. (*GS*, vol. 13, p. 7ff.).
43 The concept of fetish-character is taken from Karl Marx's *Critique of Political Economy*. What he means by it is not just the overvaluation of an object (fetishism), but that, when translated into the form of money, commodities acquire a social function, a social character. As the products of labour, they exercise power over their producers, who are fixated on the money value of what they have themselves produced. By operating as a mediating factor, money thus becomes independent, the autonomous goal of the social process.
   In psychoanalysis regression refers to the reversion to an earlier stage of functioning, e.g., to a prior libidinal stage, to earlier object relations,

identifications. Freud first made use of the concept in *The Interpretation of Dreams* (1900), where he explains that the energy which in waking life would be discharged in action is compelled by the inhibitions operative in sleep to 'regress' to the sense-organs, provoking hallucinations.

44 See Lucia Sziborsky, *Adornos Musikphilosophie*, chs 5 and 6, p. 113ff.; Max Paddison, *Adorno's Aesthetics of Music*, p. 184ff.

45 Adorno, 'On the Fetish-Character in Music and the Regression of Listening', in *Essays on Music*, p. 293.

46 Ibid., p. 292.

47 Ibid., p. 307.

48 A year after the essay was published, Adorno confessed to Benjamin that, if it had a weakness, it 'consists, to put it crudely, in the tendency to indulge in Jeremiads and polemics' (Benjamin and Adorno, *The Complete Correspondence 1928–1940*, p. 305).

49 Adorno, 'Scientific Experiences of a European Scholar in America', in *Critical Models*, p. 224.

50 Ibid., p. 219.

51 Ibid., p. 221.

52 See David Morrison, 'Kultur and Culture: The Case of Theodor W. Adorno and Paul F. Lazarsfeld', p. 343ff.

53 Adorno, 'Scientific Experiences of a European Scholar in America', in *Critical Models*, p. 223.

54 See Paul Lazarsfeld, 'Eine Episode in der Geschichte der empirischen Sozialforschung', p. 203. Lazarsfeld subsequently reproached himself for not having tried harder to integrate Adorno's theoretical and methodological innovations into the empirical research process.

55 Horkheimer, *Briefwechsel, GS*, vol. 16, p. 534f.

56 Paul Lazarsfeld, 'Eine Episode in der Geschichte der empirischen Sozialforschung', p. 202.

57 Lazarsfeld to Marshall, 9 June 1941, Rockefeller Archives.

58 Theodor W. Adorno Archive, Frankfurt am Main, Ts 49863.

59 Ibid., Ts 50500.

60 The English-language explanation of 'right listening' was as follows: 'Right listening means above all the overcoming of the current false listening. This current false listening may be roughly defined as atomistic or gustatory listening: as the dwelling on individual "tunes" out of which a piece is built or as the tasting of individual harmonic or instrumental stimuli' (ibid., Ts 50429).

61 Ibid., Ts 50102; cf. Adorno, 'Theory of Pseudo-Culture', p. 31ff.; see also Adorno, *Zu einer Theorie der musikalischen Reproduktion, NaS*, vol. 2.

62 See Adorno, 'Über die musikalische Verwendung des Radios', *GS*, vol. 15, p. 369ff. Two decades later, he judged his study as follows: 'Indeed one of the central ideas proved to be obsolete: my thesis that the radio symphony was not a symphony any more, which I derived from the technological transformations of sound quality due to the recording tape still prevalent in radio at the time and which has since largely been overcome by the techniques of high fidelity and stereophonics. Yet I believe that this affects neither the theory of atomistic listening nor that of the particular "image character" of music on the radio, which has survived the earlier distortion of sound' (Adorno, 'Scientific Experiences of a European Scholar in America', in *Critical Models*, p. 227).

63 The text was first published in the *Kenyon Review* in 1945. See also Thomas Y. Levin and Michael von der Linn, 'Elements of a Radio Theory: Adorno and the Princeton Radio Research Project'.
64 See ibid., p. 316ff., as well as Adorno, 'Die gewürdigte Musik', *GS*, vol. 15, p. 163ff.
65 Adorno, 'Scientific Experiences of a European Scholar in America', in *Critical Models*, p. 227.
66 See Horkheimer, 'Der neueste Angriff auf die Metaphysik', *GS*, vol. 4, p. 103ff.
67 Horkheimer to Benjamin, 23 February 1939. Horkheimer, *Briefwechsel*, *GS*, vol. 16, p. 567.
68 Horkheimer to Ernst Bloch, 17 March 1938, ibid., p. 413.
69 Horkheimer to Adorno, 11 September 1938, ibid., p. 478.
70 Ferdinand Kramer (1898–1985) was a member of the Deutscher Werkbund and belonged to an influential group associated with the chief architect in Frankfurt, Ernst May. In 1937, he was expelled from his profession by the Nazis and he emigrated to New York with his Jewish wife Beate. In the early 1950s, he returned to Frankfurt at the urging of Max Horkheimer and played an important part in the reconstruction of Frankfurt University. Between 1952 and 1964 Kramer and his associates were responsible for the planning and building of twenty-one university buildings. Ferdinand and Beate Kramer were both on friendly terms with Adorno. The two families remained in touch even after Kramer's second marriage, to Lore Koehn. I have this information from a conversation with Lore Kramer in May 2002.
71 See Ferdinand Kramer, *Der Charme des Sytematischen*, p. 53ff.
72 Adorno, *Minima Moralia*, p. 88.
73 Rainer Erd (ed.), *Reform und Resignation: Gespräche über Franz L. Neumann*, p. 99.
74 Henryk Grossmann (1881–1950) was not involved in any of the institute's empirical projects. He devoted his entire life to researching the laws governing the accumulation of capital and the collapse of the capitalist system. In 1949 he was appointed to a chair in political economy at the University of Leipzig. Karl August Wittfogel (1890–1988) had been the China expert of the KPD since 1920. After the Stalin–Hitler Pact he left the party and became an American citizen in 1941. In 1947 he was appointed to a chair in Chinese history in Seattle.
75 According to Pollock, for the period between 1933 and 1942, some $200,000 was disbursed in the form of grants, chiefly to émigré scholars. See Pollock, 'Memorandum for P. T. [Paul Tillich] on Certain Questions Regarding the Institute of Social Research', Max Horkheimer Archive, Stadt- und Universitätsbibliothek, Frankfurt am Main.
76 See Franz Neumann, *Behemoth*; Otto Kirchheimer, *Politische Herrschaft*, and *Von der Weimarer Republik zum Faschismus*; see also Alfons Söllner, *Geschichte und Herrschaft*, p. 86ff.
77 Marcuse's writings during the New York years, and which he was able to publish in the *Zeitschrift für Sozialforschung*, have been collected and republished in Marcuse, *Kultur und Gesellschaft*, and also *Ideen zu einer kritischen Theorie der Gesellschaft*.
78 As originally planned, the book was to be titled *Charles Baudelaire: A Lyric Poet in the Era of High Capitalism*. The book was never completed,

but Benjamin produced two essays, 'The Paris of the Second Empire in Baudelaire' and 'Some Motifs in Baudelaire'. The latter appeared in the *Zeitschrift für Sozialforschung* in 1940. See Tiedemann and Schweppenhäuser, 'Anmerkungen der Herausgeber', in Benjamin, *GS*, vol. 1.3, p. 509ff.; Susan Buck-Morss, *The Dialectics of Seeing*, pp. 49ff and 177ff.

79 See Benjamin, *Gesammelte Briefe*, vol. VI, pp. 164ff., 162f. and 168ff.

80 Benjamin and Adorno, *The Complete Correspondence 1928–1940*, p. 277f.

81 Ibid., p. 282.

82 Ibid., p. 283.

83 Ibid., p. 284.

84 Ibid., p. 282.

85 Ibid., p. 284.

86 Ibid., p. 283.

87 Benjamin, *Gesammelte Briefe*, vol. VI, p. 217.

88 Benjamin and Adorno, *The Complete Correspondence 1928–1940*, p. 294.

89 Ibid., p. 291.

90 Adorno, 'On the Fetish-Character in Music and the Regression of Listening', *Essays on Music*, p. 295f.

91 Benjamin and Adorno, *The Complete Correspondence 1928–1940*, p. 295f.

92 Adorno, 'On the Fetish-Character in Music and the Regression of Listening', *Essays on Music*, p. 314.

93 Benjamin and Adorno, *The Complete Correspondence 1928–1940*, p. 296.

94 Adorno, 'Interimsbescheid', *GS*, vol. 20.1, p. 185.

95 These suggestions referred *inter alia* to the historical interpretations of the arcades and the *flâneur*, the subterranean relations between Poe, Balzac and Daumier, and the decline of the bourgeois type in mass society which has its complement in the caricatures of typical characters. For the first version, see Benjamin, 'The Paris of the Second Empire in Charles Baudelaire', in *Charles Baudelaire: A Lyric Poet in the Era of High Capitalism*, pp. 9–106.

96 See Benjamin and Adorno, *The Complete Correspondence 1928–1940*, p. 299ff.; see also Benjamin, 'Some Motifs in Baudelaire', in *Charles Baudelaire: A Lyric Poet in the Era of High Capitalism*, pp. 107–54. The editor's note points out that 'Adorno's incisive criticism was immensely productive for the further development of Benjamin's Baudelaire project' (Benjamin, *GS*, vol. 1.3, p. 1064).

97 In *Minima Moralia*, Adorno described this mode of theory construction as specific to a dialectical form of presentation: 'In a philosophical text all the propositions ought to be equally close to the centre' (*Minima Moralia*, p. 71). Adorno uses analogous formulations to describe the style of modern music (see *Philosophie der modernen Musik*, *GS*, vol. 12, p. 73). The letter to Benjamin contains another passage used later on by Adorno in his book of aphorisms: 'I am convinced that our own best thoughts are invariably those that we cannot entirely think through' (Benjamin and Adorno, *The Complete Correspondence 1928–1940*, p. 321). In *Minima Moralia* he writes: 'True thoughts are those alone which do not understand themselves' (*Minima Moralia*, p. 192).

98 This essay consisted essentially of a contrast between 'two modes of cognition' which led to two contrasting 'types of knowledge'. 'On the one hand stood "traditional" [theory], i.e., bourgeois science, which according

to Horkheimer traced its lineage back to Descartes' rational model of knowledge and which continued down to the present in the form of scientific theory. On the other hand stood "critical" or "materialist" theory, as developed by Karl Marx in the *Critique of Political Economy*, as a mode of knowledge that comprehends both theory and practice' (Wolfgang Bonß, *Die Einübung des Tatsachenblicks*, p. 189).

99 See Horkheimer, 'Diskussionen über die Differenz zwischen Positivismus und materialistischer Dialektik', *GS*, vol. 12, pp. 437ff. and 494ff.
100 Horkheimer, *Briefwechsel*, *GS*, vol. 16, p. 734.
101 Ibid., p. 745.
102 See Benjamin and Adorno, *The Complete Correspondence 1928–1940*, p. 323f.
103 The present author learnt about this from Elisabeth Reinhuber-Adorno.
104 Benjamin, *Gesammelte Briefe*, vol. VI, pp. 335ff. and 341ff.
105 See Adrienne Monnier, *Aufzeichnungen aus der Rue de l'Odéon*, pp. 149ff. and 243ff.
106 Horkheimer, *Briefwechsel*, *GS*, vol. 16, p. 764.
107 Ibid., p. 726. For Adorno's use of the metaphor of the message in a bottle, see *The Philosophy of Modern Music*, p. 133, where it is translated as a 'surviving message of despair from the shipwrecked'.
108 See *Studies in Philosophy and Social Science*, VIII, 3, p. 413ff.; quoted in Horkheimer, *GS*, vol. 2, p. 217ff.
109 Even before his internment in summer 1939, Benjamin had accepted an invitation from Horkheimer and agreed to go to New York for an extended stay. A visitor's visa was already waiting for him in the American consulate. Encouraged by Gretel, he had begun to take English lessons in a small private circle. His fellow students included Hannah Arendt and her future husband Heinrich Blücher – the couple lived quite close to Benjamin. See Benjamin, *Gesammelte Briefe*, vol. VI, p. 379.
110 The photographer Henny Gurland was related through her second husband, Raffael Gurland, to the economist Arkady R. L. Gurland, who was for some time active in the institute in New York. Henny's third husband was Erich Fromm.
111 See Lisa Fittko, *Mein Weg über die Pyrenäen: Erinnerungen 1940/41*, p. 130ff.
112 See Rolf Tiedemann, 'Zeugnisse zur Entstehungsgeschichte', in Benjamin, *GS*, vol. V.2, p. 1183ff.
113 Benjamin and Adorno, *The Complete Correspondence 1928–1940*, p. 342.
114 See Adorno, 'Zu Benjamins Gedächtnis', *GS*, vol. 20.1, p. 170.
115 Adorno to Scholem, 19 November 1940, *Frankfurter Adorno Blätter*, V, 1998, p. 150ff.
116 Their last meeting lay two years in the past and had taken place on the mole at San Remo. See Adorno, *Interimsbescheid*, *GS*, vol. 20.1, p. 186.
117 Adorno, 'Erinnerungen', *GS*, vol. 20.1, p. 178.
118 Adorno, 'Zu Benjamins Gedächtnis', *GS*, vol. 20.1, p. 169.
119 Adorno to Scholem, 19 November 1940, *Frankfurter Adorno Blätter*, V, 1998, p. 151.
120 Horkheimer, *Briefwechsel*, *GS*, vol. 16, p. 96.
121 See *ZfS*, IX, 1941, p. 121ff.; Horkheimer, 'Zur Tätigkeit des Instituts: Forschungsprojekt über Antisemitismus', *GS*, vol. 4, p. 373ff.

122 Horkheimer, *Briefwechsel, GS*, vol. 17, p. 82.
123 Ibid., p. 95.
124 Horkheimer, *Briefwechsel, GS*, vol. 16, p. 761ff. Adorno's ideas about the prehistory of anti-Semitism were later integrated into the final chapter of *Dialectic of Enlightenment.*
125 Adorno had doubts about Pollock's assertion that totalitarian state capitalism would be the form of rule of future societies and that there was no alternative to this. He remarked that Pollock's theory was 'an inversion of Kafka. . . . Kafka had depicted the hierarchy of offices as hell. Here hell is transformed into a hierarchy of offices.' Horkheimer, *Briefwechsel, GS*, vol. 17, p. 54.
126 Helmut Dubiel points out that 'for Adorno and Horkheimer the advantage of Pollock's theory was that, whereas they had failed to discriminate between politics and economics, his analysis suggested that rule in highly developed industrial societies no longer assumed economic forms – as under liberalism – but instead was directly political in form – as in the pre-bourgeois era.' Dubiel, *Wissenschaftsorganisation und politische Erfahrung*, p. 99ff; see also pp. 61ff. and 94ff. For the debate on theories of fascism, see also Alfons Söllner, *Geschichte und Herrschaft*, p. 88ff.; Rolf Wiggershaus, *The Frankfurt School*, p. 280ff.; Dubiel and Söllner (eds), *Wirtschaft, Recht und Staat im Nationalsozialismus*, p. 7ff; Barbara Brick and Moishe Postone, 'Kritischer Pessimismus und die Grenzen des traditionellen Marxismus', p. 179ff.
127 Horkheimer, 'Die Juden in Europa', *GS*, vol. 4, p. 308f.
128 Horkheimer, 'Der Autoritäre Staat', *GS*, vol. 5, p. 300.
129 Horkheimer, 'Vernunft und Selbsterhaltung', *GS*, vol. 5, p. 348.
130 The paper 'Reflexionen zur Klassentheorie' of 1942 was not published at the time and only appeared posthumously, in *GS*, vol. 8, p. 373ff., here p. 376.
131 Adorno later expressed his diagnosis of the problem of the working class in the form of an ironic question: 'Sociologists, however, find themselves confronted with the grimly comic riddle: just where is the proletariat?' The aphorism entitled 'Puzzle Picture' in *Minima Moralia* is directly related to the 'Reflections on Class Theory'. Adorno, *Minima Moralia*, p. 193f.
132 Adorno, *Dialectic of Enlightenment*, p. xi.
133 Horkheimer to Adorno, 12 June 1941, Horkheimer–Pollock Archive, Stadt- und Universitätsbibliothek, Frankfurt am Main.
134 See Cornelius Schnauber, *Hollywood Haven: Homes and Haunts of the European Emigrés and Exiles in Los Angeles*, and *German-Speaking Artists in Hollywood: Emigration between 1910 and 1945.*
135 Horkheimer, *Briefwechsel, GS*, vol. 17, p. 147.
136 Ibid., p. 167.
137 Ibid., p. 171.
138 Ibid., p. 172. Forty years later, under the heading 'Communicative Rationality', Jürgen Habermas set out to explore systematically which validity claims are connected with language. This enabled him to prepare the ground for the so-called linguistic turn of critical theory. The central concept of communicative rationality is defined as follows: 'A particular rationality inhabits not language per se, but the communicative use of linguistic expressions. . . . This *communicative rationality* is expressed in

the unifying power of communication-orientated speech which simultaneously secures for the speakers involved a life-world that is distributed intersubjectively and hence the horizon within which everyone can relate to one and the same objective world' (Habermas, *Wahrheit und Rechtfertigung*, p. 10).

139   That Adorno had some sort of theory of linguistic disintegration in mind can be confirmed by his mention of the Chandos letter of Hugo von Hofmannsthal, in which the latter expresses his fear of the loss of language and his sceptical view of the ability of language to express ideas. See Adorno's letter to Horkheimer, 2 November 1941. Horkheimer, *Briefwechsel, GS*, vol. 17, p. 176; cf. Christoph Demmerling, *Sprache und Verdinglichung: Wittgenstein, Adorno und das Projekt einer kritischen Theorie*, p. 117ff.

140   Horkheimer, *Briefwechsel, GS*, vol. 17, p. 176.

141   Ibid.

142   Benjamin, *Briefwechsel*, vol. VI, p. 436.

143   Three months later Adorno received more of Benjamin's papers from his lawyer, Martin Domke, who had known Benjamin since his student days. While Benjamin was in Lourdes he had left his papers with his sister Dora, who passed them on to Domke after her brother's death. Domke was on the point of leaving France for the USA and he was to hand them over to Adorno, whom Benjamin had named as executor. In Adorno's letter to Gershom Scholem on 19 February 1942, he speaks of 'two suit cases [*sic*] with manuscripts and books of Walter.... I made a complete catalogue of the content of these suit cases' (*Frankfurter Adorno Blätter*, V, 1998, p. 153f.). Benjamin had entrusted further manuscripts to Georges Bataille in Paris. These formed part of the arcades project. On the history of Benjamin's literary estate, see *Walter Benjamin 1892–1940*, p. 329ff.; Susan Buck-Morss, *The Dialectics of Seeing*, p. 331ff.

144   Horkheimer, *Briefwechsel, GS*, vol. 17, p. 60.

145   David M. Kennedy, *Freedom from Fear*, pp. 426ff. and 465ff.

146   Horkheimer, *Briefwechsel, GS*, vol. 17, p. 195.

147   Ibid., p. 225.

148   Adorno to Horkheimer, 26 October 1941, Horkheimer–Pollock Archive, Stadt- und Universitätsbibliothek, Frankfurt am Main.

149   Horkheimer, *Briefwechsel, GS*, vol. 17, p. 182.

150   Ibid., p. 111. Towards the end of 1940, the American government pledged support to Great Britain as a nation whose defence was in the American interest, and delivered war material on the lend lease principle. Moreover, after Germany had attacked the Soviet Union on 22 June 1941, Russia too was declared to be of vital importance. Ever since 1941, German nationals had been interned in the USA and German capital was confiscated. Henceforth, the US navy sank German U-boats without prior warning. As for Japan, which aimed at the domination of Asia, Roosevelt blocked important exports. On 7 December 1941, the Japanese attacked a large part of the American fleet anchored off Pearl Harbor. After this, the American public abandoned its resistance to the war. On 8 December Britain and the USA declared war on Japan.

151   Adorno to Horkheimer, 20 August 1941, Horkheimer–Pollock Archive, Stadt- und Universitätsbibliothek, Frankfurt am Main.

152 Horkheimer, *Briefwechsel, GS*, vol. 17, p. 211.
153 *The Revolutionary Ideas of the Marquis de Sade*, London, 1934.
154 Horkheimer, *Briefwechsel, GS*, vol. 17, p. 211.
155 Ibid., p. 57.
156 Adorno to Horkheimer, 17 August 1941, Horkheimer–Pollock Archive, Stadt- und Universitätsbibliothek, Frankfurt am Main. [For 'lammergeiering', see p. 57, above.]

Chapter 15 Adorno's Years in California

1 Adorno to Horkheimer, 11 August 1941, Horkheimer–Pollock Archive, Stadt- und Universitätsbibliothek, Frankfurt am Main.
2 On the situation of the German emigrants in Hollywood and Los Angeles, see Joachim Radkau, *Die deutsche Emigration in die USA: Ihr Einfluß auf die amerikanische Europapolitik 1933–1945*, p. 107ff.
3 Adorno wrote these notes in August–September 1941. See Theodor W. Adorno Archive, Frankfurt am Main (Ts 51864). In them Adorno developed a theory of the basic elements of the decline of the individual: a theory of the subject without a self. He notes the reification of human beings who place themselves on the same level as things. At the psychological level, the unconscious is on the point of dissolving, just as repression and the censor are being replaced by defiance and universal hostility. In the absence of an ego, the concept of egoism is just as obsolete as the psychoanalytical theory of the Oedipus complex. The image of the body is essentially desexualized, 'either by the cult of functioning . . . as such, or by the particular way in which sexuality is released.' Theodor W. Adorno Archive, Frankfurt am Main (Ts 51873).
4 See Adorno, 'Spengler Today' and 'Veblen's Attack on Culture', in *Prisms*, pp. 51–94. These essays appeared originally in English in the *ZfS*; whether these are Adorno's original texts or unattributed translations is unclear; the versions in *Prisms* seem to be retranslations from the German translations, although they are inevitably influenced by the English originals in the *ZfS* [trans.].
5 Adorno, 'Veblen's Attack on Culture', in *Prisms*, p. 84. This statement on appearance [*Schein*] highlights the central importance of the salvaging of appearance in Adorno's aesthetic theory. Cf. Peter Bürger, *Zur Kritik der idealistischen Ästhetik*.
6 Horkheimer, *Briefwechsel, GS*, vol. 17, p. 146f.
7 Ibid., p. 163.
8 Adorno to Horkheimer, 23 September 1941, Horkheimer–Pollock Archive, Stadt- und Universitätsbibliothek, Frankfurt am Main.
9 Adorno, *The Philosophy of Modern Music*, p. 64f. This study did not appear in book form in Germany until 1949, when it was published in an expanded version in which Adorno added the chapter 'Stravinsky and Restoration' as a contrast to the original chapter, 'Schoenberg and Progress'. In his controversy with Stravinsky, Adorno assumed the existence of two musical cultures. He attempted to show that Stravinsky's neo-classicism was incompatible with the idea of the complete rational organization of the work. His music was music about music. It took up

older music and polished it up. See *GS*, vol. 12, p. 10f.; cf. also Giselher Schubert, 'Adornos Auseinandersetzung mit der Zwölftontechnik Schönbergs', p. 242ff.; Martin Hufner, *Adorno und die Zwölftontechnik*, p. 111ff.

10 Adorno, *The Philosophy of Modern Music*, p. 53.
11 Ibid., p. 54.
12 Ibid., p. 59.
13 Ibid., p. 73.
14 Ibid., p. 60.
15 Ibid., p. 67.
16 Ibid., p. 65. Martin Hufner points out that Adorno had 'recognized earlier on that "the rationality of twelve-tone technique" "organizes" the natural material, but "undialectically" regards this process as that of the emancipation of man from the coercions of nature. In *The Philosophy of Modern Music*, he draws attention to the reverse side of this process of emancipation' (Martin Hufner, *Adorno und die Zwölftontechnik*, p. 120).
17 Adorno, *Philosophy of Modern Music*, p. 117.
18 Ibid., p. 71 (translation amended).
19 Ibid., pp. 118 and 123.
20 Ibid., p. 30.
21 Adorno and Krenek, *Briefwechsel*, p. 133.
22 Modifications of twelve-tone methods can be seen in the *Four Songs based on Poems by Stefan George for Voice and Piano*, op. 7, which were completed in 1944. In the fourth poem, for example, he divided the row into three four-note groups, and at the same time the sequence of the notes is not fixed. See Martin Hufner, *Adorno und die Zwölftontechnik*, pp. 139ff. and 168. In a letter to Eduard Steuermann some six years after the publication of *The Philosophy of Modern Music*, Adorno claimed that 'one must attempt to forgo all "ties"; one must try to make the experience of twelve-tone technique useful to the listener, but at the same time one must free oneself from the tyranny of the row, not to mention everything else' (Adorno to Steuermann, 14 October 1955, in Rolf Tiedemann, *Adorno-Noten*, p. 52).
23 Adorno, *Philosophy of Modern Music*, p. 126.
24 Ibid., p. 128.
25 Ibid., p. 133.
26 Adorno and Horkheimer, *Dialectic of Enlightenment*, p. 256.
27 Ibid., p. 219.
28 Horkheimer, *Briefwechsel*, *GS*, vol. 17, p. 153. Schmid Noerr rightly points out that 'gestures taken from concepts' does not 'refer to the subliminal connotations that promote communication, but, on the contrary, it is a reference to the practice of life in its totality within which discursive language, especially that of academic disciplines, is a factor that (necessarily) entails abstraction' (Gunzelin Schmid Noerr, *Gesten aus Begriffen: Konstellationen der kritischen Theorie*, p. 68).
29 Adorno and Horkheimer, *Dialectic of Enlightenment*, p. 218.
30 Ibid., p. 30.
31 See Jürgen Habermas, *Der philosophische Diskurs der Moderne*, p. 146; Norbert Rath, 'Zur Nietzsche-Rezeption Horkheimers und Adornos', p. 73; Hauke Brunkhorst, 'Die Welt als Beute', p. 154ff.

32 Adorno and Horkheimer, *Dialectic of Enlightenment*, p. xiii.
33 In line with their general epistemological stance, the two authors developed a chain of increasingly tightly linked arguments that they would try out on a number of disparate objects and that would increase in density as their discussion advanced. Adorno and Horkheimer declined to explain their procedure in their notes. Not until later did Adorno attempt to ground the rationale of 'binding statements without a system' in *Negative Dialectics* and to explain the particular nature of a type of knowledge based on dialectical thought conceived as 'an ensemble of analytical models'. *Negative Dialectics*, p. 29f.
34 Adorno and Horkheimer, *Dialectic of Enlightenment*, p. ix.
35 See Gunzelin Schmid Noerr, 'Die Stellung der "Dialektik der Aufklärung" in der Entwicklung der kritischen Theorie', in Horkheimer, *GS*, vol. 5, p. 423ff., especially p. 429. Jürgen Habermas, too, after talking to Gretel Adorno, reported that 'the authorship of the individual chapters was not undivided . . . the title essay and the Sade chapter were largely written by Horkheimer; the chapters on *The Odyssey* and the culture industry were mainly Adorno's. Moreover, the differences were not merely stylistic' (Jürgen Habermas, *Texte und Kontexte*, p. 101).
36 See Horkheimer, 'Idee, Aktivität und Programm des Instituts für Sozialforschung', *GS*, vol. 1, p. 156f.
37 There is a mention of the 'age of concentration camps' as early as an essay Adorno wrote between 1939 and 1940 and published in 1942 in the memorial volume for Walter Benjamin. Adorno, 'George und Hofmannsthal', in *Prisms*, p. 198.
38 See *SPSS*, IX, 3, 1941, p. 366ff.
39 A typescript (Ts 52107) in the Theodor W. Adorno Archive refers to both Adorno and Horkheimer as authors.
40 The attorney William J. Donovan, who had been appointed by President Roosevelt as the director of the secret service section known as the Coordination of Information (COI) in 1941, had approached the Institute of Social Research in the summer of that year in order to obtain recommendations for recruiting personnel for the Research and Analysis branch of the Intelligence Service. The key figure here was Franz Neumann, who, as the author of *Behemoth*, deservedly enjoyed the reputation of being an expert on the Nazi system of rule. In fact, he took up a position on the Board of Economic Warfare. In spring 1943, Neumann, together with Herbert Marcuse and Otto Kirchheimer, became a member of the Office of Strategic Services (OSS). See John H. Herz, *Vom Überleben. Wie ein Weltbild entstand*, p. 136; Barry M. Katz, 'The Criticism of Arms: The Frankfurt School Goes to War'.
41 See Adorno to Scholem, 19 February 1942, in *Frankfurter Adorno Blätter*, V, 1998, p. 153ff.
42 In the Preface Horkheimer had announced: 'For the duration of the war the "Studies" will be published as a yearbook instead of three times per annum'. *SPSS*, IX, 1941, p. 365.
43 Benjamin, *Gesammelte Briefe*, vol. VI, p. 435f.
44 Benjamin, 'Theses on the Philosophy of History', in *Illuminations*, p. 265.
45 Ralf Konersmann rightly remarks that Benjamin's comments are closely related to the age in which they were written: 'There can be no doubt that

the "theses", without constituting a finished programme, were nevertheless related to their own time in a concrete fashion. They reformulated politics as the philosophy of history, the history of philosophy as politics. . . . For Benjamin, fascism was the event that fundamentally and definitively refutes the optimism that was most effectively expressed in the profane form of traditional expectations about progress' (Ralf Konersmann, *Erstarrte Unruhe: Walter Benjamins Begriff der Geschichte*, p. 174). Adorno was of the opinion that Benjamin's 'Theses' 'summed up the epistemological considerations that accompanied his thinking about the design of the arcade project' (Adorno, 'Charakteristik Walter Benjamins', *GS*, vol. 10.1, p. 250).

46 Adorno, 'George und Hofmannsthal', in *Prisms*, p. 225.
47 *Frankfurter Adorno Blätter*, V, 1998, p. 37.
48 This first publication was in fact a revised version of the original text of 1944. For publication Adorno and Horkheimer reformulated a number of concepts that had originally been taken from Marx's analysis of capitalism, and translated them into more clearly sociological terms. The chapter on 'Elements of Anti-Semitism' was supplemented by a seventh thesis. The authors then undertook a second revision for the first publication by Fischer Verlag (Frankfurt am Main, 1969), and in the course of this they softened a number of provocative statements about the function of religion. The entire publication history has been described in detail by Gunzelin Schmid Noerr, 'Die Stellung der "Dialektik der Aufklärung" in der Entwicklung der kritischen Theorie', Horkheimer, *GS*, vol. 5, p. 423ff. Schmid Noerr's edition of the *Dialektik der Aufklärung* for Horkheimer's *Collected Works* is the first to have satisfied the criteria of a historical-critical edition. The present author, however, has used the version in Adorno's *Gesammelte Schriften* (*GS*, vol. 3).
49 When the book appeared in 1947 it made no impact on the public. The first edition was still obtainable from bookshops until the early 1960s. The sensational success of the volume set in after a delay of two decades. When Adorno and Horkheimer offered their manuscript to Fritz H. Landshoff, the director of Querido Verlag, their intention was to create closer ties to the publishing house. They would have liked to see the revived *Zeitschrift für Sozialforschung* appearing there. Moreover, Adorno offered the text of his *Minima Moralia* to the same publisher. See *Marbacher Magazin*, 'Fritz H. Landshoff und der Querido-Verlag 1933–1950'.
50 Horkheimer, *Briefwechsel*, *GS*, vol. 17, p. 385.
51 Ibid.
52 Ibid., p. 274.
53 Adorno and Horkheimer left it in no doubt that the human species depends on appropriating nature through purposive activity. It follows that not 'all acts characterized by ends–means rationality . . . mean "labour", and social labour does not inevitably amount to the plundering and destruction of nature' (Jürgen Ritsert, *Ästhetische Theorie als Gesellschaftskritik: Umrisse der Dialektik in Adornos Spätwerk*, p. 15). Ritsert points out that, for Adorno, ends–means rationality has the rank of a positive norm in the sphere of social labour since it is a form of self-preservation. It is only because of this normative value that it is possible

to understand the dual nature of ends–means rationality at all. See Ritsert, *Die Rationalität Adornos*, p. 7ff.

54 Adorno and Horkheimer, *Dialectic of Enlightenment*, p. 4.
55 Ibid., p. 9.
56 Ibid., p. 8.
57 Ibid., p. 13 (translation amended). For the importance of *Dialectic of Enlightenment* as a contribution to the critique of rationality, see Anke Thyen, *Negative Dialektik und Erfahrung: Rationalität des Nichtidentischen bei Adorno*, p. 65ff.; Albrecht Wellmer, *Zur Dialektik von Moderne und Postmoderne*; Herbert Schnädelbach, 'Die Aktualität der "Dialektik der Aufklärung"', p. 231ff. For a critique of the implications of *Dialectic of Enlightenment* for the philosophy of history, see Axel Honneth, *Kritik der Macht*, p. 110ff.; Jürgen Habermas, *Der philosophische Diskurs der Moderne*, p. 130ff.; Hans-Klaus Keul, *Kritik der emanzipatorischen Vernunft*, p. 181ff.
58 Adorno and Horkheimer, *Dialectic of Enlightenment*, p. 28.
59 Ibid., p. 155.
60 Adorno's posthumous papers contain an older version of the chapter on *The Odyssey*, probably written early in 1943. This version expresses ideas that Adorno later published independently ('On Epic Naiveté', *Notes to Literature*, vol. 1, p. 24ff.). I owe this reference to Rolf Tiedemann, who again makes it clear that Adorno was responsible for this section of the book. See *Frankfurter Adorno Blätter*, V, 1998, p. 37ff.
61 Adorno and Horkheimer, *Dialectic of Enlightenment*, p. 21.
62 Doris Kolesch maintains that 'Adorno's and Horkheimer's interpretation of the Siren episode relies on the customary topos of woman as the mirror of the masculine self' (Doris Kolesch, 'Sich schwach zeigen dürfen, ohne Stärke zu provozieren: Liebe und die Beziehung der Geschlechter', p. 193ff.).
63 Adorno and Horkheimer, *Dialectic of Enlightenment*, p. 33f. (translation slightly modified).
64 Ibid., p. 95.
65 Ibid., p. 123.
66 Ibid., p. 148.
67 Ibid., p. 134.
68 Ibid., p. 121.
69 See Dan Diner, 'Aporie der Vernunft: Horkheimers Überlegungen zu Antisemitismus und Massenvernichtung', p. 30ff.; Moishe Postone, 'Nationalismus und Antisemitismus: Ein theoretischer Versuch', p. 242.
70 Adorno and Horkheimer, *Dialectic of Enlightenment*, p. 199.
71 Ibid., p. 171.
72 Ibid., p. 168.
73 Ibid., p. 179.
74 Ibid., p. 200.
75 In the *Dialectic of Enlightenment*, Adorno and Horkheimer preferred the concept of fascism to that of National Socialism. One reason for this was that they did not see anti-Semitism as a national phenomenon. 'Totalitarian anti-Semitism is by no means a specifically German phenomenon. Attempts to deduce it from such a dubious entity as national character, the pathetic dregs of what used to be the spirit of the nation,

renders harmless the incomprehensible thing that we are trying to comprehend' ('On the German edition of Paul Massing's *Rehearsal for Destruction: A Study of Political Anti-Semitism in Imperial Germany*', *GS*, vol. 20.2, p. 652).

76 See Adorno, 'Scientific Experiences of a European Scholar in America', in *Critical Models*, p. 230.

77 Jürgen Habermas, *Der philosophische Diskurs der Moderne*, p. 130ff.

78 Adorno, *Minima Moralia*, p. 74.

79 Later, Adorno explicitly discussed the rhetorical aspect of his philosophy: 'In philosophy, rhetoric represents that which cannot be thought except in language.... Dialectic – literally: language as the organon of thought, would mean to attempt a critical rescue of the rhetorical element, a mutual approximation of thing and expression, to the point where difference fades' (*Negative Dialectics*, p. 55f.).

80 Horkheimer and Adorno, 'Rettung der Aufklärung', Horkheimer, *GS*, vol. 12, p. 294.

81 Ibid., p. 596f.

82 Ibid., p. 601.

83 Adorno, 'Einleitung zum "Positivismusstreit" in der deutschen Soziologie', *GS*, vol. 8, p. 318.

84 This is evident from Adorno's letters to his parents, as well as from a letter from Horkheimer to Paul Tillich in August 1942 and one from Adorno to Horkheimer in September 1942. Horkheimer, *Briefwechsel*, *GS*, vol. 17, pp. 313ff. and 328ff.

85 The project was coordinated by the Department of Scientific Research that was specially set up in New York and directed by Horkheimer and Samuel H. Flowerman. The anti-Semitism studies were subdivided into nine separate projects. The research was staffed by a dozen social researchers who, over a period of five years, explored such complex questions as attitudes of the population towards Jews, the conditions required for racist propaganda to have an effect, the contents of anti-Semitic caricatures in the print media, the links between fear and social aggression, and early childhood experiences as a factor predisposing people towards anti-Semitic views in adulthood.

86 This special study was planned as a representative survey, based not on questionnaires but on oral interviews. 'The interviewers consisted ... of 270 workers who were recruited via the JLC and who had to learn by heart a complex of twenty-five open questions with which to interrogate their workmates.... The final report presented to the JLC ... came to four volumes of over 1300 pages altogether, and, despite attempts to shorten it, the authors never managed to reduce it to a publishable size' (Wolfgang Bonß, *Die Einübung des Tatsachenblicks*, p. 209).

87 See Rolf Wiggershaus, *The Frankfurt School*, p. 359ff.; Martin Jay, *The Dialectical Imagination*, p. 239ff. Sanford (1911–1995) had made his name as an empirical social psychologist who introduced psycho-dynamic ideas into American academic psychology. Levinson (born 1920) was a psychologist and psychiatrist. Frenkel-Brunswik (1908–1958) worked as a social psychologist with a strong leaning towards psychoanalysis; she had been born in Vienna and had studied with Charlotte and Karl Bühler.

88 This was the study by Nathan W. Ackerman and Marie Jahoda whose final title was 'Anti-Semitism and Emotional Disorder'. The authors sought to discover how the distinction between your own group and alien groups is transmitted in the course of education. They showed how feelings of hostility were projected onto the out-group of Jews.

89 These memoranda are to be found in the Theodor W. Adorno Archive, Frankfurt am Main, as well as in the Horkheimer–Pollock Archive, Stadt- und Universitätsbibliothek, Frankfurt am Main.

90 See Michael Werz, 'Untrennbarkeit von Material und Methode: Zur wechselvollen Rezeption der Authoritarian Personality', p. 48.

91 Adorno, 'Scientific Experiences of a European Scholar in America', in *Critical Models*, p. 232.

92 See Horkheimer, *Briefwechsel*, GS, vol. 17, p. 535.

93 See Adorno, 'Anti-Semitism and Fascist Propaganda', *GS*, vol. 8, p. 397; Adorno, 'Freudian Theory and the Pattern of Fascist Propaganda', *GS*, vol. 8, p. 408; Adorno, *The Psychological Technique of Martin Luther Thomas' Radio Addresses*, GS, vol. 9.1, p. 7ff.; Ernst Simmel (ed.), *Antisemitismus*, p. 148ff.; Leo Löwenthal and Norbert Gutermann, *Falsche Propheten: Studien zur faschistischen Agitation*, Löwenthal, *Schriften*, vol. 3.

94 Horkheimer, *Briefwechsel*, GS, vol. 17, p. 535f.

95 Adorno, 'Die Freudsche Theorie und die Struktur der faschistischen Propaganda', p. 41f.; Adorno, 'Freudian Theory and the Pattern of Fascist Propaganda', *GS*, vol. 8, p. 414.

96 Adorno, 'Antisemitismus und faschistische Propaganda', in Ernst Simmel (ed.), *Antisemitismus*, p. 149f.; Adorno, 'Anti-Semitism and Fascist Propaganda', *GS*, vol. 8, p. 398.

97 Adorno, 'Die Freudsche Theorie und die Struktur der faschistischen Propaganda', p. 56.

98 Ibid., p. 61.

99 Adorno, *Minima Moralia*, p. 164.

100 Ibid.

101 Adorno, 'Scientific Experiences of a European Scholar in America', in *Critical Models*, p. 230.

102 The various titles considered included *The Potential Fascist*. See Adorno to Horkheimer, 26 May 1948, Horkheimer–Pollock Archive, Stadt- und Universitätsbibliothek, Frankfurt am Main.

103 Adorno, 'Scientific Experiences of a European Scholar in America', in *Critical Models*, p. 235.

104 Adorno et al., *The Authoritarian Personality*, p. 733.

105 Adorno to Horkheimer, 26 October 1944, Horkheimer–Pollock Archive, Stadt- und Universitätsbibliothek, Frankfurt am Main.

106 Adorno et al., *The Authoritarian Personality*, p. 16.

107 This is a projective technique in which the subject is presented with a series of open-ended dramatic pictures and asked to tell a story about them. When evaluated, these stories can reveal a great deal about his internal psychological mechanisms.

108 Adorno to Horkheimer, 9 November 1944, Horkheimer–Pollock Archive, Stadt- und Universitätsbibliothek, Frankfurt am Main.

109 Adorno, 'Scientific Experiences of a European Scholar in America', in *Critical Models*, p. 233f.

110 Adorno et al., *The Authoritarian Personality*, p. 751. In a lecture with the title 'Lessons of Fascism', Horkheimer summed up the essential elements of the authoritarian personality as follows: 'A mechanical abandonment to conventional values; blind submission to authority accompanied by blind hatred of all opponents and outsiders; rejection of introverted behaviour; strict stereotyped thinking; a tendency to superstition; a half moral, half cynical devaluation of human nature; projectivity' (Horkheimer, *GS*, vol. 8, p. 10).

111 Adorno et al., *The Authoritarian Personality*, p. 753.

112 Ibid., p. 771. 'The subject in whom it [genuine liberalism] is pronounced has a strong sense of personal autonomy and independence. He cannot stand any outside interference with his personal convictions and beliefs, and he does not want to interfere with those of others either. His ego is quite developed but not libidinized. . . . One of his conspicuous features is moral courage' (ibid., p. 781). See ibid., pp. 346ff., here p. 383.

113 Ibid., p. 767.

114 Adorno, 'Scientific Experiences of a European Scholar in America', in *Critical Models*, p. 234.

115 Ibid., p. 235. It may be pointed out that the appearance of *The Authoritarian Personality* triggered a whole series of empirical studies of authoritarianism in the USA. Up to 1989, something over 2000 publications on the subject have been recorded. On the response to the book, see Michael Werz, 'Untrennbarkeit von Material und Methode', p. 40ff.

116 The thirty-page long undated typescript is preserved in the Horkheimer–Pollock Archive, Frankfurt am Main. The text as given here derives from that manuscript.

117 Cf. Adorno, 'Vorurteil und Charakter', *GS*, vol. 9.2, p. 360ff.

118 Adorno, *Minima Moralia*, p. 200.

119 Gert Raeithel, *Geschichte der nordamerikanischen Kultur*, vol. 3, p. 146.

120 Herbert Sirois, *Zwischen Illusion und Krieg: Deutschland und die USA 1933–1941*, p. 229ff.

121 Adorno expressed his regret to his parents that he had renounced the name Wiesengrund, and even the W., as well as his additional forename Ludwig. See his letter to his parents, 20 December 1943, *Briefe an die Eltern*, p. 234.

122 Horkheimer, 'Einige Betrachtungen zum Curfew', *GS*, vol. 5, p. 251ff. On the exile paper *Aufbau*, see Joachim Radkau, *Die deutsche Emigration in den USA*, p. 126ff.

123 Löwenthal to Adorno, 14 April 1942, Horkheimer–Pollock Archive, Stadt- und Universitätsbibliothek, Frankfurt am Main.

124 See Adorno, *Briefe an die Eltern*, p. 139ff.

125 Horkheimer, *Briefwechsel*, *GS*, vol. 17, p. 335.

126 See Adorno, *Briefe an die Eltern*, p. 164ff.

127 Adorno to Horkheimer, 9 February 1944, Horkheimer–Pollock Archive, Stadt- und Universitätsbibliothek, Frankfurt am Main.

128 Adorno, *Minima Moralia*, p. 170.

129 Ibid.

130 He played Kommissar Gruber in *Hangmen Also Die!*, a film on which Bertolt Brecht had also worked.

131 Adorno, *Minima Moralia*, p. 190.

132 See Adorno, *Briefe an die Eltern*, p. 186ff.
133 Adorno kept a record of his dreams his whole life long; only a portion of them have been published (cf. *GS*, vol. 20.2, p. 572ff.). Further examples are preserved in the Theodor W. Adorno Archive.
134 Adorno, *Traumprotokolle*, *GS*, vol. 20.2, p. 574f. (For 'Chatterhole', see p. 29 above [trans.].)
135 See letter from Adorno to his parents of 21 December 1942, *Briefe an die Eltern*, p. 175.
136 See Horkheimer, *Briefwechsel*, *GS*, vol. 16, p. 413ff., and also vol. 17., p. 334f.
137 Ernst Bloch, *Briefe*, vol. 2, p. 443ff.
138 Adorno, 'Für Ernst Bloch', *GS*, vol. 20.1, p. 190ff.
139 Ernst Bloch, *Briefe*, vol. 2, p. 446.
140 He wrote the poems in February, May and June 1943. Theodor W. Adorno Archive, Frankfurt am Main (Ts 51833).
141 Adorno to his mother, 10 February 1943, *Briefe an die Eltern 1939–1951*, p. 180ff.
142 Ibid., p. 181 ('sense of proportion' was in English [trans.]).
143 Adorno to Grab, 27 October 1945, Theodor W. Adorno Archive, Frankfurt am Main (Br 497/39, 40).
144 Adorno to Grab, 2 May 1946, Theodor W. Adorno Archive, Frankfurt am Main (Br 497/41, 42).
145 Adorno to Grab, 4 and 25 October 1945, Theodor W. Adorno Archive, Frankfurt am Main (Br 497/36/39).
146 Adorno to Grab, 2 May 1946, Theodor W. Adorno Archive, Frankfurt am Main (Br 497/41, 42). Charlotte later remarried and became Mrs Violin, while her husband married Anita Seligmann in 1948. Adorno had known Anita in the 1930s in Frankfurt, where she had intended to write a dissertation on Robert Walser.
147 Adorno to Luli von Bodenhausen, 8 July 1951, Theodor W. Adorno Archive, Frankfurt am Main (Br 154/18).
148 Theodor W. Adorno Archive, Frankfurt am Main (Ts 1396/1515).
149 Adorno, *Minima Moralia*, p. 18.
150 In Nietzsche's writings, like those of Adorno, aphorisms are accorded an intermediate place between philosophy and literature. The works of Nietzsche that Adorno referred to were *Beyond Good and Evil*, and the collections *Human, All Too Human, Daybreak* and *The Gay Science*. See Heinz Krüger, *Über den Aphorismus als philosophische Form*.
151 Adorno, *Minima Moralia*, p. 16ff.
152 Ibid., p. 33.
153 Ibid., p. 33f.
154 According to the archivists, the Theodor W. Adorno Archive in Frankfurt has preserved handwritten diaries that have not yet been catalogued and are therefore not available for scrutiny. It may be assumed that in part they contain early versions both of his philosophical essays and of the aphorisms that have been collected in *Minima Moralia*. He had planned to publish more aphorisms and had already written and arranged texts for a future book.
155 Adorno, *Minima Moralia*, p. 49. In Carl Maria von Weber's opera *Der Freischütz* (The Sharpshooter), the hero sells his soul for magic bullets which never miss their mark [trans.].

156 Ibid., p. 54.
157 Ibid., p. 25.
158 Ibid., p. 39.
159 Ibid., p. 40.
160 Ibid., p. 48.
161 Ibid., p. 27.
162 Ibid., p. 34 (translation altered).
163 'O avalanche, will you take me with you when you fall?' This was the last line of *Le goût du néant* (The Longing for Nothingness), from Baudelaire's *Les Fleurs du mal*.
164 Adorno, *Minima Moralia*, p. 164f.
165 Ibid., p. 165.
166 Ibid., p. 166.
167 Ibid., p. 167f.
168 Ibid., p. 170.
169 Ibid., p. 172.
170 See Raoul Hilberg, *Die Vernichtung der europäischen Juden*, p. 811ff.; Michael Burleigh, *The Third Reich*, p. 769ff.
171 Adorno, *Minima Moralia*, p. 234.
172 Ibid.
173 Ibid., p. 103.
174 Ibid. On the role of Auschwitz in Adorno's diagnosis of the contemporary world, see Lars Rensmann, *Kritische Theorie über den Antisemitismus*.
175 In *Minima Moralia*, he wrote: 'Things have come to a pass where lying sounds like truth, truth like lying. . . . Every horror necessarily becomes in the enlightened world, a horrific fairy-tale. For the untruth of truth has a core which finds an avid response in the unconscious' (p. 108).
176 Letter to his parents, 1 May 1945, *Briefe an die Eltern 1939–1951*, p. 309ff.
177 Horkheimer, *Briefwechsel, GS*, vol. 17, p. 634.
178 Adorno, *Minima Moralia*, p. 106f.
179 The view that fascist tendencies would gain the upper hand in American politics and society was by no means uncommon among intellectuals there, particularly among some groups of refugees. Such a trend was seen as a consequence of the brutality of the war with Japan and the collapse of the wartime alliance with the Soviet Union, as well as the intensification of the Cold War. These developments came to the surface after the death of President Roosevelt in April 1945, when the wartime understanding with the USSR was abandoned and was replaced by the anti-communist climate which became dominant under the presidency of Harry S. Truman. On the domestic scene a move in the direction of fascism became evident in McCarthyism and the actions of the Committee on Un-American Activities. Thomas Mann was aware of these aspirations to 'the rule of fascist violence'. In his diary he noted: 'The confrontation with Russia seems to lead inexorably towards fascism' (Mann, *Tagebücher 1946–1948*, pp. 162 and 165). Cf. Jost Hermand and Wigand Lange, '*Wollt Ihr Thomas Mann wiederhaben?*', p. 11ff.
180 When Horkheimer's father had died in January 1945 at the age of eighty-five, Adorno wrote to his friend: 'Everything to do with the lives of our parents has something indescribably sad about it, as well as something conciliatory . . . I believe that no one can understand better than I what it

means to lose the last vestige of security that lies in thinking about our parents' (Horkheimer, *Briefwechsel*, *GS*, vol. 17, p. 624).
181 Adorno to his mother, 9 July 1946, *Briefe an die Eltern 1939–1951*, p. 367ff.
182 Thomas Mann, *Die Entstehung des Doktor Faustus*, chapter 5.
183 Thomas Mann, *Doctor Faustus*, p. 53ff. The passage contains Mann's playful tribute to Adorno, since the musical illustration 'mead-ow-land' ('Wie-sengrund') is of course an allusion to Adorno's surname [trans.].
184 See Horkheimer, *Briefwechsel*, *GS*, vol. 17, p. 634.
185 Adorno, *Minima Moralia*, p. 188.
186 Adorno referred to the film in his essay on Kafka in order to illustrate the gulf between individuality and social character. See Adorno, 'Notes on Kafka', in *Prisms*, p. 255.
187 Adorno, 'Zweimal Chaplin', *GS*, vol. 10.1, p. 365f. In an essay that Habermas wrote in memory of Adorno, he pointed out quite rightly that this story tells us more about Adorno than about Chaplin. See Jürgen Habermas, 'Urgeschichte der Subjektivität und verwilderte Selbstbehauptung', p. 167.
188 Adorno, *Minima Moralia*, p. 145.
189 Ibid., p. 137. Charlie McCarthy was a popular ventriloquist dummy of the 1940s operated by Edgar Bergen [trans.].
190 Ibid., p. 25.
191 Adorno, *Kompositionen für den Film*, *GS*, vol. 15, p. 46ff.
192 Ibid., p. 77.
193 Ibid., p. 144.
194 Adorno to his mother, 13 June 1947, *Briefe an die Eltern 1939–1951*, p. 405ff., especially p. 407.
195 See Adorno and Mann, *Briefwechsel*, p. 17. It is not impossible that Thomas Mann may have noticed his young admirer. He notes in his diary on 17 September 1921 that he had been 'the object of curiosity in Kampen and Wenningstedt'. Cf. Reinhard Pabst, *Seesucht*.
196 Adorno and Mann, *Briefwechsel*, p. 17.
197 See Hermann Kurzke, *Thomas Mann*, p. 444ff. and 490ff.; Thomas Mann, *Die Entstehung des Doktor Faustus*.
198 Thomas Mann was the best-known and most highly respected German writer to have emigrated to the USA. His fame stemmed not just from the Nobel Prize he had been awarded in 1929, and from the fact that his books had been published in English translation by Alfred A. Knopf, but also from the honorary doctorate he had received from Harvard University and his extended lecture tours in the United States, in which his antifascist views were clearly articulated. His reputation was so great that he was invited to visit the White House, where he was received by President and Mrs Roosevelt. See Jost Hermand and Wigand Lange, '*Wollt ihr Thomas Mann wiederhaben?*', p. 17ff.; Kurzke, *Thomas Mann*, p. 470ff.
199 Having read the MS of *The Philosophy of Modern Music*, Mann was in no doubt that he had learnt something that would be of use to him for the novel he had planned. 'I discovered an artistic, sociological critique of the greatest progressiveness, subtlety and depth, one that had a peculiar affinity with the idea of my own work, with the "composition" in which I lived and on which I was working. I decided at once that "this was my man".' Thomas Mann, *Die Entstehung des Doktor Faustus*, p. 33.

200 'Late Style in Beethoven', *Essays on Music*, p. 564.
201 Adorno and Mann, *Briefwechsel*, pp. 9 and 20.
202 Ibid., p. 9.
203 Ibid., p. 21.
204 Adorno, 'Toward a Portrait of Thomas Mann', *Notes to Literature*, vol. 2, p. 17. Cf. Tiedemann, 'Mitdichtende Einfühlung', *Frankfurter Adorno Blätter*, I, 1992, p. 9ff.
205 Adorno to Erika Mann, 19 April 1962, Erika Mann, *Briefe und Antworten*, p. 109ff.
206 Thomas Mann, *Die Entstehung des Doktor Faustus*, p. 105.
207 Ibid., p. 106.
208 Thomas Mann, *Tagebücher 1946–1948*, p. 950.
209 Adorno and Mann, *Briefwechsel*, p. 158ff.
210 Rolf Tiedemann, 'Mitdichtende Einfühlung', *Frankfurter Adorno Blätter*, I, 1992, p. 23.
211 See Ibid., p. 26; Lieselotte Voss, *Die Entstehung von Thomas Manns Roman 'Doktor Faustus'*, p. 184ff.
212 See Donald Prater, *Thomas Mann, Deutscher und Weltbürger*, p. 551ff.
213 Thomas Mann, *Doctor Faustus*, p. 319ff.
214 Adorno and Mann, *Briefwechsel*, p. 76.
215 Michael Maar, 'Der kalte Schatten großer Männer'. Maar argues persuasively that the portrait of the Devil in *Faustus* has a very strong resemblance to Gustav von Aschenbach in *Death in Venice*, whose character was based on Gustav Mahler.
216 Hermann Kurzke, *Thomas Mann*, p. 503.
217 The accusation had been made by a film distribution company, who claimed that Thomas Mann had been guilty of plagiarism in *Doktor Faustus* and *Felix Krull*. The plaintiff had referred in his statement of claim to Adorno as both a victim and a witness. The content of the statutory declaration had essentially been formulated by Katia Mann, and Adorno felt duty bound to back her up. All the more incomprehensible, therefore, is the verbal invective directed against Adorno by both Katia and Erika Mann. (The present author owes this information to Christoph Gödde of the Theodor W. Adorno Archive, Frankfurt am Main.)
218 This statutory declaration has been preserved in both the Thomas Mann Archive in Zurich and the Theodor W. Adorno Archive in Frankfurt am Main.
219 Adorno, 'Toward a Portrait of Thomas Mann', *Notes to Literature*, vol. 2, p. 12ff.
220 Adorno to Bräutigam, 18 March 1968, *Frankfurter Adorno Blätter*, I, 1992, p. 31.
221 Thomas Mann, *Briefe*, vol. 3, p. 266f.
222 In Katia Mann's memoirs we can read the following: 'It is a great error for Adorno to imagine with hindsight that it was essentially he who had written the book on the grounds that music plays a significant role in it. He was at times quite beside himself with arrogance and complacency. That was highly amusing and there were a few curious anecdotes about "his" *Faustus*' (Katia Mann, *Meine ungeschriebenen Memoiren*, p. 146f.). And Erika Mann, having written two letters to Adorno in 1963 which struck the wrong note and contained unjust accusations, wrote about her

former companion in exile: 'In my own definite experience, he is not only pathologically conceited, and not only does his conceit go hand in hand, logically enough, with a high degree of paranoia – but in addition he is a great bluffer. He consciously throws sand in people's eyes; he quite consciously and intentionally writes incomprehensibly and quite often his highly concentrated and all-embracing expertise merely hides his total ignorance' (Erika Mann, *Briefe und Antworten*, p. 166). Marcel Reich-Ranicki rightly points out in his commentary on this malicious description of Adorno that these statements 'say more about the writer than their subject' (M. Reich-Ranicki, *Thomas Mann und die Seinen*, p. 183).

223　See Donald Prater, *Thomas Mann, Deutscher und Weltbürger*, p. 558ff.
224　Adorno, *Minima Moralia*, p. 56.
225　In spring 1947, the Arts Faculty of the University of Frankfurt had discussed the circumstances in which Horkheimer and also Adorno might be able to return to the faculty. The dean informed the rector of the University that Horkheimer had had a special chair and that Adorno could only be offered the post of a *Privatdozent*. However, since the rector, Walter Hallstein, had already invited Horkheimer to rebuild the Institute of Social Research at the end of 1946, the latter had decided to make the journey to Europe. See Horkheimer, *Briefwechsel, GS*, vol. 17, p. 765; Notker Hammerstein, *Die Johann Wolfgang Goethe-Universität*, p. 810ff.
226　Adorno, *Vier Lieder nach Gedichten von Stefan George für Singstimme und Klavier, GS*, vol. 18, p. 552.
227　Adorno, 'Amorbach', *GS*, vol. 10, p. 304.
228　Horkheimer, *Briefwechsel, GS*, vol. 18, p. 67f.

Part IV　The Explosive Power of Saying No

1　Adorno, *Negative Dialectics*, p. 404f. (translation slightly altered).
2　Clemens Albrecht et al., *Die intellektuelle Gründung der Bundesrepublik*.
3　Adorno, *Minima Moralia*, p. 217.
4　Adorno, 'On the Question: "What is German?"', *Critical Models*, p. 212.
5　Ibid.
6　The essay containing this sentence was written in 1949 and first published in 1951 in the volume *Soziologische Forschung in unserer Zeit*. See Adorno, 'Cultural Criticism and Society', *Prisms*, p. 34. For responses to this statement, see Petra Kiedaisch (ed.), *Lyrik nach Auschwitz?: Adorno und die Dichter*.
7　Adorno, 'Scientific Experiences of a European Scholar in America', *Critical Models*, p. 239.

Chapter 16　Change of Scene: Surveying the Ruins

1　For Adorno's assessment of Heuss, see 'Worte zum Gedenken an Theodor Heuss', *GS*, vol. 20.2, p. 7ff.
2　On these 'voices from the beginning', see Helmut Dubiel, *Niemand ist frei von der Geschichte*, p. 37ff.

3   See Christoph Kleßmann, *Die doppelte Staatsgründung*; Norbert Frei, *Vergangenheitspolitik*; Helmut Dubiel, *Niemand ist frei von der Geschichte*.
4   The intellectual climate, the specific tone of the age that Adorno called 'the Heidegger fashion', has been ably captured, right down to and including the aesthetics of everyday life, by Christoph Marthaler in his play *Stunde Null oder Die Kunst des Servierens: Ein Gedenktraining für Führungskräfte* (Zero Hour, or, The Art of Serving: Memory Training for Managers). In this he makes use of Ernst Wiechert's 'Speech to German Youth', Hans Leip's 'Address to Young Poets', the declarations of concerned politicians of East and West, but also Thomas Mann's radio talks to Germany during the war. (Ernst Wiechert and Hans Leip were writers who were in some ways close to National Socialism. Wiechert's books were recommended reading for young people, though Wiechert himself served a term in Buchenwald concentration camp. Leip, a writer of popular fiction and sentimental poems, is best known as the author of *Lili Marleen* [trans.].)
5   Horkheimer travelled to Europe in spring 1948. He spent a few weeks in Frankfurt in order to discuss with the university authorities the re-establishment of the Institute of Social Research, which had been destroyed in the war. In a letter to his wife, he described what he felt when he first met his former colleagues: 'I was respectfully welcomed by the rector [Franz Böhm] and the two deans [Otto Vossler of the Arts Faculty and Erich Gutenberg of Social Sciences] and others. They were all as sweet as pie, smooth as eels and hypocritical. They are not sure whether to regard me as a relatively influential American tourist or as the brother of their victims who is bent on remembering the past. They will have to choose the latter. . . . I attended a faculty meeting yesterday and found it too friendly by half and enough to make you want to throw up. All these people sit there as they did before the Third Reich . . . just as if nothing had happened. . . . They are acting out a Ghost Sonata that leaves Strindberg standing' (Horkheimer, *Briefwechsel, GS*, vol. 17, pp. 976 and 980).
6   Ibid., vol. 18, p. 35.
7   Adorno, 'Im Flug erhascht', *GS*, vol. 20.2, p. 548.
8   Adorno to Else Herzberger, 8 February 1950, Theodor W. Adorno Archive, Frankfurt am Main (Br 613/4). Adorno tried to help his friend and former co-author Carl Dreyfus, who was living in Buenos Aires, with both advice and practical assistance on compensation issues. As late as October 1955, Adorno wrote to Dreyfus to say that he (Adorno) had still not received any money for what he had lost through his dismissal from the university. Two years later, he wrote that he had still not received compensation for the money his father had had to pay as a 'Jew tax' and the 'tax on leaving the Reich' when he had emigrated from Germany in 1939. Adorno to Dreyfus, 29 September 1957 and 12 January 1962, Theodor W. Adorno Archive, Frankfurt am Main (Br 331/3/4/9/13).
9   The present author owes this information to Hartmut Wolf, who lived in the house in Oberrad as a tenant for a long time after the war.
10 Walter Dirks (1901–91) was a politically active left-wing Catholic who published the *Frankfurter Hefte* together with Eugen Kogon after the war. The journal debated the question of how to come to terms with the past and discussed pan-European politics in the spirit of a humanist, libertarian

socialism. In the 1950s he worked for a time at the Institute of Social Research, but in 1956 he went on to Westdeutscher Radio in Cologne, where he was in charge of the Culture Section (Br 331/3/4/9/13). (Eugen Kogon (1903–87) was a Catholic journalist and writer who had written on fascism before the war. He was arrested in Austria after the Nazi takeover and following sojourns in Gestapo prisons was sent to Buchenwald, where he remained until 1945, one of the few people to have survived. His classic book *Der SS-Staat* (1946) was the first attempt at a systematic account of the world of concentration camps [trans.].)

11 This literary group was founded on the initiative of Hans Werner Richter on 16 September 1947. It was an association of writers and publicists who had belonged to the journal *Der Ruf*, which had been founded by Richter together with Alfred Andersch and had been closed down by the US military government. The Gruppe 47 was the most representative grouping of critical contemporary literature in Germany, having brought together writers such as Heinrich Böll, Max Frisch, Günter Eich, Ilse Aichinger, Jürgen Becker, Martin Walser, Ingeborg Bachmann and Hans Magnus Enzensberger. See Karl Brieglieb, *Mißachtung und Tabu*.

12 He wrote to Thomas Mann about Ernst Jünger that Jünger 'was acting out the role of a miserable kitschy writer in the process of transforming himself from an unpleasant man of steel into what is if possible an even more unpleasant second-hand Stefan George with bronze foliage, coloured scales and concrete descriptions that miss the point' (Adorno and Mann, *Briefwechsel*, p. 47f.).

13 Adorno, 'Peter Suhrkamp', *GS*, vol. 20.2, p. 491.

14 Marie Luise Kaschnitz, *Orte*, p. 519; cf. Dagmar von Gersdorff, *Marie Luise Kaschnitz: Eine Biographie*, p. 174.

15 Ibid., p. 189.

16 The contents of this lecture course have been preserved thanks to the notes taken by Kraft Bretschneider. They show that Adorno had already started to develop the core themes of his philosophy in a programmatic way. For example, there was his critique of Martin Heidegger, which was not fully worked out until the middle 1960s, and also his conception of philosophical hermeneutics and dialectics. See *Frankfurter Adorno Blätter*, II, 1993, p. 11ff.

17 Adorno, 'Die auferstandene Kultur', *GS*, vol. 20.2, p. 456. At the same time as Adorno, Hannah Arendt, the philosopher and the author of *The Origins of Totalitarianism*, also returned to Germany for the first time since her emigration. She had come under the auspices of the Jewish Cultural Reconstruction, an organization which had been set up in 1948 (see Elizabeth Young-Bruehl, *Hannah Arendt*, p. 270ff.). She gave detailed descriptions of her experiences (including meetings with Karl Jaspers and Martin Heidegger, among others) in letters to Hilde Fränkel and to her own husband, Heinrich Blücher, and she published an article in *Commentary* on her impressions of Germany with the title 'The Aftermath of Nazi Rule: Report from Germany'. In a striking parallel to Adorno, she came to the conclusion that the frenetic activity of the Germans served to blot out the reality of the past. A general apathy was the dominant mood, and totalitarianism continued to have an afterlife even in the democratic state. She thought that the de-Nazification process introduced by the

Allies obscured the nature of Nazi Party membership, since people joined the party from necessity and fear, as well as voluntarily from conviction. Furthermore, it helped to create a politically dangerous community of compromised people. Hannah Arendt, *Besuch in Deutschland*.

18 His report on his journey appeared on 25 September 1949 in the *New York Times Magazine* under the title 'Germany Today: A Famous Exile's Impression of a Ruined, Vanquished Land and Unchanging People'. In it Mann expressed his horror at the 'brazen nationalism' of the German population which had not been prepared to come to grips with the atrocities of the Nazi regime. Thomas Mann, *Essays*, vol. VI, p. 131ff.

19 Adorno and Mann, *Briefwechsel*, p. 45.

20 Ibid.

21 Kurt Mautz, *Der Urfreund*, p. 175.

22 Ibid., p. 180.

23 Adorno to Horkheimer, 23 December 1949, Horkheimer, *Briefwechsel*, *GS*, vol. 18, p. 85.

24 Ibid., p. 80.

25 This was the Darmstadt study on local government that the institute carried out at the request of the US military government between 1949 and 1952. In December Adorno was invited to a colloquium at the Technical University of Darmstadt at which he gave a talk on 'Town Planning and the Social Order' (*GS*, vol. 20.2, p. 605). This study, on which Adorno acted as consultant, resulted in the production of nine monographs which exercised a significant influence on the sociology of German local government.

26 Adorno and Mann, *Briefwechsel*, p. 49.

27 Adorno to his mother, 24 September 1950, *Briefe an die Eltern 1939–1951*, p. 537.

28 Cf. the short essay *Auf die Frage, warum sind Sie zurückgekehrt* (Answer to the Question: Why Did You Come Back?) (*GS*, vol. 20.1, p. 394), in which Adorno wrote that he belonged in Europe and in Germany: 'I am dependent on the language that I can write as my own, whereas the English I learnt in the long years of emigration only enabled me to write like other people. In Germany I feel no pressure from the market and public opinion, forcing me to adjust the expression of what I have in mind.'

29 Max Bense, 'Hegel und die kalifornische Emigration'.

30 Horkheimer, *Briefwechsel*, *GS*, vol. 18, p. 73.

31 Horkheimer was in Frankfurt at the time. His wife told him in a letter about Hallstein's visit to the house in D'Este Drive and of the evening spent with the Mann, Adorno and Dieterle families. 'Teddie behaved throughout so utterly narcissisticly that no one could compete with him. . . . Teddie talked the whole evening. . . . He is the greatest narcissist to be found in either the Old or the New World' (Horkheimer, *Briefwechsel*, *GS*, vol. 18, p. 37).

32 Hans-Georg Gadamer was still interested in collaborating with Adorno and Horkheimer even after his move to Heidelberg. 'It is a crying shame', he wrote to Horkheimer in March 1950, 'that my departure from Frankfurt has nullified, or at least made much more difficult, some very concrete

opportunities for genuine communication and interaction.' He pointed to the affinities between his way of thinking and the writings of Horkheimer and Adorno. Furthermore, he would welcome it if Adorno were to succeed to his chair in Frankfurt. 'I would gladly offer to use what influence I have' (Horkheimer, *Briefwechsel, GS*, vol. 18, p. 123). In 1950 Gadamer had taken part in a radio broadcast to commemorate the fiftieth anniversary of Nietzsche's death. Habermas disputes the assertion that Gadamer retained his respect for the philosophy of Horkheimer and Adorno throughout his long life despite their disagreements. It is true that he thought well of Horkheimer's *Critique of Instrumental Reason*, but he did not regard Adorno as a professional philosopher. Gadamer used his position in Heidelberg to entice talented thinkers away from Frankfurt (conversation of the present author with Jürgen Habermas in December 2001). Cf. Jean Grondin, *Hans-Georg Gadamer: Eine Biographie.*

33 Horkheimer to Adorno, 9 November 1949, Horkheimer–Pollock Archive, Stadt- und Universitätsbibliothek, Frankfurt am Main.

34 This emerges from a preliminary decision about reparations on the part of the finance committee of the university. Archive of the Dean of the Arts Faculty of the Johann Wolfgang Goethe University.

35 Horkheimer, *Briefwechsel, GS*, vol. 18, p. 94.

36 Ibid., p. 124.

37 Institute of Social Research, *Ein Bericht über die Feier seiner Wiedereröffnung, seiner Geschichte und seiner Arbeiten*, p. 12.

38 Adorno, 'Notes on Kafka', *Prisms*, p. 262.

39 Horkheimer, *Briefwechsel, GS*, vol. 18, pp. 120f. and 193ff. In his letter of 2 March 1951, Horkheimer set out a detailed plan for the joint research programme.

40 Adorno and Mann, *Briefwechsel*, p. 104.

41 Adorno, 'Zur gegenwärtigen Stellung der empirischen Sozialforschung', *GS*, vol. 8, p. 481f.

42 Ibid., p. 482.

43 Adorno's view of the value of empirical methods changed along with his experience of the field. As a researcher on the radio research project he had retained his scepticism, whereas he came to accept the benefits of both qualitative and quantitative methods during his work on *The Authoritarian Personality*. For this reason he came to see himself in postwar Germany as the representative of an approach to social research that in many respects anticipated the 'grounded theory' of Anselm L. Strauss. This aims at the production of a theory without being tied to particular types of data. (Cf. Anselm L. Strauss, *Grundlagen qualitativer Sozialforschung*, p. 29f.) Where standard empirical methods such as questionnaires are treated as general panaceas, Adorno criticized the identification of sociology with the discovery of facts, the 'hypostatization' of the empirical, analytical model in sociology, i.e., the dissolving of sociological problems into hypotheses, isolated variables and measurements. See Adorno, 'Teamwork in der Sozialforschung', *GS*, vol. 8, p. 494.

44 See König, *Briefwechsel*, vol. 1, p. 423. Not until the 1960s and the so-called Positivist Dispute did the differences in approach between the schools or paradigms emerge more clearly. Thus König distinguished between sociology which was supposed to concentrate on the empirical

study of specific social problems and the philosophical theory of society which was concerned with the interpretation of social life as a totality. See König, *Soziologie*, p. 8ff.

45 Continuity can be seen not just in the careers of Arnold Gehlen and Helmut Schelsky, but also in the fact that former Nazis occupied important posts in postwar German sociology. Examples are Werner Brepohl, Karl Valentin-Müller and Karl-Heinz Pfeffer, whose work has direct links with so-called national (*völkisch*) thinking. Cf. Carsten Klingemann, 'Vergangenheitsbewältigung oder Geschichtsschreibung?'; Alex Demirović, 'Die Hüter der Gesellschaft: Zur Professionalisierung der Soziologie in Westdeutschland 1945–1950'; Johannes Weyer, *Westdeutsche Soziologie 1945–1950: Deutsche Kontinuitäten und nordamerikanischer Einfluß*.

46 Horkheimer to René König, 22 June 1952, Horkheimer–Pollock Archive, Stadt- und Universitätsbibliothek, Frankfurt am Main.

47 See Gerd Schäfer, 'Wider die Inszenierung des Vergessens: Hans Freyer und die Soziologie in Leipzig 1925–1945', p. 121ff.

48 See Gerd Schäfer, 'Die nivellierte Mittelstandsgesellschaft – Strategien der Soziologie in den 50er-Jahren'; Schäfer, 'Soziologie auf dem Vulkan – Zur Stellung René Königs in der Dreieckskonstellation der westdeutschen Nachkriegssoziologie', p. 378ff.

49 Adorno to Mauss, 14 September 1955, Heinz Mauss's Literary Estate, Hessisches Staatsarchiv, Marburg (NL 340). I am indebted to Gerhard Schäfer for drawing my attention to this letter.

50 Adorno to Anders, 24 June 1963, Theodor W. Adorno Archive, Frankfurt am Main (Br 23/13/14).

51 Adorno to Anders, 31 October 1963, Theodor W. Adorno Archive, Frankfurt am Main (Br 23/22–25); cf. Konrad Paul Liessmann, 'Hot Potatoes: Zum Briefwechsel zwischen Günther Anders und Theodor W. Adorno', p. 29ff.

52 Adorno to Schelsky, 28 May 1954. Archive of the Sozialforschungsstelle, Dortmund. Adorno subsequently cultivated relations with Arnold Gehlen, the cultural anthropologist who had also incriminated himself through his open sympathy for National Socialism. But in both cases he knew very well whom he was dealing with. As early as 3 September 1951, he wrote to Horkheimer, warning him against Schelsky's attempts to persuade the German Trades Union League to adopt an affirmative policy of restraint and social partnership. Horkheimer, *Briefwechsel, GS*, vol. 18, p. 214.

53 Adorno to Abendroth, 6 November 1954, Archive of the Institut für Sozialforschung, quoted in Alex Demirović, *Der nonkonformistische Intellektuelle*, p. 238.

54 See the study *Betriebsklima: Eine industriesoziologische Untersuchung aus dem Ruhrgebiet*, published by the institute in 1955.

55 Adorno to his mother, 21 October 1951, *Briefe an die Eltern 1939–1951*, p. 540.

56 Wolfgang Steinecke had studied music in Kiel with Fritz Stein, a pupil of Max Reger. He obtained his doctorate in 1934 with a thesis on 'Parody in Music'. In Darmstadt, where he was active at first on an honorary basis, he conducted courses on atonal and dodecaphonic music and arranged for performances of works by Schoenberg together with the composer and conductor René Leibowitz. He died in December 1961; Adorno wrote an

appreciation of his work in 'Nachruf für einen Organisator', _GS_, vol. 10.1, p. 346ff.
57 See Rolf Tiedemann, 'Nur ein Gast in der Tafelrunde', p. 177.
58 Hans Gerhard Evers (ed.), _Darmstädter Gespräch: Das Menschenbild in unserer Zeit_, p. 193.
59 Peter Suhrkamp (1891–1959) founded his publishing house in the summer of 1950. As editor of the literary magazine the _Neue Rundschau_, which he had tried to maintain as a bulwark of independent thinking free of National Socialist ideas, he had arrived at S. Fischer Verlag in 1932 when Gottfried Bermann Fischer was forced into exile. He succeeded in bringing the publishing house through the Nazi period despite being arrested by the Gestapo in 1944, during which he suffered from pneumonia and heart problems. As Carl Zuckmayer, with whom he was friendly, wrote in his _Geheimreport_: 'Suhrkamp rejected the idea of emigration for himself, above all, because, like many others, he was convinced that there were good people in Germany who should not simply be abandoned, that some people should stay to defend what should be defended and to save what could be saved, and that Germany was the responsible place to be for people who were not forced to flee.... Personally, Suhrkamp is a very profound character, a somewhat brooding, eccentric, difficult person, more depressive than optimistic' (Carl Zuckmayer, _Geheimreport_, p. 20ff.). After the war, because of a series of disagreements with Bermann Fischer, Suhrkamp, encouraged by writers such as Hermann Hesse, set up his own publishing house on 1 July 1950. The programme of 1950 and 1951 revealed a definite character that became even more marked in the years to follow. Books he published include T. S. Eliot, _Ausgewählte Essays_; Max Frisch, _Tagebuch 1946–1949_; Theodor W. Adorno, _Minima Moralia_; Walter Benjamin, _Berliner Kindheit um 1900_; Bertolt Brecht, _Versuche_ 10 & 11; and Hermann Hesse, _Späte Prosa_. The University of Frankfurt conferred on him an honorary doctorate in 1951. See Siegfried Unseld, _Peter Suhrkamp: Zur Biographie eines Verlegers in Daten, Dokumenten und Bildern_; Friedrich Voit, _Der Verleger Peter Suhrkamp_.
60 See Adorno, '_So müßte ich ein Engel und kein Autor sein': Theodor W. Adorno und die Frankfurter Verleger_.
61 See Adorno, 'Dank an Peter Suhrkamp', _GS_, vol. 20.2, p. 488ff.
62 Gershom Scholem, _Briefe_, vol. II, p. 239.
63 See Alex Demirović, _Der nonkonformistische Intellektuelle_, p. 537; Demirović, 'Zwischen Nihilismus und Aufklärung', p. 153ff.
64 Ibid., p. 154.
65 Quoted in ibid., p. 156.
66 Ibid., p. 538.
67 Adorno and Mann, _Briefwechsel_, p. 97.
68 Kracauer to Adorno, 4 July 1951, Newspaper Archive of Suhrkamp Verlag, quoted in Demirović, _Der nonkonformistische Intellektuelle_, p. 539.
69 Adorno, _Minima Moralia_, p. 74f.
70 Ibid., p. 50.
71 Ibid., p. 39.
72 Ibid., p. 126f. According to Habermas, 'Adorno regarded the striking aphorism as the appropriate form of representation; as a _form_, the aphorism can express Adorno's secret ideal of knowledge, a Platonic idea that cannot

be expressed in logical speech or at least not without contradiction: namely that knowledge must burst asunder the prison of discursive thought and terminate in pure intuition [*Anschauung*]' (Jürgen Habermas, *Nachmetaphysiches Denken*, p. 262).

73 Adorno, *Minima Moralia*, p. 86.
74 Ibid., p. 192.
75 See Jürgen Habermas, *Philosophisch-politische Profile*, p. 162.
76 Adorno, *Minima Moralia*, p. 110.
77 See *Unser Liederbuch: Die beliebtesten Kinderlieder.*
78 Adorno, *Minima Moralia*, p. 200.
79 See Albrecht Wellmer, 'Die Bedeutung der Frankfurter Schule heute', p. 224f.
80 Adorno, *Minima Moralia*, p. 247.
81 Ibid., p. 156.
82 Ibid., p. 102.
83 This paper was run by the US occupation authorities, while editorial control was in the hands of the writer Erich Kästner.
84 Adorno, 'A Title', *Notes to Literature*, vol. 2, p. 301.
85 Adorno and Mann, *Briefwechsel*, p. 98f.
86 Adorno, 'Unrat and Angel', *Notes to Literature*, vol. 2, p. 304. ('I did not wish for this' was supposed to have been said by the Emperor Franz Joseph about the First World War [trans.].)
87 Adorno to Grzimek, 1 February 1955, Theodor W. Adorno Archive, Frankfurt am Main (Br 518/1).
88 Adorno to Grzimek, 8 February 1955, Theodor W. Adorno Archive, Frankfurt am Main (Br 518/2).
89 Adorno to Grzimek, 23 April 1955, Theodor W. Adorno Archive, Frankfurt am Main (Br 518/4). Zoos, no matter where, were one of Adorno's passions. Many of the animals he loved were associated with private fantasies. His mother, Maria, who had great talents as an actor, could do a convincing imitation of a mother chimpanzee de-lousing her offspring. In his personal bestiary, however, she was not a primate, but a female hippopotamus. Her son was known as Archibald, the Hippopotamus King, and called himself just Hippo (and sometimes just a great fool [*großes Rindvieh*, literally, 'cattle' = 'a great ass']), one of the pachyderms which, according to Brehm's *Life of the Animals*, is a gregarious animal that spends much time dozing dreamily but is also immensely greedy, so that it can easily become a pest. Aunt Agathe was a tigress which, again according to Brehm, commonly attacked the largest animals but was also content with the smallest ones; it was bold and cheeky. Gretel was called a gazelle by her husband, an animal well known for its long legs, graceful head and large clear eyes.
90 Monika Plessner, *Die Argonauten auf Long Island: Begegnungen mit Hannah Arendt, Theodor W. Adorno, Gershom Scholem und anderen*, p. 48.
91 Ibid., p. 49.
92 Benjamin, *GS*, vol. 1.2, p. 697. Dorothea Razumovsky, who with her husband was a frequent guest of the Adornos in the mid-1950s, remembers the picture. The original was in the possession of Gershom Scholem and is now in the Israel Museum in Jerusalem.

93 Monika Plessner, *Die Argonauten auf Long Island*, p. 47ff.
94 The present author owes this information to research by Reinhard Pabst.
95 The present author owes this information to a letter of 27 November 1952 from Helene Calvelli-Adorno to her daughter Elisabeth Reinhuber, the present owner of the letter, extracts from which have been transcribed by Reinhard Pabst.
96 Adorno, *Negative Dialectics*, p. 371.
97 Adorno to Horkheimer, 19 April 1953, Horkheimer–Pollock Archive, Stadt- und Universitätsbibliothek, Frankfurt am Main.
98 Adorno to Horkheimer, 20 October 1952, Horkheimer–Pollock Archive, Stadt- und Universitätsbibliothek, Frankfurt am Main.
99 Friedrich (Frederick) Hacker (1914–89) had been born in Austria and emigrated in 1938 to Switzerland, from where he moved on via Britain in 1939 to the USA in 1940. There he emerged in the mid-1940s as a psychiatrist and psychoanalyst and director of the Hacker Clinic in Beverly Hills. He made a name as a researcher on aggression and as a crisis counsellor. In 1968 he created the Siegmund Freud Society in Vienna and became its president. His best-known book is *Aggression: Die Brutalisierung der modernen Welt* (1971).
100 Adorno, 'Scientific Experiences of a European Scholar in America', *Critical Models*, p. 238.
101 See Adorno, *The Stars Down to Earth*, GS, vol. 9.2, p. 11ff.; Adorno, 'Aberglaube aus zweiter Hand', *GS*, vol. 8, p. 147ff.
102 Adorno, 'Fernsehen als Ideologie', *GS*, vol. 10.2, p. 519. Adorno brought together the findings of this study of the contents of American television in two essays which are integral parts of his theory of the culture industry. See 'Fernsehen als Ideologie' and 'Prolog zum Fernsehen', *GS*, vol. 10.2, pp. 518ff and 507ff. (For an English-language essay on television, incorporating some of the ideas in these pieces, see 'How to Look at Television', in *The Culture Industry*, p. 136ff. [trans.].)
103 Adorno, 'Prologue to Television', in *Critical Models*, p. 51.
104 Ibid., p. 50.
105 Adorno, 'Résumé über Kulturindustrie', *GS*, vol. 10.1, p. 342.
106 Adorno, 'Free Time', in *The Culture Industry*, p. 170.
107 Adorno, 'Theory of Pseudo-Culture', pp. 15–38.
108 Ibid., p. 20f.
109 Ibid., p. 22.
110 Ibid., p. 26f. (translation modified).
111 Adorno and Mann, *Briefwechsel*, p. 97f.
112 Ibid., p. 85.
113 Thomas Mann, *Der Erwählte, Gesammelte Werke*, vol. VII, p. 152; Hermann Kurzke, *Thomas Mann*, p. 548ff.
114 Adorno, 'Auf die Frage: Warum sind Sie zurückgekehrt?', *GS*, vol. 20.1, p. 395.
115 Adorno used the English word [trans.].
116 Adorno to Horkheimer, 12 November 1952, Horkheimer–Pollock Archive, Stadt- und Universitätsbibliothek, Frankfurt am Main.
117 Horkheimer, *Briefwechsel*, *GS*, vol. 18, p. 247.
118 Adorno to Horkheimer, 20 October 1952, Horkheimer–Pollock Archive, Stadt- und Universitätsbibliothek, Frankfurt am Main.

119 Horkheimer, *Briefwechsel, GS*, vol. 18, p. 248. Horkheimer is known to have liked a glass of kirsch liqueur. As for Adorno, as the son of a wine-merchant who knew how to distil his own liqueurs, he had grown up knowing about drinks. The Schlagbaum public house at the Bockenheimer Warte was a favourite meeting place in the 1950s for all types of academic staff. The American academic David Riesman had recently achieved great success with *The Lonely Crowd* (1950), whose subject, not unlike that of *The Authoritarian Personality*, was changes in the social character of personality.

120 In his letter to Horkheimer of 19 April, Adorno described the difficulties of the situation in detail: 'On Wednesday evening at a staff meeting, there was the first public row between Hacker and me. I wanted to discuss with the staff how we might achieve closer cooperation between the therapists and the foundation, despite the huge handicap that the therapists are labouring under since they are overloaded with their clinical work . . . , the fact that they mostly have to perform analyses in the evenings and literally have no time for research. Hacker suddenly launched an all-out attack on me. If people had had time for research it would not have been necessary to recruit big shots like us. He said that all I was doing was to advance the projects that you and I would have pursued anyway and that I had failed to identify with the clinic. What I should be doing was to initiate projects that were in line with the interests of members of staff, however stupid they were (he literally said that). When I responded that decisions about the content of research were exclusively a matter for us, he simply denied that it was so. What he expected from us was to make the impossible possible, and to inspire the therapists to the point where they would undertake research without extra payment and even though they did not have the time. The fact that I had not done this meant that I was a dismal failure. I was being paid by the majority of the staff, and this could not be justified. . . . The entire discussion was conducted in the most shameless, rude and aggressive manner imaginable' (Adorno to Horkheimer, 19 April 1953, Horkheimer–Pollock Archive, Stadt- und Universitätsbibliothek, Frankfurt am Main.

121 Adorno to Horkheimer, 25 April 1953, Horkheimer–Pollock Archive, Stadt- und Universitätsbibliothek, Frankfurt am Main.

122 Adorno, 'Im Flug erhascht', *GS*, vol. 20.2, p. 550.

123 See Kersten Schüßler, *Helmuth Plessner: Eine intellektuelle Biographie*, p. 180ff.

124 Monika Plessner, *Die Argonauten auf Long Island*, p. 63.

125 Adorno, 'Notes on Philosophical Thinking', *Critical Models*, p. 132.

126 These were brought together and published in a final version with the title *Franz Kafka: On the Tenth Anniversary of his Death*. See *Illuminations*, p. 111ff. See also 'Franz Kafka', in *Selected Writings*, vol. 2, pp. 794–818.

127 Benjamin and Adorno, *The Complete Correspondence*, p. 67f.

128 Adorno, 'Notes on Kafka', *Prisms*, p. 246.

129 Ibid., p. 246.

130 Ibid., p. 249. For the concepts of 'gesture' and 'the gestural' in Adorno, see Michael Esders, *Begriffs-Gesten: Philosophie als kurze Prosa von Friedrich Schlegel bis Adorno*, p. 276ff.

131 Adorno, 'Notes on Kafka', *Prisms*, p. 252.

132 Ibid., p. 251.
133 Ibid., p. 265.
134 Ibid., p. 255.
135 Ibid., p. 260.
136 Ibid., p. 268.
137 Ibid.
138 Ibid., p. 270.
139 Ibid.
140 Rudolf Hirsch (1905–96) had been forced to emigrate to Holland after 1933. In 1950 he was put in charge of the literary department of S. Fischer Verlag and at the same time assumed editorial responsibility for the *Neue Rundschau*.
141 Adorno to Rudolf Hirsch, 13 August 1953, Theodor W. Adorno Archive, Frankfurt am Main (Br 634/2).
142 Adorno to Scholem, 6 January 1954, *Frankfurter Adorno Blätter*, V, 1998, p. 176.
143 Kracauer to Adorno, 28 August 1954, Kracauer's Literary Estate, Deutsches Literaturarchiv, Marbach.
144 See Alex Demirović, *Der nonkonformistische Intellektuelle*, p. 585ff.
145 Adorno to Baronin Dora von Bodenhausen, 12 February 1955, Theodor W. Adorno Archive, Frankfurt am Main (Br 153/4).
146 Alex Demirović, *Der nonkonformistische Intellektuelle*, p. 603.
147 Adorno and Mann, *Briefwechsel*, p. 140.
148 Ibid., p. 135.
149 Walter Höllerer (born 1922) was a professor of literature who became a key figure in the literary life of the Federal Republic. *Akzente*, founded by Hans Bender, was the forum of the Gruppe 47, which had been set up by Hans Werner Richter. The magazine was one of the few that refused to follow the fashion 'of cultural rebellion with its slogan of "death to bourgeois literature" and its demands for political action instead of producing literature' (Heinz Ludwig Arnold, 'Über Kulturzeitschriften nach 1945', p. 501f.).
150 Adorno, 'From a Letter to Thomas Mann on his *Die Betrogene*', *Notes to Literature*, vol. 2, p. 318f.
151 Adorno, 'On Lyric Poetry and Society', *Notes to Literature*, vol. 1, p. 50.
152 Ibid., p. 40.
153 Adorno, 'In Memory of Eichendorff', *Notes to Literature*, vol. 1, p. 57.
154 Adorno, 'On Lyric Poetry and Society', *Notes to Literature*, vol. 1, p. 44.
155 Ibid., pp. 39 and 43.
156 He stayed at the Hotel Erzherzzog Rainer in the Fourth District. The previous year, too, he had spent Easter in Vienna in order to give some lectures; he lived in the no less luxurious Parkhotel Schönbrunn in the Thirteenth District, Hietzinger Hauptstraße 12. Likewise, in April 1956, he had visited Vienna, where he had met Helene Berg for lunch in the Hotel Sacher. It was presumably through her that he met Andreas Razumovsky, a Viennese born in 1929. They shared interests in music theory and this led to a close friendship. When Razumovsky, who had been recommended to Adorno by Karl Korn of the *Frankfurter Zeitung*, returned the visit in Frankfurt in 1956, Adorno introduced him to his pupil Princess Dorothea Solms-Lich, who later became Razumovsky's wife.

157 Adorno to Horkheimer, 17 April 1958, Horkheimer–Pollock Archive, Stadt- und Universitätsbibliothek, Frankfurt am Main.
158 Horkheimer, *Späne: Notizen über Gespräche mit Max Horkheimer*, GS, vol. 14, p. 338f.
159 There were five (documented) meetings in all between Adorno and Beckett: in addition to November 1958 in Paris, meetings took place in February 1961 in Frankfurt, September 1967 in Berlin (in the Savoy Hotel in the Fasanenstraße), and in January 1968, once again in Paris. The Theodor W. Adorno Archive contains a letter from Adorno to Beckett, dated 1 March 1965, in which he announces his arrival in Paris and suggests a meeting in the Hotel Port Royal. Elizabeth Lenk insists that this meeting took place. 'Adorno forgot everything around him when Beckett entered the room. "Did you notice?", he whispered to me in the Hotel Port Royal, "He took his spectacles off for my sake?"' (Adorno and Lenk, *Briefwechsel 1962–1969*, pp. 55 and 125).
160 Rolf Tiedemann, 'Gegen den Trug der Frage nach dem Sinn', p. 23.
161 See James Knowlson, *Samuel Beckett*, p. 480ff.
162 Rolf Tiedemann has documented these notes in a highly illuminating essay. A comparison between them and the printed essay shows clearly the different stages in the development of Adorno's thinking. What is striking is that he begins by noting ideas simply as they come to him. These notes then form the foundation from which he dictates the first draft. Once this had been typed out, it was subjected to a number of thorough revisions. See Tiedemann, 'Gegen den Trug der Frage nach dem Sinn', p. 26ff.
163 There were four volumes of the *Notes to Literature*. The second volume to which the author refers here is Part II of vol. 1 of the English edition [trans.].
164 See Knowlson, *Samuel Beckett*, p. 601; Adorno, 'Trying to Understand *Endgame*', *Notes to Literature*, vol. 1, p. 267.
165 Adorno was well aware that Beckett had reservations not just about his interpretation of his work, but about all interpretations. Thus in November 1964 he wrote to Elisabeth Lenk, who intended to write a dissertation on surrealism under his supervision: 'Beckett was someone who embodied a truly indescribably advanced consciousness and at the same time he strictly rejected every interpretation of his works, including mine. In this respect he seems quite exemplary.' – 'Exemplary' of the fact that it was not possible 'simply to pump ideas into the works and then to imagine that this was their substantial meaning' (Adorno and Lenk, *Briefwechsel*, p. 39).
166 Adorno and Mann, *Briefwechsel*, pp. 128 and 141.
167 Adorno, 'Trying to Understand *Endgame*', *Notes to Literature*, vol. 1, p. 241.
168 Ibid., p. 248.
169 Ibid., p. 244.
170 Ibid., p. 250.
171 Ibid., p. 249.
172 Ibid.
173 Ibid., p. 250; see also 'Amorbach', *GS* vol. 10.1, p. 305.
174 Samuel Beckett, *The Beckett Trilogy*, p. 381.

175 Benjamin had met Kraft (1896–1991) while studying in Berlin. In the early 1920s they fell out and only resumed their friendship during their exile in Paris.

176 Adorno to Werner Kraft, 21 May 1952, quoted by Rolf Tiedemann, 'Gegen den Trug der Frage nach Sinn', p. 34. ('Indian Summer' = *Der Nachsommer* by the Austrian writer Adalbert Stifter, a lengthy elegiac novel of 1857 [trans.].)

177 Tiedemann has included a transcription of these notes in his essay, together with a facsimile of Adorno's manuscript. Ibid., p. 60ff. Adorno also commented on Beckett's novel in the *Aesthetic Theory*: 'The "*Il faut continuer*", the conclusion of Beckett's *The Unnameable*, condenses this antinomy into its essence: that externally art appears impossible while immanently it must be pursued' (*Aesthetic Theory*, p. 320).

178 Rolf Tiedemann, 'Gegen den Trug der Frage nach dem Sinn', pp. 65 and 67.

179 Adorno et al., 'Optimistisch zu denken ist kriminell', *Frankfurter Adorno Blätter*, III, 1994, p. 91.

180 Ibid., p. 122.

181 Adorno, 'Trying to Understand *Endgame*', *Notes to Literature*, vol. 1, p. 262.

182 Adorno to Marcuse, 12 December 1963, Herbert Marcuse Archive, Stadt- und Universitätsbibliothek, Frankfurt am Main.

183 *Hölderlin Jahrbuch*, vol. 13; cf. Gerhard van den Bergh, *Adornos philosophisches Deuten von Dichtung*, p. 143ff.; Pierre Bertaux, *Friedrich Hölderlin*, p. 119ff.

184 There was every reason for this essay to have been placed right at the beginning of the *Notes to Literature*, vol. 1, p. 3ff.

185 Adorno, 'Parataxis: On Hölderlin's Late Poetry', *Notes to Literature*, vol. 2, p. 110.

186 See, for example, the notes he made for his Darmstadt lecture of 1954 on the interpretation of music: 'Music – mediated by the text – has a right of its own as against the author. . . . How little of a work, conceived as the unity of material and the objective context of meaning, belongs to the author. For the most part, no more than the spontaneous act of synthesis. The author is indeed decisive – but he can only be discovered through the *text*, not from something beyond it' (Adorno, *Zu einer Theorie der musikalischen Reproduktion*, NaS, vol. 2, p. 122).

187 Adorno always resisted the idea that the task of the critic is to discover what the author meant to say with one statement or another. He made it a rule to insist on 'the consistency of the interpretation with the text'. Theodor W. Adorno Archive, Frankfurt am Main (Ts 52026).

188 Adorno, 'Parataxis', *Notes to Literature*, vol. 2, p. 110.

189 Ibid., p. 112f.

190 Ibid., p. 128.

191 Ibid., p. 131.

192 Ibid., p. 477.

193 Ibid.

194 Ibid., p. 143.

195 Adorno to Habermas, 22 July 1963, Theodor W. Adorno Archive, Frankfurt am Main (Br 536/14).

196 Jürgen Habermas, *Philosophisch-politische Profile*, p. 161.
197 Adorno, 'The Essay as Form', *Notes to Literature*, vol. 1, p. 13f.
198 Horkheimer, *Briefwechsel, GS*, vol. 18, p. 387.
199 Ibid., p. 389.
200 Adorno, 'Progress', *Critical Models*, p. 148.
201 Ibid., p. 147.
202 Ibid., p. 150.
203 Ibid.
204 Jürgen Ritsert rightly notes that Adorno attempts to retain the dual character of ends–means rationality as the foundation of all self-preserving rational action, and at the same time to expose the social conditions in which this principle contributes to the irrationalization (destruction) of the social conditions in which the individual lives. Ritsert, *Die Rationalität Adornos*.
205 Adorno, 'Progress', *Critical Models*, p. 154.
206 Ibid., p. 157.
207 Ibid., p. 159.
208 Ibid., p. 148 (translation modified).
209 See Adorno, 'Trying to Understand *Endgame*', *Notes to Literature*, vol. 1, p. 263.
210 Adorno, 'Parataxis', *Notes to Literature*, vol. 2, p. 121.

Chapter 17 Gaining Recognition for Critical Theory

1 From these lectures only a few survive in note form in the Theodor W. Adorno Archive. From the winter semester 1957–8 on, Adorno recorded his lectures on tape and then had them copied. Of the thirty-five lecture courses that he gave altogether in the course of his teaching career, some fifteen have survived. See Rolf Tiedemann, 'Editor's Afterword', in Adorno, *Kant's Critique of Pure Reason*, p. 282f.
2 Herbert Schnädelbach, 'Philosophieren lernen', p. 56ff.
3 Oskar Negt, 'Denken als Gegenproduktion', p. 77.
4 See Adorno, 'Einleitung zum *Positivisumusstreit in der deutschen Soziologie*'; 'Einleitung zu Émile Durkheim, *Soziologie und Philosophie*', *GS*, vol. 8, pp. 280ff. and 245ff.
5 See Adorno, *Introduction to Sociology*.
6 See ibid., p. 15.
7 Hauser to Adorno, 'Arnold Hauser und Theodor W. Adorno. Zeugnisse einer Freundschaft', in *Der Aquädukt 1763–1988: Ein Almanach aus dem Verlag C. H. Beck im 225. Jahr seines Bestehens*, p. 508.
8 Ibid., p. 511.
9 Weischedel himself had refused an offer of a post at Frankfurt University in 1957. See Horkheimer, *Briefwechsel, GS*, vol. 18, p. 378.
10 Ibid., p. 514.
11 See Elmar Schübl, *Jean Gebser und die Frage der Astrologie*. The correspondence between Adorno and Gebser is preserved in the Archive for Swiss Literature in Berne.
12 On 5 December, Adorno received notification from the university administration that a decision had been reached in connection with his application

for compensation. This was an initial 'compensation for acts of National Socialist injustice for members of the public service'. This decision declared, *inter alia*, 'The withdrawal of the licence to teach . . . is an oppressive measure on the part of the National Socialist regime and an act of persecution.' The law required that 'a *Privatdozent* who has been dismissed from university service on account of his Jewish origins be granted the legal status and salary to which he would have been entitled in the normal course of his academic career.' Thus, together with the title of full professor, he received 'the appropriate emoluments with effect from 1 January 1954', and furthermore, for the period between 1 April 1950 and 31 March 1951, 'compensation at the rate of the emoluments due to a full professor in retirement'. Moreover, it was resolved that 'the period between the withdrawal of the licence to teach and the reappointment . . . was to be treated as a period of service as far as salary and other entitlements were concerned.' According to the final decision on compensation of 1 February 1957, Adorno received an annual salary of DM 18,424 as from 1 January 1954, and as from 1 January 1956 an annual salary of DM 20,164. The sum for the one-year compensation amounted to DM 11,600. Archive of the Dean of the Arts Faculty of the Johann Wolfgang Goethe University (Adorno File No. 104/106); *Wiedergutmachungs-Teilbescheid*, 5 December 1956 and *Wiedergutmachung ltd. Bescheid*, 1 February 1957 (signed Dr. Rau).

13 Adorno to Hacker, 30 October 1957, Theodor W. Adorno Archive, Frankfurt am Main (Br 537/26, 27).
14 Notker Hammerstein, *Die Johann Wolfgang Goethe-Universität*, p. 801f.
15 Ibid., p. 802.
16 Institute of Social Research, *Soziologische Exkurse*, p. 18.
17 Adorno, *Traumprotokolle, GS*, vol. 20.2, p. 578.
18 The present writer is indebted to the account given by Ludwig von Friedeburg during an interview in May 1999. See also Friedeburg, 'Anspruch und Schwierigkeiten kritischer Sozialforschung', p. 71.
19 Ibid.
20 See Alex Demirović, *Der nonkonformistische Intellektuelle*, pp. 348ff. and 367ff.
21 Martin Jander, *Theo Pirker über 'Pirker': Ein Gespräch*, p. 57ff.
22 Adorno to Horkheimer, 25 February 1955, Horkheimer–Pollock Archive, Stadt- und Universitätsbibliothek, Frankfurt am Main.
23 Ralf Dahrendorf, *Über Grenzen: Lebenserinnerungen*, p. 169f.
24 Adorno to Horkheimer, 17 August 1954, Horkheimer–Pollock Archive, Stadt- und Universitätsbibliothek, Frankfurt am Main.
25 Horkheimer, *Briefwechsel, GS*, vol. 18, p. 274.
26 See Bernhard Koßmann (ed.), *Vertreter der Frankfurter Schule in den Hörfunkprogrammen 1950–1992*; Conrad Lay, 'Viele Beiträge waren urspünglich Rundfunkarbeiten', p. 173ff.; Adorno, *Erziehung zur Mündigkeit: Vorträge und Gespräche mit Hellmut Becker, 1959–1969*, p. 8f.
27 Adorno to Andersch, 31 August 1955, Theodor W. Adorno Archive (Br 24/14). Adorno said that Benn was the living proof that there was no such thing as 'the ideal instance of a unified, integral human being'. His life showed 'the degree to which the discontinuity of the individual has become necessary today – and the precondition of all things worthy

of being called human.' Adorno to Bühler, 23 September 1960 (Br 223/ 67).

28 Gottfried Benn, *Briefe an F. W. Oelze, 1950–1959*, p. 209.

29 Peter Rühmkorf, *Die Jahre, die ihr kennt*, p. 153.

30 See Clemens Albrecht et al., *Die intellektuelle Gründung der Bundesrepublik*, pp. 220ff. and 228ff.

31 For example, on Saturday, 26 September, Adorno, introduced by René König, gave the introductory talk on 'The Individual and Organization'. This was followed by discussion with such luminaries as José Ortega y Gasset (Madrid), Ernst von Schenk (Basel), Franco Lombardi (Rome), Robert Jungk (Los Angeles) and Alexander Mitscherlich (Heidelberg).

32 Adorno, 'Zur Bekämpfung des Antisemitismus heute', *GS*, vol. 20.1, p. 360.

33 Adorno, 'Notes on Philosophical Thinking', *Critical Models*, p. 132 (translation adjusted).

34 Adorno, *Minima Moralia*, p. 21.

35 Hartmut Paffrath, *Die Wendung aufs Subjekt*.

36 Adorno, 'Theory of Pseudo-Culture', pp. 15–39.

37 Adorno, 'Zur Demokratisierung der deutschen Universitäten', *GS*, vol. 20.1, pp. 335 and 336f.

38 See Institute of Social Research, *Mitteilungen*, no. 10, 1999, p. 31ff.

39 Thorsten Bonacker has tried to show that the criticism that Habermas aimed at Schelling's attempt to ground identity in the infinity of history was the starting-point for Habermas's own contribution to the further development of critical theory. 'Against this background of a turning away from Schelling, but while retaining his approach, the entire future development of critical theory can be understood as the attempt to tackle the unity of the unconditioned and the uncertain, but this time in a post-metaphysical manner and with quasi-transcendental methods' (Bonacker, 'Ungewißheit und Unbedingtheit', p. 113f.).

40 In his review Habermas had asked: 'Is it possible for the planned murder of millions of human beings about which we all now know to be made comprehensible by explaining it ontologically as an arbitrary blow of fate? Is it not in fact a crime committed by people who acted while in full command of their faculties – and is it not at the same time the bad conscience of an entire nation? . . . Is it not the primary task of all reflective people to clarify the actions of a nation that were carried out in full consciousness, and to ensure that this knowledge is kept alive?' (Jürgen Habermas, *Philosophisch-Politische Profile*, p. 65ff.).

41 Jürgen Habermas, *Die neue Unübersichtlichkeit*, pp. 167ff. and 214ff. In this interview of 1981, as well as in two further conversations with the present writer, Habermas emphasized that, outside Frankfurt in the early 1950s, there was no such thing as an unambiguous position called 'critical theory': 'To my mind, there was no such thing as critical theory, there was no coherent doctrine. Adorno wrote critical essays on cultural matters and apart from that he taught seminars on Hegel. He brought a specific Marxist background into play – that's how it was' (ibid., p. 171). Demirović's scrupulous reconstruction of Adorno's practice as a teacher led him to a different conclusion: 'The central themes of critical theory were discussed in great detail in the seminars. And with the *Dialectic of*

Enlightenment, the participants also had the opportunity to discuss a central text from the period before the return from exile. There was constant talk about Marx, the Marxist tradition, the history of the workers' movement and the theoretical problems of critical theory. Marx's theory set the standard by which to judge other sociological theories' (Alex Demirović, *Der nonkonformistische Intellektuelle*, p. 477).

42 According to Demirović, these objections were based on the claim that the study had relied on 'too narrow a link between politics, democracy and education'. This had led to talk of a 'political society'. In a letter to Adorno, Horkheimer asked, 'If it is the case that the nation is "imprisoned in a bourgeois society by the shackles of a liberal constitution and the rule of law", how is it to make the transition to a so-called political society for which it is "long-since ready", according to Habermas, if not by the use of force? Such statements in the research report of an institute that is financed out of the public funds of this shackling society are impossible' (Horkheimer, *Briefwechsel*, *GS*, vol. 18, p. 447); see Demirović, *Der nonkonformistische Intellektuelle*, p. 257ff.

43 Jürgen Habermas, *Student und Politik*, p. 44.

44 Abendroth gave his talks within the framework of an internal institute lecture series on 'Politics and Sociology'. See the letter from Adorno to Abendroth, 14 November 1957, Theodor W. Adorno Archive, Frankfurt am Main (Br 1/15); Abendroth, *Antagonistische Gesellschaft und politische Demokratie*.

45 Jürgen Habermas, *Student und Politik*, p. 156.

46 This agreement can be seen in his letter to Horkheimer, 15 March 1960, Horkheimer–Pollock Archive, Stadt- und Universitätsbibliothek, Frankfurt am Main. See also Demirović, *Der nonkonformistische Intellektuelle*, p. 253ff.

47 See Horkheimer's letter to Adorno, 27 September 1958, Horkheimer, *Briefwechsel*, *GS*, vol. 18, p. 437ff. Adorno's marginal comments on the original letter in the Theodor W. Adorno Archive make it clear that he by no means shared Horkheimer's general settling of accounts with Habermas's Marxist position as that had been expounded in his report on the literature 'Zur philosophischen Diskussion um Marx und den Marxismus', in Habermas, 'Between Philosophy and Science: Marxism as Critique', in *Theory and Practice*, p. 195ff.

48 Adorno to Horkheimer, 15 March 1960, Horkheimer–Pollock Archive, Stadt- und Universitätsbibliothek, Frankfurt am Main.

49 See René Görtzen, 'Habermas: Bi(bli)ographische Bausteine', p. 543ff.

50 Adorno's artistic and academic interests were so extensive that he tended to accept very many invitations to conferences, discussion forums and congresses. In addition to those already mentioned – the *Darmstädter Gespräche* and the legendary Summer Courses for New Music – he took part, for example, in the Forum on Art in Baden-Baden in summer 1959 where the topic discussed was 'Is Modern Art being "Managed"?' Or, in 1967, he attended the 'Rencontres internationales de Genève', which addressed the subject of 'Art in Society Today'. See Adorno, 'Vorschlag zur Ungüte', *GS*, vol. 10.1, p. 330; 'Die Kunst und die Künste', *GS*, vol. 10.1, p. 432; see also Jutta Held, 'Adorno und die kunsthistorische Diskussion der Avantgarde vor 1968'.

51 A draft by Horkheimer with revisions in Adorno's handwriting as well as a version of the report in two and a half pages are preserved in the Horkheimer–Pollock Archive of the Stadt- und Universitätsbibliothek, Frankfurt am Main.

52 See Clemens Albrecht et al., *Die intellektuelle Gründung der Bundesrepublik*, p. 194. Albrecht points out that, 'underlying the dispute about the appointment of Golo Mann, there were profound disagreements about the nature of anti-Semitism and its anthropological and sociopsychological causes. This was not merely a question of different theories being advanced to explain a historical phenomenon of central importance, but in the heated atmosphere of the 1960s there were also considerations of the political and educational consequences at stake.' Ibid., p. 198.

53 See Christoph von Schwerin, *Als sei nichts gewesen*, p. 122f. Adorno's dislike of Golo Mann persisted. He regarded Mann as a key figure in the attempt to smear him in 1963 by disinterring his review of Müntzel in 1933–4 (see the account in chapter 11: 'Hibernating with Dignity?'). In 1963 a meeting between him and Golo Mann was supposed to take place in Vienna, but Adorno went out of his way to avoid it. He wrote to Arnold Gehlen, saying that he wished to avoid such a meeting. 'Since my relations with him are so fraught, the situation would have been embarrassing' (Adorno to Gehlen, 19 June 1963, Gehlen Archive, TU Dresden). The correspondence between Adorno and Gehlen is preserved in the Gehlen Archive administered by Karl-Siegberg Rehberg in the Technical University, Dresden. There are thirty-nine letters there in all, eleven from Adorno. The present writer has read the correspondence.

54 Adorno to Gehlen, 2 December 1960, Gehlen Archive, TU Dresden; see also Christian Thies, *Die Krise des Individuums*, p. 45ff.

55 Gehlen to Adorno, 18 October 1961, Gehlen Archive, TU Dresden.

56 See Adorno, *Philosophische Terminologie*, vol. 1, p. 190ff.

57 See Christian Thies, *Die Krise des Individuums*, p. 51.

58 Talk on Radio Free Berlin, *Literarisches Wort*, 9 March 1956, quoted by Demirović, *Der nonkonformistische Intellektuelle*, p. 500.

59 Adorno, *Aesthetic Theory*, p. 257.

60 Adorno, *Minima Moralia* (Appendix), GS, vol. 4, p. 288f.

61 Adorno, 'Schuld und Abwehr', GS, vol. 9.2, p. 143; cf. R. Wiggershaus, *The Frankfurt School*, p. 472ff.; Demirović, *Der nonkonformistische Intellektuelle*, p. 353ff.

62 For Adorno what emerged from chance conversations in a train was the terrorism of a society that compels conformism: 'There is nothing innocuous left', he remarks in one of the first aphorisms in *Minima Moralia*. 'The chance conversation in the train, when, to avoid dispute, one consents to a few statements that one knows ultimately to implicate murder, is already a betrayal; no thought is immune against communication, and to utter it in the wrong place and in wrong agreement is enough to undermine its truth' (*Minima Moralia*, p. 25).

63 Ibid., p. 233.

64 Ibid., p. 108.

65 Adorno, 'Schuld und Abwehr', GS, vol. 9.2, p. 136; Institute of Social Research, *Gruppenexperiment*. The section written by Adorno includes pp. 275–426 of the original text revised by Fritz Pollock.

66 Adorno, 'Schuld und Abwehr', *GS*, vol. 9.2, p. 150.
67 Ibid., pp. 155 and 158.
68 Ibid., p. 184.
69 Ibid., p. 294f.
70 Ibid., p. 312.
71 Adorno to Böhm, 14 January 1957, Adorno, *Ontologie und Dialektik*, *NaS*, vol. 7, p. 367.
72 Hofstätter, 'Zum "Gruppenexperiment" von Pollock', p. 103.
73 See König, *Briefwechsel*, vol. 1, p. 448.
74 Adorno, 'Hofstätter-Replik', *GS*, vol. 9.2, p. 392f.
75 This was a talk Adorno gave at the First European Conference on Education, which took place at Wiesbaden, 30 October–30 November 1962.
76 Adorno, 'The Meaning of Working Through the Past', *Critical Models*, p. 90.
77 Unknown vandals had defaced the monument for the victims of National Socialism and also the synagogue in Cologne with swastikas and anti-Semitic slogans. (See Wolfgang Kraushaar (ed.), *Frankfurter Schule und Studentenbewegung*, vol. 1, p. 157.) Right-wing radicals carried out similar anti-Semitic daubings and there was a wave of graveyard desecrations. Against this background, Horkheimer wrote to Wolf Jost Siedler, the editor of the culture section of *Der Tagesspiegel*, who had invited him to list the most significant cultural events since 1945: 'I am astonished that life can go on so merrily after all the horrors that have taken place. Wherever something of the insanity of this situation makes itself felt in the despairing works of avant-garde art, I have felt some sort of affinity' (Horkheimer, *Briefwechsel*, *GS*, vol. 18, p. 456).
78 The psychoanalyst Alexander Mitscherlich regarded this lack of moral sensitivity as part of a general 'inability to mourn'. The principal thesis of his psycho-social analysis in the book he wrote with this title was 'that there is a cause-and-effect relation between the political and social immobilism and provincialism that prevails in the Federal Republic and the obstinate resistance to memories, and in particular the refusal to share feelings towards events of the past that are currently being denied' (Mitscherlich, *Die Unfähigkeit zu trauern*, p. 9).
79 See Thorsten Bonacker, 'Theodor W. Adorno – Die Zukunft des Erinnerns', p. 173ff.; Lars Rensmann, *Kritische Theorie über den Antisemitismus*, p. 231ff.; Helmut Dubiel, *Niemand ist frei von der Geschichte*, p. 81ff.
80 Adorno, *Critical Models*, p. 93.
81 Ibid., p. 98. See also Adorno, 'Education after Auschwitz', *Critical Models*, p. 191ff.
82 The idea that parliamentary democracy threatened to turn into pseudo-democracy because the political form assumed by the sovereignty of the people was in contradiction with the social and economic system was a fear that inspired many of the books on politics in the mid-1960s. See Schäfer and Nedelmann (eds), *Der CDU-Staat*; Agnoli and Brückner, *Die Transformation der Demokratie*.
83 Adorno, 'Education after Auschwitz', *Critical Models*, p. 98f.
84 Ibid., p. 102.
85 Ibid., p. 103.
86 See Adorno, 'Critique', *Critical Models*, p. 281f. On the question, not discussed here, of the normative content of democratic societies and the

criteria of social criticism 'that attempts to fix or transcend locally practised values', see Axel Honneth, 'Rekonstruktive Gesellschaftskritik unter genealogischem Vorbehalt', p. 729ff.; also Thorsten Bonacker, 'Hat die Moderne einen normativen Gehalt?', p. 159ff.; Michael Walzer, *Kritik und Gemeinsinn*; Ulrich Oevermann, 'Der Intellektuelle – Soziologische Strukturbestimmung des Komplementär von Öffentlichkeit', p. 13ff.

87 See Clemens Albrecht et al., *Die intellektuelle Gründung der Bundesrepublik*.

88 'Interventions' (*Eingriffe*) is the title of an essay collection. It forms one half of the volume that has appeared in English with the title of *Critical Models* [trans.].

89 Adorno, *Minima Moralia*, p. 50.

90 Adorno to Hacker, 29 June 1956, Theodor W. Adorno Archive, Frankfurt am Main (Br 537/13, 14).

91 Institute of Social Research, *Freud in der Gegenwart*, p. x.

92 Adorno to Andersch, 22 October 1955, Theodor W. Adorno Archive, Frankfurt am Main (Br 24/17).

93 Adorno's diagnosis was as follows: 'Modern character types are those who neither have an ego nor really act unconsciously, but who mirror an objective feature reflexively. Together they carry out a senseless ritual, follow the compulsive rhythm of repetition, and become emotionally deprived: the destruction of the ego is accompanied by the growth in narcissism or its collectivist derivatives' (Adorno, 'Zum Verhältnis von Soziologie und Psychologie', *GS*, vol. 8, p. 83); cf. Bonacker, 'Ohne Angst verschieden sein können: Individualität in der integralen Gesellschaft', p. 117ff.

94 Adorno, 'Die revidierte Psychoanalyse', *GS*, vol. 8, p. 20ff.

95 Theodor W. Adorno Archive, Frankfurt am Main (Ts 51864ff.); see also Stefan Breuer, 'Adornos Anthropologie', p. 336ff.

96 See, for example, 'The Health unto Death' (p. 58ff.); 'This Side of the Pleasure Principle' (p. 60ff.); 'Invitation to the Dance' (p. 62f.); 'Monad' (p. 148ff.); 'Novissimum Organum' (p. 228ff.).

97 Theodor W. Adorno Archive, Frankfurt am Main (Ts 51959).

98 Ibid. (Ts 51873); see also Adorno, 'Sexual Taboos and Law Today', *Critical Models*, p. 71ff.

99 Adorno, 'Individuum und Organisation', *GS*, vol. 8, p. 450.

100 In his account of Adorno's critique of the subject, Bonacker establishes that the particular nature of Adorno's critical theory is 'that it focuses on the immanent meanings of individuality as they have been developed by modern society – albeit not in the sense that it simply contrasts this individuality with the individuality that has failed to materialize.' Instead, he is concerned 'to show how in the individual modern society creates its own opposite, one that only obtains the strength to live from the tension with society' (Bonacker, 'Ohne Angst verschieden sein können', p. 141).

101 Adorno and Gehlen, 'Ist die Soziologie eine Wissenschaft vom Menschen?', p. 228.

102 Adorno, *Minima Moralia*, p. 135.

103 Adorno, 'Zum Verhältnis von Soziologie und Psychologie', *GS*, vol. 8, p. 65.

104 Ibid., p. 55ff.

105 Ibid., p. 83.
106 Adorno, *Minima Moralia*, p. 150.
107 Adorno and Gehlen, 'Ist die Soziologie eine Wissenschaft vom Menschen?', p. 250.
108 Ibid.
109 See *Negative Dialectics*, p. 374.
110 Adorno, 'Postscriptum', *GS*, vol. 8, p. 92.
111 Ibid.
112 Ibid., p. 91.
113 See Adorno, 'Late Capitalism or Industrial Society?', '*Can One Live after Auschwitz?*', p. 123f.
114 See Adorno, *Introduction to Sociology*, p. 153; Adorno, 'Free Time', *Critical Models*, p. 174f.
115 Ibid., p. 175. It may be pointed out that Adorno's death prevented him from carrying out his intention of bringing together his various texts on sociological theory into a volume that would bear the title *Integration – Disintegration*, preceded by an introductory essay on this theme. See Rolf Tiedemann, 'Editorische Nachbemerkung', *GS*, vol. 9.2, p. 404.
116 Adorno, 'Theory of Pseudo-Culture', p. 35 (translation slightly changed).
117 Adorno, 'Vers une musique informelle', *Quasi una fantasia*, p. 269.
118 He had been invited originally in 1948 by René Leibowitz through the good offices of Wolfgang Steinecke. In the summer courses, the young composers who were present became increasingly preoccupied with Schoenberg's twelve-tone technique. 'In 1949 the Second Viennese School made its début in the concert programmes. Olivier Messiaen was active as a teacher in Darmstadt and wrote the piano piece "Mode de valeurs et d'intensités", which is said to be the first piece of serial music. In 1950 Edgar Varèse taught in Kranichstein; the sound waves of electronic music attracted attention, Luigi Nono's op. 1 was given its premiere – and provoked a furious scandal. In 1951, the summer courses joined forces with the 24th Music Festival of the IGNM, while the Second International Twelve-Tone Congress witnessed the world premiere of Schoenberg's "Dance round the Golden Calf". Herbert Eimert and Pierre Schaeffer debated the problems of electronic music and musique concrète' (Wulf Konold, 'Adorno – Metzger: Rückblick auf eine Kontroverse', p. 93).
119 See Adorno to Frederick Goldbeck, 30 April 1954, Theodor W. Adorno Archive, Frankfurt am Main (Br 483/19); Rolf Tiedemann, 'Nur ein Gast in der Tafelrunde', p. 178.
120 The notes for this lecture have been reprinted in Adorno, *Zu einer Theorie der musikalischen Reproduktion*, *NaS*, vol. 2, p. 319ff.
121 Adorno to Kolisch, 4 June 1954, ibid., p. 383.
122 Adorno, 'Für die Kranchsteiner Idee', *GS*, vol. 19, p. 630ff.
123 Carla Henius, *Schnebel, Nono, Schoenberg oder Die wirkliche und erdachte Musik*, pp. 81 and 83.
124 Adorno, 'The Ageing of the New Music', *Essays on Music*, p. 182 (translation altered). Claus-Steffen Mahnkopf has summed up Adorno's criticisms as follows: 'Serialism, in Adorno's view, hypostatizes the pre-artistic, purely physical material, fetishizes autonomized techniques; replaces composition with handicraft and the mere, atomized arrangement of material, instead of configuring it in a musically qualified way;

neutralizes it and levels it down to the integral, rational denominator of abstract time; destroys meaning of every kind by refusing all logic and context; abandons subjectivity in favour of a so-called being in itself; confuses the integral coherence of material with an integral coherent meaning; and consistently denies the immanent historical aspect of the material' (Claus-Steffen Mahnkopf, 'Adornos Kritik der Neueren Musik', p. 253ff.).

125 Adorno, *Dissonanzen*, p. 7; cf. the revised preface in *GS*, vol. 13, p. 12.

126 Adorno, 'The Ageing of the New Music', *Essays on Music*, p. 195.

127 In his polemic, Adorno succinctly formulated one of his chief criticisms: 'Infatuation with the material along with blindness toward what is made out of it resulting from the fiction that the material speaks for itself, from an effectively primitive symbolism. To be sure, the material does speak but only in those constellations in which the artwork positions it' (ibid., p. 189).

128 Adorno to Kolisch, 4 June 1954, quoted in Tiedemann, 'Nur ein Gast in der Tafelrunde', p. 180.

129 Heinz-Klaus Metzger had studied with Max Deutsch and Rudolf Kolisch, among others, and had met Adorno in the International Summer Courses in Darmstadt. He and Adorno had been on friendly terms, and the friendship was even strengthened by the debate in the mid-1950s. At the turn of the year 1957–8, he and Adorno took part in a debate on the radio with the title 'Recent Music – Progress or Regression?'. See Hans-Klaus Jungheinrich, ' "Ich halte jedenfalls an der Idee der Moderne fest": Von Adorno lernen: Ein Gespräch mit Heinz-Klaus Metzger', p. 68ff.

130 Ibid., p. 70; cf. Metzger, 'Musik wozu: Literatur zu Noten', p. 61ff. and also p. 90ff.; Konold, 'Adorno – Metzger: Blick auf eine Kontroverse', p. 91ff.

131 Adorno to Marcuse, 24 November 1964, Herbert Marcuse Archive, Stadt- und Universitätsbibliothek, Frankfurt am Main; Adorno to Henius, 8 December 1964, Theodor W. Adorno Archive, Frankfurt am Main (Br 592/46); cf. Adorno, 'Nach Steuermanns Tod', *GS*, vol. 17, p. 311ff.

132 See Rolf Tiedemann, 'Vorrede, Editorische Nachbemerkung', in Adorno, *Beethoven: The Philosophy of Music*, pp. ix and 249ff.

133 Ibid., p. 14.

134 Ibid., p. 39.

135 Ibid., p. 76f.

136 See Adorno, *Mahler: A Musical Physiognomy*, p. ix.

137 Ibid., p. 129.

138 Theodor W. Adorno Archive, Frankfurt am Main (Ts 52004).

139 Christine Eichel has clarified the concept of 'physiognomy'. Adorno 'traces the hidden impulses of the music and their expressive language by interpreting the music anthropomorphically; by treating the structure of the works as an analogy to the face with all its individual features, he explores the expression of the work through an analogy with the mimicry that comes to form an image of collective mimetic historiography which lies beyond the rational analysis of reality.... The concept of physiognomy points in two directions: on the one hand, the physiognomical expression of a work of art is taken to exist independently of individual listeners; on the other, it is assumed that this physiognomical expression can be translated into a linguistic description – without the imponderabilia

inseparable from a consideration of the listeners' responses' (Eichel, *Vom Ermatten der Avantgarde zur Vernetzung der Künste*, pp. 197 and 188).

140   Adorno to Helms, 12 September 1960, Theodor W. Adorno Archive, Frankfurt am Main (Br 588/64).

141   Eichel interprets this personal note as a function of the logic of Adorno's imagination. He 'unfolds the elements of his philosophy in images and metaphors as in a microcosm. They not only render visible the epistemo- logical content of the music, but also situate the music within a spectrum of the arts and works of art. This takes place through the medium of analogy' (Eichel, *Vom Ermatten der Avantgarde zur Vernetzung der Künste*, p. 197).

142   Adorno to Gehlen, 2 December 1960, Gehlen Archive, TU Dresden.

143   Adorno, *Mahler*, p. 146.

144   In the context of a discussion of the Fourth Symphony, Adorno remarks: 'After the development, at the dictate of the fanfare, has dwindled away, masking the beginning of the recapitulation, the music is swept from the scene by a general pause, until suddenly, the main theme continues from the middle of the restatement; this moment is like the child's joy at being abruptly transported from the forest to the old-fashioned market place of Miltenberg' (ibid., p. 54f.). The relation between the childhood of Adorno's imagination and his view of Mahler's music is even more intimate when he observes that 'Mahler's music passes a maternal hand over the hair of those to whom it turns' (ibid., p. 29).

145   Ibid., p. 154.

146   Ibid., p. 39.

147   Ibid., p. 46.

148   Ibid., p. 22.

149   Ibid., p. 125.

150   Ibid., p. 56.

151   Adorno, 'Mahler: A Centenary Address', *Quasi una fantasia*, p. 85f. The Mahler monograph was the basis of a commemorative speech that Adorno had given in June 1960 at the invitation of the Mahler Society in Vienna. As he remarked, the text aimed to facilitate access to Mahler's works.

152   Adorno, 'Vers une musique informelle', *Quasi una fantasia*, p. 282.

153   According to Mahnkopf, 'Vers une musique informelle' is the 'metatheory of the *Philosophy of Modern Music* whose rationalizing diagnosis anti- cipates the problems of serialism in so far as serialism generalizes the structure of dodecaphonic thinking about the row.' Mahnkopf sums up Adorno's intentions with the comment that 'musique informelle seeks a way out from the techniques of dodecaphony, serialism and aleatorics, all of which refuse a return to free atonality' (Mahnkopf, 'Adornos Kritik der Neueren Musik', pp. 259 and 261).

154   Adorno, 'Vers une musique informelle', *Quasi una fantasia*, p. 288.

155. Ibid., p. 292.

156   Ibid., p. 318ff.

157   Mahnkopf, 'Adornos Kritik der Neueren Musik', p. 266. Mahnkopf con- cludes that even today 'Vers une musique informelle' is a text that will be among the first that the philosopher of music will wish to consult. At the same time, he recommends a 'deconstructive reading' (ibid., p. 276f.). See also the interesting interpretation in Günter Seubold, 'Die Erinnerung retten und dem Kitsch die Zunge lösen', p. 141ff.

158 Adorno, 'Vers une musique informelle', *Quasi una fantasia*, p. 282f.
159 Adorno, *Alban Berg: Master of the Smallest Link*, p. 38.
160 The present writer has based this account on the research of Reinhard Pabst. See Pabst, 'Der Vogel, der da sang', p. 16.
161 Adorno, 'Amorbach', *GS*, vol. 10.1, p. 303ff. (Neidhard von Reuental was a Middle High German troubadour who lived in the first half of the thirteenth century, until around 1230 [trans.].)
162 Ibid., p. 307. (Gottfried von Berlichingen was a robber baron from the Peasants' War of the 1520s. He was immortalized in Goethe's play *Götz von Berlichingen* (1773)[trans.].)
163 Adorno, 'Wien, nach Ostern 1967', *GS*, vol. 10.1, p. 426.
164 Adorno, *Negative Dialectics*, p. 373.
165 Lore Kramer has told the present author about these excursions to Amorbach, which usually featured a good luncheon or dinner in a country inn.
166 Adorno to Bührer, 31 January 1968, Theodor W. Adorno Archive, Frankfurt am Main (Br 20/6).
167 See Christoph von Schwerin, *Als sei nichts gewesen*, p. 293. Having first met Count Andreas Razumovsky in Vienna in 1955, he introduced him to a pupil of his, Dorothea Princess zu Solms-Lich, the following year. This meeting finally led to the marriage of the couple. (The present writer is indebted to Dorothea Razumovsky for this information.)
168 Adorno, 'Wien, nach Ostern 1967', *GS*, vol. 10.1, p. 424.
169 Adorno, 'Konzeption eines Wiener Operntheaters', *GS*, vol. 19, p. 501.
170 Adorno, 'Wien, nach Ostern 1967', *GS*, vol. 10.1, p. 425.
171 Adorno, 'Konzeption eines Wiener Operntheaters', *GS*, vol. 19, p. 498.
172 Ibid., p. 499.
173 Adorno, 'Wien, nach Ostern 1967', *GS*, vol. 10.1, p. 430.
174 Ibid., p. 428.
175 Ibid., p. 429.
176 Adorno, 'Luccheser Memorial', *GS*, vol. 10.1, p. 396.
177 See Friedrich Nietzsche, *Sämtliche Briefe*, vol. 6, letters to Peter Gast, 7 July, 8 July, 9 July 1881 and 3 September 1883. With his poem *Sils Maria*, he ensured that its name would live on. See also Werner Ross, *Der ängstliche Adler*, pp. 577, 592 and 681.
178 Heinz Steinert, *Adorno in Wien*, p. 141. Steinert had a conversation with Lotte Tobisch which he quotes in his book. Urs Kienberger, then the owner of the Hotel Waldhaus, told the present author about having Adorno as a guest. On rare occasions, when the mood took him, Adorno would play the piano late into the night. He played pieces from the popular songs and jazz repertoire of the 1920s. The Adornos spent altogether almost 400 nights at the Waldhaus. Every summer, they always insisted on occupying the same table by the window for dinner. As a hotel guest, Adorno was said to be difficult and demanding.
179 Adorno, 'Aus Sils Maria', *GS*, vol. 10.1, p. 326.
180 Ibid., p. 328.
181 Jean Bollack, Celan's biographer, commented on this failed encounter: 'The meeting was destined not to happen. This was to make it possible for an idea to take its place, without the obstacles that usually block its path.' We can endorse Bollack's view that this imagined meeting helped the

poet 'discover his own, historically based identity'. Jean Bollack, *Paul Celan: Poetik der Fremdheit*, pp. 25 and 208.

182 Adorno and Celan, *Briefwechsel*, p. 23ff.; Joachim Seng, *Auf den Kreis-Wegen der Dichtung*, p. 260ff.; Seng, 'Von der Musikalität einer "graueren" Sprache: Zu Celans Auseinandersetzung mit Adorno', p. 419ff.; Bollack believes that Celan's letter to Adorno is not without irony. After all, it contains the statement that 'in this text he is represented by a figure that is very different from him, his opposite in fact, namely a "Jew", the very thing Adorno wasn't. He was neither great as a Jew, nor a great Jew (like Scholem). Celan may have visited him in Frankfurt in order to explain the significance of this substitution' (Bollack, *Paul Celan*, p. 211).

183 In his biography of Celan, Felstiner describes this poem, which Celan wrote towards the end of the war, as 'the Guernica of postwar European literature' (John Felstiner, *Paul Celan: Poet, Survivor, Jew*, p. 3).

184 The seventeen letters that passed between the two men make this quite clear.

185 Paul Celan, *Gesammelte Werke*, vol. 3, pp. 169 and 172f. (The allusion to Lenz going through the mountains is a reference – evidently apposite in the light of the award to Celan of the Büchner Prize – to the first sentence of Georg Büchner's *Lenz*, a story of the mental breakdown of the Sturm und Drang poet Johann Michael Reinhold Lenz [trans.].)

186 Celan to Adorno, 23 May 1960, *Briefwechsel*, p. 27f.

187 Dagmar von Gersdorff, *Marie Luise Kaschnitz*, p. 176ff.

188 Paul Celan, 'Der Meridian: Rede anläßlich der Verleihung des Georg-Büchner Preises', *Gesammelte Werke*, vol. 3, p. 187.

189 Adorno to Celan, 13 June 1960, *Briefwechsel*, p. 29f.

190 Adorno, 'Those Twenties', *Critical Models*, p. 48.

191 Claire Goll was the widow of the poet Yvan Goll, the friend of Paul Celan who was younger than him by thirty years. She had publicly accused Celan of having plagiarized her late husband's poems. Together with Kaschnitz and Bachmann, Peter Szondi had leapt to Celan's defence. He published a refutation in the *Neue Züricher Zeitung*. See Barbara Wiedemann, *Paul Celan: Die Goll-Affäre: Dokumente zu einer 'Infamie'*. In the meantime, it has become clear that Claire Goll staged the entire affair. Celan, who was unable properly to defend himself against the accusations, experienced them as a theft of his own identity.

192 See Adorno and Lenk, *Briefwechsel*, pp. 113f. and 128ff.; see also Adorno to Celan, 9 February 1968, *Briefwechsel*, p. 44f. The *Aesthetic Theory*, however, contains a lengthy passage on Celan's poetry; cf. Adorno, *Aesthetic Theory*, p. 321f.; cf. Jean Bollack, *Paul Celan*, p. 190.

193 Adorno, *Negative Dialectics*, p. 362.

194 Ibid., p. 367.

195 See Petra Kiedaisch (ed.), *Lyrik nach Auschwitz?: Adorno und die Dichter*, p. 9ff.

196 See Enzensberger, *Einzelheiten*, p. 249ff.; Hildesheimer, *Gesammelte Werke*, vol. 7, p. 57ff.

197 Adorno, *Minima Moralia*, p. 44.

198 Alfred Andersch (1914–80) had been interned in Dachau as a communist. After the war he became the editor of *Der Ruf*, a magazine that was at first licensed and then banned by the occupation authorities. He founded

the Evening Studio on Frankfurt Radio and until 1958 he was the chairman of 'Radio Essay' on South-West German Radio. His most important literary works include *Die Kirschen der Freiheit* (1952), *Sansibar oder Der letzte Grund* (1957), and *Die Rote* (1960). See also Stephan Reinhardt, *Alfred Andersch: Eine Biographie*; W. G. Sebald, *On the Natural History of Destruction*, p. 109ff.

199　Petra Kiedaisch, *Lyrik nach Auschwitz?*, p. 76ff.
200　In his illuminating essay on Adorno's verdict on poetry after Auschwitz, Peter Stein points out that Andersch to all intents and purposes whitewashes the period of Nazi rule in Germany by describing it as an 'experiment' about 'how to live in a society from which literature is completely absent.' He goes on to interpret the period after 1945 as the 'attempt to create a literature after the end of literature'. Adorno's own statement is said to be a fitting comment on such efforts. In effect, Andersch turns everything on its head: '"Auschwitz" as a metaphor for uncultured fascism (without the genocide of the Jews), and Adorno's aphorism as critique of anti-fascist literature! With this argument Andersch helped to establish a trend in which an ignorant argument was turned against Adorno on the following pattern: the great philosopher A. has indeed stated that after Auschwitz . . . no poetry should be written; but the writers have refuted him' (Peter Stein, 'Darum mag falsch gewesen sein . . .'). See also Burkhardt Lindner, 'Was heißt: Nach Auschwitz?'
201　Hans Magnus Enzensberger, *Einzelheiten*, p. 491. (*In the dwellings of death* is the title of a collection of poems by Nelly Sachs, the winner of the Nobel Prize for literature in 1966 [trans.].)
202　Wolfgang Hildesheimer, *Gesammelte Werke*, vol. 7, p. 57.
203　Adorno, 'Commitment', Ernst Bloch et al., *Aesthetics and Politics*, p. 188. See also *Notes to Literature*, vol. 2, p. 87. Rolf Tiedemann has pointed out that Adorno's statement was misunderstood not just by those poets who feared that their vocation was being called into question. He was misunderstood also by the likes of Günther Anders, who read into it the *prohibition* on writing more poetry. Adorno, *'Can One Live After Auschwitz?'*, p. xv.
204　Adorno, *Negative Dialectics*, p. 365.
205　See Adorno to Steuermann, 29 October 1961 and 2 January 1962, Rolf Tiedemann (ed.), *Adorno-Noten*, pp. 64 and 68. Adorno had suggested to Eduard Steuermann that he should persuade Bachmann to write a libretto based on Balzac's *Peau de chagrin*, but she had refused. 'You write with such love and respect for your friend that I find it truly difficult to explain why it is quite impossible for me to write a libretto for Steuermann. But let me try to do so: for months now I have been unable to do or write anything, and without wishing to impress you or myself with talk of a "crisis", I feel that this not being able and not wanting is not something that will go away tomorrow or even the day after.' Quoted in Sigrid Weigel, *Ingeborg Bachmann: Hinterlassenschaften unter Wahrung des Briefgeheimnisses*, p. 473.
206　The allusion is to Hölderlin's question in *Bread and Wine*: 'And why poets in desolate times?' [trans.].
207　Adorno, 'Valéry's Deviations', *Notes to Literature*, vol. 1, p. 143.
208　Marie Luise Kaschnitz, *Steht noch dahin: Neue Prosa*, p. 7.

209 Letter from Carla Henius to Adorno, 18 May 1961, Theodor W. Adorno Archive, Frankfurt am Main (Br 592/36).
210 Marie Luise Kaschnitz, *Tagebücher aus den Jahren 1936–1966*, vol. 1, p. 843f.
211 See Sigrid Weigel, *Ingeborg Bachmann*, p. 473.
212 See Scholem, *Briefe*, vol. III, pp. 85 and 335; also vol. II, p. 156; cf. Sigrid Weigel, *Ingeborg Bachmann*, p. 6ff.
213 See Adorno and Lenk, *Briefwechsel*, p. 12ff.
214 On 29 March 1956, Adorno wrote to Alfred Andersch that after his return from America he felt overwhelmed by Paris, and in particular 'by the way in which when you return home late at night in Paris you hear the echo of your own steps on the pavement – a sound that is quite inconceivable in America. And this led me to the reflection that the difference between New York and Paris was far greater than between Paris and Amorbach. . . . This was an observation I made when returning home very late at night from the home of my friend René Leibowitz on the quai Voltaire, to the Hotel Lutétia on boulevard Raspail' (Adorno to Andersch, 29 March 1956, Theodor W. Adorno Archive, Frankfurt am Main [Br 24/46]). Adorno later worked this experience into his essay on Amorbach.; cf. 'Amorbach', *GS*, vol. 10.1, p. 304.
215 Adorno started work on the German-language version of the lectures at the end of 1960. At that time, he completed the lecture on 'Ontological Need' and also the second one on 'Being and Existence'. The notes on the third lecture, on *Negative Dialectics*, were probably finished by the time he was due to travel on 13 March 1961. The French-language versions were produced by Gabrielle Wittkop-Ménardeau, and were given the titles: 'Le besoin ontologique', 'Être et existence' and 'Vers une dialectique négative'.
216 See Rolf Tiedemann, 'Editorische Nachbemerkung', Adorno, *Ontologie und Dialektik*, *NaS*, vol. 7, p. 426. After the lectures at the Collège de France, the Adornos flew on to Rome, where he lectured on questions of the aesthetics of music and, at the request of Franco Lombardi, repeated two of the Paris lectures.
217 See Helms, *Die Ideologie der anonymen Gesellschaft*, and 'Musik zwischen Geschäft und Unwahrheit'.
218 See Adorno, 'Art and the Arts', *'Can One Live After Auschwitz?'*, p. 370; see also Christine Eichel, *Vom Ermatten der Avantgarde zur Vernetzung der Künste*.
219 Helms's 'FA: M'AHNIESGWOW' is a very difficult, more or less untranslatable piece of hermetic prose in the tradition of experimental modernism. Both Adorno and Stefan Müller-Doohm refer to it in the same context as James Joyce's *Finnegans Wake*, by which it was no doubt influenced [trans.].
220 Eichel comments that Adorno's examination of Helms 'leads among other things to his abandoning the old concept of the avant-garde and this crucially influenced Adorno's attitude towards the newer forms of modernism' (Eichel, *Vom Ermatten der Avantgarde zur Vernetzung der Künste*, p. 141); cf. Peter Bürger, *Das Altern der Moderne*, and *Theorie der Avantgarde*.
221 Adorno, 'Presuppositions', *Notes to Literature*, vol. 2, p. 97.

222 In his essay 'Valéry's Deviations' (1960), which Adorno wrote in response to the publication of a selection of Valéry's works in German translation by Bernhard Böschenstein, Hans Staub and Peter Szondi, he pointed to Valéry's insight into the adventitious, the irregular, and his understanding of 'the tension in art between contingency and the law of construction'. (See 'Valéry's Deviations', *Notes to Literature*, vol. 1, p. 143.) Later, in *Aesthetic Theory*, in his discussion of the trend to aleatory music, he pointed to John Cage's Piano Concerto as one of the 'key events' that 'impose on themselves a law of inexorable aleatoriness and thereby achieve a sort of meaning: the expression of horror' (*Aesthetic Theory*, p. 154).

223 Adorno, 'Presuppositions', *Notes to Literature*, pp. 101 and 104.

224 Ibid., p. 103f.

225 Adorno, *Negative Dialectics*, p. 205 (translation altered).

226 Adorno, 'Transparencies on Film', *The Culture Industry*, p. 156.

227 Adorno, 'Fantasia sopra *Carmen*', *Quasi una fantasia*, p. 54.

228 Alexander Kluge, 'Ein imaginärer Opernführer'.

229 Alexander Kluge and Gertrud Koch, 'Die Funktion des Zerrwinkels in zertrümmernder Absicht', p. 109.

230 Adorno to Enzensberger, 6 September 1956, Theodor W. Adorno Archive, Frankfurt am Main (Br 361/3).

231 Alexander Kluge and Hans Magnus Enzensberger, 'Deutscher sein ist kein Beruf', p. 2. Of course, Adorno did in fact think well of a number of writers in the *Gruppe 47* – Ingeborg Bachmann, Max Frisch, Alfred Andersch, among others. To that extent, this statement was a conscious exaggeration, designed to emphasize his high opinion of Enzensberger, as Kluge confirmed in a conversation with the present writer.

232 This emerged in the course of a conversation with the present author in Enzensberger's home in Munich in December 2001.

233 Hans Magnus Enzensberger, *Blindenschrift*, p. 58f.

Chapter 18 A Theory Devoured by Thought

1 Adorno, *Negative Dialectics*, p. 48.

2 In a letter to Horkheimer, 27 February 1957, he talks of an inquiry from the American consulate about his citizenship. He wrote: 'I myself would say simply that I have become a German once again, but would of course be only too pleased if some way could be found of allowing me to retain my American citizenship.' Horkheimer–Pollock Archive, Stadt- und Universitätsbibliothek, Frankfurt am Main.

3 According to Adorno, 'crypto-anti-Semitism' was 'a function of authority that stands behind the prohibition on open manifestations of anti-Semitism. This concealed anti-Semitism contains a dangerous potential; the whispering, the rumours (I once remarked that anti-Semitism consists of rumours about the Jews), opinions that are not quite exposed to public view have always been the medium in which are to be found social disaffections of the most varied kind which do not quite trust themselves to face up to the light of day in society. . . . This is one of the essential tricks that modern anti-Semites rely on. They present themselves as the persecuted, they behave as if public opinion rendered it impossible to express one's

anti-Semitic opinions today. It is the anti-Semite at whom the barbs of society are aimed, whereas in general it is the anti-Semites who have the greatest and cruellest success in wielding the barbs of society' (Adorno, 'Zur Bekämpfung des Antisemitismus heute', *GS*, vol. 20.1, p. 363).

4   Adorno's prominence was due in no small measure to his frequent presence on the radio, whether as studio guest or as speaker and contributor to debates. In the New Year broadcast in 1953, 'The Good Fairy's Gifts for the Future – What Prominent Celebrities Want', Adorno was asked for his contribution along with Rudolf Augstein, Dieter Borsche, Gottfried Benn, Fritz Kortner and Ina Seidel. See Conrad Lay, '"Viele Beiträge waren ursprünglich Rundfunkarbeiten": Über das wechselseitige Verhältnis von Frankfurter Schule und Rundfunk', p. 177.

5   Adorno, 'Auf die Frage: Warum sind Sie zurückgekehrt', *GS*, vol. 20.1, p. 394f. Helmut Dubiel notes that the slogan of Zero Hour [i.e., Germany in 1945] was highly misleading since the military destruction of the Third Reich did not also imply the destruction of the mentalities and attitudes of the period which underpinned the Third Reich. Dubiel's interpretation of the first speeches and debates in the West German Bundestag makes it clear that 'the ideas of the Third Reich had survived not just in the minds and hearts of incorrigible Nazis, but also in those of democratic politicians, and that they endured well into the history of the Federal Republic' (Helmut Dubiel, *Niemand ist frei von der Geschichte*, p. 67f.).

6   Adorno, 'Max Horkheimer', *GS*, vol. 20.1, p. 151.

7   Adorno and Mann, *Briefwechsel*, p. 153.

8   Adorno to Andersch, 18 April 1956, Theodor W. Adorno Archive, Frankfurt am Main (Br 24/49).

9   Ebbinghaus was a philosopher at the University of Marburg and a member of the board of trustees of the International Association of the Philosophy of Law and Social Philosophy.

10 Max Horkheimer, *Briefwechsel*, *GS*, vol. 18, p. 377.

11 This volume was conceived as a kind of sequel to *Minima Moralia*, one which would reflect his 'experiences on his return' from exile. 'What he had in mind was a rehabilitation of those Graeculi, the "little Greeks" of the Rome of the first pre-Christian century who were mocked by Cicero and Juvenal because they chattered about all the things they knew nothing about. . . . Adorno wished to defend them because these Graeculi were the very same people who acted as tutors to prosperous Romans and can be credited with transmitting classical culture to them' (Rolf Tiedemann, Preface to Adorno, 'Graeculus', *Frankfurter Adorno Blätter*, VII, 2001, p. 10).

12 Theodor W. Adorno Archive, Frankfurt am Main (Ts 520022).

13 Thus they comment in the new preface to the *Dialectic of Enlightenment* in 1969: 'In a period of political division into immense power blocs, set objectively upon collision, the sinister trend continues.' Adorno and Horkheimer, *Dialectic of Enlightenment*, p. ix.

14 Alex Demirović, *Der nonkonformistische Intellektuelle*, p. 367.

15 Jürgen Habermas, 'Eine Generation von Adorno getrennt', p. 48.

16 Horkheimer, *Briefwechsel*, *GS*, vol. 18, p. 478.

17 Adorno and Horkheimer to Herbert Marcuse, 12 February 1960, Horkheimer, *Briefwechsel*, *GS*, vol. 18, p. 467ff.

18 Adorno and Sohn-Rethel, *Briefwechsel*, p. 120 and also p. 127. In the event, Sohn-Rethel's experience was quite different from what Adorno had predicted. The select audience in East Berlin to whom he expounded his efforts to derive the forms of thought from the commodity form understood him perfectly. 'I can best give you an idea of the nature of the discussion if I tell you that criticism was directed not at my thesis but simply focused on the exclusive nature of the true economic root. This is because, depending on that, it will be possible to decide whether we will be able to hope that the disappearance of a commodity economy will lead to the elimination of the antagonism between intellectual and manual labour. And unless that opposition does disappear, there can be no classless society. In my opinion, it is the conditions of the liquidation of democracy that are at stake' (Sohn-Rethel to Adorno, 9 November 1958, ibid., p. 129f.). Relations between Adorno and Sohn-Rethel were broken off – though, as Adorno emphasized, this breach was not politically motivated – and were not resumed until the beginning of 1962, when they continued until Adorno's death.

19 Horkheimer, *Briefwechsel*, GS, vol. 18, p. 387.

20 Wolfgang Kraushaar (ed.), *Frankfurter Schule und Studentenbewegung: Von der Flaschenpost zum Molotowcocktail*, vol. 1, p. 134ff.

21 Ibid., p. 139; see also Wolfgang Kraushaar, *Die Protestchronik 1949–1959*, vol. 3, p. 1889ff.

22 Adorno, 'Why Still Philosophy?', *Critical Models*, p. 6.

23 Wolfgang Kraushaar, *Frankfurter Schule und Studentenbewegung*, vol. 1, p. 110. Seven years later, Adorno gave the article as a talk on Hessen Radio with the now definitive title of 'Why Still Philosophy?', and published the text in the *Merkur*. See Adorno, 'Why still Philosophy?', *Critical Models*, pp. 3–17.

24 Horkheimer, *Briefwechsel*, GS, vol. 18, pp. 441 and 444. What Horkheimer objected to was that Habermas had lacked the minimal sense of responsibility that could reasonably be expected even from a dissident. His constantly reiterated commitment to revolution in his article 'On the Philosophical Debate about Marx and Marxism' was not just a sign of political blindness, but 'promoted the affairs of the gentlemen in the East' and thus 'played into the hands of potential fascists at home'. Ibid.

25 Jürgen Habermas, 'Eine Generation von Adorno getrennt', p. 49.

26 Adorno to Horkheimer, 25 October 1957, Horkheimer, *Briefwechsel*, GS, vol. 18, p. 399.

27 Ibid., p. 397.

28 Ibid., p. 448.

29 In the 1961 elections, the CDU/CSU suffered a loss of support. Adenauer was forced to resign as federal chancellor in 1963 by pressure from within his own party. He was succeeded by Ludwig Erhard, the previous minister of economics, who was himself brought down by the first major recession of the postwar period. To revive both the economy and the government, a Grand Coalition was formed in December 1966, in which Georg Kiesinger, who had previously been prime minister of Baden-Württemberg, became federal chancellor, and Willy Brandt, who up until then had been chairman of the SPD and mayor of West Berlin, was made vice-chancellor and foreign minister.

30 In his brief but instructive historical survey of West German cultural magazines, Heinz Ludwig Arnold describes the *Kursbuch*, which was published by Wagenbach from 1970 on, and then by Rotbuch Verlag, as the 'flagship of the student movement. . . . Whether or not that was true, it undoubtedly captured the mood of the new generation and continued it into the 1970s. It not only opened their eyes to abuses in their own country, but a series of well-researched articles and dossiers introduced them to the problems of the Third World. . . . If one were to sum up the stance adopted by the *Kursbuch* in three expressions, they would have to be: belligerence, curiosity about theory, and international orientation' (Heinz Ludwig Arnold, 'Über Kulturzeitschriften nach 1945', p. 504).

31 See Ralf Bentz (ed.), *Protest! Literatur um 1968*, p. 36f.

32 Horkheimer, *Briefwechsel, GS*, vol. 18, p. 629ff. (The NPD was an extreme right-wing splinter group that emerged at the same time as the Grand Coalition and had some electoral success at regional level, thus raising fears of a resurgence of National Socialism. However, it never gained any seats in the Bundestag [trans.].)

33 Adorno to Grass, 4 November 1968, *Frankfurter Adorno Blätter*, VI, 2000, p. 80.

34 Adorno to Horkheimer, 15 December 1966, in Horkheimer, *Briefwechsel, GS*, vol. 18, p. 633. A letter to John Slawson of the American Jewish Committee makes it quite clear that Horkheimer too had his doubts about the new government of the Grand Coalition. For many Germans, he wrote, 'it represented a new national strength . . . the first obvious step to a greater, more powerful Germany. We must be aware that this new nationalist wave . . . in continental Europe derives in essence from hostility towards the USA. . . . The mistakes and the false background knowledge about the American intervention in Vietnam as well as a dislike in principle of an open society favour a powerful consensus about the USA between people who otherwise think very differently from one another. . . . What shall we do? The question is hard to answer because at the moment it is much easier to make serious mistakes than to do good.' Ibid., p. 637f.

35 Adorno to Enzensberger, 10 September 1965, Theodor W. Adorno Archive, Frankfurt am Main (Br 361/14, 15). Adorno wanted to begin his incisive critique of positivism right away, but it was not finished until the end of 1968, when it appeared as the introduction to the volume *Der Positivismusstreit in der deutschen Soziologie*, which appeared in 1969.

36 Adorno to Enzensberger, 23 September 1965, Theodor W. Adorno Archive, Frankfurt am Main (Br 361/22).

37 Adorno and Haselberg, 'Über die geschichtliche Angemessenheit des Bewußtseins', p. 487ff.

38 Ibid., p. 492.

39 Ibid., p. 494.

40 Ibid., p. 497.

41 See Rüdiger Safranski, *Martin Heidegger*. (The reference in Safranski and here is to Paul Celan's verse in the *Todesfuge* [Death Fugue] that 'Death is a master from Germany' [trans.].)

42 Adorno to Horkheimer, 13 March 1960, Horkheimer–Pollock Archive, Stadt- und Universitätsbibliothek, Frankfurt am Main.

43 Ernst Bloch, *Briefe 1903–1975*, vol. 2, p. 451.

44 Telegram from Adorno to Bloch, 8 July 1965, Theodor W. Adorno Archive, Frankfurt am Main (Br 142/38).
45 Adorno and Bloch, 'Etwas fehlt . . . Glück und Utopie', p. 412; cf. Gunzelin Schmid-Noerr, 'Bloch und Adorno: Bildhafte und bilderlose Utopie', p. 25ff.
46 Adorno et al., *The Positivist Dispute in German Sociology*, p. 35.
47 Theo Pirker, the Berlin sociologist, said of this second conference that it was 'an Adorno congress'; Adorno was actively involved in all the debates. 'The future confrontation with the student movement was already fore-shadowed here. At that time, Adorno did not seek to fight, but to con-vince' (Martin Jander, *Theo Pirker über 'Pirker': Ein Gespräch*, p. 59).
48 Between 1954 and 1959, Horkheimer spent some time as visiting pro-fessor in Chicago. His premature retirement from Frankfurt was officially explained on grounds of health. Even after his retirement he continued to give regular courses in both sociology and philosophy. See Gunzelin Schmid Noerr, 'Eine Geschichte der "Frankfurter Schule" in Briefen', in Horkheimer, *Briefwechsel, GS*, vol. 18, p. 825f.
49 Taken as a whole, Adorno's sociological texts may be regarded as the core works of what was meant by the epithet of 'Frankfurt School' – along with the reprint of Horkheimer's older essays from the *Zeitschrift für Sozialforschung* under the title of *Kritische Theorie* in 1968, and books of Herbert Marcuse such as *Kultur und Gesellschaft* (1965) and, above all, *One-Dimensional Man* (1964) [German edition 1967] and *Eros and Civilization* (1955) [German edition 1965].
50 Ludwig von Friedeburg emphasized this point in a conversation with the present author. See also von Friedeburg, 'Anspruch und Schwierigkeiten kritischer Forschung', p. 73.
51 Herbert Marcuse, 'Industrialization and Capitalism in the Work of Max Weber', in *Negations*, p. 201ff.
52 Adorno to Marcuse, 24 September 1963, Herbert Marcuse Archive, Stadt-und Universitätsbibliothek, Frankfurt am Main.
53 Herbert Marcuse, *Negations*, p. 204f.
54 Adorno remained unimpressed by these critical objections when he proposed a visiting professorship for Marcuse in the Philosophical Faculty of Frankfurt University. Nelson took Marcuse's lecture as the occasion for a review of the Heidelberg conference in the form of a reader's letter to the *New York Times* (3 January 1965). Adorno replied to this attack with a letter of his own to the same newspaper: 'It would be impossible to conceal basic antagonisms such as that between a critical theoretical approach to society and a more positivistic one. Both positions, by the way, have roots in the works of Max Weber himself. However, nobody has, to the best of my knowledge, attempted a "scapegoating" of Max Weber, or made him in any manner responsible for the Third Reich, or charged his theory of scientific value neutrality with guilt for the con-centration camps. The truth is that Professor Herbert Marcuse, against whom obviously the letter of Mr Nelson is directed, has printed out in his paper, which drew considerable attention from all sides, that the socio-logical thought of Max Weber contains, among other and quite different historical tendencies, certain elements of German thinking that proved later disastrous. I do not think that one does injustice to the significance of

Max Weber by bringing to the fore those aspects of his work.' English original of Adorno's letter to the editor of the *New York Times* book review of 26 March 1965. Herbert Marcuse Archive, Stadt- und Universitätsbibliothek, Frankfurt am Main.

55 König, *Briefwechsel*, vol. 1, p. 539. Demirović comments: 'Unlike König, who continually proclaimed a unified sociological method by which he wished to measure the progress of sociology as a science, Adorno regarded the different sociologies as rational. He believed that, since they were woven into the fabric of the various interest-groups of society, they represented objective contradictions' (Alex Demirović, *Der nonkonformistische Intellektuelle*, p. 832).

56 *Frankfurter Adorno Blätter*, IV, 1995, p. 7; cf. Udo Tietz, *Ontologie und Dialektik: Heidegger und Adorno über das Sein, das Nichtidentische, die Synthesis und die Kopula*, p. 90ff; cf. also Christoph Demmerling, *Sprache und Verdinglichung: Wittgenstein, Adorno und das Projekt einer kritischen Theorie*, p. 118ff.

57 Horkheimer and Adorno, *Sociologica II, Reden und Vorträge*, p. 2.

58 Horkheimer, *Briefwechsel*, GS, vol. 18, p. 521; cf. also Adorno's draft enclosed with his letter, Horkheimer–Pollock Archive, Stadt-und Universitätsbibliothek, Frankfurt am Main; cf. also Wiggershaus, *The Frankfurt School*, p. 564ff. Wiggershaus remarks accurately enough that, in his attempts to justify the absence of a developed theory of society, Adorno 'arrived unexpectedly at an idealization of "marginalia" they were presenting into the actual goal of their collaboration.' Ibid., p. 565.

59 Adorno, 'Empirische Sozialforschung', *GS*, vol. 9.2, p. 359.

60 Alongside the investigation of such statistical data as income and educational qualifications, the methods of social research were confined to the study of short-term social guides to action in order to throw light on the subjective dimension of society. Here Adorno distinguished between three categories: conscious opinions and their motivations, attitudes as generalized ways of seeing, and actual patterns of behaviour.

61 Adorno, 'Einleitung zu Émile Durkheim, *Soziologie und Philosophie*', *GS*, vol. 8, p. 264.

62 The concept of positivism goes back to Auguste Comte (1798–1857), a French tutor in mathematics and physics at the École Polytechnique in Paris. He introduced the concept of sociology for the positive philosophy he had founded which was based on the exact methods of the natural sciences. For the principles and different currents in positivism, see Georg Hendrik von Wright, *Explanation and Understanding*. Wright explains there that one of its basic assumptions is 'methodological monism, i.e., the idea of the unity of scientific method amidst the variety of the objects of scientific investigation. A second basic assumption consists in the belief that the exact sciences, especially mathematical physics, posit a methodological ideal . . . by which the state of development and perfection of all other sciences . . . is to be measured. . . . Such explanations are "causal" in a broad sense. They consist . . . in the subsumption of individual facts under hypothetically assumed universal laws of nature.' Ibid., p. 18.

63 Cf. Wolfgang Bonß, *Die Einübung des Tatsachenblicks*, p. 118ff. Bonß distinguishes between two types of empirical knowledge: totalizing and factual. While the emphasis on factual knowledge has triumphed in

sociology, a second tradition has survived, as Bonß shows, which is recognizable by its emphasis on the monograph as a form. Either model can be based on one or the other conception of the empirical. This means that the equation of the empirical with factual knowledge is mistaken: 'The expression "monographic form" points to strategies of constructing and appropriating reality in which empirical entities are defined and delimited not by number and measurement, but by so-called qualitative procedures that amount to a subject-specific and situation-specific construction of empirical reality by a set of inductive generalizations.' Ibid., p. 98.

64 Karl Popper was born in Vienna in 1902, and after a colourful youth became a lecturer in philosophy at the University of New Zealand at the age of thirty-five. He was forced into emigration because of the threat posed to Jewish left-wing intellectuals in Austria by the rise of National Socialism. On the strength of the publication of the *Logik der Forschung* in 1934, he was given a chair at the London School of Economics, where he stayed until his retirement in 1969. Popper's theory of scientific knowledge developed through a critical engagement with logical positivism. It is linked to his anti-dogmatic approach and his espousing of an open, pluralistic society. He attacked the foundational positivist conception of scientific knowledge, according to which a number of hypotheses can be derived from particular observations and can themselves be made to yield laws. On the one hand, he objects that induction from a number of individual observations cannot be made to serve as the foundation of universal laws. On the other hand, he rejects the idea that there could be observations that are not themselves in part the product of theory. Popper assumes furthermore that there is no absolutely certain starting-point for knowledge, and nor is there a single possible method for finding it. Scientific theories are distinguished by the fact that they may be falsified by further knowledge. The scientist is under an obligation to look for facts that refute his theories. The progress of scientific knowledge is the product of successful problem-solving through the elimination of mistakes by a process of trial and error. Popper, 'Die Logik der Sozialwissenschaften'. [English original: *The Logic of Scientific Discovery*, London, 1959. This was a translation with additional appendices and footnotes of the *Logik der Forschung* of 1934.]; cf. Manfred Geier, *Karl Popper*.

65 See Hans-Joachim Dahms, *Positivismusstreit*; Rainer M. Lepsius, 'Die Entwicklung der Soziologie nach dem Zweiten Weltkrieg 1945 bis 1967'; Weyer, *Westdeutsche Soziologie 1945–1960*.

66 See Michael Schmid, 'Der Positivismusstreit in der deutschen Soziologie dreißig Jahre danach', p. 37.

67 This is an argument advanced by Jürgen Habermas later on in his statement on the logic of the social sciences. He maintained that 'the research process instigated by human subjects belongs, through the act of cognition itself, to the objective context that is to be apprehended.' Habermas, 'The Analytical Theory of Science and Dialectics'; Adorno et al., *The Positivist Dispute in German Sociology*, p. 132.

68 Ibid., p. 111.

69 Ibid., p. 114. Popper too claims criticism for his own scientific model. In his presentation, 'The Logic of the Social Sciences', he states: 'Thus the method of science is one of tentative attempts to solve our problems; by

conjectures which are controlled by severe criticism. It is a consciously critical development of the method of "trial and error".... The so-called objectivity of science lies in the objectivity of the critical method. This means, above all, that no theory is beyond attack by criticism.' Popper, in *The Positivist Dispute in German Sociology*, p. 89f.

70 Adorno, 'On the Logic of the Social Sciences', in *The Positivist Dispute in German Sociology*, p. 120.

71 Hans-Joachim Dahms maintains that both Adorno and Horkheimer used the concept of positivism 'really quite loosely' even in the initial phase of their first discussion of this philosophical trend in the late 1930s. 'The label "positivist"... frequently means nothing more than a scientist who devotes himself or has devoted himself at some time in the past... to the serious individual pursuit of scientific research' (Dahms, *Positivismusstreit*, p. 92f.). However, Habermas has shown in his own contributions to the debate that Adorno had a very clear idea of positivism. His critique of positivism is indebted for many of its ideas to an essay by Horkheimer, 'Der neueste Angriff auf die Metaphysik', that appeared in the *Zeitschrift für Sozialforschung* in 1937. Horkheimer wrote this essay in close cooperation with Adorno, who had written a number of detailed letters with a large number of suggestions about the line of argument to be taken. See the letters from Adorno to Horkheimer, 28 November 1963 and 23 March 1937, Horkheimer, *Briefwechsel*, *GS*, vol. 15, p. 752ff., and also vol. 16, p. 96ff.; Horkheimer, 'Der neueste Angriff auf die Metaphysik', *GS*, vol. 4, p. 108ff.

72 Adorno, 'Introduction' to *The Positivist Dispute in German Sociology*, p. 3.

73 This critical offensive, which is based on a contrast between 'positivist' and 'dialectical' conceptions, makes it clear that Adorno had 'changed his opinion about Popper after 1961' (Hans-Joachim Dahms, *Positivismusstreit*, p. 353); for Habermas's subsequent view of the dispute, see Habermas, *Logik der Sozialwissenschaften*, p. 7ff.; for a general account of the dispute about the nature of sociology, see Alex Demirović, *Der nonkonformistische Intellektuelle*, p. 741ff.

74 Nominalism holds that there is no objective reality corresponding to cognitive forms of thought. Concepts are regarded as the subjective contents of consciousness or as linguistic names (*nomina*). In the history of philosophy, nominalism is regarded as a forerunner of empiricism.

75 Karl Popper, 'The Logic of the Social Sciences', p. 96.

76 Adorno, 'Introduction' to *The Positivist Dispute in German Sociology*, p. 28.

77 Adorno, *Introduction to Sociology*, p. 159.

78 Adorno, 'Introduction' to *The Positivist Dispute in German Sociology*, p. 55f.; cf. also *Introduction to Sociology*, p. 102f.

79 Adorno, 'Introduction' to *The Positivist Dispute in German Sociology*, p. 23.

80 Ibid., p. 32.

81 Adorno, 'Anmerkungen zum sozialen Konflikt heute', *GS*, vol. 8, p. 194.

82 Adorno, *Philosophische Terminologie*, vol. 1, p. 83.

83 Adorno, draft for *Sociologica* II. See p. 4 of the attachment to the letter to Horkheimer, 31 January 1962, Horkheimer–Pollock Archive, Stadt- und

Universitätsbibliothek, Frankfurt am Main; cf. also Rolf Wiggershaus, *The Frankfurt School*, p. 565ff. In *Negative Dialectics* Adorno took up the image of the eater and the bread in a slightly different form. There he was arguing against thought relying too much on a particular standpoint. If critical theory is asked to produce a standpoint, 'it would be that of the diner regarding the roast. Experience lives by consuming the standpoint; not until the standpoint is submerged in it would there be philosophy' (Adorno, *Negative Dialectics*, p. 30); cf. also Adorno, 'Anmerkungen zum philosophischen Denken', *GS*, vol. 10.2, p. 599ff.

84   Adorno, 'On Subject and Object', *Critical Models*, p. 254.
85   Ibid. (translation changed).
86   Adorno, *Philosophische Terminologie*, vol. 1, pp. 86, 94 and 133.
87   Adorno, *Negative Dialectics*, p. 17f.
88   Ibid., p. 163.
89   Ibid.
90   Max Weber, *Gesammelte Aufsätze zur Wissenschaftslehre*, p. 192. For Weber, the ideal type has 'the meaning of a pure ideal marginal concept . . . by which reality can be measured in order to clarify particular significant components of its empirical content with which it is being compared' (ibid., p. 194). Whether the construction of an ideal type is intellectually productive cannot be decided in advance, but can be ascertained only by the success with which 'the ideal type has facilitated the cognition of concrete manifestations of culture in their context, their causal conditioning and their meaning' (ibid., p. 193). The formation of ideal types arises from 'the one-sided intensification of one or more points of view and through the confluence of a plethora of individual phenomena that join those one-sided points of view to form a unified intellectual structure' (ibid., p. 191). 'Intensification' means that specific characteristics are singled out and brought together in a concept with greater clarity.
91   Adorno, *Negative Dialectics*, p. 53.
92   Adorno, *The Positivist Dispute in German Sociology*, p. 44.
93   Max Weber introduced the idea of value freedom or ethical neutrality in science in 1909 in order to make a strict distinction between 'is' and 'ought'. Value judgements cannot be established with empirical methods. An empirical science must treat social and cultural values as the objects of cognition. It must limit itself to stating the means that can be employed to achieve specific ends, and to describing their consequences. Over and above this, the social sciences are in a particularly good position to shed light on a consciousness of desired values. The researcher's choice of subject is dictated and limited by his own values. For this reason, Weber thought that it was important for scholars to reflect upon their own values in order to eliminate bias.
94   Adorno, *The Positivist Dispute in German Sociology*, p. 59.
95   See also Adorno, 'Critique', *Critical Models*, p. 281ff.; Stefan Müller-Doohm, 'Kritik in kritischen Theorien', p. 71ff.
96   Adorno, *Introduction to Sociology*, p. 85f.
97   Adorno, *The Positivist Dispute in German Sociology*, p. 66.
98   Adorno, *Ontologie und Dialektik*, *NaS*, vol. 7, p. 147.
99   Adorno began to write down his critique of Heidegger in summer 1951. 'The radical gesture, combined with the total absence of any socially

critical content, the sympathy for the concept of "origin" as such and in the abstract (a concept that could all too easily be filled with racial theory), as well as the concept of the culture of "attitude" [*Haltung*] as such, without any content, so that it amounted to a self-sufficient ideal of heroism – all that is an authentic component of National Socialist ways of thinking. . . . Heidegger falls entirely into the category of philosophers criticized by Nietzsche who claim that truth and timelessness are identical.' Theodor W. Adorno Archive, Frankfurt am Main (Ts 51942 and Ts 51944).

100 Adorno, 'Der Begriff der Philosophie', transcript by Kraft and Bretschneider, *Frankfurter Adorno Blätter*, II, 1993, p. 28.
101 Walter Benjamin, *Gesammelte Briefe*, vol. III, p. 522.
102 Adorno to Minder, 25 June 1959, in Adorno, *Ontologie und Dialektik*, *NaS*, vol. 7, p. 424.
103 Ibid., p. 425.
104 Heidegger's student Hermann Mörchen has written two studies on the differences between Adorno and Heidegger and, more particularly, on what they have in common: Mörchen, *Adorno und Heidegger*, and *Macht und Herrschaft im Denken von Heidegger und Adorno*. Mörchen interprets Adorno's social theory as a necessary complement to Heidegger's analysis of being-there (*Dasein*). What the two share is the critique of domination and the domination of instrumental reason. In fact, Adorno, who had made his own reckoning with progress, nevertheless continued to embrace the idea of progress, whose material and cultural successes were in his view the prerequisites of emancipation. (Cf. Adorno, *Negative Dialectics*, p. 91). Brunkhorst remarks that 'Adorno's negative view of modern society stems from a no less consistent affirmation of its cultural modernism'. '*This* affirmation is reconcilable with negativism. For the reflective potential of a methodical negativism has long since been *institutionalized*' (Hauke Brunkhorst, *Adorno and Critical Theory*, p. 67). See also Rüdiger Safranski, *Martin Heidegger*, p. 413ff.
105 Adorno, *Ontologie und Dialektik*, *NaS*, vol. 7, p. 10.
106 Ibid., p. 122.
107 Ibid., p. 149.
108 Adorno, *The Jargon of Authenticity*, p. 40.
109 Ibid. (translation altered).
110 Ibid., p. 12.
111 Adorno to Marcuse, 15 December 1964, Herbert Marcuse Archive, Stadt- und Universitätsbibliothek, Frankfurt am Main.
112 See Hermann Mörchen, *Adorno und Heidegger*, pp. 13 and 207; Mörchen refers to comments by Horkheimer. Cf. Horkheimer, *Briefwechsel*, *GS*, vol. 18, p. 79ff.
113 It is likewise wrong to believe that Adorno had provided some of the ideas for a highly critical article on Heidegger that appeared in the weekly magazine *Der Spiegel* in 1966. It was claimed in that article that Heidegger had forbidden his former teacher Husserl to enter Freiburg University and that he had stopped visiting Karl Jaspers because Jaspers's wife was Jewish. It was Hannah Arendt who claimed that these rumours had their origins in Frankfurt. 'I have no proof, but am fairly convinced that the real behind-the-scenes manipulators here are the Wiesengrund-Adorno people in Frankfurt. . . . For years now, he and Horkheimer have accused

anyone in Germany who opposed them of being anti-Semites, or have threatened to do so' (Arendt and Jaspers, *Briefwechsel 1926–1969*, p. 670).

114 See Hermann Mörchen, *Adorno und Heidegger*, p. 13.

115 'It is easier to raise a shrine than bring the deity down to haunt it.' Samuel Beckett, *The Unnameable*, in *The Beckett Trilogy*, p. 316.

116 After his return to Germany, in a house belonging to one of Heidegger's friends, Adorno is said to have remarked before all the guests present: 'In five years I have cut Heidegger down to size.' Hermann Mörchen, *Adorno und Heidegger*, p. 13.

117 Adorno, *The Jargon of Authenticity*, pp. 3 and 59. Safranski notes with some justice that Adorno's critique of existentialist jargon is settling accounts with 'the spirit of an epoch that, by the time the book appeared in the mid-1960s, was no longer in existence.' By then, a 'new matter-of-factness' had made its appearance. 'The charm of naked reality was being discovered, in philosophy as much as in the sex shops, and it was not long before unmasking, criticism, and relentless questioning governed the world of discourse' (Rüdiger Safranski, *Martin Heidegger*, p. 411).

118 Adorno, *The Jargon of Authenticity*, p. xix (translation altered).

119 Ibid., p. 39.

120 Ibid., p. 40.

121 Ibid., p. xvii.

122 In the author's note accompanying the first edition, Adorno suggests that the book was conceived as 'part of a philosophical "work in progress"'; later he spoke of it as 'part of *Negative Dialectics*'. Ibid., p. xvii.

123 Adorno, *Negative Dialectics*, p. 377f.

124 In March 1965, Adorno spent some more time in Paris, where he renewed contact with Beckett and again gave some lectures and talks in French. See Adorno to Marcuse, 18 March 1965, Herbert Marcuse Archive, Stadt- und Universitätsbibliothek, Frankfurt am Main.

125 Adorno to Helms, 7 November 1966, Theodor W. Adorno Archive, Frankfurt am Main (Br 588/112).

126 Adorno to Marcuse, 2 December 1965 and 21 December 1965, Herbert Marcuse Archive, Stadt- und Universitätsbibliothek, Frankfurt am Main.

127 Adorno to Helene Berg, 6 December 1966, Theodor W. Adorno Archive, Frankfurt am Main (Br 101/53).

128 See Adorno, *Problems of Moral Philosophy*, pp. 2 and 100.

129 In addition to these three lecture courses, two earlier ones, 'Philosophische Terminologie I and II', are also connected with his work on *Negative Dialectics*, which was closely linked to his teaching activities during these years. Cf. Alex Demirović, *Der nonkonformistische Intellektuelle*, p. 632ff.

130 Adorno, *Negative Dialectics*, p. xx.

131 Ibid., p. 13.

132 Anke Thyen interprets *Negative Dialectics* 'as the epistemological foundation of Adorno's philosophy'. With it he attempts 'to reflect on the aporias of *Dialectic of Enlightenment*'. 'With the concept of the non-identical Adorno implies that the equation of the rational preservation of the self with subjective, instrumental reason is not tenable' (Thyen, *Negative Dialektik und Erfahrung*, p. 109). She therefore describes *Negative Dialectics* as 'the attempt to treat the epistemological problem of a subject/object dialectics in post-idealist conditions' (ibid., p. 170).

133 Adorno, *Negative Dialectics*, p. 127.
134 Ibid., p. 10 (translation altered).
135 Jürgen Ritsert is the latest commentator to try and clarify the concept of the non-identical. He notes that non-identity 'includes the idea of a "reconciled society" even though this idea can only ever be experienced indirectly, through the criticism of social negativity'. His conclusion is that 'the non-identical is not a mysterious substance, but shorthand for a variety of problems with which Adorno's critical theory is concerned and which it partly makes visible' (Ritsert, 'Das Nichtidentische bei Adorno: Substanz- oder Problembegriff?' pp. 45 and 48); cf. also Anke Thyen, *Negative Dialektik und Erfahrung*, p. 198ff.
136 Adorno, *Negative Dialectics*, p. 12.
137 Ibid., p. 175.
138 Ibid., p. 219.
139 Ibid., p. xx.
140 Ibid., p. 366.
141 Adorno told Kaschnitz about his own encounter with a child and suggested that she should use this as the basis for a second story about a child in her volume *Tage, Tage, Jahre*. This told the story of 'the visit from a "seemingly demonic" child who had come to him with the demand that he rescue his ball from the roof guttering, an episode that almost ended in death' (Kaschnitz, *Tage, Tage, Jahre: Aufzeichnungen*, p. 68ff.). The short story *The Fat Child* appears in the volume *Lange Schatten* (1960). It deals with a very pushy girl who is always hungry and who, without admitting it, feels neglected in favour of her older sister. This unhappy child longs to shine like her sister and be generally admired. There are at least two letters in which Adorno refers to the fat child. See Horkheimer, *Briefwechsel, GS*, vol. 18, p. 633f.; see also Adorno to Dreyfus, 31 January 1967, Theodor W. Adorno Archive, Frankfurt am Main (Br 331/47).
142 Adorno to Dreyfus, 6 September 1966, Theodor W. Adorno Archive, Frankfurt am Main (Br 331/41, 42).
143 Adorno and Lenk, *Briefwechsel*, p. 95ff.
144 Adorno to Horkheimer, 5 December 1966, Horkheimer–Pollock Archive, Stadt- und Universitätsbibliothek, Frankfurt am Main.
145 See Horkheimer, *Briefwechsel, GS*, vol. 18, p. 634.
146 Adorno to Scholem, 14 March 1967, quoted by Rolf Tiedemann, 'Editorisches Nachwort', *Ontologie und Dialektik, NaS*, vol. 7, p. 422.
147 Adorno to Scholem, 14 March 1967, Scholem, *Briefe*, vol. II, p. 302.
148 Ibid., p. 177.
149 Adorno to Scholem, 14 March 1967, ibid., p. 302.
150 Ibid., p. 178.
151 Ibid., p. 179.
152 Ibid., p. 302. The great respect in which Adorno held Scholem can be seen from the two little essays he wrote about the Jewish scholar. See Adorno, 'Gershom G. Scholem', *GS*, vol. 20.2, p. 477f., and also 'Gruß an Gershom Scholem', ibid., p. 478ff. At the end of the article Adorno wrote for the *Neue Zürcher Zeitung* for Scholem's seventieth birthday, he said: 'A while ago I had a dream that seems to me to be quite an apt parable for Scholem . . . He was said to have told me this story: "There is an old Nordic saga in which a knight makes off with a maiden with the aid of a

silken ladder. This leads to all sorts of complications. This saga is the basis for the old German folksong *Fox, you have stolen the goose"'* (ibid., p. 486).

153 Adorno and Sohn-Rethel, *Briefwechsel*, p. 150f.
154 Ibid., p. 152.
155 Ibid., p. 152f.
156 Adorno, *Negative Dialectics*, p. 203.
157 Ibid., p. 408.
158 Ibid., p. 405.
159 Ibid., p. 52.
160 Ibid., p. 5.
161 Ibid., p. 52.
162 Alex Demirović, *Der nonkonformistische Intellektuelle*, p. 662.
163 Dieter Henrich, 'Diagnose der Gegenwart'.
164 Alex Demirović, *Der nonkonformistische Intellektuelle*, p. 665.
165 Adorno, 'Diskussionsbeitrag zu "Spätkapitalismus oder Industriegesell-schaft"', *GS*, vol. 8, p. 580ff.
166 Alex Demirović, *Der nonkonformistische Intellektuelle*, p. 656.
167 Adorno, 'Marginalia to Theory and Praxis', in *Critical Models*, p. 260. (The lines in Goethe's *Faust* are: 'My friend, all theory is grey, and green / The golden tree of life.' *Faust*, part I, trans. David Luke. Oxford and New York, 1987, p. 61, lines 2038f.)
168 Adorno, 'Scientific Experiences of a European Scholar in America', in *Critical Models*, p. 216.
169 Adorno, *Negative Dialectics*, p. 29.
170 Adorno, *Introduction to Sociology*, pp. 49, 84ff., and 136ff. This course of lectures, the last that Adorno gave from beginning to end, not only contains important aspects of his conception of sociology, but also reproduces his approach to thinking about sociology in a highly authentic manner.
171 Adorno devoted seminars to both these topics in the summer semester 1965 and winter semester 1965–6. Cf. Adorno, 'Anmerkungen zum sozialen Konflikt heute', *GS*, vol. 8, p. 177ff.; see also Alex Demirović, *Der nonkonformistische Intellektuelle*, p. 429.
172 Adorno, 'Soziologie und empirische Forschung', *GS*, vol. 8, p. 196.
173 The typescript of the lecture course is in the Theodor W. Adorno Archive in Frankfurt am Main (Vo 5456ff.). In the course of these lectures Adorno spoke of his own philosophical training. Under Hans Cornelius, his studies were limited to Aristotle and Plato. Later on, this was extended to include Kant, then Kierkegaard and Husserl and, finally, Hegel, Fichte and Schelling. What Adorno considered important was to think philosophically rather than to learn the history of philosophy. He attacked the 'men with beards' who insisted on eternal values and also the 'complacent positivists' who were busy making themselves at home in a meaningless world (Vo 5517).
174 See ibid. (Vo 5548).
175 See ibid. (Vo 5610).
176 See ibid. (Vo 5609).
177 When Adorno gave his paper, he and von Friedeburg had already given up their posts in the German Sociological Society. Dahrendorf was elected chairman as successor to Adorno in November 1967.

178 A helpful survey of the theories arising from Marx's analysis of capitalism can be found in Gerhard Brandt, 'Ansichten kritischer Sozialforschung 1930–1980', p. 40ff.; Hans-Georg Backhaus, *Dialektik der Wertform*, especially the appendix, 'Theodor W. Adorno on Marx and the basic concepts of sociological theory', p. 501ff.

179 Adorno (ed.), *Verhandlungen des 16. Deutschen Soziologentages*, p. 4.

180 No less remarkable was the critical solidarity with the student movement shown by Jürgen Habermas as long as the symbolic acts of protest during demonstrations were aimed at securing fundamental reforms, e.g., in the universities, and as long as they did not go beyond argument. This call for reform was much less spectacular than Herbert Marcuse's call for revolution. Marcuse had allowed himself to be nominated the true theoretician of the 'New Left' (see Marcuse, *An Essay on Liberation*). Marcuse told the New Left that they 'had awakened the spectre of revolution which had subordinated the development of the forces of production and a higher standard of living to the demands of creating solidarity for the human race, eliminating poverty and deprivation beyond all national frontiers, and bringing about peace' (ibid.). He was convinced that a new subject was in the making that was capable of a new sensibility that would constitute a politically emancipated force.

181 See Wolfgang Kraushaar (ed.), *Frankfurter Schule und Studentenbewegung*, vol. 1, p. 302.

182 Adorno, 'Spätkapitalismus oder Industriegesellschaft?', *GS*, vol. 8, p. 368. (Evidently a parody of Schopenhauer's *magnum opus*: *The World as Will and Idea* [trans.].)

183 Ibid., p. 354.

184 Adorno, *Anmerkungen zum sozialen Konflikt heute*, *GS*, vol. 8, p. 187.

185 The structural characteristics of capitalism are the production of commodities with surplus value, private ownership of the means of production, the free signing of contracts, the antagonism of labour and capital, and the competition of capital for the best rates of profit.

186 Adorno, 'Spätkapitalismus oder Industriegesellschaft?', *GS*, vol. 8, p. 361.

187 Ibid., p. 365.

188 Ibid., p. 362.

189 Ibid., p. 363f.

190 Ibid., p. 363.

191 Stefan Breuer has drawn attention to the similarity between Adorno's conception of social totality and the systems theory of Niklas Luhmann. A comparison between the two is said to show 'that critical theory . . . is no antiquated theory which has lost its object, but very up to date. Its conceptual apparatus may be less polished than that of systems theory, but . . . it possesses a conception that permits more elegant solutions from a structural point of view than the . . . organization of systems theory' (Stefan Breuer, *Die Gesellschaft des Verschwindens: Von der Selbstzerstörung der technischen Zivilisation*, p. 96).

192 Adorno, 'Spätkapitalismus oder Industriegesellschaft?', *GS*, vol. 8, p. 364.

193 Ibid., p. 369.

194 Adorno (ed.), *Verhandlungen des 16. Deutschen Soziologentages*, p. 91ff.

195 Ibid., p. 93f.

196 Adorno, 'Diskussionsbeitrag zu "Spätkapitalismus oder Industriegesell-schaft?"', *GS*, vol. 8, p. 582.
197 Ibid., p. 587.

Chapter 19 With his Back to the Wall

1 Adorno to Horkheimer, 12 July 1967, *Frankfurter Adorno Blätter*, VI, 2000, p. 55.
2 Adorno to Dreyfus, 16 March 1965, Theodor W. Adorno Archive, Frankfurt am Main (Br 331/37, 38).
3 Adorno to Andersch, 23 April 1965, Theodor W. Adorno Archive, Frankfurt am Main (Br 23/35).
4 Adorno to Marcuse, 2 June 1965 and 10 March 1966, Herbert Marcuse Archive, Stadt- und Universitätsbibliothek, Frankfurt am Main.
5 The *Spiegel* affair raised issues of press freedom and the defence of the state; the metal workers' strike provoked questions about the public's acceptance of the right to strike in defence of workers' interests. In the case of the Eichmann trial, the survey considered the prevalence of anti-Semitic prejudice in the German population.
6 See Regina Schmidt and Egon Becker, *Reaktionen auf politische Vorgänge: Drei Meinungstudien*, p. 81.
7 Ibid., p. 137f.
8 Adorno to Marcuse, 14 September 1965, Herbert Marcuse Archive, Stadt- und Universitätsbibliothek, Frankfurt am Main.
9 The concept of a 'fully-formed society' (*formierte Gesellschaft*) was essentially devised by Rüdiger Altmann, an adviser to Erhard. It proposed a strengthening of state power so as to be able to integrate divergent social groups. This was a reaction to what was held to be an over-exuberant pluralism and the excessive growth of organized interest groups. See Gert Schäfer and Carl Nedelmann, *Der CDU-Staat*.
10 Adorno, 'Gegen die Notstandsgesetze', *GS*, vol. 20.1, p. 396f.
11 Adorno to Marcuse, 1 June 1967, *Frankfurter Adorno Blätter*, VI, 2000, p. 44f. Adorno defended Horkheimer's statements against Marcuse, who had learnt of them in the press. See Marcuse to Horkheimer, 17 June 1967, Horkheimer, *Briefwechsel*, *GS*, vol. 18, p. 655ff.
12 Wolfgang Kraushaar (ed.), *Frankfurter Schule und Studentenbewegung*, vol. 1, p. 252f.
13 Adorno, *Metaphysics: Concepts and Problems*, p. 101.
14 Wolfgang Kraushaar (ed.), *Frankfurter Schule und Studentenbewegung*, vol. 1, p. 254.
15 Ibid.
16 *Frankfurter Adorno Blätter*, III, 1994, p. 145.
17 Jürgen Habermas, *Protestbewegung und Hochschulreform*, p. 141f.
18 Wolfgang Kraushaar (ed.), *Frankfurter Schule und Studentenbewegung*, vol. 1, p. 258f.
19 Habermas distinguished between three phases in the protest movement of the time. To begin with, there was a reform movement confined to the university that underwent an initial politicization through the debates about the Vietnam War. A second, more radical politicization took place with

the protests against the shah's visit, the death of Benno Ohnesorg and the anti-Springer campaign, as well as the resistance to the emergency laws and the Grand Coalition. In its final phase of direct action, matters escalated to the murderous 'special path' of the terrorism of the Red Army Faction, from which there was 'a return to the university' where the supporters of direct action maintained their position, partly in the shape of dogmatic sectarian groups. Habermas, *Protestbewegung und Hochschulreform*, p. 10ff.

20 *Frankfurter Adorno Blätter*, III, 1994, p. 146f.
21 Horkheimer, *Briefwechsel, GS*, vol. 18, p. 652.
22 See Wolfgang Kraushaar (ed.), *Frankfurter Schule und Studentenbewegung*, vol. 2, p. 231.
23 Monika Steffen, 'Tiere an Ketten', p. 263ff.
24 Rolf Tiedemann, 'Iphigenie bei den Berliner Studenten', p. 124ff.
25 Wolfgang Kraushaar (ed.), *Frankfurter Schule und Studentenbewegung*, vol. 1, p. 264f.
26 Ibid., vol. 2, p. 265ff.
27 Adorno, 'On the Classicism of Goethe's *Iphigenie*', *Notes to Literature*, vol. 2, p. 161.
28 Wolfgang Kraushaar (ed.), *Frankfurter Schule und Studentenbewegung*, vol. 2, p. 267.
29 Adorno to Kolisch, 17 July 1967, *Frankfurter Adorno Blätter*, VI, 2000, p. 58.
30 Adorno to Helge Pross, 13 July 1967, ibid., p. 55. Even if Adorno played down the whole incident, it is clear, as Tiedemann points out, that it was a situation in which Adorno was confronted with brutish behaviour. 'He interpreted the *Iphigenie* as the adversary of such behaviour which he had now experienced directly probably for the first time since 1933, when the police had searched his house in Frankfurt and he had witnessed the first Jewish boycott in Berlin' (Rolf Tiedemann, 'Iphigenie bei den Berliner Studenten', p. 125).
31 Adorno to Hellmut Becker, 13 July 1967, *Frankfurter Adorno Blätter*, VI, 2000, p. 55f.
32 Adorno, 'Gespräch mit Peter Szondi über die "Unruhen der Studenten"', quoted in Wolfgang Kraushaar (ed.), *Frankfurter Schule und Studentenbewegung*, vol. 2, p. 304ff.
33 Ibid., p. 327.
34 Ibid., p. 237.
35 In a letter of 17 July 1967 to Rudolf Kolisch, Adorno described Marcuse as a 'kind of sacred cow of the rebellious students . . . , and sacred animals are never good, whatever the constellation.' He reacted to Marcuse's 'commitment for Mao' with a kind of distanced irony. *Frankfurter Adorno Blätter*, VI, 2000, p. 59.
36 Adorno to Marcuse, 1 June 1967, ibid., p. 44f.
37 Adorno to Beckett, 4 February 1969, Theodor W. Adorno Archive, Frankfurt am Main (Br 76/5).
38 Adorno to Szondi, 9 May 1968, *Frankfurter Adorno Blätter*, VI, 2000, p. 65.
39 Adorno and Lenk, *Briefwechsel*, p. 148.
40 The publication of Benjamin's *Schriften*, edited by Adorno and his wife with the assistance of Friedrich Podszus in 1955, was followed by

Illuminationen: Ausgewählte Schriften in 1961 and *Angelus Novus* in 1966.

41 See *alternative: Zeitschrift für Literatur und Diskussion*, October–December 1967.

42 Arendt published her strictures in a three-part essay in three successive issues of *Merkur*. They were entitled: 'The Hunchback', 'Dark Times' and 'The Pearlfisher'.

43 See Heißenbüttel, 'Vom Zeugnis des Fortlebens in Briefen', and 'Zu Walter Benjamins Spätwerk'. Adorno wrote directly to Heißenbüttel on 14 March: 'You seem to suspect that I wished, for whatever reason, to dilute Benjamin's Marxist intentions. My motive in the controversy was far more complex. While on the one hand I wanted to defend Benjamin's metaphysical impulses against himself, I wished also to defend dialectical materialism against him, since he seemed to me to have a mistaken idea of it. And this misunderstanding was not just his alone, but was shared by Brecht. I fancy that I have a very precise knowledge of Marx, as indeed you implicitly concede. This means that I could not fail to see that, while Benjamin felt committed to Marxism, he had missed the point of the essential contents of Marxist theory. God knows how highly I think of Brecht, but his ignorance of Marxism . . . was indescribable. Neither had made a serious study of Marx, but . . . they had swallowed him like a pill. This was what struck me as being so dubious; their view of Marx was heteronomous and irrational, in contrast to materialist dialectics as a theory. If Benjamin had understood this, it would have been a better fit with his own ideas. But the fact is that he clung to his metaphysical ideas to the last, and for the truth of this I would ask you to trust both my memory and that of Gershom Scholem.' Adorno to Heißenbüttel, 14 March 1968, quoted in Ralf Bentz (ed.), *Protest! Literatur um 1968*, p. 132.

44 See Wolfgang Kraushaar (ed.), *Frankfurter Schule und Studentenbewegung*, vol. 1, p. 292.

45 Adorno, 'Interimsbescheid', *GS*, vol. 20.1, p. 182ff.

46 Shortly before he took his own life, Benjamin had named Adorno as the trustee of his intellectual legacy and left instructions that his papers should be handed over to him.

47 Adorno, 'Interimsbescheid', *GS*, vol. 20.1, p. 185f.; cf. Rolf Tiedemann, 'Zur "Beschlagnahme" Walter Benjamins', p. 74ff.

48 Adorno, 'Zur Interpretation Benjamins', quoted by Rolf Tiedemann in his notes to *Über Walter Benjamin*, p. 97ff.

49 Adorno to Hartung, 8 May 1968, ibid., p. 99.

50 Gershom Scholem, *Briefe*, vol. II, p. 309.

51 Ibid., p. 201.

52 Ibid.

53 Ibid., p. 209f. Scholem had written to Paeschke as early as 7 March 1968, to say that Hannah Arendt's criticisms arose from her own 'inexactitudes'. He had the feeling that 'she felt a hatred of Adorno that must have its source elsewhere. It must have been building up over years and she was using this pretext to get it off her chest.' Ibid., p. 313.

54 Ibid.

55 Adorno to Kaufmann, 27 February 1968, quoted in Otto Kolleritsch, 'Adorno und Graz', p. 158.

56 See Adorno to Stefan Benjamin, 8 January 1968 and 22 January 1968, Theodor W. Adorno Archive, Frankfurt am Main (Br 92/39 and 92/43). The copyright of Benjamin's works had passed after his death to his son, who had given Adorno full powers of attorney in all matters concerning Benjamin's literary estate. See Rolf Tiedemann, *Die Abrechnung: Walter Benjamin und sein Verleger*, p. 12ff.

57 Adorno to Gabriele Henkel, 20 February 1968, Theodor W. Adorno Archive, Frankfurt am Main (Br 594/12, 13).

58 Adorno, *Introduction to Sociology*, p. 153f.

59 Horkheimer and Adorno, 'Diskussionen über Theorie und Praxis', *GS*, vol. 19, p. 61.

60 Adorno to Gabriele Henkel, 17 May 1968, Theodor W. Adorno Archive, Frankfurt am Main (Br 594/15).

61 Wolfgang Kraushaar (ed.), *Frankfurter Schule und Studentenbewegung*, vol. 2, p. 326.

62 Adorno, 'Diskussionsbeitrag am 23. September 1968', *Frankfurter Adorno Blätter*, VI, 2000, p. 77.

63 Adorno to Szondi, 14 June 1968, Theodor W. Adorno Archive, Frankfurt am Main.

64 Wolfgang Kraushaar (ed.), *Frankfurter Schule und Studentenbewegung*, vol. 2, p. 471.

65 Adorno to Grass, 4 November 1968, *Frankfurter Adorno Blätter*, VI, 2000, p. 78ff.

66 Adorno, 'Marginalia to Theory and Praxis', in *Critical Models*, p. 261.

67 Ibid., p. 263.

68 Ibid., p. 277.

69 Ibid., p. 267 (translation amended).

70 Ibid., p. 269.

71 Ibid., p. 276 (note added [trans.]).

72 Ibid., p. 274.

73 Adorno to Marcuse, 19 June 1969, *Frankfurter Adorno Blätter*, VI, 2000, p. 111.

74 Adorno, 'Marginalia to Theory and Praxis', *Critical Models*, p. 269.

75 Adorno, 'Resignation', *Critical Models*, p. 292.

76 Adorno, 'Konzeption eines Wiener Operntheaters', *GS*, vol. 19, p. 496ff.; cf. Otto Kolleritsch, 'Adorno und Graz', p. 156ff.

77 Kaufmann to Adorno, 13 November 1968, quoted in Kolleritsch, 'Adorno und Graz', p. 161. The correspondence between Adorno and Kaufmann is in the Institut für Wertungsforschung in Graz.

78 Towards the end of 1968, Marcuse had received anonymous threats and kept out of sight for a week. See Horkheimer, *Briefwechsel, GS*, vol. 18, p. 702f.

79 Adorno to Marcuse, 17 December 1968, Wolfgang Kraushaar (ed.), *Frankfurter Schule und Studentenbewegung*, vol. 2, p. 519f.

80 Ibid., p. 499.

81 Ibid., p. 555.

82 'Aktennotiz', February 1969, *Frankfurter Adorno Blätter*, VI, 2000, p. 93f. Adorno wrote to Alexander Kluge that he would proceed with the charges against Krahl. He did not see 'why I should make a martyr of myself to Herr Krahl, whom I picture putting a knife to my throat and getting ready

to use it and when I utter a mild protest, he responds by saying, "But, Herr Professor, it's wrong to take these things personally".' Adorno to Kluge, 1 April 1969, ibid., p. 100.

83 'Aktennotiz', ibid., p. 94.
84 Adorno to Marcuse, 28 February 1969, ibid., p. 97.
85 Adorno to Hans Heinz Stuckenschmidt, 25 February 1969, ibid., p. 96.
86 Adorno, *Aesthetic Theory*, p. 119.
87 Adorno, 'Free Time', *Critical Models*, p. 168.
88 At the end of March, in a letter to Siegfried Unseld, Adorno expressed his 'pride' in having contributed to Suhrkamp's success over the years. Adorno to Unseld, 27 March 1969, in Adorno, *'So müßte ich Engel und kein Autor sein': Theodor W. Adorno und die Frankfurter Verleger*, p. 388.
89 For his activities as director of the Institute of Social Research, Adorno obtained only the refund of his expenses. The only benefits he received from his position took the form of a number of assistants, a secretary and other clerical help.
90 See Rolf Tiedemann, 'Gegen den Trug der Frage nach Sinn', p. 76.
91 Theodor W. Adorno Archive, Frankfurt am Main (Ts 52028).
92 Ibid. (Ts 52029).
93 Adorno, 'Resignation', *Critical Models*, p. 293.
94 Adorno, *Minima Moralia*, p. 200.
95 Marie-Luise Borchardt was a niece of Rudolf Alexander Schröder; she lived in Italy with her husband, who had been born in Königsberg in 1877 into a prosperous Protestant family of Jewish origin. In 1944 Borchardt was arrested there by a German unit and taken to Innsbruck and put in prison. He succumbed to a heart attack shortly after his release. After his death, his widow devoted herself to the publication of his works for forty-four years. She died on 31 January 1989.
96 Adorno to Marie-Luise Borchardt, 18 April and 13 June 1967, Theodor W. Adorno Archive, Frankfurt am Main (Br 171/7, 8 and 14).
97 Adorno to Marie-Luise Borchardt, 1 September 1967, Theodor W. Adorno Archive, Frankfurt am Main (Br 171/ 17, 18).
98 Dieter Schnebel, 'Komposition von Sprache', p. 144f.
99 The volume *Ausgewählte Gedichte* appeared with an introduction and a comment on the choice of poems in the Bibliothek Suhrkamp in 1968; see also Adorno, 'Charmed Language', *Notes to Literature*, vol. 2, p. 193ff.
100 Ibid., p. 200.
101 Ibid., p. 209.
102 *Frankfurter Allgemeine Zeitung*, 11 September 1968.
103 Horkheimer, *Briefwechsel, GS*, vol. 18, p. 700ff.
104 Adorno, *Aesthetic Theory*, p. 130.
105 Adorno's preoccupation with aesthetics dates back to his activities as a *Privatdozent* in 1931–2. After his return to Germany, he lectured on aesthetics in 1950–1 and 1955–6. He lectured again on the subject in the winter semester of 1958–9 and then, in two parts, in the summer semester 1961 and winter semester 1961–2. By this time he had written a first draft of the *Aesthetic Theory* which was still subdivided into different paragraphs. See *Frankfurter Adorno Blätter*, I, 1992, p. 35.
106 A non-authorized partial transcription of the winter lectures was published in a pirated edition.

107　Adorno and Lenk, *Briefwechsel*, p. 157f.
108　Adorno to Marcuse, 24 January 1969, Herbert Marcuse Archive, Stadt- und Universitätsbibliothek, Frankfurt am Main.
109　Adorno and Lenk, *Briefwechsel*, p. 160.
110　See the Editor's Afterword in *Aesthetic Theory*, p. 361ff.
111　Since publication the volume, which appeared in the series suhrkamp taschenbuch wissenschaft, has sold 68,000 copies.
112　See Adorno, *Aesthetic Theory*, p. 259.
113　Ibid., p. 107 and p. 129f.; cf. Adorno and Lenk, *Briefwechsel*, p. 163. The planning of a volume on aesthetics to appear in Suhrkamp goes back to 1960. Publication was envisaged for 1964. See Siegfried Unseld to Adorno, 29 December 1960. See Adorno, *'So müßte ich ein Engel und kein Autor sein'*, p. 223.
114　Adorno, *Aesthetic Theory*, p. 129.
115　Ibid., p. 226.
116　Ibid., p. 136.
117　Ibid., p. 83.
118　Adorno, *Negative Dialectics*, p. 15.
119　Adorno, *Aesthetic Theory*, p. 53ff. Neither in the *Dialectic of Enlightenment* nor in the *Aesthetic Theory* did Adorno really elaborate the concept of mimesis. See Jürgen Habermas, *Theorie des kommunikativen Handelns*, vol. 1, p. 512. For the concept of mimesis, see Josef Früchtl, *Mimesis: Konstellation eines Zentralbegriffs bei Adorno*; Britta Scholze, *Kunst als Kritik: Adornos Weg aus der Dialektik*, p. 136ff. Jürgen Ritsert claims that the opposing concepts 'mimesis' and 'ratio' run through Adorno's *Aesthetic Theory* like a red thread. In the *Dialectic of Enlightenment* the defining pair of concepts is myth and enlightenment; for *Negative Dialectics* it is identity and non-identity. According to him, mimesis 'consists in the subject's practice of surrendering to the stubbornness and particularity of the object, seeking as it were closeness to the individual object.' Alternatively, mimesis can be understood as 'the sensitivity of the senses (aesthesis) and hence the receptivity of the subject to the inexhaustible plenitude of individual impressions.' Ritsert concludes that Adorno links mimetic experience with the 'thinking in configurations' that makes its appearance in *Negative Dialectics*. Jürgen Ritsert, *Ästhetische Theorie als Gesellschaftskritik*, p. 29ff.; cf. Christoph Menke, *Die Souveränität der Kunst*, p. 109ff.
120　Adorno, *Aesthetic Theory*, p. 289.
121　Ibid., p. 54.
122　Ibid., p. 110.
123　Ibid., p. 39.
124　Ibid., p. 135.
125　Ibid., p. 73.
126　Ibid., p. 71f.
127　Ibid., p. 66.
128　Ibid., p. 12; cf. p. 84.
129　See especially ibid., p. 182; cf. also Adorno, 'Die Kunst und die Künste', *GS*, vol. 10.1, p. 432ff.; see also 'Über einige Relationen zwischen Musik und Malerei', *GS*, vol. 16, p. 28ff.; furthermore, Christine Eichel, *Vom Ermatten der Avantgarde zur Vernetzung der Künste*, p. 27ff. On Adorno's

philosophy and sociology of art, see Günter Seubold, *Das Ende der Kunst und der Paradigmenwechsel in der Ästhetik*.

130 Adorno, 'Die Kunst und die Künste', *GS*, vol. 10.1, p. 438.

131 Adorno, *Negative Dialectics*, p. 33.

132 Adorno, 'Notizheft ß', *Frankfurter Adorno Blätter*, VI, 2000, p. 7.

133 Adorno to Tilly Dreyfus, 17 April 1969, Theodor W. Adorno Archive, Frankfurt am Main (Br 332/3).

134 Adorno to Carla Henius, 27 March 1969, Theodor W. Adorno Archive, Frankfurt am Main (Br 592/57); see also *Frankfurter Adorno Blätter*, VI, 2000, p. 42.

135 After Hans-Jürgen Krahl had been taken into custody for questioning, Adorno had telephoned Fritz Bauer, the state prosecutor, with whom he was on friendly terms, in order to tell him that Krahl was a sensitive person who ought to be set free quickly. See Rudolf zur Lippe, 'Die Frankfurter Studentenbewegung und das Ende Adornos', p. 116.

136 The present author has benefited from a number of personal accounts from those who witnessed the disruption of this lecture. See also Kraushaar (ed.), *Frankfurter Schule und Studentenbewegung*, vol. 1, p. 418; Alex Demirović, *Der nonkonformistische Intellektuelle*, p. 856ff., and especially p. 945ff.; Hans-Klaus Jungheinrich, who was present at the lecture, wrote a report about it for the *Frankfurter Rundschau* on 24 April 1969 with the title 'Adorno as an Institution is Dead: How the Consciousness Changer was Driven out of the Lecture Hall'. In this article, the author, a pupil of Adorno, wrote: 'Anyone who has direct experience of fascism will necessarily feel allergic towards the slightest hint of terrorism. . . . The disrupting of the philosophy lecture . . . was an own goal, for the left at any rate. The rowdy treatment of Adorno, far from signalling the emergence of a new post-bourgeois style, as one commentator claimed, points to a pre-bourgeois, indeed pre-civilized, relapse into barbarism.'

137 Adorno, 'Keine Angst vor dem Elfenbeinturm', *GS*, vol. 20.1, p. 406f.

138 Adorno to Eduard Grosse, 5 May 1969, *Frankfurter Adorno Blätter*, VI, 2000, p. 101.

139 Adorno, 'Kritische Theorie und Protestbewegung', *GS*, vol. 20.1, p. 399ff.

140 Adorno, 'Keine Angst vor dem Elfenbeinturm', *GS*, vol. 20.1, p. 402.

141 Ibid., p. 404. As to the question of the influence of the representatives of critical theory on the New Left, see Günter C. Behrmann's study. He concludes: 'If we look through the notable theoretical publications and indeed through the entire New Left before the mid-sixties, we look in vain for any sign that critical theory formed a significant reference point for the discussion of theory. Even later on, when the traces of Marcuse's ideas can be found and followed up, there is no general turn to Frankfurt critical theory either in the Frankfurt *Neue Kritik* or in the Berlin *Argument*.' Clemens Albrecht et al., *Die intellektuelle Gründung der Bundesrepublik*, p. 333f.

142 Adorno, 'Keine Angst vor dem Elfenbeinturm', *GS*, vol. 20.1, p. 405f.

143 Adorno to the dean of the Arts Faculty, 13 June 1969, *Frankfurter Adorno Blätter*, VI, 2000, p. 108f.

144 On 5 April 1969, Marcuse wrote to Adorno: 'I believe that if I were to accept the institute's invitation without also speaking to the students, I would identify myself with a position . . . that I do not share politically.

To put it brutally, if the alternative is to choose between the police or the left-wing students, then I am with the students – with one decisive exception, of course, namely if I am threatened or there is a threat to use force against me or my friends, and if the threat is meant seriously. The occupation of rooms (outside my house) without any such threat of violence is in my view no reason to call the police. . . . The alternative for me is to come to Frankfurt and discuss with the students, or not to come at all.' Wolfgang Kraushaar (ed.), *Frankfurter Schule und Studentenbewegung*, vol. 2, p. 601f.

145 Marcuse to Adorno, 4 June 1969, Horkheimer, *Briefwechsel*, *GS*, vol. 18, p. 732ff.
146 Adorno to Marcuse, 19 June 1969, *Frankfurter Adorno Blätter*, VI, 2000, p. 111.
147 Ibid.
148 Ibid., p. 112.
149 Rudolf zur Lippe, who had been friendly with the Adornos since 1968, knew from conversations with Adorno's doctor, who was also his doctor, just how risky a 3000-metre mountain was for Adorno, who had heart trouble. See Lippe, 'Die Frankfurter Studentenbewegung und das Ende Adornos', p. 116.
150 Adorno, 'Uromi', *GS*, vol. 20.2, p. 571.
151 Horkheimer, 'Theodor W. Adorno zum Gedächtnis', *GS*, vol. 7, p. 289f.

Epilogue: Thinking Against Oneself

1 Adorno to Plessner, 11 February 1958, Institut für Sozialforschung, Ordner Korrespondenzen, quoted in Alex Demirović, *Der nonkonformistische Intellektuelle*, p. 673.
2 Adorno and Mann, *Briefwechsel*, p. 134.
3 Adorno and Ernst Bloch, 'Etwas fehlt . . . Glück und Utopie: Ein Gespräch mit Theodor W. Adorno', p. 411.
4 Theodor W. Adorno Archive, Frankfurt am Main (Ts 52018).
5 Adorno, *Negative Dialectics*, p. 371.
6 Ibid.
7 Rolf Tiedemann, 'Editor's Preface', in Adorno, *Beethoven: The Philosophy of Music*, p. viii.
8 Adorno to his parents, 11 June 1940, *Briefe an die Eltern 1939–51*, p. 87.
9 The volume *Beethoven: The Philosophy of Music*, ed. Rolf Tiedemann, is a fragment from his posthumous papers, assembled from the various manuscripts and individual pieces of text that Adorno wrote on the composer.
10 See Adorno, *Zu einer Theorie der musikalischen Reproduktion*, *NaS*, vol. 2.
11 Adorno, *Problems of Moral Philosophy*.
12 Adorno, *Minima Moralia*, p. 39; Edmund Jephcott has translated this: 'Wrong life cannot be lived rightly' [trans.].
13 Adorno, *Negative Dialectics*, p. 365.
14 See Rolf Tiedemann, 'Editorische Nachbemerkung', in Adorno, *GS*, vol. 9.2, p. 404.
15 See Rudolf zur Lippe, 'Die Frankfurter Studentenbewegung und das Ende Adornos', p. 123ff.

16 Cf. *Frankfurter Adorno Blätter*, VII, 2001, p. 9f.
17 Theodor W. Adorno Archive, Frankfurt am Main (Ts 51905); cf. *Frankfurter Adorno Blätter*, VII and VIII.
18 Ibid. (Ts 52021).
19 Ibid.
20 Ibid. (Ts 51755).
21 Ibid. (Ts 51795).
22 This was the Corso Internazionale of the Cini Foundation on the Isola San Giorgio Maggiore.
23 Adorno to Elisabeth Lenk, 18 July 1969, Adorno and Lenk, *Briefwechsel*, p. 162.
24 Scholem to Adorno, 22 April 1969, Gershom Scholem, *Briefe*, vol. II, p. 221.
25 See Rudolf zur Lippe, 'Die Frankfurter Studentenbewegung und das Ende Adornos', p. 124.
26 Paul Lüth, 'Brief aus einer Landpraxis', p. 122.
27 Marie Luise Kaschnitz, *Gesammelte Werke*, vol. 2, p. 723.
28 Adorno to Carla Henius, 27 March 1969, Theodor W. Adorno Archive, Frankfurt am Main (Br 592/57).
29 Adorno and Lenk, *Briefwechsel*, p. 166f.
30 Rolf Tiedemann, 'Gretel Adorno zum Abschied', *Frankfurter Adorno Blätter*, III, 1994, p. 148.
31 Alexander Kluge wrote in his *Chronicle of the Feelings*: 'She, the experienced chemist, took poison as soon as she had dealt with the funeral, the burial of the dead man, some writings and the will. Impatiently, she embarked on her own death. Only at this point did her attention flag. The poison, wrongly dosed, paralysed a part of her soul, the other part lived on, without memory, for many years' (Kluge, *Chronik der Gefühle*, vol. 1, p. 863).
32 See Adorno, 'Resignation', *Critical Models*, p. 289ff.
33 Horkheimer, 'Himmel, Ewigkeit und Schönheit', *GS*, vol. 7, p. 291ff.
34 Cf. 'Nach dem Tode Theodor W. Adornos', in Hermann Schweppenhäuser (ed.), *Theodor W. Adorno zum Gedächtnis*, p. 22ff.; Wolfgang Kraushaar (ed.), *Frankfurter Schule und Studentenbewegung*, vol. 2, p. 676.
35 Ibid., p. 676ff.
36 Hans-Jürgen Krahl, 'Der politische Widerspruch der kritischen Theorie Adornos', p. 673.
37 Herbert Marcuse, 'Reflexionen zu Theodor W. Adorno', in Hermann Schweppenhäuser (ed.), *Theodor W. Adorno zum Gedächtnis*, p. 679ff.
38 Iring Fetscher, Adorno's departmental colleague, also succeeded in giving a picture of Adorno as man: 'His eyes gazed at the world in terror. They saw too much to allow him to remain content, calm and peaceful. He could become excited and yet there was nothing over-excited about him. He suffered and yet was able to transform his lament into sharp, analytic insight. He loved and knew how hopeless his love – his love for the possibilities of human beings – really was' (Fetscher, 'Ein Kämpfer ohne Illusion', p. 90).
39 Jürgen Habermas, 'Theodor W. Adorno wäre am 11. September 66 Jahre alt geworden'; see also Habermas, *Philosophisch-politische Profile*, p. 175.
40 Adorno, 'Critique', *Critical Models*, p. 281f. (translation altered).
41 Jürgen Habermas, *Die Einbeziehung des Anderen*, p. 7.

42 Jürgen Habermas, *Philosophisch-politische Profile*, p. 175.
43 Various trends came together in the history of the reception and the productive appropriation of Adorno's philosophy and sociology. There is no doubt that they have demonstrated their ability to make themselves acceptable. Worth mentioning here are, on the one hand, cultural theory, the different variants of the paradigms of interpretation and the Anglo-Saxon developments in cultural studies. On the other, we find Habermas's idea of communication free from domination, Axel Honneth's conception of the ethics of recognition, and the post-structuralist critique of logocentrism in Foucault and Derrida. See David Couzens Hoy and Thomas McCarthy, *Critical Theory*.
44 Adorno, *Negative Dialectics*, p. 365.
45 See Barbara Merker, 'Wozu noch Adorno?', p. 489ff. and, especially, p. 502ff.
46 Adorno, *Hegel: Three Studies*, p. 9.

References and Bibliography

I.1 Theodor W. Adorno

Gesammelte Schriften, 20 vols, ed. Rolf Tiedemann with Gretel Adorno, Susan Buck-Morss and Klaus Schultz. Frankfurt am Main: Suhrkamp, 1970–86 [*GS*].
1   *Philosophische Frühschriften*, 1973.
2   *Kierkegaard: Konstruktion des Ästhetischen*, 1979.
3   *Dialektik der Aufklärung: Philosophische Fragmente*, 1981.
4   *Minima Moralia: Reflexionen aus dem beschädigten Leben*, 1980.
5   *Zur Metakritik der Erkenntnistheorie*, 1971.
6   *Negative Dialektik*, 1973.
7   *Ästhetische Theorie*, 1970.
8   *Soziologische Schriften* I, 1972.
9.1 *Soziologische Schriften* II, 1975.
9.2 *Soziologische Schriften* II, 1975.
10.1 *Kulturkritik und Gesellschaft* I. *Prismen: Ohne Leitbild*, 1977.
10.2 *Kulturkritik und Gesellschaft* II. *Eingriffe: Stichworte*, 1977.
11   *Noten zur Literatur*, 1974.
12   *Philosophie der neuen Musik*, 1975.
13   *Die musikalischen Monographien*, 1971.
14   *Dissonanzen: Einleitung in die Musiksoziologie*, 1973.
15   *Komposition für den Film: der getreue Korrepetitor*, 1976.
16   *Musikalische Schriften* I–III: *Klangfiguren* (I); *Quasi una fantasia* (II); *Musikalische Schriften* (III), 1978.
17   *Musikalische Schriften* IV. *Moments musicaux: Impromptus*, 1982.
18   *Musikalische Schriften* V, 1984.
19   *Musikalische Schriften* VI, 1984.
20.1 *Vermischte Schriften* I, 1986.
20.2 *Vermischte Schriften* II, 1986.

Nachgelassene Schriften, ed. Theodor W. Adorno Archive. Frankfurt am Main: Suhrkamp, 1993–2002 [*NaS*].
Division I: Incomplete Works
1   *Beethoven: Philosophie der Musik*, ed. Rolf Tiedemann, 1993.
2   *Zu einer Theorie der musikalischen Reproduktion*, ed. Henri Lonitz, 2001.
Division IV: Lecture Courses
4   *Kants 'Kritik der reinen Vernunft'* (1959), ed. Rolf Tiedemann, 1995.

7   *Ontologie und Dialektik* (1960–1), ed. Rolf Tiedemann, 2002.
10   *Probleme der Moralphilosophie* (1963), ed. Thomas Schröder, 1996.
13   *Zur Lehre von der Geschichte und von der Freiheit* (1964–5), ed. Rolf Tiedemann, 2001.
14   *Metaphysik* (1965), ed. Rolf Tiedemann, 1998.
15   *Einleitung in die Soziologie* (1968), ed. Christoph Gödde, 1993.

Writings in English (monographs or essay collections only)

Walter Benjamin and Theodor Adorno, *The Complete Correspondence 1928–1940*, ed. Henri Lonitz, trans. Nicholas Walker. Cambridge: Polity 1999.
Aesthetic Theory, trans. Robert Hullot-Kentor. London: Athlone Press; Minneapolis: University of Minnesota Press, 1997 [*GS*, vol. 7].
Against Epistemology: A Metacritique – Studies in Husserl and the Phenomenological Antinomies, trans. Willis Domingo. Oxford: Blackwell, 1982 [*Zur Metakritik der Erkenntnistheorie, GS*, vol. 5, pp. 7–245].
Alban Berg: Master of the Smallest Link, trans. Juliane Brand and Christopher Hailey. Cambridge: Cambridge University Press, 1991 [*GS*, vol. 13, pp. 321–494].
Aspects of Sociology, trans. John Viertel. Boston: Beacon Press, 1972.
The Authoritarian Personality (with Else Frenkel-Brunswik, Daniel J. Levinson and R. Nevitt Sanford). New York: Harper & Brothers, 1950 [*GS*, vol. 9.1, pp. 143–509].
Beethoven: The Philosophy of Music, trans. Edmund Jephcott. Cambridge: Polity, 1998 [*NaS*, vol. 1].
'Can One Live After Auschwitz?', ed. Rolf Tiedemann, trans. Rodney Livingstone et al. Stanford, CA: Stanford University Press, 2003.
Composing for the Films (with Hanns Eisler), ed. Graham McCann. London: Athlone Press, 1994 [*GS*, vol. 15, pp. 7–155].
Critical Models: Interventions and Catchwords, trans. and with a preface by Henry W. Pickford. New York: Columbia University Press, 1998 [a translation of *Eingriffe* (1963) and *Stichworte* (1969), *GS*, vol. 10.2, pp. 455–799].
The Culture Industry: Selected Essays on Mass Culture, ed. J. M. Bernstein. London: Routledge, 1991.
Dialectic of Enlightenment (with Max Horkheimer), trans. John Cumming. London: Allen Lane, 1973 [*GS*, vol. 3].
Essays on Music, ed. Richard Leppert, trans. Susan H. Gillespie. Berkeley, Los Angeles and London: University of California Press, 2002.
Hegel: Three Studies, trans. Shierry Weber Nicholsen. Cambridge, MA: MIT Press, 1993 [*GS*, vol. 5, pp. 245–380].
In Search of Wagner, trans. Rodney Livingstone. London: NLB, 1981 [*GS*, vol. 13, pp. 7–148].
Introduction to Sociology (1968), trans. Edmund Jephcott. Cambridge: Polity, 1999 [*NaS*, vol. 15].
Introduction to the Sociology of Music, trans. E. B. Ashton. New York: Seabury Press, 1976 [*GS*, vol. 14, pp. 168–463].
The Jargon of Authenticity, trans. Knut Tarnowski and Frederic Will. London and New York: Routledge, 1973 [*GS*, vol. 6, pp. 413–531].
Kant's Critique of Pure Reason (1959), trans. Rodney Livingstone. Cambridge: Polity, 2001 [*NaS*, vol. 4].

Kierkegaard: Construction of the Aesthetic, trans. Robert Hullot-Kentor. Minneapolis: University of Minnesota Press, 1989 [*GS*, vol. 2].

Mahler: A Musical Physiognomy, trans. Edmund Jephcott. Chicago: University of Chicago Press, 1992 [*GS*, vol. 13, pp. 149–319].

Metaphysics: Concepts and Problems (1965), trans. Edmund Jephcott. Stanford, CA: Stanford University Press, 2000 [*NaS*, vol. 14].

Minima Moralia: Reflections from Damaged Life, trans. Edmund Jephcott. London: NLB, 1974 [*GS*, vol. 4].

Negative Dialectics, trans. E. B. Ashton. London: Routledge; New York: Seabury Press, 1973 [*GS*, vol. 6, pp. 7–412].

Notes to Literature, trans. Shierry Weber Nicholsen. 2 vols., New York: Columbia University Press, 1991–2 [*GS*, vol. 11].

The Philosophy of Modern Music, trans. Anne G. Mitchell and Wesley V. Bloomster. London: Sheed & Ward, 1973 [*GS*, vol. 12].

The Positivist Dispute in German Sociology (with others), trans. Glyn Adey and David Frisby. London: Heinemann, 1976.

Prisms, trans. Samuel Weber and Shierry Weber. Cambridge, MA: MIT Press, 1981 [*GS*, vol. 10.1, pp. 9–287].

Problems of Moral Philosophy (1963), trans. Rodney Livingstone. Cambridge: Polity, 2000 [*NaS*, vol. 10].

The Psychological Technique of Martin Luther Thomas' Radio Addresses. Stanford, CA: Stanford University Press, 2000 [*GS*, vol. 9.1].

Quasi una fantasia, trans. Rodney Livingstone. London: Verso, 1992 [*GS*, vol. 16, pp. 249–540].

Sound Figures, trans. Rodney Livingstone. Stanford, CA: Stanford University Press, 1999 [*GS*, vol. 16, pp. 7–248].

The Stars down to Earth, ed. Stephen Crook. London and New York: Routledge, 1994.

Correspondence

Briefe und Briefwechsel, ed. Theodor W. Adorno Archive. Frankfurt am Main: Suhrkamp, 1994–2003.
1 Theodor W. Adorno and Walter Benjamin: *Briefwechsel 1928–1940*, ed. Henri Lonitz, 1994.
2 Theodor W. Adorno and Alban Berg: *Briefwechsel 1925–1935*, ed. Henri Lonitz, 1997.
3 Theodor W. Adorno and Thomas Mann: *Briefwechsel 1943–1955*, ed. Christoph Gödde and Thomas Sprecher, 2002.
4 Theodor W. Adorno and Max Horkheimer: *Briefwechsel*. vol. I, ed. Henri Lonitz and Christoph Gödde, 2003.
5 Theodor W. Adorno: *Briefe an die Eltern 1939–1951*, ed. Christoph Gödde and Henri Lonitz, 2003.

Theodor W. Adorno and Ernst Krenek: *Briefwechsel*, ed. Wolfgang Rogge. Frankfurt am Main, 1974.

Theodor W. Adorno and Alfred Sohn-Rethel: *Briefwechsel 1936–1969*, ed. Christoph Gödde. Munich, 1991.

Theodor W. Adorno and Elisabeth Lenk: *Briefwechsel 1962–1969*, ed. Elisabeth Lenk. Munich, 2002.

Theodor W. Adorno and Paul Celan: *Briefwechsel 1960–1968*, ed. Joachim Seng. *Frankfurter Adorno Blätter*, VIII, 2003, pp. 26–49.

'So müßte ich ein Engel und kein Autor sein': Adorno und die Frankfurter Verleger: Der Briefwechsel mit Peter Suhrkamp und Siegfried Unseld, ed. Wolfgang Schopf. Frankfurt am Main, 2003.

Individual Editions/Essays/Conversations

Adorno, Theodor W.: *Dissonanzen: Musik in der verwalteten Welt*. Göttingen, 1956.

Adorno, Theodor W., and Bloch, Ernst: 'Etwas fehlt . . . Glück und Utopie', in Apel, Karl-Otto, Böhler, Dietrich, Berlich, Alfred, and Pumpe, Gerhard (eds): *Praktische Philosophie*. Frankfurt am Main, 1964, pp. 405–13.

Adorno, Theodor W.: *Jargon der Eigentlichkeit: Zur deutschen Ideologie*. Frankfurt am Main, 1964.

Adorno, Theodor W., and Haselberg, Peter von: 'Über die geschichtliche Angemessenheit des Bewußtseins', *Akzente*, no. 6, 1965, pp. 487–97.

Adorno, Theodor W.: 'Erinnerungen an Paul Tillich', Sendung des Süddeutschen Rundfunk Stuttgart, 21 August 1966, in *Werk und Wirken Paul Tillichs: Ein Gedenkbuch*. Stuttgart, 1967.

Adorno, Theodor W. (ed.): *Verhandlungen des 16. Deutschen Soziologentages: Spätkapitalismus oder Industriegesellschaft?: Im Auftrag der Deutschen Gesellschaft für Soziologie*. Stuttgart, 1969.

Adorno, Theodor W.: *Erziehung zur Mündigkeit: Vorträge und Gespräche mit Hellmut Becker 1959–1969*, ed. Gerd Kadelbach. Frankfurt am Main, 1970.

Adorno, Theodor W.: 'Die Freudsche Theorie und die Struktur der faschistischen Propaganda', in *Kritik: Kleine Schriften zur Gesellschaft*, ed. Rolf Tiedemann. Frankfurt am Main, 1971.

Adorno, Theodor W.: *Philosophische Terminologie*, ed. Rudolf zur Lippe. 2 vols., Frankfurt am Main, 1973.

Adorno, Theodor W.: *Studien zum autoritären Charakter*. Frankfurt am Main, 1973.

Adorno, Theodor W., and Gehlen, Arnold: 'Ist die Soziologie eine Wissenschaft vom Menschen?', in Grenz, Friedmann: *Adornos Philosophie in Grundbegriffen: Auflösung einiger Deutungsprobleme*. Frankfurt am Main, 1975, pp. 224–51.

Adorno, Theodor W.: *Der Schatz des Indianer-Joe: Singspiel nach Mark Twain*, ed. Rolf Tiedemann. Frankfurt am Main, 1979.

Adorno, Theodor W.: *Kompositionen*, vol. 1: *Alle Klavierliederzyklen*, ed. Heinz-Klaus Metzger and Rainer Riehn. Munich, 1989.

Adorno, Theodor W.: *Kompositionen*, vol. 2: *Kammermusik, Chor- und Orchesterwerke*, ed. Heinz-Klaus Metzger and Rainer Riehn. Munich, 1989.

Adorno, Theodor W.: *Über Walter Benjamin*, ed. and with notes by Rolf Tiedemann. Rev. edn, Frankfurt am Main, 1990.

Adorno, Theodor W.: 'Aufzeichnungen zur Ästhetik-Vorlesung von 1931/32', *Frankfurter Adorno Blätter*, I, 1992, pp. 35–90.

Adorno, Theodor W.: 'Theory of Pseudo-Culture', *Telos*, 95, spring 1993.

Adorno, Theodor W., Boehlich, Walter, Esslin, Martin, Falkenberg, Hans-Geert, and Fischer, Ernst: 'Optimistisch zu denken ist kriminell', *Frankfurter Adorno Blätter*, III, 1994, pp. 78–122.

Adorno's seminar of the summer semester 1932 on Benjamin's *Ursprünge des deutschen Trauerspiels*, *Frankfurter Adorno Blätter*, IV, 1995, pp. 52–77.
Adorno, Theodor W.: 'Graeculus (I). Musikalische Notizen', *Frankfurter Adorno Blätter*, VII, 2001, pp. 9–36.
Adorno, Theodor W.: 'Musik im Rundfunk: Zwei unveröffentlichte Texte', *Frankfurter Adorno Blätter*, VII, 2001.
Zwieback, Castor: 'Lesestücke', *Akzente: Zeitschrift für Dichtung*, 10, 1963, pp. 405–15.

Frankfurter Adorno Blätter, ed. Theodor W. Adorno Archiv (from issue V, ed. Rolf Tiedemann on behalf of the Theodor W. Adorno Archive). Munich, 1992–2003.
Frankfurter Adorno Blätter I, 1992.
Frankfurter Adorno Blätter II, 1993.
Frankfurter Adorno Blätter III, 1994.
Frankfurter Adorno Blätter IV, 1995.
Frankfurter Adorno Blätter V, 1998.
Frankfurter Adorno Blätter VI, 2000.
Frankfurter Adorno Blätter VII, 2001.
Frankfurter Adorno Blätter VIII, 2003.

I.2 Walter Benjamin

Gesammelte Schriften (Werkausgabe), ed. Rolf Tiedemann and Hermann Schweppenhäuser, with the assistance of Theodor W. Adorno and Gershom Scholem. Frankfurt am Main, 1980.
I.1–3   *Abhandlungen.*
II.1–3   *Aufsätze, Essays, Vorträge.*
III   *Kritiken und Rezensionen.*
IV.1–2   *Kleine Prosa, Baudelaire-Übertragungen.*
V.1–2   *Das Passagen-Werk.*
VI.   *Fragmente vermischten Inhalts, Autobiographische Schriften.*
VII.1–2   *Nachträge.*
Gesammelte Briefe, ed. Theodor W. Adorno Archiv, Christoph Gödde and Henri Lonitz. Frankfurt am Main: Suhrkamp, 1995–2000.
I   *Briefe 1910–1918*, 1995.
II   *Briefe 1919–1924*, 1996.
III   *Briefe 1925–1930*, 1997.
IV   *Briefe 1931–1934*, 1998.
V   *Briefe 1935–1937*, 1999.
VI   *Briefe 1938–1941*, 2000.

Individual Publications

Benjamin, Walter: *Briefe*, ed. Gershom Scholem and Theodor W. Adorno. Frankfurt am Main, 1966.
Benjamin, Walter: *Illuminations*, trans. Harry Zohn. London, 1970.
Benjamin, Walter: *Drei Hörmodelle*. Frankfurt am Main, 1971.

Benjamin, Walter: *Charles Baudelaire: A Lyric Poet in the Era of High Capitalism*, trans. Harry Zohn. London, 1973.
Benjamin, Walter: *The Origin of German Tragic Drama*, trans. John Osborne. London, 1977.
Benjamin, Walter: *The Arcades Project*, trans. H. Eiland and K. McClaughlin. Cambridge, MA, and London, 1999.
Benjamin, Walter: *Berliner Kindheit um neunzehnhundert*, ed. Rolf Tiedemann. Frankfurt am Main, 2000.
Benjamin, Walter: *Selected Writings*, trans. E. Jephcott, H. Eiland et al., vol. 3. Cambridge, MA, and London, 2003.
Benjamin, Walter, and Scholem, Gershom: *Briefwechsel 1933–1940*, ed. Gershom Scholem. Frankfurt am Main, 1980.

I.3 Max Horkheimer

Gesammelte Schriften, ed. Alfred Schmidt and Gunzelin Schmid Noerr. Frankfurt am Main, 1985–96 [*GS*]
1 *Aus der Pubertät – Novellen und Tagebuchblätter 1914–1918*, 1988.
2 *Philosophische Frühschriften 1922–1932*, 1987.
3 *Schriften 1931–1936*, 1988.
4 *Schriften 1936–1941*, 1988.
5 *Dialektik der Aufklärung und Schriften 1940–1950*, 1987.
6 *Zur Kritik der instrumentellen Vernunft und Notizen 1949–1969*, 1991.
7 *Vorträge und Aufzeichnungen 1949–1973*, 1985.
8 *Vorträge und Aufzeichnungen 1949–1973*, 1985.
9 *Nachgelassene Schriften 1914–1931*, 1987.
10 *Nachgelassene Schriften 1914–1931*, 1990.
11 *Nachgelassene Schriften 1912–1931*, 1987.
12 *Nachgelassene Schriften 1931–1949*, 1985.
13 *Nachgelassene Schriften 1949–1972*, 1989.
14 *Nachgelassene Schriften 1949–1972*, 1988.
15 *Briefwechsel 1913–1936*, 1995.
16 *Briefwechsel 1937–1940*, 1995.
17 *Briefwechsel 1941–1948*, 1996.
18 *Briefwechsel 1949–1973*, 1996.
19 *Nachträge, Verzeichnisse und Register*, 1996.

Individual Publications

Horkheimer, Max: *Zeugnisse: Theodor W. Adorno zum sechzigsten Geburtstag*. Frankfurt am Main, 1963.
Horkheimer, Max: *Dawn and Decline*, trans. Michael Shaw. New York, 1978.
Horkheimer, Max: *Critical Theory and Society*, ed. S. E. Bronner and D. M. Kellner. London and New York, 1989.
Horkheimer, Max: 'Art and Mass Culture', *Studies in Philosophy and Social Science*, 9, 1991, pp. 290–304.
Horkheimer, Max: *Between Philosophy and Social Science*, trans. E. F. Hunter et al. Cambridge, MA, 1993.

Horkheimer, Max, and Adorno, Theodor W.: *Sociologica II: Reden und Vorträge.* Frankfurt am Main, 1962.
Horkheimer, Max, and Flowerman, Samuel H. (eds): *Studies in Prejudice.* New York 1949–50.

I.4 Siegfried Kracauer

Schriften. Frankfurt am Main, 1971–90.
1   *Soziologie als Wissenschaft,* 1971.
2   *Von Caligari zu Hitler: Eine psychologische Geschichte des deutschen Films,* 1979.
3   *Theorie des Films: Die Errettung der äußeren Wirklichkeit,* ed. Karsten Witte, 1973.
4   *Geschichte – Vor den letzten Dingen,* trans. from the American by Karsten Witte, 1971.
5.1 *Aufsätze (1915–1925),* ed. Inka Mülder-Bach, 1990.
5.2 *Aufsätze (1926–1932),* ed. Inka Mülder-Bach, 1990.
5.3 *Aufsätze (1932–1965),* ed. Inka Mülder-Bach, 1990.
7   *Ginster. Georg,* 1973.
8   *Jacques Offenbach und das Paris seiner Zeit,* ed. Karsten Witte, 1976.

Individual Works

Kracauer, Siegfried: *The Mass Ornament,* trans. T. Y. Levin. Cambridge, MA, and London, 1995.

I.5 Leo Löwenthal

Schriften, ed. Helmut Dubiel. Frankfurt am Main 1980–7.
1 *Literatur und Massenkultur,* 1980.
2 *Das bürgerliche Bewusstsein in der Literatur,* 1981.
3 *Falsche Propheten: Studien zum Autoritarismus,* 1982.
4 *Judaica, Vorträge, Briefe,* 1984.
5 *Philosophische Frühschriften,* 1987.

Individual Works

Löwenthal, Leo: *Mitmachen wollte ich nie.* Frankfurt am Main, 1980.
Löwenthal, Leo: 'Erinnerungen an Theodor W. Adorno', in von Friedeburg, Ludwig, and Habermas, Jürgen (eds): *Adorno-Konferenz 1983.* Frankfurt am Main, 1983, pp. 388–401.
Löwenthal, Leo: *An Unmastered Past,* ed. M. Jay. Berkeley, Los Angeles and London, 1987.
Löwenthal, Leo: 'Individuum und Terror', in Löwenthal: *Untergang der Dämonologien.* Leipzig, 1990.

I.6 Publications of the Institute of Social Research

Ein Bericht über die Feier seiner Wiedereröffnung, seine Geschichte und seine Arbeiten. Frankfurt am Main, 1951.

Betriebsklima: Eine industriesoziologische Untersuchung aus dem Ruhrgebiet. Frankfurt am Main, 1955.

Gruppenexperiment: Ein Studienbericht, ed. Friedrich Pollock. Frankfurt am Main, 1955.

Sociologica I: Aufsätze: Max Horkheimer zum sechzigsten Geburtstag gewidmet. Frankfurt am Main, 1955.

Friedrich Pollock, *Automation: Materialien zur Beurteilung der ökonomischen und sozialen Folgen.* Frankfurt am Main, 1956.

Soziologische Exkurse: Nach Vorträgen und Diskussionen. Frankfurt am Main, 1956.

Freud in der Gegenwart: Ein Vortragszyklus der Universitäten Frankfurt und Heidelberg zum hundertsten Geburtstag. Frankfurt am Main, 1957.

Massing, Paul W.: *Vorgeschichte des politischen Antisemitismus.* Frankfurt am Main, 1959.

Horkheimer, Max, and Adorno, Theodor W.: *Sociologica II: Reden und Vorträge.* Frankfurt am Main, 1962.

Schmidt, Regina, and Becker, Egon: *Reaktionen auf politische Vorgänge: Drei Meinungsstudien aus der Bundesrepublik.* Frankfurt am Main, 1967.

Der autoritäre Charakter. Amsterdam, 1968.

Mitteilungen, no. 10, 1999.

Zeitschrift für Sozialforschung [*ZfS*]
Zeitschrift für Sozialforschung, ed. Institut für Sozialforschung. I, 1932, nos. 1–2, no. 3 (Leipzig).
Zeitschrift für Sozialforschung, II, 1933, no. 1 (Leipzig), no. 2, no. 3 (Paris).
Zeitschrift für Sozialforschung, III, 1934, no. 1, no. 2, no. 3 (Paris).
Zeitschrift für Sozialforschung, IV, 1935, no. 1, no. 2, no. 3 (Paris).
Zeitschrift für Sozialforschung, V, 1936, no. 1, no. 2, no. 3 (Paris).
Zeitschrift für Sozialforschung, VI, 1937, no. 1, no. 2, no. 3 (Paris).
Zeitschrift für Sozialforschung, VII, 1938, nos. 1–2, no. 3 (Paris).
Zeitschrift für Sozialforschung, VIII, 1939, nos. 1–2 (Paris).
Studies in Philosophy and Social Science, pubd by the Institute of Social Research, VIII, 1939, no. 3 (New York) [*SPSS*]
Studies in Philosophy and Social Science, pubd by the Institute of Social Research, IX, 1941, no. 1, no. 2, no. 3 (New York).

II Secondary Literature

Abendroth, Wolfgang: *Antagonistische Gesellschaft und politische Demokratie: Aufsätze zur politischen Soziologie.* Neuwied and Berlin, 1967.

Ackerman, Nathan W., and Jahoda, Marie: *Anti-Semitism and Emotional Disorder: A Psychoanalytic Interpretation.* New York, 1950.

Adler, Hans G.: *Der verwaltete Mensch: Studien zur Deportation der Juden aus Deutschland.* Tübingen, 1974.

Agnoli, Johannes, and Brückner, Peter: *Die Transformation der Demokratie.* Berlin, 1967.

Ahrens, Jörn: 'Zur Faschismusanalyse Hannah Arendts und Theodor W. Adornos', *Leviathan*, no. 1, 1995, pp. 27–40.

Albrecht, Clemens, Behrmann, Günter C., Bock, Michael, Homann, Harald, and Tenbruck, Friedrich: *Die intellektuelle Gründung der Bundesrepublik: Eine Wirkungsgeschichte der Frankfurter Schule.* Frankfurt am Main and elsewhere, 1999.

Der Aquädukt 1763–1988: Ein Almanach aus dem Verlag C. H. Beck im 225. Jahr seines Bestehens. Munich, 1988.

Arendt, Hannah: *Elemente und Ursprünge totaler Herrschaft.* Munich, 1986.

——: *Besuch in Deutschland.* Berlin, 1993.

Arendt, Hannah, and Jaspers, Karl: *Briefwechsel 1926–1969.* Munich, 1985.

Arnold, Heinz Ludwig: 'Über Kulturzeitschriften nach 1945', in *Der Aquädukt 1763–1988: Ein Almanach aus dem Verlag C. H. Beck im 225. Jahr seines Bestehens.* Munich, 1988, pp. 494–507.

Asiáin, Martin: *Theodor W. Adorno: Dialektik des Aporetischen: Untersuchungen zur Rolle der Kunst in der Philosophie Theodor W. Adornos.* Freiburg (Breisgau) and elsewhere, 1996.

Auer, Dirk: 'Daß die Naturbefangenheit nicht das letzte Wort behalte: Fortschritt, Vernunft und Aufklärung', in Auer, Dirk, Bonacker, Thorsten, and Müller-Doohm, Stefan (eds): *Die Gesellschaftstheorie Adornos: Themen und Grundbegriffe.* Darmstadt, 1998, pp. 21–40.

——: 'Paria wider Willen: Adornos und Arendts Reflexionen auf den Ort des Intellektuellen', in Auer, Dirk, Schulze Wessel, Julia, and Rensmann, Lars (eds): *Arendt und Adorno.* Frankfurt am Main, 2003.

Ayer, Alfred: *Part of my Life: The Memoirs of a Philosopher.* London and New York, 1977.

Backhaus, Hans-Georg: *Dialektik der Wertform: Untersuchungen zur Marxschen Ökonomiekritik.* Freiburg, 1997.

Baudelaire, Charles: *Les Fleurs du mal.* Paris, 1989.

Bauer, Karin: *Adorno's Nietzschean Narratives: Critiques of Ideology, Readings of Wagner.* Albany, NY, 1999.

Becker-Schmidt, Regina: 'Wenn die Frauen erst einmal Frauen sein könnten', in Früchtl, Josef, and Calloni, Maria (eds): *Geist gegen den Zeitgeist: Erinnern an Adorno.* Frankfurt am Main 1991, pp. 206–24.

Beckett, Samuel: *The Beckett Trilogy.* London, 1979.

Benhabib, Seyla: *Critique, Norm and Utopia: A Study of the Foundations of Critical Theory.* New York, 1986.

Benn, Gottfried: *Briefe an F. W. Oelze, 1950–1959.* Munich, 1980.

Bense, Max: 'Hegel und die kalifornische Emigration', *Merkur*, 4, no. 5, 1950, pp. 118–25.

Bentz, Ralf (ed.): *Protest! Literatur um 1968. Eine Ausstellung des Deutschen Literaturarchivs in Verbindung mit dem Germanistischen Seminar der Universität Heidelberg und dem Deutschen Rundfunkarchiv im Schiller-Nationalmuseum Marbach am Neckar.* Marbach am Neckar, 1998.

Benz, Wolfgang: 'Die jüdische Emigration', in Krohn, Claus-Dieter, Mühlen, Patrik von der, Paul, Gerhard, and Winkler, Lutz (eds): *Handbuch der Deutschsprachigen Emigration 1933–1945.* Darmstadt, 1998, pp. 5–16.

Benz, Wolfgang, Graml, Hermann, and Weiß, Hermann (eds): *Enzyklopädie des Nationalsozialismus.* Munich, 1997.

Bergh, Gerhard van den: *Adornos philosophisches Deuten von Dichtung*. Bonn, 1989.

Bertaux, Pierre: *Friedrich Hölderlin*. Frankfurt am Main, 1978.

Berthold, Werner, Eckert, Brita, and Wende, Frank: *Deutsche Intellektuelle im Exil*. Munich, London, New York and Paris, 1993 [exhibition catalogue].

Bloch, Ernst: *Geist der Utopie*. Frankfurt am Main, 1975.

—— : *Briefe 1903–1975*. 2 vols., ed. Karola Bloch et al. Frankfurt am Main, 1985.

—— : *Das Prinzip Hoffnung*. 3 vols., Frankfurt am Main, 1986.

Bloch, Ernst, et al.: *Aesthetics and Politics*. London, 1977.

Blumentritt, Martin: 'Adorno, der Komponist als Philosoph', *Musik-Konzepte*, 63–4, 1989, pp. 8–25.

Bog, Ingomar: 'Die Industrialisierung in Hessen', in Schultz, Uwe (ed.), *Die Geschichte Hessens*. Stuttgart, 1983.

Bollack, Jean: *Paul Celan: Poetik der Fremdheit*. Vienna, 2000.

Bonacker, Thorsten: 'Ohne Angst verschieden sein können: Individualität in der integralen Gesellschaft', in Auer, Dirk, Bonacker, Thorsten, and Müller-Doohm, Stefan (eds): *Die Gesellschaftstheorie Adornos: Themen und Grundbegriffe*. Darmstadt, 1998, pp. 117–44.

—— : 'Theodor W. Adorno – Die Zukunft des Erinnerns', in Fröhlich, Claudia, and Kohlstruck, Michael (eds): *Engagierte Demokraten: Vergangenheitspolitik in kritischer Absicht*. Münster, 1999, pp. 170–84.

—— : *Die normative Kraft der Kontingenz: Nichtessentialistische Gesellschaftskritik nach Weber und Adorno*. Frankfurt am Main, 2000.

—— : 'Ungewißheit und Unbedingtheit: Zu den Möglichkeitsbedingungen des Normativen', in Müller-Doohm, Stefan (ed.): *Das Interesse der Vernunft: Rückblicke auf das Werk von Jürgen Habermas seit 'Erkenntnis und Interesse'*. Frankfurt am Main, 2000, pp. 107–43.

—— : 'Hat die Moderne einen normativen Gehalt? Zur Möglichkeit einer kritischen Gesellschaftstheorie unter Kontingenzbedingungen', *Berliner Journal für Soziologie*, 2, 2001, pp. 159–78.

Bonß, Wolfgang: *Die Einübung des Tatsachenblicks*. Frankfurt am Main, 1982.

—— : 'Psychoanalyse als Wissenschaft und Kritik: Zur Freudrezeption der Frankfurter Schule', in Bonß, Wolfgang and Honneth, Axel (eds): *Sozialforschung als Kritik*. Frankfurt am Main, 1982, pp. 367–425.

—— : 'Empirie und Dechiffrierung von Wirklichkeit: Zur Methodologie bei Adorno', in Friedeburg, Ludwig von, and Habermas, Jürgen (eds): *Adorno-Konferenz 1983*. Frankfurt am Main, 1983, pp. 201–25.

Bonß, Wolfgang, and Schindler, Norbert: 'Kritische Theorie als interdisziplinärer Materialismus', in Bonß, Wolfgang, and Honneth, Axel (eds): *Sozialforschung als Kritik*. Frankfurt am Main, 1982, pp. 31–66.

Braach, Mile: *Rückblende: Erinnerungen einer Neunzigjährigen*. Frankfurt am Main, 1992.

Brandt, Gerhard: 'Ansichten kritischer Sozialforschung 1930–1980', in Institut für Sozialforschung: 'Gesellschaftliche Arbeit und Rationalisierung: Neuere Studien aus dem Institut für Sozialforschung in Frankfurt am Main', *Leviathan*, no. 4, 1981 [special issue], pp. 9–56.

Brecht, Bertolt: *Journals 1934–1955*, trans. H. Rorrison. London, 1993.

Breuer, Stefan: 'Adornos Anthropologie', *Leviathan*, no. 3, 1984, pp. 336–53.

—— : *Die Gesellschaft des Verschwindens: Von der Selbstzerstörung der technischen Zivilisation.* Hamburg, 1992.

Brick, Barbara, and Postone, Moishe: 'Kritischer Pessimismus und die Grenzen des traditionellen Marxismus', in Bonß, Wolfgang, and Honneth, Axel (eds): *Sozialforschung als Kritik.* Frankfurt am Main, 1982, pp. 179–239.

Brieglieb, Karl: *Mißachtung und Tabu: Eine Streitschrift zur Frage: Wie antisemitisch war die Gruppe 47?.* Berlin, 2003.

Brodersen, Momme: *Spinne im eigenen Netz: Walter Benjamin, Leben und Werk.* Darmstadt, 1990.

—— : *Siegfried Kracauer.* Hamburg, 2001.

Brumlik, Micha: 'Theologie und Messianismus im Denken Adornos', in Schröter, Hartmut, and Gürtler, Sabine (eds): *Ende der Geschichte: Abschied von der Geschichtskonzeption der Moderne?.* Münster, 1986, pp. 36–52.

Brunkhorst, Hauke: 'Die Welt als Beute: Rationalisierung und Vernunft in der Geschichte', in Reijen, Willem van, and Schmid Noerr, Gunzelin (eds): *Vierzig Jahre Flaschenpost: 'Dialektik der Aufklärung' 1947 bis 1987.* Frankfurt am Main, 1987, pp. 154–91.

—— : *Adorno and Critical Theory.* Cardiff, 1999.

Bubner, Rüdiger: *Dialektik als Topik: Bausteine zu einer lebensweltlichen Theorie der Rationalität.* Frankfurt am Main, 1989.

Buckmiller, Michael: 'Die "Marxistische Arbeitswoche" 1923 und die Gründung des Instituts für Sozialforschung', in Reijen, Willem van, and Schmid Noerr, Gunzelin (eds): *Grand Hotel Abgrund.* Hamburg, 1988, pp. 141–82.

Buck-Morss, Susan: *The Origin of Negative Dialectics.* Hassocks, Sussex, 1977.

—— : *The Dialectics of Seeing.* Cambridge, MA, 1990.

Bürger, Peter: *Theorie der Avantgarde.* Frankfurt am Main, 1974.

—— : *Zur Kritik der idealistischen Ästhetik.* Frankfurt am Main, 1983.

—— : *Das Altern der Moderne: Schriften zur bildenden Kunst.* Frankfurt am Main, 2001.

Burleigh, Michael: *The Third Reich.* London, 2000.

Cahn, Peter: *Das Hoch'sche Konservatorium in Frankfurt am Main.* Frankfurt am Main, 1979.

Cantril, Hadley, and Allport, Gordon W.: *The Psychology of Radio.* Salem, NH, 1986 [orig. pubd 1935].

Celan, Paul: *Gesammelte Werke.* 3 vols., ed. Beda Allemann and Stefan Reichert. Frankfurt am Main, 1983.

Chadwick, Nick: 'Mátyás Seiber's Collaboration in Adorno's Jazz Project, 1936', *British Library Journal*, 21, 1995, pp. 259–88.

Champion, James: 'Tillich and the Frankfurt School: Parallels and Differences in Prophetic Criticism', *Soundings: An Interdisciplinary Journal*, 69, 1986, p. 529ff.

Claussen, Detlev: 'Nach Auschwitz: Ein Essay über die Aktualität Adornos', in Diner, Dan (ed.): *Zivilisationsbruch: Denken nach Auschwitz.* Frankfurt am Main, 1988, pp. 54–68.

Cobet, Christoph (ed.): *Einführung in Fragen an die Soziologie in Deutschland nach Hitler 1945–1950.* Frankfurt am Main, 1988.

Coing, Helmut: 'Der Wiederaufbau und die Rolle der Wissenschaft', in Coing, Helmut (ed.): *Wissenschaftsgeschichte seit 1900.* Frankfurt am Main, 1992, pp. 85–99.

Cornelius, Hans: 'Leben und Lehre', in Schmidt, Raymund (ed.): *Die Philosophie der Gegenwart in Selbstdarstellungen*. 2nd rev. edn, Leipzig, 1923, pp. 83–102.

Dahms, Hans-Joachim: *Positivismusstreit: Die Auseinandersetzung der Frankfurter Schule mit dem logischen Positivismus, dem amerikanischen Pragmatismus und dem kritischen Rationalismus*. Frankfurt am Main, 1994.

Dahrendorf, Ralf: 'Die drei Soziologien: Zu Helmut Schelskys "Ortsbestimmung der deutschen Soziologie"', *Kölner Zeitschrift für Soziologie und Sozialpsychologie*, 12, 1960, pp. 120–33.

——: *Pfade aus Utopia*. Munich, 1967.

——: *Über Grenzen: Lebenserinnerungen*. Munich, 2002.

Demirović, Alex: 'Die Hüter der Gesellschaft: Zur Professionalisierung der Soziologie in Westdeutschland 1945–1950', in Cobet, Christoph (ed.): *Einführung in Fragen an die Soziologie in Deutschland nach Hitler 1945–1950*. Frankfurt am Main, 1988, pp. 48–75.

——: 'Das Glück der Wahrheit: Die Rückkehr der Frankfurter Schule', in: *Die Neue Gesellschaft, Frankfurter Hefte* 36, 1989, pp. 700–7.

——: 'Zwischen Nihilismus und Aufklärung: Publizistische Reaktionen auf die "Minima Moralia"', in Erd, Rainer, Hoß, Dieter, Jacobi, Otto, and Noller, Peter (eds): *Kritische Theorie und Kultur*. Frankfurt am Main, 1989, pp. 153–72.

——: *Der nonkonformistische Intellektuelle: Die Entwicklung der Kritischen Theorie zur Frankfurter Schule*. Frankfurt am Main, 1999.

Demmerling, Christoph: *Sprache und Verdinglichung: Wittgenstein, Adorno und das Projekt einer kritischen Theorie*. Frankfurt am Main, 1994.

Deuser, Hermann: *Dialektische Theologie: Studien zu Adornos Metaphysik und zum Spätwerk Kierkegaards*. Munich, 1980.

Diner, Dan: 'Aporie der Vernunft: Horkheimers Überlegungen zu Antisemitismus und Massenvernichtung', in Diner, Dan (ed.): *Zivilisationsbruch: Denken nach Auschwitz*. Frankfurt am Main, 1988, pp. 30–53.

Dubiel, Helmut: 'Kritische Theorie und politische Ökonomie', in Pollock, Friedrich: *Stadien des Kapitalismus*, ed. Helmut Dubiel. Munich, 1975, pp. 7–19.

——: *Wissenschaftsorganisation und politische Erfahrung*. Frankfurt am Main, 1978.

——: 'Die Aufhebung des Überbaus', in Bonß, Wolfgang, and Honneth, Axel (eds): *Sozialforschung als Kritik*. Frankfurt am Main, 1983, pp. 456–81.

——: *Niemand ist frei von der Geschichte: Die nationalsozialistische Herrschaft in den Debatten des Deutschen Bundestages*. Munich, 1999.

Dubiel, Helmut, and Söllner, Alfons (eds): *Wirtschaft, Recht und Staat im Nationalsozialismus: Analysen des Instituts für Sozialforschung 1939–1942*. Frankfurt am Main, 1984.

Dufraisse, Roger: *Napoleon: Revolutionär und Monarch*. Munich, 1994.

Ehlers, Lisbeth, and Krohn, Helga: *Juden in Bockenheim: Die vergessenen Nachbarn*. Frankfurt am Main, 1990.

Eichel, Christine: *Vom Ermatten der Avantgarde zur Vernetzung der Künste: Perspektiven einer interdisziplinären Ästhetik im Spätwerk Theodor W. Adornos*. Frankfurt am Main, 1993.

Eissler, Kurt Robert: *Goethe: Eine psychoanalytische Studie*. 2 vols., Munich, 1987.

Ellwein, Thomas: *Krisen und Reformen: Die Bundesrepublik seit den sechziger Jahren.* Munich, 1989.

Emrich, Wilhelm: 'Ladenhüter', in: *Zeugnisse: Theodor W. Adorno zum sechzigsten Geburtstag,* ed. Max Horkheimer. Frankfurt am Main, 1963, pp. 213–24.

Engelhardt, Ulrich: *'Bildungsbürgertum': Begriffs- und Dogmengeschichte eines Etiketts.* Stuttgart, 1986.

'Entartete Kunst': Das Schicksal der Avantgarde im Nazi-Deutschland. Munich and Los Angeles, 1992.

Enzensberger, Hans Magnus: *Einzelheiten.* Frankfurt am Main, 1962.

—— : *Blindenschrift.* Frankfurt am Main, 1964.

Erd, Rainer (ed.): *Reform und Resignation: Gespräche über Franz L. Neumann.* Frankfurt am Main, 1980.

Esders, Michael: *Begriffs-Gesten: Philosophie als kurze Prosa von Friedrich Schlegel bis Adorno.* Frankfurt am Main, 2000.

Evers, Hans Gerhard (ed.): *Darmstädter Gespräch: Das Menschenbild in unserer Zeit.* Darmstadt, 1950.

Farías, Victor: *Heidegger und der Nationalsozialismus.* Frankfurt am Main, 1987.

Felstiner, John: *Paul Celan: Poet, Survivor, Jew.* New Haven, CT, 1995.

Fetscher, Iring: 'Ein Kämpfer ohne Illusion', in Schweppenhäuser, Hermann (ed.): *Theodor W. Adorno zum Gedächtnis.* Frankfurt am Main, 1971, pp. 90–4.

Fink, Wolfgang: ' "... in jener richtigen, höheren Art einfach": Anmerkungen zu Adornos kurzen Orchesterstücken op. 4', *Musik-Konzepte,* 63–4, 1989, pp. 100–10.

Fischer, Karsten: *'Verwilderte Selbsterhaltung': Zivilisationstheoretische Kulturkritik bei Nietzsche, Freud, Weber und Adorno.* Berlin, 1999.

Fittko, Lisa: *Mein Weg über die Pyrenäen: Erinnerungen 1940/41.* Munich, 1988.

Floros, Constantin: 'Alban Berg und Hanna Fuchs: Briefe und Studien' *Österreichische Musikzeitschrift,* Special issue, 1995, pp. 30–69.

—— : *Alban Berg und Hanna Fuchs: Die Geschichte einer Liebe in Briefen.* Zurich and Hamburg, 2001.

Forstmann, Wilfried: 'Frankfurt am Main in Wilhelminischer Zeit 1866–1918', in Frankfurter Historische Kommission (ed.): *Frankfurt am Main: Die Geschichte der Stadt in neun Beiträgen.* Sigmaringen, 1991, pp. 349–422.

Fox, John P.: 'Das nationalsozialistische Deutschland und die Emigration nach Großbritannien', in Hirschfeld, Gerhard (ed.): *Exil in Großbritannien: Zur Emigration aus dem nationalsozialistischen Deutschland, Veröffentlichungen des Deutschen Historischen Instituts London.* Stuttgart, 1983, pp. 14–43.

Frankfurter Historische Kommission (ed.): *Frankfurt am Main: Die Geschichte der Stadt in neun Beiträgen.* Sigmaringen, 1991.

Frei, Norbert: *Vergangenheitspolitik: Die Anfänge der Bundesrepublik und die NS-Vergangenheit.* Munich, 1997.

Freud in der Gegenwart: Ein Vortragszyklus der Universitäten Frankfurt und Heidelberg zum hundertsten Geburtstag. Frankfurt am Main, 1957.

Friedeburg, Ludwig von: 'Frankfurt – die Stadt und ihre Soziologie', in Zapf, Wolfgang (ed.): *Die Modernisierung moderner Gesellschaften.* Frankfurt and Main and New York, 1990, pp. 151–64.

——: 'Anspruch und Schwierigkeiten kritischer Sozialforschung', in Früchtl, Josef, and Calloni, Maria (eds): *Geist gegen den Zeitgeist: Erinnern an Adorno*. Frankfurt am Main, 1991, pp. 68–75.

Friedeburg, Ludwig von, and Habermas, Jürgen (eds): *Adorno Konferenz 1983*. Frankfurt am Main, 1983.

Friedländer, Saul: *Nazi Germany and the Jews: The Years of Persecution 1933–1939*. London, 1997.

Fromm, Erich: 'Sozialpsychologischer Teil, Studien über Autorität und Familie', in Horkheimer, Max (ed.): *Studien über Autorität und Familie*. Paris, 1936, pp. 75–135.

——: *Der moderne Mensch und seine Zukunft*. Frankfurt am Main, 1967.

——: *Analytische Sozialpsychologie und Gesellschaftstheorie*. Frankfurt am Main, 1970.

——: *Arbeiter und Angestellte am Vorabend des Dritten Reiches*, ed. Wolfgang Bonß. Stuttgart, 1980.

Frost, Robert: *The Poetry of Robert Frost*, ed. Edward Connery Latham. London, 1971.

Früchtl, Josef: *Mimesis: Konstellation eines Zentralbegriffs bei Adorno*. Würzburg, 1986.

Früchtl, Josef, and Calloni, Maria (eds): *Geist gegen den Zeitgeist: Erinnern an Adorno*. Frankfurt am Main, 1991.

Fuld, Werner: *Walter Benjamin: Zwischen den Stühlen*. Munich, 1979.

García Düttmann, Alexander: *Das Gedächtnis des Denkens: Versuch über Heidegger und Adorno*. Frankfurt am Main, 1991.

Geier, Manfred: *Der Wiener Kreis mit Selbstzeugnissen und Bilddokumenten*. Reinbek bei Hamburg, 1992.

——: *Karl Popper*. Reinbek bei Hamburg, 1994.

Gersdorff, Dagmar von: *Marie Luise Kaschnitz: Eine Biographie*. Frankfurt am Main, 1997.

Glaser, Hermann: *Die Kulturgeschichte der Bundesrepublik Deutschland*. 3 vols., Frankfurt am Main, 1990.

Gorer, Geoffrey: *The Revolutionary Ideas of the Marquis de Sade*. London, 1934.

Görtzen, René: 'Theodor W. Adorno: Vorläufige Bibliographie seiner Schriften und die Sekundärliteratur', in Friedeburg, Ludwig von, and Habermas, Jürgen (eds): *Adorno-Konferenz 1983*. Frankfurt am Main, 1983, pp. 402–71.

——: 'Habermas: Bi(bli)ographische Bausteine', in Müller-Doohm, Stefan (ed.): *Das Interesse der Vernunft: Rückblicke auf das Werk von Jürgen Habermas seit 'Erkenntnis und Interesse'*. Frankfurt am Main, 2000, pp. 543–97.

Grab, Hermann: *Hochzeit in Brooklyn*. Frankfurt am Main, 1995.

Greffrath, Mathias (ed.): *Die Zerstörung einer Zukunft: Gespräche mit emigrierten Sozialwissenschaftlern*. Reinbek bei Hamburg, 1979.

Gregor-Dellin, Martin: *Richard Wagner: Sein Leben, sein Werk, sein Jahrhundert*. Munich, 1989.

Grenz, Friedemann: *Adornos Philosophie in Grundbegriffen*. Frankfurt am Main, 1975.

Gripp, Helga: *Theodor W. Adorno: Erkenntnisdimensionen negativer Dialektik*. Paderborn, 1986.

Grondin, Jean: *Hans-Georg Gadamer: Eine Biographie*. Tübingen, 1999.

Guz, Tadeusz: *Der Zerfall der Metaphysik: Von Hegel zu Adorno*. Frankfurt am Main, 2000.

Habermas, Jürgen: *Student und Politik: Eine soziologische Untersuchung zum politischen Bewußtsein Frankfurter Studenten*. Neuwied, 1967.

—— : *Erkenntnis und Interesse*. Frankfurt am Main, 1968.

—— : 'Gegen einen positivistisch halbierten Rationalismus', in *Der Positivismusstreit in der deutschen Soziologie*. Neuwied and Berlin, 1969, pp. 235–66.

—— : *Protestbewegung und Hochschulreform*. Frankfurt am Main, 1969.

—— : 'Theodor W. Adorno wäre am 11 September 66 Jahre alt geworden', *Die Zeit*, 12 September 1969; repr. in Schweppenhäuser, Hermann (ed.): *Theodor W. Adorno zum Gedächtnis*. Frankfurt am Main, 1971, pp. 26–38.

—— : *Theory and Practice*, trans. J. Viertel. London, 1974.

—— : 'The Analytical Theory of Science and Dialectics', in Adorno et al.: *The Positivist Dispute in German Sociology*. London, 1976.

—— : *Philosophisch-politische Profile*. Frankfurt am Main, 1981.

—— : *Theorie des kommunikativen Handelns*. 2 vols., Frankfurt am Main, 1981.

—— : 'Urgeschichte der Subjektivität und verwilderte Selbstbehauptung', in Habermas: *Philosophisch-politische Profile*. Frankfurt am Main, 1981, pp. 167–79.

—— : *Logik der Sozialwissenschaften*. Frankfurt am Main, 1982.

—— : *Die neue Unübersichtlichkeit: Kleine politische Schriften*, V. Frankfurt am Main, 1985.

—— : *Der philosophische Diskurs der Moderne*. Frankfurt am Main, 1985.

—— : *Nachmetaphysisches Denken: Philosophische Aufsätze*. Frankfurt am Main, 1988.

—— : 'Eine Generation von Adorno getrennt', in Früchtl, Josef, and Calloni, Maria (eds): *Geist gegen den Zeitgeist: Erinnern an Adorno*. Frankfurt am Main, 1991, pp. 47–53.

—— : 'Soziologie in der Weimarer Republik', in Habermas: *Texte und Kontexte*, Frankfurt am Main, 1992, pp. 184–204.

—— : 'Das Falsche im Eigenen: Der Briefwechsel zwischen Theodor W. Adorno und Walter Benjamin', *Die Zeit*, 23 September 1994.

—— : *Die Einbeziehung des Anderen*. Frankfurt am Main, 1999.

—— : *Wahrheit und Rechtfertigung*. Frankfurt am Main, 1999.

Hammerstein, Notker: *Die Johann Wolfgang Goethe-Universität: Von der Stiftungsuniversität zur staatlichen Hochschule 1914–1950*. Frankfurt am Main, 1989.

—— : 'Zur Geschichte der Johann Wolfgang Goethe Universität zu Frankfurt am Main', in *Wissenschaftsgeschichte seit 1900: 75 Jahre Universität Frankfurt*. Frankfurt am Main, 1992, pp. 124–40.

Hansert, Andreas: *Bürgerkultur und Kulturpolitik in Frankfurt am Main: Eine historisch-soziologische Rekonstruktion*. Frankfurt am Main, 1992.

Haselbach, Dieter: 'Franz Oppenheimer', in Steinert, Heinz (ed.): *Die (mindestens) zwei Sozialwissenschaften in Frankfurt und ihre Geschichte*. Frankfurt am Main, 1989, pp. 55–71.

Haselberg, Peter von: 'Wiesengrund-Adorno', *Text und Kritik: Zeitschrift für Literatur*, special issue, 1983, pp. 7–21.

—— : 'Geist und Aristokratie', in Früchtl, Josef, and Calloni, Maria (eds): *Geist gegen den Zeitgeist: Erinnern an Adorno*. Frankfurt am Main, 1991, pp. 11–22.

Hässlin, Johann Jakob (ed.): *Frankfurt*. Stuttgart, 1959.
Heilbrunn, Rudolf M.: 'Erinnerungen an das Frankfurt Max Beckmanns', in Gallwitz, Hans (ed.): *Max Beckmann in Frankfurt am Main*. Frankfurt am Main, 1984, pp. 16–25.
Heilbut, Anthony: *Exiled in Paradise: German Refugee Artists and Intellectuals in America from the 1930s to the Present*. New York, 1983.
Heine, Heinrich: *Schriften über Deutschland, Werke*, vol. 4, ed. Helmut Schanze. Frankfurt am Main, 1968.
Heißenbüttel, Helmut: 'Vom Zeugnis des Fortlebens in Briefen', *Merkur*, 21, 1967, pp. 232–44.
——: 'Zu Walter Benjamins Spätwerk', *Merkur*, 22, 1968, pp. 179–85.
Held, Jutta: 'Adorno und die kunsthistorische Diskussion der Avantgarde vor 1968', in Berndt, Andreas, Kaiser, Peter, Rosenberg, Angela, and Trinkner, Diana (eds): *Frankfurter Schule und Kunstgeschichte*. Berlin, 1992, pp. 41–58.
Heller, Agnes: *Der Affe auf dem Fahrrad*. Berlin, 1999.
Helms, Hans G.: *Die Ideologie der anonymen Gesellschaft: Max Stirners 'Einziger' und der Fortschritt des demokratischen Selbstbewußtsein vom Vormärz bis zur Bundesrepublik*. Cologne, 1966.
——: 'Musik zwischen Geschäft und Unwahrheit', in Metzger, Heinz-Klaus, and Riehn, Rainer: *Musik-Konzepte*. Munich, 2001, pp. 5–26.
Henius, Carla: *Schnebel, Nono, Schönberg oder Die wirkliche und erdachte Musik: Essays und Autobiographisches*. Hamburg, 1993.
Henrich, Dieter: 'Diagnose der Gegenwart', *Frankfurter Allgemeine Zeitung*, 10 October 1967.
Hermand, Jost, and Lange, Wigand: *'Wollt Ihr Thomas Mann wiederhaben?': Deutschland und die Emigranten*. Hamburg, 1999.
Herz, John H.: *Vom Überleben: Wie ein Weltbild entstand*. Düsseldorf, 1984.
Hilberg, Raul: *Die Vernichtung der europäischen Juden: Die Gesamtgeschichte des Holocaust*. Berlin, 1982.
Hildesheimer, Wolfgang: *Gesammelte Werke*, vol. 7: *Vermischte Schriften*, ed. Christiaan Lucas Hart Nibbrig and Volker Jehle. Frankfurt am Main, 1991.
Hirschfeld, Gerhard: '"The Defence of Learning and Science . . ." Der Academic Assistance Council in Großbritannien und die wissenschaftliche Emigration aus Nazi-Deutschland', *Exilforschung*, 8, 1988, pp. 28–43.
Hofstätter, Peter R.: 'Zum "Gruppenexperiment" von Pollock', *Kölner Zeitschrift für Soziologie und Sozialpsychologie*, 1, 1957, pp. 97–104.
Hohendahl, Peter Uwe: *Prismatic Thought: Theodor W. Adorno*. Lincoln, NE, 1995.
Hölderlin Jahrbuch: Begründet von Friedrich Beissner und Paul Kluckhohn, ed. Wolfgang Binder and Alfred Kellert. Vol. 13 (1963–1964), Tübingen, 1965.
Holl, Hans Günther: 'Emigration in die Immanenz', *Neue Deutsche Hefte*, 163, 1978, pp. 535–56.
——: 'Theodor W. Adorno: Elemente einer intellektuellen Biographie', *Konkursbuch 5*, 1980, pp. 307–43.
Honneth, Axel: *Kritik der Macht: Reflexionsstufen einer kritischen Gesellschafts-theorie*. Frankfurt am Main, 1985.
——: 'Kritische Theorie: Vom Zentrum zur Peripherie einer Denktradition', *Leviathan*, no. 1, 1989, pp. 1–32.

—— : 'Rekonstruktive Gesellschaftskritik unter genealogischem Vorbehalt: Zur Idee der "Kritik" in der Frankfurter Schule', *Deutsche Zeitschrift für Philosophie*, 5, 2000, pp. 729–37.

Honneth, Axel, and Wellmer, Albrecht (eds): *Die Frankfurter Schule und die Folgen*. Berlin and New York, 1986.

Hoy, David Couzens, and McCarthy, Thomas: *Critical Theory*. Cambridge, MA, 1994.

Hufner, Martin: *Adorno und die Zwölftontechnik*. Regensburg, 1996.

Hughes, Richard: *A High Wind in Jamaica*. Leipzig, 1931.

Huhn, Tom, and Zuidervaart, Lambert (eds): *The Semblance of Subjectivity: Essays in Adorno's Aesthetic Theory*. Cambridge, MA, 1997.

Hullot-Kentor, Robert: 'Critique of the Organic', in Adorno, Theodor W.: *Kierkegaard: Construction of the Aesthetic*. Minneapolis and London, 1989, pp. 10–23.

Huyssen, Andreas: *Twilight Memories*. New York, 1995.

Ingram, David: *Critical Theory and Philosophy*. New York, 1990.

Jäckel, Eberhard (ed.): *Der Mord an den Juden im Zweiten Weltkrieg*. Frankfurt am Main, 1987.

Jander, Martin: *Theo Pirker über 'Pirker': Ein Gespräch*. Marburg, 1988.

Janz, Marlies: *Vom Engagement absoluter Poesie: Zur Lyrik und Ästhetik Paul Celans*. Frankfurt am Main, 1976.

Jardin, André, and Tudesq, André-Jean: *La France des notables*. Paris, 1973.

Jay, Martin: *The Dialectical Imagination*. London, 1973.

—— : 'Positive und negative Totalität', in Bonß, Wolfgang, and Honneth, Axel (eds): *Sozialforschung als Kritik*. Frankfurt am Main, 1982, pp. 67–86.

—— : *Marxism and Totality: The Adventures of a Concept from Lukács to Habermas*. Berkeley, CA: 1984.

—— : *Permanent Exiles: Essays on the Intellectual Migration from Germany to America*. New York, 1985.

—— : 'Massenkultur und deutsche intellektuelle Emigration: Der Fall Max Horkheimer und Siegfried Kracauer', in Srubar, Ilja (ed.): *Exil, Wissenschaft, Identität: Die Emigration deutscher Sozialwissenschaftler 1933–1945*. Frankfurt am Main, 1988, pp. 227–51.

Jungheinrich, Hans-Klaus: 'Adorno als Institution ist tot: Wie der Bewußtseinsveränderer aus dem Hörsaal gejagt wurde', *Frankfurter Rundschau*, 24 April 1969.

—— : ' "Ich halte jedenfalls an der Idee der Moderne fest": Von Adorno lernen: Ein Gespräch mit Heinz-Klaus Metzger', in Jungheinrich (ed.): *Nicht versöhnt: Musikästhetik nach Adorno*. Kassel, 1987, pp. 68–90.

—— : 'Wie kompositorische Praxis in Sprachkunst übergeht', *Musik-Konzepte*, 63–4, 1989, pp. 138–43.

Kager, Reinhard: *Herrschaft und Versöhnung*. Frankfurt am Main and New York, 1988.

—— : 'Einheit in der Zersplitterung: Überlegungen zu Adornos Begriff des "musikalischen Materials" ', in Klein, Richard, and Mahnkopf, Claus-Steffen (eds): *Mit den Ohren denken: Adornos Philosophie der Musik*. Frankfurt am Main, 1998, pp. 92–114.

Kamphausen, Georg: *Die Erfindung Amerikas in der Kulturkritik der Generation von 1890*. Weilerswist, 2002.

Kappner, Hans-Hartmut: *Die Bildungstheorie Adornos als Theorie der Erfahrung von Kultur und Kunst*. Frankfurt am Main, 1984.

Karádi, Eva, and Erzsébet, Vezér (eds): *Georg Lukács, Karl Mannheim und der Sonntagskreis*. Frankfurt am Main, 1985.

Kaschnitz, Marie Luise: *Steht noch dahin: Neue Prosa*. Frankfurt am Main, 1969.

—— : *Orte: Aufzeichnungen*. Frankfurt am Main, 1973.

—— : *Gesammelte Werke*. Frankfurt am Main, 1981–9.

— : *Tage, Tage, Jahre: Aufzeichnungen*. Frankfurt am Main, 1985.

—— : *Tagebücher aus den Jahren 1936–1966*, vol. I, ed. Christian Büttrich, Marianne Büttrich and Iris Schnebel-Kaschnitz. Frankfurt am Main, 2000.

Käsler, Dirk: *Die frühe deutsche Soziologie 1909 bis 1934 und ihre Entstehungs-Milieus: Eine wissenschaftssoziologische Untersuchung*. Opladen, 1984.

Katz, Barry M.: 'The Criticism of Arms: The Frankfurt School goes to War', *Journal of Modern History*, 59, 1987, pp. 439–78.

Kausch, Michael: *Kulturindustrie und Populärkultur*. Frankfurt am Main, 1988.

Kennedy, David M.: *Freedom from Fear: The American People in Depression and War 1929–1945*. Oxford and New York, 1999.

Kershaw, Ian: *The Hitler Myth: Image and Reality in the Third Reich*. Oxford, 1987.

Keul, Hans-Klaus: *Kritik der emanzipatorischen Vernunft*. Frankfurt am Main, 1997.

Keval, Susanne: *Widerstand und Selbstbehauptung in Frankfurt am Main*. Frankfurt am Main, 1988.

Kiedaisch, Petra (ed.): *Lyrik nach Auschwitz?: Adorno und die Dichter*. Stuttgart, 1995.

Kierkegaard, Sören: *Either/Or*, ed. H. V. Hong and E. H. Hong. 2 vols, Princeton, NJ, 1987.

Kirchheimer, Otto: *Politische Herrschaft: Fünf Beiträge zur Lehre vom Staat*. Frankfurt am Main, 1967.

—— : *Von der Weimarer Republik zum Faschismus*. Frankfurt am Main, 1976.

Klein, Richard: 'Der Kampf mit dem Höllenfürst, oder, Die vielen Gesichter des "Versuch über Wagner"', in Klein, Richard, and Mahnkopf, Claus-Steffen (eds): *Mit den Ohren denken: Adornos Philosophie der Musik*. Frankfurt am Main, 1998, pp. 167–205.

Kleßmann, Christoph: *Die doppelte Staatsgründung: Deutsche Geschichte 1945–1955*. Bonn, 1951.

Klingemann, Carsten: 'Vergangenheitsbewältigung oder Geschichtsschreibung? Unerwünschte Traditionsbestände deutscher Soziologie zwischen 1939 und 1945', in Papcke, Sven (ed.): *Ordnung und Theorie: Beiträge zur Geschichte der Soziologie in Deutschland*. Darmstadt, 1986, pp. 223–79.

Kluge, Alexander: 'Ein imaginärer Opernführer', *Jahrbuch der Hamburgischen Staatsoper 1984–1988*. Hamburg, 1988.

—— : *Chronik der Gefühle*. 2 vols., Frankfurt am Main, 2000.

Kluge, Alexander, and Enzensberger, Hans Magnus: 'Deutscher sein ist kein Beruf: Spaziergang durch die Zeit: Alexander Kluge im Gespräch mit Hans Magnus Enzensberger', *DU*, no. 699, 1999, p. 2.

Kluge, Alexander, and Koch, Gertrud: 'Die Funktion des Zerrwinkels in zertrümmernder Absicht: Ein Gespräch zwischen Alexander Kluge und

Gertrud Koch', in Erd, Rainer, Hoß, Dieter, Jacobi, Otto, and Noller, Peter (eds): *Kritische Theorie und Kultur*. Frankfurt am Main, 1989, pp. 106–24.

Kluke, Paul: *Die Stiftungsuniversität Frankfurt am Main 1914–1932*. Frankfurt am Main, 1972.

Knoll, Manuel: *Theodor W. Adorno: Ethik als erste Philosophie*. Munich, 2002.

Knowlson, James: *Samuel Beckett: Eine Biographie*. Frankfurt am Main, 2001.

Koestler, Arthur: *Arrow in the Blue: An Autobiography*. London, 1952.

Kohlmann, Ulrich: *Dialektik der Moral: Untersuchungen zur Moralphilosophie Adornos*. Lüneburg, 1997.

Kohse, Petra: *Marianne Hoppe: Eine Biografie*. Berlin, 2001.

Kolesch, Doris: *Das Schreiben des Subjekts: Zur Inszenierung ästhetischer Subjektivität bei Baudelaire, Barthes und Adorno*. Vienna, 1996.

—— : 'Sich schwach zeigen dürfen, ohne Stärke zu provozieren: Liebe und die Beziehung der Geschlechter', in Auer, Dirk, Bonacker, Thorsten, and Müller-Doohm, Stefan: *Die Gesellschaftstheorie Adornos: Themen und Grundbegriffe*. Darmstadt, 1998, pp. 187–206.

Kolleritsch, Otto: 'Adorno und Graz: Kontakte und Wirkungsgeschichte unter Berücksichtigung des Einflusses auf das wertungsanalytische Verfahren Harald Kaufmanns', in Kolleritsch, Otto (ed.): *Adorno und die Musik*. Graz, 1979, pp. 156–69.

Konersmann, Ralf: *Erstarrte Unruhe: Walter Benjamins Begriff der Geschichte*. Frankfurt am Main, 1992.

König, René: *Soziologie*. Frankfurt am Main, 1964.

—— : *Briefwechsel*, vol. 1, ed. Mario and Oliver König. Opladen, 2000.

Konold, Wulf: 'Adorno – Metzger: Rückblick auf eine Kontroverse', in Jungheinrich, Hans-Klaus (ed.): *Nicht versöhnt: Musikästhetik nach Adorno*. Kassel, 1987, pp. 91–100.

Korn, Karl: *Lange Lehrzeit: Ein deutsches Leben*. Frankfurt am Main, 1975.

Korthals, Michael: 'Die kritische Gesellschaftstheorie des frühen Horkheimer', *Zeitschrift für Soziologie*, 4, 1985, pp. 315–29.

Koßmann, Bernhard (ed.): *Vertreter der Frankfurter Schule in den Hörfunkprogrammen 1950–1992* [Hessischer Rundfunk, Bestandsverzeichnis 9]. Frankfurt am Main, 1992.

Krahl, Hans-Jürgen: 'Der politische Widerspruch der kritischen Theorie Adornos: Nachruf', *Frankfurter Rundschau*, 13 August 1969; repr: in Kraushaar, Wolfgang: *Frankfurter Schule und Studentenbewegung*, vol. 2. Hamburg 1969, pp. 673–5.

Kramer, Andreas, and Wilcock, Evelyn: ' "A Preserve for Professional Philosophers": Adornos Husserl-Dissertation 1934–37 und ihr Oxforder Kontext', *Deutsche Vierteljahrsschrift für Literaturwissenschaft und Geistesgeschichte*, 73, special issue, 1999, pp. 115–61.

Kramer, Beate: '36 Jahre mit Ferdinand Kramer', in Lichtenstein, Claude (ed.): *Ferdinand Kramer: Der Charme des Systematischen*. Giessen, 1991, pp. 12–19.

Kraushaar, Wolfgang: *Die Protestchronik 1949–1959: Eine illustrierte Geschichte von Bewegung, Widerstand und Utopie*, vol. 3. Hamburg, 1996.

—— (ed.): *Frankfurter Schule und Studentenbewegung: Von der Flaschenpost zum Molotowcocktail 1946–1995*. 3 vols., Hamburg, 1998.

Krenek, Ernst: *Die Amerikanischen Tagebücher 1937–1942: Dokumente aus dem Exil*, ed. Claudia Maurer Zenk. Zürich, Vienna, Cologne and Weimar, 1992.

—— : *Im Atem der Zeit: Erinnerungen an die Moderne*. Hamburg, 1998.

Krockow, Christian von: *Die Deutschen in ihrem Jahrhundert 1890–1990*. Reinbek bei Hamburg, 1990.

Krüger, Heinz: *Über den Aphorismus als philosophische Form*. Munich, 1988.

Kuhlmann, Anne: 'Das Exil als Heimat: Über jüdische Schreibweisen und Metaphern', *Exilforschung: Ein internationales Jahrbuch*, 17, 1999, pp. 198–213.

Kuhn, Axel: *Das faschistische Herrschaftssystem und die moderne Gesellschaft*. Hamburg, 1973.

Kurzke, Hermann: *Thomas Mann: Das Leben als Kunstwerk*. Munich, 1999.

Laqueur, Walter: *Was niemand wissen wollte*. Frankfurt am Main, 1992.

Lay, Conrad: '"Viele Beiträge waren ursprünglich Rundfunkarbeiten": Über das wechselseitige Verhältnis von Frankfurter Schule und Rundfunk', in Erd, Rainer, Hoß, Dieter, Jacobi, Otto, and Noller, Peter (eds): *Kritische Theorie und Kultur*. Frankfurt am Main, 1989, pp. 173–88.

Lazarsfeld, Paul: 'Eine Episode in der Geschichte der empirischen Sozialforschung', in Parsons, Talcott, Shils, Edward and Lazarsfeld, Paul: *Soziologie autobiographisch*. Stuttgart, 1975, pp. 147–210.

Lazarsfeld, Paul, and Stanton, Frank (eds): *Radio Research*. New York, 1944.

Lefebvre, Georges: *Napoleon*. London, 1969.

Lepenies, Wolf: *Die drei Kulturen: Soziologie zwischen Literatur und Wissenschaft*. Munich, 1985.

—— : *Sainte-Beuve: auf der Schwelle zur Moderne*. Munich and elsewhere, 1997.

Lepsius, Rainer M.: 'Die Entwicklung der Soziologie nach dem Zweiten Weltkrieg 1945 bis 1967', in Lüschen, Günther (ed.): *Deutsche Soziologie seit 1945*. Opladen, 1979, pp. 25–70.

—— : 'Soziologie in Deutschland und in Österreich 1918–1945', *Kölner Zeitschrift für Soziologie und Sozialpsychologie*, special issue 23, 1981, pp. 25–70.

Levin, Thomas Y., and Linn, Michael von der: 'Elements of a Radio Theory: Adorno and the Princeton Radio Research Project', *Musical Quarterly*, 78, 1994, pp. 316–77.

Levin, Walter: 'Adornos Zwei Stücke für Streichquartett op. 2', *Musik-Konzepte*, 63–4, 1989, pp. 74–99.

Lichtenstein, Claude (ed.): Ferdinand Kramer: *Der Charme des Systematischen: Architektur, Einrichtung, Design: Katalogbuch zur gleichnamigen Ausstellung*. Giessen, 1991.

Liessmann, Konrad Paul: 'Hot Potatoes: Zum Briefwechsel zwischen Günther Anders und Theodor W. Adorno', *Zeitschrift für kritische Theorie*, 6, 1998, pp. 29–38.

Lindner, Burkhardt: 'Was heißt: Nach Auschwitz? Adornos Datum', in Braese, Stephan, Gehle, Holger, Kiesel, Doron, and Loewy, Hanno (eds): *Deutsche Nachkriegsliteratur und der Holocaust*. Frankfurt am Main and New York, 1998, pp. 283–300.

Lindner, Burkhardt, and Lüdke, Martin (eds): *Materialien zur ästhetischen Theorie: Theodor W. Adornos Konstruktion der Moderne*. Frankfurt am Main, 1980.

Lippe, Rudolf zur: 'Die Frankfurter Studentenbewegung und das Ende Adornos: Ein Zeitzeugnis', in Wolfgang Kraushaar (ed.): *Frankfurter Schule und Studentenbewegung*, vol. 3. Hamburg, 1998, pp. 112–25.

Luhr, Geret (ed.): *'Was noch begraben lag': Zu Walter Benjamins Exil: Briefe und Dokumente*. Berlin, 2000.

Lukács, Georg: *Die Theorie des Romans*. Berlin, 1920.
——: *History and Class Consciousness*, trans. Rodney Livingstone. London, 1971.
——: *Gelebtes Leben: Eine Autobiographie im Dialog*. Frankfurt am Main, 1981.
Lüschen, Günther (ed.): *Deutsche Soziologie seit 1945*. Opladen, 1979.
Lüth, Paul: *Nächte in Alexandria: Roman einer Ägyptenreise*. Düsseldorf and Cologne, 1963.
——: 'Brief aus einer Landpraxis', in Schweppenhäuser, Hermann (ed.): *Theodor W. Adorno zum Gedächtnis*. Frankfurt am Main, 1971, pp. 116–23.
Maar, Michael: 'Der kalte Schatten großer Männer: Über den Teufel in Thomas Manns *Doktor Faustus*', *Frankfurter Allgemeine Zeitung*, 13 June 1992.
Mahnkopf, Claus-Steffen: 'Adornos Kritik der Neueren Musik', in Mahnkopf, Claus-Steffen, and Klein, Richard (eds): *Mit den Ohren denken: Adornos Philosophie der Musik*. Frankfurt am Main, 1998, pp. 251–80.
Makropoulos, Michael: 'Haltlose Souveränität: Benjamin, Schmitt und die Klassische Moderne in Deutschland', in Gangl, Manfred, and Raulet, Gérard (eds): *Intellektuellendiskurse in der Weimarer Republik: Zur politischen Kultur einer Gemengelage*. Frankfurt am Main and New York, 1994, pp. 198–214.
Mann, Erika: *Briefe und Antworten*. 2 vols., ed. Anna Zanco Prestel. Munich, 1985.
Mann, Golo: *Deutsche Geschichte*. Frankfurt am Main, 1992.
Mann, Katia: *Meine ungeschriebenen Memoiren*. Frankfurt am Main, 1976.
Mann, Klaus: *Der Wendepunkt: Ein Lebensbericht*. Munich, 1969.
Mann, Thomas: *Dr Faustus*, trans. H. T. Lowe-Porter. London, 1959.
——: *Briefe*, vol. 3, ed. Erika Mann. Frankfurt am Main, 1965.
——: *Gesammelte Werke*, vol. 7. Frankfurt am Main, 1974.
——: *Die Entstehung des Doktor Faustus*. Frankfurt am Main, 1984.
——: *Tagebücher 1944–1946*, ed. Inge Jens. Frankfurt am Main, 1986.
——: *Tagebücher 1946–1948*, ed. Inge Jens. Frankfurt am Main, 1989.
——: *Tagebücher 1949–1950*, ed. Inge Jens. Frankfurt am Main, 1993.
——: *Tagebücher 1951–1952*, ed. Inge Jens. Frankfurt am Main, 1993.
——: *Essays*, vol. VI: *Meine Zeit 1945–1955*, ed. Hermann Kurzke and Stephan Stachorski. Frankfurt am Main, 1997.
Mannheim, Karl: *Die Gegenwartsaufgaben der Soziologie: Ihre Lehrgestalt*. Tübingen, 1932.
——: 'Heidelberger Briefe', in Karádi, Éva (ed.): *Georg Lukács, Karl Mannheim und der Sonntagskreis*. Frankfurt am Main, 1985.
——: *Ideologie und Utopie*. Frankfurt am Main, 1985; Eng. trans. as *Ideology and Utopia*. London and New York, 1946.
Marbacher Magazin: 'Siegfried Kracauer 1889–1966', ed. Ingrid Belke and Irina Renz, 47, 1988.
Marbacher Magazin: 'Walter Benjamin 1892–1940', ed. Rolf Tiedemann, Christoph Gödde and Henri Lonitz, 1990.
Marbacher Magazin: 'Fritz H. Landshoff und der Querido-Verlag 1933–1950', 78, 1997.
Marcuse, Herbert: 'Zum Begriff des Wesens', *Zeitschrift für Sozialforschung*, 5, 1936, pp. 1–39.
——: 'Über den affirmativen Charakter in der Kultur', *Zeitschrift für Sozialforschung*, 6, 1937, pp. 54–94.

—— : *One-Dimensional Man: Studies in the Ideology of Advanced Industrial Society.* Boston, 1964.

—— : 'Repressive Tolerance', in Marcuse, Herbert, Wolff, Robert Paul, and Moore, Barrington: *A Critique of Pure Tolerance*, Boston, 1965.

—— : *Kultur und Gesellschaft.* 2 vols., Frankfurt am Main, 1965.

—— : *Negations*, trans. J. J. Shapiro. Harmondsworth, 1968.

—— : *An Essay on Liberation.* Boston, 1969.

—— : *Ideen zu einer kritischen Theorie der Gesellschaft.* Frankfurt am Main, 1969.

—— : 'Reflexionen zu Theodor W. Adorno: Aus einem Gespräch mit Michaela Seiffe', in Schweppenhäuser, Hermann (ed.): *Theodor W. Adorno zum Gedächtnis*, Frankfurt am Main, 1971, pp. 47–51.

—— : *Zeit-Messungen.* Frankfurt am Main, 1975.

Marx, Karl: *Das Kapital, Kritik der politischen Ökonomie*, vol. 1. [Marx–Engels Werke, vol. 23]. Berlin, 1965.

—— : *The Eighteenth Brumaire of Louis Bonaparte*, in *Political Writings*, vol. 2: *Surveys from Exile.* Harmondsworth, 1973, pp. 143–259.

Matthiesen, Ulf: 'Kontrastierungen/Kooperationen: Karl Mannheim in Frankfurt (1930–1933)', in Steinert, Heinz (ed.): *Die (mindestens) zwei Sozialwissenschaften in Frankfurt und ihre Geschichte.* Frankfurt am Main, 1989, pp. 72–87.

Mauser, Siegfried: 'Adornos Klavierlieder', *Musik-Konzepte*, 63–4, 1989, pp. 45–55.

Mautz, Kurt: *Der Urfreund.* Paderborn, 1996.

Mayer, Hans: *Außenseiter.* Frankfurt am Main, 1975.

—— : *Ein Deutscher auf Widerruf: Erinnerungen.* 2 vols., Frankfurt am Main, 1982.

—— : *Wir Außenseiter.* Aachen, 1983.

Mehring, Reinhard: *Thomas Mann: Künstler und Philosoph.* Munich, 2001.

Menke, Christoph: *Die Souveränität der Kunst: Ästhetische Erfahrung nach Adorno und Derrida.* Frankfurt am Main, 1991.

Menke, Christoph, and Seel, Martin (eds): *Zur Verteidigung der Vernunft gegen ihre Liebhaber und Verächter.* Frankfurt am Main, 1993.

Mérimée, Prosper: *Colomba.* Stuttgart, 1988.

Merker, Barbara: 'Wozu noch Adorno?' *Deutsche Zeitschrift für Philosophie*, 3, 1999, pp. 489–504.

Merton, Robert K.: *On the Shoulders of Giants: A Shandean Postscript.* Chicago and London, 1993.

Metzger, Heinz-Klaus: *Musik wozu: Literatur zu Noten*, ed. Rainer Riehn. Frankfurt am Main, 1980.

—— : 'Das Ende der Musikgeschichte', in Früchtl, Josef, and Calloni, Maria: *Geist gegen den Zeitgeist: Erinnern an Adorno.* Frankfurt am Main, 1991, pp. 163–78.

Metzger, Heinz-Klaus, and Riehn, Rainer: 'T. W. Adorno: Der Komponist', *Musik-Konzepte*, 63–4, 1989.

Migdal, Ulrike: *Die Frühgeschichte des Frankfurter Instituts für Sozialforschung.* Frankfurt am Main and New York, 1981.

Millington, Barry (ed.): *The Wagner Compendium: A Guide to Richard Wagner's Life and Music.* London, 1992.

Mitscherlich, Alexander, and Mitscherlich, Margarete: *Die Unfähigkeit zu trauern.* Munich, 1967.

Mohr, Albert Richard: *Musikleben in Frankfurt am Main*. Frankfurt am Main, 1976.
Monnier, Adrienne: *Aufzeichnungen aus der Rue de l'Odéon*. Frankfurt am Main, 1995.
Mörchen, Hermann: *Macht und Herrschaft im Denken von Heidegger und Adorno*. Stuttgart, 1980.
—— : *Adorno und Heidegger: Untersuchung einer philosophischen Kommunikationsverweigerung*. Stuttgart, 1981.
Morgenstern, Soma: *Alban Berg und seine Idole: Erinnerungen und Briefe*, ed. Ingolf Schulte. Berlin, 1999.
Morrison, David E.: 'Kultur and Culture: The Case of Theodor W. Adorno and Paul F. Lazarsfeld', *Social Research*, 45, 1978, pp. 331–59.
Mülder, Inka: *Siegfried Kracauer: Grenzgänger zwischen Theorie und Literatur*. Stuttgart, 1985.
Müller, Thomas: *Die Musiksoziologie Theodor W. Adornos: Ein Modell ihrer Interpretation am Beispiel Alban Bergs*. Frankfurt am Main and New York, 1990.
Müller, Ulrich, and Wapnewski, Peter (eds): *Richard-Wagner-Handbuch*. Stuttgart, 1986.
Müller-Doohm, Stefan: 'Kritik in kritischen Theorien, oder, Wie kritisches Denken selber zu rechtfertigen sei', in Müller-Doohm, Stefan (ed.): *Das Interesse der Vernunft: Rückblicke auf das Werk von Jürgen Habermas seit 'Erkenntnis und Interesse'*. Frankfurt am Main, 2000, pp. 71–106.
—— : *Die Soziologie Theodor W. Adornos*. Frankfurt am Main, 2001.
—— : 'Theodor W. Adorno', in Kaesler, Dirk (ed.): *Klassiker der Soziologie*, vol. II. Munich, 2002, pp. 51–71.
Münz-Koenen, Ingeborg: *Konstruktion des Nirgendwo: Die Diskursivität des Utopischen bei Bloch, Adorno, Habermas*. Berlin, 1997.
Naeher, Jürgen (ed.): *Die Negative Dialektik Adornos*. Opladen, 1984.
Negt, Oskar: *Politik als Protest*. Frankfurt am Main, 1971.
—— : 'Denken als Gegenproduktion', in Früchtl, Josef, and Calloni, Maria (eds): *Geist gegen den Zeitgeist: Erinnern an Adorno*. Frankfurt am Main, 1991, pp. 76–93.
Neumann, Franz: *Behemoth: Struktur und Praxis des Nationalsozialismus 1933–1944*. Frankfurt am Main, 1977.
Nietzsche, Friedrich: *Sämtliche Briefe*, vol. 6, ed. Giorgio Colli and Mazzino Montinari. Berlin and Munich, 1986.
Noth, Ernst Erich: *Erinnerungen eines Deutschen*. Hamburg and Düsseldorf, 1971.
Oevermann, Ulrich: 'Der Intellektuelle – Soziologische Strukturbestimmung des Komplementär von Öffentlichkeit', in Franzmann, Andreas, Liebermann, Sascha, and Tykwer, Jörg (eds): *Die Macht des Geistes: Soziologische Fallanalysen zum Strukturtyp des Intellektuellen*. Frankfurt am Main, 2001, pp. 13–76.
Offe, Claus: *Strukturprobleme des kapitalistischen Staates*. Frankfurt am Main, 1972.
Oppenheimer, Franz: *Erlebtes, Erstrebtes, Erreichtes: Lebenserinnerungen*, ed. L. Y. Oppenheimer. Düsseldorf, 1964.
Osborne, Peter (ed.): *A Critical Sense: Interviews with Intellectuals*. London and New York, 1996.

638   *References and Bibliography*

Pabst, Reinhard: 'Der Vogel, der da sang', *Süddeutsche Zeitung*, 25 October 2002.
——: *Seesucht: Thomas Manns Sommerreisen nach Litauen*. Marburg, 2003.
Paddison, Max: *Adorno's Aesthetics of Music*. Cambridge and New York, 1993.
——: *Adorno, Modernism and Mass Culture: Essays on Critical Theory and Music*. London, 1996.
Paffrath, Hartmut F.: *Die Wende aufs Subjekt*. Weinheim, 1992.
Parsons, Talcott, Shils, Edward, and Lazarsfeld, Paul F.: *Soziologie autobiographisch. Drei kritische Berichte zur Entwicklung einer Wissenschaft*, Stuttgart, 1975.
Pauen, Michael: 'Der Protest ist Schweigen: Zur Benjamin-Rezeption Theodor W. Adornos', in Garber, Klaus, and Rehm, Ludger (eds): *Global Benjamin: Internationaler Walter-Benjamin-Kongreß 1992*. 3 vols., Munich, 1999, pp. 1428–52.
Pensky, Max (ed.): *The Actuality of Adorno: Critical Essays on Adorno and the Postmodern*. New York, 1997.
Perels, Joachim: 'Verteidigung der Erinnerung im Angesicht ihrer Zerstörung – Theodor W. Adorno', in Buckmiller, Michael, Heimann, Dietrich, and Perels, Joachim (eds): *Judentum und politische Existenz: Siebzehn Porträts deutsch-jüdischer Intellektueller*. Hannover, 2000, pp. 271–91.
Peukert, Detlev J. K.: *Die Weimarer Republik: Krisenjahre der klassischen Moderne*. Frankfurt am Main, 1987.
Pfeiffer-Belli, Erich: *Junge Jahre im alten Frankfurt*. Wiesbaden and Munich, 1986.
Piven, Frances Fox, and Cloward, Richard A.: *Aufstand der Armen*. Frankfurt am Main, 1986.
Plessner, Monika: *Die Argonauten auf Long Island: Begegnungen mit Hannah Arendt, Theodor W. Adorno, Gershom Scholem und anderen*. Berlin, 1995.
Pollock, Friedrich: *Stadien des Kapitalismus*, ed. Helmut Dubiel. Munich, 1975.
Popper, Karl R.: *Objektive Erkenntnis*. Hamburg, 1973.
——: 'The Logic of the Social Sciences', in Adorno et al.: *The Positivist Dispute in German Sociology*. London, 1976.
Postone, Moishe: 'Nationalismus und Antisemitismus: Ein theoretischer Versuch', in Diner, Dan (ed.): *Zivilisationsbruch: Denken nach Auschwitz*. Frankfurt am Main, 1988, pp. 242–54.
Prater, Donald A.: *Thomas Mann, Deutscher und Weltbürger: Eine Biographie*. Munich, 1995.
Prigge, Walter: 'Geistesgeschichte und Stadtgeschichte', in Prigge, Walter (ed.): *Städtische Intellektuelle: Urbane Milieus im 20. Jahrhundert*. Frankfurt am Main, 1929.
Pross, Helge: *Die deutsche akademische Emigration nach den Vereinigten Staaten 1933–1941*. Berlin, 1955.
Rademacher, Claudia: *'Nach dem versäumten Augenblick': Zur Konstruktion des Utopischen in Adornos essayistischer Sozialphilosophie*. Opladen, 1997.
Radkau, Joachim: *Die deutsche Emigration in den USA: Ihr Einfluß auf die amerikanische Europapolitik 1933–1945*. Düsseldorf, 1971.
Raeithel, Gert: *Geschichte der nordamerikanischen Kultur*, vol. 3. Frankfurt am Main, 1995.
Rammstedt, Otthein: *Deutsche Soziologie 1933–1945: Die Normalität einer Anpassung*. Frankfurt am Main, 1986.

Rath, Norbert: 'Zur Nietzsche-Rezeption Horkheimers und Adornos', in Reijen, Willem van, and Schmid Noerr, Gunzelin (eds): *Vierzig Jahre Flaschenpost: 'Dialektik der Aufklärung' 1947 bis 1987*. Frankfurt am Main, 1987, pp. 73–110.

Rebentisch, Dieter: 'Frankfurt am Main in der Weimarer Republik und im Dritten Reich 1918–1945'. In Frankfurter Historische Kommission (ed.): *Frankfurt am Main: Die Geschichte der Stadt in neun Beiträgen*. Sigmaringen, 1991, pp. 423–520.

Reich, Willi: *Alban Berg: Mit Bergs eigenen Schriften und Beiträgen von Theodor Wiesengrund-Adorno*. Vienna, Leipzig and Zürich, 1937.

——: *Alban Berg: Leben und Werk*. Zürich, 1963.

Reich-Ranicki, Marcel: *Thomas Mann und die Seinen*. Frankfurt am Main, 1990.

Reijen, Willem van, and Schmid Noerr, Gunzelin (eds): *Vierzig Jahre Flaschenpost: 'Dialektik der Aufklärung' 1947 bis 1987*. Frankfurt am Main, 1987.

Reinfelder, Konrad: 'Zur Geschichte der Juden in Dettelbach. Teil 1: Das 17. Jahrhundert; Teil 2: Die Zeit vor und nach 1800', *Dettelbacher Geschichtsblätter: Mitteilungen des Stadtarchivs*, 23, 1997, nos. 191–4.

Reinhardt, Stephan: *Alfred Andersch: Eine Biographie*. Zürich, 1990.

Rensmann, Lars: *Kritische Theorie über den Antisemitismus: Studien zu Struktur, Erklärungspotential und Aktualität*. Berlin and elsewhere, 1998.

Riha, Karl: 'Die Prosa Castor Zwiebacks: Noten und Notizen', *Frankfurter Adorno Blätter*, III, 1992, pp. 123–34.

Rilke, Rainer Maria: *Briefwechsel mit Regina Ullmann und Ellen Delp*, ed. Walter Simon. Frankfurt am Main, 1987.

Ritsert, Jürgen: *Die Rationalität Adornos*. Frankfurt am Main, 1995.

——: *Ästhetische Theorie als Gesellschaftskritik: Umrisse der Dialektik in Adornos Spätwerk*. Frankfurt am Main, 1996.

——: 'Das Nichtidentische bei Adorno: Substanz- oder Problembegriff?', *Zeitschrift für kritische Theorie*, 4, 1997, pp. 29–52.

——: *Drei Studien zu Adorno*. Frankfurt am Main, 1998.

Rode, Susanne: *Alban Berg und Karl Kraus: Zur geistigen Biographie des Komponisten der 'Lulu'*. Frankfurt am Main, Bern, New York and Paris, 1988.

Roh, Franz: *'Entartete' Kunst: Kunstbarbarei im Dritten Reich*. Hannover, 1962.

Röhrich, Wilfried: *Die Demokratie der Westdeutschen: Geschichte und politisches Klima einer Republik*. Munich, 1988.

Ross, Werner: *Der ängstliche Adler: Friedrich Nietzsches Leben*. Munich, 1984.

Roth, Joseph: *Die Flucht ohne Ende: Ein Bericht*. Lüneburg, 1994.

Roth, Ralf: *Stadt und Bürgertum in Frankfurt am Main: Ein besonderer Weg von der ständischen zur modernen Bürgergesellschaft*. Munich, 1996.

Rühmkorf, Peter: *Die Jahre, die Ihr kennt: Anfälle und Erinnerungen*. Reinbek bei Hamburg, 1972.

Safranski, Rüdiger: *Martin Heidegger*. Cambridge, MA, and London, 1998.

Sahl, Hans: *Das Exil im Exil*. Frankfurt am Main, 1990.

Sander, Gerhard (ed.): *Die Bücherverbrennung*. Berlin, 1972.

Schäfer, Gerd: 'Wider die Inszenierung des Vergessens: Hans Freyer und die Soziologie in Leipzig 1925–1945', *Jahrbuch für Soziologiegeschichte*, 1, 1990, pp. 22–175.

640 References and Bibliography

——: 'Soziologie auf dem Vulkan – Zur Stellung René Königs in der Dreieckskonstellation der westdeutschen Nachkriegssoziologie', in Deppe, Frank, Fülberth, Georg, and Rilling, Rainer (eds): *Antifaschismus*. Heilbronn, 1996, pp. 370–87.

——: 'Die nivellierte Mittelstandsgesellschaft – Strategien der Soziologie in den 50er-Jahren', in Bollenbeck, Georg, and Kaiser, Gerhard (eds): *Die janusköpfigen 50er Jahre: Kulturelle Moderne und bildungsbürgerliche Semantik III*. Opladen, 2002, pp. 115–42.

Schäfer, Gerd, and Nedelmann, Carl (eds): *Der CDU-Staat: Analysen zur Verfassungswirklichkeit der Bundesrepublik*. 2 vols., Frankfurt am Main, 1969.

Schäfer, Hans Dieter: *Das gespaltene Bewußtsein: Deutsche Kultur- und Lebenswirklichkeit 1933–1945*. Berlin, 1984.

Schärf, Christian: *Geschichte des Essays von Montaigne bis Adorno*. Göttingen, 1999.

Scheible, Hartmut: '"Dem Wahren Schönen Guten": Adornos Anfänge im Kontext', in Weber, Gerd Wolfgang (ed.): *Idee, Gestalt, Geschichte: Festschrift Klaus von See*. Odense, 1988, pp. 627–712.

——: *Theodor W. Adorno*. Reinbek bei Hamburg, 1989.

Schivelbusch, Wolfgang: *Intellektuellendämmerung: Zur Lage der Intelligenz in den zwanziger Jahren*. Frankfurt am Main, 1982.

Schiwy, Günther: 'Arnold Hauser und Theodor W. Adorno: Zeugnisse einer Freundschaft', in *Der Aquädukt 1763–1988: Ein Almanach aus dem Verlag C. H. Beck im 225. Jahr seines Bestehens*. Munich, 1988, pp. 507–14.

Schmid, Michael: 'Der Positivismusstreit in der deutschen Soziologie dreißig Jahre danach', *Logos*, new ser., 1, 1, 1993, pp. 35–81.

Schmid Noerr, Gunzelin: 'Flaschenpost: Die Emigration Max Horkheimers und seines Kreises im Spiegel des Briefwechsels', in Srubar, Ilja (ed.): *Exil, Wissenschaft, Identität: Die Emigration deutscher Sozialwissenschaftler 1933–1945*. Frankfurt am Main, 1988, pp. 252–80.

——: *Das Eingedenken der Natur im Subjekt: Zur Dialektik von Vernunft und Natur in der Kritischen Theorie Horkheimers, Adornos und Marcuses*. Darmstadt, 1990.

——: 'Frankfurter Geschichten 1933: Aus den Akten eines Gleichschalters', *Institut für Sozialforschung, Mitteilungen*, 5, 1995, pp. 66–81.

——: *Gesten aus Begriffen: Konstellationen der kritischen Theorie*. Frankfurt am Main, 1997.

——: 'Bloch und Adorno: Bildhafte und bilderlose Utopie', *Zeitschrift für kritische Theorie*, 7, 13, 2001, pp. 25–56.

Schmidt, Alfred: *Die Zeitschrift für Sozialforschung: Geschichte und gegenwärtige Bedeutung*. Munich, 1980.

——: 'Materialismus als nachmetaphysisches und metaphysisches Denken', in Früchtl, Josef, and Calloni, Maria (eds): *Geist gegen den Zeitgeist: Erinnern an Adorno*. Frankfurt am Main, 1991, pp. 33–46.

Schmidt, Regina, and Becker, Egon: *Reaktionen auf politische Vorgänge: Drei Meinungsstudien*. Frankfurt am Main, 1967.

Schmuhl, Hans-Walter: 'Rassismus unter den Bedingungen charismatischer Herrschaft', in Bracher, Karl Dieter, Funke, Manfred, and Jacobsen, Hans A. (eds): *Deutschland 1933–1945: Neue Studien zur nationalsozialistischen Herrschaft*. Bonn, 1993, pp. 182–97.

Schnädelbach, Herbert: *Reflexion und Diskurs*. Frankfurt am Main, 1977.

———: *Vernunft und Geschichte*. Frankfurt am Main, 1987.

———: 'Philosophieren lernen', in Früchtl, Josef, and Calloni, Maria (eds): *Geist gegen den Zeitgeist: Erinnern an Adorno*. Frankfurt am Main, 1991, pp. 54–67.

———: 'Die Aktualität der "Dialektik der Aufklärung"', in Schnädelbach, Herbert: *Zur Rehabilitierung des animal rationale: Vorträge und Abhandlungen 2*. Frankfurt am Main, 1992, pp. 231–76.

Schnauber, Cornelius: *German-Speaking Artists in Hollywood: Emigration between 1910 and 1945*. Bonn, 1996.

———: *Hollywood Haven: Homes and Haunts of the European Emigrés and Exiles in Los Angeles*. Riverside, CA, 1997.

Schnebel, Dieter: 'Komposition von Sprache: Sprachliche Gestaltung von Musik in Adornos Werk', in Schuleppenhäuser, Hermann (ed.): *Theodor W. Adorno zum Gedächtnis*. Frankfurt am Main, 1971.

———: 'Einführung in Adornos Musik', in Kolleritsch, Otto (ed.): *Adorno und die Musik*. Graz, 1979, pp. 15–19.

Scholem, Gershom: *Walter Benjamin: Die Geschichte einer Freundschaft*. Frankfurt am Main, 1990.

———: *Briefe II, 1948–1970*, ed. Thomas Sparr. Frankfurt am Main, 1995.

———: *Briefe III, 1971–1982*, ed. Itta Shedletzky. Munich, 1999.

Scholze, Britta: *Kunst als Kritik: Adornos Weg aus der Dialektik*. Würzburg, 2000.

Schorske, Carl E.: *Wien: Geist und Gesellschaft im 'Fin de siècle'*. Frankfurt am Main, 1982.

Schramm, Wilbur: *Grundfragen der Kommunikationsforschung*. Munich, 1970.

Schubert, Giselher: 'Adornos Auseinandersetzung mit der Zwölftontechnik Schönbergs', *Archiv für Musikwissenschaft*, 45, 1989, pp. 235–54.

Schübl, Elmar: *Jean Gebser und die Frage der Astrologie: Eine philosophisch-geistesgeschichtliche Studie*. PhD dissertation, University of Graz, 2001.

Schüßler, Kersten: *Helmuth Plessner: Eine intellektuelle Biographie*. Berlin, 2000.

Schweppenhäuser, Gerhard: *Emanzipationstheorie und Ideologiekritik*. Cuxhaven, 1990.

———: *Ethik nach Auschwitz: Adornos negative Moralphilosophie*. Hamburg, 1993.

———: *Soziologie im Spätkapitalismus: Zur Gesellschaftstheorie Theodor W. Adornos*. Darmstadt, 1995.

———: *Theodor W. Adorno zur Einführung*. Hamburg, 2000.

Schweppenhäuser, Gerhard, and Wischke, Mirko: *Impuls und Negativität Ethik und Ästhetik bei Adorno*. Hamburg, 1995.

Schweppenhäuser, Hermann (ed.): *Theodor W. Adorno zum Gedächtnis*. Frankfurt am Main, 1971.

Schwerin, Christoph von: *Als sei nichts gewesen: Erinnerungen*. Berlin, 1997.

Sebald, Winfried G.: *On the Natural History of Destruction*. London, 2003.

Seng, Joachim: 'Von der Musikalität einer "graueren" Sprache: Zu Celans Auseinandersetzung mit Adorno', *Germanisch-Romanische Monatshefte*, new ser., 45, 1995, pp. 419–30.

———: *Auf den Kreis-Wegen der Dichtung: Zyklische Komposition bei Paul Celan am Beispiel der Gedichtbände bis 'Sprachgitter'*. Heidelberg, 1998.

Seubold, Günter: *Das Ende der Kunst und der Paradigmenwechsel in der Ästhetik: Philosophische Untersuchungen zu Adorno, Heidegger und Gehlen in systematischer Absicht*. Freiburg (Breisgau), 1998.

——— : 'Die Erinnerung retten und dem Kitsch die Zunge lösen: Adornos Mahler-und Berg-Interpretation – gehört als Kritik des (Post-)Modernismus', in Klein, Richard, and Mahnkopf, Claus-Steffen (eds): *Mit den Ohren denken: Adornos Philosophie der Musik*. Frankfurt am Main 1998, pp. 134–66.

Sieg, Ulrich: *Jüdische Intellektuelle in Ersten Weltkrieg*. Berlin, 2001.

Simmel, Ernst (ed.): *Antisemitismus*. Frankfurt am Main, 1993.

Sirois, Herbert: *Zwischen Illusion und Krieg: Deutschland und die USA 1933–1941*. Paderborn and elsewhere, 2000.

Sohn-Rethel, Alfred: *Warenform und Denkform: Aufsätze*. Frankfurt am Main, 1971.

——— : *Warenform und Denkform*. Frankfurt am Main, 1978.

——— : 'Einige Unterbrechungen waren wirklich unnötig', in Greffrath, Mathias: *Die Zerstörung einer Zukunft: Gespräche mit emigrierten Sozialwissenschaftlern*. Reinbek bei Hamburg, 1979, pp. 249–98.

——— : *Portrait eines Menschen für den Denken Leben ist: Film von Günther Hörmann*. Bremen, 1988.

——— : *Geistige und körperliche Arbeit: Zur Epistemologie der abendländischen Geschichte*. Weinheim, 1989.

Söllner, Alfons: *Geschichte und Herrschaft: Studien zur materialistischen Sozialwissenschaft 1929–1942*. Frankfurt am Main, 1979.

——— (ed.): *Zur Archäologie der Demokratie in Deutschland*. 2 vols., Frankfurt am Main, 1986.

Städelsches Kunstinstitut Frankfurt am Main: *Max Beckmann: Eisgang*. Frankfurt am Main, 1994.

Steffen, Monika: 'Tiere an Ketten: SDS und Horkheimer', in Kraushaar, Wolfgang (ed.): *Frankfurter Schule und Studentenbewegung*, vol. 2, Hamburg, 1997, pp. 263–5.

Stein, Erwin: 'Neue Formprinzipien', *Anbruch*, special Schöenberg issue, 1924.

Stein, Peter: ' "Darum mag falsch gewesen sein . . .": Wirkung eines Verdikts: Ein Zitat und seine Verkürzung', *Weimarer Beiträge*, 4, 1996, pp. 485–508.

Steinert, Heinz: *Adorno in Wien: Über die (Un-)Möglichkeit von Kunst, Kultur und Befreiung*. Vienna, 1989.

——— : *Die Entdeckung der Kulturindustrie, oder, Warum Professor Adorno Jazz-Musik nicht ausstehen konnte*. Vienna, 1992.

Stephan, Rudolf (ed.): *Von Kranichstein zur Gegenwart: 50 Jahre Darmstädter Ferienkurse*. Stuttgart, 1996.

Strauss, Anselm L.: *Grundlagen qualitativer Sozialforschung: Datenanalyse und Theoriebildung in der empirischen und soziologischen Forschung*. Munich, 1991.

Strzelewicz, Willy: 'Diskurse im Institut für Sozialforschung um 1930', in Papcke, Sven (ed.): *Ordnung und Theorie: Beiträge zur Geschichte der Soziologie in Deutschland*. Darmstadt, 1986, pp. 147–67.

Stuckenschmidt, Hans Heinz: *Schönberg: Leben – Umwelt – Werk*. Zürich and Freiburg, 1974.

Sziborsky, Lucia: *Adornos Musikphilosophie: Genese – Konstitution – pädagogische Perspektiven*. Munich, 1979.

——— : *Rettung des Hoffnungslosen: Untersuchungen zur Ästhetik und Musikphilosophie Theodor W. Adornos*. Würzburg, 1994.

Thalmann, Rita: 'Das Protokoll der Wannsee-Konferenz – Vom Antisemitismus zur "Endlösung der Judenfrage" ', in Grosser, Alfred (ed.): *Wie war es möglich? Die Wirklichkeit des Nationalsozialismus*. Munich, 1977, pp. 147–67.

Theunissen, Michael, and Greve, Wilfried (eds): *Materialien zur Philosophie Sören Kierkegaards*. Frankfurt am Main, 1979.

Thies, Christian: *Die Krise des Individuums: Zur Kritik der Moderne bei Adorno und Gehlen*. Reinbek bei Hamburg, 1997.

Thyen, Anke: *Negative Dialektik und Erfahrung: Rationalität des Nichtidentischen bei Adorno*. Frankfurt am Main, 1989.

Tiedemann, Rolf: 'Zur "Beschlagnahme" Walter Benjamins, oder, Wie man mit der Philologie Schlitten fährt', *Das Argument*, no. 46, 1968.

——: *Studien zur Philosophie Walter Benjamins*. Frankfurt am Main, 1973.

——: *Dialektik im Stillstand: Versuche zum Spätwerk Walter Benjamins*. Frankfurt am Main, 1983.

—— (ed.): *Adorno-Noten*. Berlin, 1984.

——: 'Gegen den Trug der Frage nach dem Sinn: Eine Dokumentation zu Adornos Beckett-Lektüre', *Frankfurter Adorno Blätter*, III, 1994, pp. 18–77.

——: 'Gretel Adorno zum Abschied', *Frankfurter Adorno Blätter*, III, 1994, pp. 148–52.

——: (ed.): *'Ob nach Auschwitz noch sich leben lasse': Ein philosophisches Lesebuch*. Frankfurt am Main, 1997.

——: 'Iphigenie bei den Berliner Studenten: Notiz zu dem Vortrag am 17. Juli in der Freien Universität', *Frankfurter Adorno Blätter*, VI, 2000, pp. 122–7.

——: 'Nur ein Gast in der Tafelrunde: Theodor W. Adorno: kritisch und kritisiert', in *Von Kranichstein zur Gegenwart: 50 Jahre Darmstädter Ferienkurse*. Stuttgart, 2001, pp. 149–55.

——: *Die Abrechnung: Walter Benjamin und sein Verleger*. Hamburg, n.d.

Tietz, Udo: *Ontologie und Dialektik: Heidegger und Adorno über das Sein, das Nichtidentische, die Synthesis und die Kopula*. Vienna, 2003.

Topitsch, Ernst (ed.): *Logik der Sozialwissenschaft*. Cologne and Berlin 1965.

Traub, Rainer, and Wieser, Harald (eds): *Gespräche mit Bloch*. Frankfurt am Main, 1975.

Unseld, Siegfried: *Peter Suhrkamp: Zur Biographie eines Verlegers in Daten, Dokumenten und Bildern*. Frankfurt am Main, 1975.

Unser Liederbuch: Die beliebtesten Kinderlieder, selected by Friederike Merck with illustrations by Ludwig von Zumbusch, set for children's voices by Fritz Volbach. Mainz, 1900–01.

Vogt, Günther: *Frankfurter Bürgerhäuser des 19. Jahrhunderts: Ein Stadtbild des Klassizismus*. Frankfurt am Main, 1970.

Voit, Friedrich: *Der Verleger Peter Suhrkamp und seine Autoren*. Typescript, 1975.

Voss, Lieselotte: *Die Entstehung von Thomas Manns Roman 'Doktor Faustus': Dargestellt anhand von unveröffentlichten Vorarbeiten*. Tübingen, 1975.

Wald, Alan M.: *The New York Intellectuals: The Rise and Decline of the Anti-Stalinist Left from the 1930s to the 1980s*. Chapel Hill, NC, 1987.

Walter Benjamin 1892–1940. Stuttgart, 1990 [exhibition catalogue].

Walzer, Michael: *Kritik und Gemeinsinn: Drei Wege der Gesellschaftskritik*. Frankfurt am Main, 1993.

Weber, Max: *Gesammelte Aufsätze zur Wissenschaftslehre*. Tübingen, 1951.

——: *Die rationalen und soziologischen Grundlagen der Musik*. Tübingen, 1972.

Weigel, Sigrid: *Ingeborg Bachmann: Hinterlassenschaften unter Wahrung des Briefgeheimnisses*. Darmstadt, 1999.

Wellmer, Albrecht: *Kritische Gesellschaftstheorie und Positivismus*. Frankfurt am Main, 1969.
——: *Zur Dialektik von Moderne und Postmoderne*. Frankfurt am Main, 1990.
——: 'Die Bedeutung der Frankfurter Schule heute', in Wellmer, Albrecht: *Endspiele: Die unversöhnliche Moderne: Essays und Vorträge*. Frankfurt am Main, 1993, pp. 224–38.
Werk und Wirken Paul Tillichs: Ein Gedenkbuch. Stuttgart, 1967.
Werz, Michael: 'Untrennbarkeit von Material und Methode: Zur wechselvollen Rezeption der Authoritarian Personality', *Philosophie und Empirie: Hannoversche Schriften*, 4, 2001, pp. 40–68.
Weyer, Johannes: *Westdeutsche Soziologie 1945–1960: Deutsche Kontinuitäten und nordamerikanischer Einfluß*. Berlin, 1984.
Wiedemann, Barbara: *Paul Celan: Die Goll-Affäre: Dokumente zu einer 'Infamie'*. Frankfurt am Main, 2000.
Wiggershaus, Rolf: *Theodor W. Adorno*. Munich, 1987.
——: *The Frankfurt School: Its History, Theories and Political Significance*, trans. Michael Robertson. Cambridge, 1994.
Wilcock, Evelyn: 'Adorno in Oxford 1: Oxford University Musical Club', *Oxford Magazine*, Hilary term, 1996, pp. 11–15.
——: 'Adorno, Jazz and Racism: "Über Jazz" and the 1934–7 British Jazz Debate', *Telos*, 107, 1996, pp. 63–80.
——: 'Adorno's Uncle: Dr. Bernhard Wingfield and the English Exile of Theodor W. Adorno', *German Life and Letters*, 49, 1996, pp. 324–38.
——: 'Alban Berg's Appeal to Edward Dent on Behalf of Theodor Adorno, 18 November 1933', *German Life and Letters*, 50, 1997, pp. 365–8.
——: 'The Dating of Seiber/Adorno Papers held by the British Library', *British Library Journal*, 2, 1997, pp. 264–7.
Wilson, Michael: *Das Institut für Sozialforschung und seine Faschismusanalysen*. Frankfurt am Main and New York, 1982.
Witkin, Robert W.: *Adorno on Music*. London and New York, 1998.
Witte, Bernd: *Walter Benjamin: Mit Selbstzeugnissen und Bilddokumenten*. Hamburg, 1985.
Wolff, Kurt H. (ed.): *Wissenssoziologie: Auswahl aus dem Werk*. Neuwied and Berlin, 1964.
Wolgast, Eike: *Die Wahrnehmung des Dritten Reiches in der unmittelbaren Nachkriegszeit*. Heidelberg, 2002.
Worbs, Dietrich: 'Bauen für den Gebrauch', in Lichtenstein, Claude (ed.): *Ferdinand Kramer: Der Charme des Systematischen*. Giessen, 1991.
Wright, Georg Hendrik von: *Explanation and Understanding*. London, 1971.
Wysling, Hans, and Fischer, Marianne (eds): *Dichter über ihre Dichtungen*. 3 vols, Zürich, Munich and Frankfurt am Main, 1975–81.
Young-Bruehl, Elisabeth: *Hannah Arendt: Leben, Werk und Zeit*. Frankfurt am Main, 1986.
Zuckmayer, Carl: *Geheimreport*, ed. Gunther Nickel and Johanna Schrön. Göttingen, 2002.
Zudeick, Peter: *Der Hintern des Teufels: Ernst Bloch – Leben und Werk*. Baden-Baden, 1989.
Zuidervaart, Lambert: *Adorno's Aesthetic Theory*. Boston, 1991.

Index